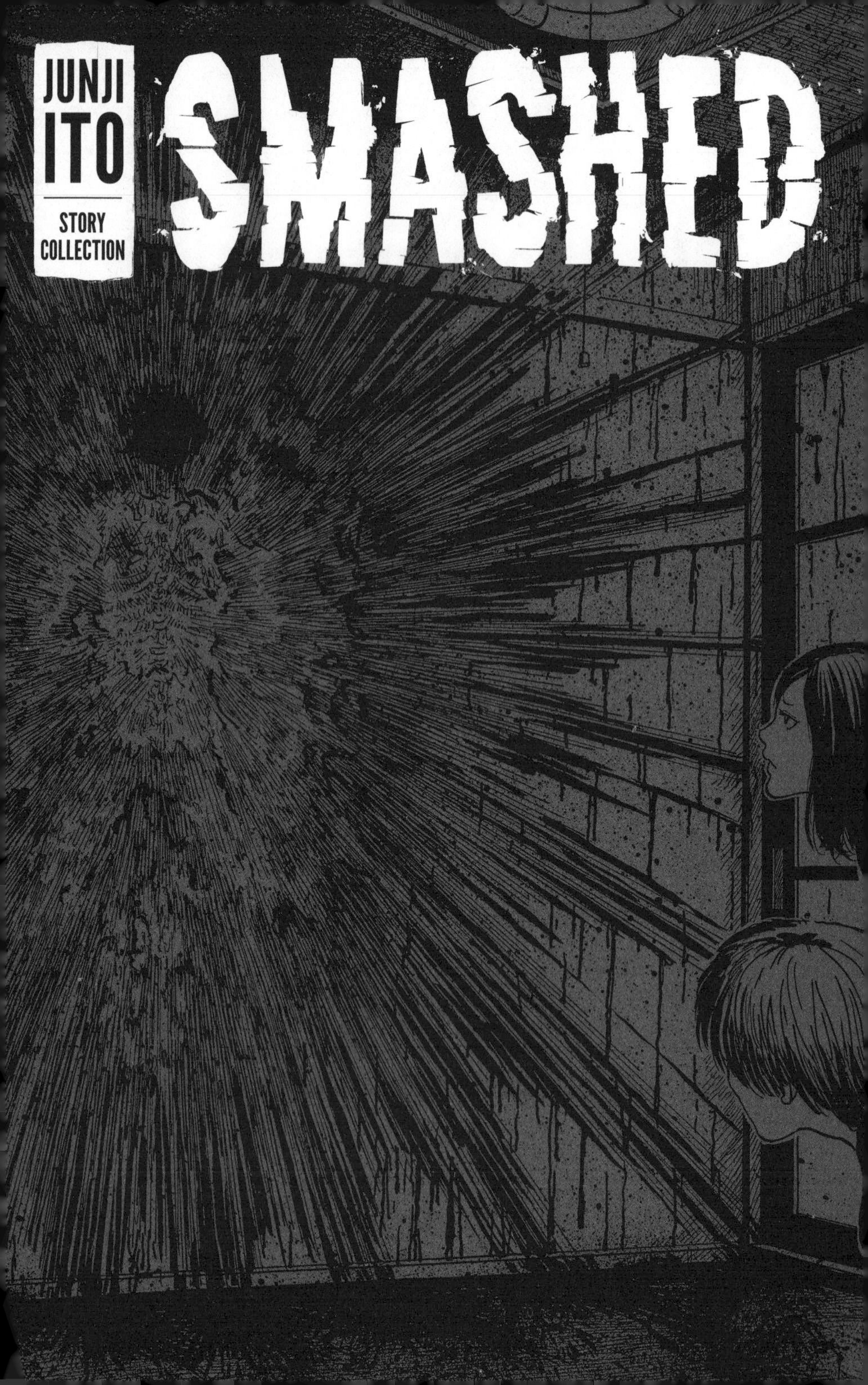
JUNJI
ITO
STORY
COLLECTION
SMASHED

CONTENTS

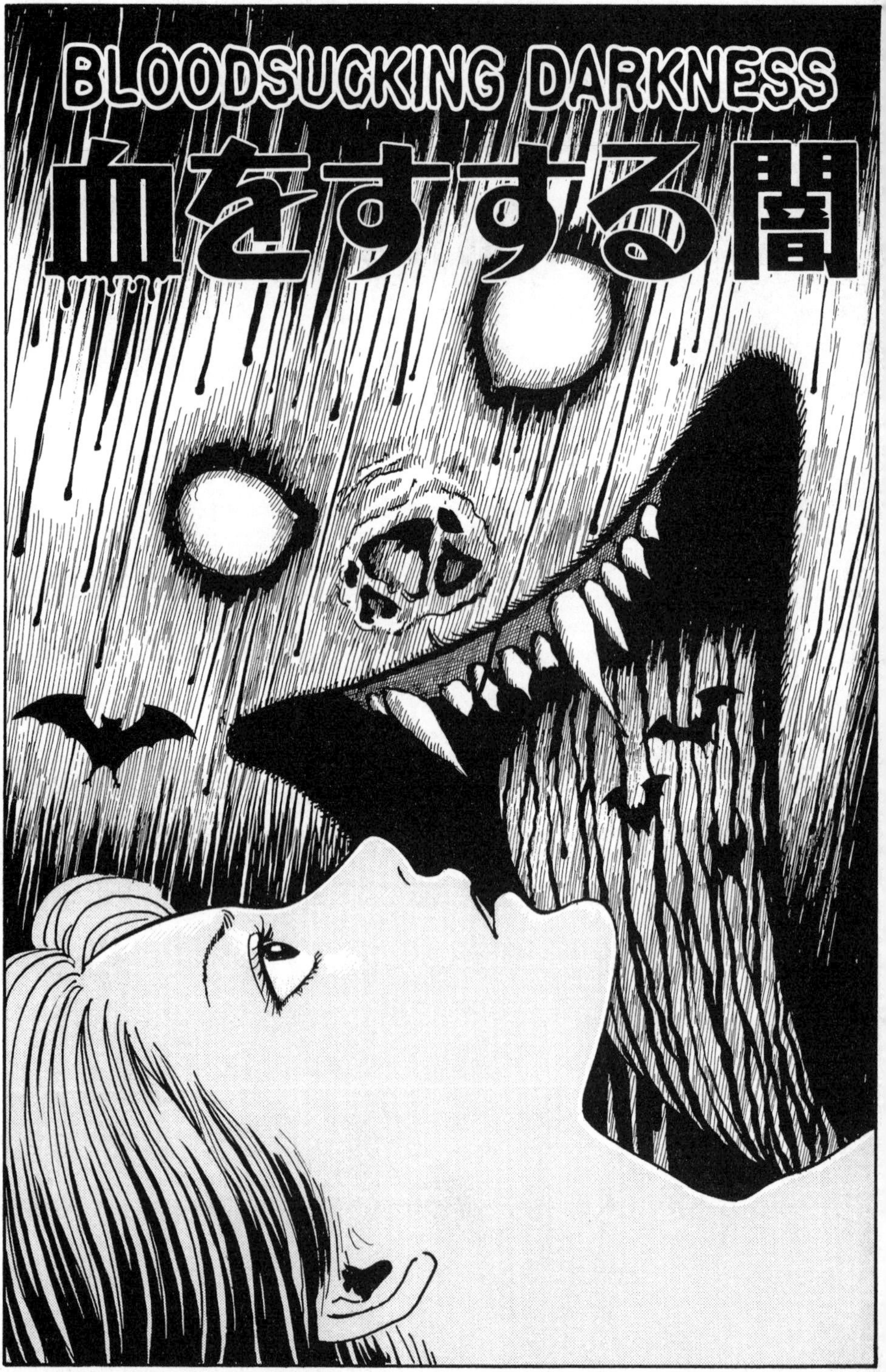
BLOODSUCKING DARKNESS
血をすする闇

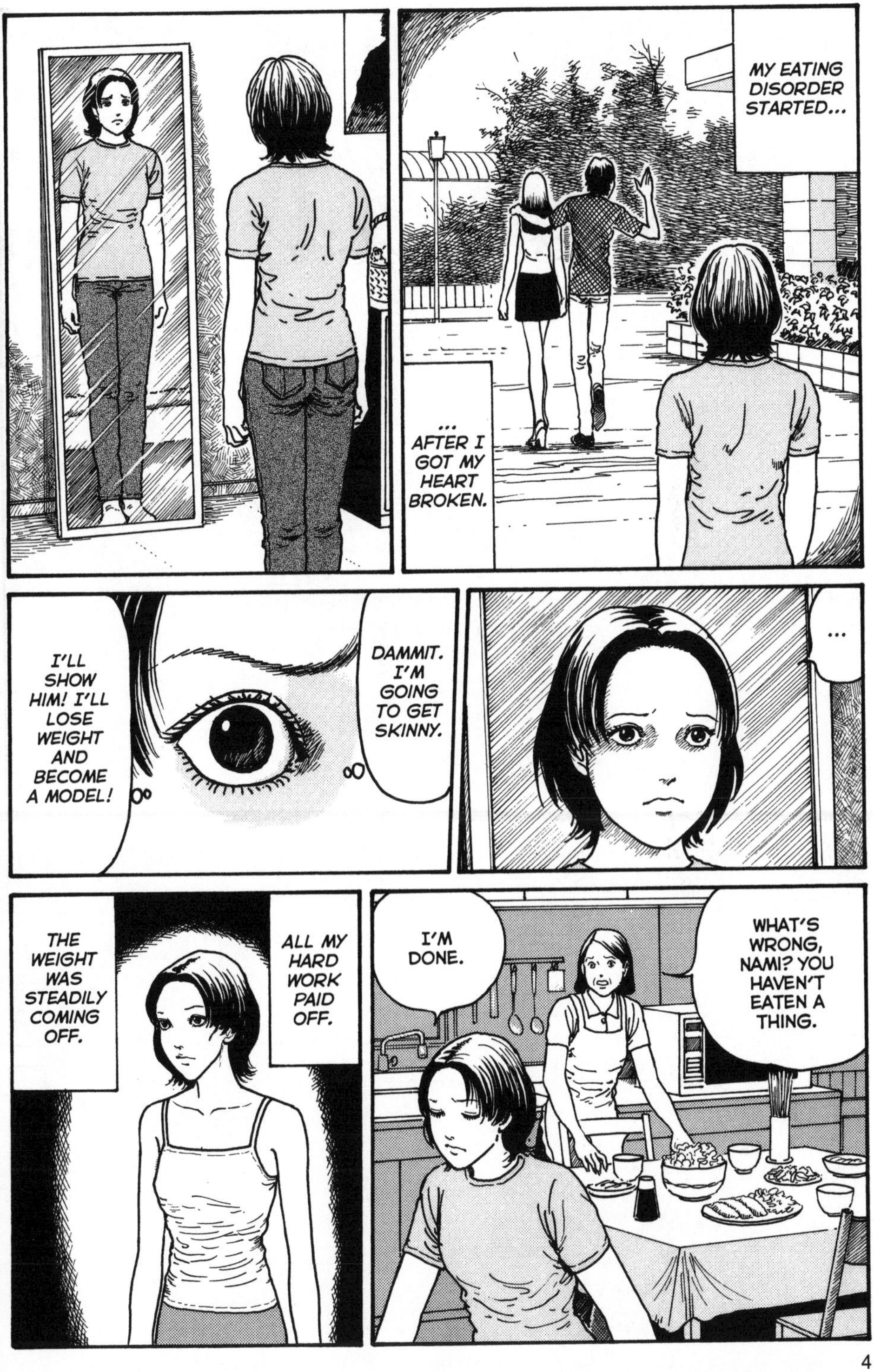
MY EATING DISORDER STARTED...
...AFTER I GOT MY HEART BROKEN.
...
DAMMIT. I'M GOING TO GET SKINNY.
I'LL SHOW HIM! I'LL LOSE WEIGHT AND BECOME A MODEL!
WHAT'S WRONG, NAMI? YOU HAVEN'T EATEN A THING.
I'M DONE.
ALL MY HARD WORK PAID OFF.
THE WEIGHT WAS STEADILY COMING OFF.

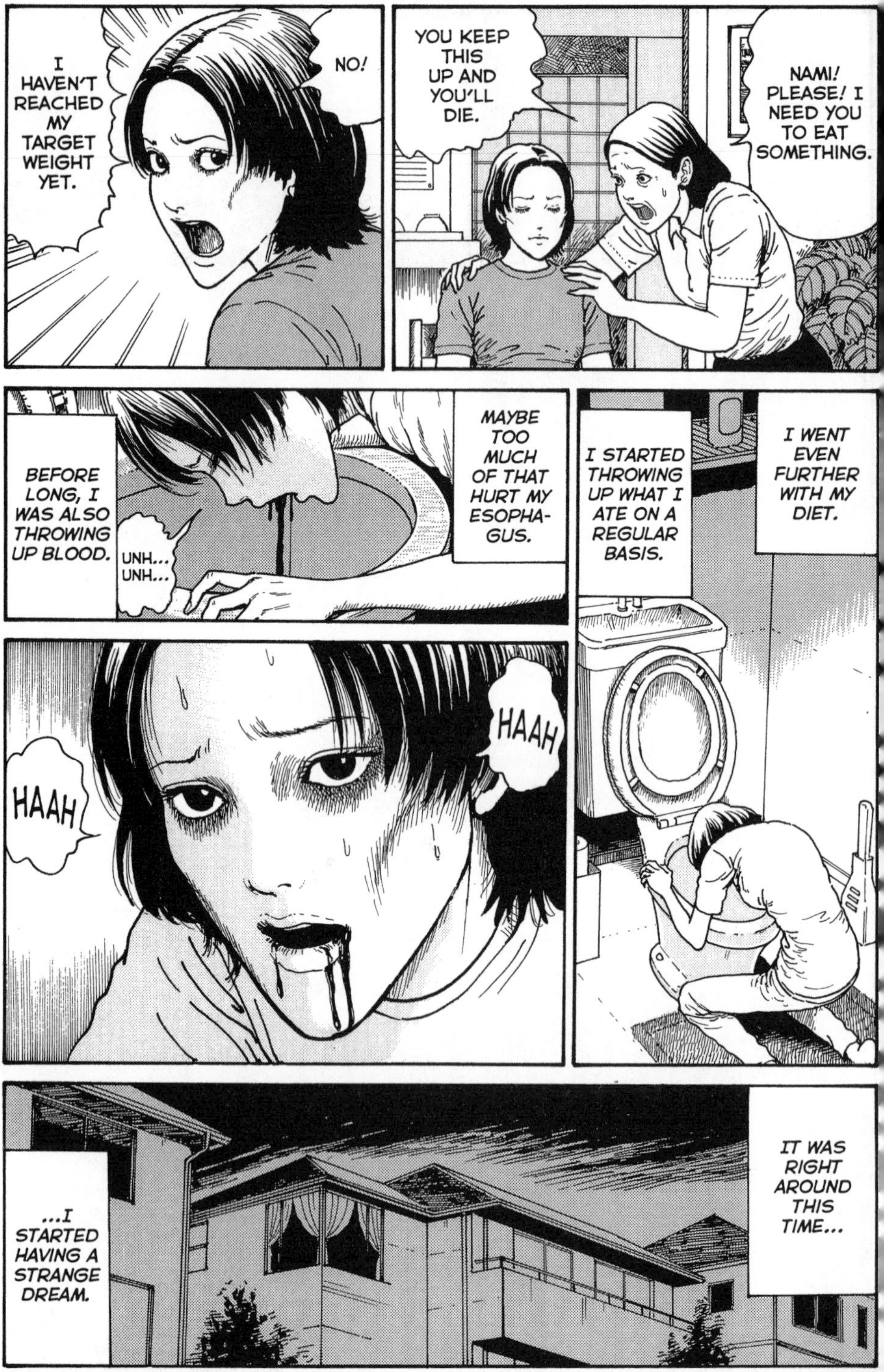
NAMI! PLEASE! I NEED YOU TO EAT SOMETHING.
YOU KEEP THIS UP AND YOU'LL DIE.
NO!
I HAVEN'T REACHED MY TARGET WEIGHT YET.
I WENT EVEN FURTHER WITH MY DIET.
I STARTED THROWING UP WHAT I ATE ON A REGULAR BASIS.
MAYBE TOO MUCH OF THAT HURT MY ESOPHAGUS.
BEFORE LONG, I WAS ALSO THROWING UP BLOOD.
UNH... UNH...
HAAH
HAAH
IT WAS RIGHT AROUND THIS TIME...
...I STARTED HAVING A STRANGE DREAM.

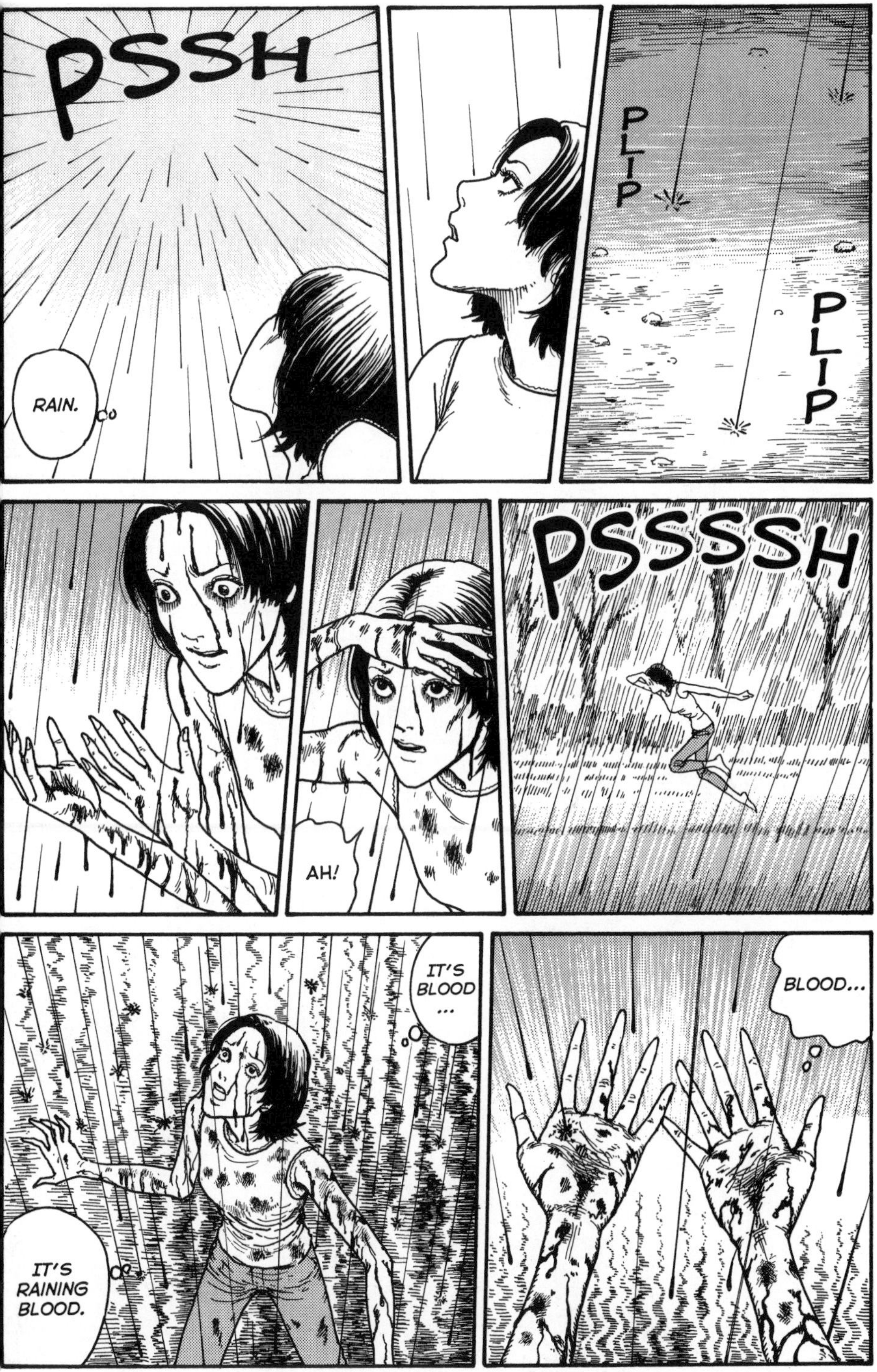
PLIP
PLIP
PSSH
RAIN.
PSSSSH
AH!
BLOOD...
IT'S BLOOD ...
IT'S RAINING BLOOD.

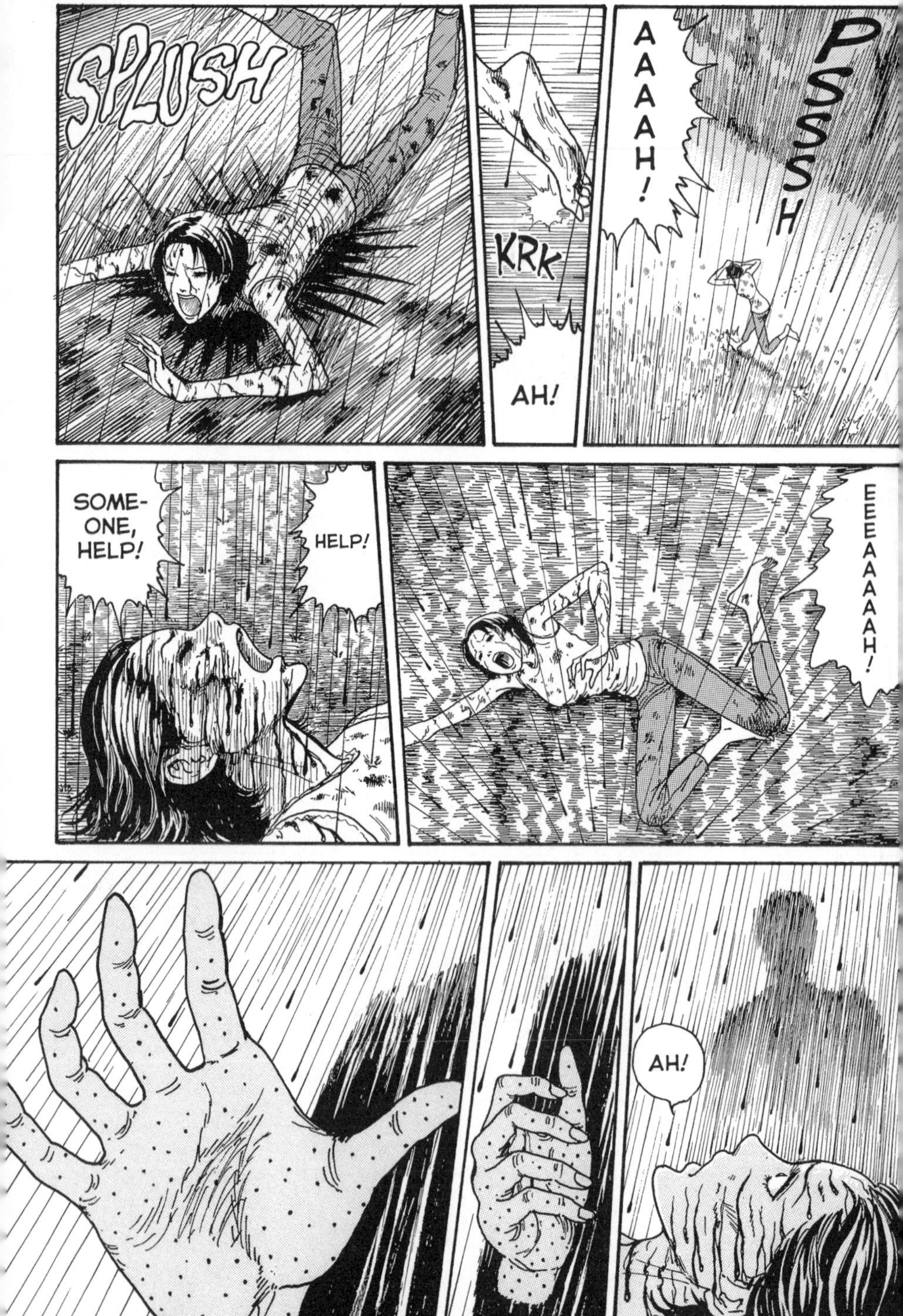
PSSSH
AAAAAH!
KRK
AH!
SPLUSH
EEEAAAAAAH!
HELP!
SOME-ONE, HELP!
AH!

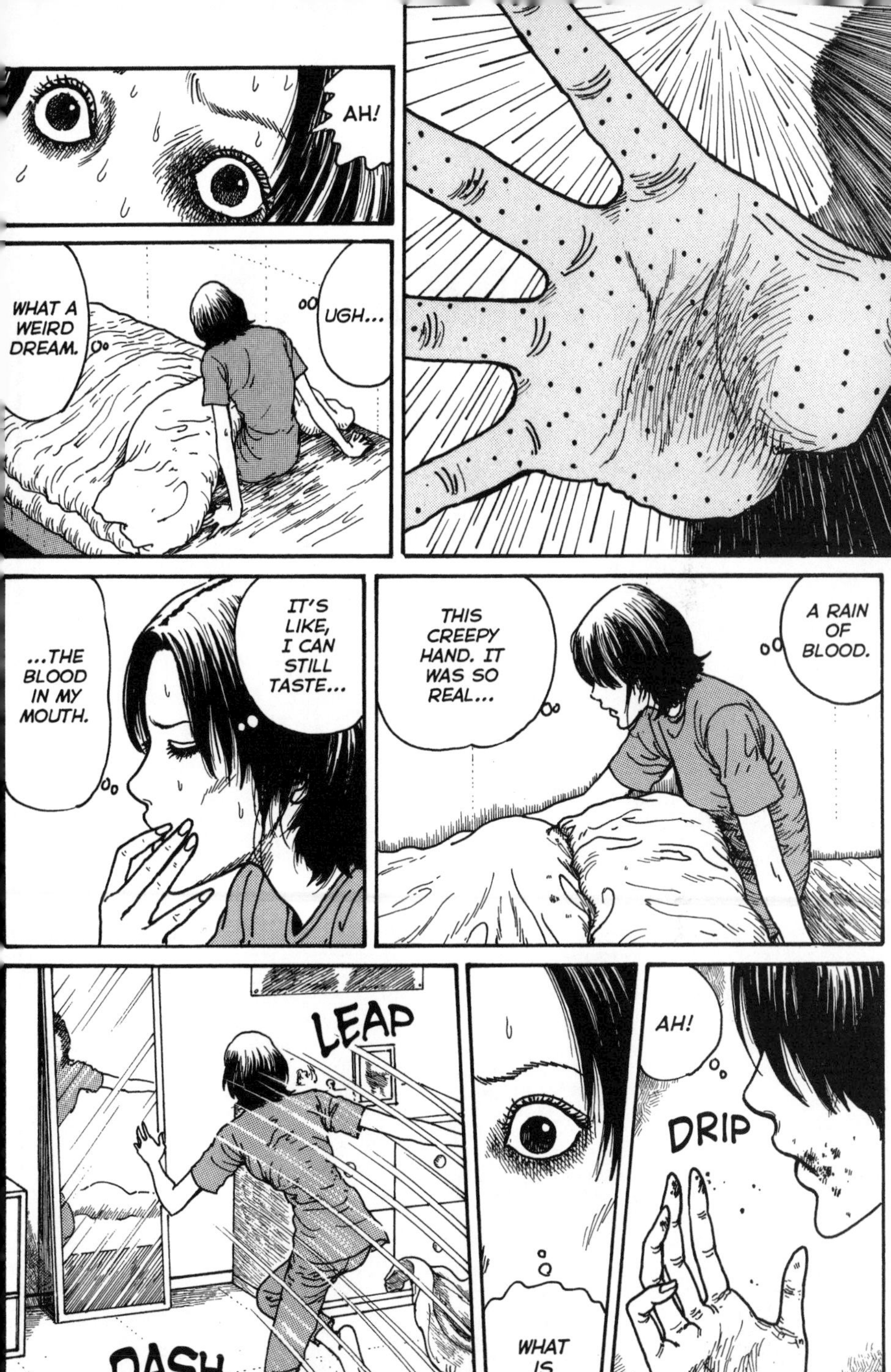
AH!
UGH...
WHAT A WEIRD DREAM.
A RAIN OF BLOOD.
THIS CREEPY HAND. IT WAS SO REAL...
IT'S LIKE, I CAN STILL TASTE...
...THE BLOOD IN MY MOUTH.
AH!
DRIP
WHAT IS THIS?
LEAP
DASH

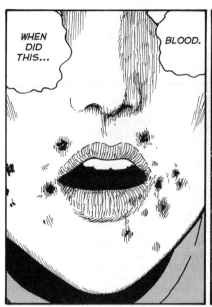

BLOOD.
WHEN DID THIS...
MAYBE I THREW UP WHILE I WAS ASLEEP?
THERE ARE SPOTS ALL OVER MY BED, TOO.
I GUESS I DID THROW UP.
GROSS.
SO THAT'S WHY I HAD THAT DREAM.

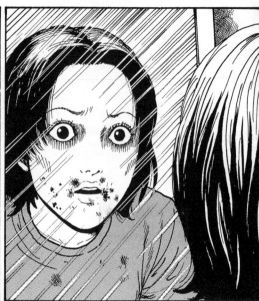

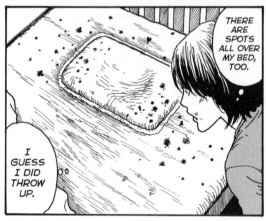

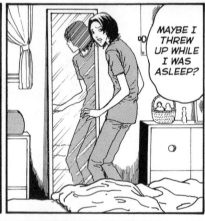

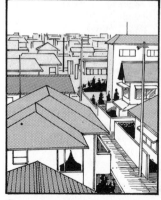

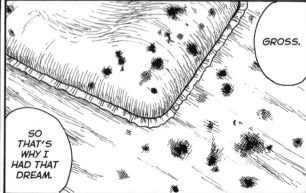

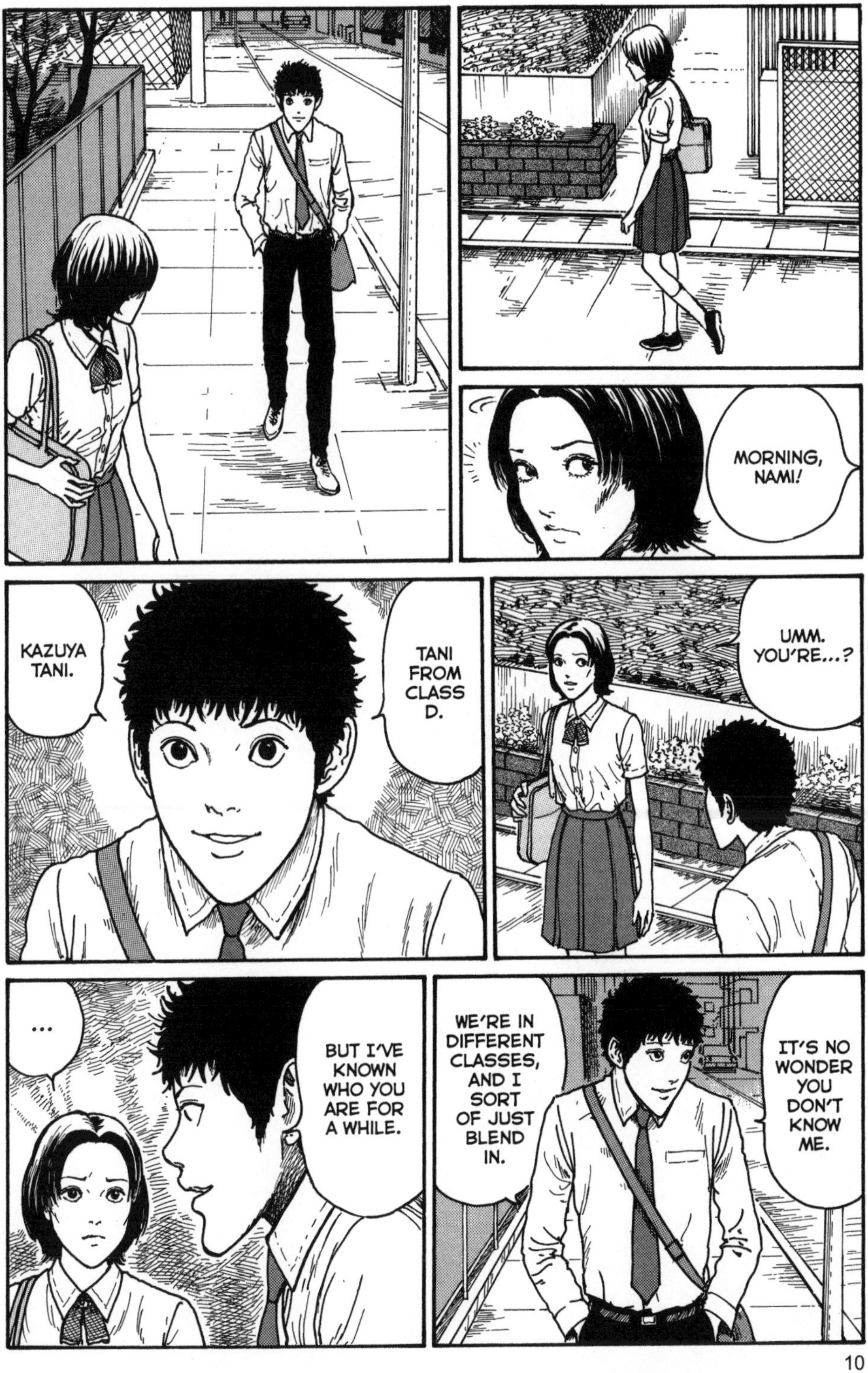
MORNING, NAMI!
UMM. YOU'RE...?
TANI FROM CLASS D.
KAZUYA TANI.
IT'S NO WONDER YOU DON'T KNOW ME.
WE'RE IN DIFFERENT CLASSES, AND I SORT OF JUST BLEND IN.
BUT I'VE KNOWN WHO YOU ARE FOR A WHILE.
...

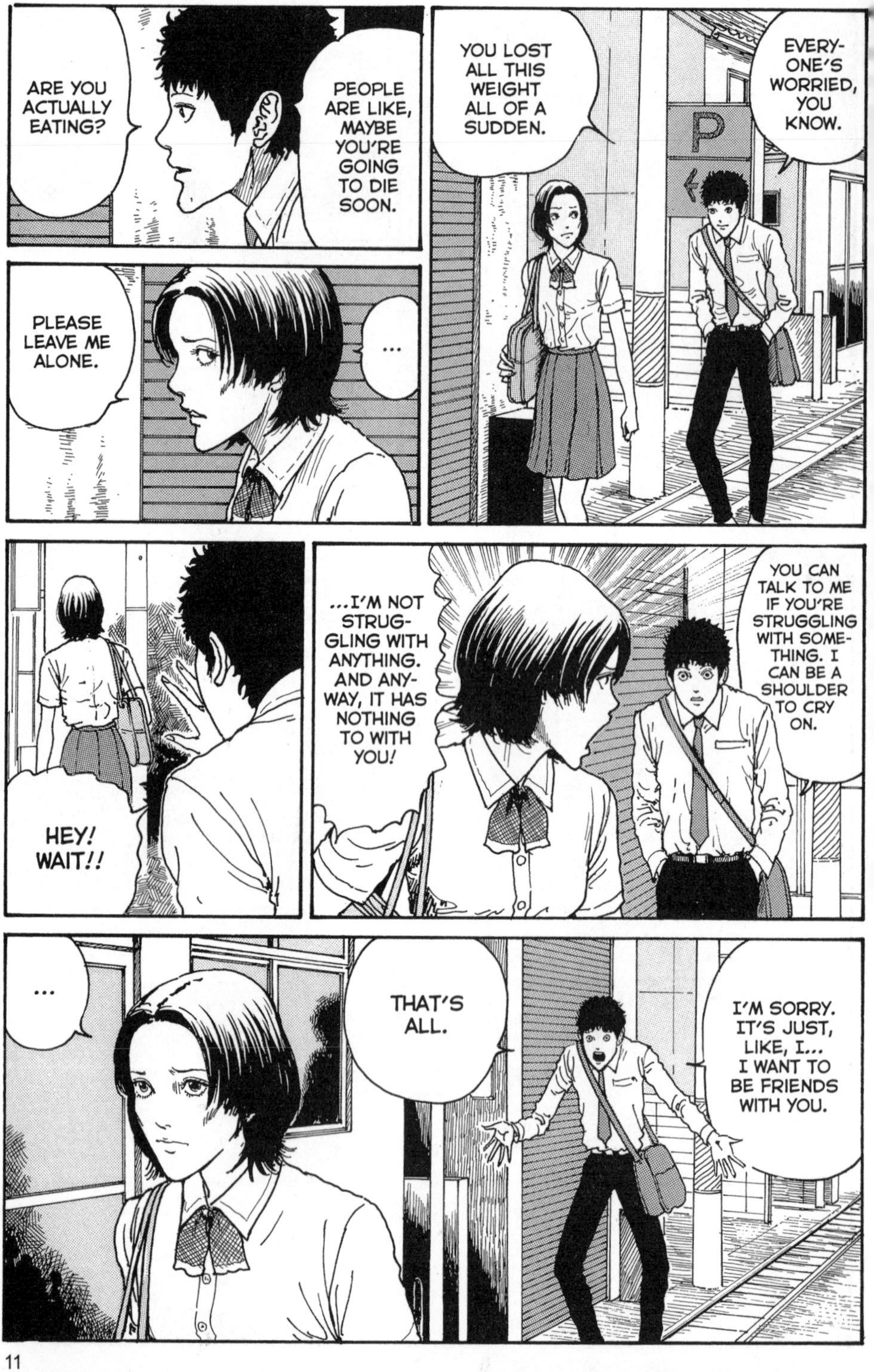
EVERYONE'S WORRIED, YOU KNOW.
YOU LOST ALL THIS WEIGHT ALL OF A SUDDEN.
PEOPLE ARE LIKE, MAYBE YOU'RE GOING TO DIE SOON.
ARE YOU ACTUALLY EATING?
...
PLEASE LEAVE ME ALONE.
YOU CAN TALK TO ME IF YOU'RE STRUGGLING WITH SOMETHING. I CAN BE A SHOULDER TO CRY ON.
...I'M NOT STRUGGLING WITH ANYTHING. AND ANYWAY, IT HAS NOTHING TO WITH YOU!
HEY! WAIT!!
I'M SORRY. IT'S JUST, LIKE, I... I WANT TO BE FRIENDS WITH YOU.
THAT'S ALL.
...

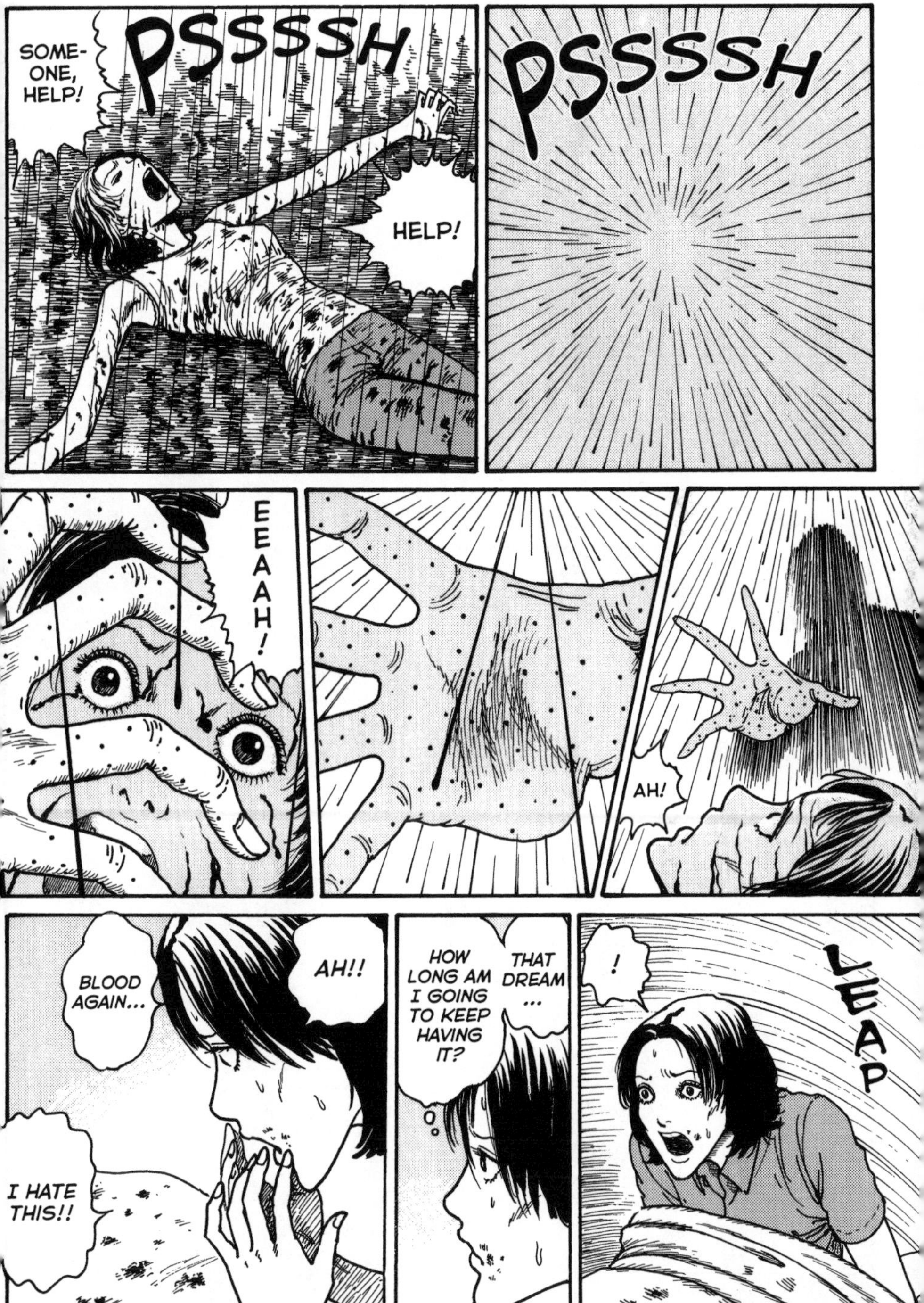
PSSSSH
PSSSSH
SOME-ONE, HELP!
HELP!
AH!
EEAAAH!
!
LEAP
THAT DREAM...
HOW LONG AM I GOING TO KEEP HAVING IT?
AH!!
BLOOD AGAIN...
I HATE THIS!!

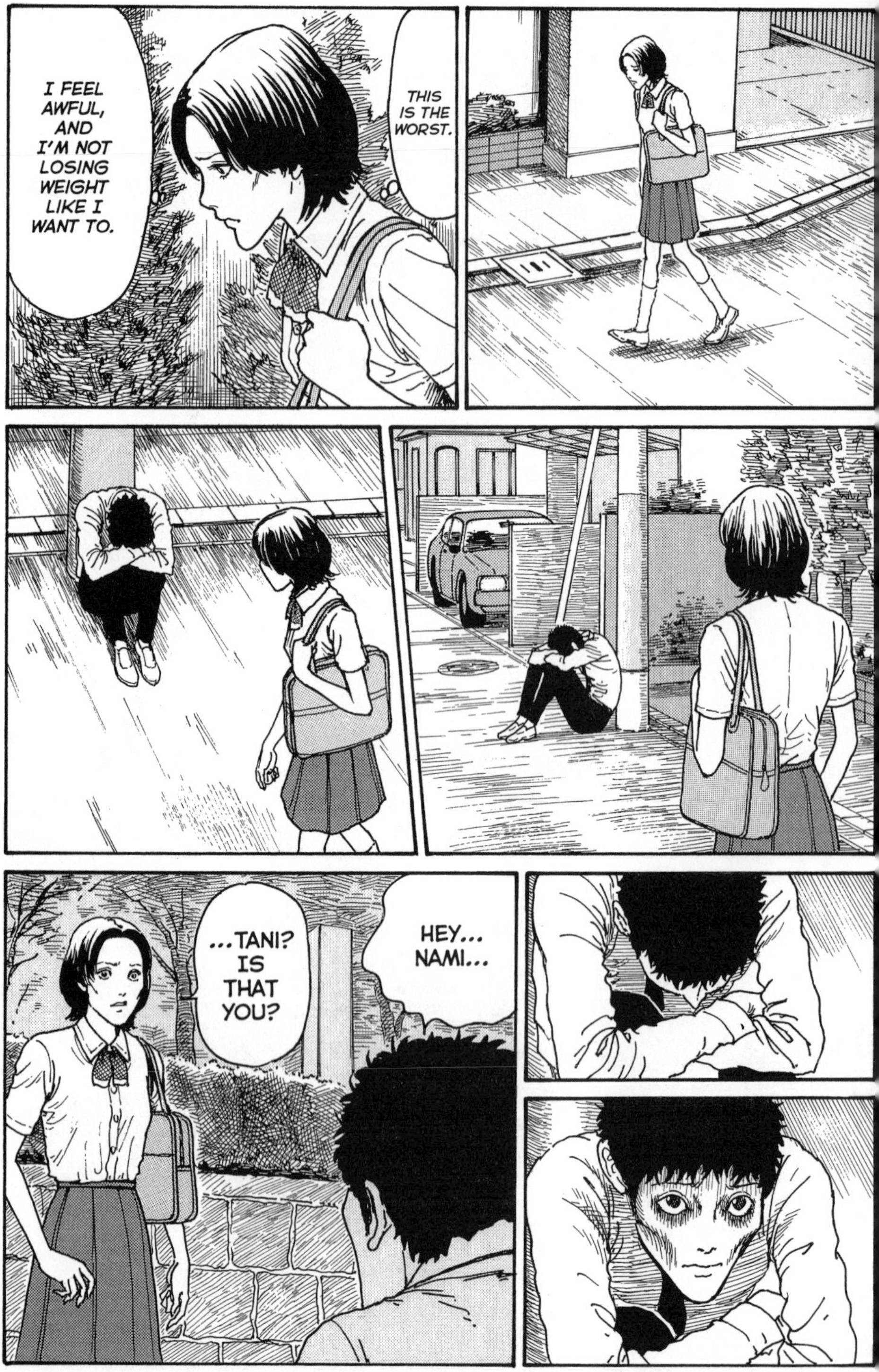
THIS IS THE WORST.
I FEEL AWFUL, AND I'M NOT LOSING WEIGHT LIKE I WANT TO.
HEY... NAMI...
...TANI? IS THAT YOU?

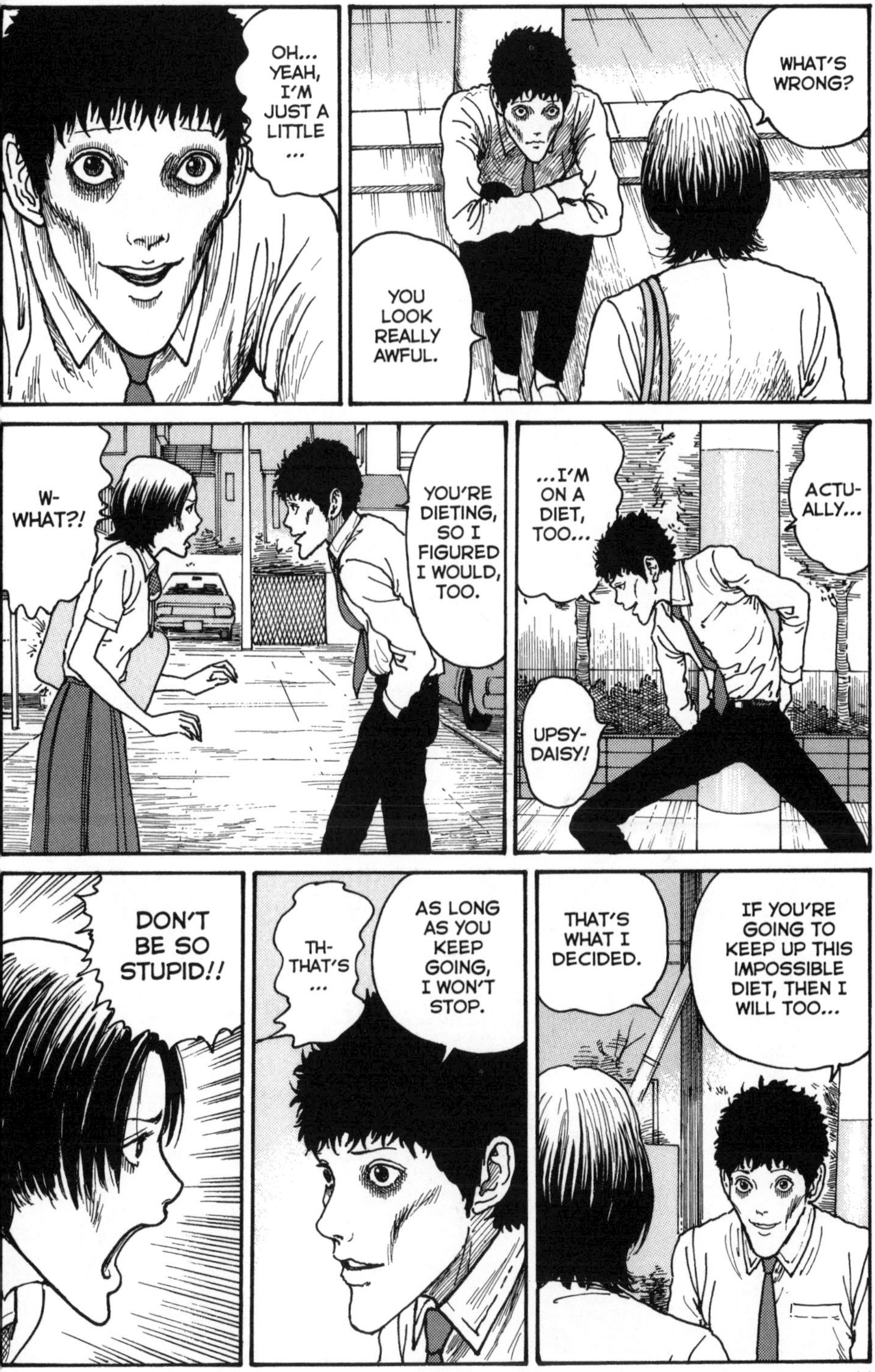
WHAT'S WRONG?
YOU LOOK REALLY AWFUL.
OH... YEAH, I'M JUST A LITTLE ...
ACTU-ALLY...
...I'M ON A DIET, TOO...
UPSY-DAISY!
YOU'RE DIETING, SO I FIGURED I WOULD, TOO.
W-WHAT?!
IF YOU'RE GOING TO KEEP UP THIS IMPOSSIBLE DIET, THEN I WILL TOO...
THAT'S WHAT I DECIDED.
AS LONG AS YOU KEEP GOING, I WON'T STOP.
TH-THAT'S ...
DON'T BE SO STUPID!!

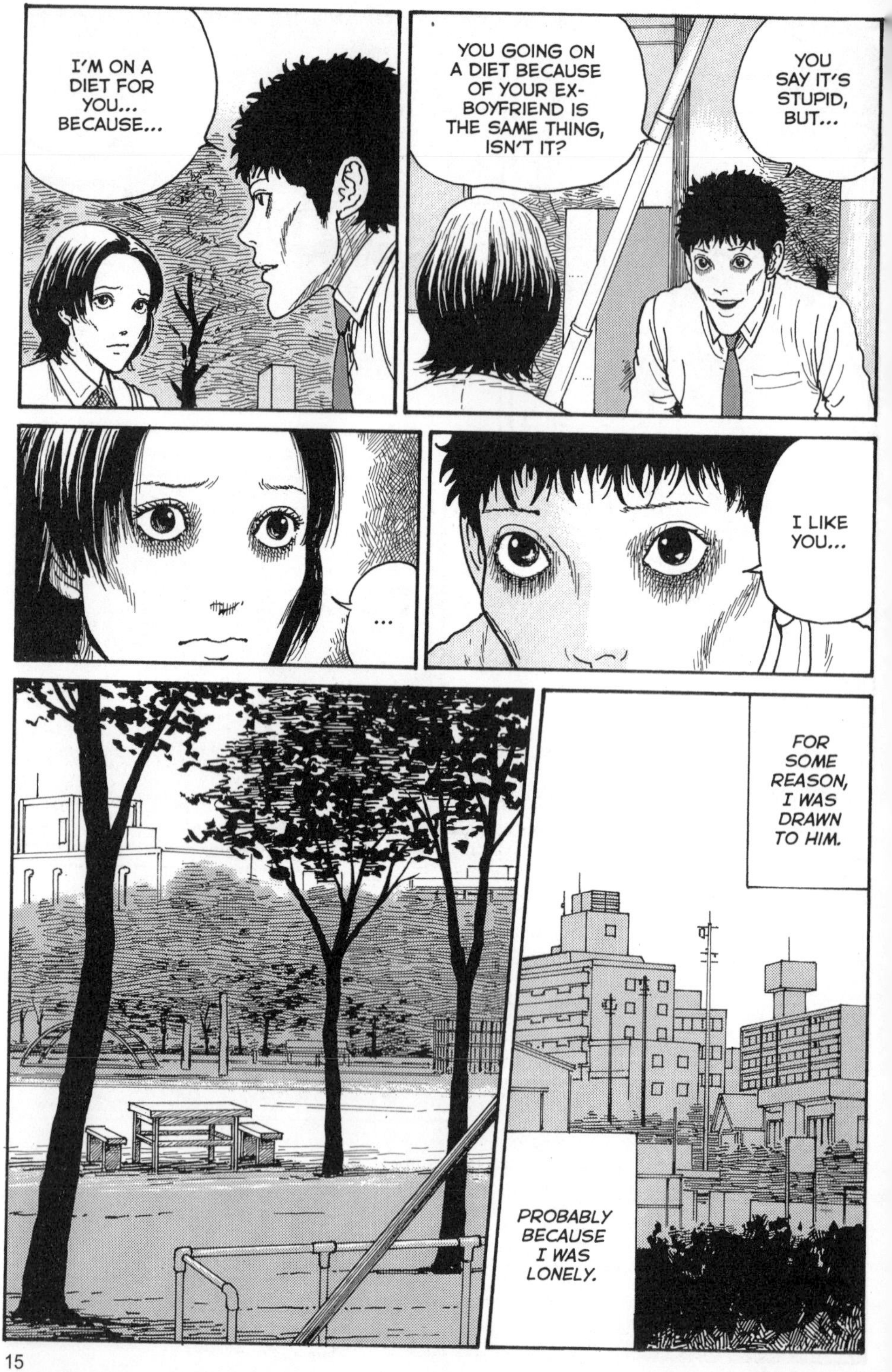
YOU SAY IT'S STUPID, BUT...
YOU GOING ON A DIET BECAUSE OF YOUR EX-BOYFRIEND IS THE SAME THING, ISN'T IT?
I'M ON A DIET FOR YOU... BECAUSE...
I LIKE YOU...
...
FOR SOME REASON, I WAS DRAWN TO HIM.
PROBABLY BECAUSE I WAS LONELY.

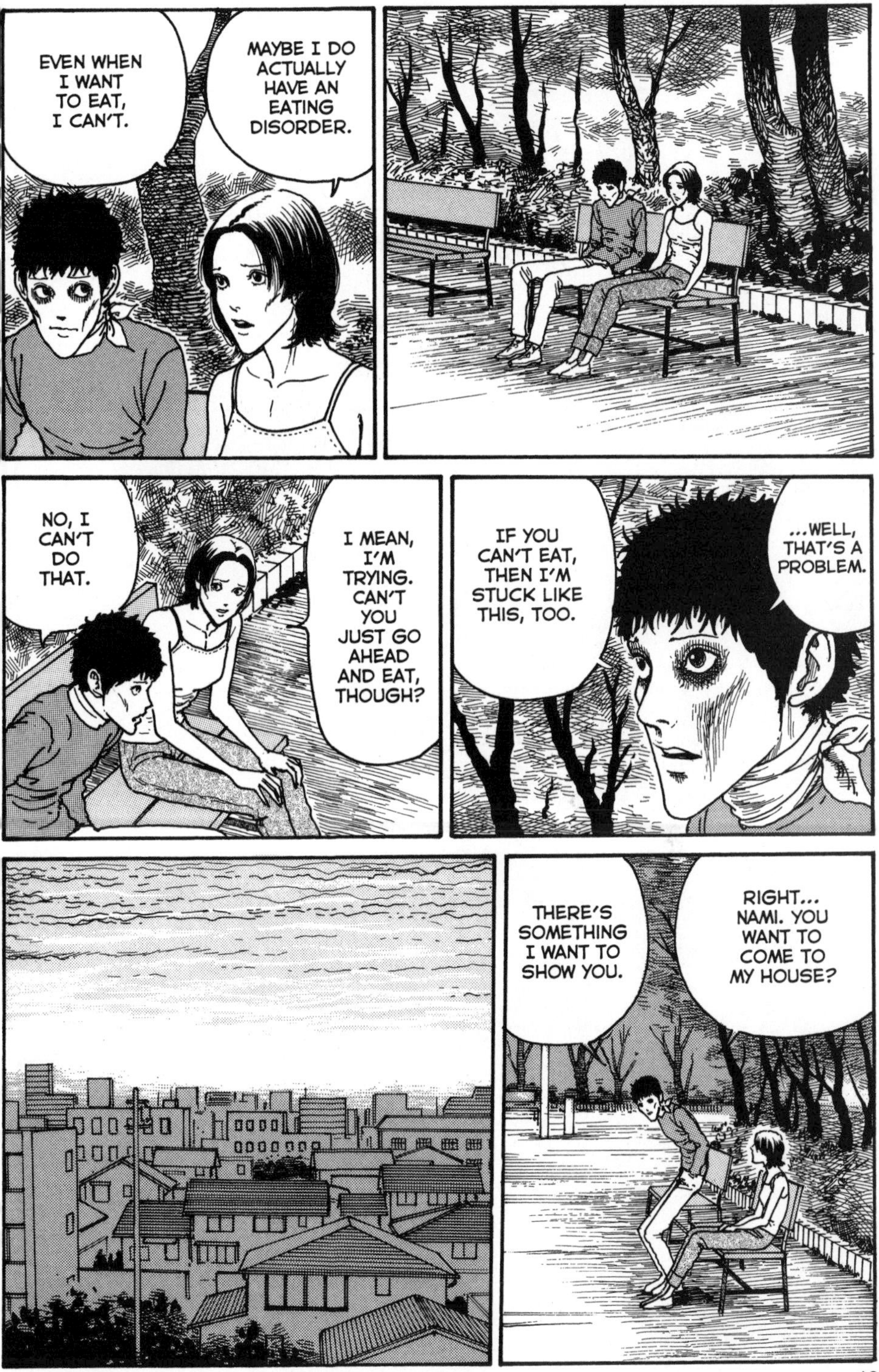
MAYBE I DO ACTUALLY HAVE AN EATING DISORDER.
EVEN WHEN I WANT TO EAT, I CAN'T.
...WELL, THAT'S A PROBLEM.
IF YOU CAN'T EAT, THEN I'M STUCK LIKE THIS, TOO.
I MEAN, I'M TRYING. CAN'T YOU JUST GO AHEAD AND EAT, THOUGH?
NO, I CAN'T DO THAT.
RIGHT... NAMI. YOU WANT TO COME TO MY HOUSE?
THERE'S SOMETHING I WANT TO SHOW YOU.

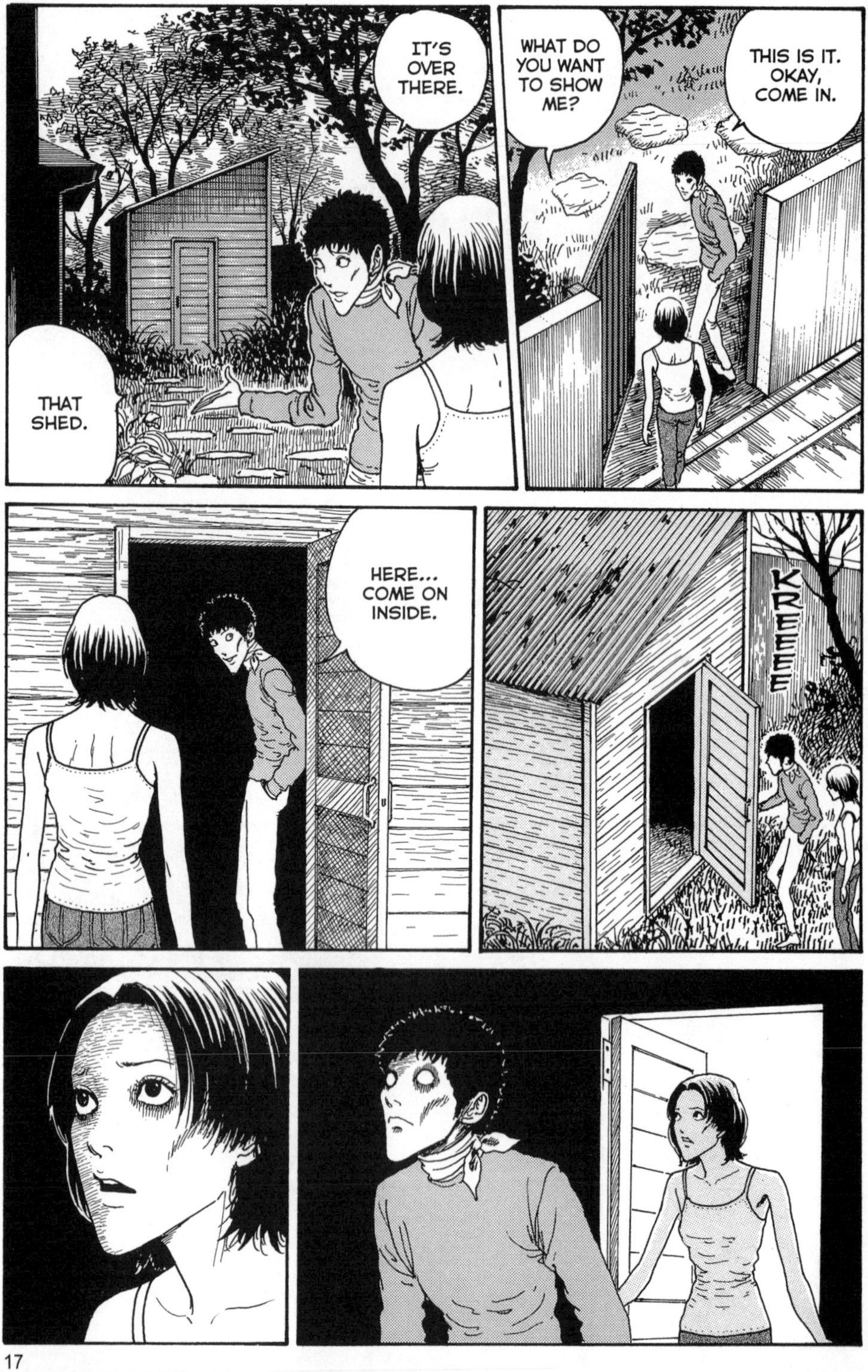
THIS IS IT. OKAY, COME IN.
WHAT DO YOU WANT TO SHOW ME?
IT'S OVER THERE.
THAT SHED.
KREEEE
HERE... COME ON INSIDE.

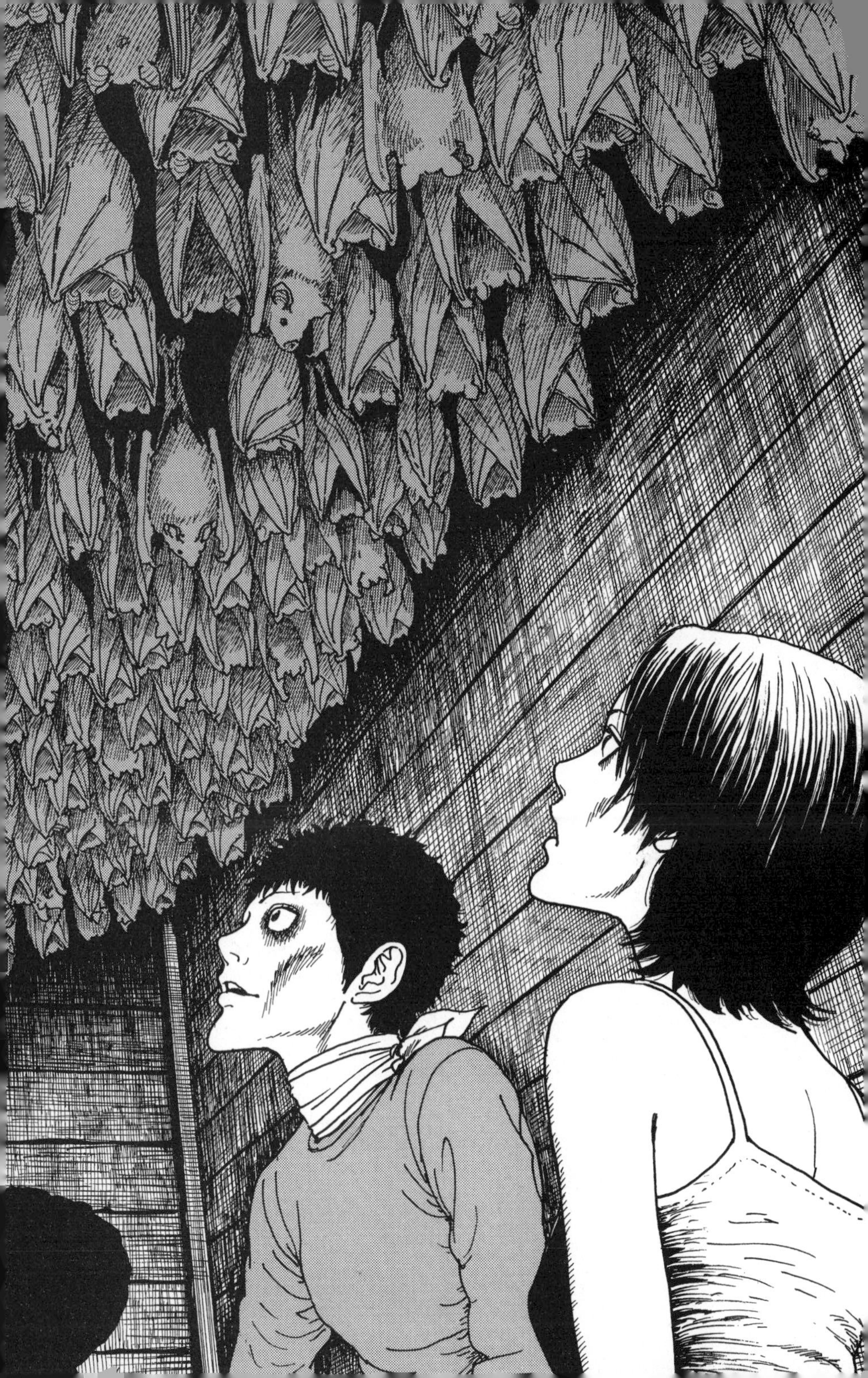

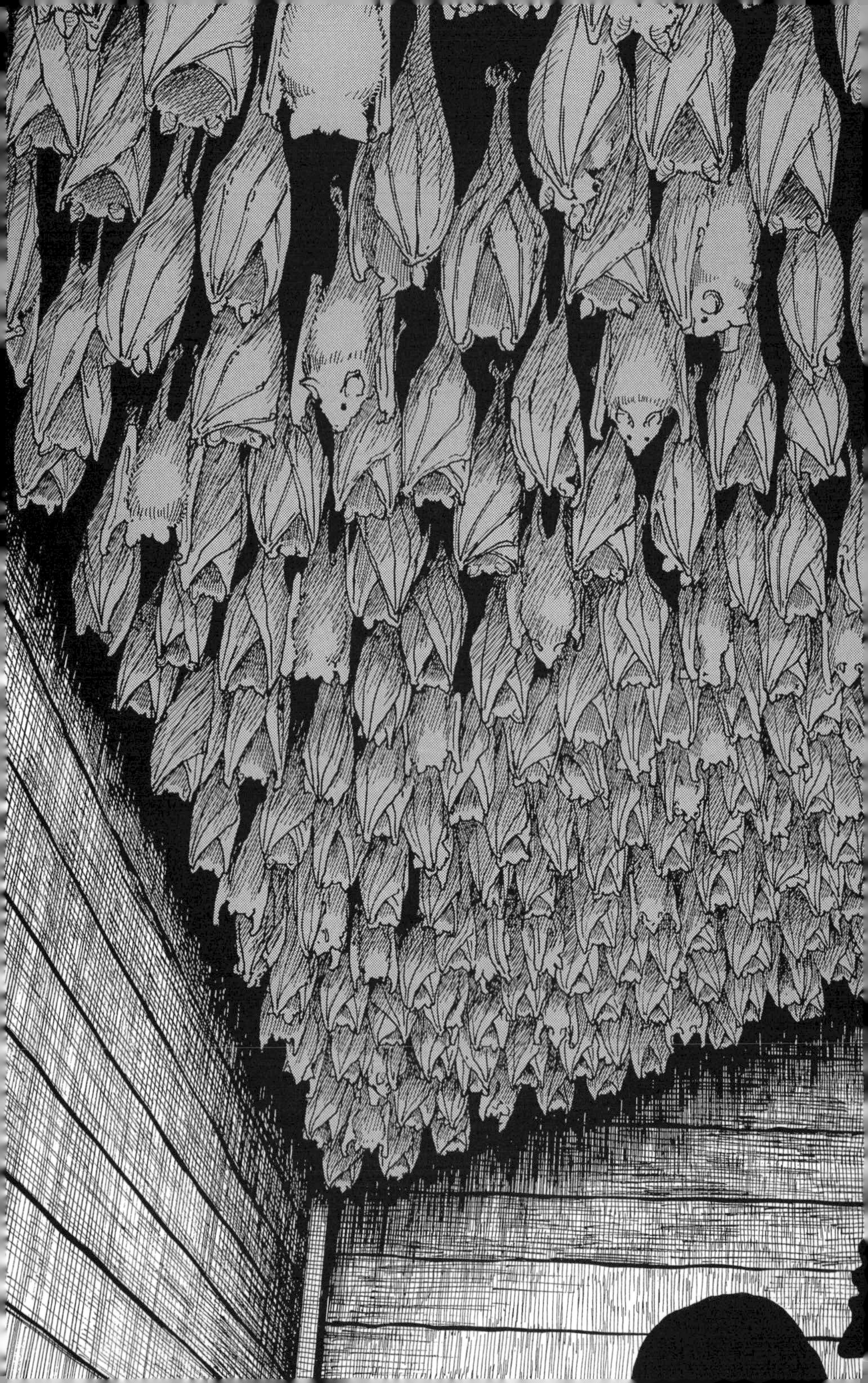

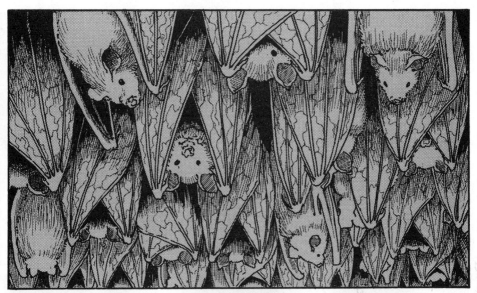

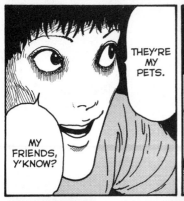

AAAH! BATS!!
IT'S OKAY!!
THEY'RE MY PETS.
MY FRIENDS, Y'KNOW?
THEY'RE RARE BATS. THEY DON'T NORMALLY LIVE IN JAPAN.
THAT'S CHUTARO.
THAT'S PERO.
THAT'S KYUSUKE...

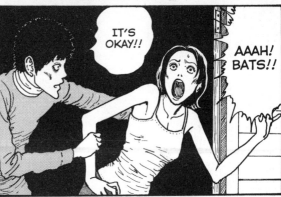

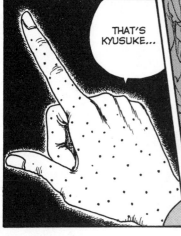

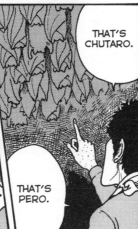

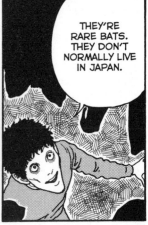

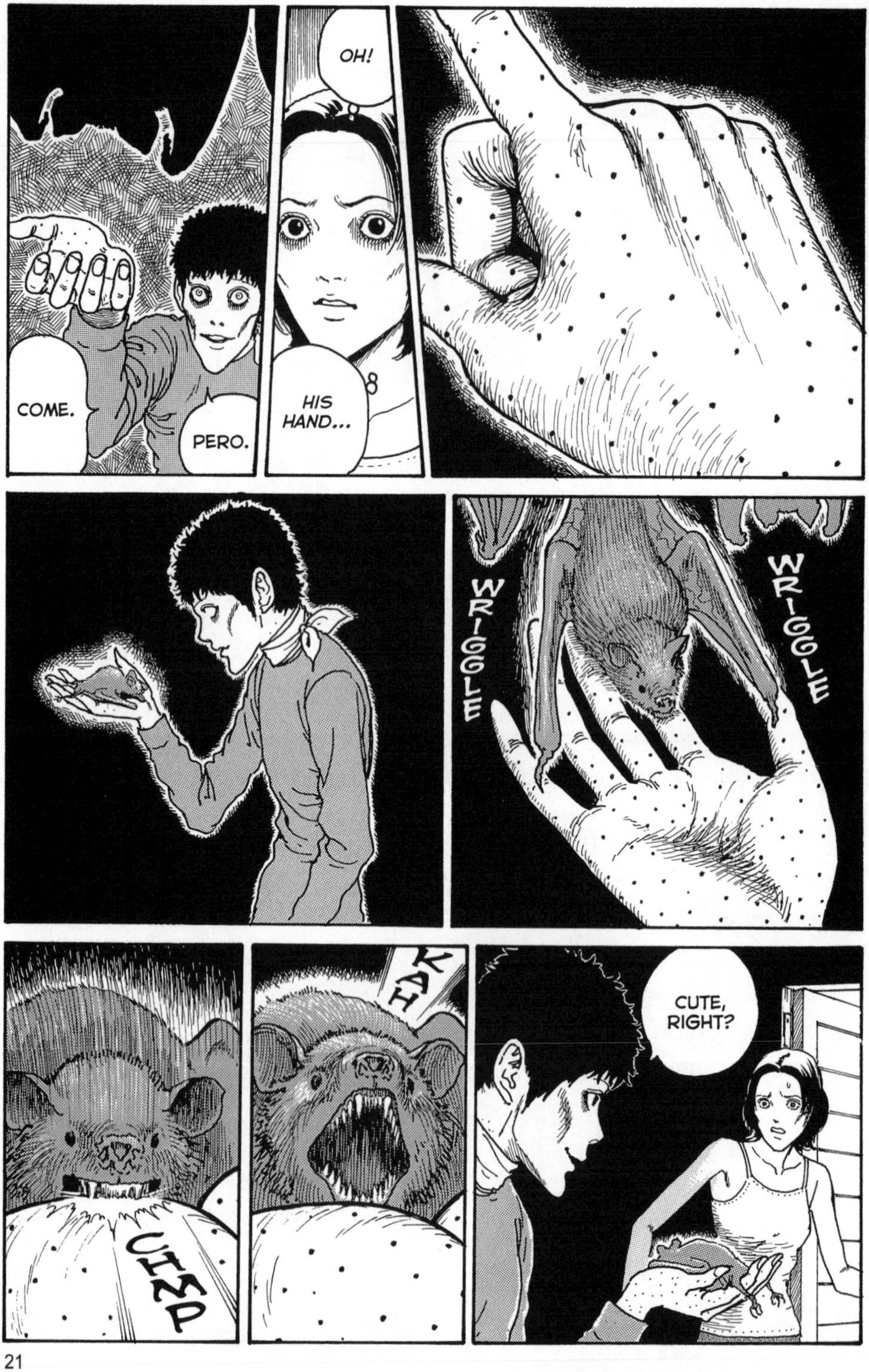
OH!
HIS HAND...
PERO.
COME.
WRIGGLE
WRIGGLE
CUTE, RIGHT?
KAH
CHMP

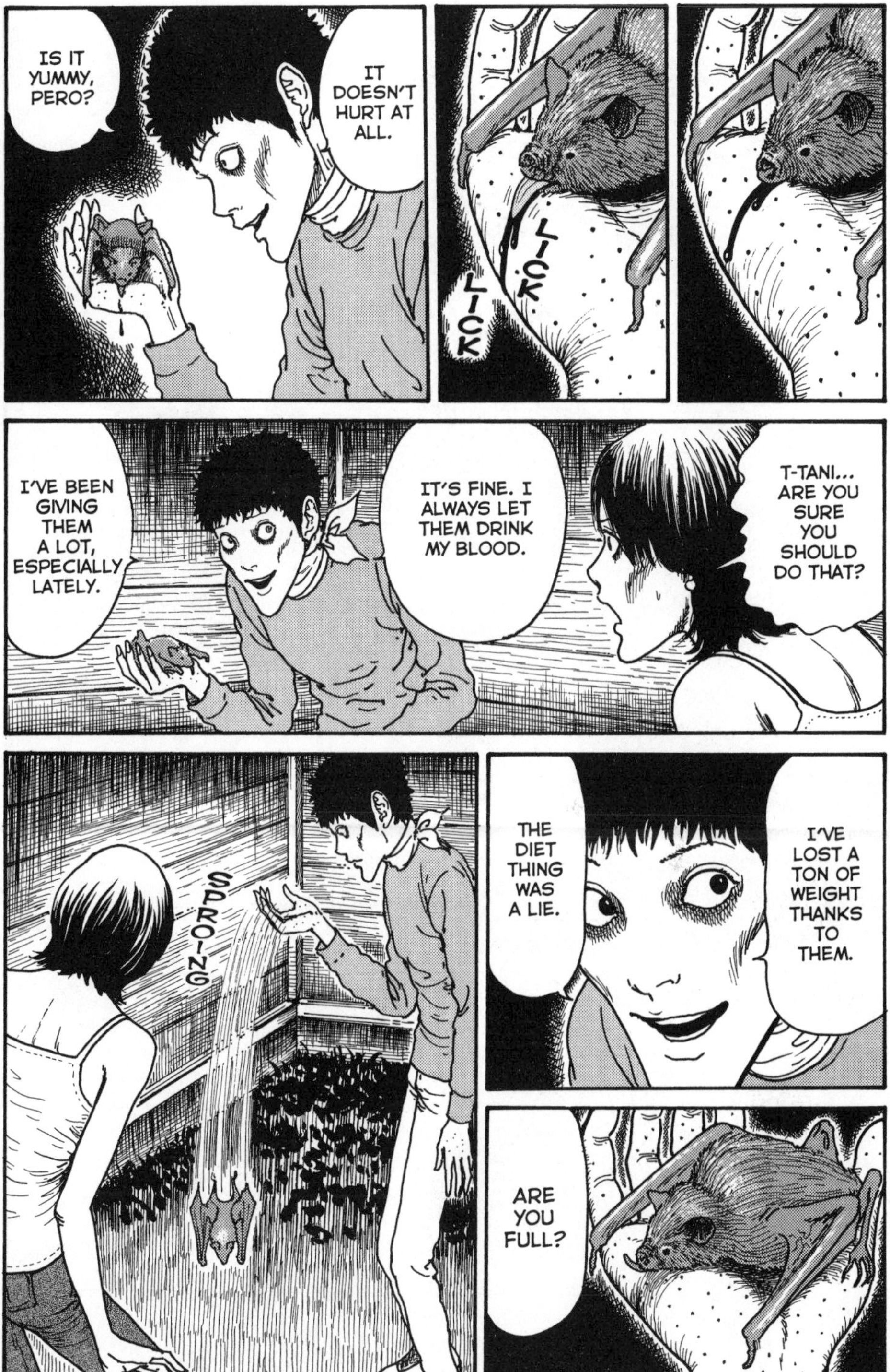
LICK
LICK
IT DOESN'T HURT AT ALL.
IS IT YUMMY, PERO?
T-TANI... ARE YOU SURE YOU SHOULD DO THAT?
IT'S FINE. I ALWAYS LET THEM DRINK MY BLOOD.
I'VE BEEN GIVING THEM A LOT, ESPECIALLY LATELY.
I'VE LOST A TON OF WEIGHT THANKS TO THEM.
THE DIET THING WAS A LIE.
ARE YOU FULL?
SPROING

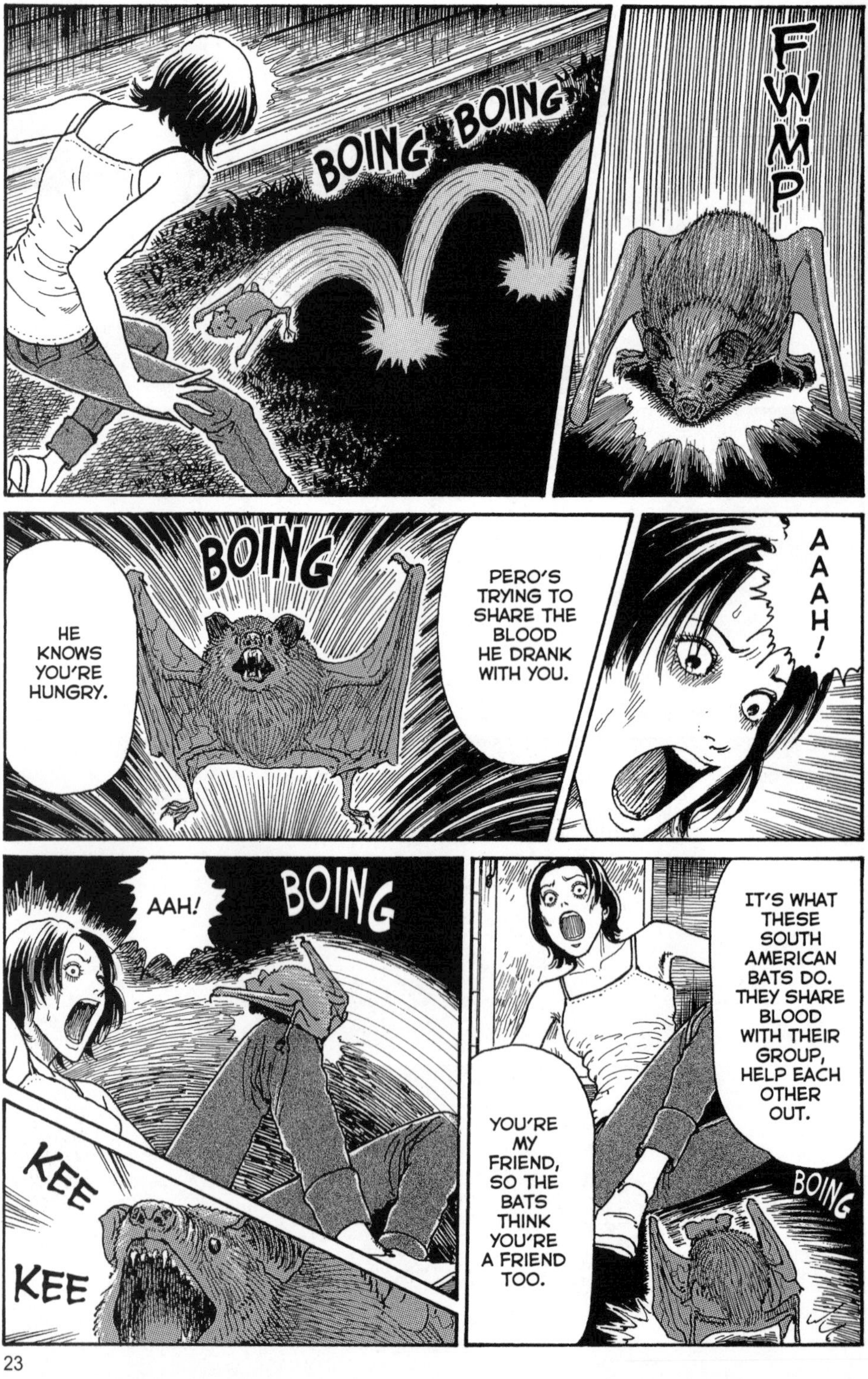
FWMP
BOING BOING
AAAAH!
PERO'S TRYING TO SHARE THE BLOOD HE DRANK WITH YOU.
BOING
HE KNOWS YOU'RE HUNGRY.
IT'S WHAT THESE SOUTH AMERICAN BATS DO. THEY SHARE BLOOD WITH THEIR GROUP, HELP EACH OTHER OUT.
YOU'RE MY FRIEND, SO THE BATS THINK YOU'RE A FRIEND TOO.
BOING
BOING
AAH!
KEE
KEE

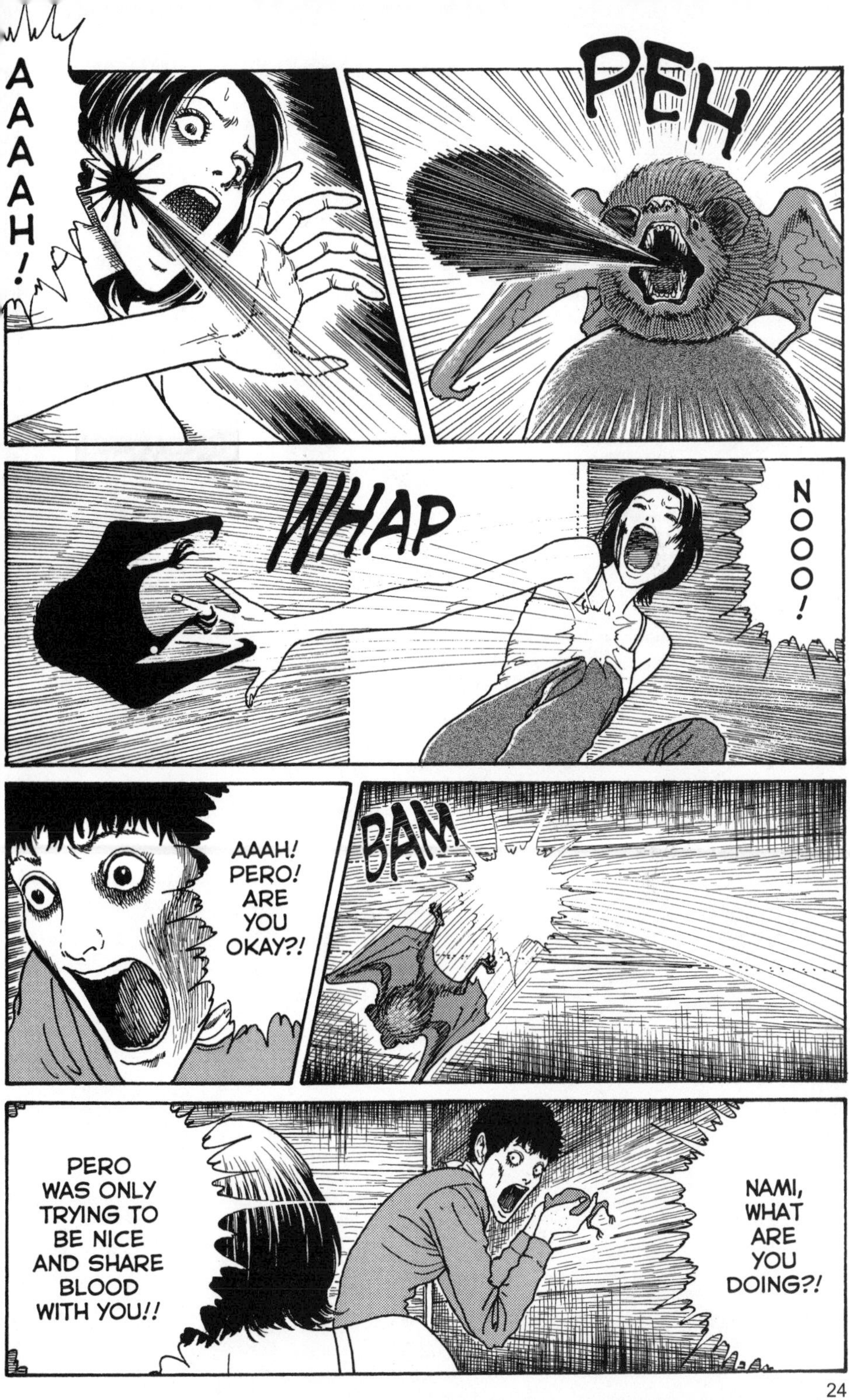
PEH
AAAAAH!
NOOO!
WHAP
BAM
AAAH! PERO! ARE YOU OKAY?!
NAMI, WHAT ARE YOU DOING?!
PERO WAS ONLY TRYING TO BE NICE AND SHARE BLOOD WITH YOU!!

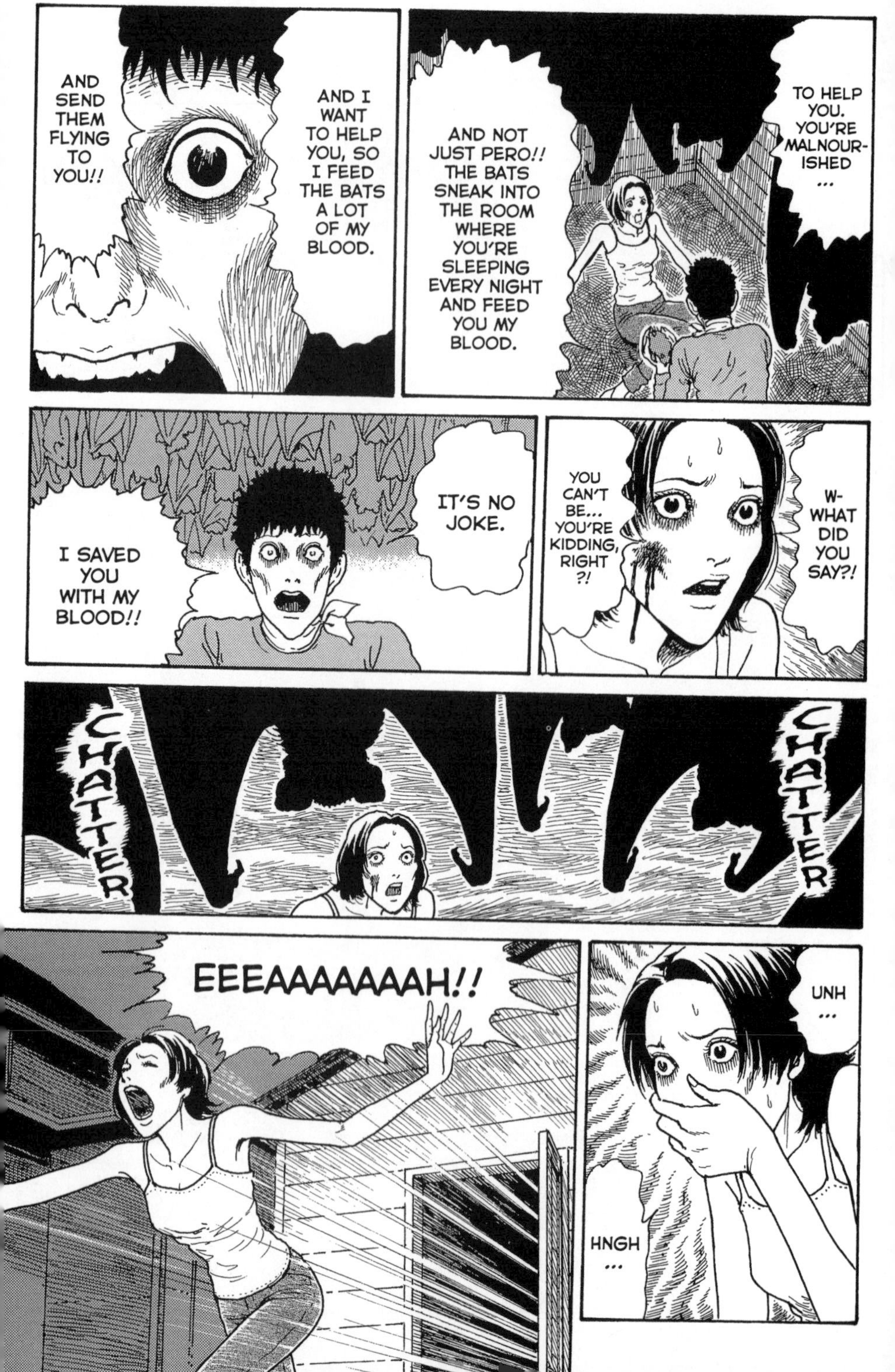
TO HELP YOU. YOU'RE MALNOURISHED...
AND NOT JUST PERO!! THE BATS SNEAK INTO THE ROOM WHERE YOU'RE SLEEPING EVERY NIGHT AND FEED YOU MY BLOOD.
AND I WANT TO HELP YOU, SO I FEED THE BATS A LOT OF MY BLOOD.
AND SEND THEM FLYING TO YOU!!
W-WHAT DID YOU SAY?!
YOU CAN'T BE... YOU'RE KIDDING, RIGHT?!
IT'S NO JOKE.
I SAVED YOU WITH MY BLOOD!!
CHATTER
CHATTER
UNH...
HNGH...
EEEAAAAAAAAH!!

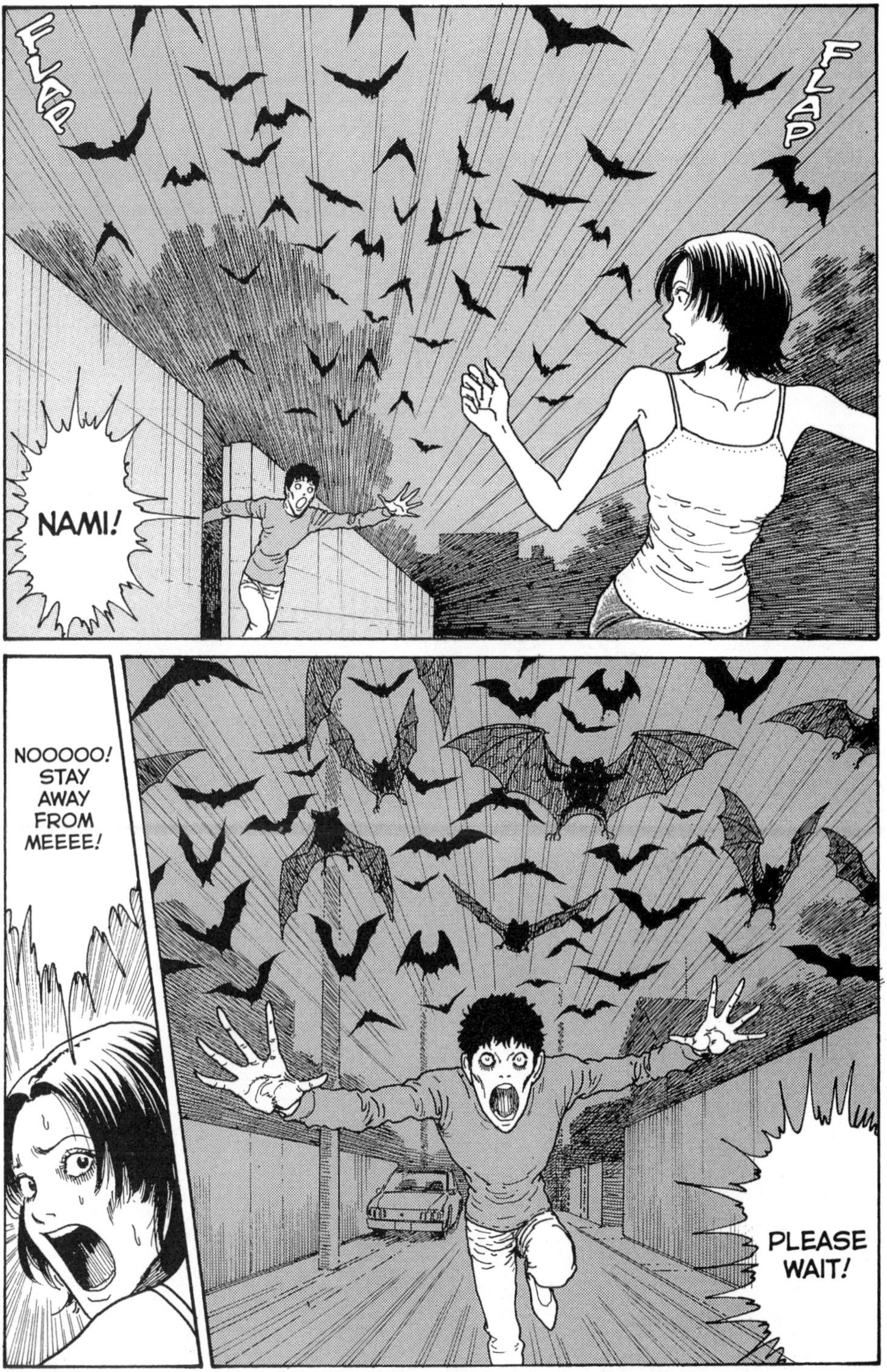
FLAP
FLAP
NAMI!
PLEASE WAIT!
NOOOOO! STAY AWAY FROM MEEEE!

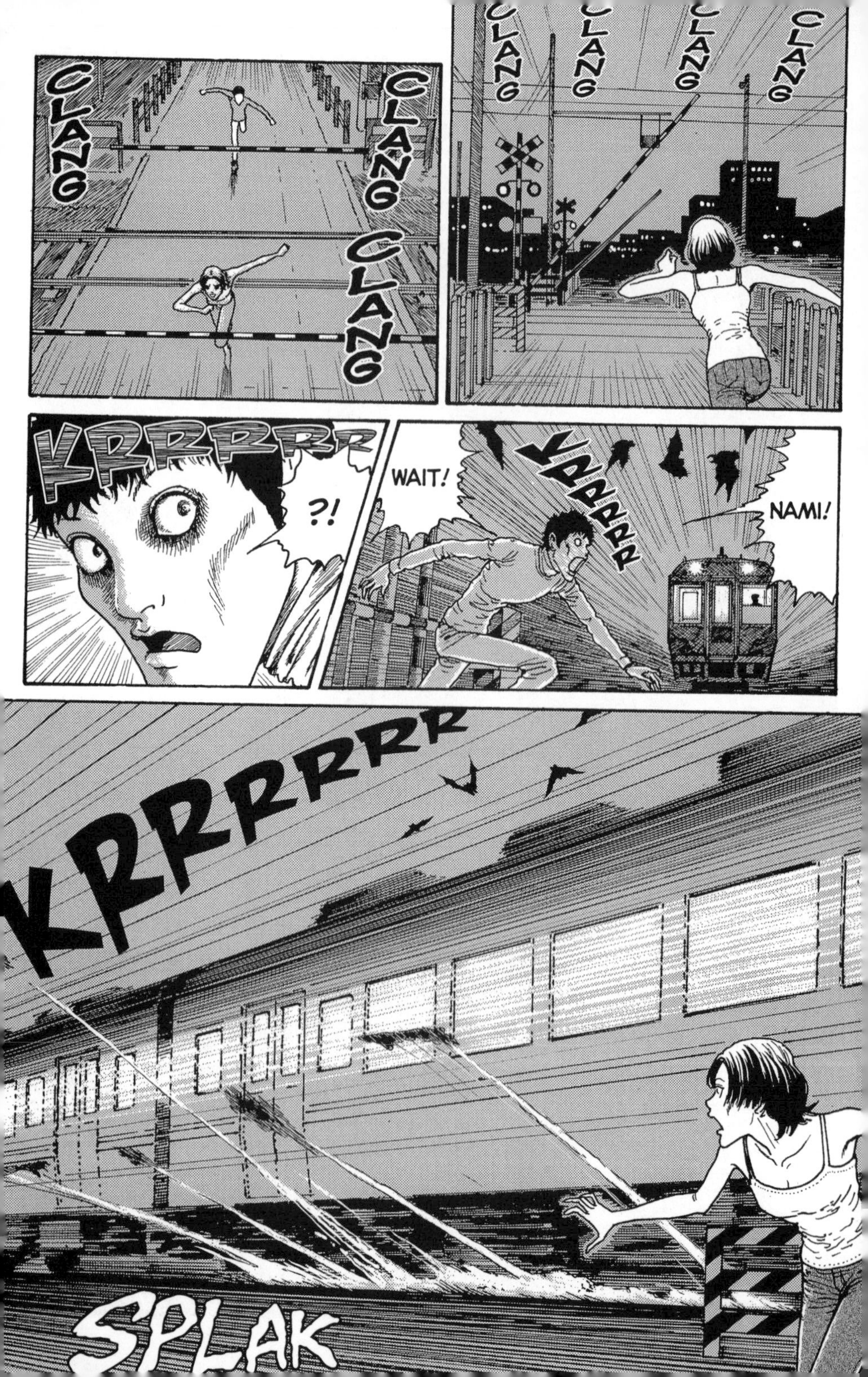
CLANG
CLANG
CLANG
CLANG
CLANG
CLANG
CLANG
NAMI!
KRRRRRR
WAIT!
KRRRRRR
?!
KRRRRRR
SPLAK

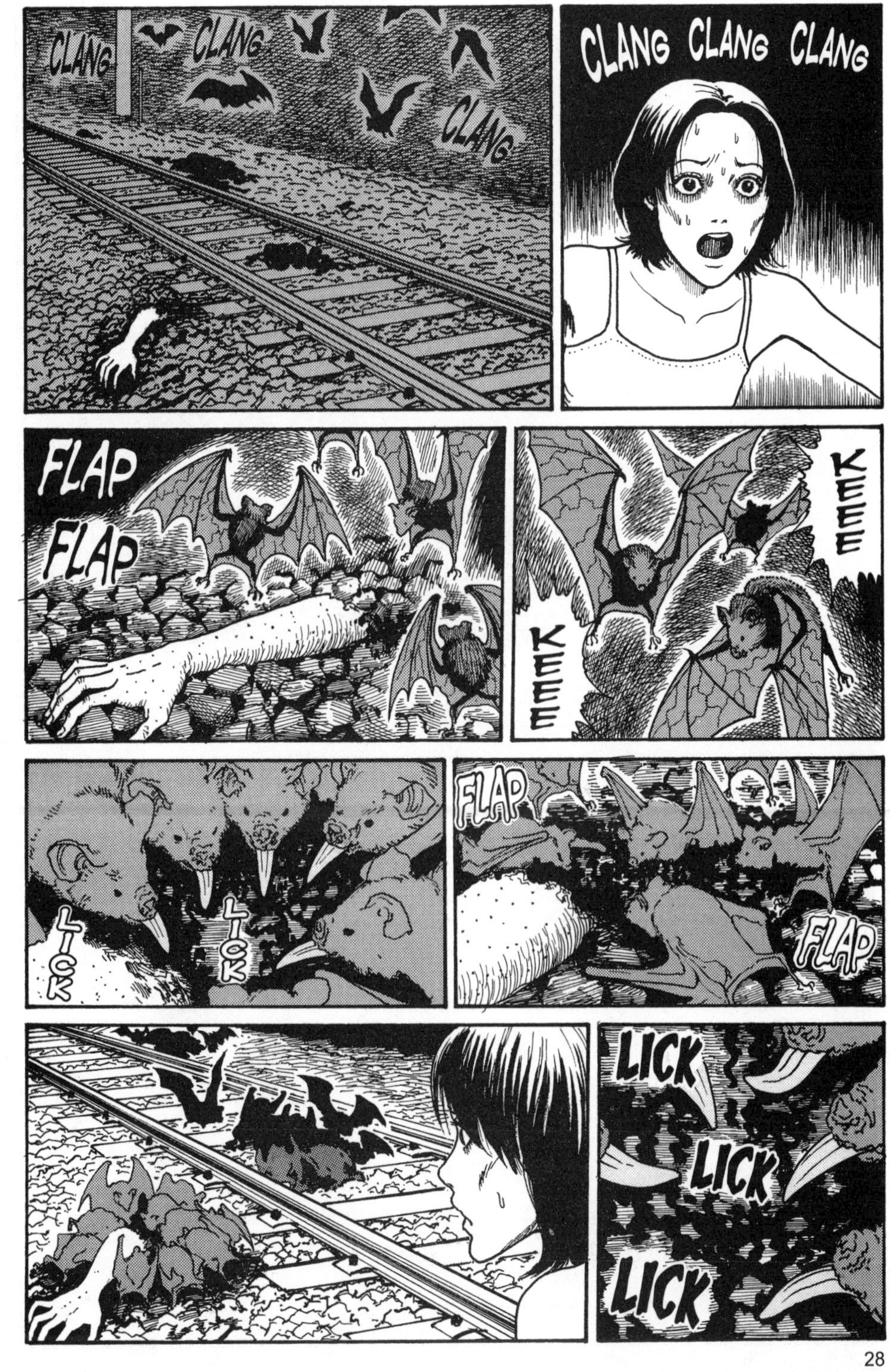
CLANG CLANG CLANG
CLANG
CLANG
CLANG
KEEE
KEEE
FLAP
FLAP
FLAP
FLAP
LICK
LICK
LICK
LICK
LICK

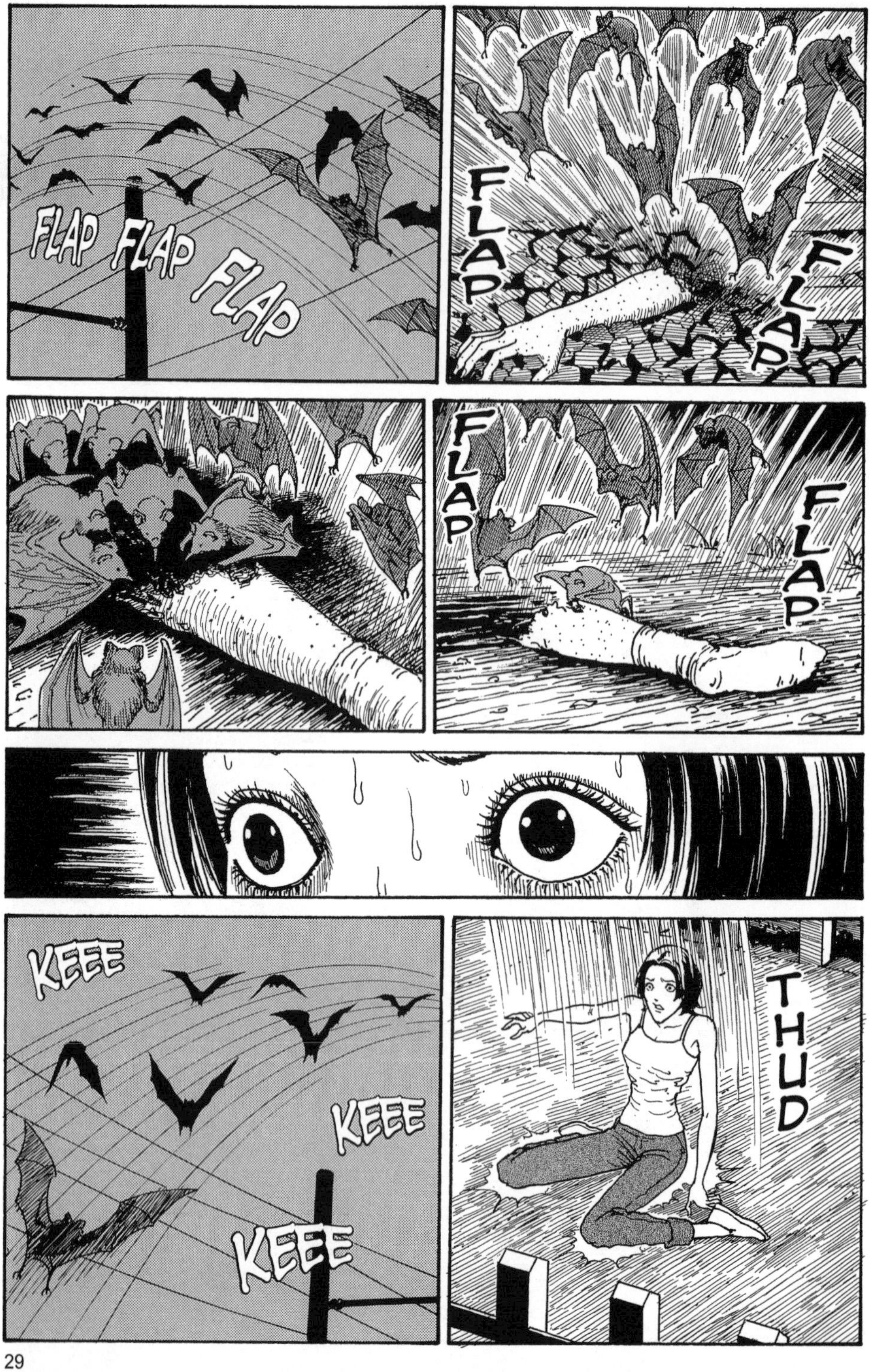
FLAP
FLAP
FLAP
FLAP
FLAP
FLAP
FLAP
FLAP
FLAP
THUD
KEEE
KEEE
KEEE

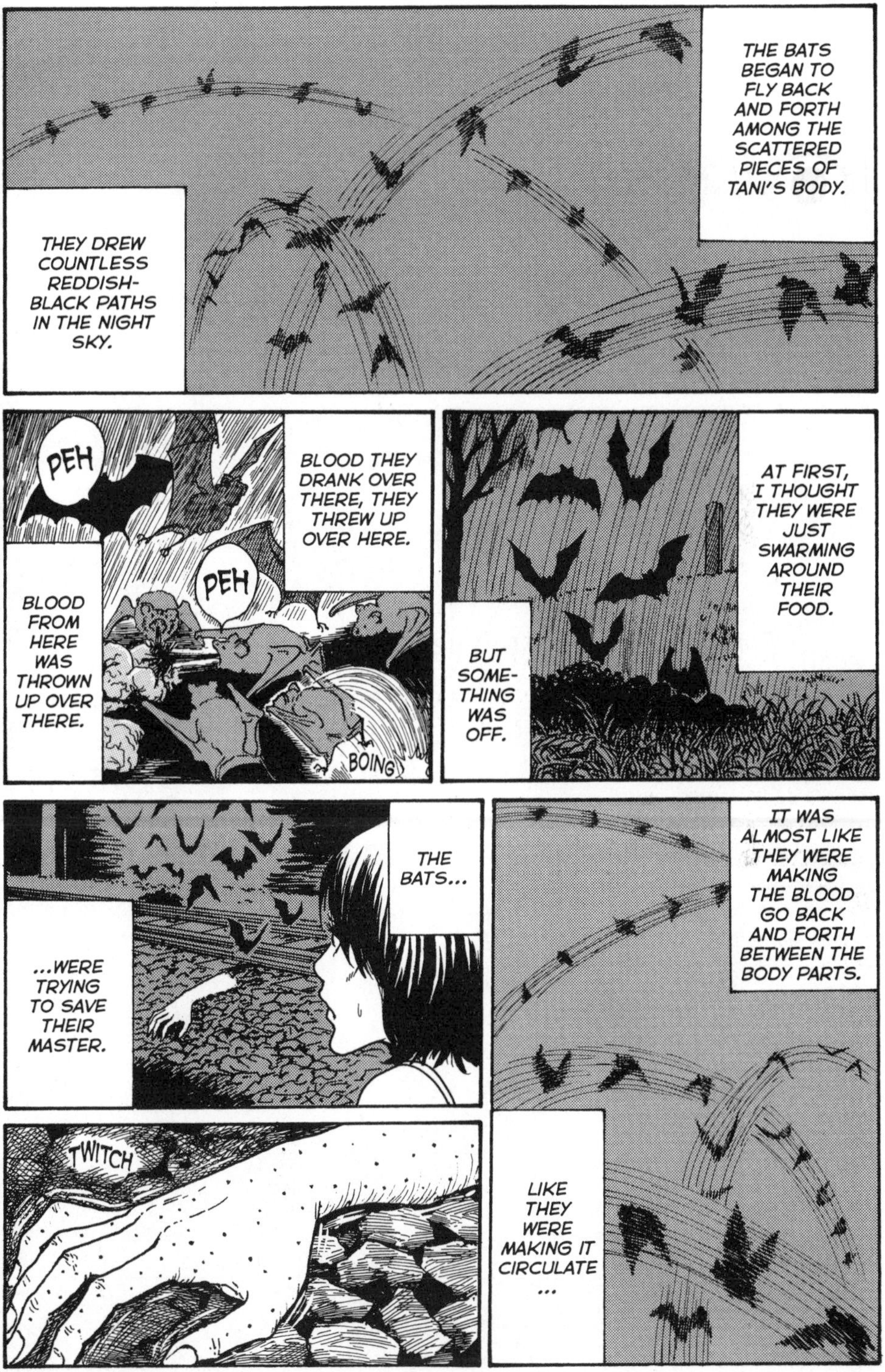
THE BATS BEGAN TO FLY BACK AND FORTH AMONG THE SCATTERED PIECES OF TANI'S BODY.
THEY DREW COUNTLESS REDDISH-BLACK PATHS IN THE NIGHT SKY.
AT FIRST, I THOUGHT THEY WERE JUST SWARMING AROUND THEIR FOOD.
BUT SOME-THING WAS OFF.
BLOOD THEY DRANK OVER THERE, THEY THREW UP OVER HERE.
PEH
PEH
BLOOD FROM HERE WAS THROWN UP OVER THERE.
BOING
IT WAS ALMOST LIKE THEY WERE MAKING THE BLOOD GO BACK AND FORTH BETWEEN THE BODY PARTS.
LIKE THEY WERE MAKING IT CIRCULATE ...
THE BATS...
...WERE TRYING TO SAVE THEIR MASTER.
TWITCH

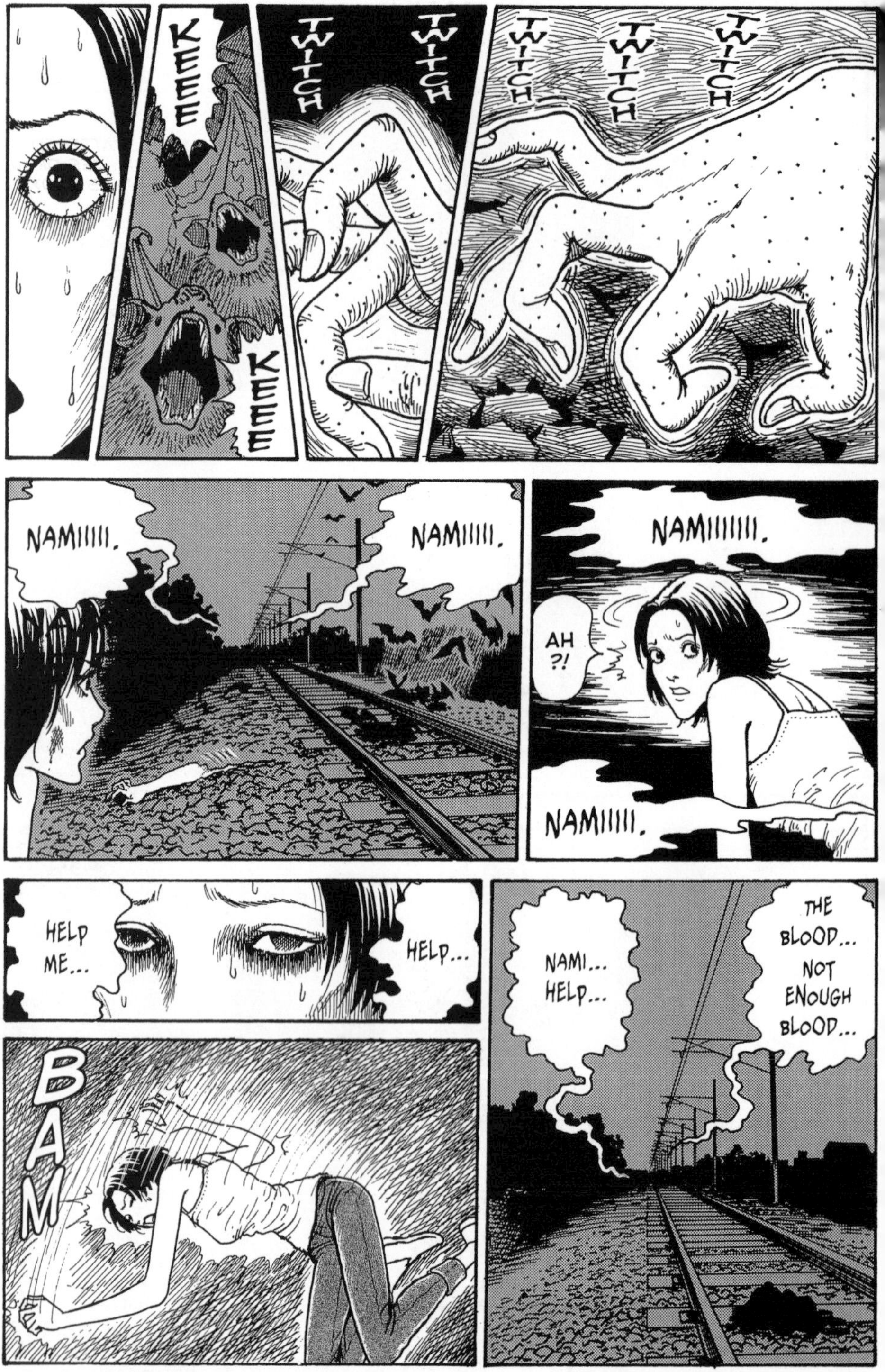
TWITCH
TWITCH
TWITCH
TWITCH
TWITCH
KEEE
KEEE
NAMIIIIIII.
AH ?!
NAMIIIII.
NAMIIIII.
NAMIIIII.
THE BLOOD... NOT ENOUGH BLOOD...
NAMI... HELP...
HELP...
HELP ME...
BAM

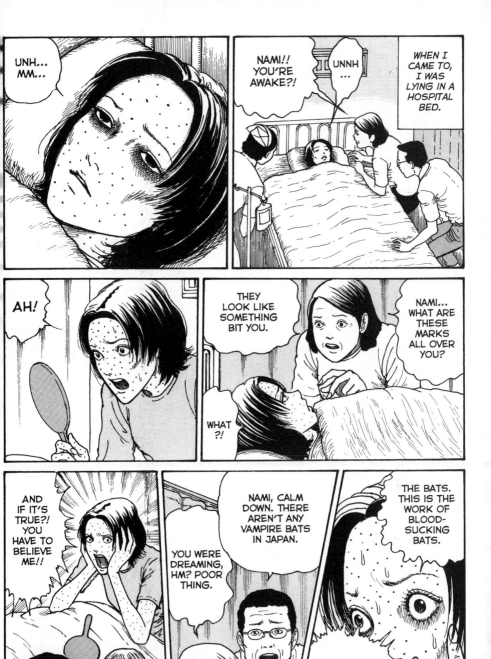

WHEN I CAME TO, I WAS LYING IN A HOSPITAL BED.
UNNH ...
NAMI!! YOU'RE AWAKE?!
UNH... MM...
NAMI... WHAT ARE THESE MARKS ALL OVER YOU?
THEY LOOK LIKE SOMETHING BIT YOU.
WHAT ?!
AH!
THE BATS. THIS IS THE WORK OF BLOOD-SUCKING BATS.
THE VAMPIRE BATS WERE DRINKING MY BLOOD!!
NAMI, CALM DOWN. THERE AREN'T ANY VAMPIRE BATS IN JAPAN.
YOU WERE DREAMING, HM? POOR THING.
AND IF IT'S TRUE?! YOU HAVE TO BELIEVE ME!!

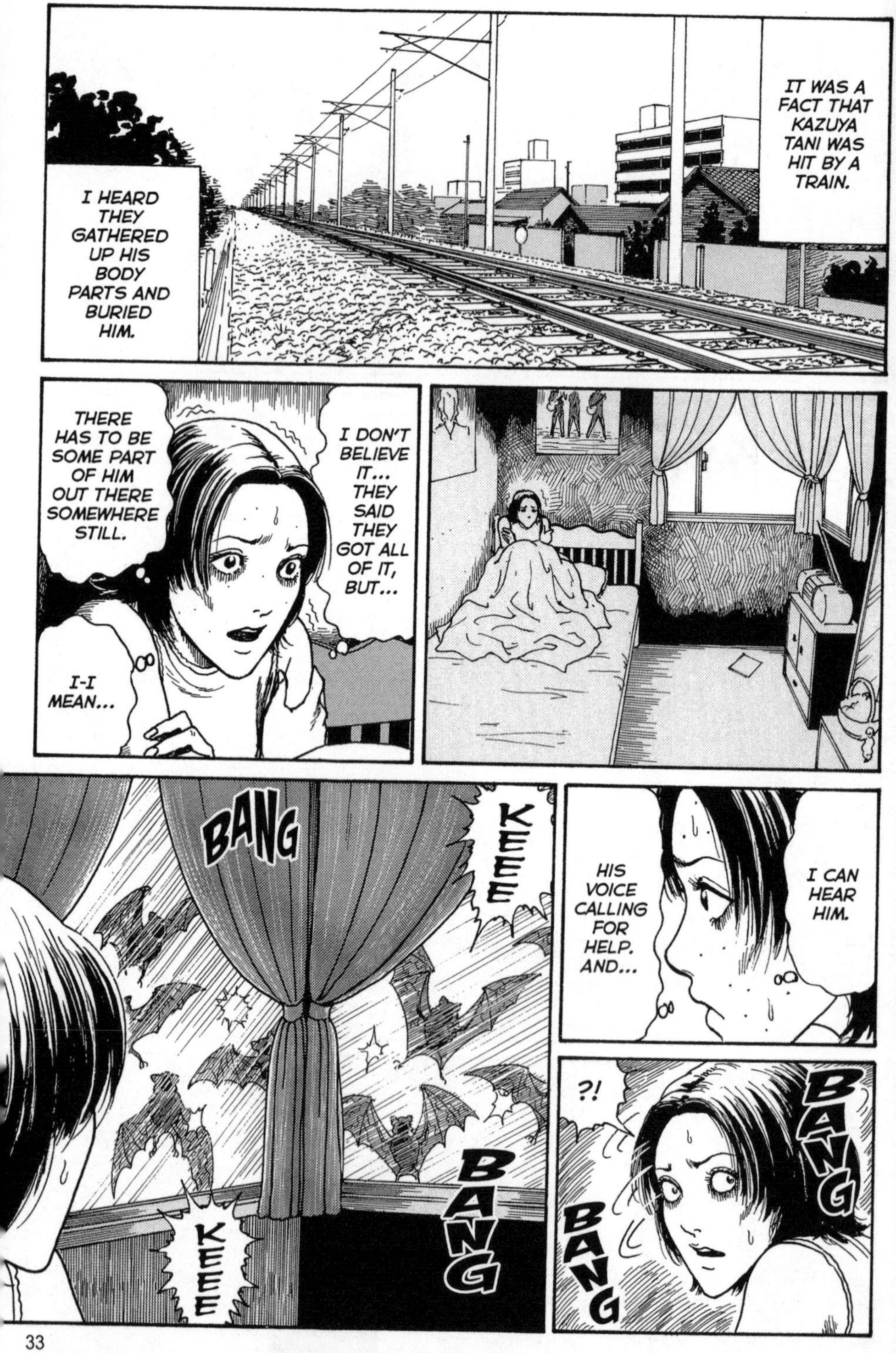
IT WAS A FACT THAT KAZUYA TANI WAS HIT BY A TRAIN.
I HEARD THEY GATHERED UP HIS BODY PARTS AND BURIED HIM.
I DON'T BELIEVE IT... THEY SAID THEY GOT ALL OF IT, BUT...
THERE HAS TO BE SOME PART OF HIM OUT THERE SOMEWHERE STILL.
I-I MEAN...
I CAN HEAR HIM.
HIS VOICE CALLING FOR HELP. AND...
BANG
?!
BANG
KEEE
BANG
BANG
KEEE

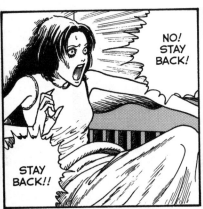

NO! STAY BACK!

STAY BACK!!

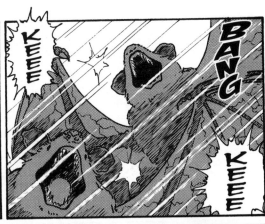

KEEE

BANG

KEEE

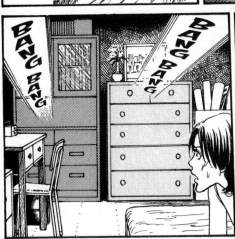

BANG BANG

BANG BANG

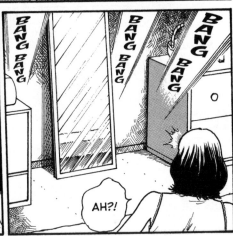

BANG BANG

BANG BANG

AH?!

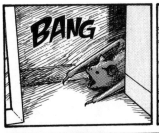

BANG

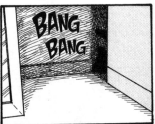

BANG BANG

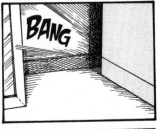

BANG

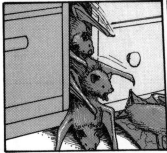

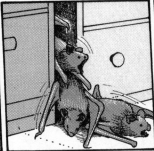

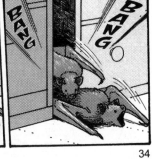

BANG

BANG

34

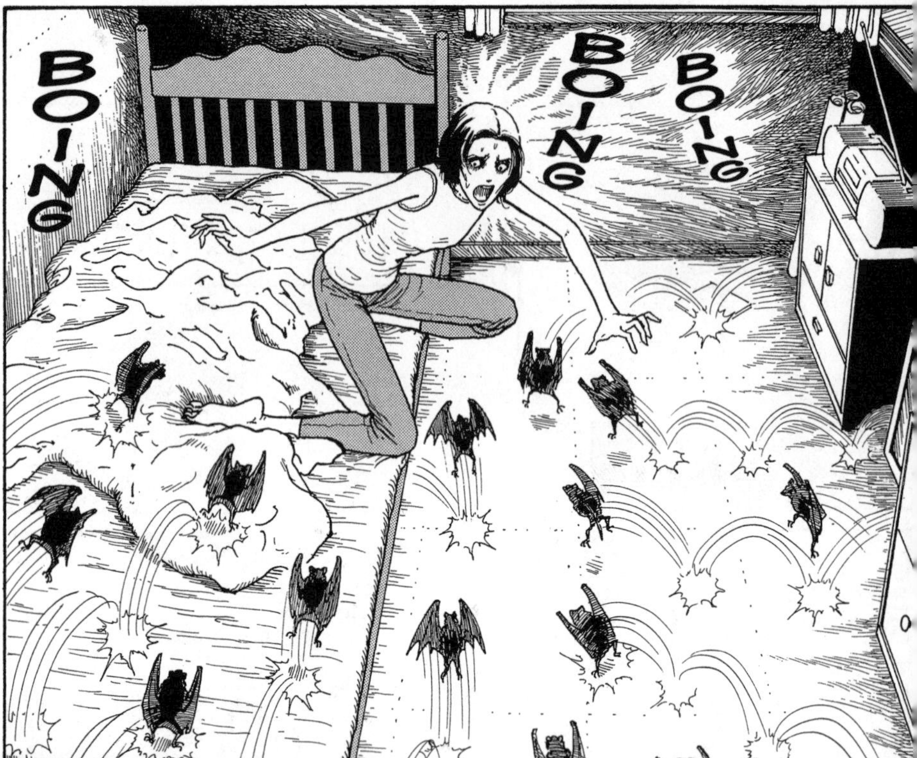
BOING
BOING
BOING

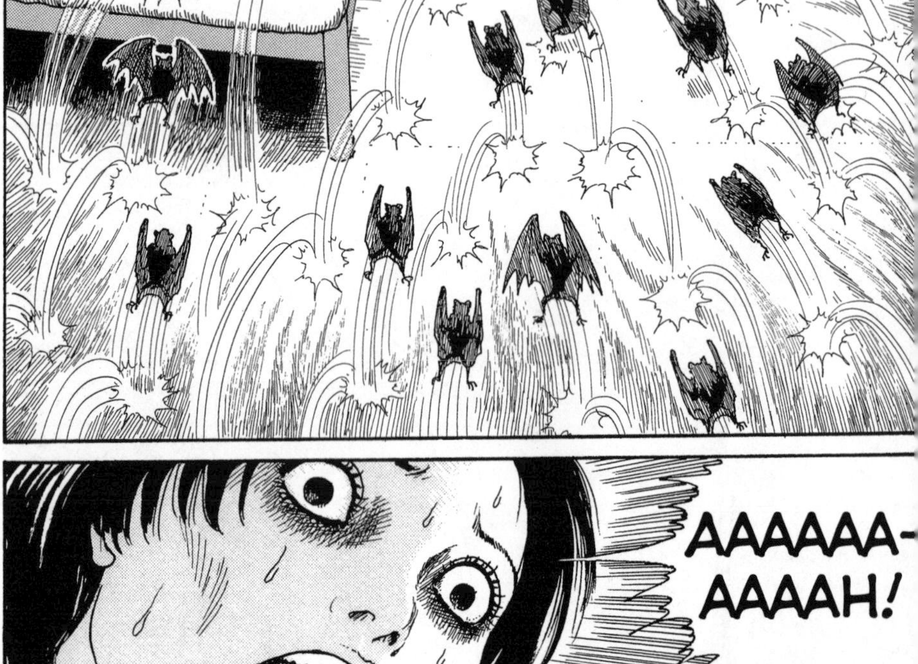
AAAAAA-
AAAAH!

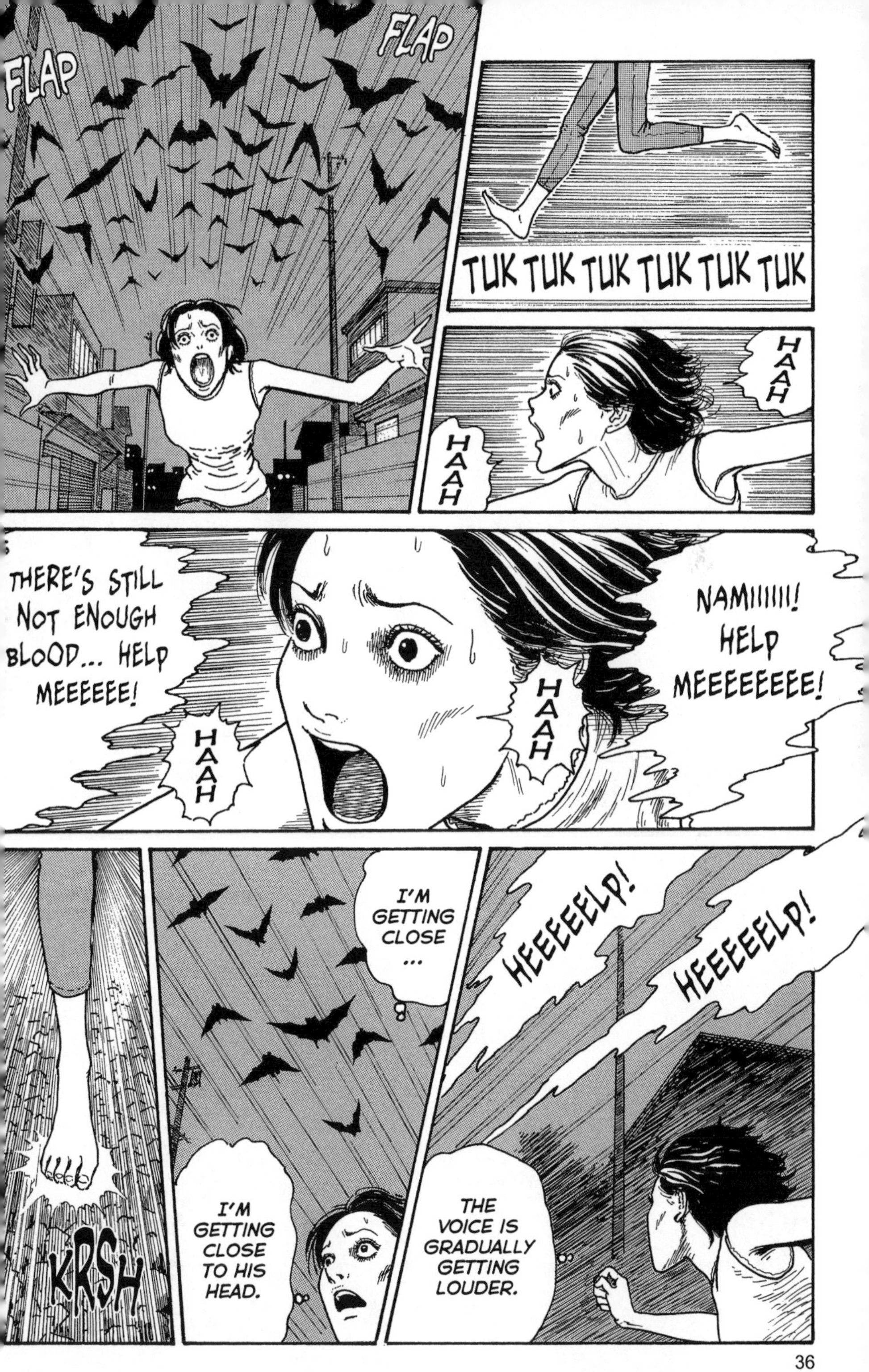
TUK TUK TUK TUK TUK TUK
HAAH
HAAH
FLAP
FLAP
NAMIIIIII! HELP MEEEEEEEE!
HAAH
THERE'S STILL NOT ENOUGH BLOOD... HELP MEEEEEE!
HAAH
HEEEEELP!
HEEEEELP!
THE VOICE IS GRADUALLY GETTING LOUDER.
I'M GETTING CLOSE ...
I'M GETTING CLOSE TO HIS HEAD.
KRSH

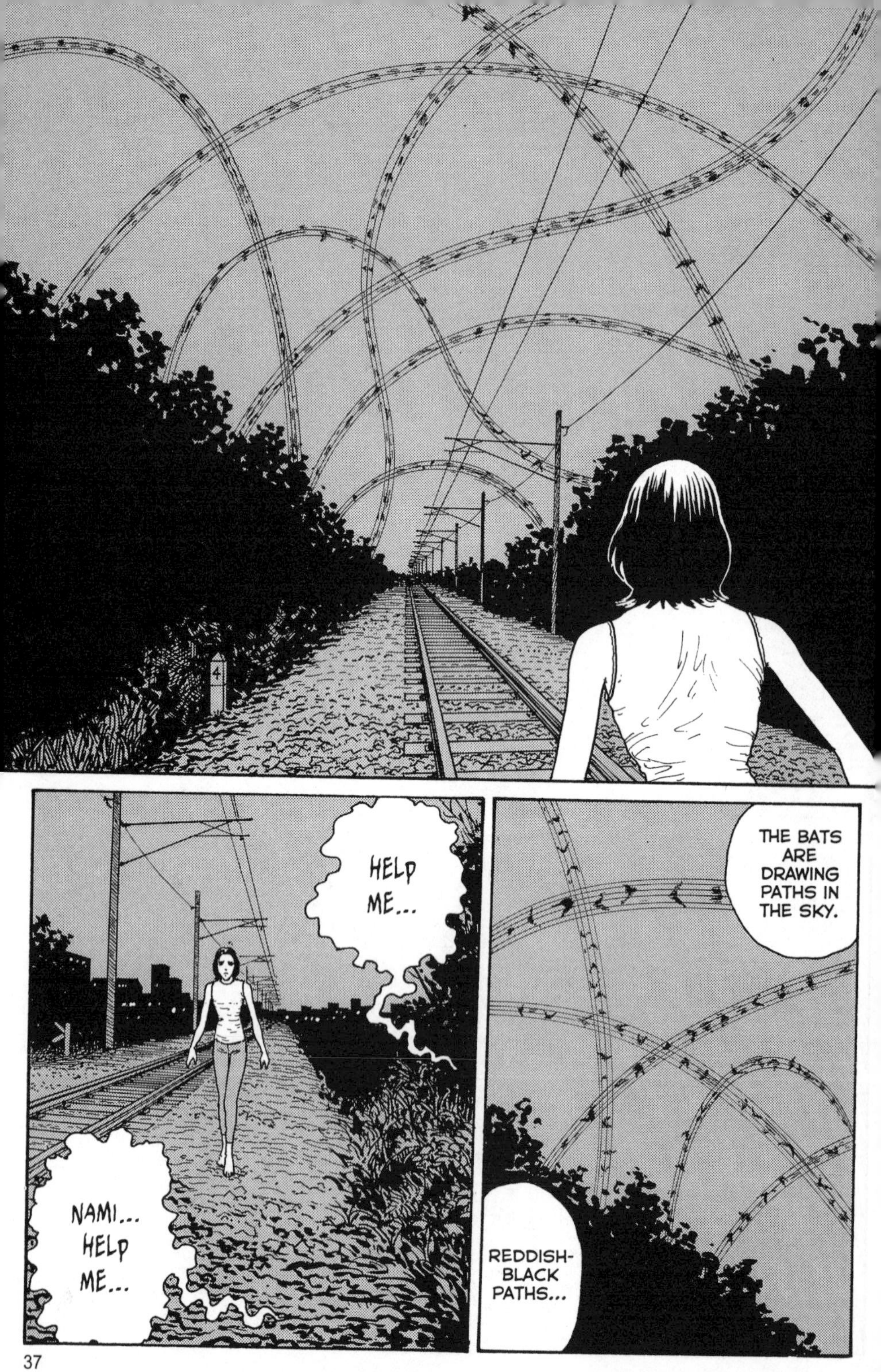
THE BATS ARE DRAWING PATHS IN THE SKY.
REDDISH-BLACK PATHS...
HELP ME...
NAMI... HELP ME...

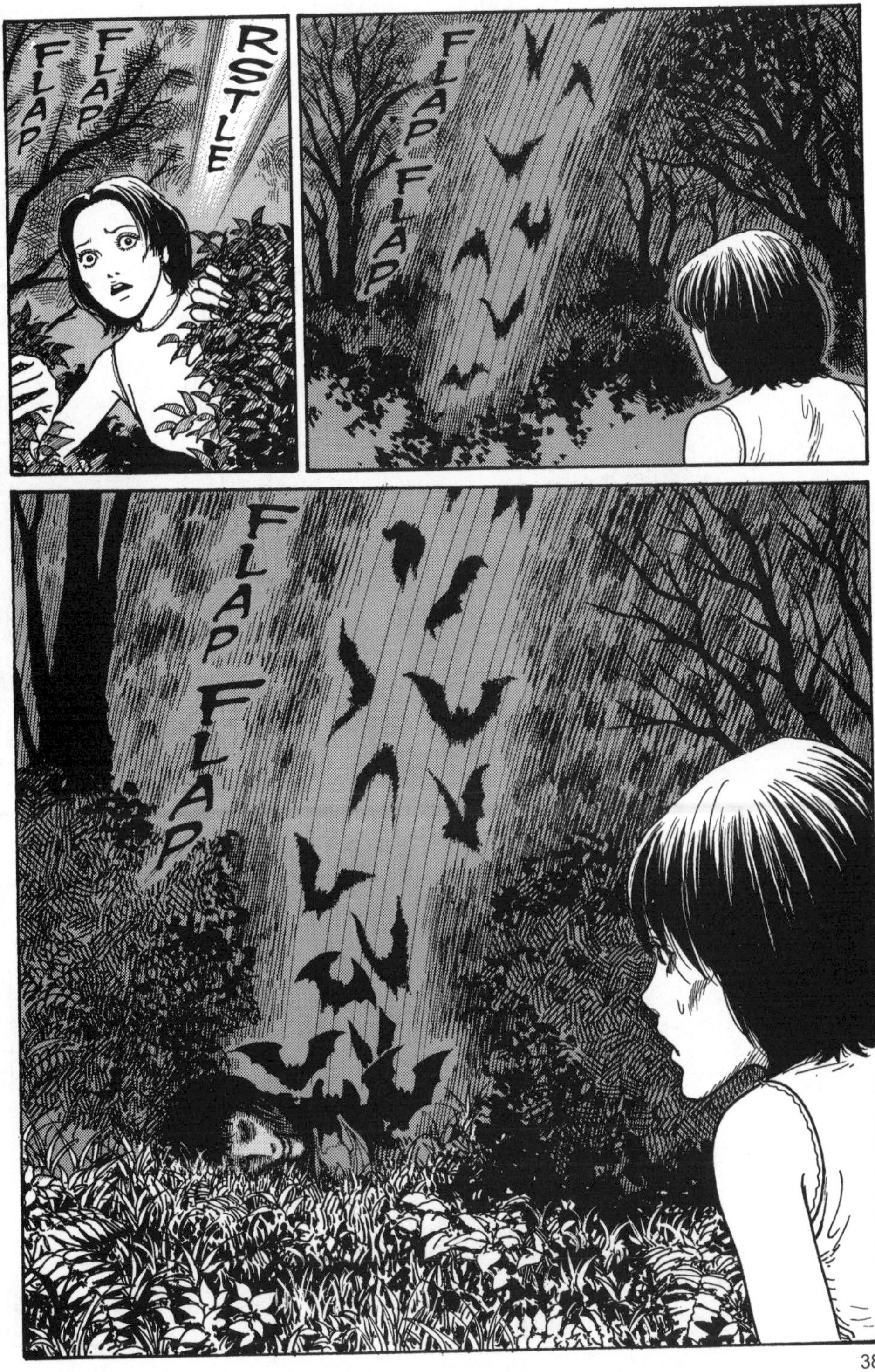
FLAP FLAP
RSTLE
FLAP FLAP
FLAP FLAP

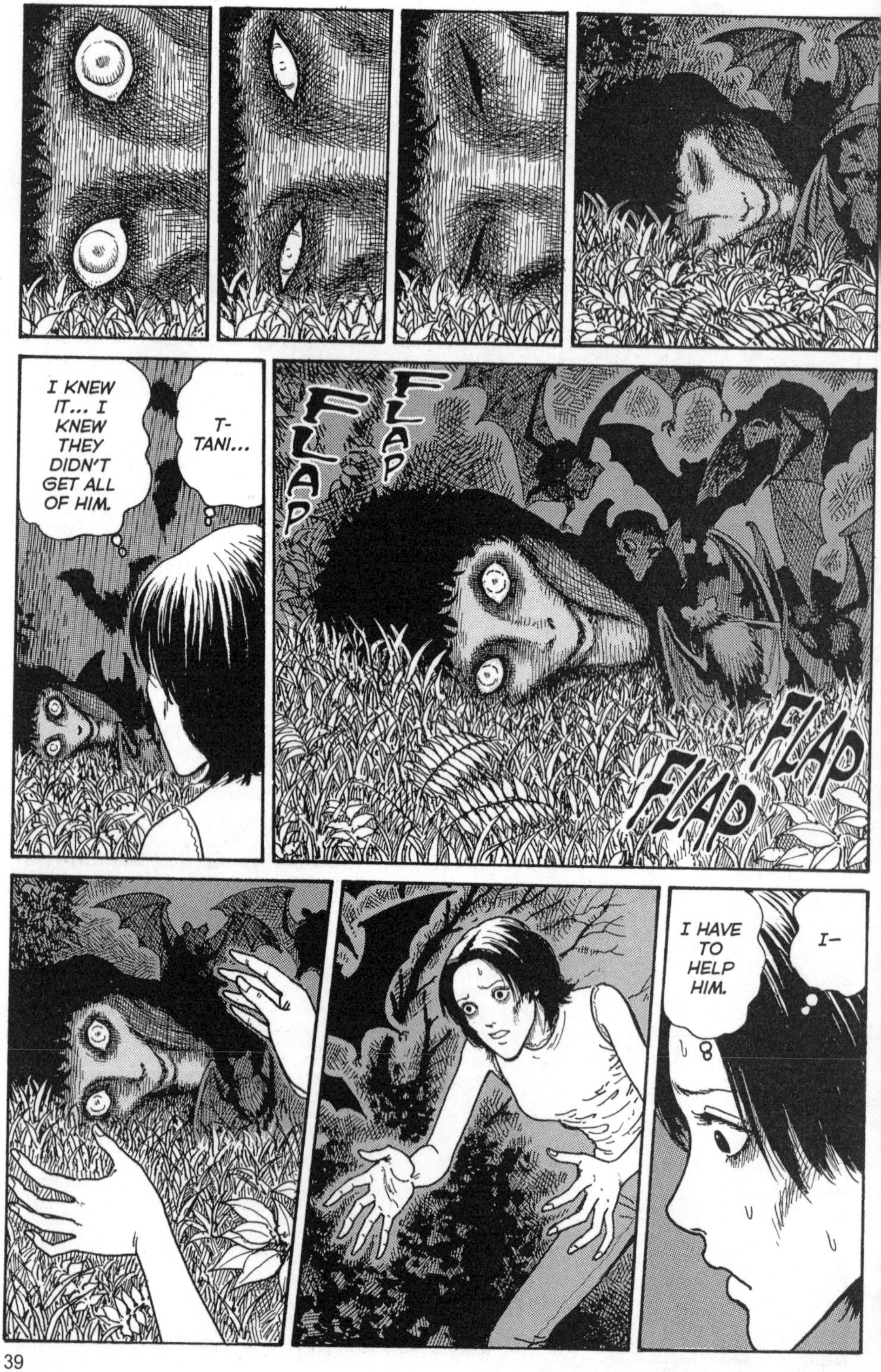
FLAP FLAP
FLAP FLAP
T-TANI...
I KNEW IT... I KNEW THEY DIDN'T GET ALL OF HIM.
I-
I HAVE TO HELP HIM.

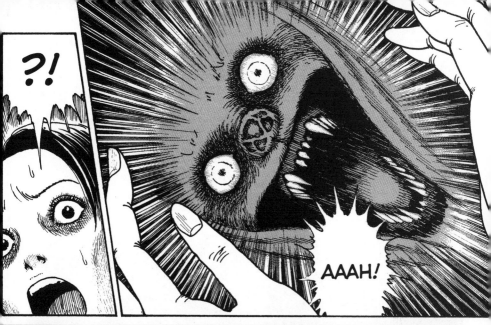

?!

AAAH!

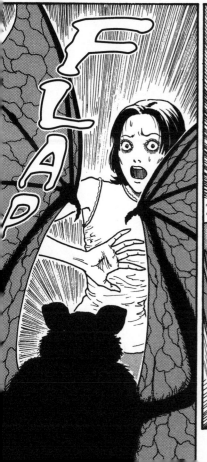

FLAP

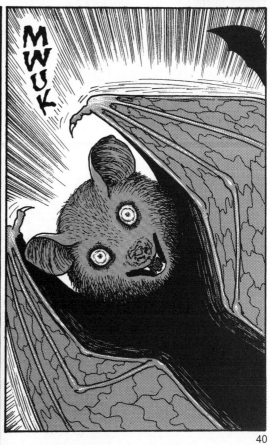

MWUK

40

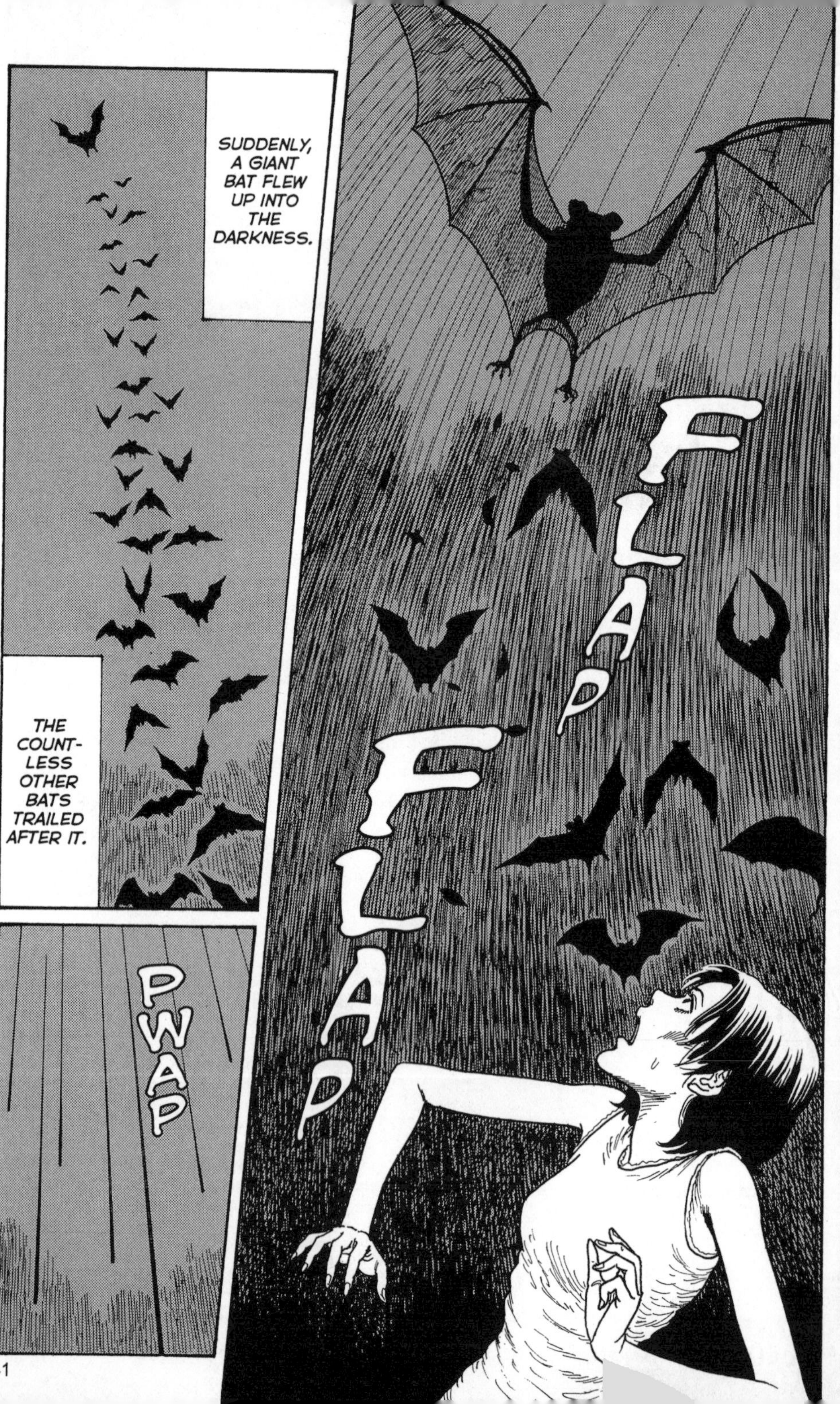
FLAP
FLAP
SUDDENLY, A GIANT BAT FLEW UP INTO THE DARKNESS.
THE COUNT-LESS OTHER BATS TRAILED AFTER IT.
PWAP

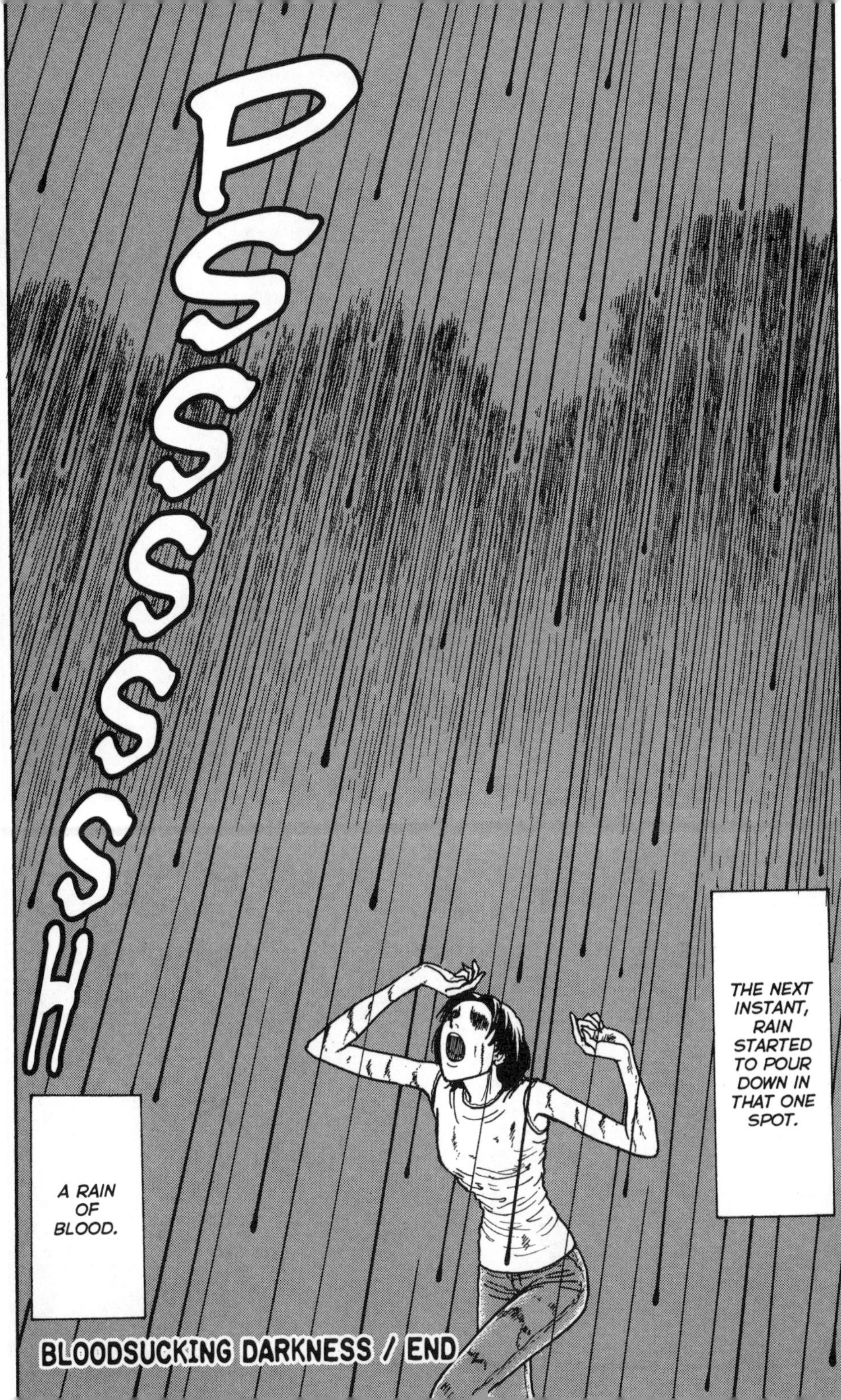
PSSSSSSH
THE NEXT INSTANT, RAIN STARTED TO POUR DOWN IN THAT ONE SPOT.
A RAIN OF BLOOD.
BLOODSUCKING DARKNESS / END

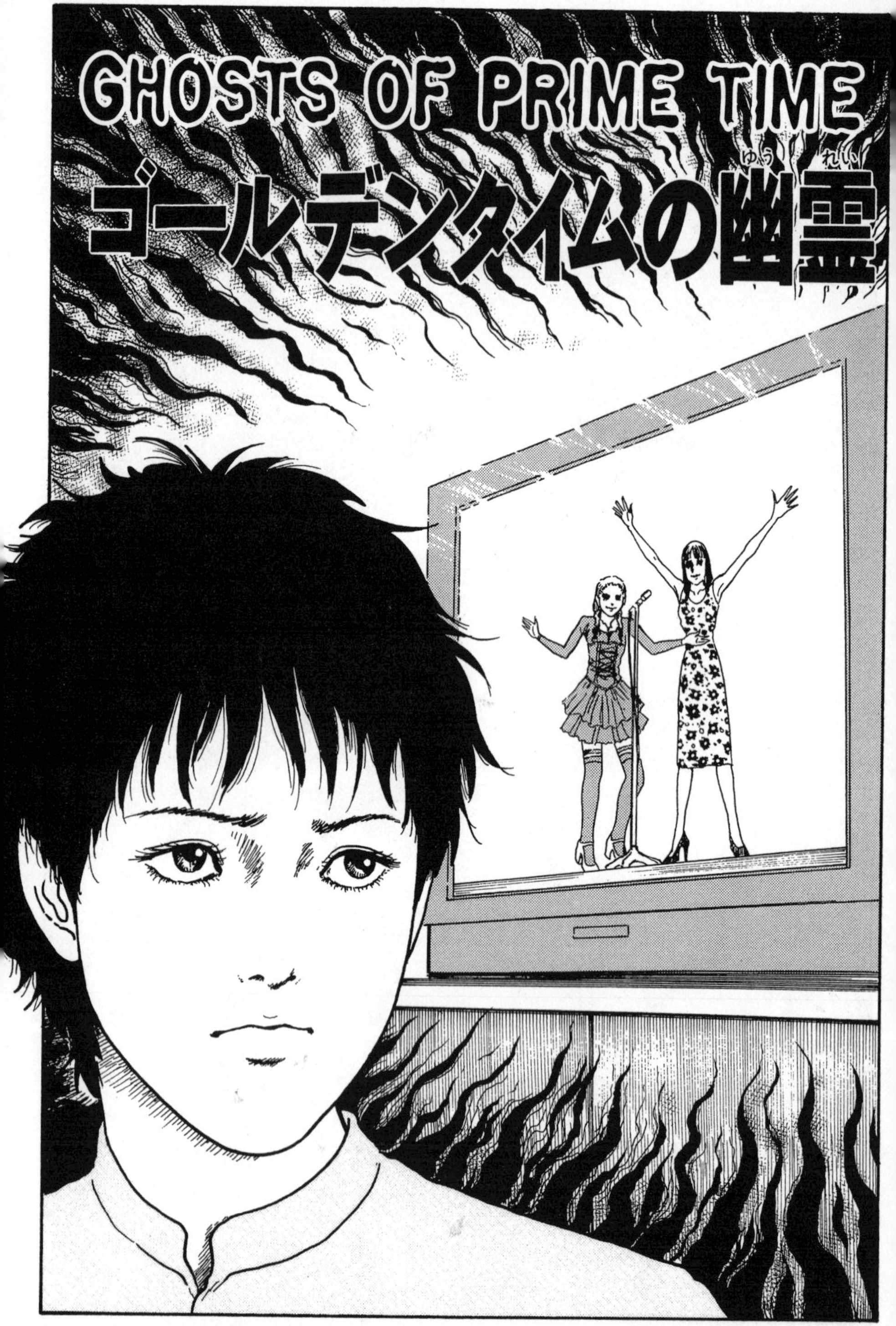
GHOSTS OF PRIME TIME
ゴールデンタイムの幽霊(ゆうれい)

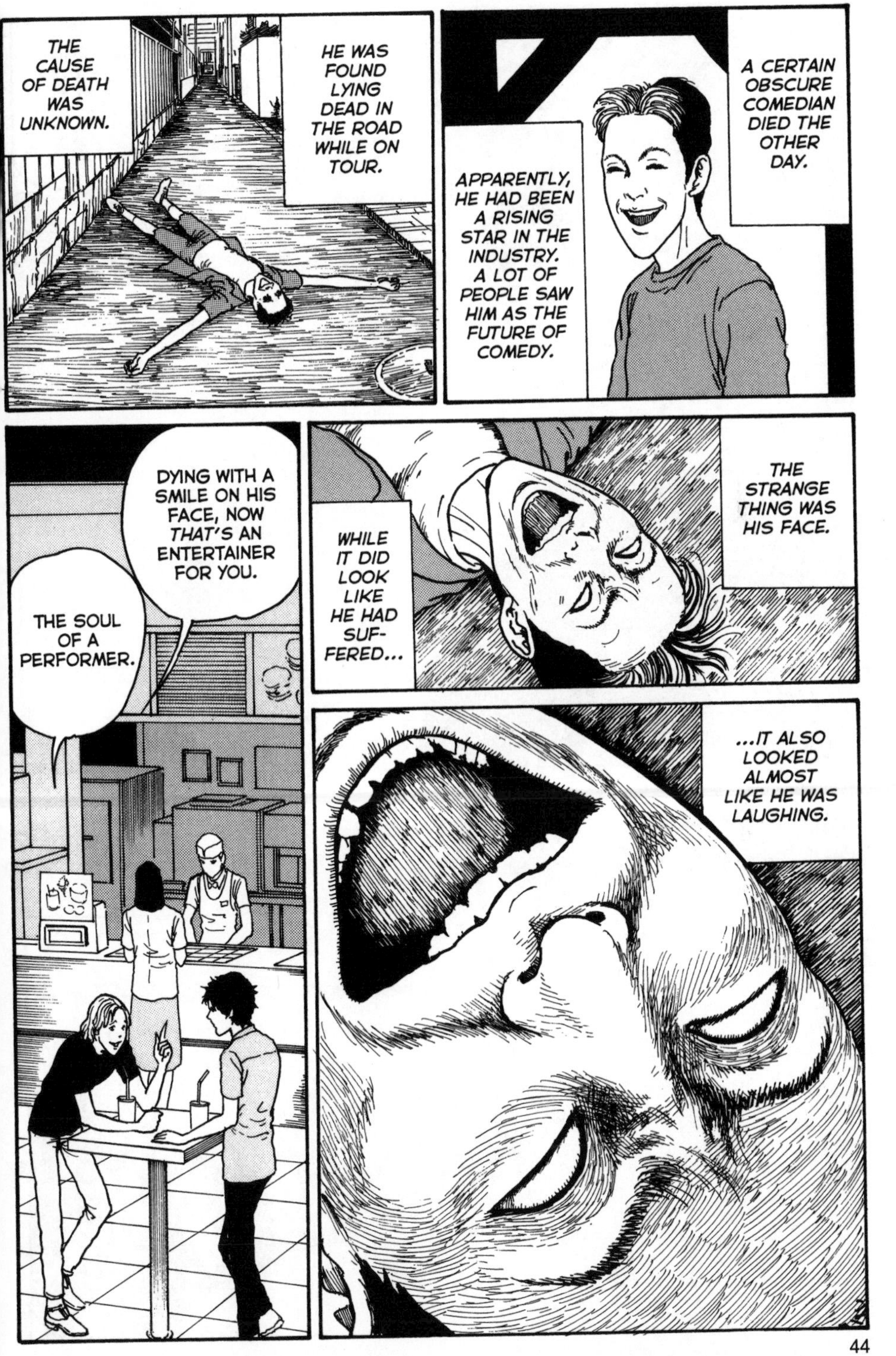
A CERTAIN OBSCURE COMEDIAN DIED THE OTHER DAY.
APPARENTLY, HE HAD BEEN A RISING STAR IN THE INDUSTRY. A LOT OF PEOPLE SAW HIM AS THE FUTURE OF COMEDY.
HE WAS FOUND LYING DEAD IN THE ROAD WHILE ON TOUR.
THE CAUSE OF DEATH WAS UNKNOWN.
THE STRANGE THING WAS HIS FACE.
WHILE IT DID LOOK LIKE HE HAD SUF-FERED...
...IT ALSO LOOKED ALMOST LIKE HE WAS LAUGHING.
DYING WITH A SMILE ON HIS FACE, NOW *THAT'S* AN ENTERTAINER FOR YOU.
THE SOUL OF A PERFORMER.

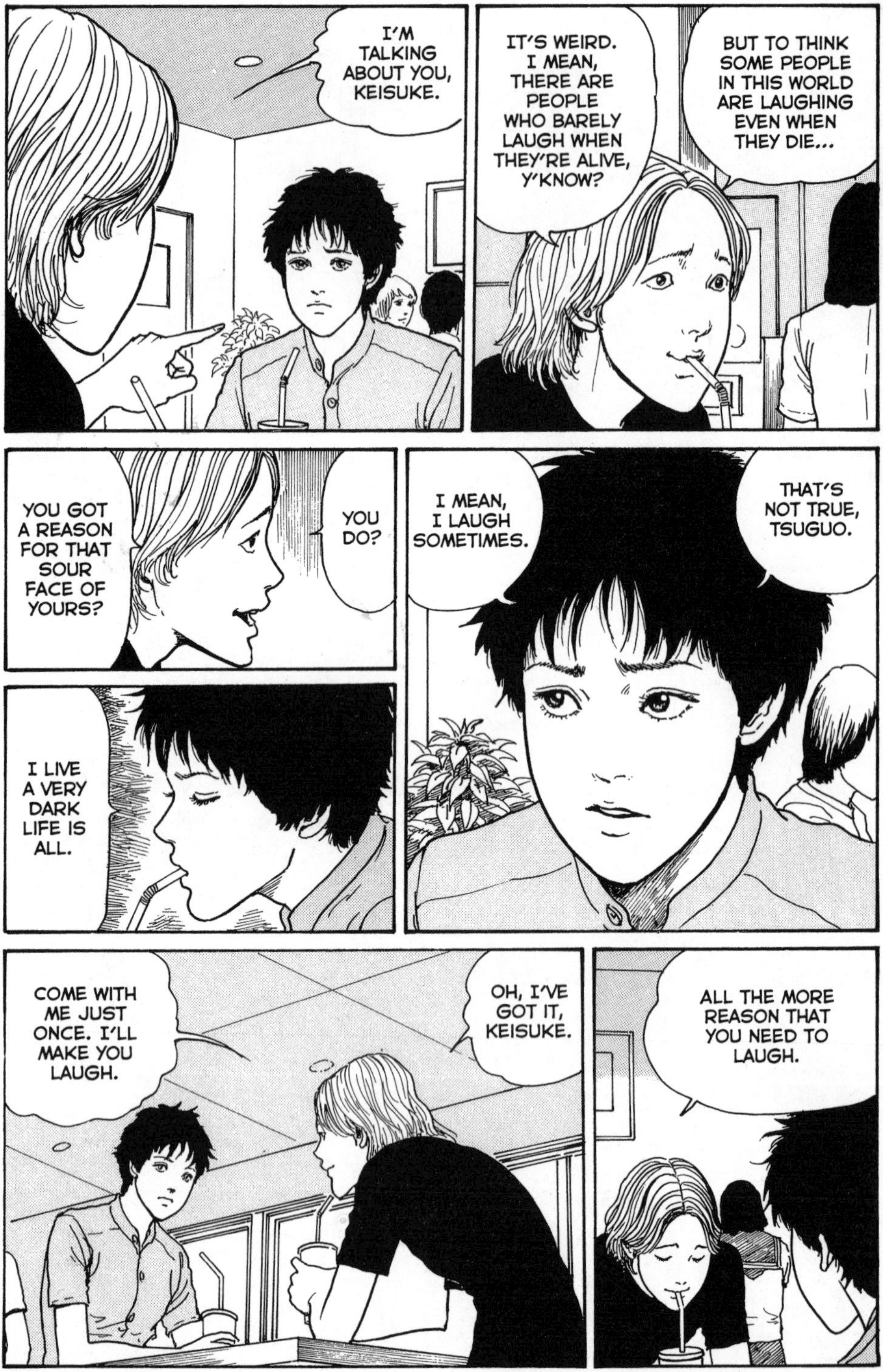
BUT TO THINK SOME PEOPLE IN THIS WORLD ARE LAUGHING EVEN WHEN THEY DIE...
IT'S WEIRD. I MEAN, THERE ARE PEOPLE WHO BARELY LAUGH WHEN THEY'RE ALIVE, Y'KNOW?
I'M TALKING ABOUT YOU, KEISUKE.
THAT'S NOT TRUE, TSUGUO.
I MEAN, I LAUGH SOMETIMES.
YOU DO?
YOU GOT A REASON FOR THAT SOUR FACE OF YOURS?
I LIVE A VERY DARK LIFE IS ALL.
ALL THE MORE REASON THAT YOU NEED TO LAUGH.
OH, I'VE GOT IT, KEISUKE.
COME WITH ME JUST ONCE. I'LL MAKE YOU LAUGH.

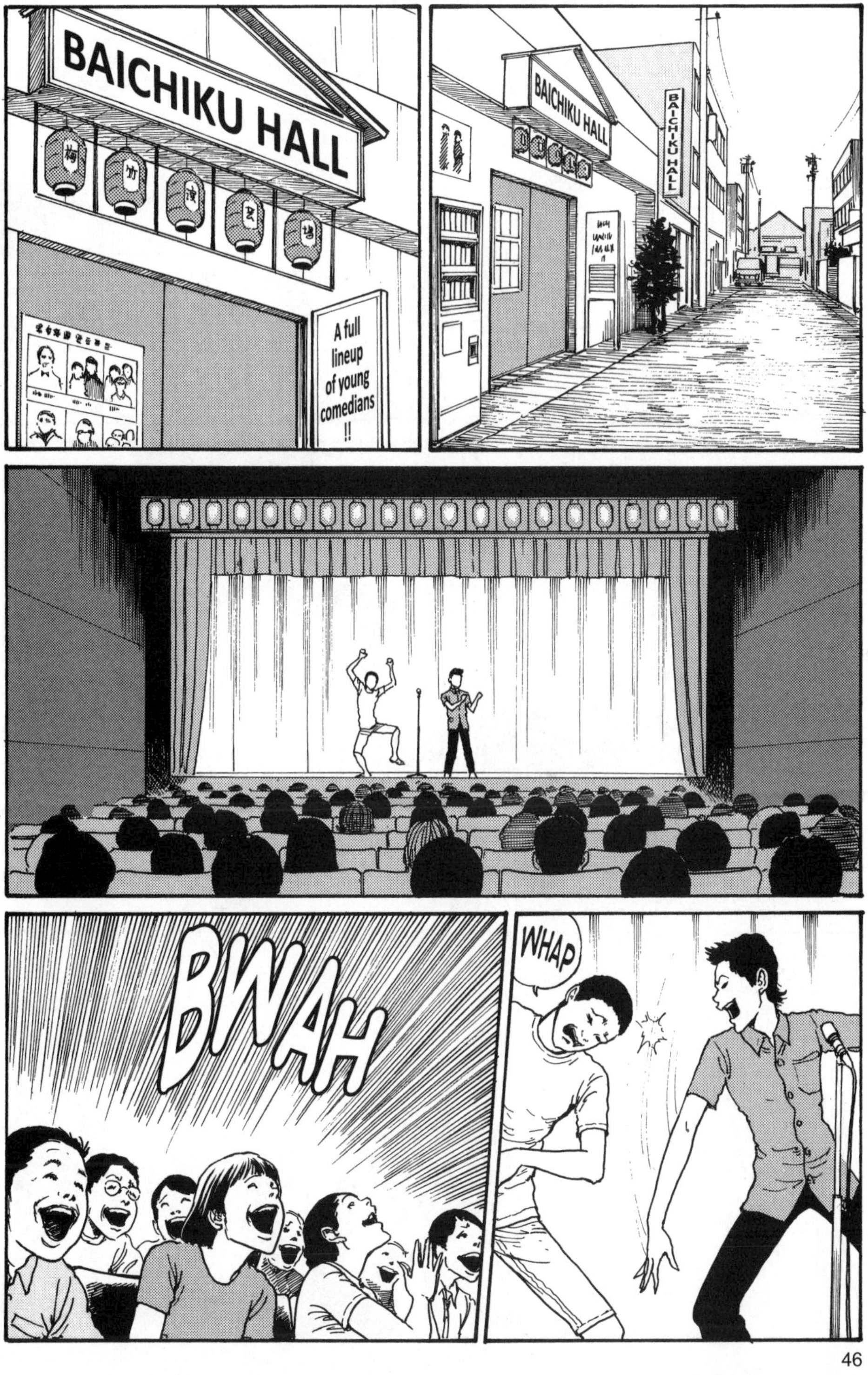
BAICHIKU HALL
BAICHIKU HALL
BAICHIKU HALL
A full lineup of young comedians !!
WHAP
BWAH

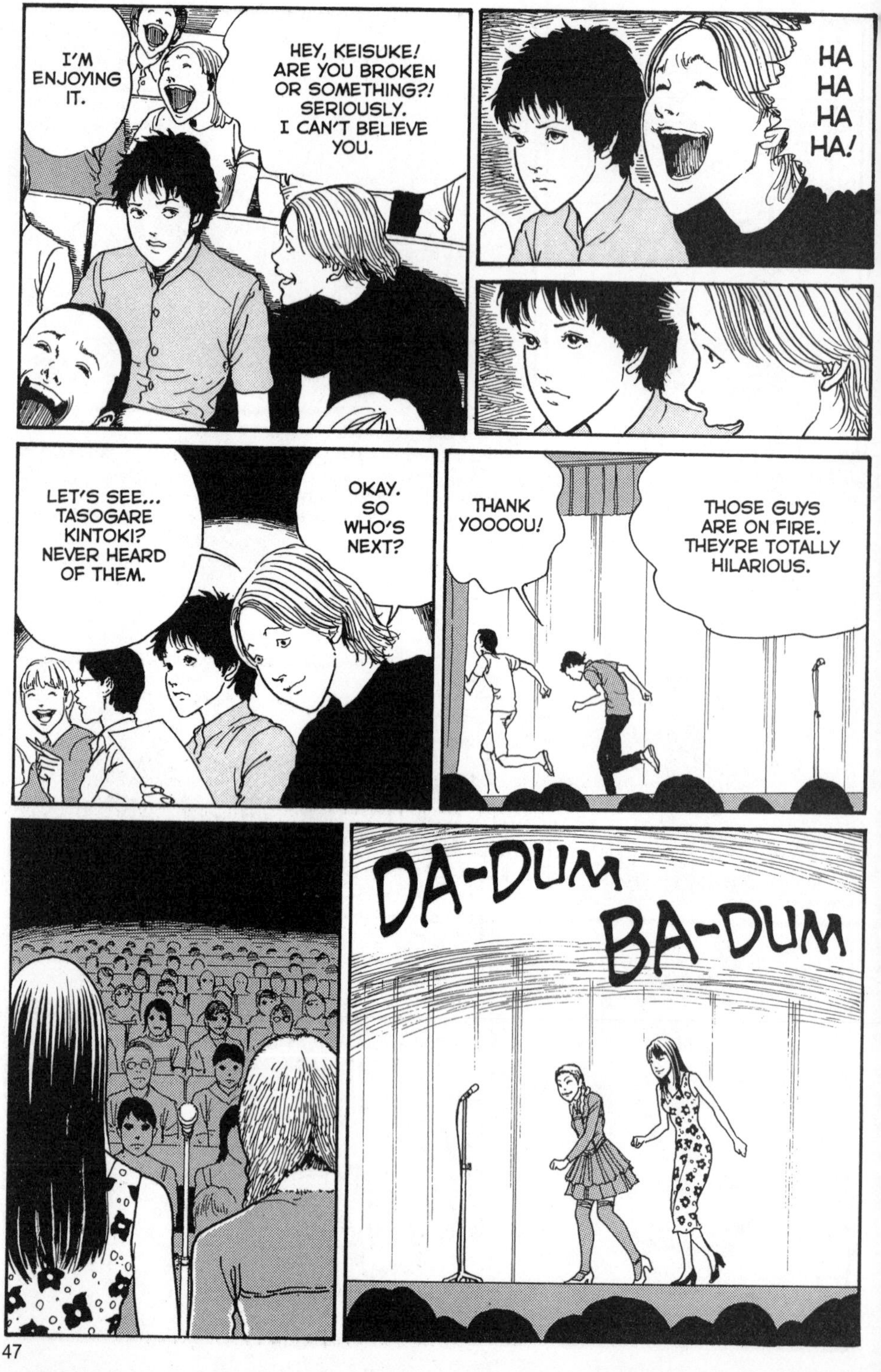
HA HA HA HA!
HEY, KEISUKE! ARE YOU BROKEN OR SOMETHING?! SERIOUSLY. I CAN'T BELIEVE YOU.
I'M ENJOYING IT.
THOSE GUYS ARE ON FIRE. THEY'RE TOTALLY HILARIOUS.
THANK YOOOOU!
OKAY. SO WHO'S NEXT?
LET'S SEE... TASOGARE KINTOKI? NEVER HEARD OF THEM.
DA-DUM
BA-DUM

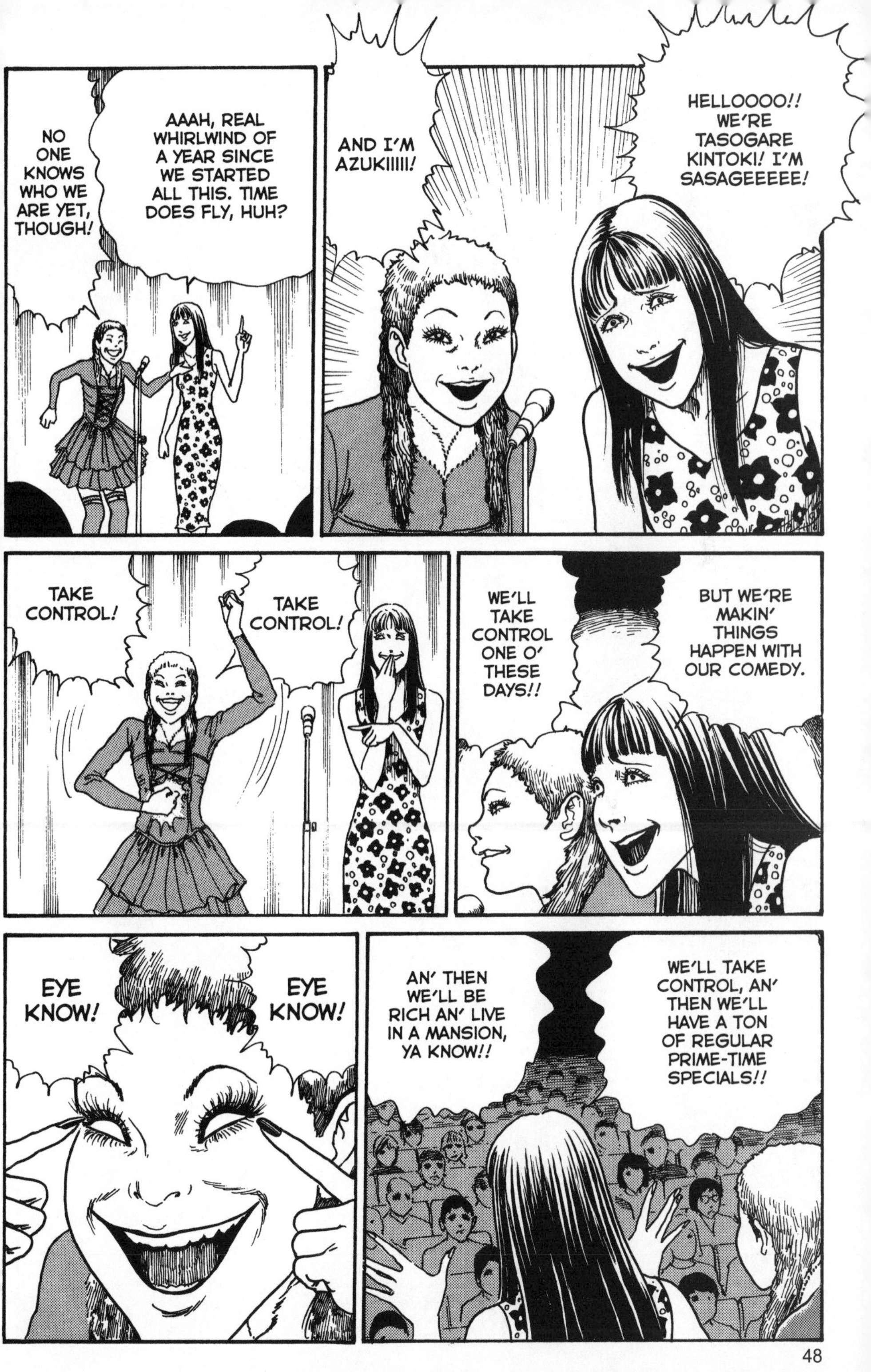
HELLOOOO!! WE'RE TASOGARE KINTOKI! I'M SASAGEEEEE!
AND I'M AZUKIIIII!
AAAH, REAL WHIRLWIND OF A YEAR SINCE WE STARTED ALL THIS. TIME DOES FLY, HUH?
NO ONE KNOWS WHO WE ARE YET, THOUGH!
BUT WE'RE MAKIN' THINGS HAPPEN WITH OUR COMEDY.
WE'LL TAKE CONTROL ONE O' THESE DAYS!!
TAKE CONTROL!
TAKE CONTROL!
WE'LL TAKE CONTROL, AN' THEN WE'LL HAVE A TON OF REGULAR PRIME-TIME SPECIALS!!
AN' THEN WE'LL BE RICH AN' LIVE IN A MANSION, YA KNOW!!
EYE KNOW!
EYE KNOW!

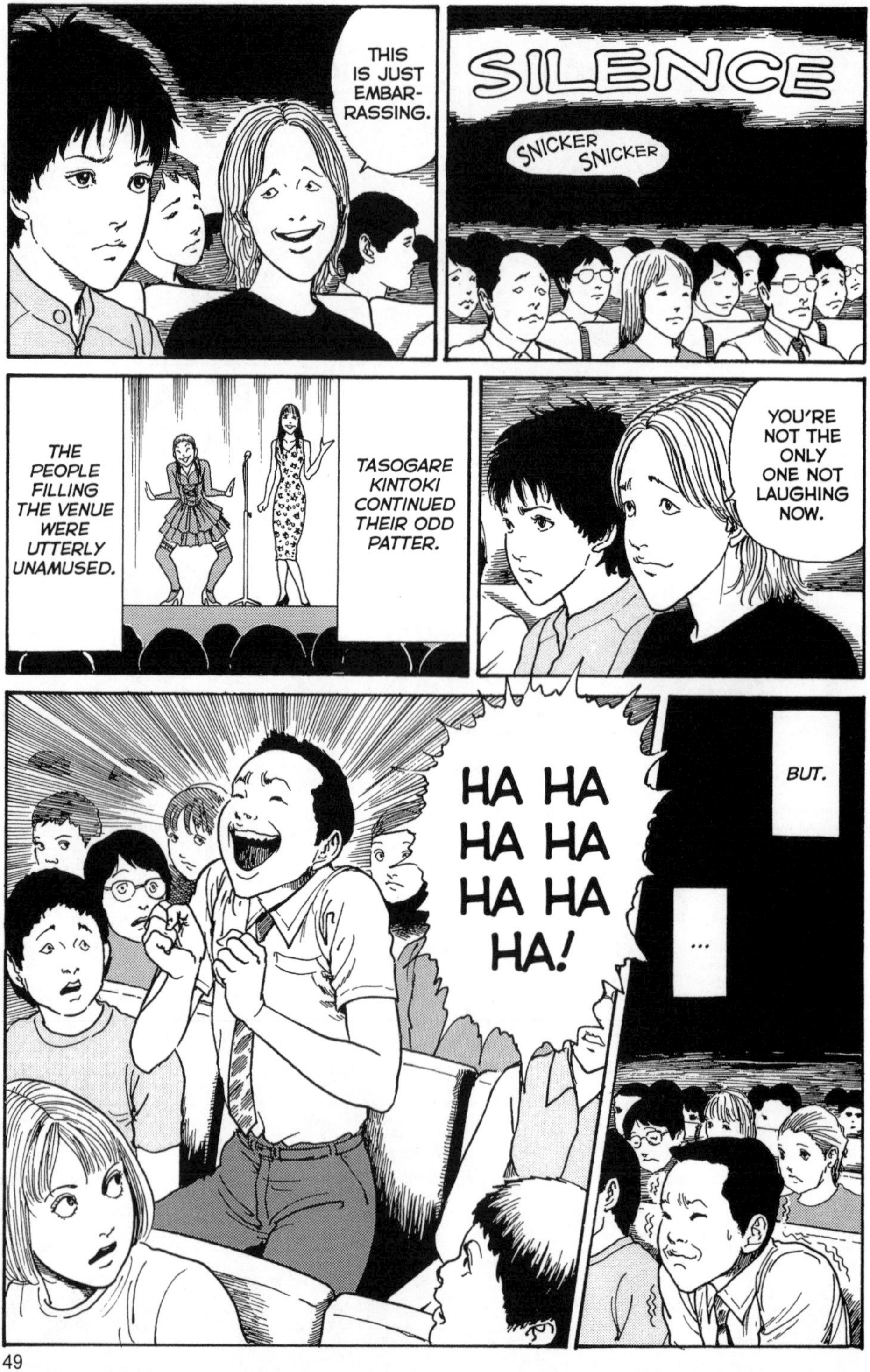
SILENCE
SNICKER SNICKER
THIS IS JUST EMBARRASSING.
YOU'RE NOT THE ONLY ONE NOT LAUGHING NOW.
TASOGARE KINTOKI CONTINUED THEIR ODD PATTER.
THE PEOPLE FILLING THE VENUE WERE UTTERLY UNAMUSED.
BUT.
...
HA HA HA HA HA HA HA!

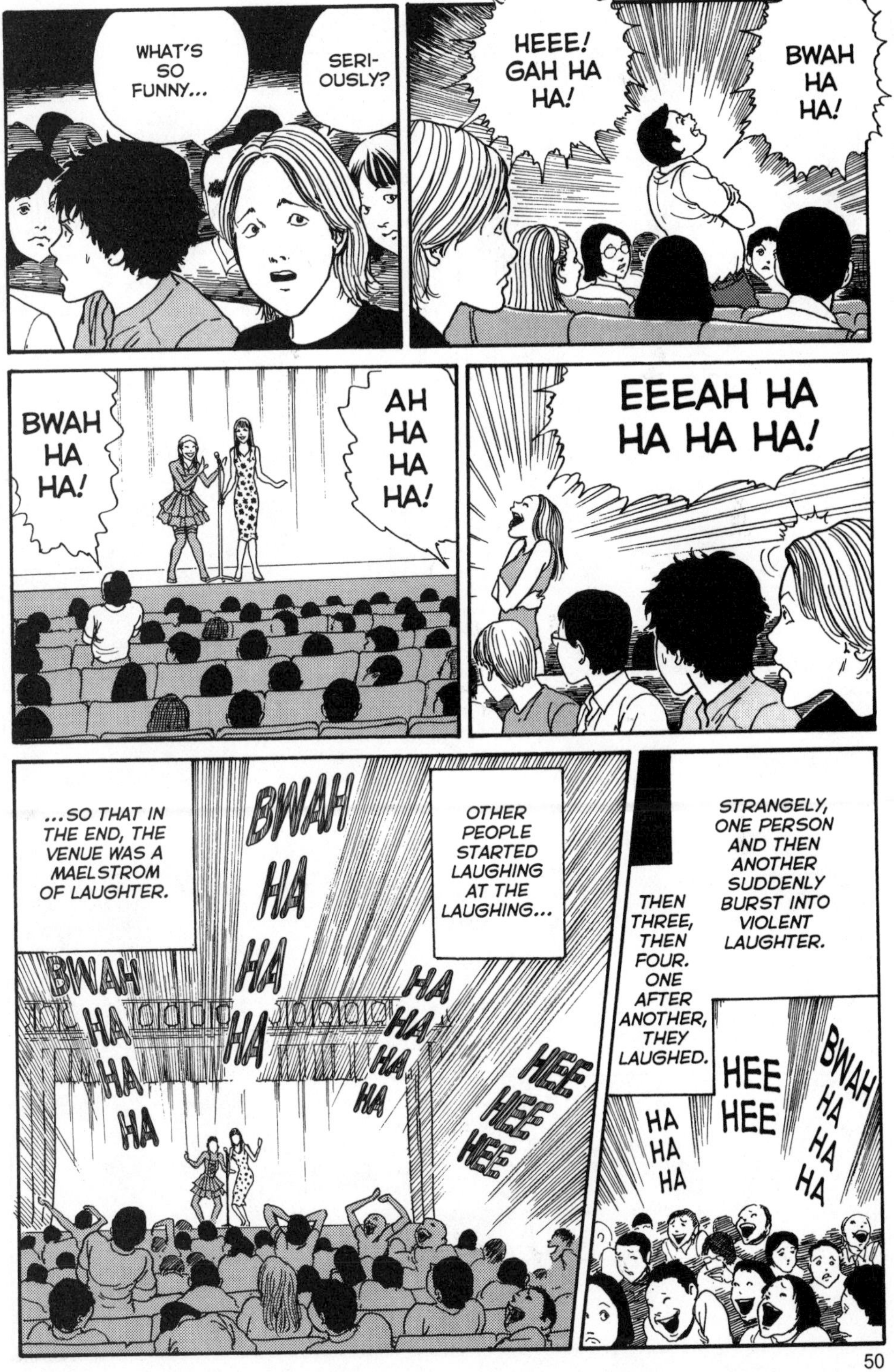
BWAH HA HA!
HEEE! GAH HA HA!
SERI-OUSLY?
WHAT'S SO FUNNY...
EEEAH HA HA HA HA!
AH HA HA HA HA!
BWAH HA HA!
STRANGELY, ONE PERSON AND THEN ANOTHER SUDDENLY BURST INTO VIOLENT LAUGHTER.
THEN THREE, THEN FOUR. ONE AFTER ANOTHER, THEY LAUGHED.
BWAH HA HA HA HA
HEE HEE
HA HA HA
OTHER PEOPLE STARTED LAUGHING AT THE LAUGHING...
BWAH HA HA HA
...SO THAT IN THE END, THE VENUE WAS A MAELSTROM OF LAUGHTER.
HEE HEE HEE
HA HA HA HA HA
BWAH HA HA HA

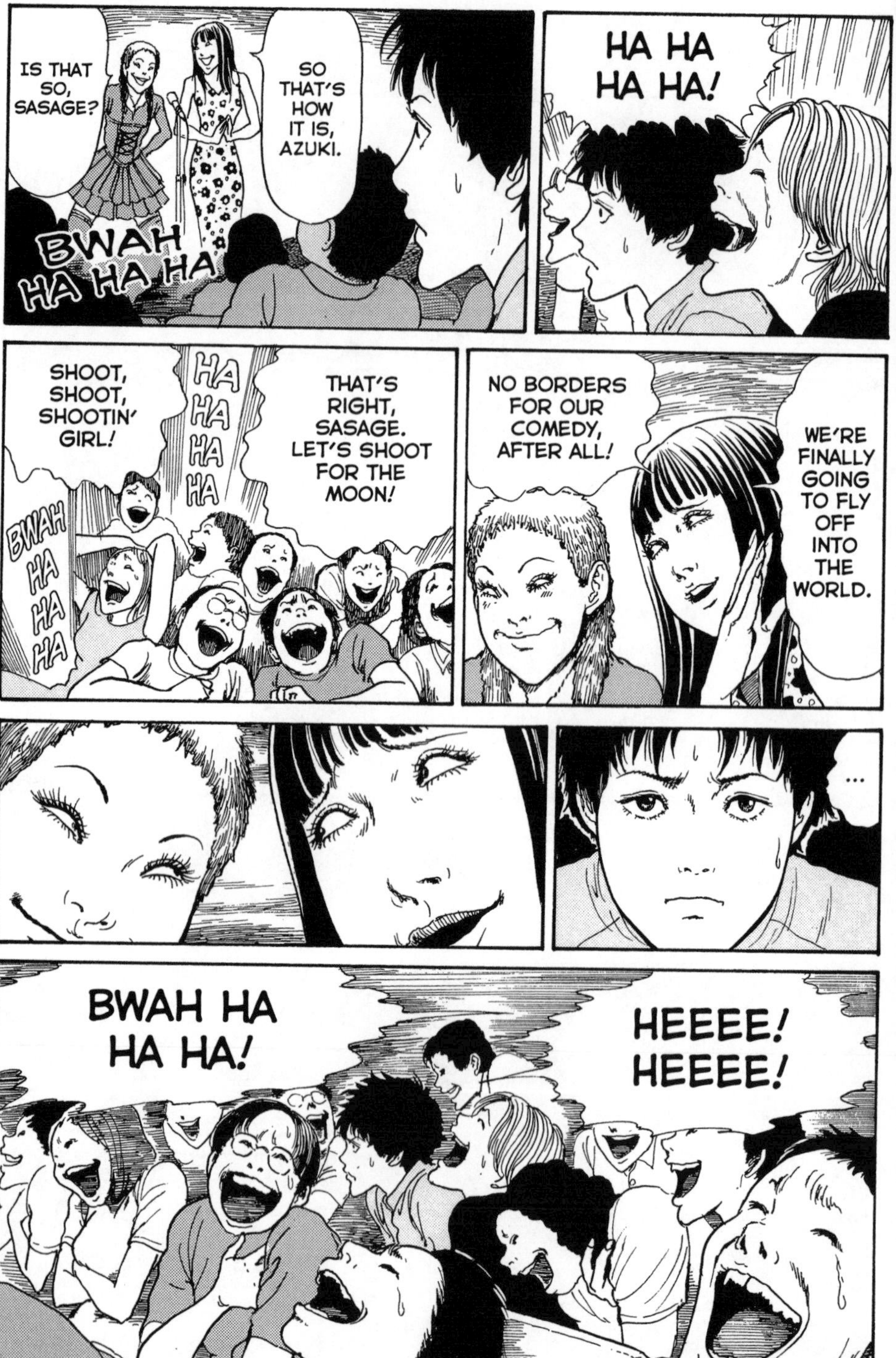
HA HA HA HA!
SO THAT'S HOW IT IS, AZUKI.
IS THAT SO, SASAGE?
BWAH HA HA HA
WE'RE FINALLY GOING TO FLY OFF INTO THE WORLD.
NO BORDERS FOR OUR COMEDY, AFTER ALL!
THAT'S RIGHT, SASAGE. LET'S SHOOT FOR THE MOON!
HA HA HA HA
SHOOT, SHOOT, SHOOTIN' GIRL!
BWAH HA HA HA
...
HEEEEE! HEEEEE!
BWAH HA HA HA!

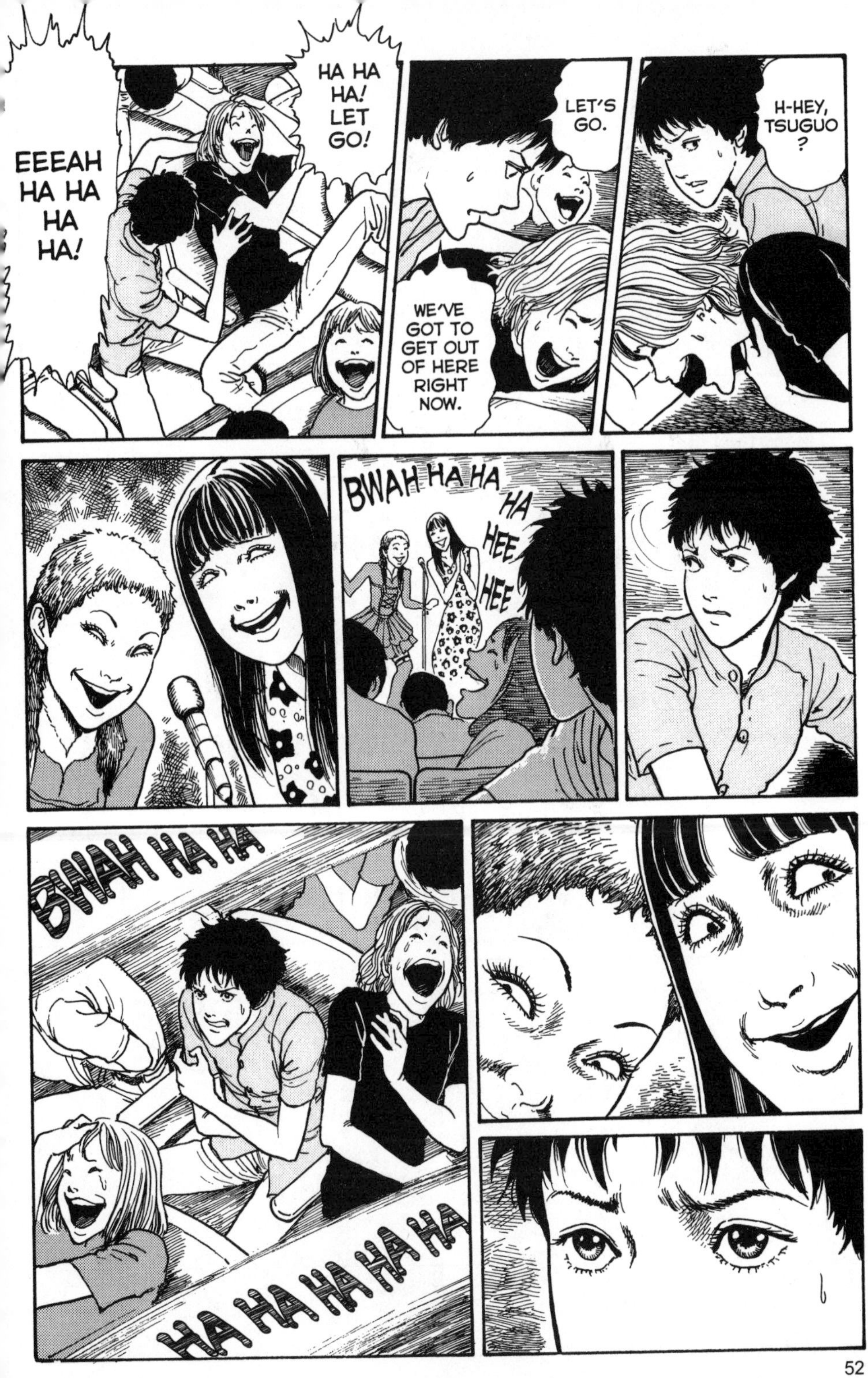
H-HEY, TSUGUO ?
LET'S GO.
WE'VE GOT TO GET OUT OF HERE RIGHT NOW.
HA HA HA! LET GO!
EEEAH HA HA HA HA!
BWAH HA HA HA HEE HEE
BWAH HA HA
HA HA HA HA HA HA

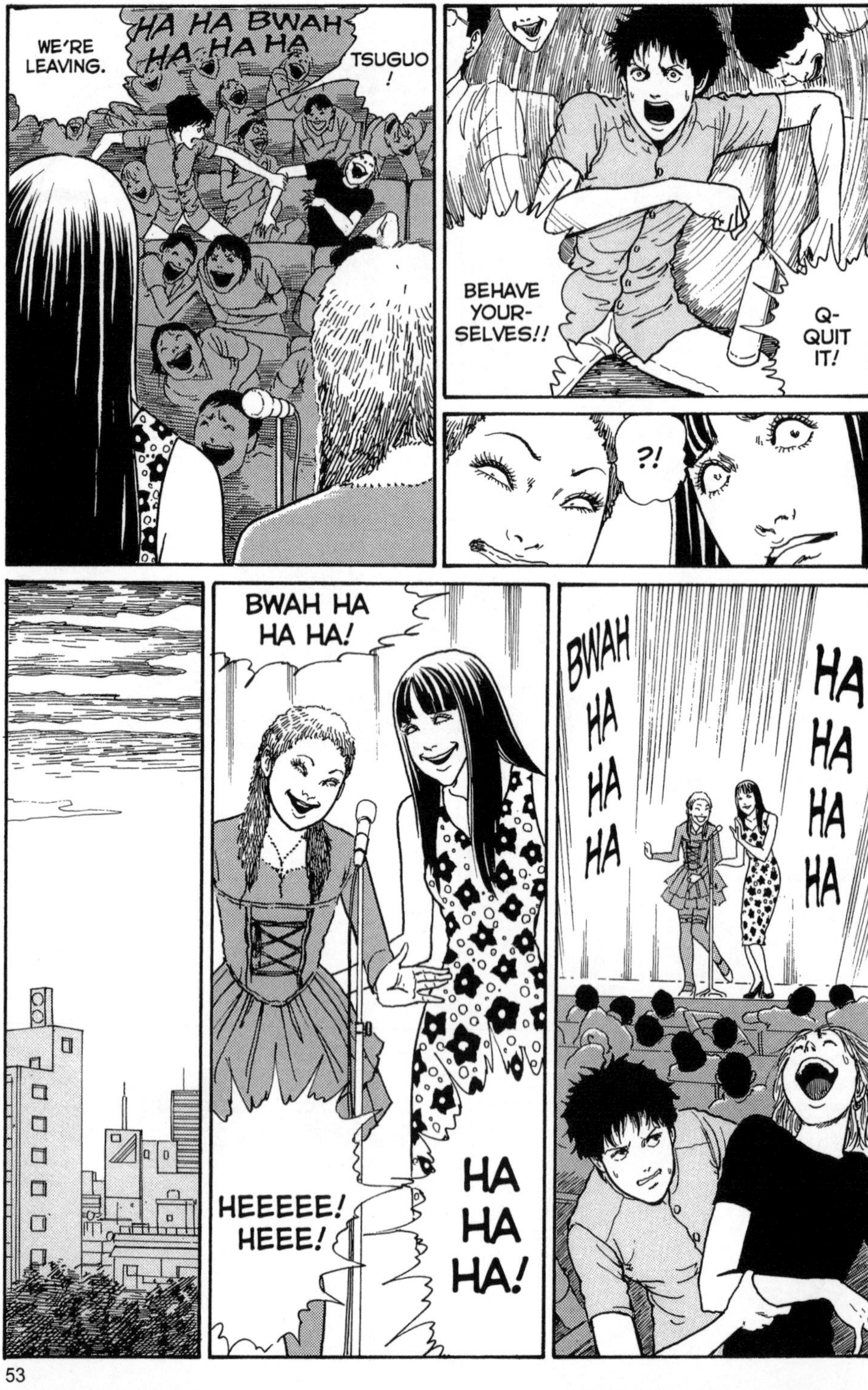

Q-QUIT IT!
BEHAVE YOURSELVES!!
?!
TSUGUO!
HA HA BWAH HA HA HA
WE'RE LEAVING.
HA HA HA HA HA
BWAH HA HA HA HA
BWAH HA HA HA!
HA HA HA HA!
HEEEEE! HEEE!

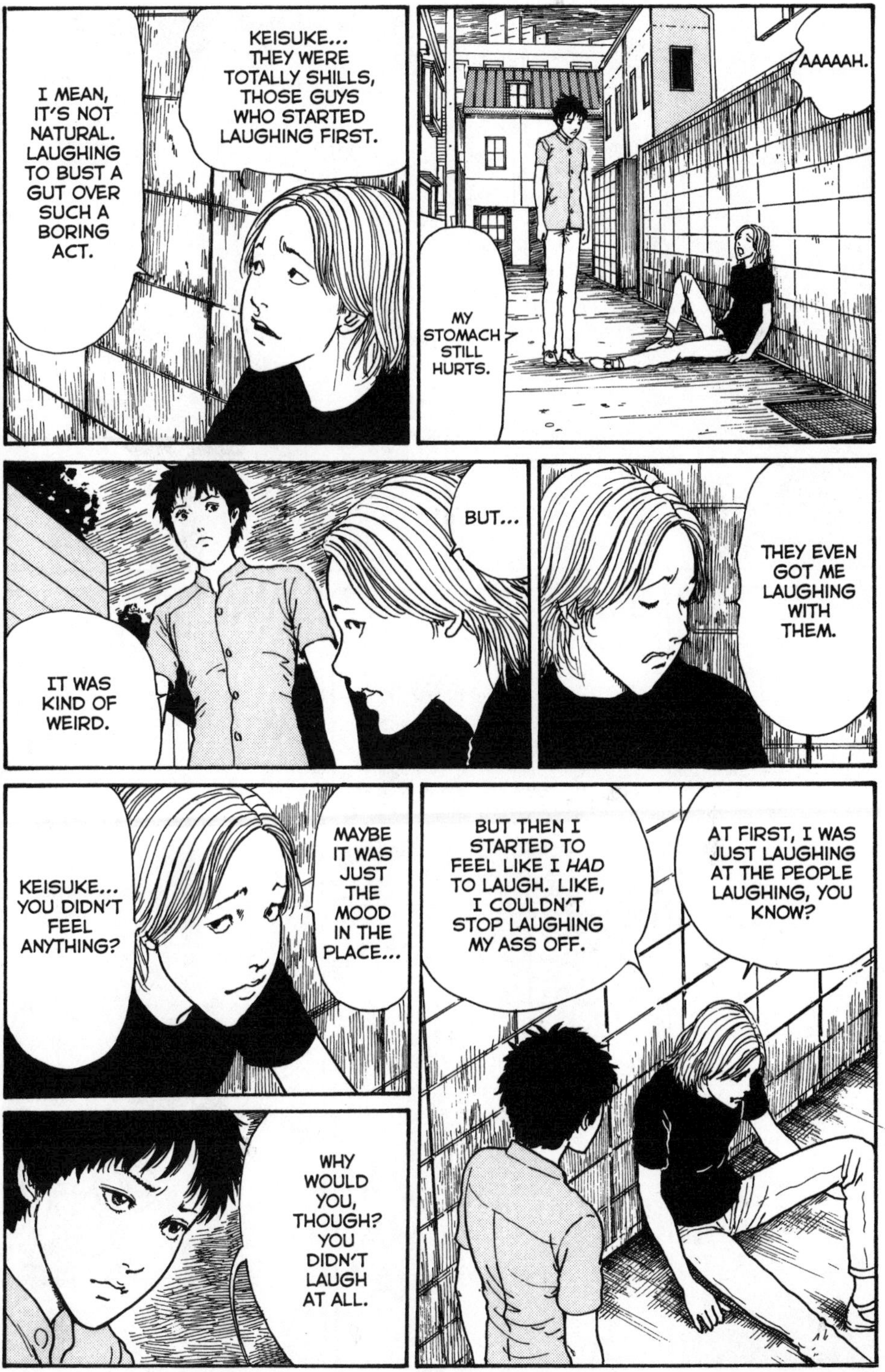
AAAAAH.
MY STOMACH STILL HURTS.
KEISUKE... THEY WERE TOTALLY SHILLS, THOSE GUYS WHO STARTED LAUGHING FIRST.
I MEAN, IT'S NOT NATURAL. LAUGHING TO BUST A GUT OVER SUCH A BORING ACT.
THEY EVEN GOT ME LAUGHING WITH THEM.
BUT...
IT WAS KIND OF WEIRD.
AT FIRST, I WAS JUST LAUGHING AT THE PEOPLE LAUGHING, YOU KNOW?
BUT THEN I STARTED TO FEEL LIKE I *HAD* TO LAUGH. LIKE, I COULDN'T STOP LAUGHING MY ASS OFF.
MAYBE IT WAS JUST THE MOOD IN THE PLACE...
KEISUKE... YOU DIDN'T FEEL ANYTHING?
WHY WOULD YOU, THOUGH? YOU DIDN'T LAUGH AT ALL.

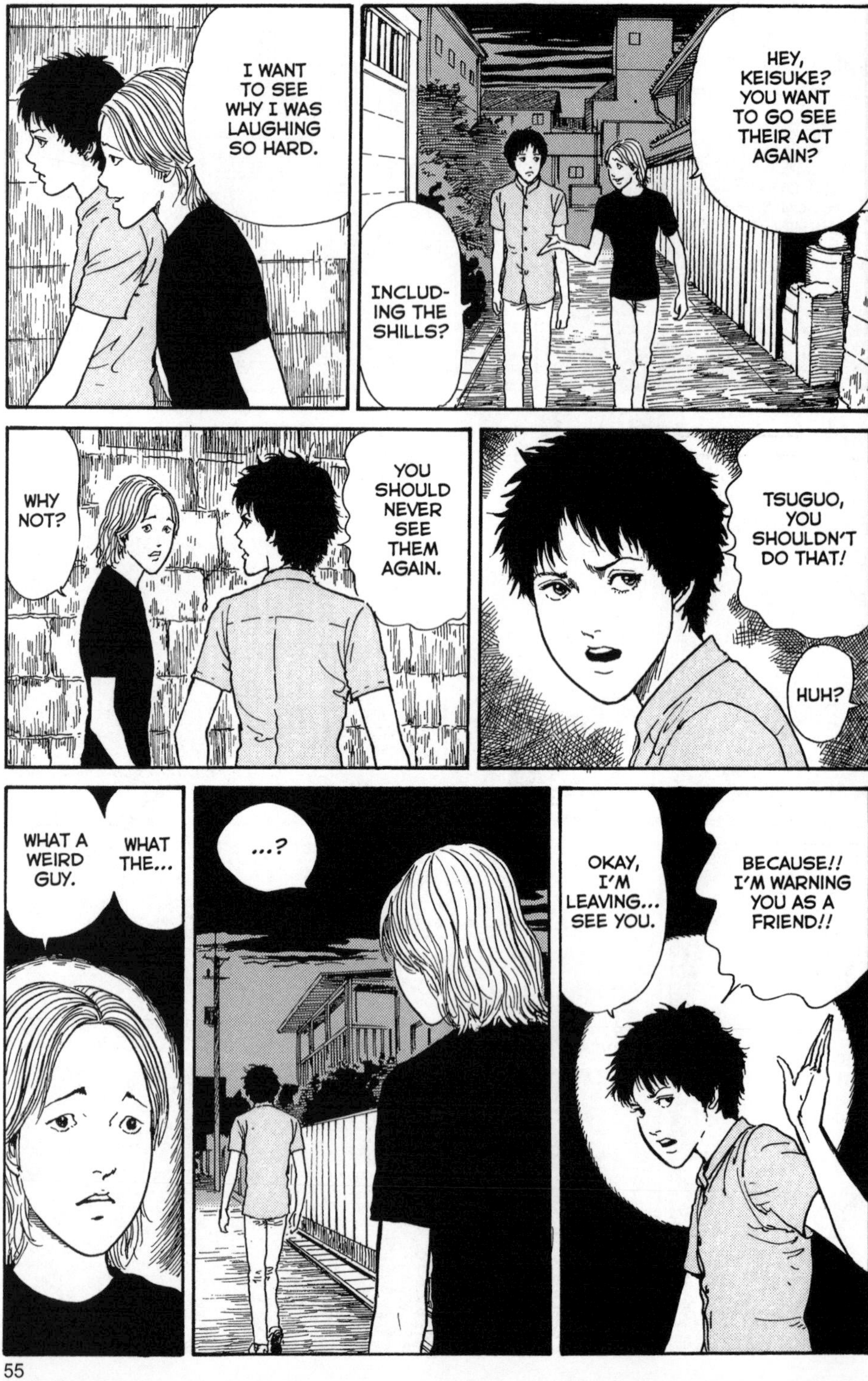
HEY, KEISUKE? YOU WANT TO GO SEE THEIR ACT AGAIN?
INCLUD-ING THE SHILLS?
I WANT TO SEE WHY I WAS LAUGHING SO HARD.
TSUGUO, YOU SHOULDN'T DO THAT!
HUH?
YOU SHOULD NEVER SEE THEM AGAIN.
WHY NOT?
BECAUSE!! I'M WARNING YOU AS A FRIEND!!
OKAY, I'M LEAVING... SEE YOU.
...?
WHAT THE...
WHAT A WEIRD GUY.

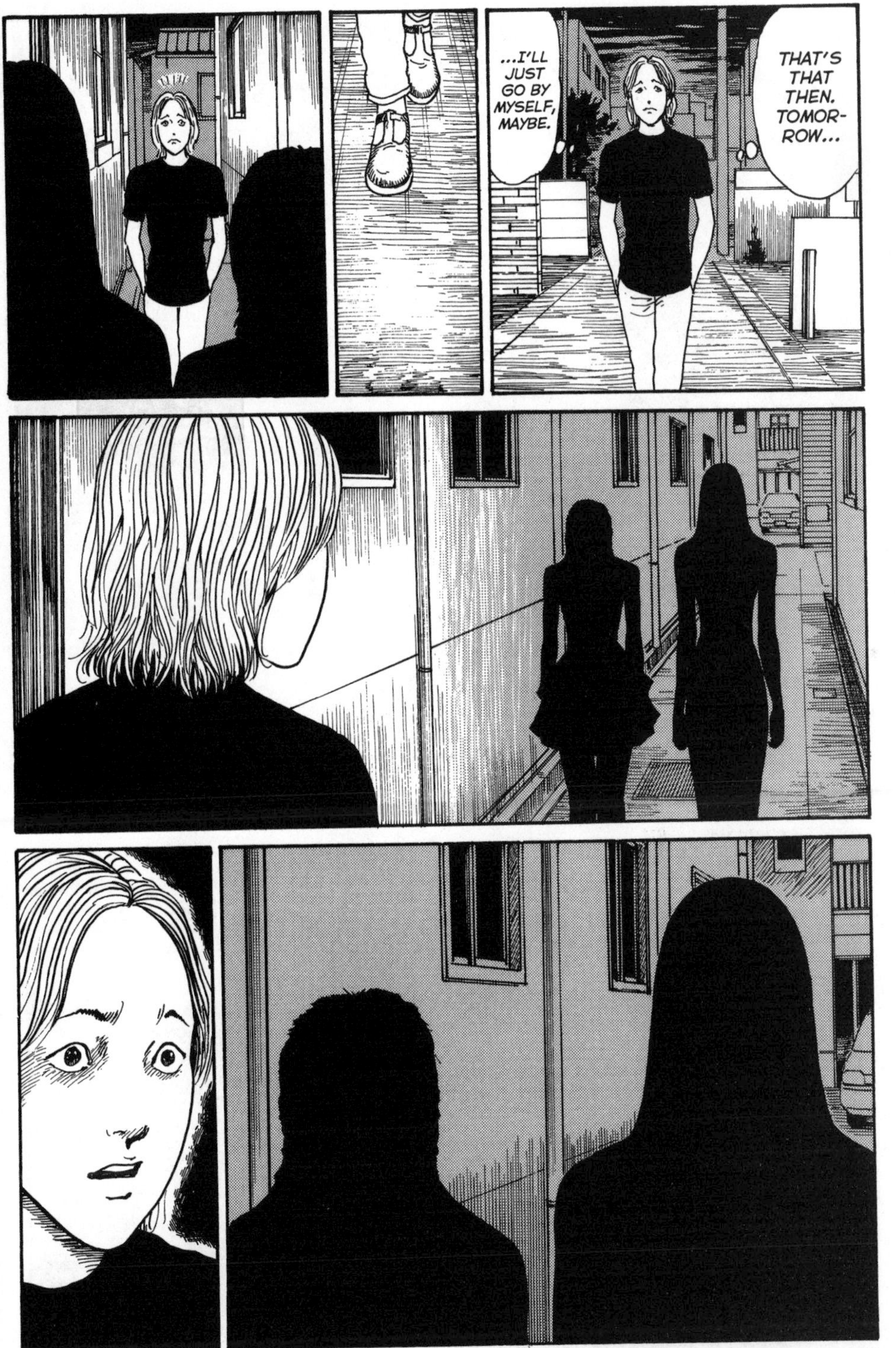
THAT'S THAT THEN. TOMORROW...
...I'LL JUST GO BY MYSELF, MAYBE.

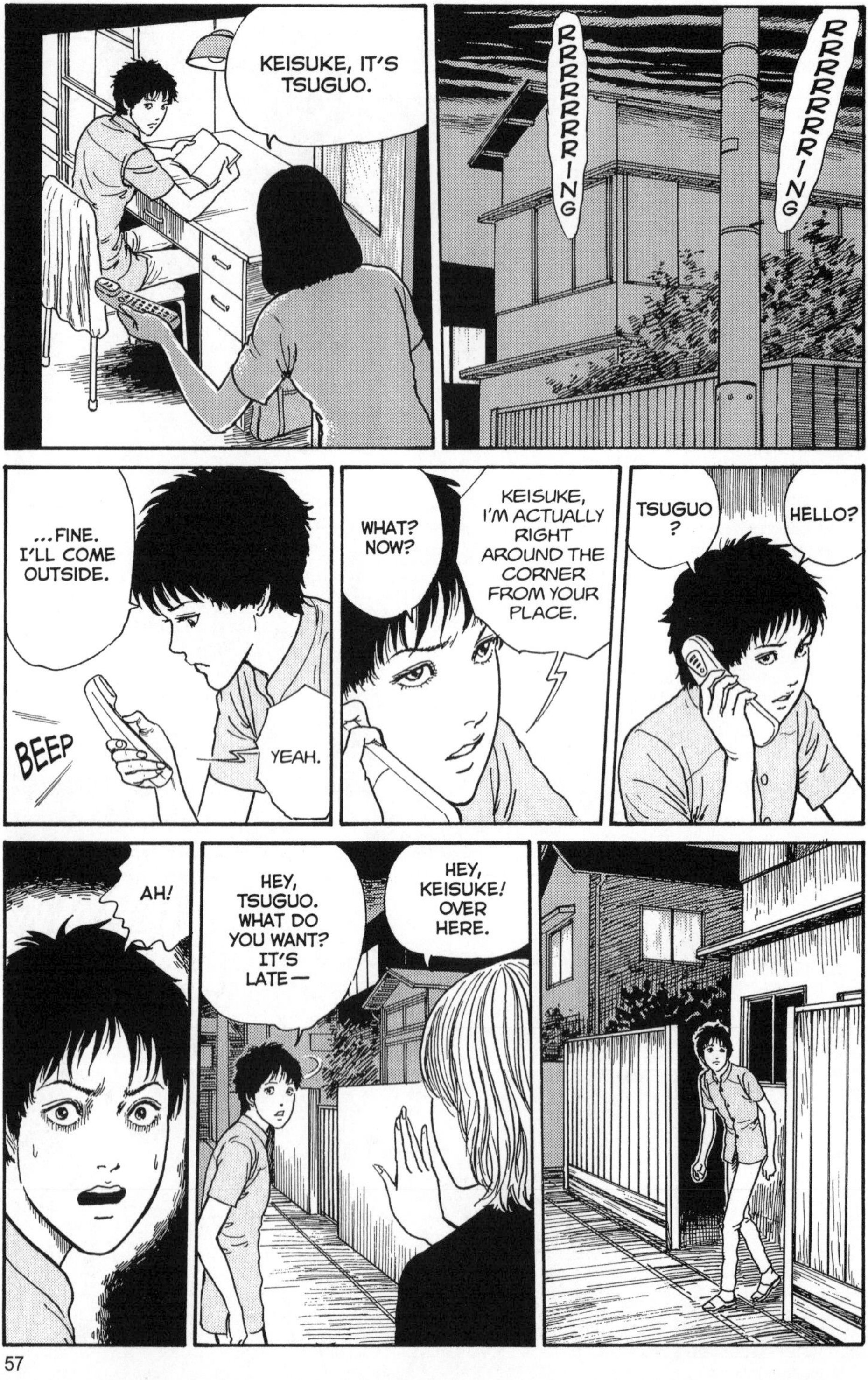
RRRRRRRING
RRRRRRRING
KEISUKE, IT'S TSUGUO.
HELLO?
TSUGUO?
KEISUKE, I'M ACTUALLY RIGHT AROUND THE CORNER FROM YOUR PLACE.
WHAT? NOW?
...FINE. I'LL COME OUTSIDE.
YEAH.
BEEP
HEY, KEISUKE! OVER HERE.
HEY, TSUGUO. WHAT DO YOU WANT? IT'S LATE—
AH!

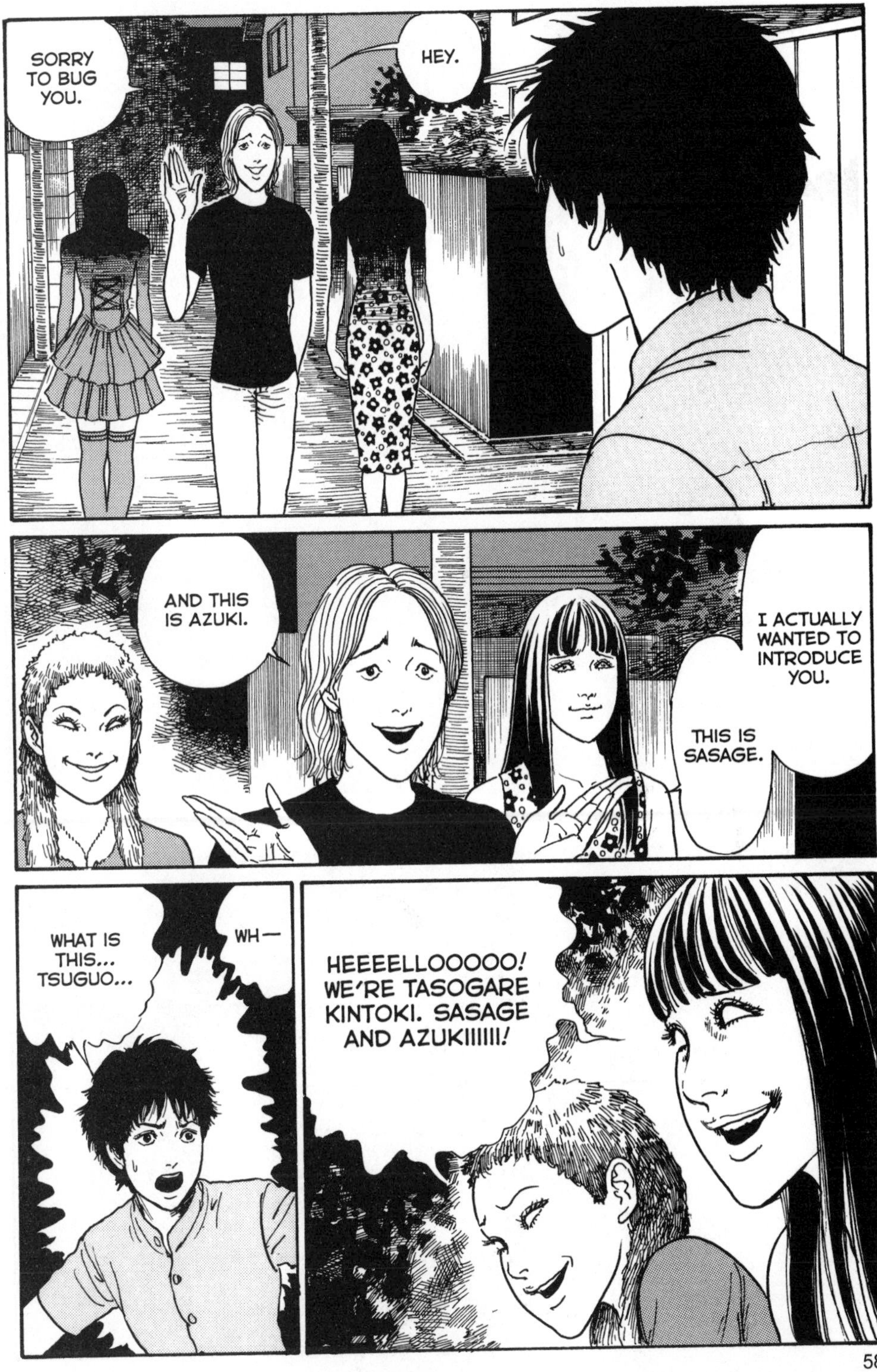
HEY.
SORRY TO BUG YOU.
I ACTUALLY WANTED TO INTRODUCE YOU.
THIS IS SASAGE.
AND THIS IS AZUKI.
HEEEELLOOOOO! WE'RE TASOGARE KINTOKI. SASAGE AND AZUKIIIIII!
WH—
WHAT IS THIS... TSUGUO...

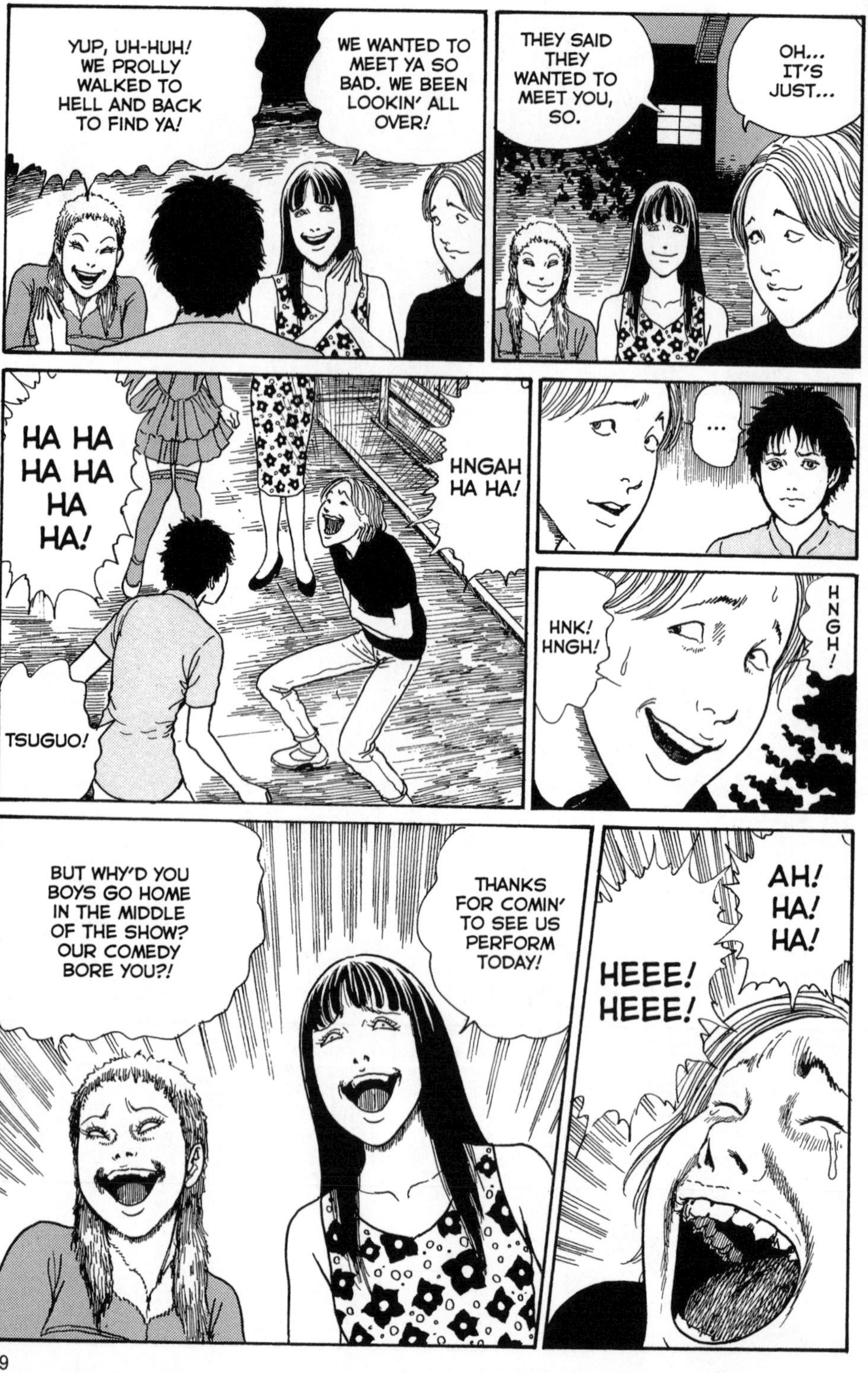
OH... IT'S JUST...
THEY SAID THEY WANTED TO MEET YOU, SO.
WE WANTED TO MEET YA SO BAD. WE BEEN LOOKIN' ALL OVER!
YUP, UH-HUH! WE PROLLY WALKED TO HELL AND BACK TO FIND YA!
...
HNGH!
HNK! HNGH!
HNGAH HA HA!
HA HA HA HA HA HA!
TSUGUO!
AH! HA! HA!
HEEE! HEEE!
THANKS FOR COMIN' TO SEE US PERFORM TODAY!
BUT WHY'D YOU BOYS GO HOME IN THE MIDDLE OF THE SHOW? OUR COMEDY BORE YOU?!

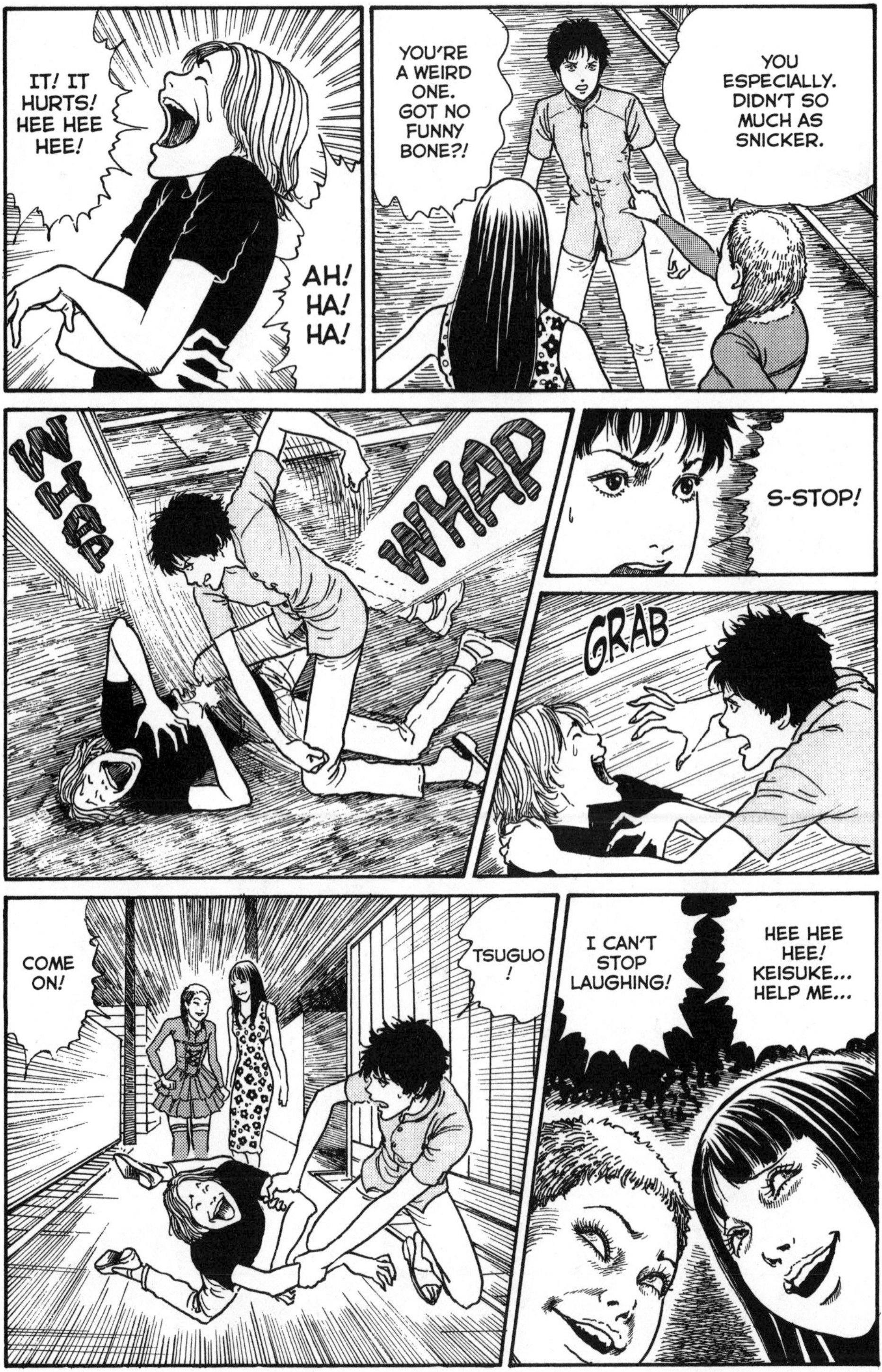
YOU ESPECIALLY. DIDN'T SO MUCH AS SNICKER.
YOU'RE A WEIRD ONE. GOT NO FUNNY BONE?!
IT! IT HURTS! HEE HEE HEE!
AH! HA! HA!
S-STOP!
GRAB
WHAP
WHAP
HEE HEE HEE! KEISUKE... HELP ME...
I CAN'T STOP LAUGHING!
TSUGUO!
COME ON!

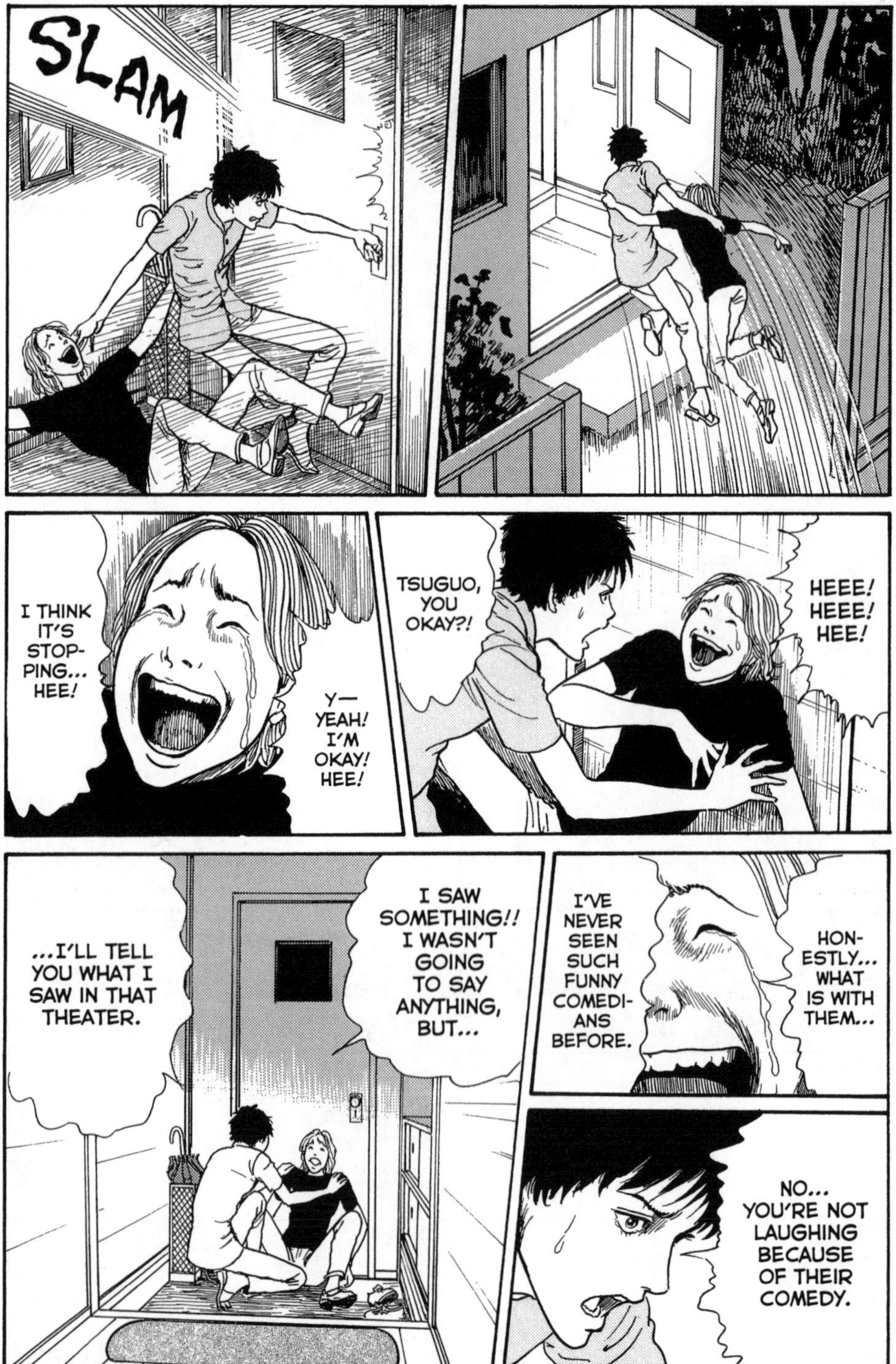
SLAM
HEEE! HEEE! HEE!
TSUGUO, YOU OKAY?!
Y— YEAH! I'M OKAY! HEE!
I THINK IT'S STOP-PING... HEE!
HON-ESTLY... WHAT IS WITH THEM...
I'VE NEVER SEEN SUCH FUNNY COMEDI-ANS BEFORE.
NO... YOU'RE NOT LAUGHING BECAUSE OF THEIR COMEDY.
I SAW SOMETHING!! I WASN'T GOING TO SAY ANYTHING, BUT...
...I'LL TELL YOU WHAT I SAW IN THAT THEATER.

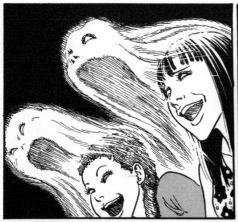

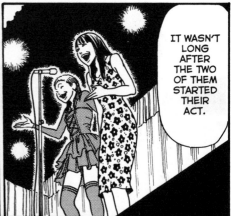

IT WASN'T LONG AFTER THE TWO OF THEM STARTED THEIR ACT.

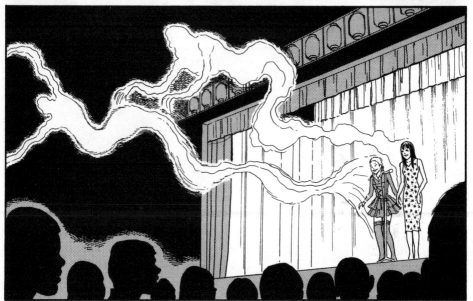

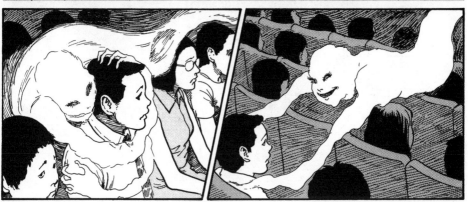

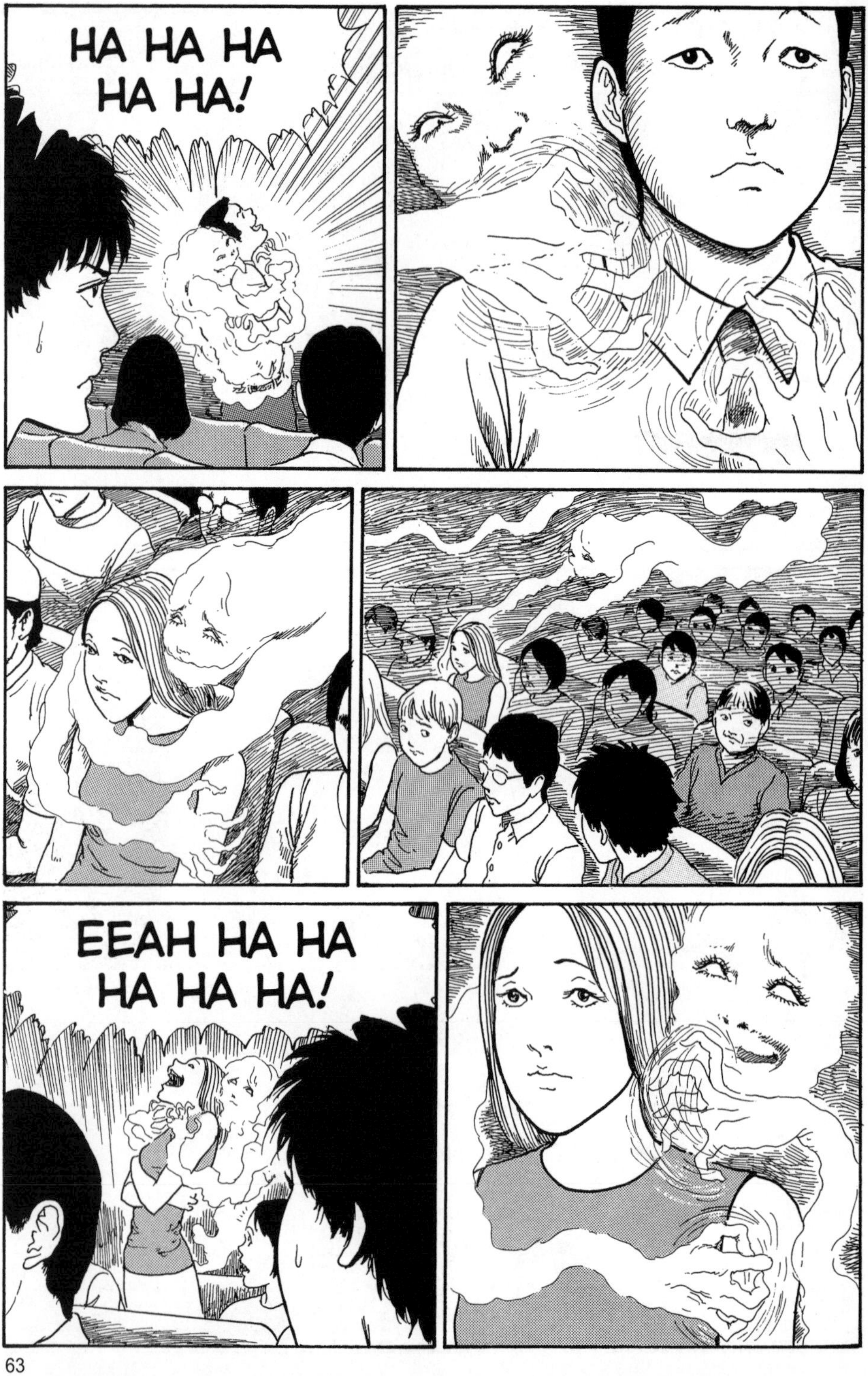
HA HA HA
HA HA!
EEAH HA HA
HA HA HA!

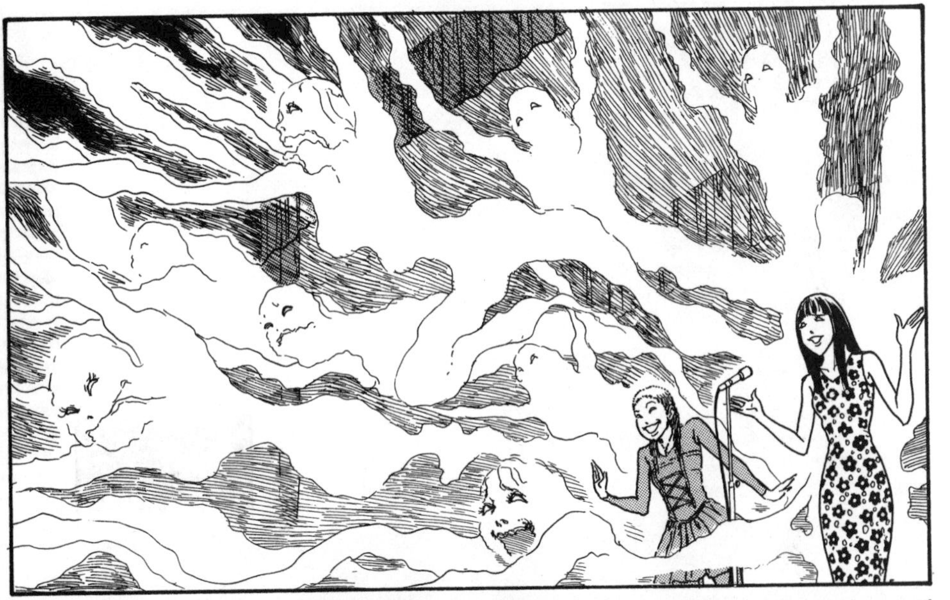

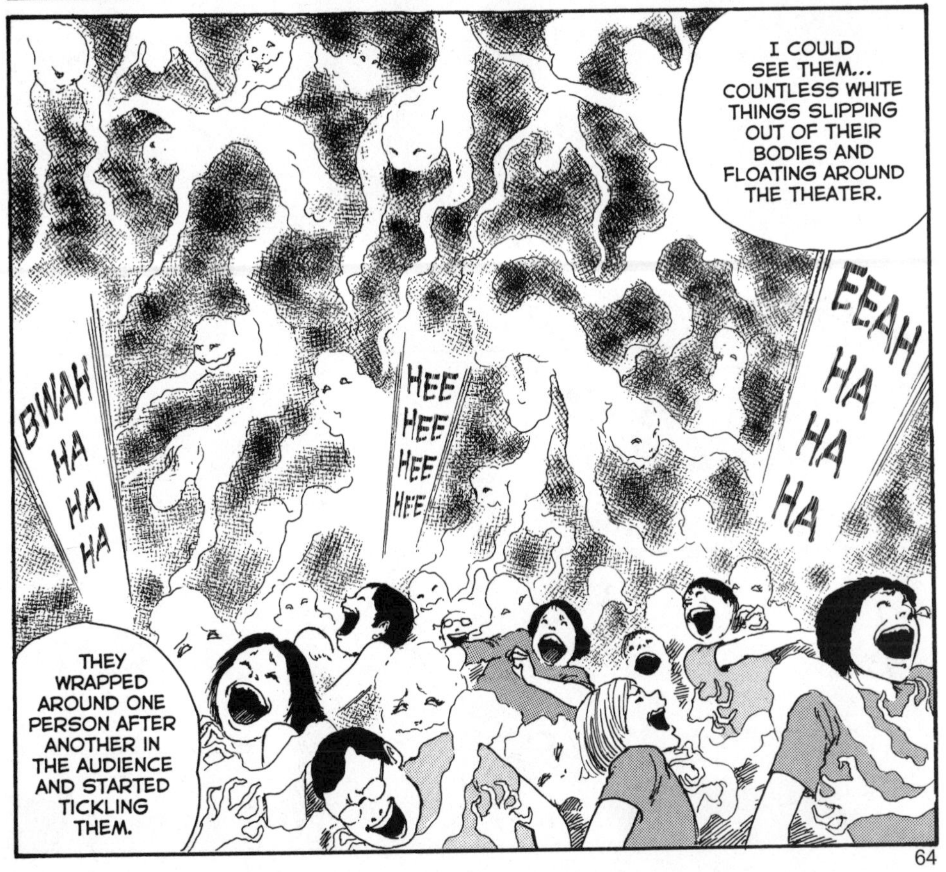
I COULD SEE THEM... COUNTLESS WHITE THINGS SLIPPING OUT OF THEIR BODIES AND FLOATING AROUND THE THEATER.
EEAH HA HA HA HA
HEE HEE HEE HEE
BWAH HA HA HA
THEY WRAPPED AROUND ONE PERSON AFTER ANOTHER IN THE AUDIENCE AND STARTED TICKLING THEM.

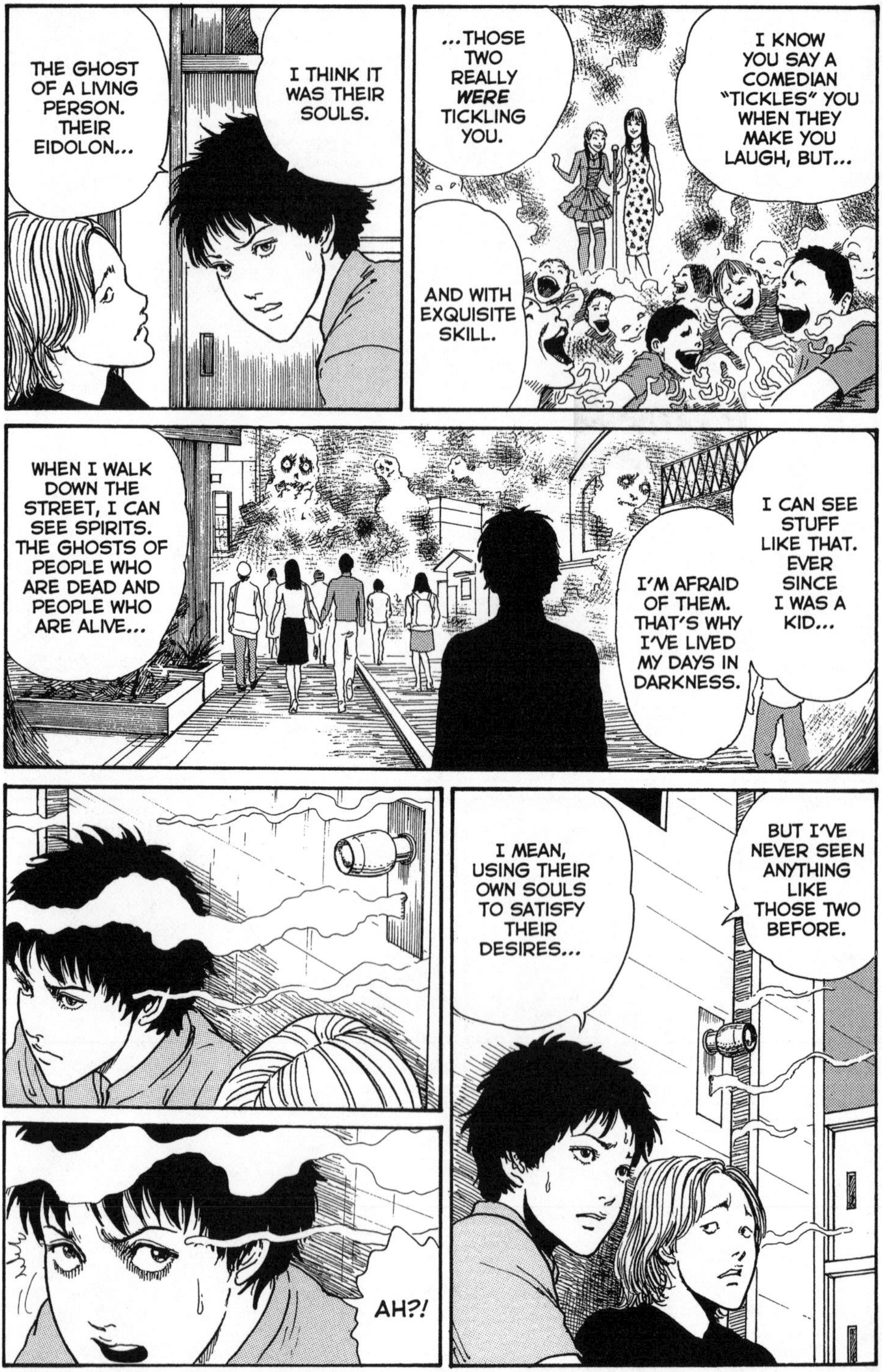
I KNOW YOU SAY A COMEDIAN "TICKLES" YOU WHEN THEY MAKE YOU LAUGH, BUT...
...THOSE TWO REALLY *WERE* TICKLING YOU.
AND WITH EXQUISITE SKILL.
I THINK IT WAS THEIR SOULS.
THE GHOST OF A LIVING PERSON. THEIR EIDOLON...
I CAN SEE STUFF LIKE THAT. EVER SINCE I WAS A KID...
I'M AFRAID OF THEM. THAT'S WHY I'VE LIVED MY DAYS IN DARKNESS.
WHEN I WALK DOWN THE STREET, I CAN SEE SPIRITS. THE GHOSTS OF PEOPLE WHO ARE DEAD AND PEOPLE WHO ARE ALIVE...
BUT I'VE NEVER SEEN ANYTHING LIKE THOSE TWO BEFORE.
I MEAN, USING THEIR OWN SOULS TO SATISFY THEIR DESIRES...
AH?!

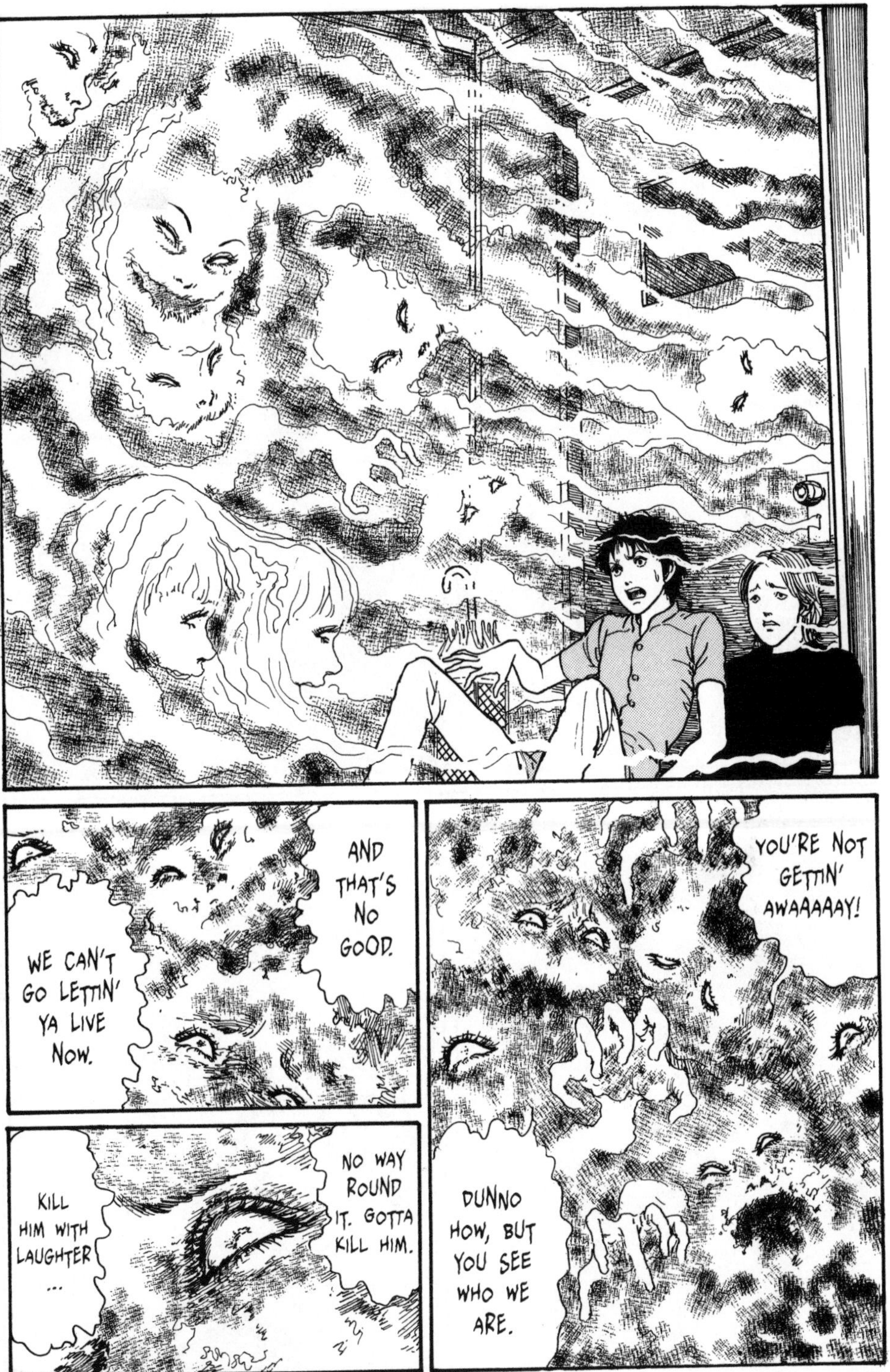
YOU'RE NOT GETTIN' AWAAAAAY!
DUNNO HOW, BUT YOU SEE WHO WE ARE.
AND THAT'S NO GOOD.
WE CAN'T GO LETTIN' YA LIVE NOW.
NO WAY ROUND IT. GOTTA KILL HIM.
KILL HIM WITH LAUGHTER ...

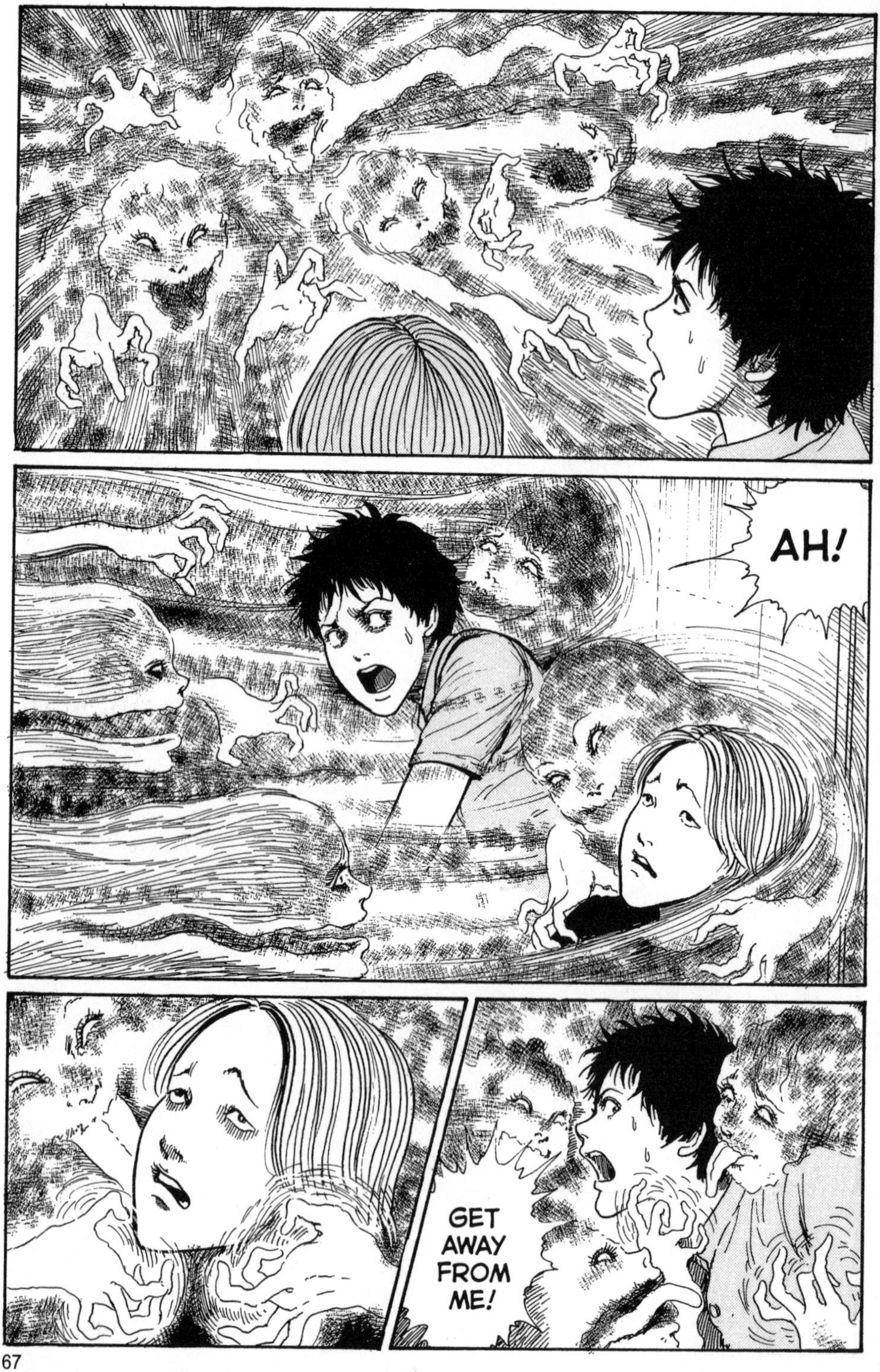
AH!
GET AWAY FROM ME!

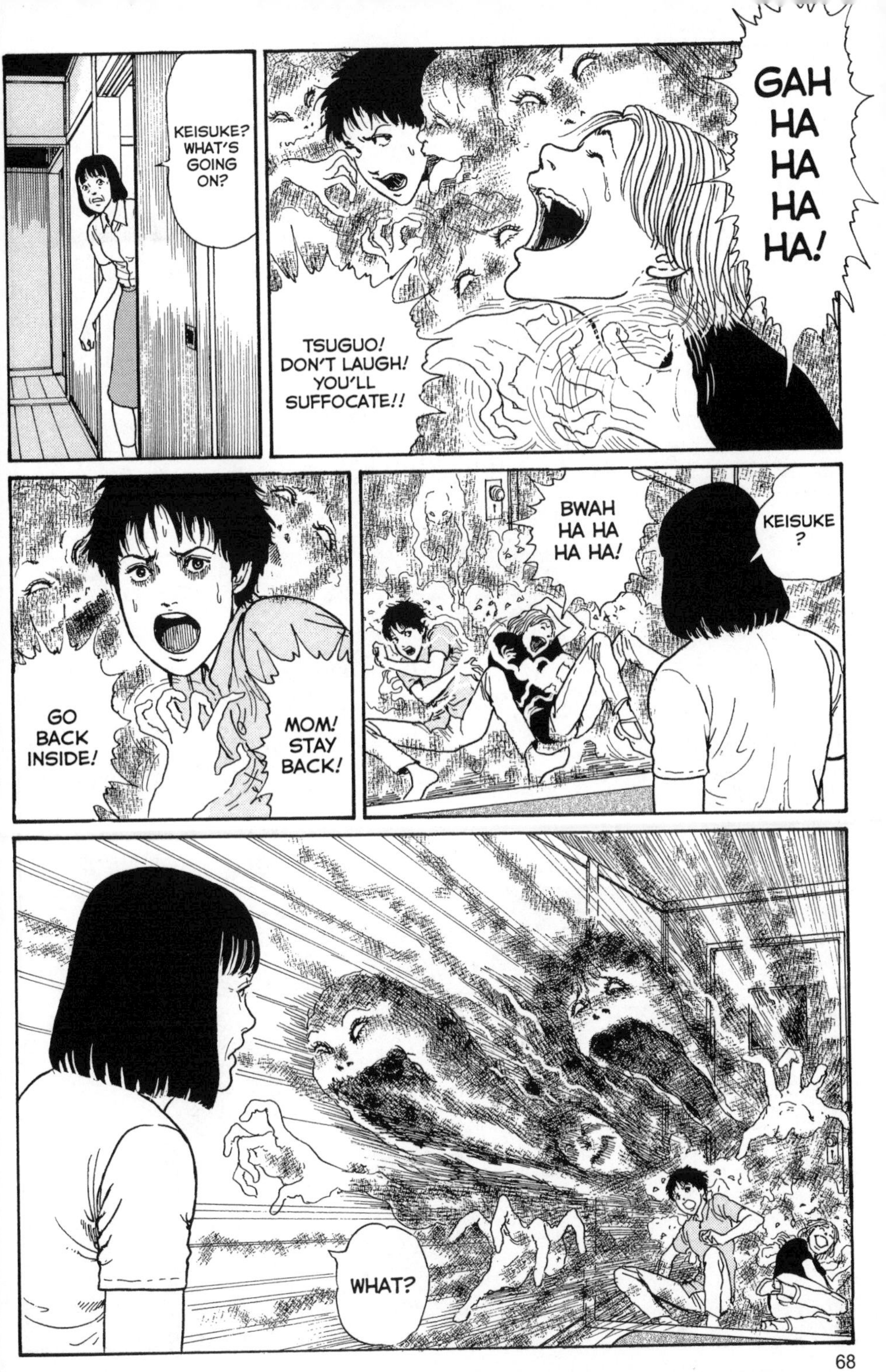
GAH HA HA HA HA!
TSUGUO! DON'T LAUGH! YOU'LL SUFFOCATE!!
KEISUKE? WHAT'S GOING ON?
KEISUKE ?
BWAH HA HA HA HA!
MOM! STAY BACK!
GO BACK INSIDE!
WHAT?

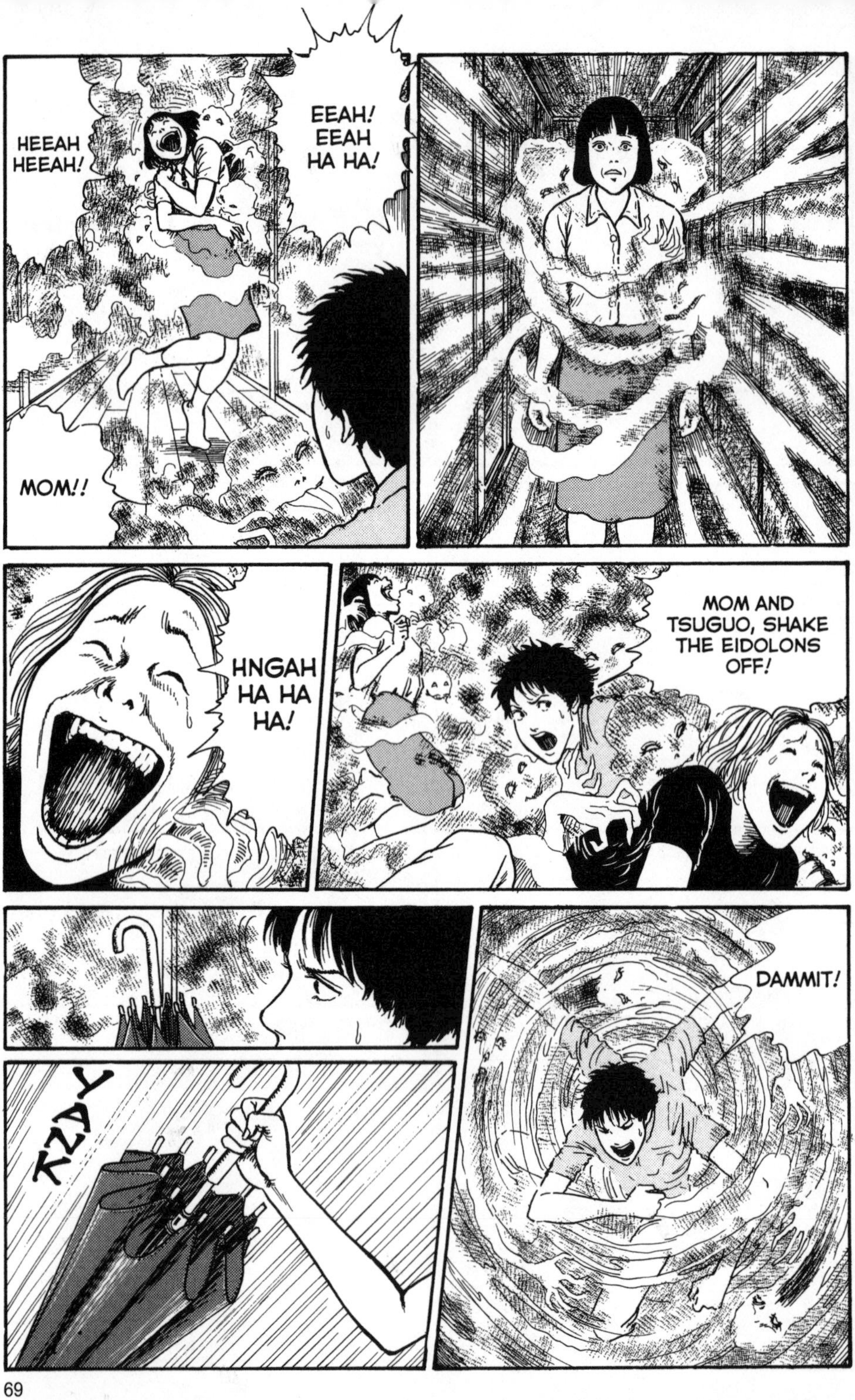
EEAH! EEAH HA HA!
HEEAH HEEAH!
MOM!!
MOM AND TSUGUO, SHAKE THE EIDOLONS OFF!
HNGAH HA HA HA!
DAMMIT!
TZAY

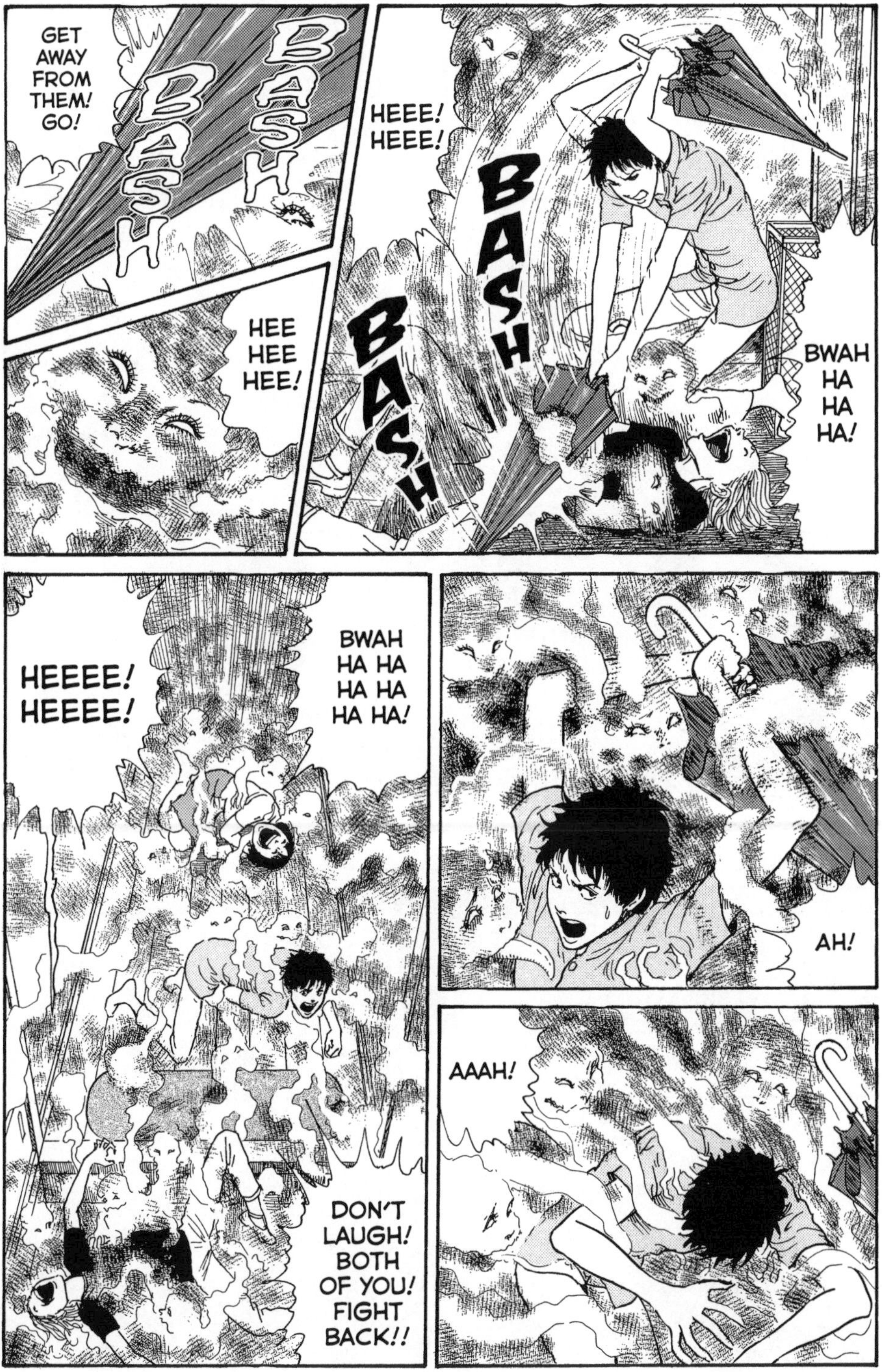
HEEE! HEEE!
BASH
BASH
BWAH HA HA HA!
BASH
BASH
GET AWAY FROM THEM! GO!
HEE HEE HEE!
AH!
AAAH!
BWAH HA HA HA HA HA HA!
HEEEE! HEEEE!
DON'T LAUGH! BOTH OF YOU! FIGHT BACK!!

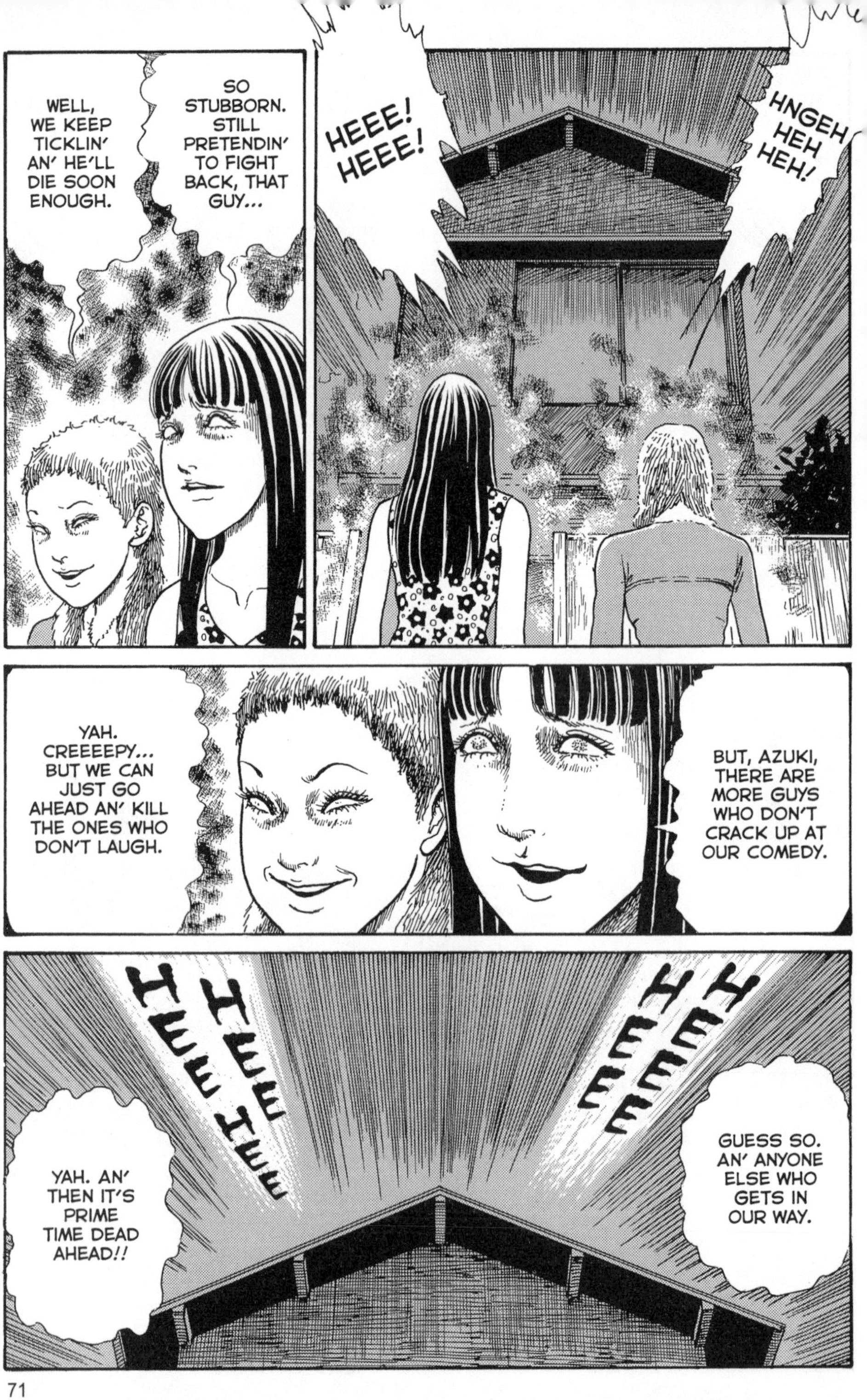
HNGEH HEH HEH!
HEEE! HEEE!
SO STUBBORN. STILL PRETENDIN' TO FIGHT BACK, THAT GUY...
WELL, WE KEEP TICKLIN' AN' HE'LL DIE SOON ENOUGH.
BUT, AZUKI, THERE ARE MORE GUYS WHO DON'T CRACK UP AT OUR COMEDY.
YAH. CREEEEPY... BUT WE CAN JUST GO AHEAD AN' KILL THE ONES WHO DON'T LAUGH.
HEEEEE
HEEE HEEE
GUESS SO. AN' ANYONE ELSE WHO GETS IN OUR WAY.
YAH. AN' THEN IT'S PRIME TIME DEAD AHEAD!!

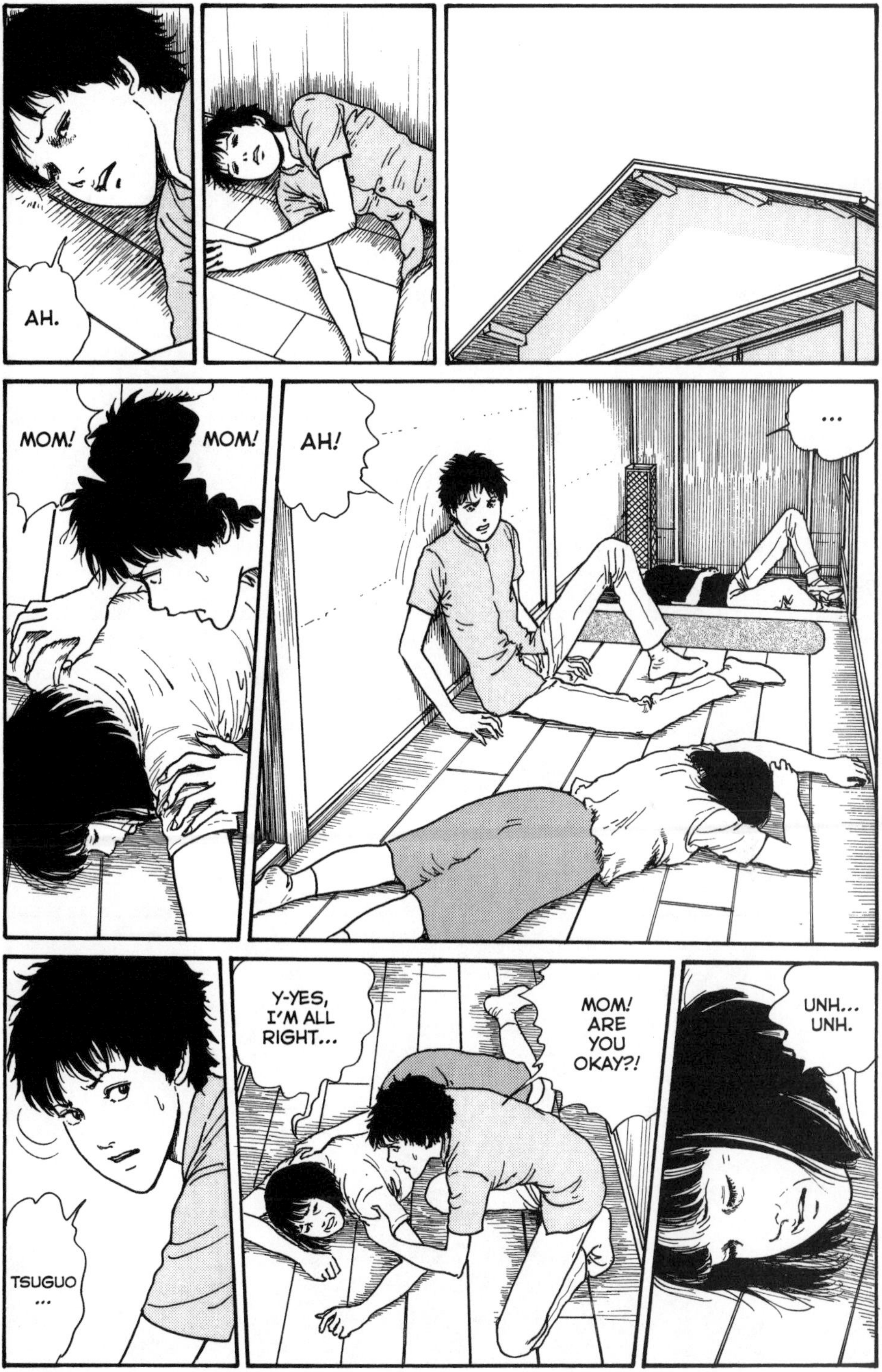
AH.
...
AH!
MOM!
MOM!
UNH... UNH.
MOM! ARE YOU OKAY?!
Y-YES, I'M ALL RIGHT...
TSUGUO ...

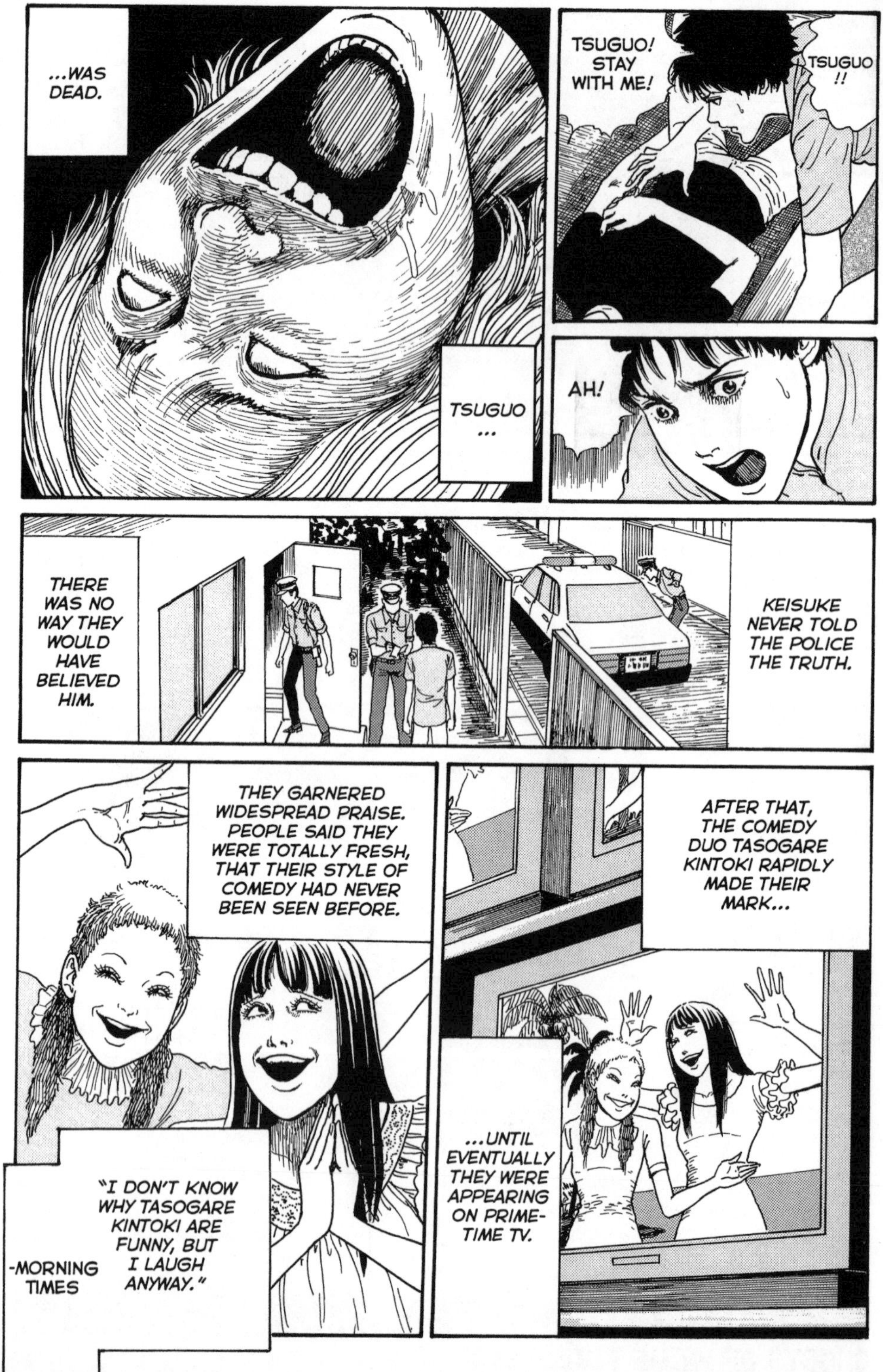
TSUGUO !!
TSUGUO! STAY WITH ME!
AH!
TSUGUO ...
...WAS DEAD.
KEISUKE NEVER TOLD THE POLICE THE TRUTH.
THERE WAS NO WAY THEY WOULD HAVE BELIEVED HIM.
AFTER THAT, THE COMEDY DUO TASOGARE KINTOKI RAPIDLY MADE THEIR MARK...
...UNTIL EVENTUALLY THEY WERE APPEARING ON PRIME-TIME TV.
THEY GARNERED WIDESPREAD PRAISE. PEOPLE SAID THEY WERE TOTALLY FRESH, THAT THEIR STYLE OF COMEDY HAD NEVER BEEN SEEN BEFORE.
"I DON'T KNOW WHY TASOGARE KINTOKI ARE FUNNY, BUT I LAUGH ANYWAY."
-MORNING TIMES

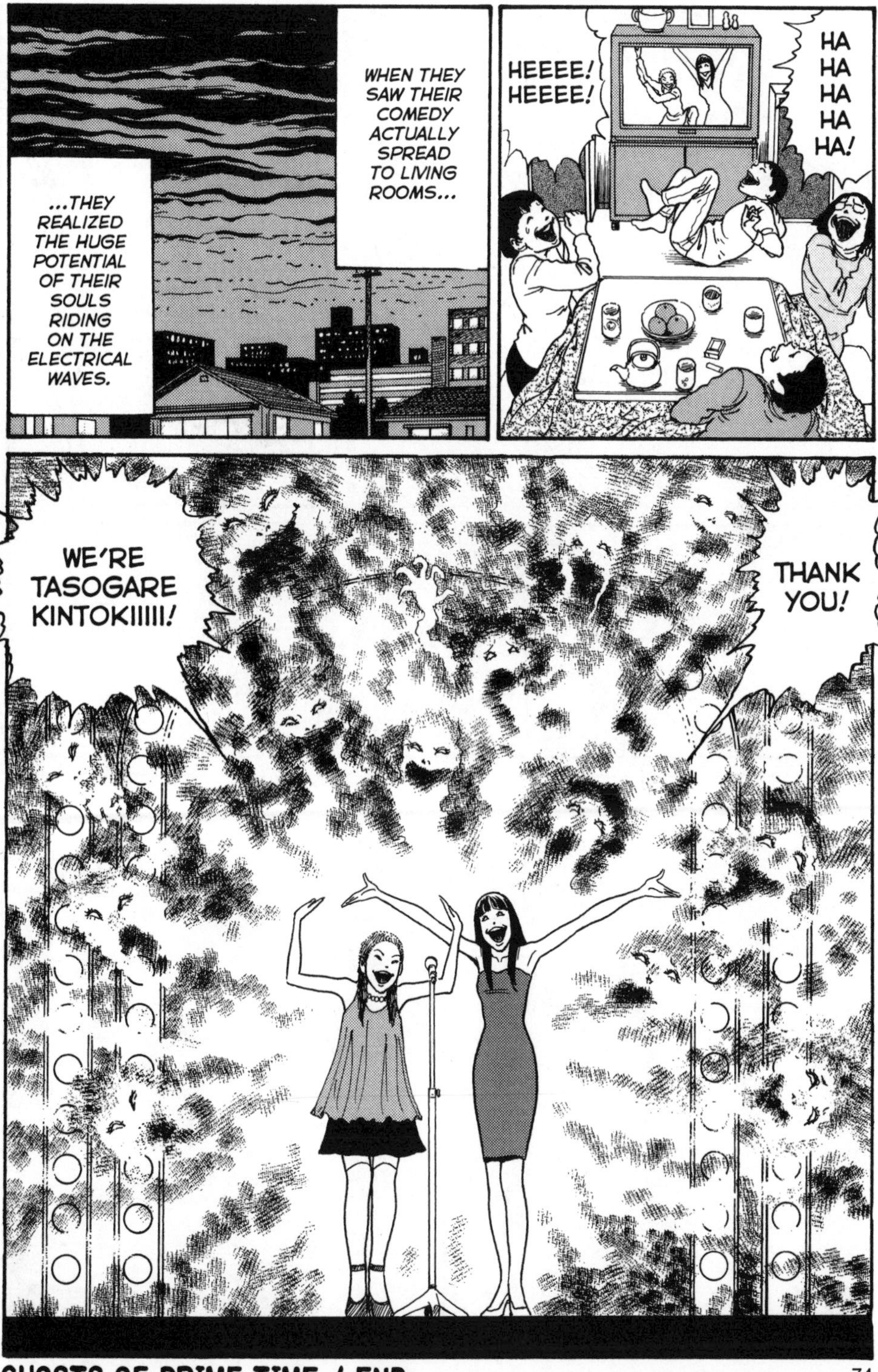
HEEEE! HEEEE!
HA HA HA HA HA!
WHEN THEY SAW THEIR COMEDY ACTUALLY SPREAD TO LIVING ROOMS...
...THEY REALIZED THE HUGE POTENTIAL OF THEIR SOULS RIDING ON THE ELECTRICAL WAVES.
THANK YOU!
WE'RE TASOGARE KINTOKIIIII!

GHOSTS OF PRIME TIME / END

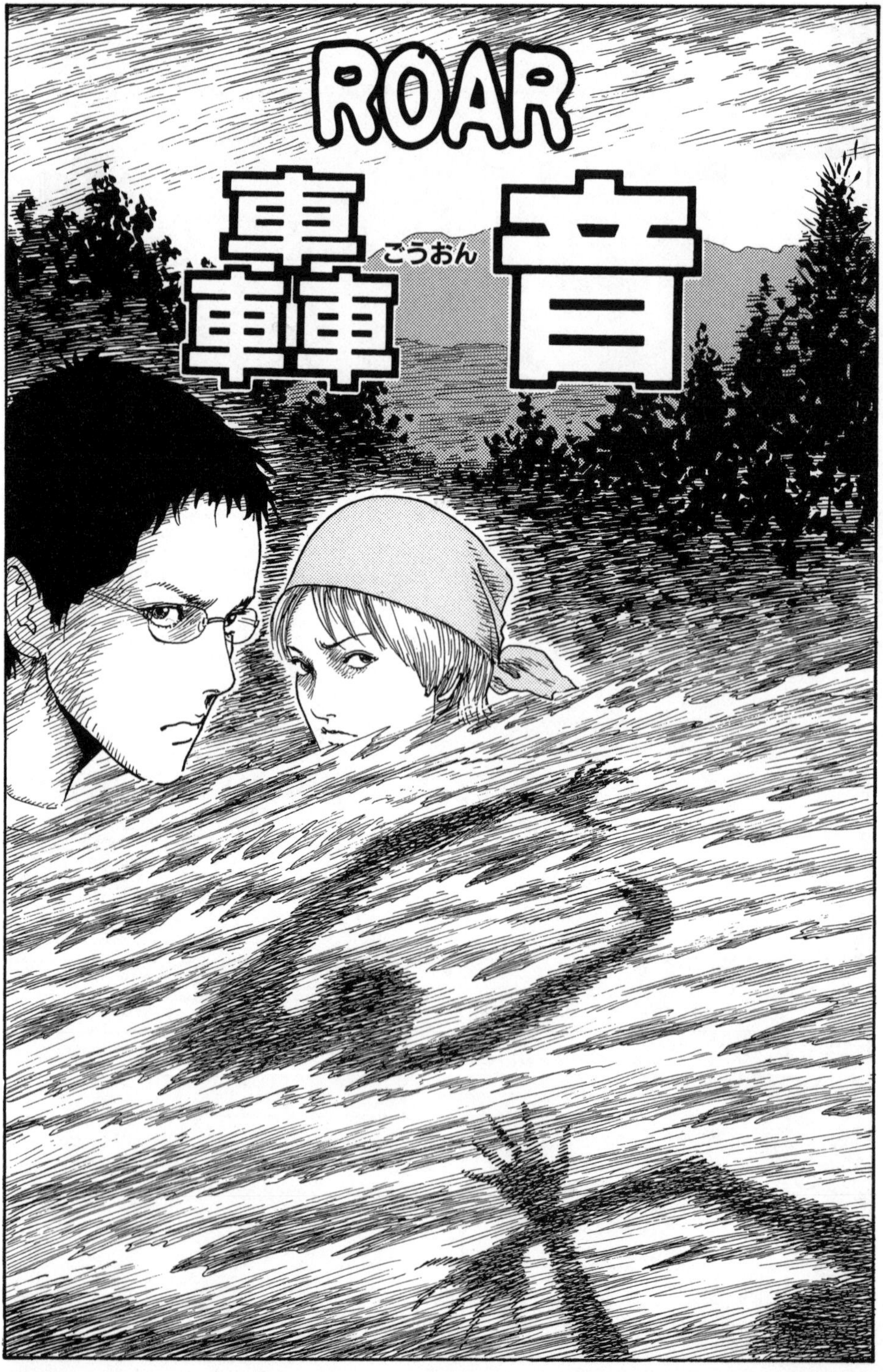
ROAR
轟音
ごうおん

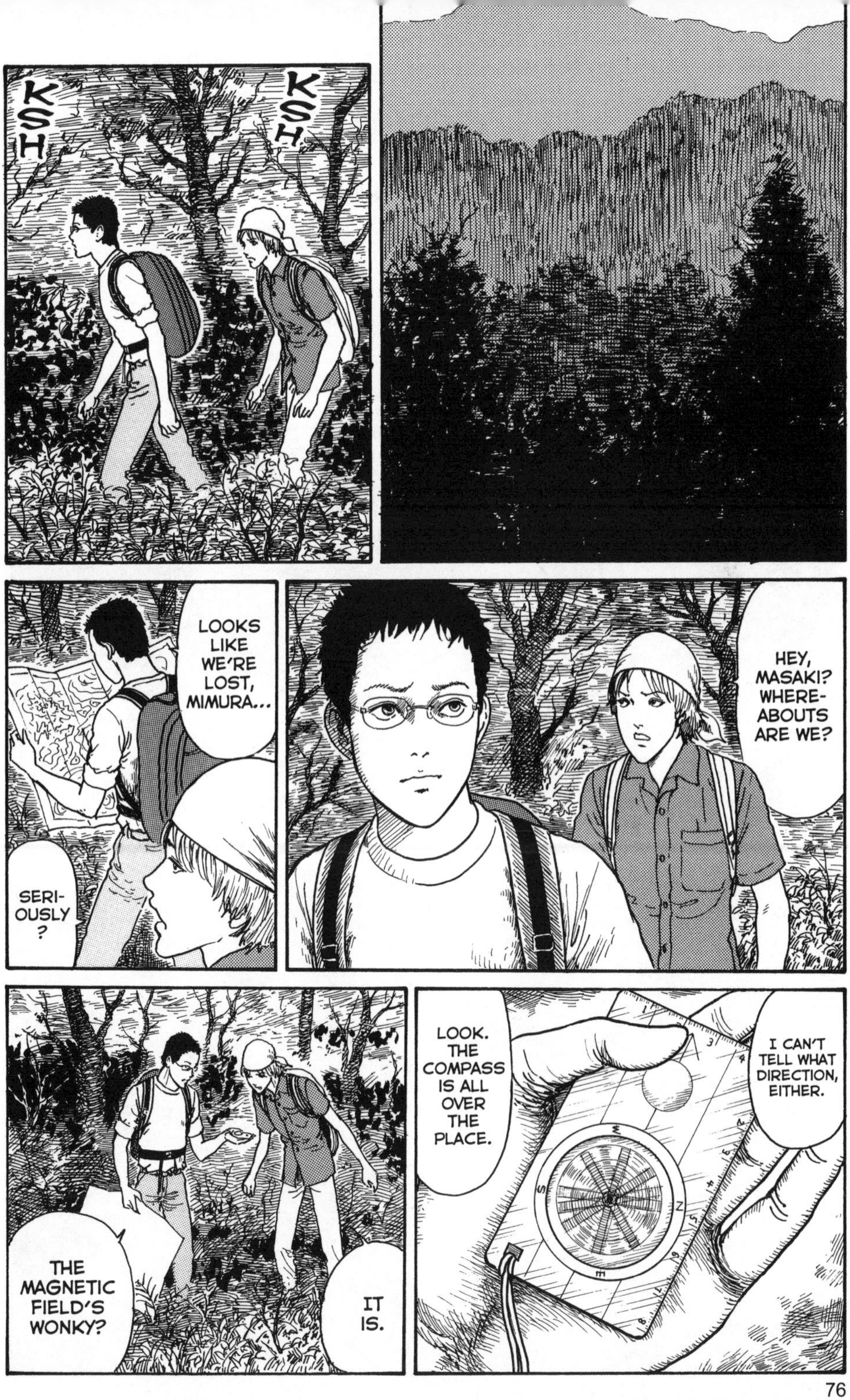
KSH
KSH
HEY, MASAKI? WHEREABOUTS ARE WE?
LOOKS LIKE WE'RE LOST, MIMURA...
SERIOUSLY?
I CAN'T TELL WHAT DIRECTION, EITHER.
LOOK. THE COMPASS IS ALL OVER THE PLACE.
THE MAGNETIC FIELD'S WONKY?
IT IS.

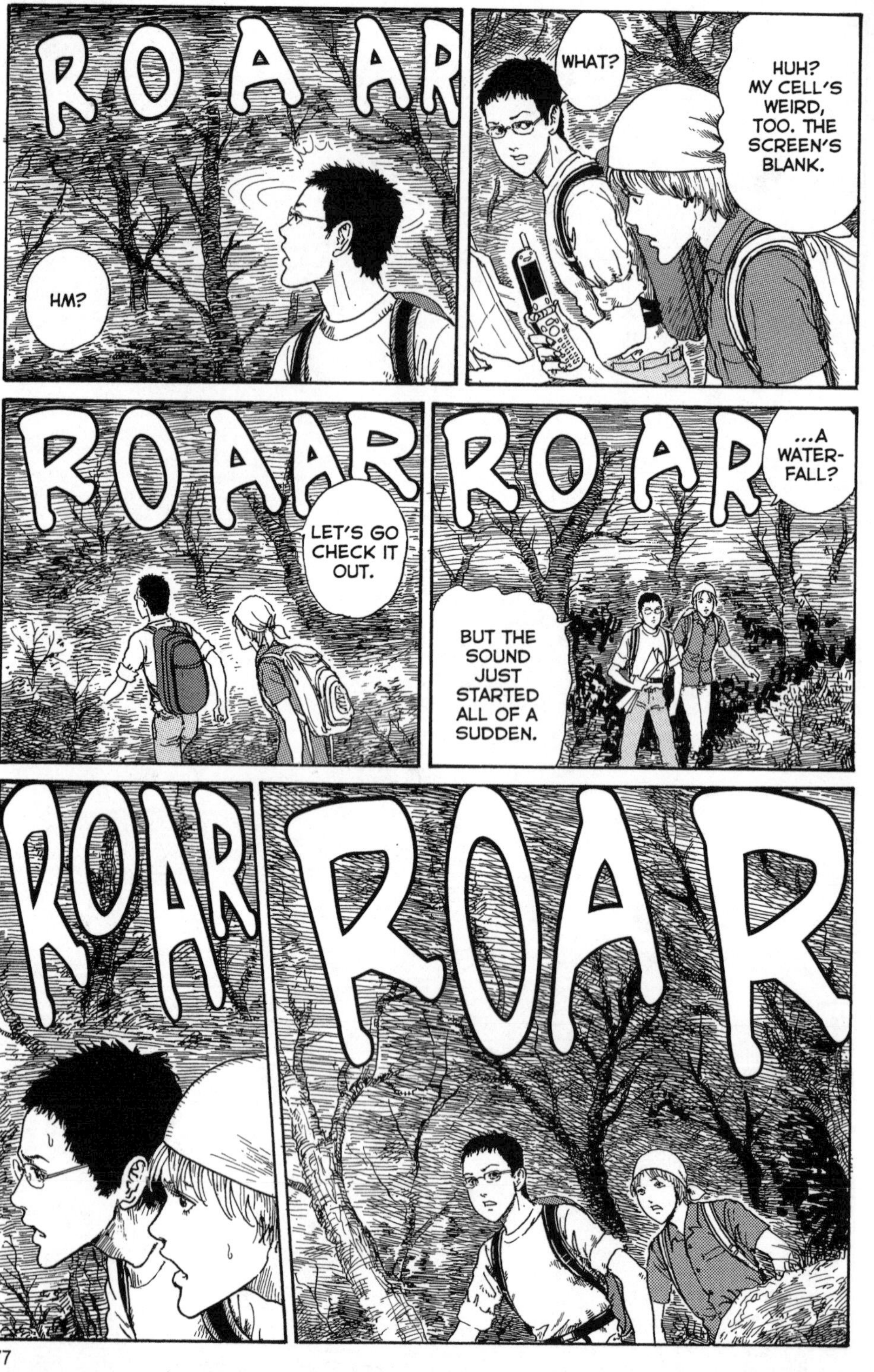
HUH? MY CELL'S WEIRD, TOO. THE SCREEN'S BLANK.
WHAT?
ROAAR
HM?
ROAR
...A WATER-FALL?
BUT THE SOUND JUST STARTED ALL OF A SUDDEN.
ROAAR
LET'S GO CHECK IT OUT.
ROAR
ROAR

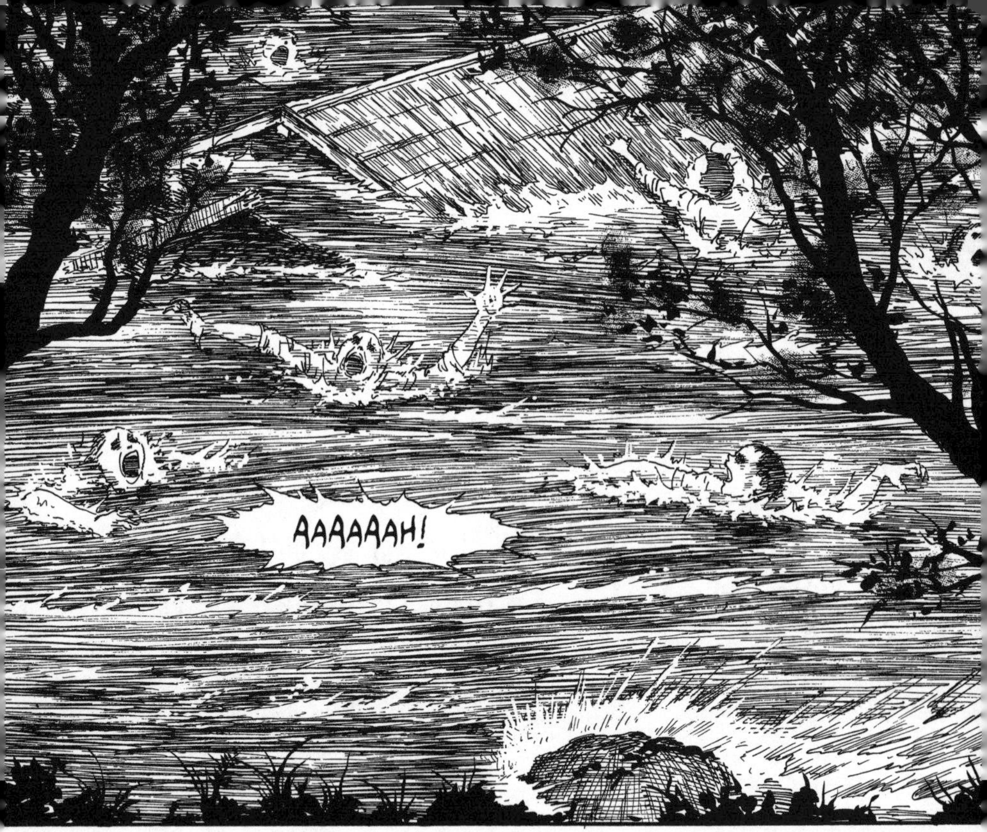
AAAAAAH!
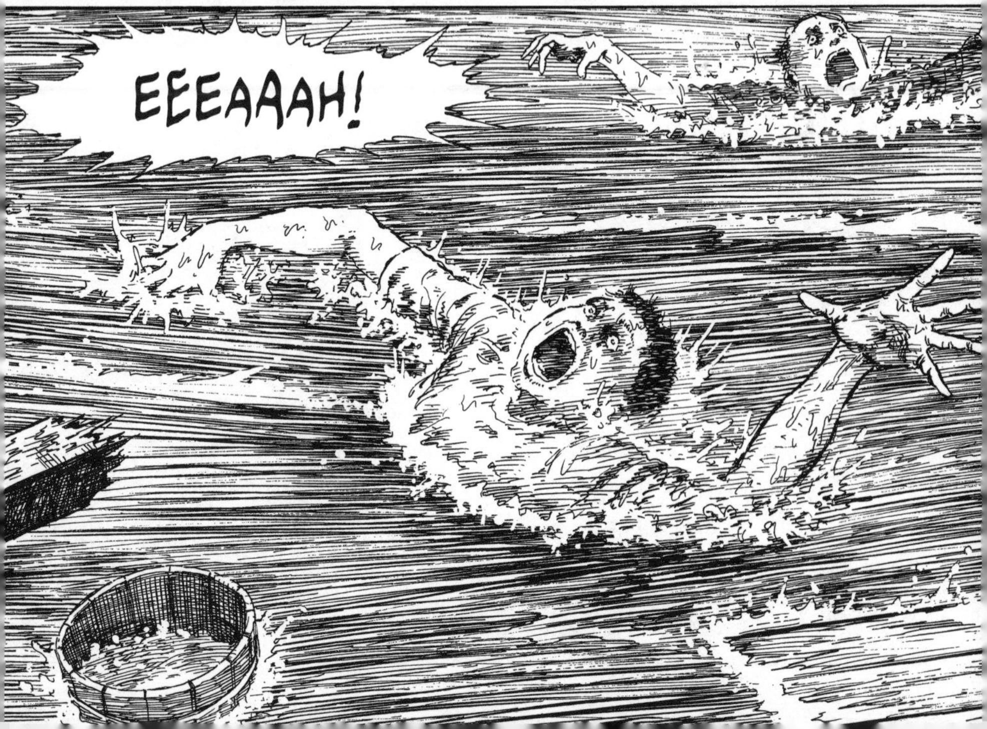
EEEAAAH!

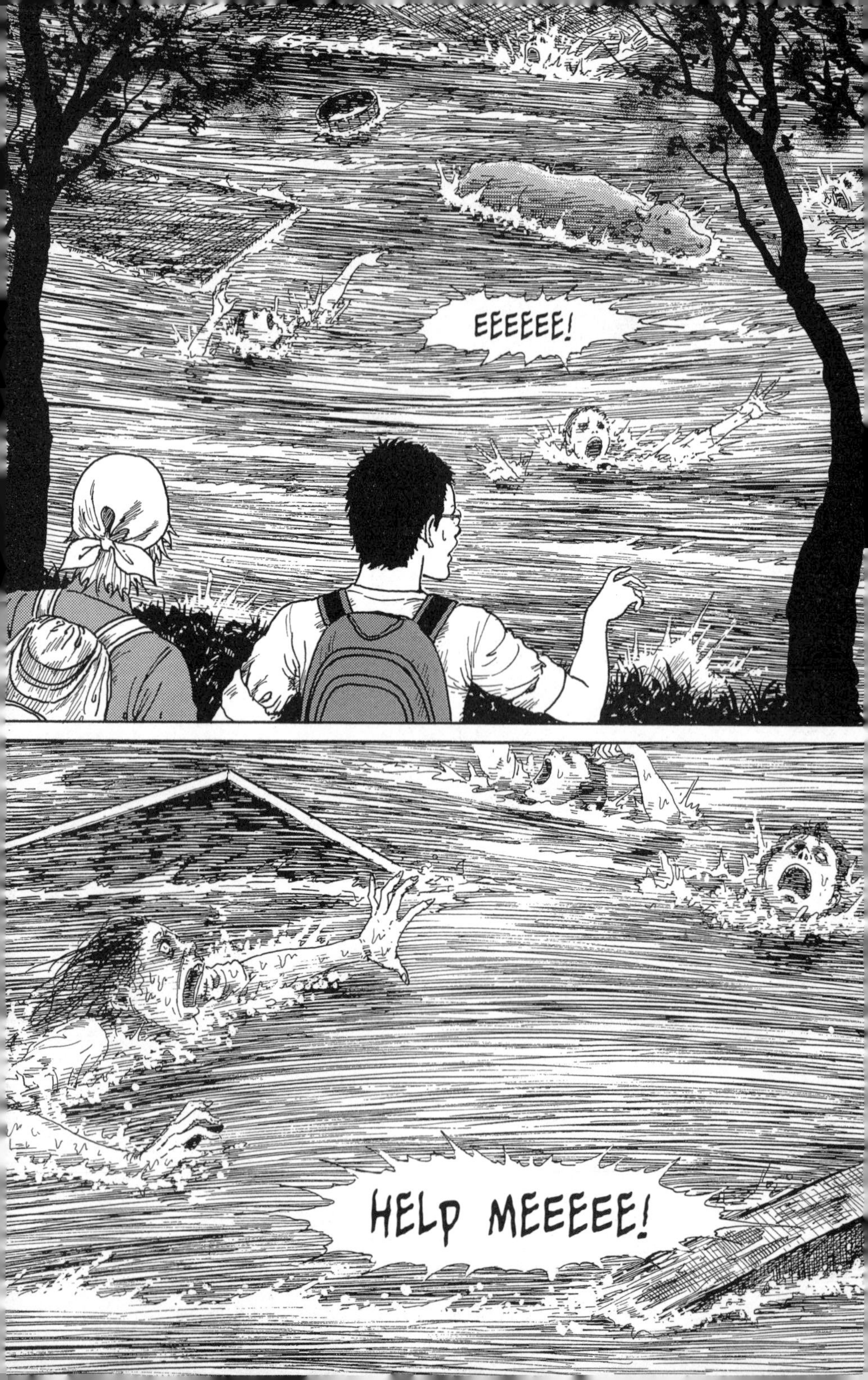
EEEEEE!
HELP MEEEEE!

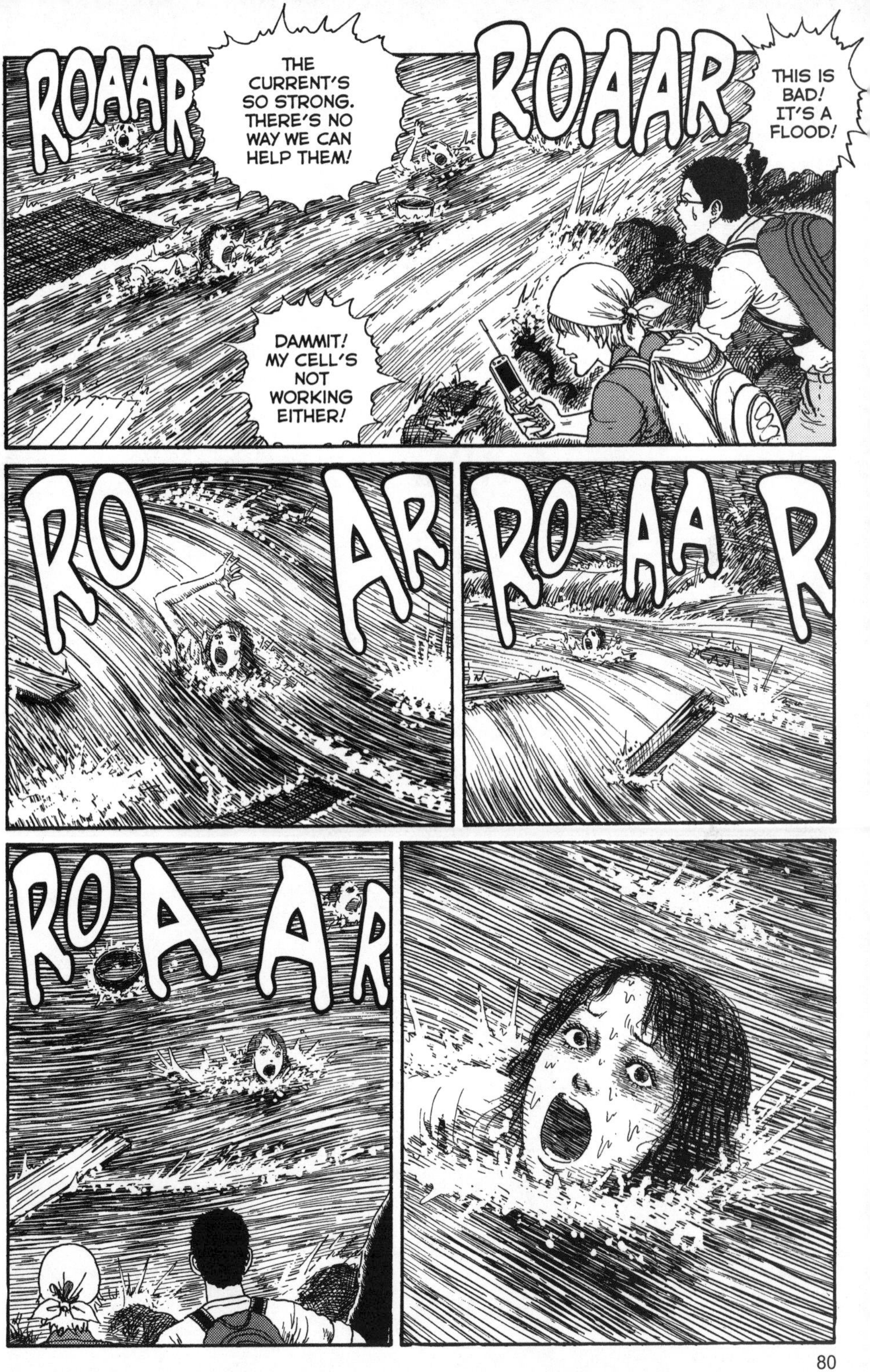
THIS IS BAD! IT'S A FLOOD!
ROAAR
THE CURRENT'S SO STRONG. THERE'S NO WAY WE CAN HELP THEM!
ROAAR
DAMMIT! MY CELL'S NOT WORKING EITHER!
ROAAR
ROAR
ROAAR

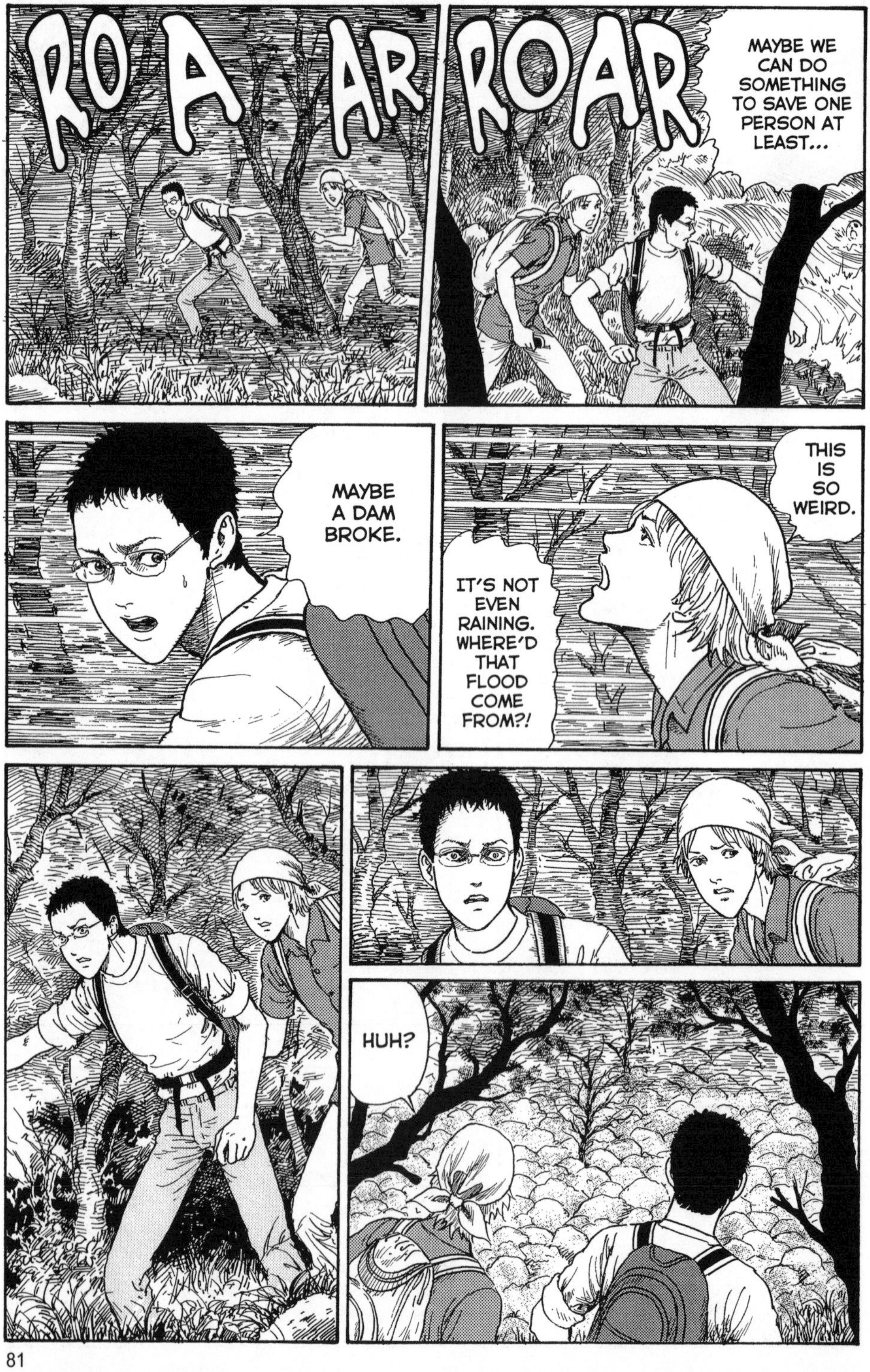
MAYBE WE CAN DO SOMETHING TO SAVE ONE PERSON AT LEAST...
ROAR
RO A AR
THIS IS SO WEIRD.
IT'S NOT EVEN RAINING. WHERE'D THAT FLOOD COME FROM?!
MAYBE A DAM BROKE.
HUH?

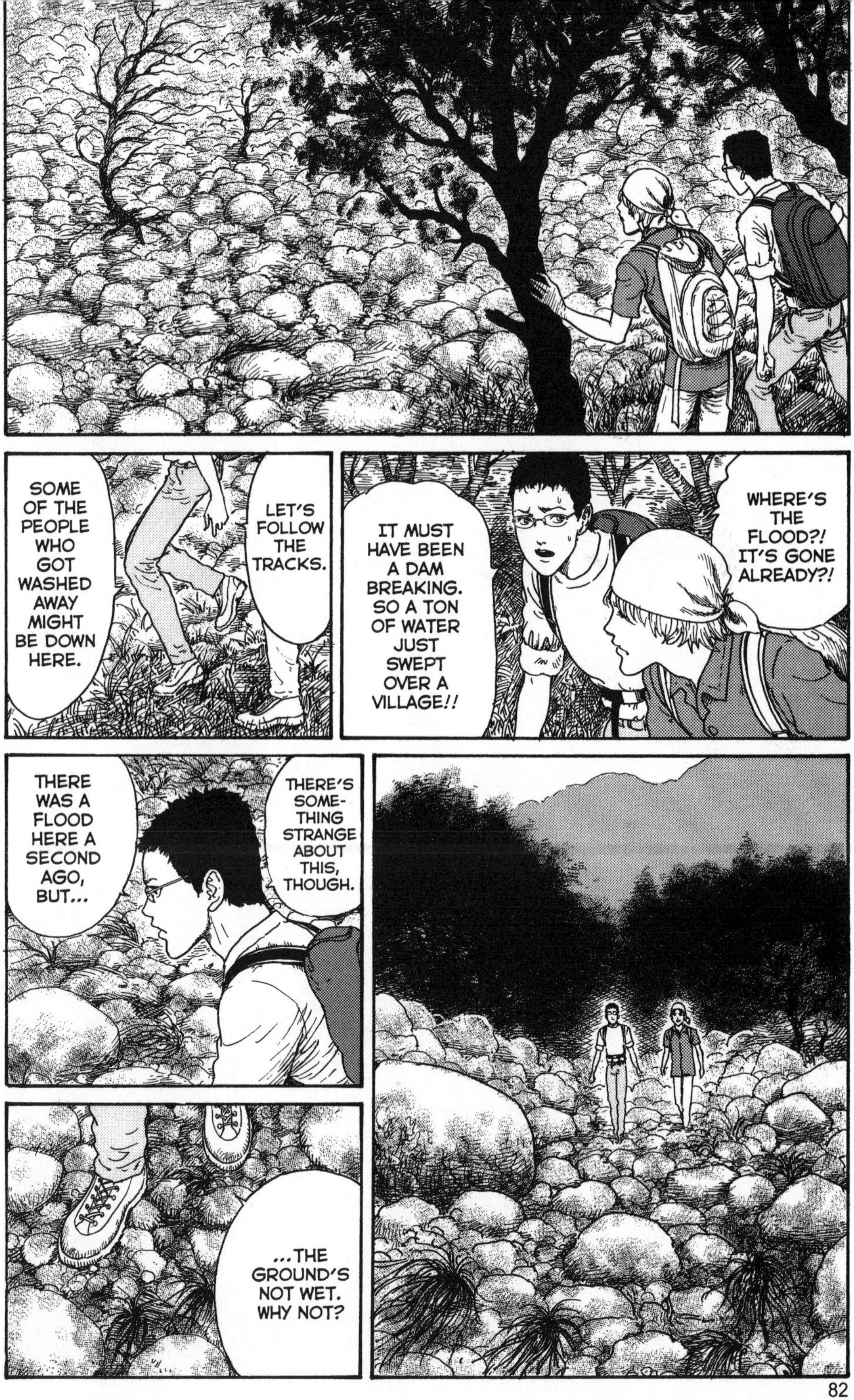
WHERE'S THE FLOOD?! IT'S GONE ALREADY?!
IT MUST HAVE BEEN A DAM BREAKING. SO A TON OF WATER JUST SWEPT OVER A VILLAGE!!
LET'S FOLLOW THE TRACKS.
SOME OF THE PEOPLE WHO GOT WASHED AWAY MIGHT BE DOWN HERE.
THERE'S SOMETHING STRANGE ABOUT THIS, THOUGH.
THERE WAS A FLOOD HERE A SECOND AGO, BUT...
...THE GROUND'S NOT WET. WHY NOT?

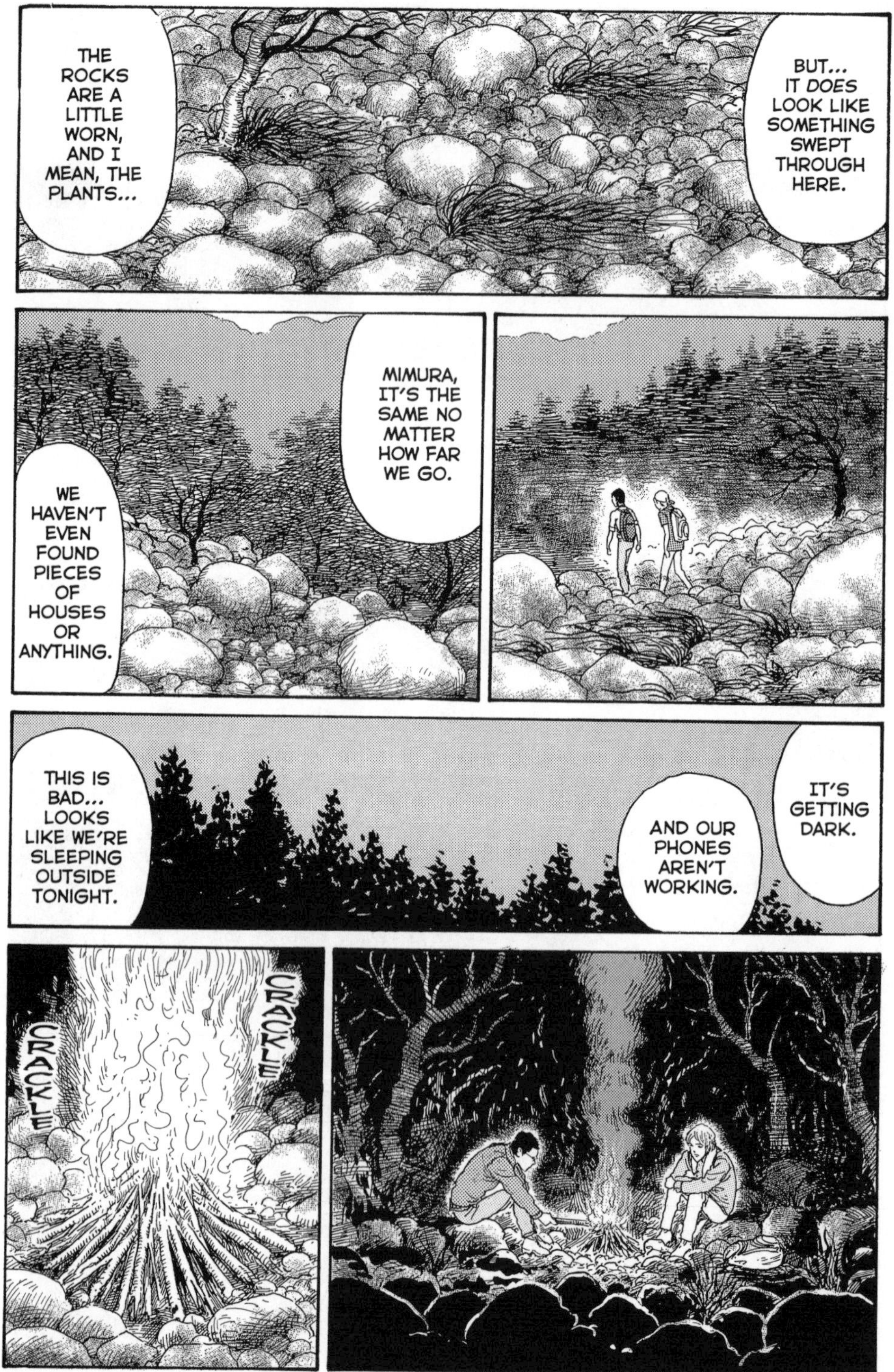
BUT... IT *DOES* LOOK LIKE SOMETHING SWEPT THROUGH HERE.
THE ROCKS ARE A LITTLE WORN, AND I MEAN, THE PLANTS...
MIMURA, IT'S THE SAME NO MATTER HOW FAR WE GO.
WE HAVEN'T EVEN FOUND PIECES OF HOUSES OR ANYTHING.
IT'S GETTING DARK.
AND OUR PHONES AREN'T WORKING.
THIS IS BAD... LOOKS LIKE WE'RE SLEEPING OUTSIDE TONIGHT.
CRACKLE
CRACKLE

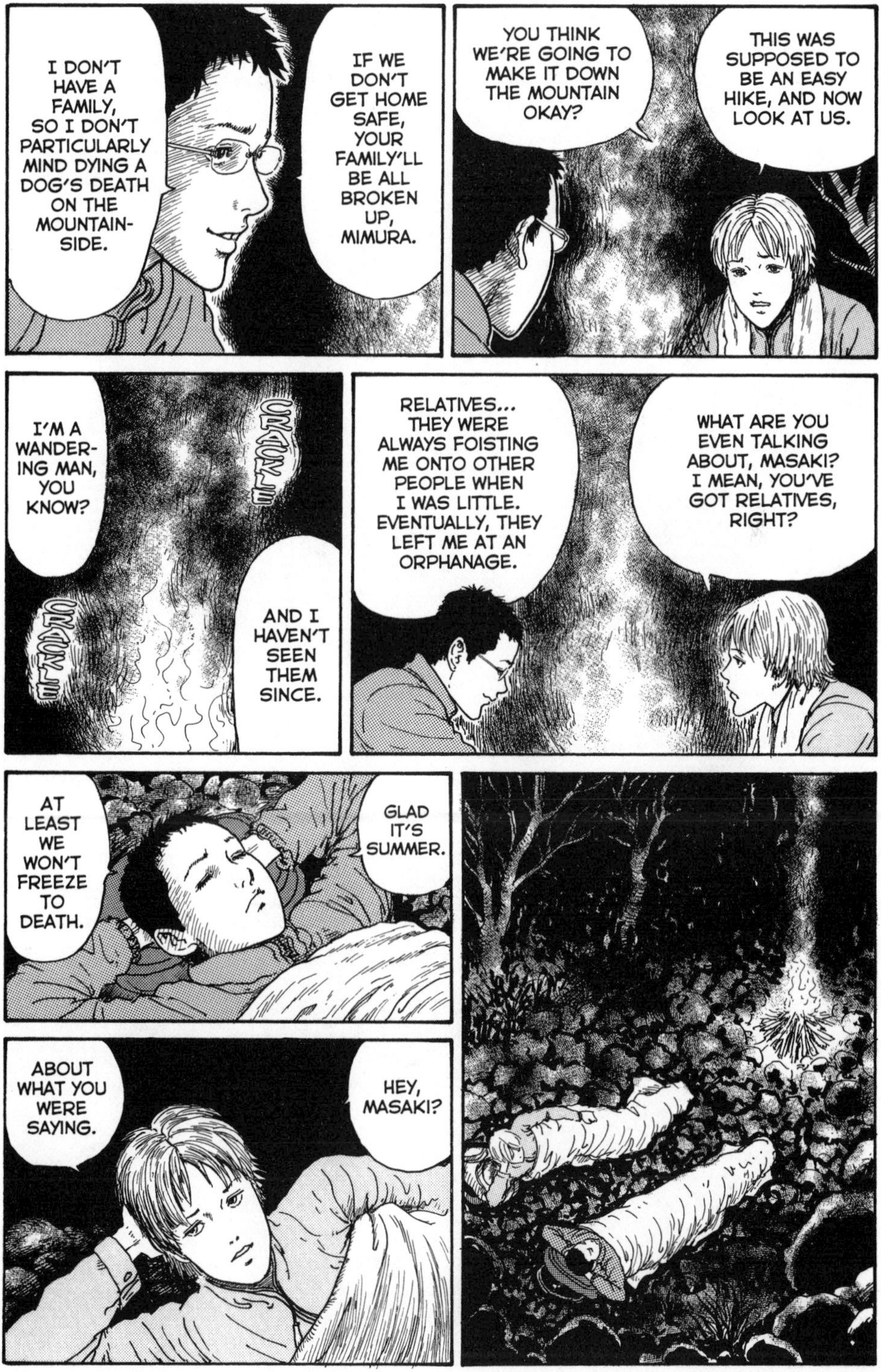
THIS WAS SUPPOSED TO BE AN EASY HIKE, AND NOW LOOK AT US.
YOU THINK WE'RE GOING TO MAKE IT DOWN THE MOUNTAIN OKAY?
IF WE DON'T GET HOME SAFE, YOUR FAMILY'LL BE ALL BROKEN UP, MIMURA.
I DON'T HAVE A FAMILY, SO I DON'T PARTICULARLY MIND DYING A DOG'S DEATH ON THE MOUNTAIN-SIDE.
WHAT ARE YOU EVEN TALKING ABOUT, MASAKI? I MEAN, YOU'VE GOT RELATIVES, RIGHT?
RELATIVES... THEY WERE ALWAYS FOISTING ME ONTO OTHER PEOPLE WHEN I WAS LITTLE. EVENTUALLY, THEY LEFT ME AT AN ORPHANAGE.
CRACKLE
AND I HAVEN'T SEEN THEM SINCE.
I'M A WANDER-ING MAN, YOU KNOW?
CRACKLE
GLAD IT'S SUMMER.
AT LEAST WE WON'T FREEZE TO DEATH.
HEY, MASAKI?
ABOUT WHAT YOU WERE SAYING.

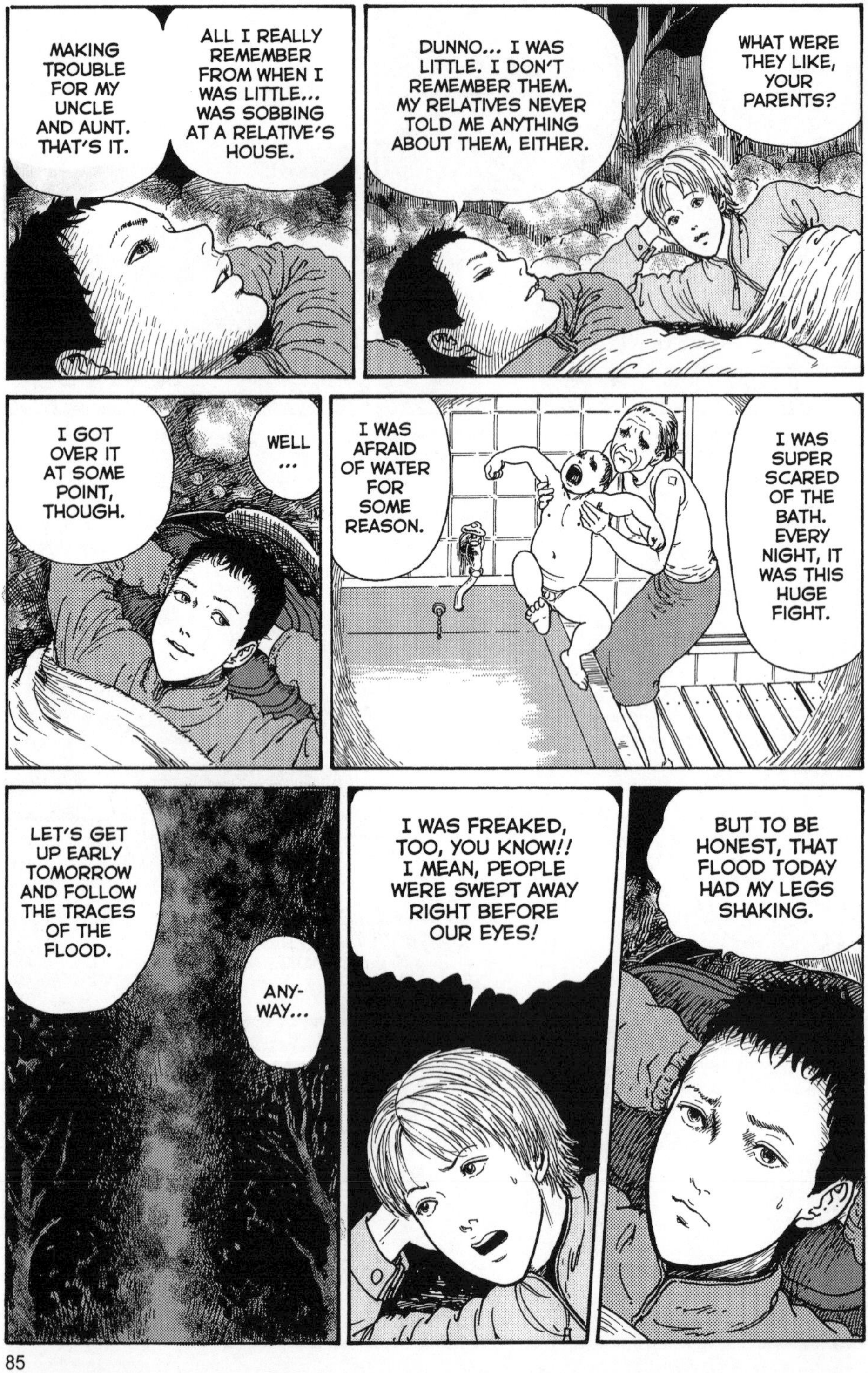
WHAT WERE THEY LIKE, YOUR PARENTS?
DUNNO... I WAS LITTLE. I DON'T REMEMBER THEM. MY RELATIVES NEVER TOLD ME ANYTHING ABOUT THEM, EITHER.
ALL I REALLY REMEMBER FROM WHEN I WAS LITTLE... WAS SOBBING AT A RELATIVE'S HOUSE.
MAKING TROUBLE FOR MY UNCLE AND AUNT. THAT'S IT.
I WAS SUPER SCARED OF THE BATH. EVERY NIGHT, IT WAS THIS HUGE FIGHT.
I WAS AFRAID OF WATER FOR SOME REASON.
WELL ...
I GOT OVER IT AT SOME POINT, THOUGH.
BUT TO BE HONEST, THAT FLOOD TODAY HAD MY LEGS SHAKING.
I WAS FREAKED, TOO, YOU KNOW!! I MEAN, PEOPLE WERE SWEPT AWAY RIGHT BEFORE OUR EYES!
ANY-WAY...
LET'S GET UP EARLY TOMORROW AND FOLLOW THE TRACES OF THE FLOOD.

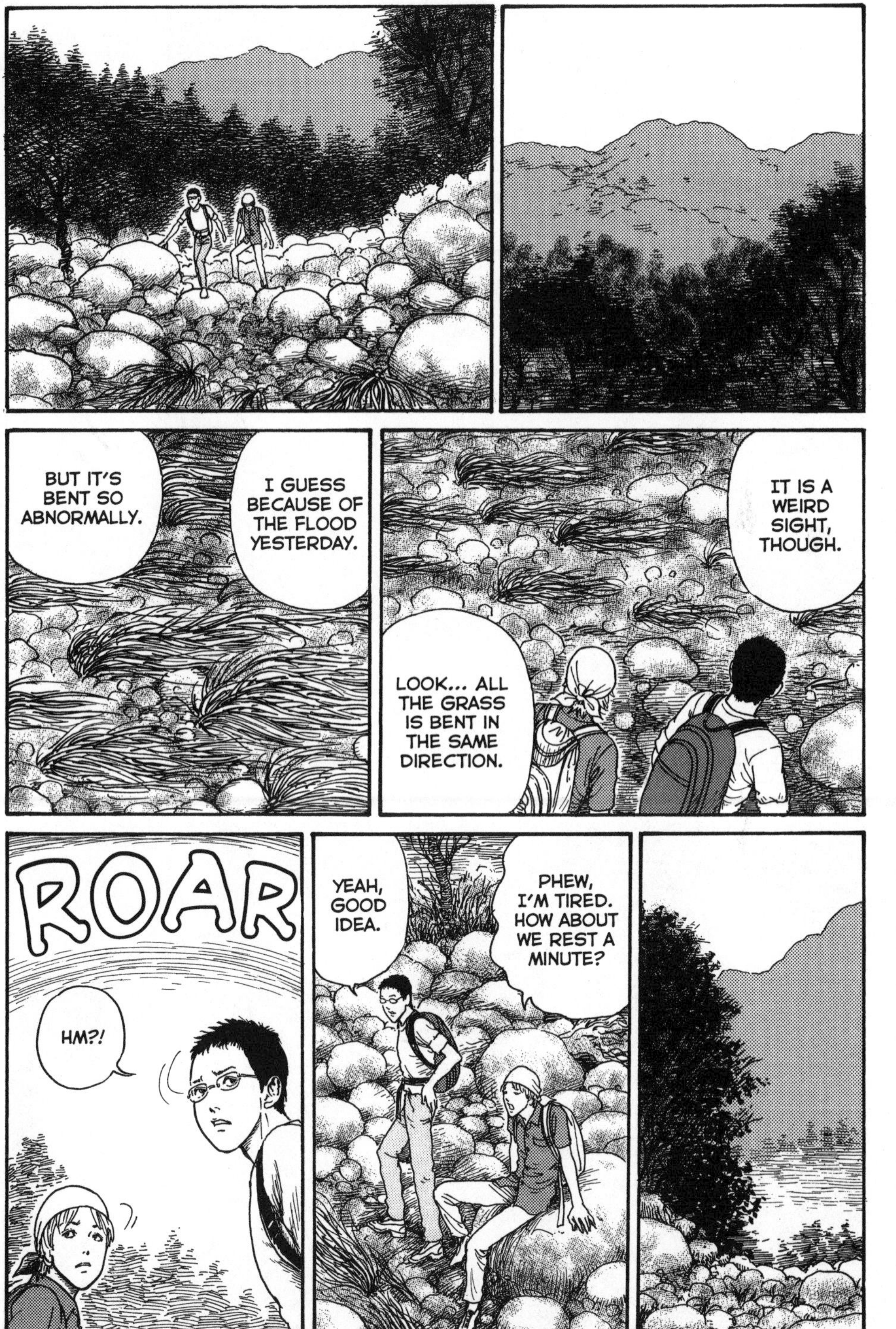
IT IS A WEIRD SIGHT, THOUGH.
LOOK... ALL THE GRASS IS BENT IN THE SAME DIRECTION.
I GUESS BECAUSE OF THE FLOOD YESTERDAY.
BUT IT'S BENT SO ABNORMALLY.
PHEW, I'M TIRED. HOW ABOUT WE REST A MINUTE?
YEAH, GOOD IDEA.
ROAR
HM?!

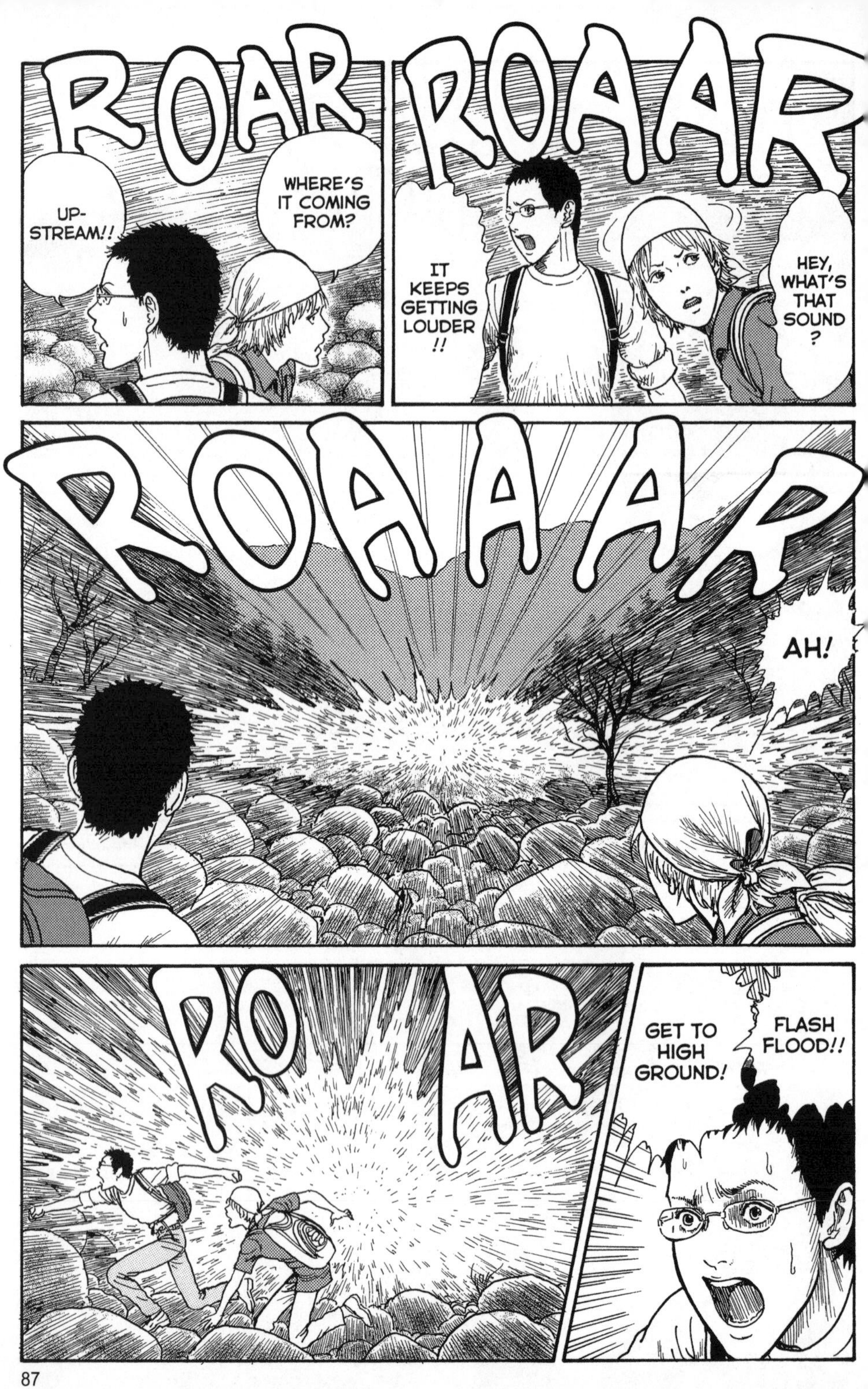
ROAAAR
HEY, WHAT'S THAT SOUND?
IT KEEPS GETTING LOUDER!!
ROAR
WHERE'S IT COMING FROM?
UP-STREAM!!
ROAAAR
AH!
FLASH FLOOD!!
GET TO HIGH GROUND!
RO AR

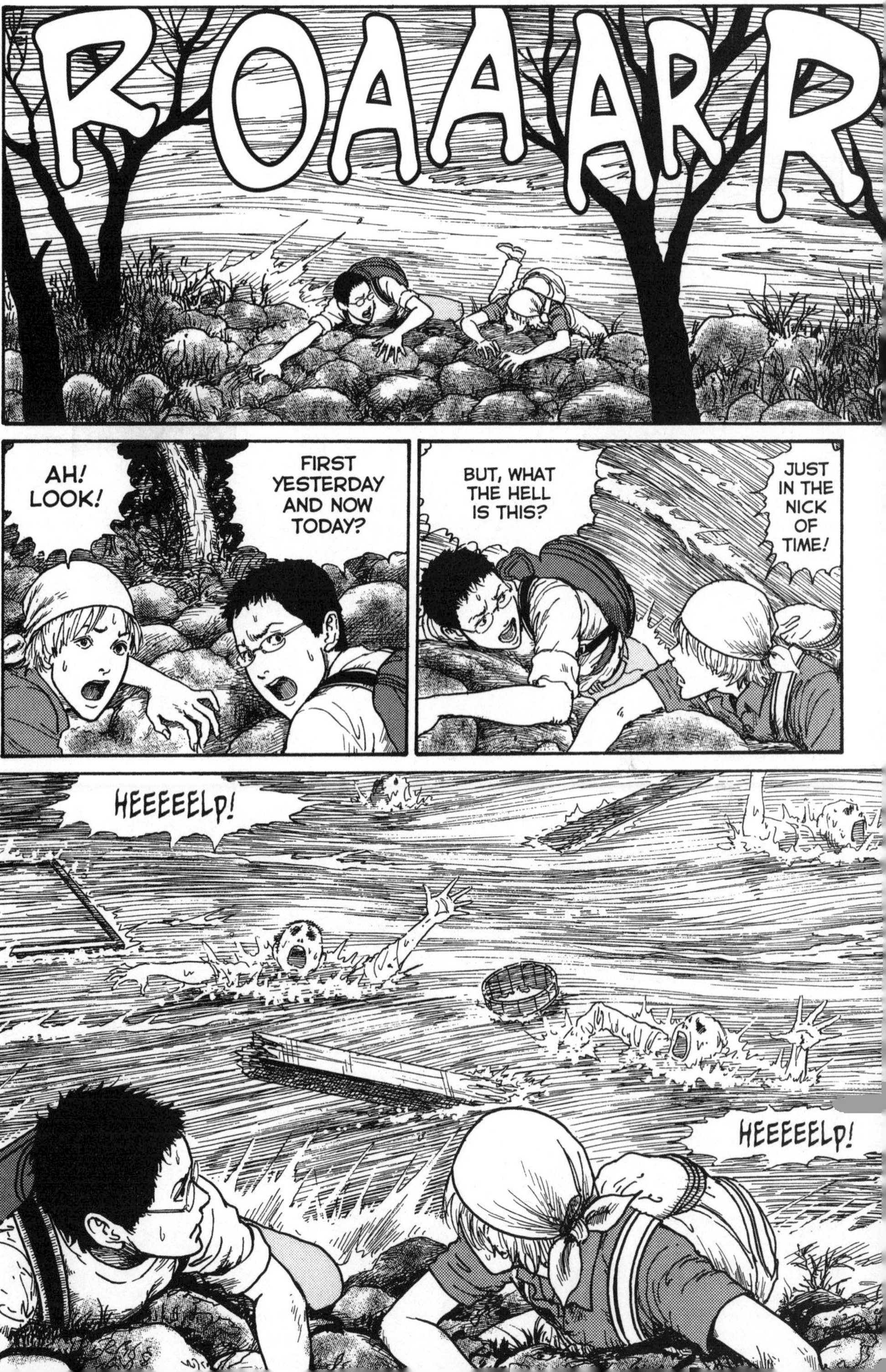
ROAAARR
JUST IN THE NICK OF TIME!
BUT, WHAT THE HELL IS THIS?
FIRST YESTERDAY AND NOW TODAY?
AH! LOOK!
HEEEEELP!
HEEEEELP!

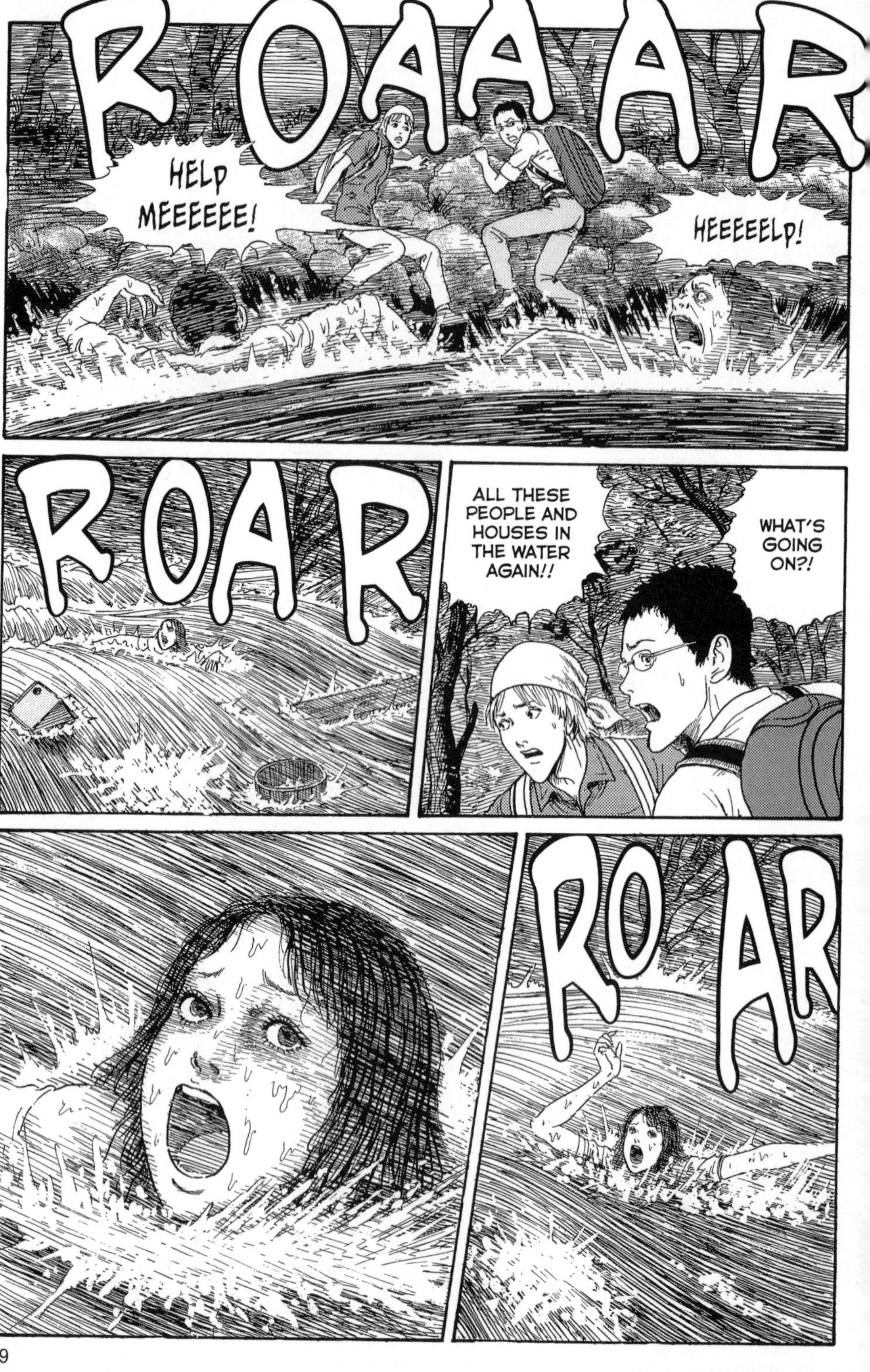
ROAAAR
HEEEEELP!
HELP MEEEEEE!
WHAT'S GOING ON?!
ALL THESE PEOPLE AND HOUSES IN THE WATER AGAIN!!
ROAR
ROAR

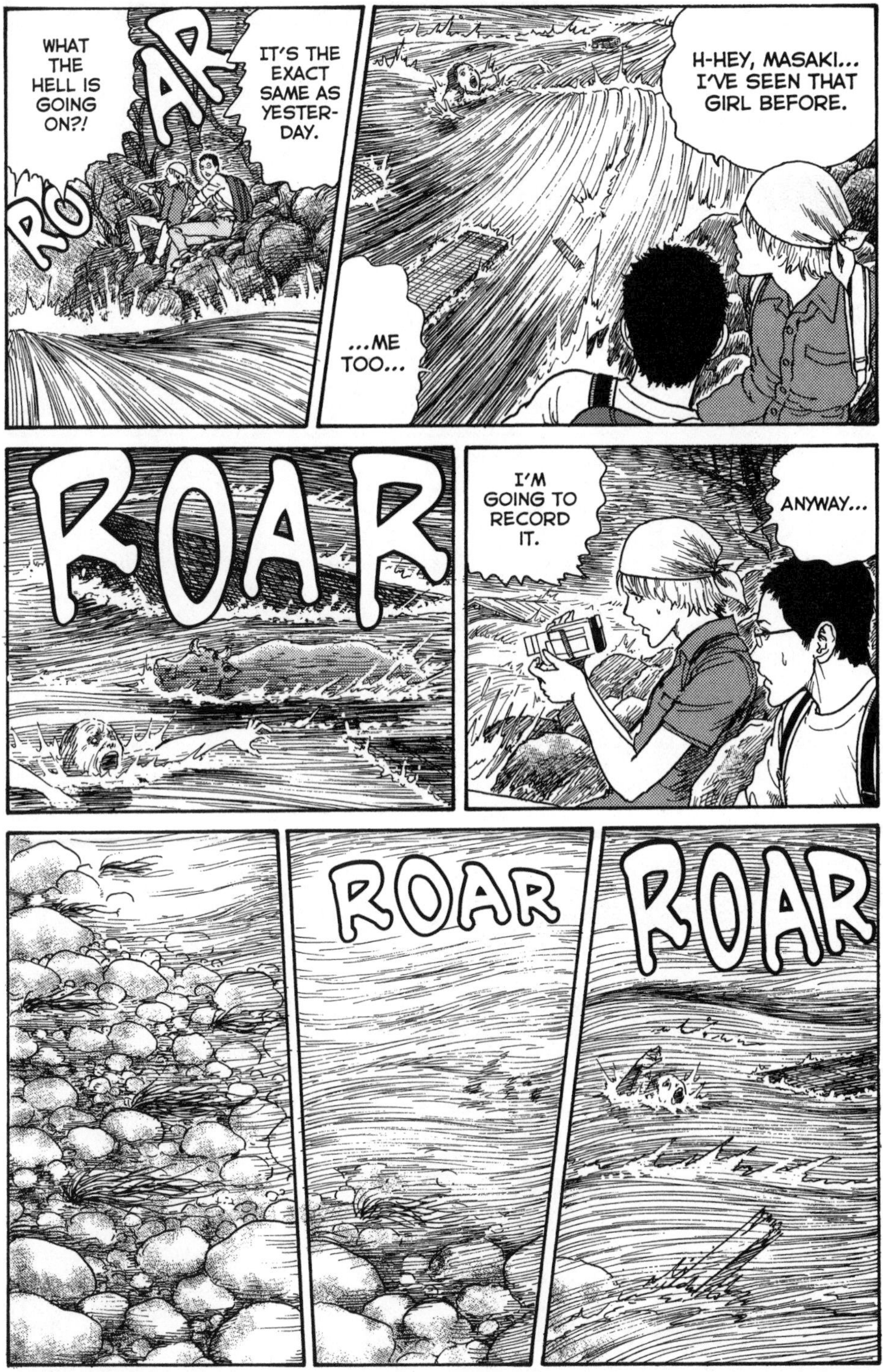
H-HEY, MASAKI... I'VE SEEN THAT GIRL BEFORE.
...ME TOO...
IT'S THE EXACT SAME AS YESTERDAY.
ROAR
WHAT THE HELL IS GOING ON?!
ANYWAY...
I'M GOING TO RECORD IT.
ROAR
ROAR
ROAR

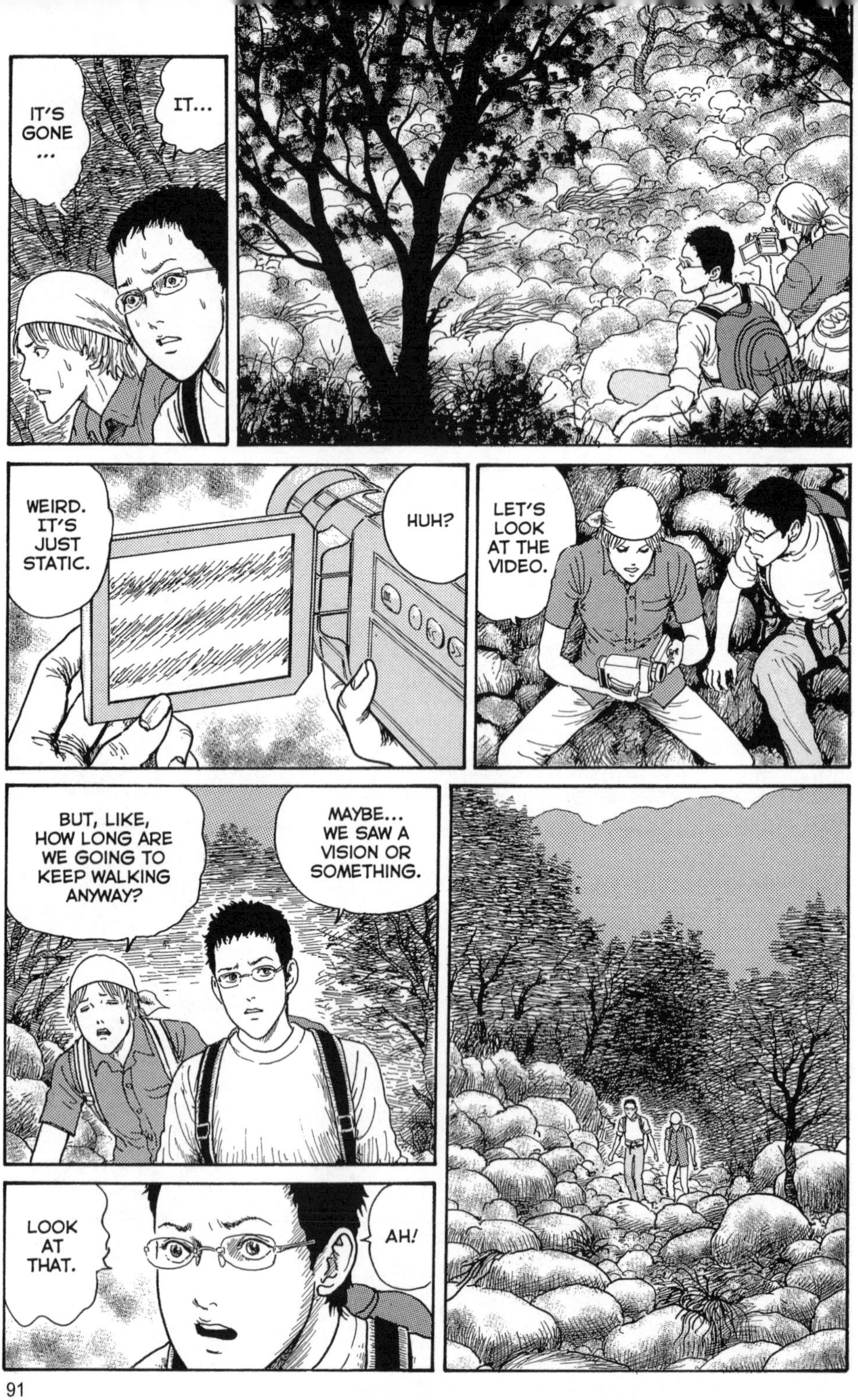
IT...
IT'S GONE ...
LET'S LOOK AT THE VIDEO.
HUH?
WEIRD. IT'S JUST STATIC.
MAYBE... WE SAW A VISION OR SOMETHING.
BUT, LIKE, HOW LONG ARE WE GOING TO KEEP WALKING ANYWAY?
AH!
LOOK AT THAT.

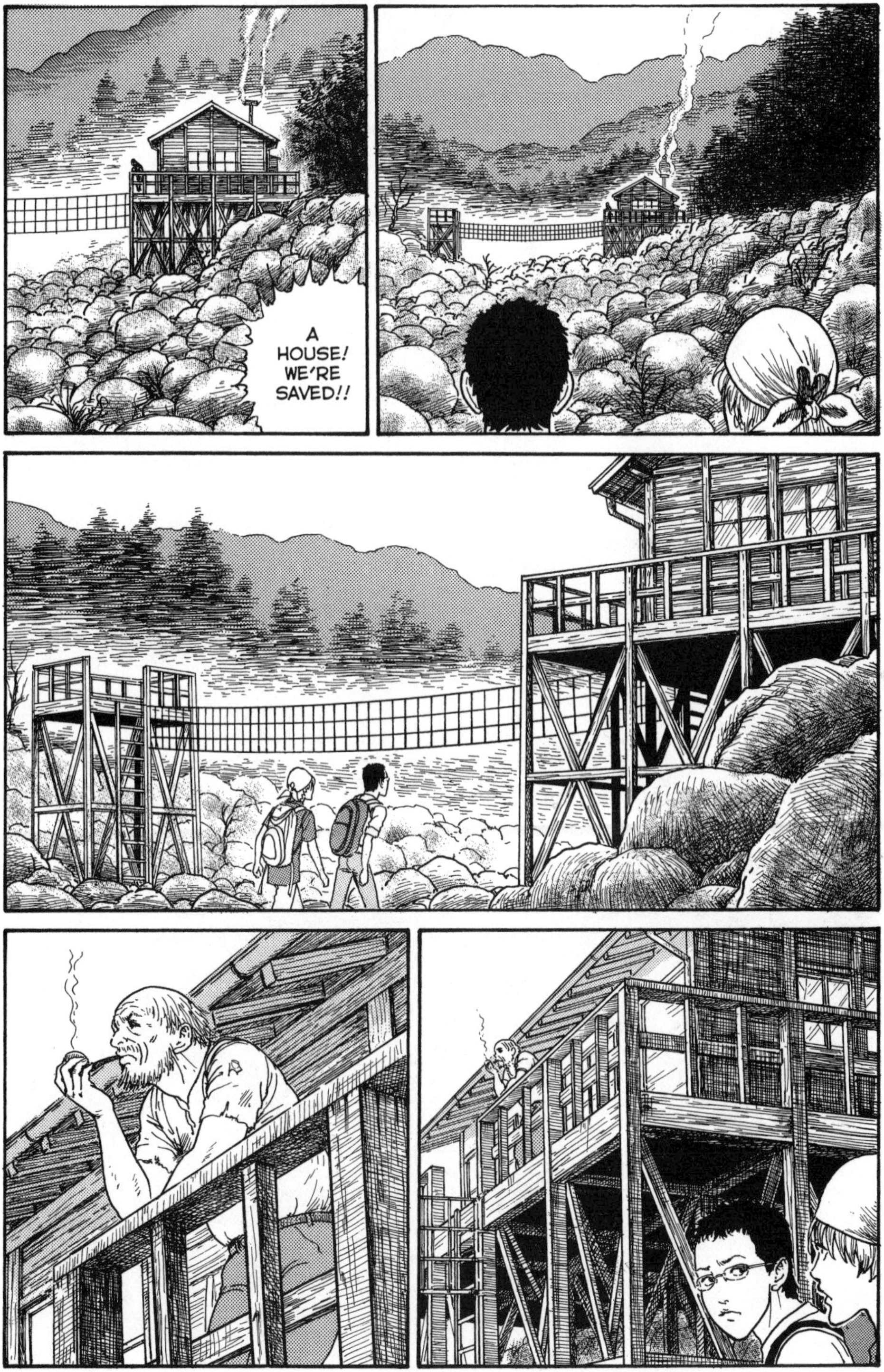
A HOUSE! WE'RE SAVED!!

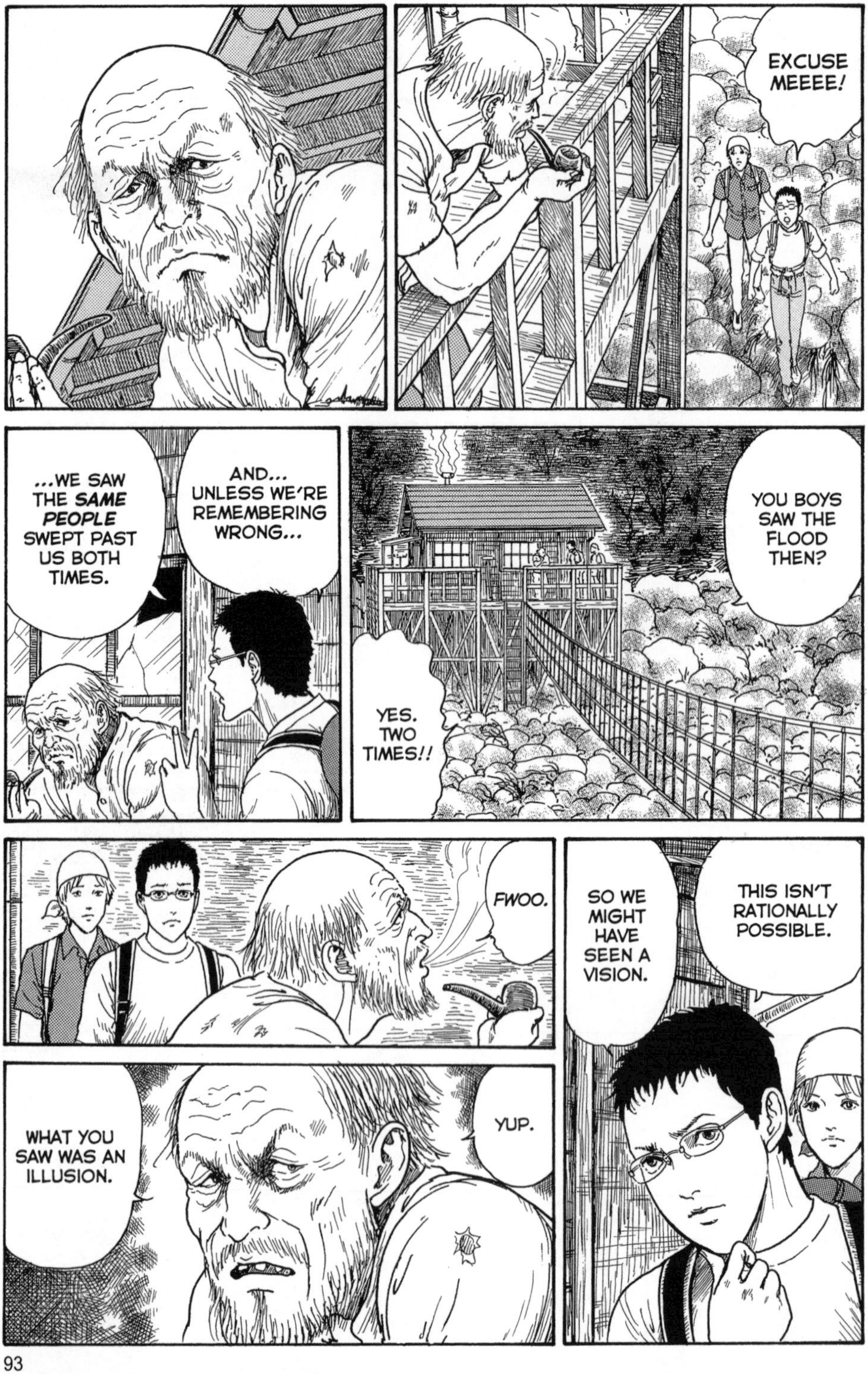
EXCUSE MEEEE!
YOU BOYS SAW THE FLOOD THEN?
YES. TWO TIMES!!
AND... UNLESS WE'RE REMEMBERING WRONG...
...WE SAW THE *SAME PEOPLE* SWEPT PAST US BOTH TIMES.
THIS ISN'T RATIONALLY POSSIBLE.
SO WE MIGHT HAVE SEEN A VISION.
FWOO.
YUP.
WHAT YOU SAW WAS AN ILLUSION.

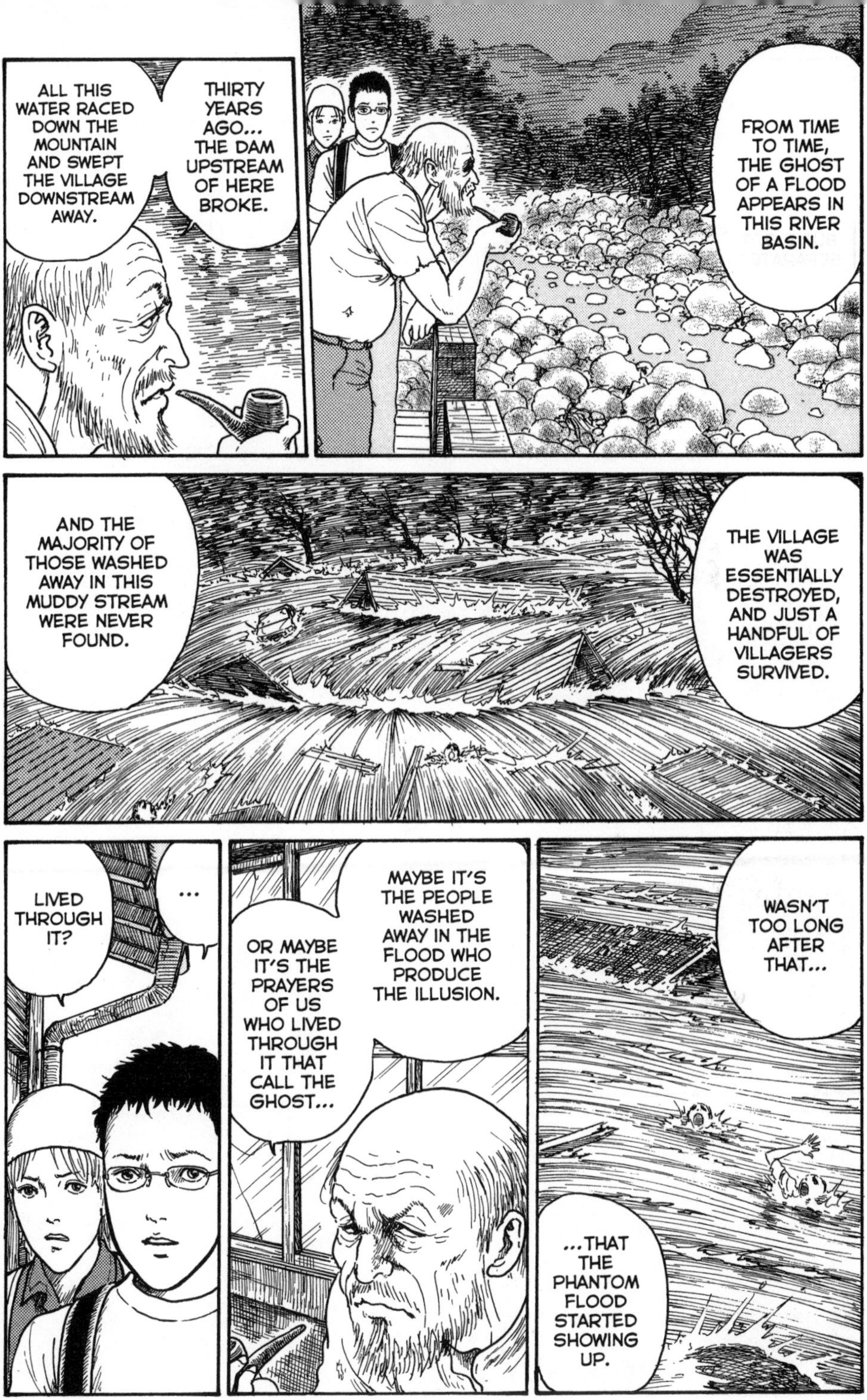
FROM TIME TO TIME, THE GHOST OF A FLOOD APPEARS IN THIS RIVER BASIN.
THIRTY YEARS AGO... THE DAM UPSTREAM OF HERE BROKE.
ALL THIS WATER RACED DOWN THE MOUNTAIN AND SWEPT THE VILLAGE DOWNSTREAM AWAY.
THE VILLAGE WAS ESSENTIALLY DESTROYED, AND JUST A HANDFUL OF VILLAGERS SURVIVED.
AND THE MAJORITY OF THOSE WASHED AWAY IN THIS MUDDY STREAM WERE NEVER FOUND.
WASN'T TOO LONG AFTER THAT...
...THAT THE PHANTOM FLOOD STARTED SHOWING UP.
MAYBE IT'S THE PEOPLE WASHED AWAY IN THE FLOOD WHO PRODUCE THE ILLUSION.
OR MAYBE IT'S THE PRAYERS OF US WHO LIVED THROUGH IT THAT CALL THE GHOST...
...
LIVED THROUGH IT?

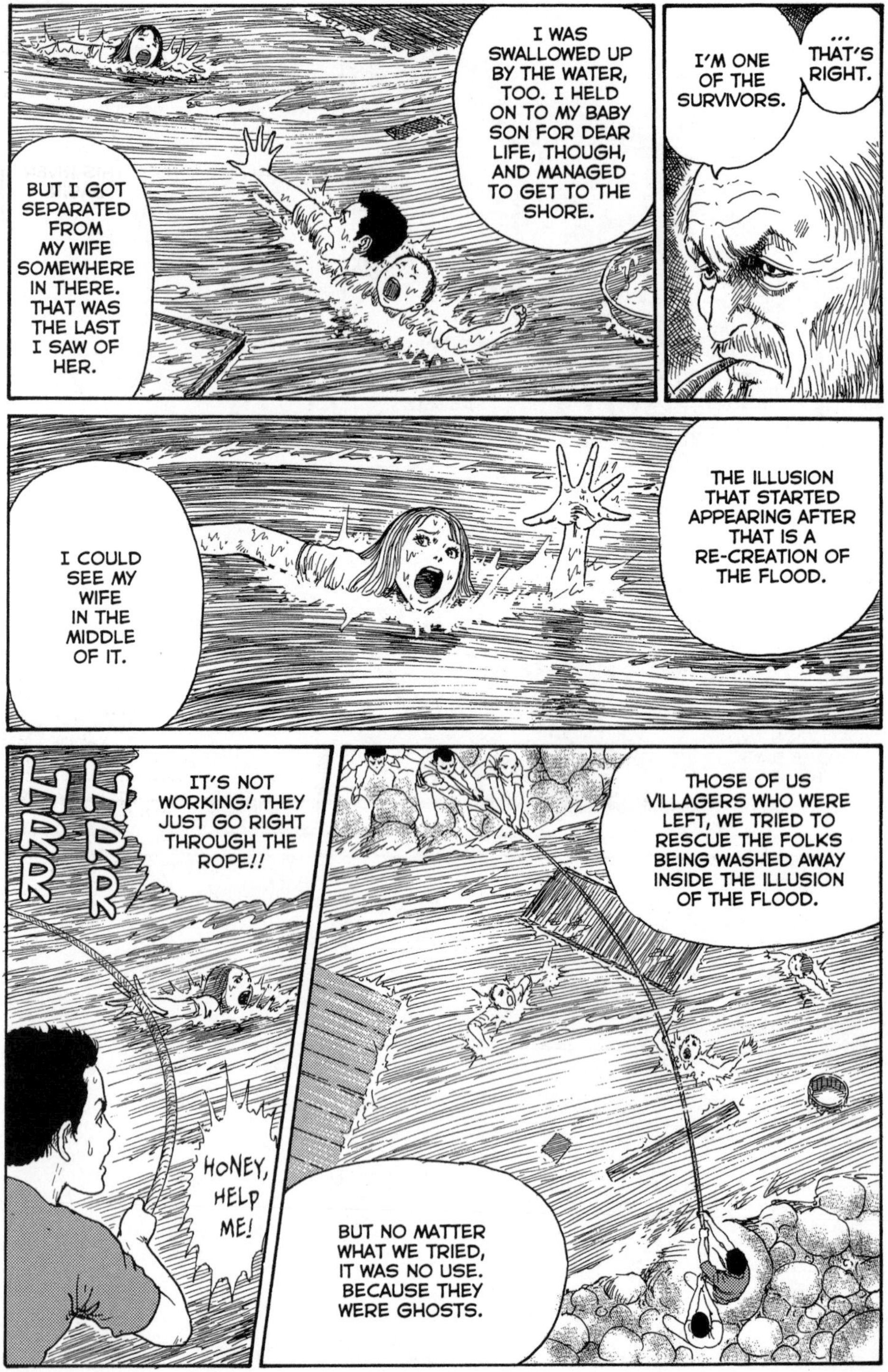
... THAT'S RIGHT.
I'M ONE OF THE SURVIVORS.
I WAS SWALLOWED UP BY THE WATER, TOO. I HELD ON TO MY BABY SON FOR DEAR LIFE, THOUGH, AND MANAGED TO GET TO THE SHORE.
BUT I GOT SEPARATED FROM MY WIFE SOMEWHERE IN THERE. THAT WAS THE LAST I SAW OF HER.
THE ILLUSION THAT STARTED APPEARING AFTER THAT IS A RE-CREATION OF THE FLOOD.
I COULD SEE MY WIFE IN THE MIDDLE OF IT.
THOSE OF US VILLAGERS WHO WERE LEFT, WE TRIED TO RESCUE THE FOLKS BEING WASHED AWAY INSIDE THE ILLUSION OF THE FLOOD.
BUT NO MATTER WHAT WE TRIED, IT WAS NO USE. BECAUSE THEY WERE GHOSTS.
HRR
HRR
IT'S NOT WORKING! THEY JUST GO RIGHT THROUGH THE ROPE!!
HONEY, HELP ME!

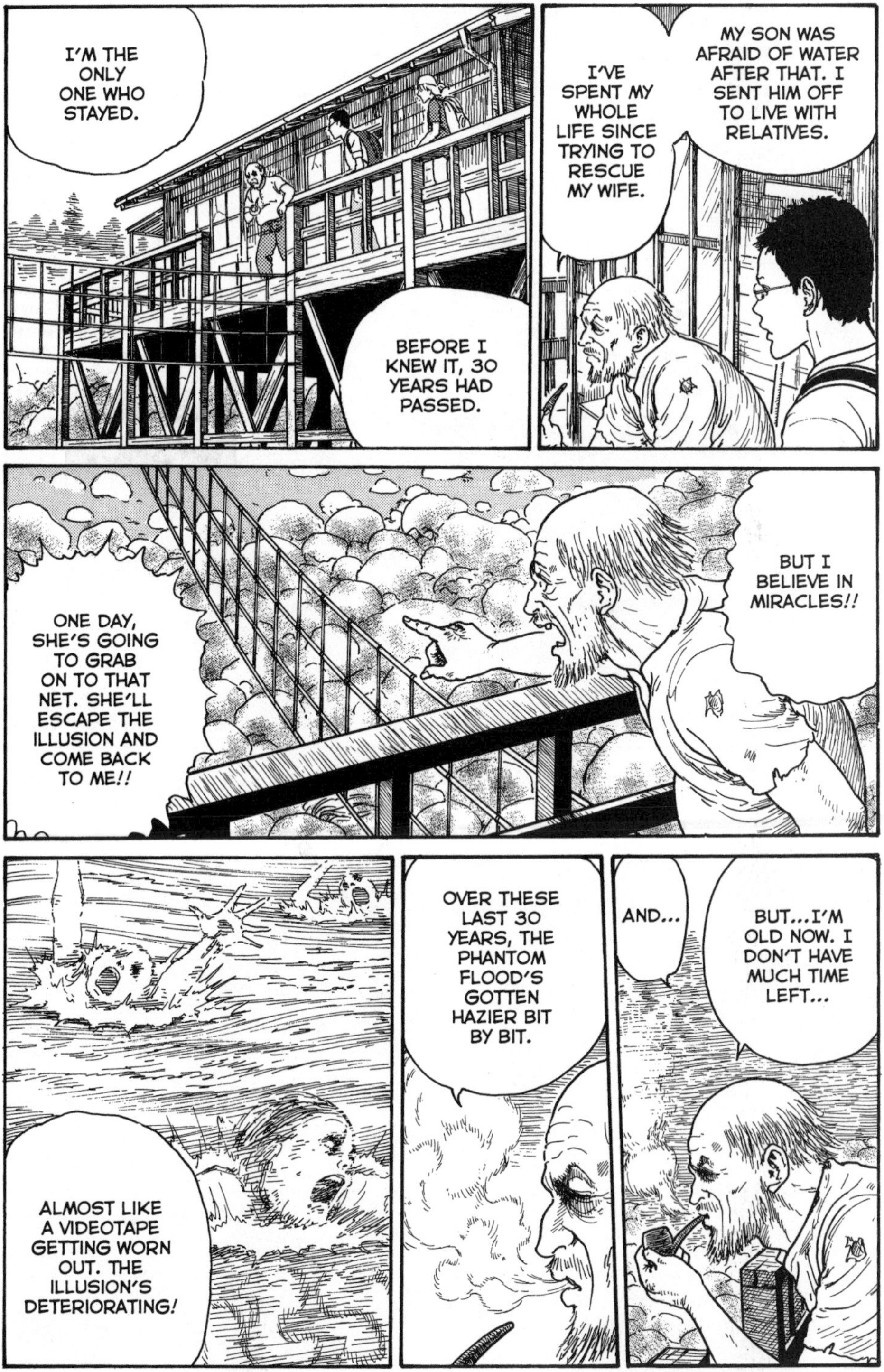
MY SON WAS AFRAID OF WATER AFTER THAT. I SENT HIM OFF TO LIVE WITH RELATIVES.
I'VE SPENT MY WHOLE LIFE SINCE TRYING TO RESCUE MY WIFE.
I'M THE ONLY ONE WHO STAYED.
BEFORE I KNEW IT, 30 YEARS HAD PASSED.
BUT I BELIEVE IN MIRACLES!!
ONE DAY, SHE'S GOING TO GRAB ON TO THAT NET. SHE'LL ESCAPE THE ILLUSION AND COME BACK TO ME!!
BUT...I'M OLD NOW. I DON'T HAVE MUCH TIME LEFT...
AND...
OVER THESE LAST 30 YEARS, THE PHANTOM FLOOD'S GOTTEN HAZIER BIT BY BIT.
ALMOST LIKE A VIDEOTAPE GETTING WORN OUT. THE ILLUSION'S DETERIORATING!

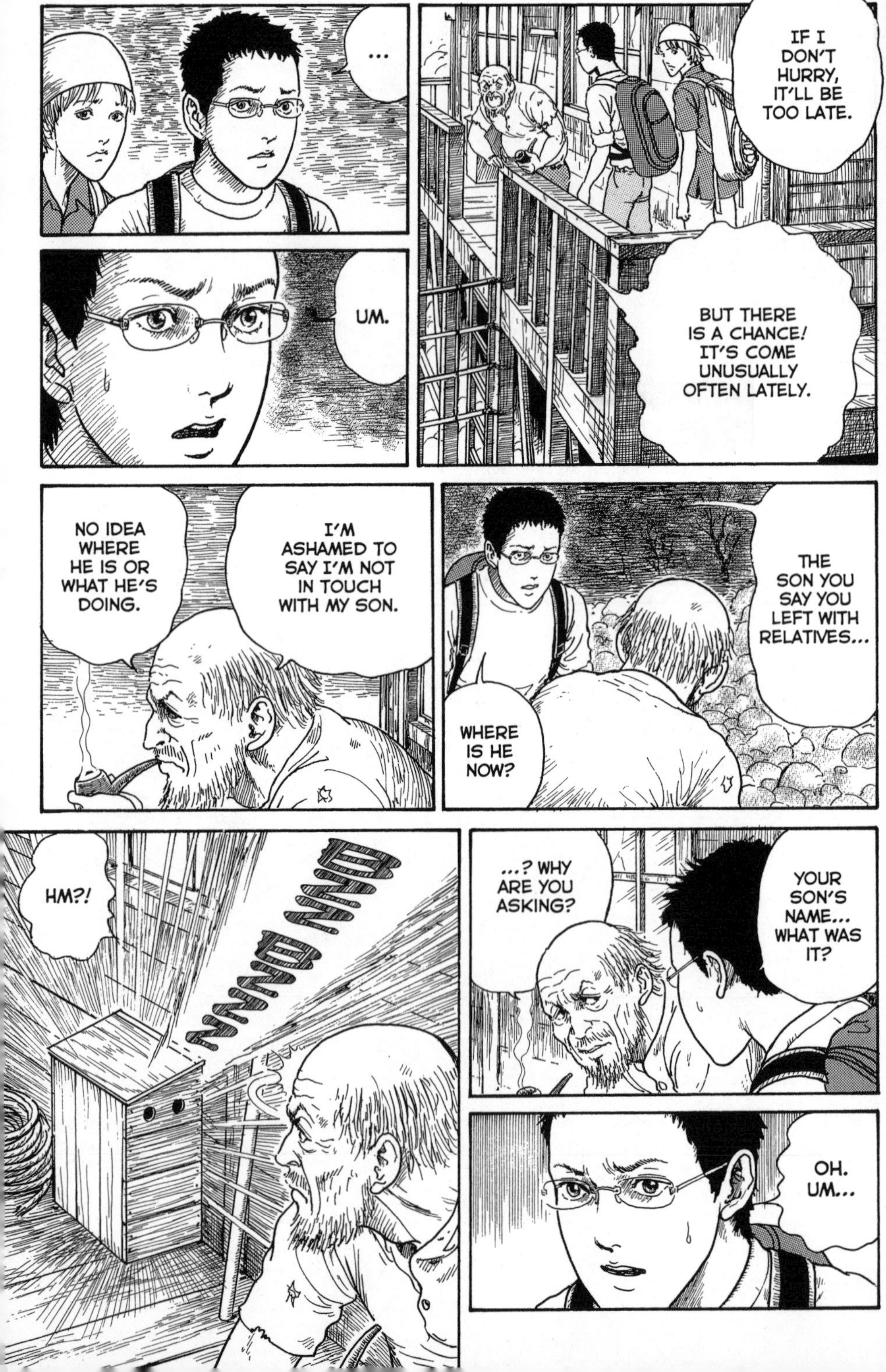
IF I DON'T HURRY, IT'LL BE TOO LATE.
BUT THERE IS A CHANCE! IT'S COME UNUSUALLY OFTEN LATELY.
...
UM.
THE SON YOU SAY YOU LEFT WITH RELATIVES...
WHERE IS HE NOW?
I'M ASHAMED TO SAY I'M NOT IN TOUCH WITH MY SON.
NO IDEA WHERE HE IS OR WHAT HE'S DOING.
YOUR SON'S NAME... WHAT WAS IT?
...? WHY ARE YOU ASKING?
OH. UM...
DNNN DNNN
HM?!

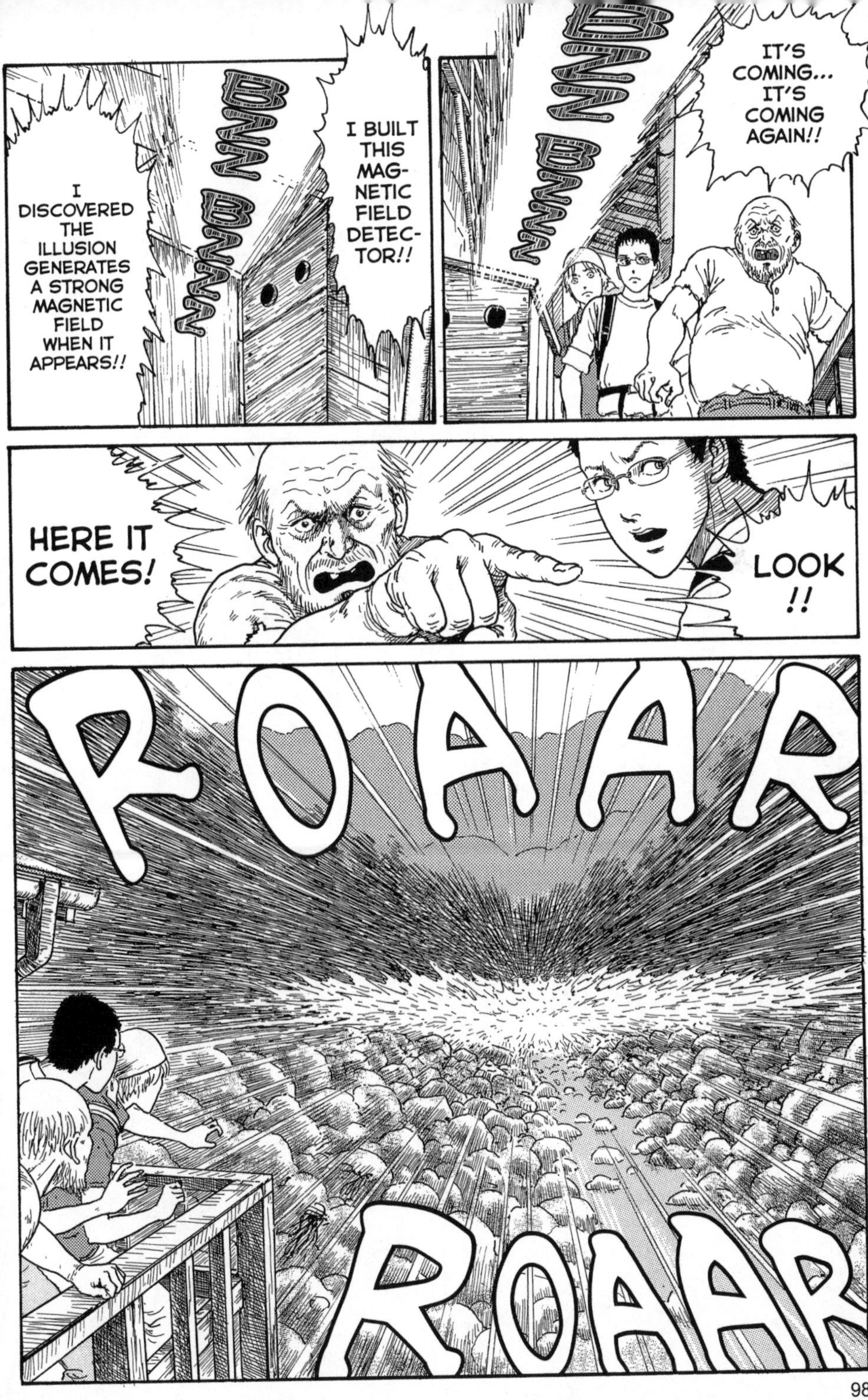
BZZN BZZN
IT'S COMING... IT'S COMING AGAIN!!
BZZN BZZN
I BUILT THIS MAG-NETIC FIELD DETEC-TOR!!
I DISCOVERED THE ILLUSION GENERATES A STRONG MAGNETIC FIELD WHEN IT APPEARS!!
LOOK!!
HERE IT COMES!
ROAAR
ROAAR

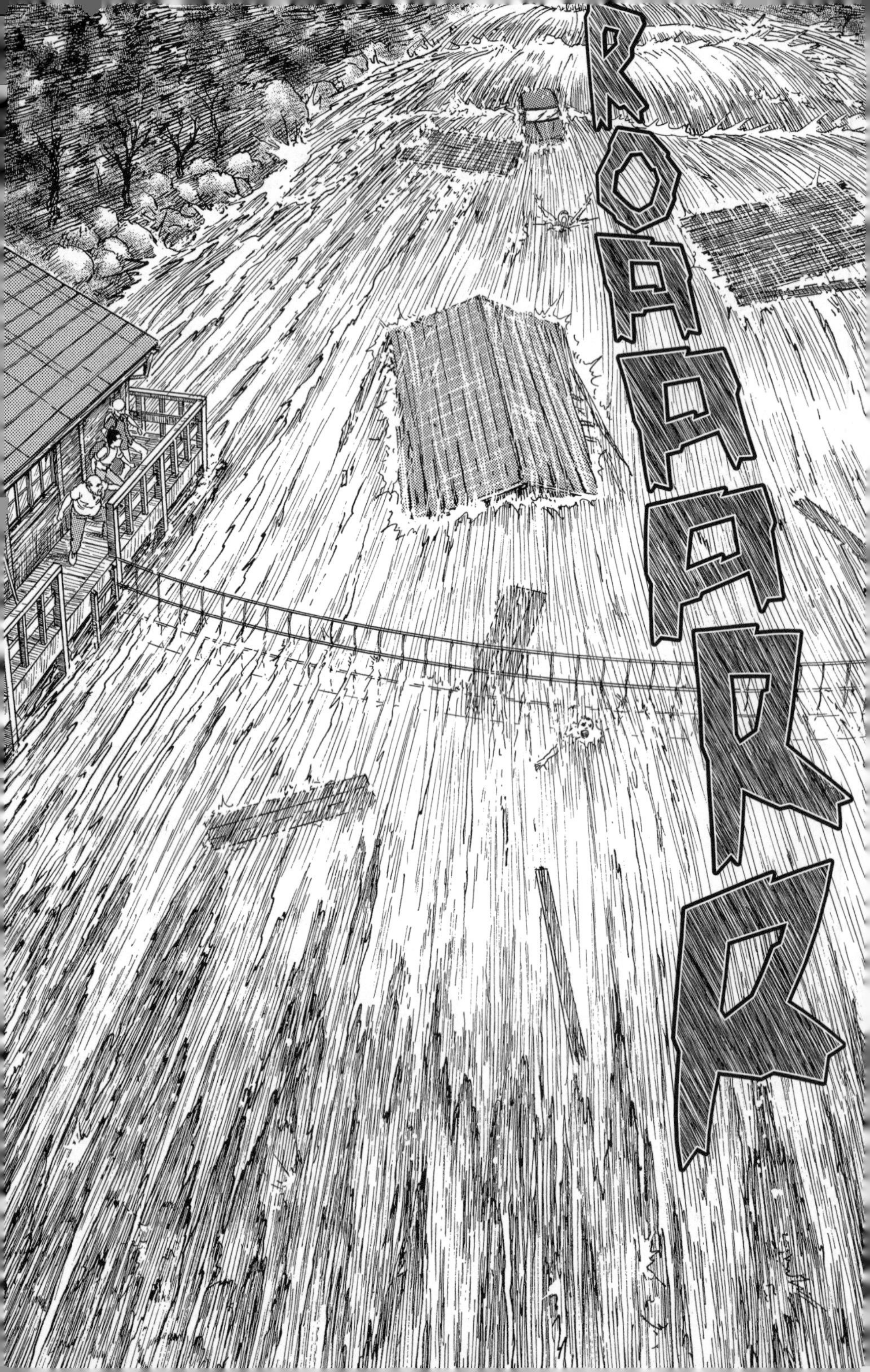
ROAAARR

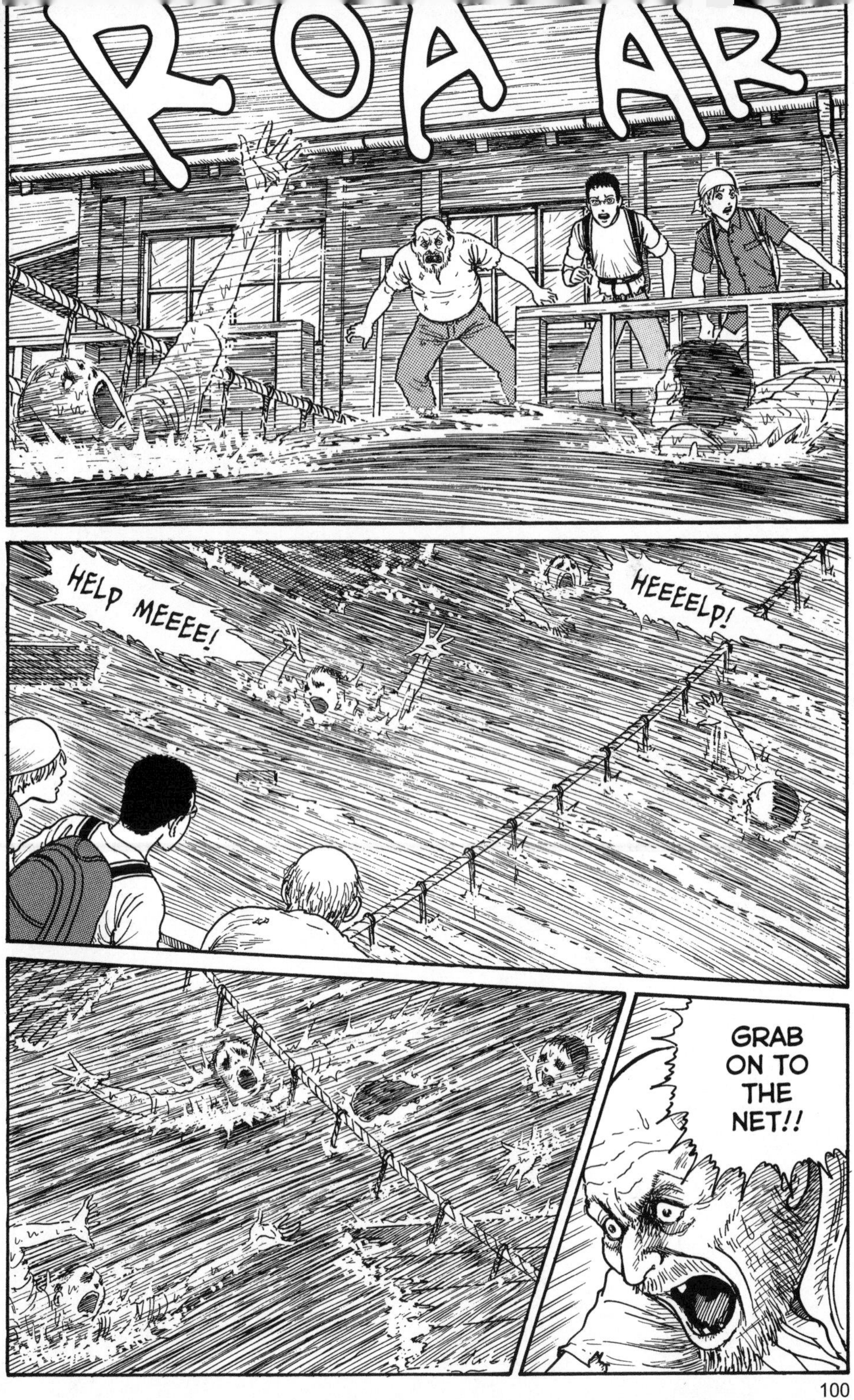
ROAAR
HEEEELP!
HELP MEEEE!
GRAB ON TO THE NET!!

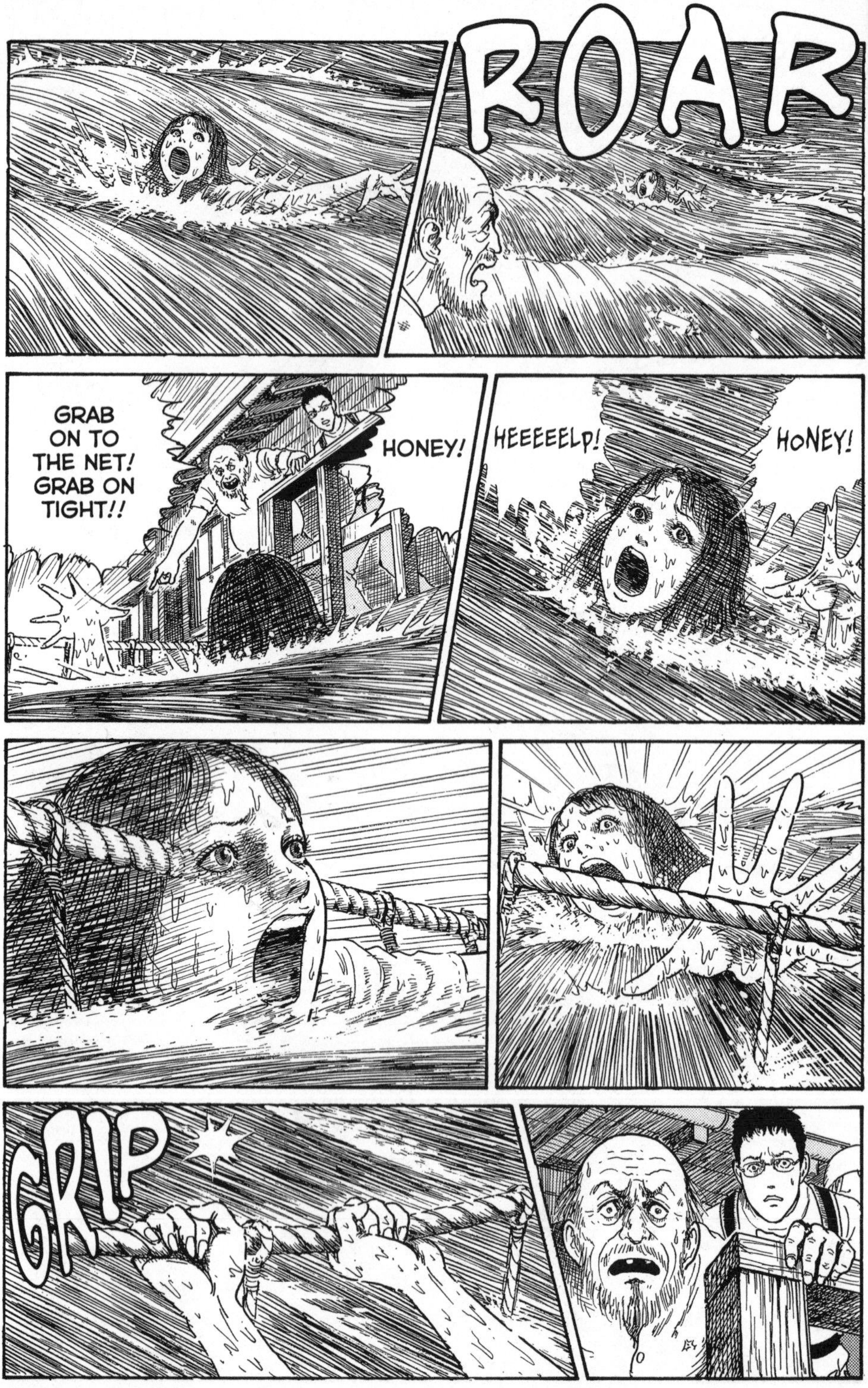
ROAR
HONEY!
HEEEEELP!
HONEY!
GRAB ON TO THE NET! GRAB ON TIGHT!!
GRIP

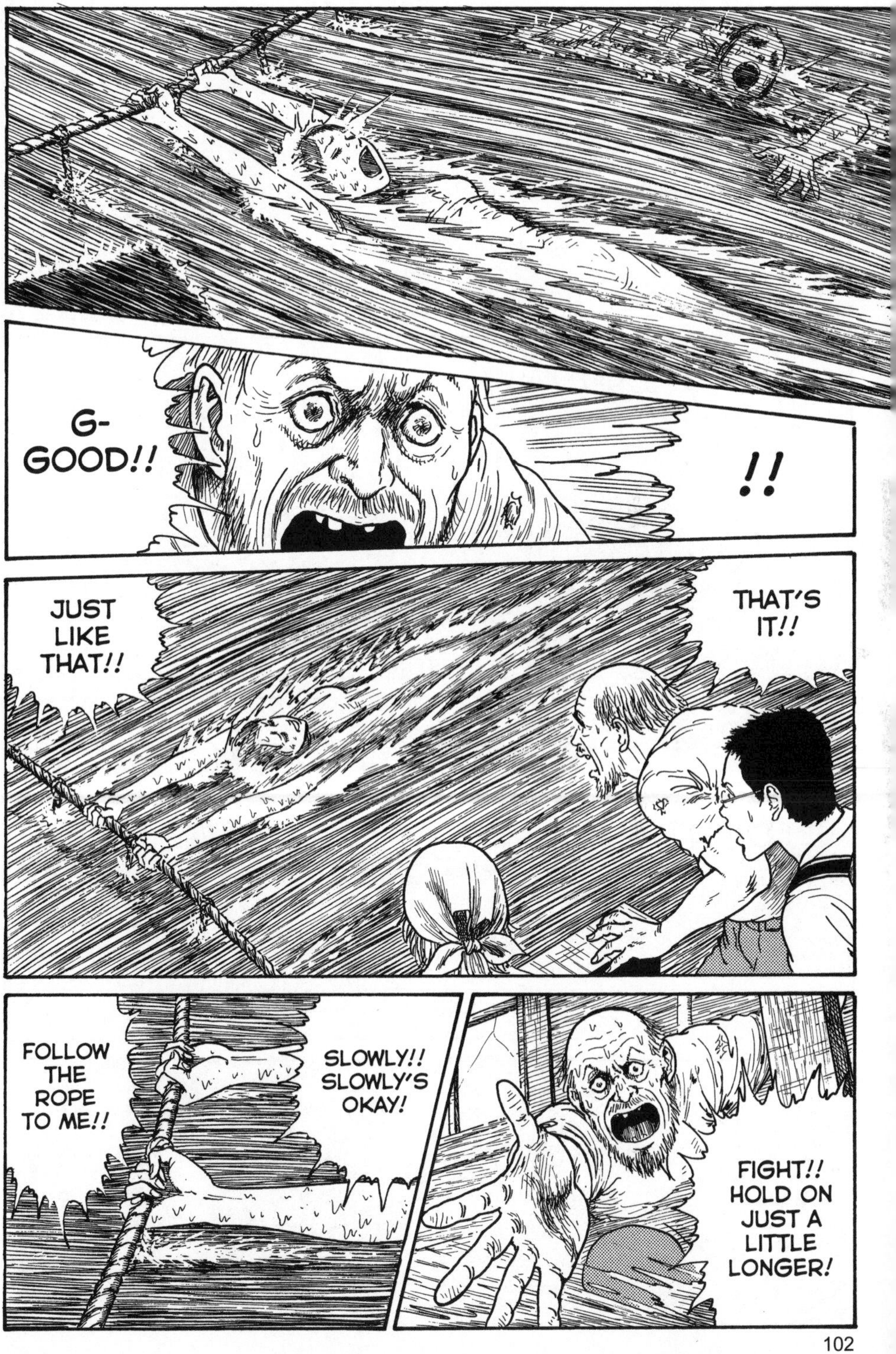
!!
G-GOOD!!
THAT'S IT!!
JUST LIKE THAT!!
FIGHT!! HOLD ON JUST A LITTLE LONGER!
SLOWLY!! SLOWLY'S OKAY!
FOLLOW THE ROPE TO ME!!

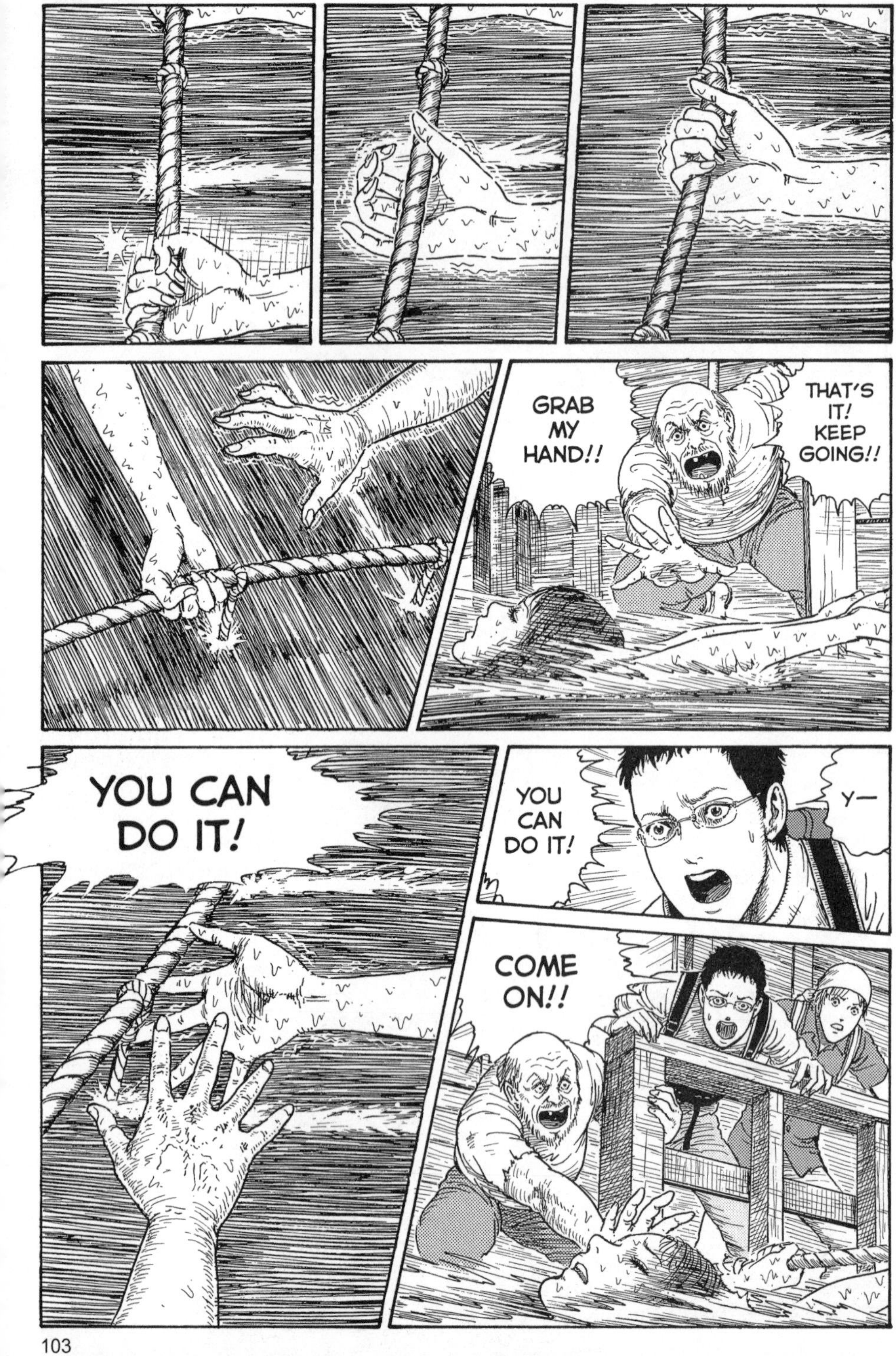
THAT'S IT! KEEP GOING!!
GRAB MY HAND!!
Y—
YOU CAN DO IT!
COME ON!!
YOU CAN DO IT!

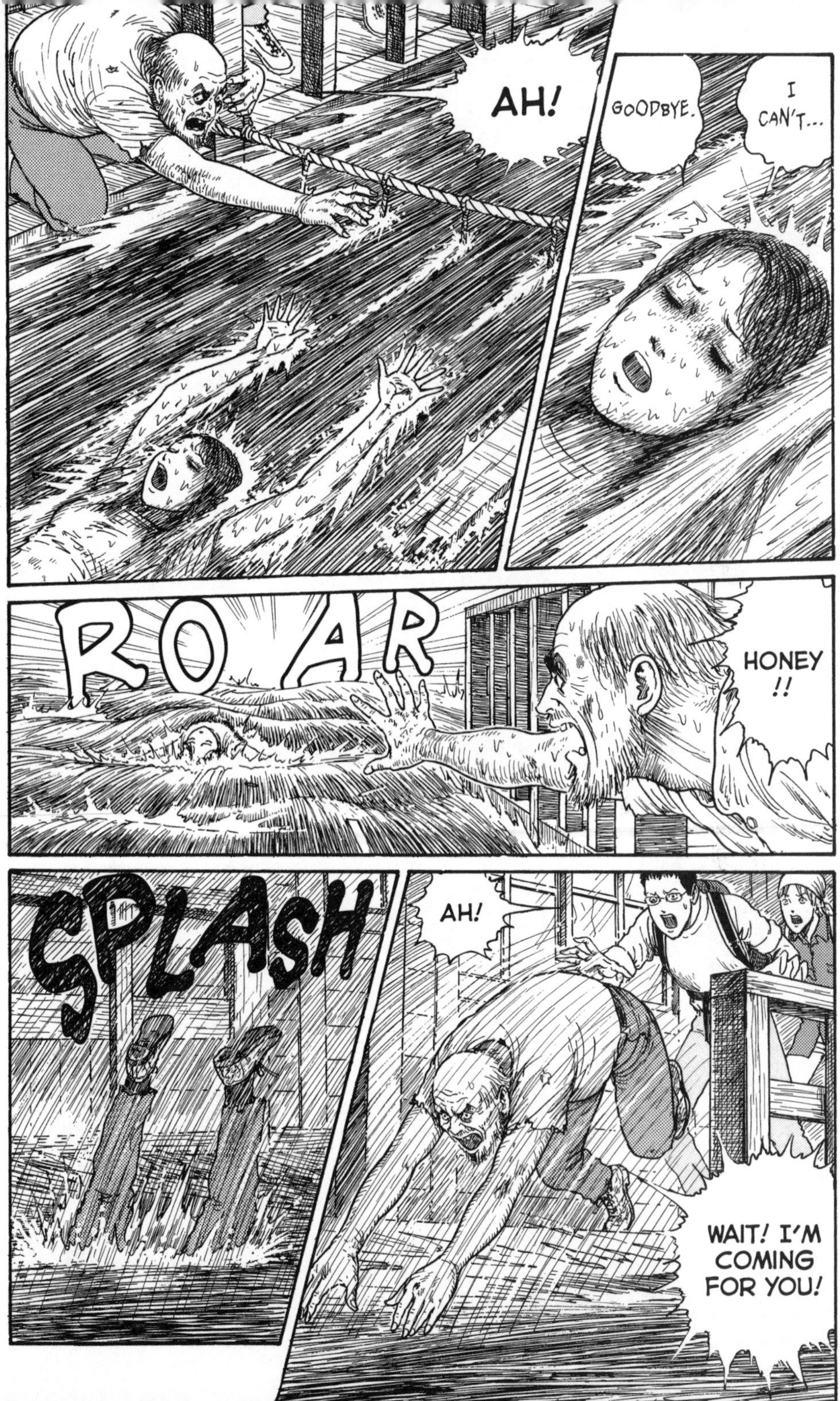
I CAN'T...
GOODBYE.
AH!
HONEY!!
RO AR
AH!
WAIT! I'M COMING FOR YOU!
SPLASH

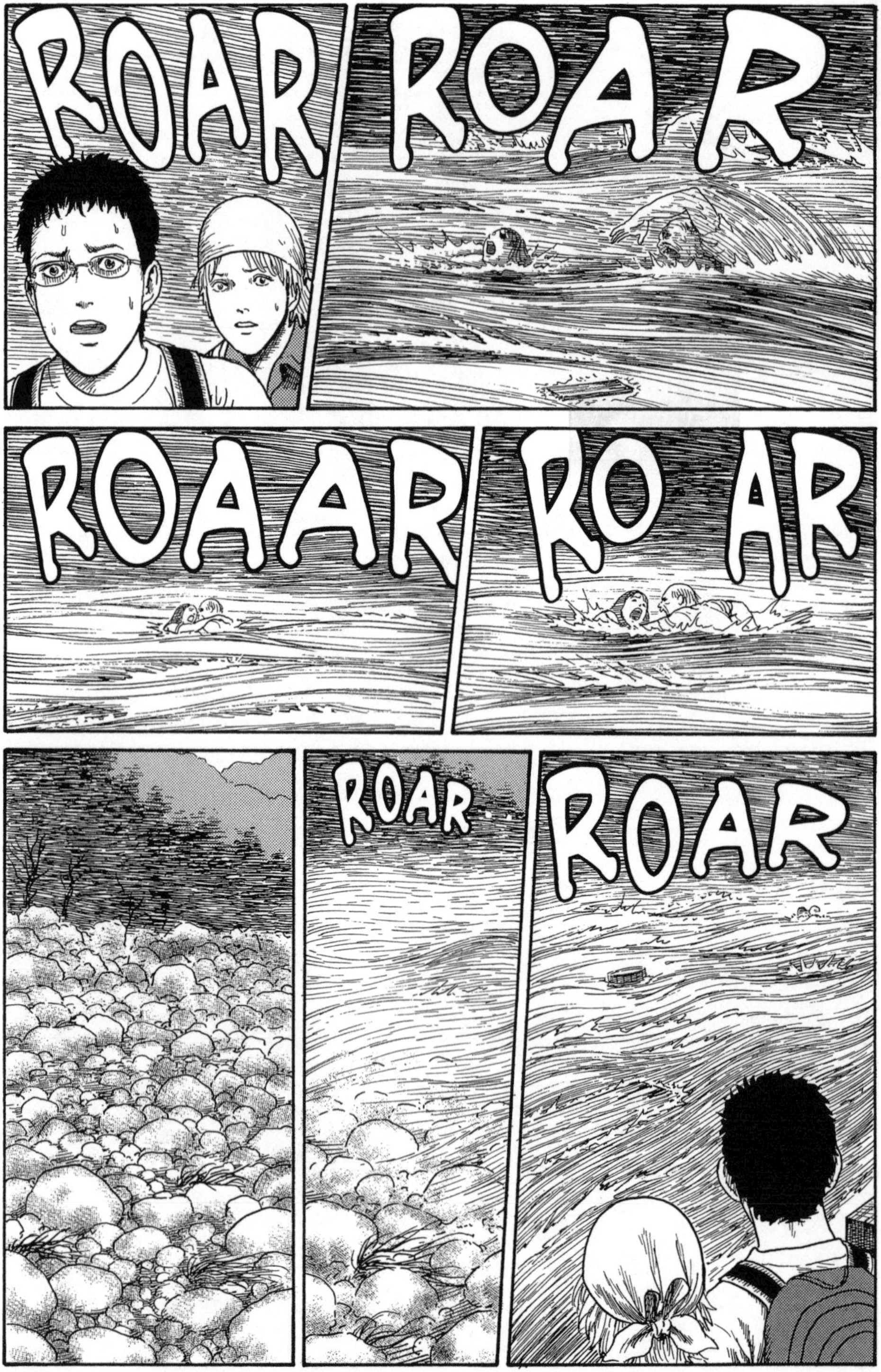
ROAR
ROAR
RO AR
ROAAR
ROAR
ROAR

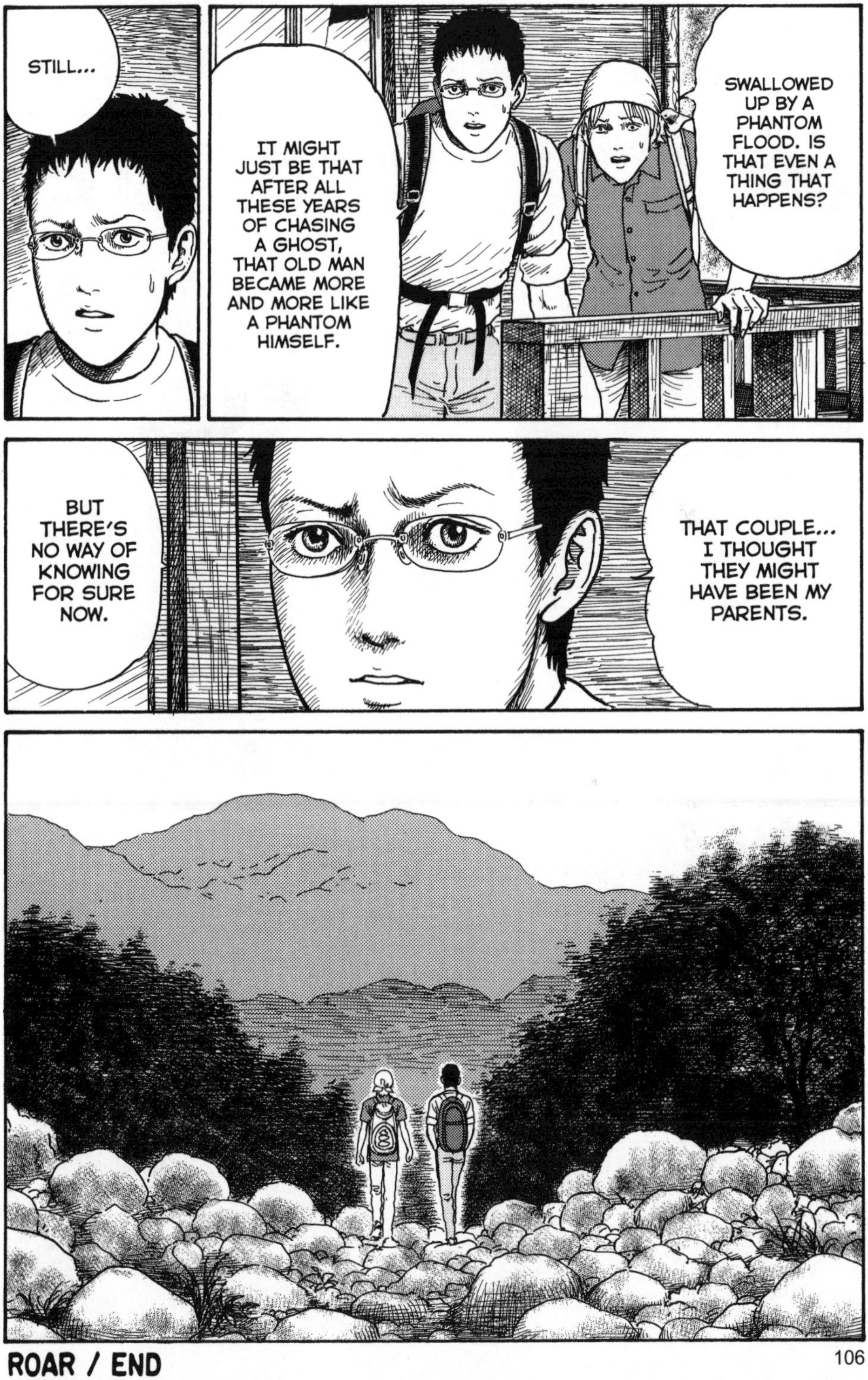
SWALLOWED UP BY A PHANTOM FLOOD. IS THAT EVEN A THING THAT HAPPENS?
IT MIGHT JUST BE THAT AFTER ALL THESE YEARS OF CHASING A GHOST, THAT OLD MAN BECAME MORE AND MORE LIKE A PHANTOM HIMSELF.
STILL...
THAT COUPLE... I THOUGHT THEY MIGHT HAVE BEEN MY PARENTS.
BUT THERE'S NO WAY OF KNOWING FOR SURE NOW.

ROAR / END

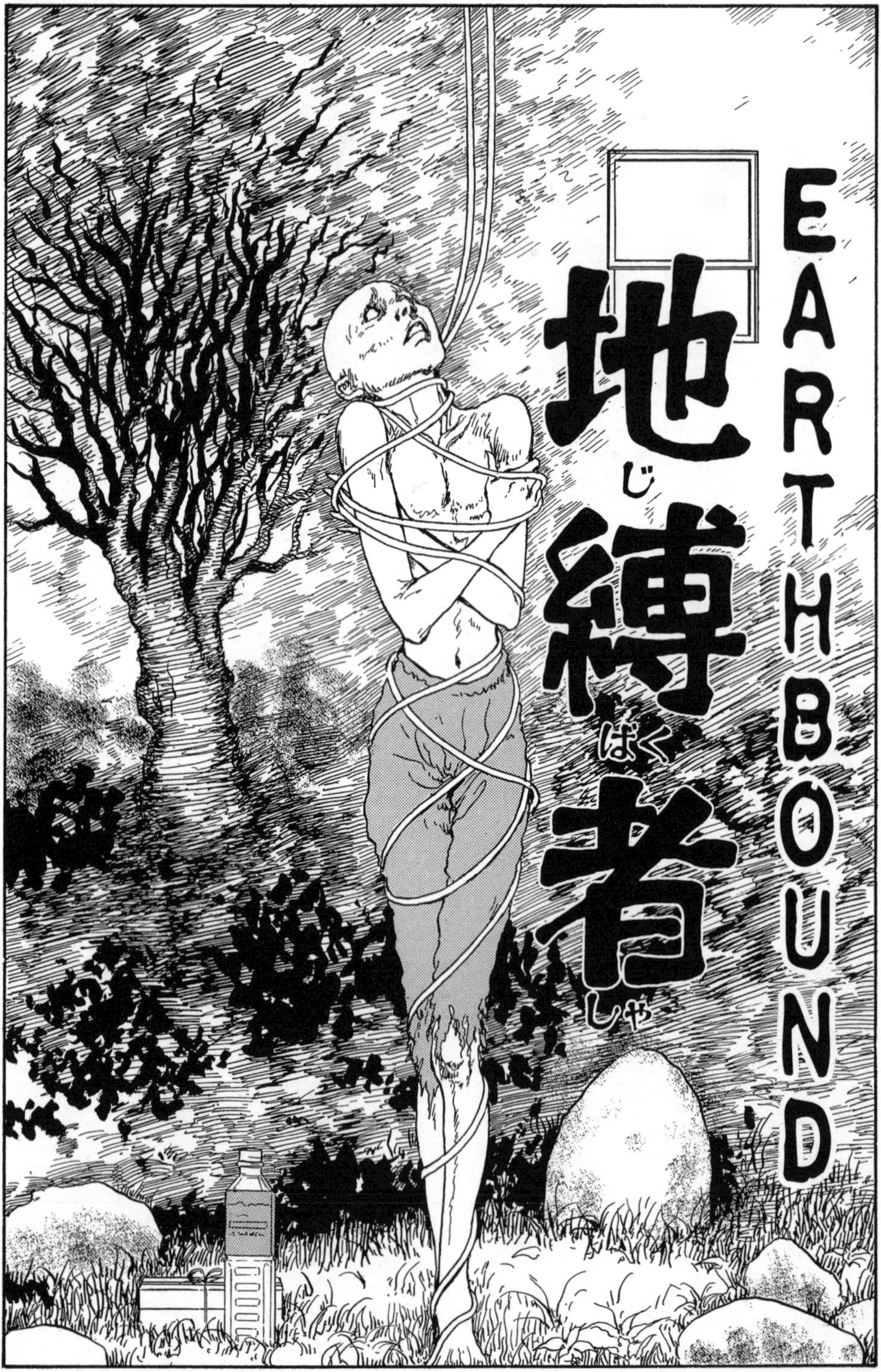

EARTHBOUND
地縛者(じばくしゃ)

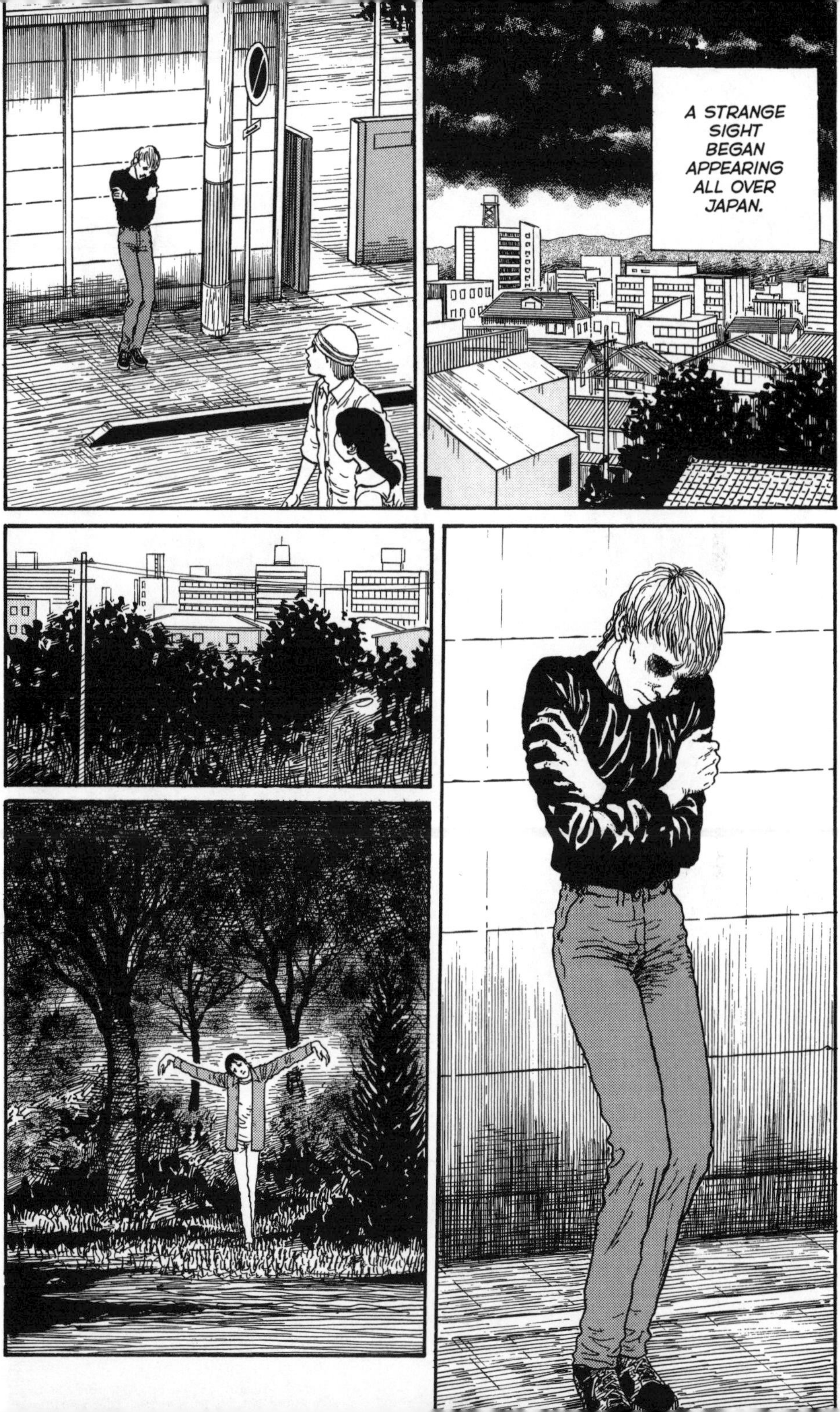
A STRANGE SIGHT BEGAN APPEARING ALL OVER JAPAN.

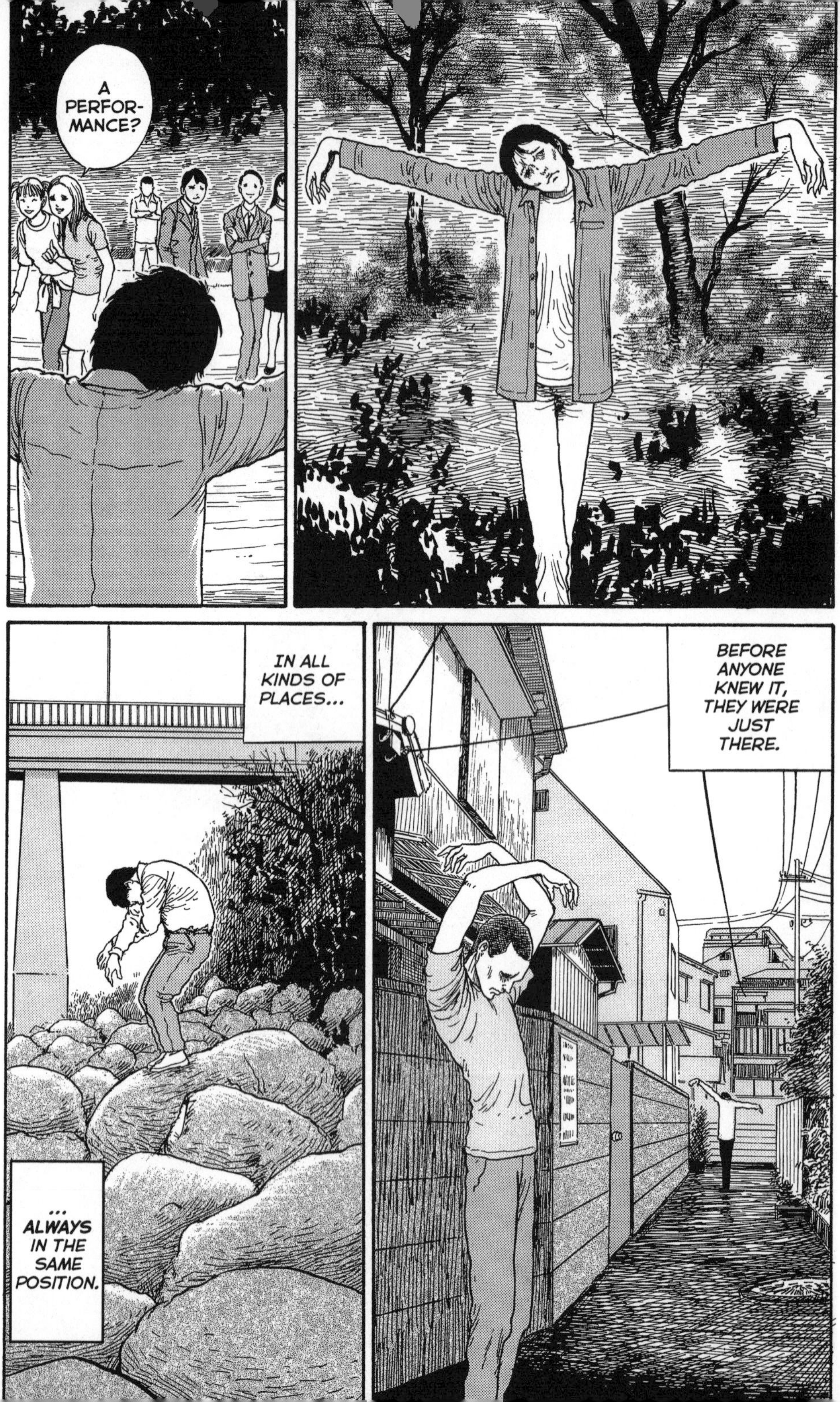
A PERFORMANCE?
BEFORE ANYONE KNEW IT, THEY WERE JUST THERE.
IN ALL KINDS OF PLACES...
...ALWAYS IN THE SAME POSITION.

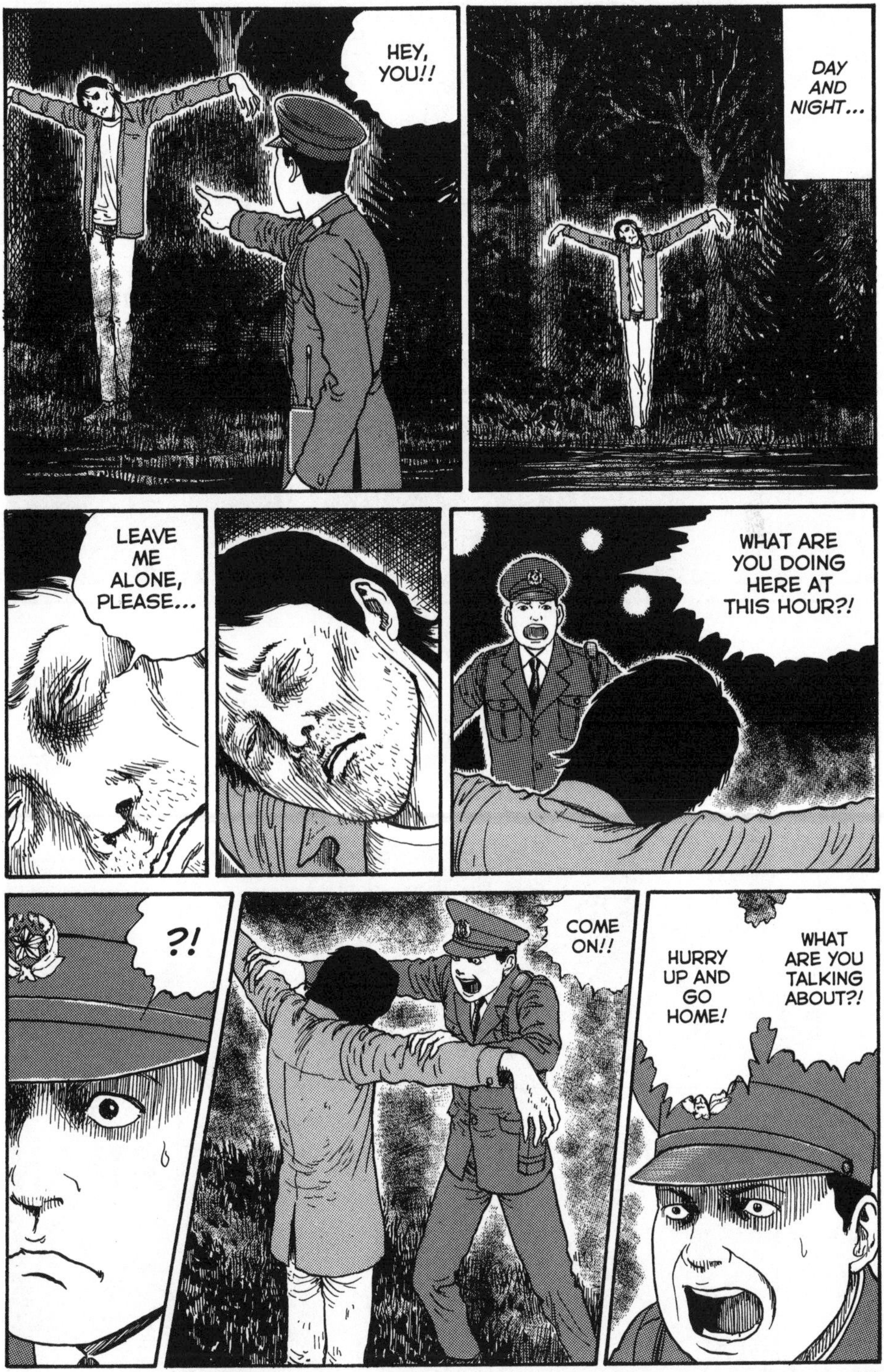
DAY AND NIGHT...
HEY, YOU!!
WHAT ARE YOU DOING HERE AT THIS HOUR?!
LEAVE ME ALONE, PLEASE...
WHAT ARE YOU TALKING ABOUT?!
HURRY UP AND GO HOME!
COME ON!!
?!

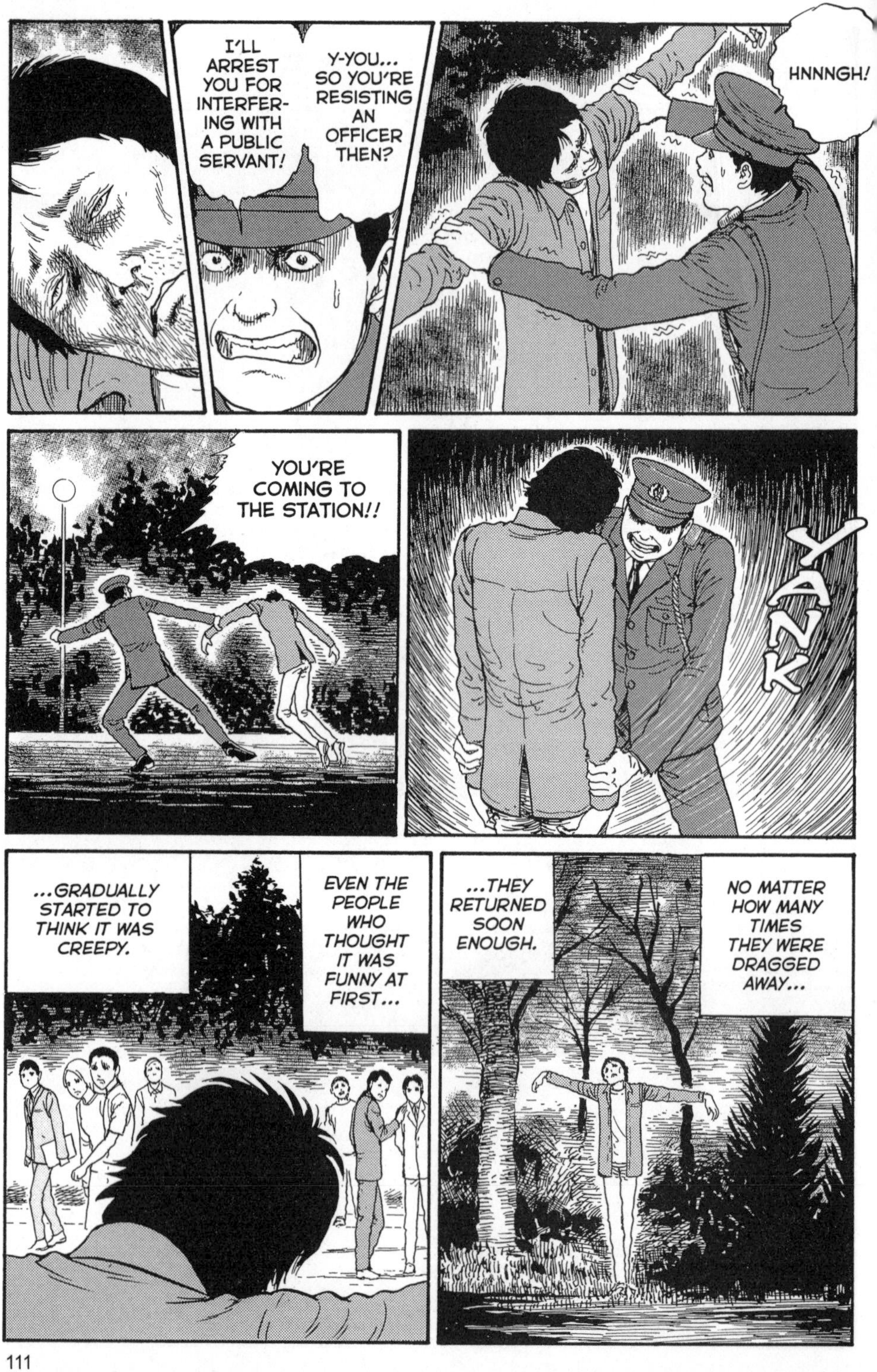
HNNNGH!
Y-YOU... SO YOU'RE RESISTING AN OFFICER THEN?
I'LL ARREST YOU FOR INTERFERING WITH A PUBLIC SERVANT!
YANK
YOU'RE COMING TO THE STATION!!
NO MATTER HOW MANY TIMES THEY WERE DRAGGED AWAY...
...THEY RETURNED SOON ENOUGH.
EVEN THE PEOPLE WHO THOUGHT IT WAS FUNNY AT FIRST...
...GRADUALLY STARTED TO THINK IT WAS CREEPY.

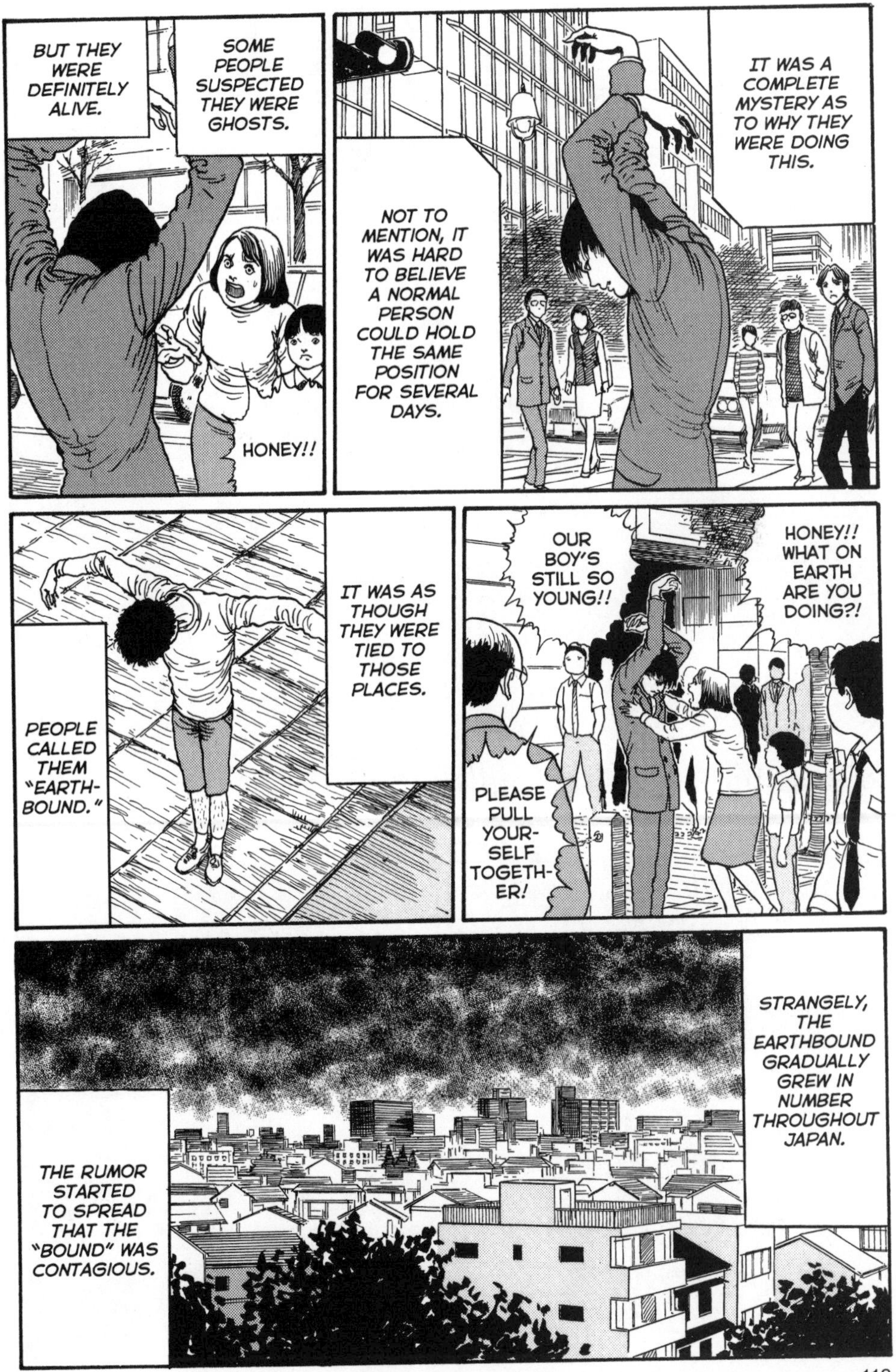
IT WAS A COMPLETE MYSTERY AS TO WHY THEY WERE DOING THIS.
NOT TO MENTION, IT WAS HARD TO BELIEVE A NORMAL PERSON COULD HOLD THE SAME POSITION FOR SEVERAL DAYS.
SOME PEOPLE SUSPECTED THEY WERE GHOSTS.
BUT THEY WERE DEFINITELY ALIVE.
HONEY!!
HONEY!! WHAT ON EARTH ARE YOU DOING?!
OUR BOY'S STILL SO YOUNG!!
PLEASE PULL YOURSELF TOGETHER!
IT WAS AS THOUGH THEY WERE TIED TO THOSE PLACES.
PEOPLE CALLED THEM "EARTHBOUND."
STRANGELY, THE EARTHBOUND GRADUALLY GREW IN NUMBER THROUGHOUT JAPAN.
THE RUMOR STARTED TO SPREAD THAT THE "BOUND" WAS CONTAGIOUS.

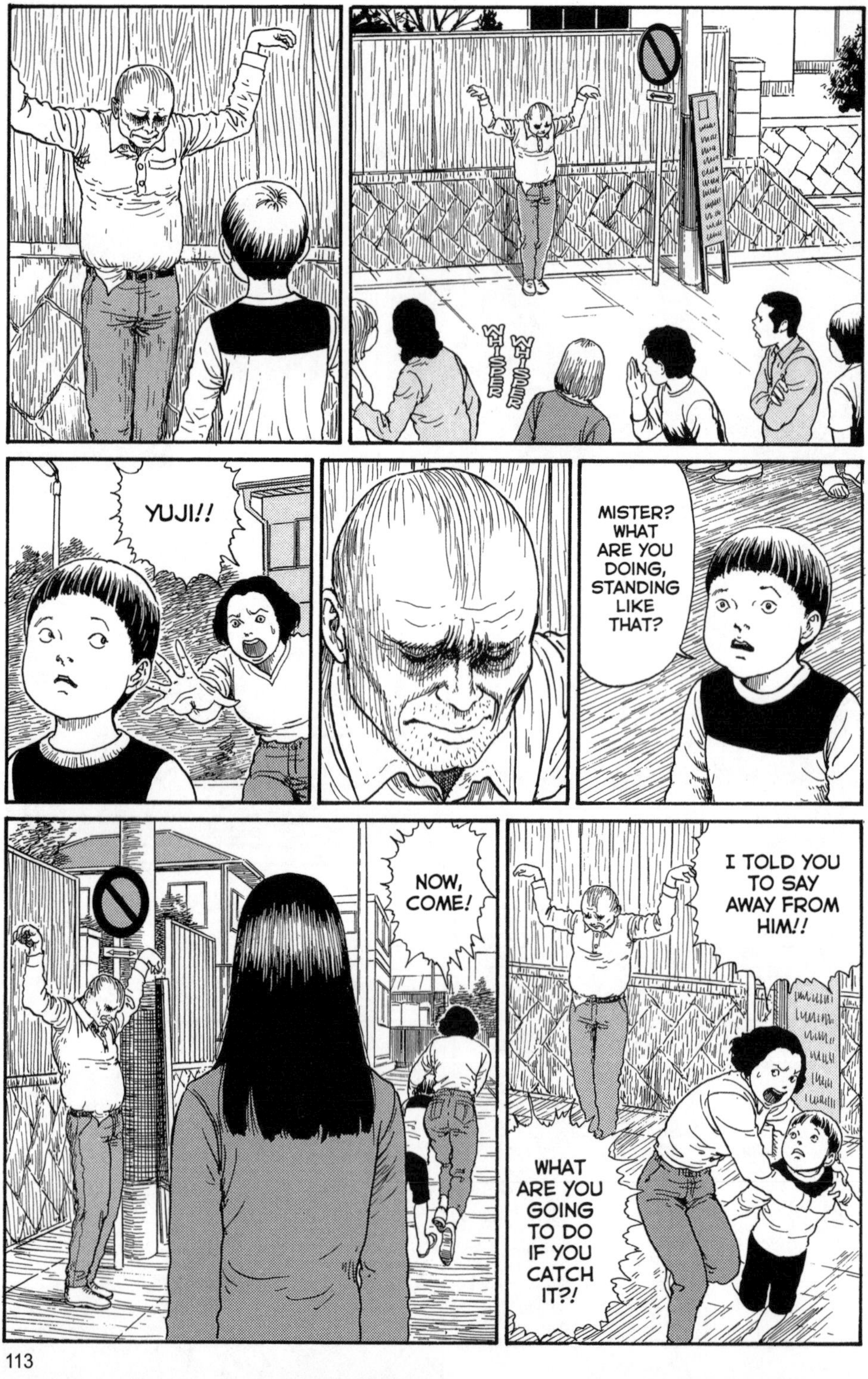
WHISPER
WHISPER
MISTER? WHAT ARE YOU DOING, STANDING LIKE THAT?
YUJI!!
I TOLD YOU TO SAY AWAY FROM HIM!!
WHAT ARE YOU GOING TO DO IF YOU CATCH IT?!
NOW, COME!

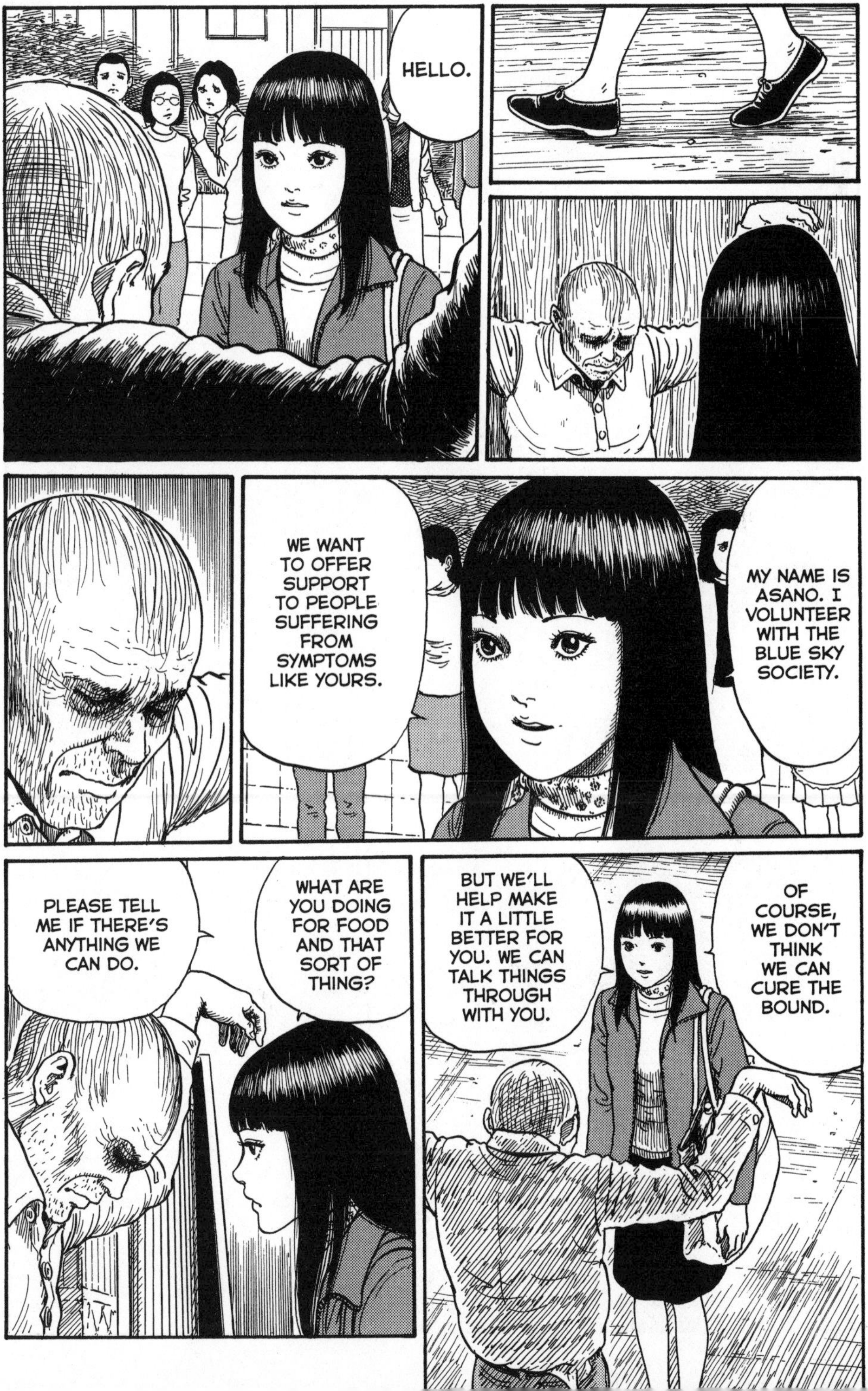
HELLO.
MY NAME IS ASANO. I VOLUNTEER WITH THE BLUE SKY SOCIETY.
WE WANT TO OFFER SUPPORT TO PEOPLE SUFFERING FROM SYMPTOMS LIKE YOURS.
OF COURSE, WE DON'T THINK WE CAN CURE THE BOUND.
BUT WE'LL HELP MAKE IT A LITTLE BETTER FOR YOU. WE CAN TALK THINGS THROUGH WITH YOU.
WHAT ARE YOU DOING FOR FOOD AND THAT SORT OF THING?
PLEASE TELL ME IF THERE'S ANYTHING WE CAN DO.

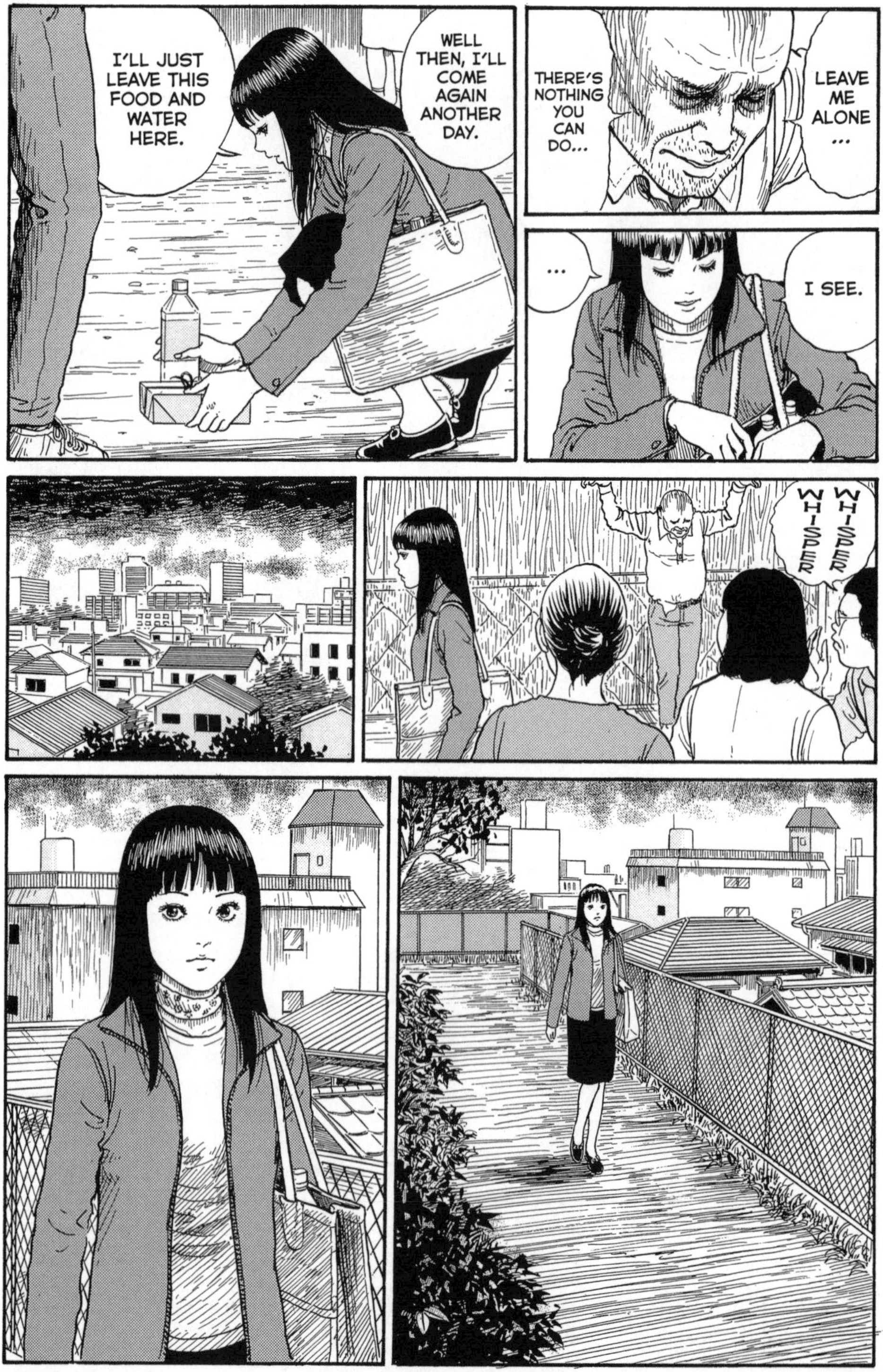
LEAVE ME ALONE ...
THERE'S NOTHING YOU CAN DO...
I SEE.
...
WELL THEN, I'LL COME AGAIN ANOTHER DAY.
I'LL JUST LEAVE THIS FOOD AND WATER HERE.
WHISPER WHISPER

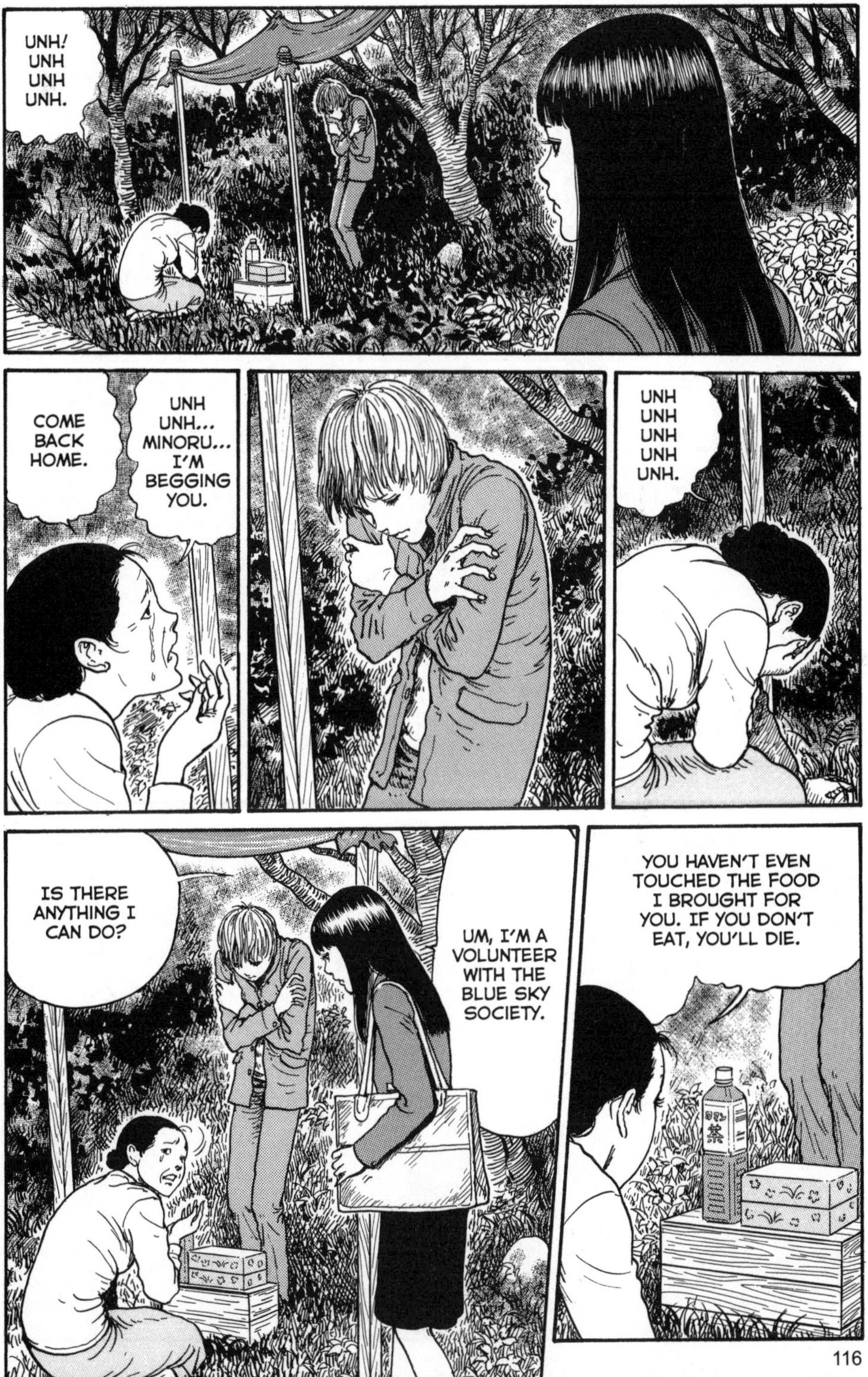
UNH! UNH UNH UNH.
UNH UNH UNH UNH UNH.
UNH UNH... MINORU... I'M BEGGING YOU.
COME BACK HOME.
YOU HAVEN'T EVEN TOUCHED THE FOOD I BROUGHT FOR YOU. IF YOU DON'T EAT, YOU'LL DIE.
UM, I'M A VOLUNTEER WITH THE BLUE SKY SOCIETY.
IS THERE ANYTHING I CAN DO?

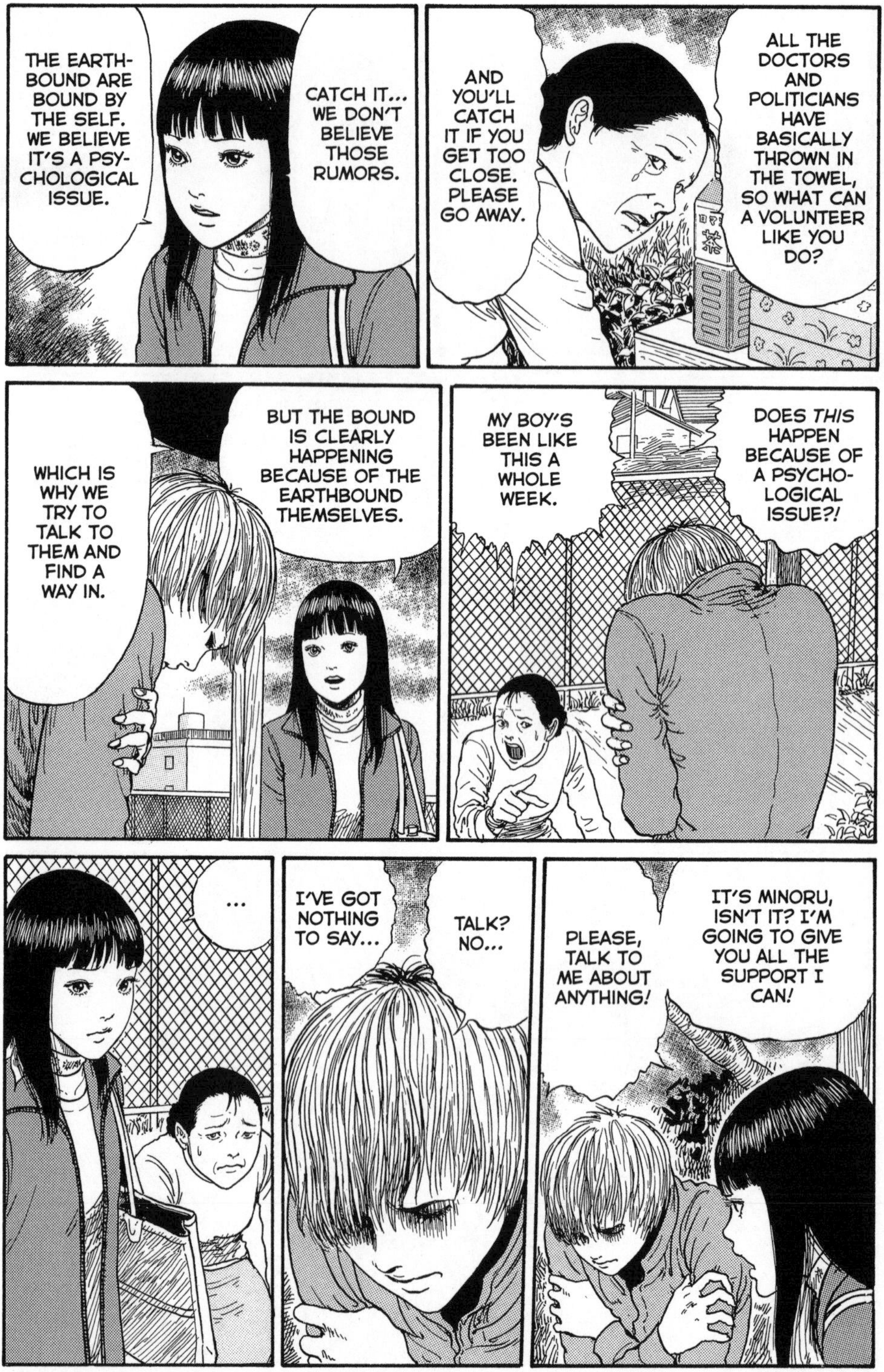
ALL THE DOCTORS AND POLITICIANS HAVE BASICALLY THROWN IN THE TOWEL, SO WHAT CAN A VOLUNTEER LIKE YOU DO?
AND YOU'LL CATCH IT IF YOU GET TOO CLOSE. PLEASE GO AWAY.
CATCH IT... WE DON'T BELIEVE THOSE RUMORS.
THE EARTH-BOUND ARE BOUND BY THE SELF. WE BELIEVE IT'S A PSY-CHOLOGICAL ISSUE.
DOES *THIS* HAPPEN BECAUSE OF A PSYCHO-LOGICAL ISSUE?!
MY BOY'S BEEN LIKE THIS A WHOLE WEEK.
BUT THE BOUND IS CLEARLY HAPPENING BECAUSE OF THE EARTHBOUND THEMSELVES.
WHICH IS WHY WE TRY TO TALK TO THEM AND FIND A WAY IN.
IT'S MINORU, ISN'T IT? I'M GOING TO GIVE YOU ALL THE SUPPORT I CAN!
PLEASE, TALK TO ME ABOUT ANYTHING!
TALK? NO...
I'VE GOT NOTHING TO SAY...
...

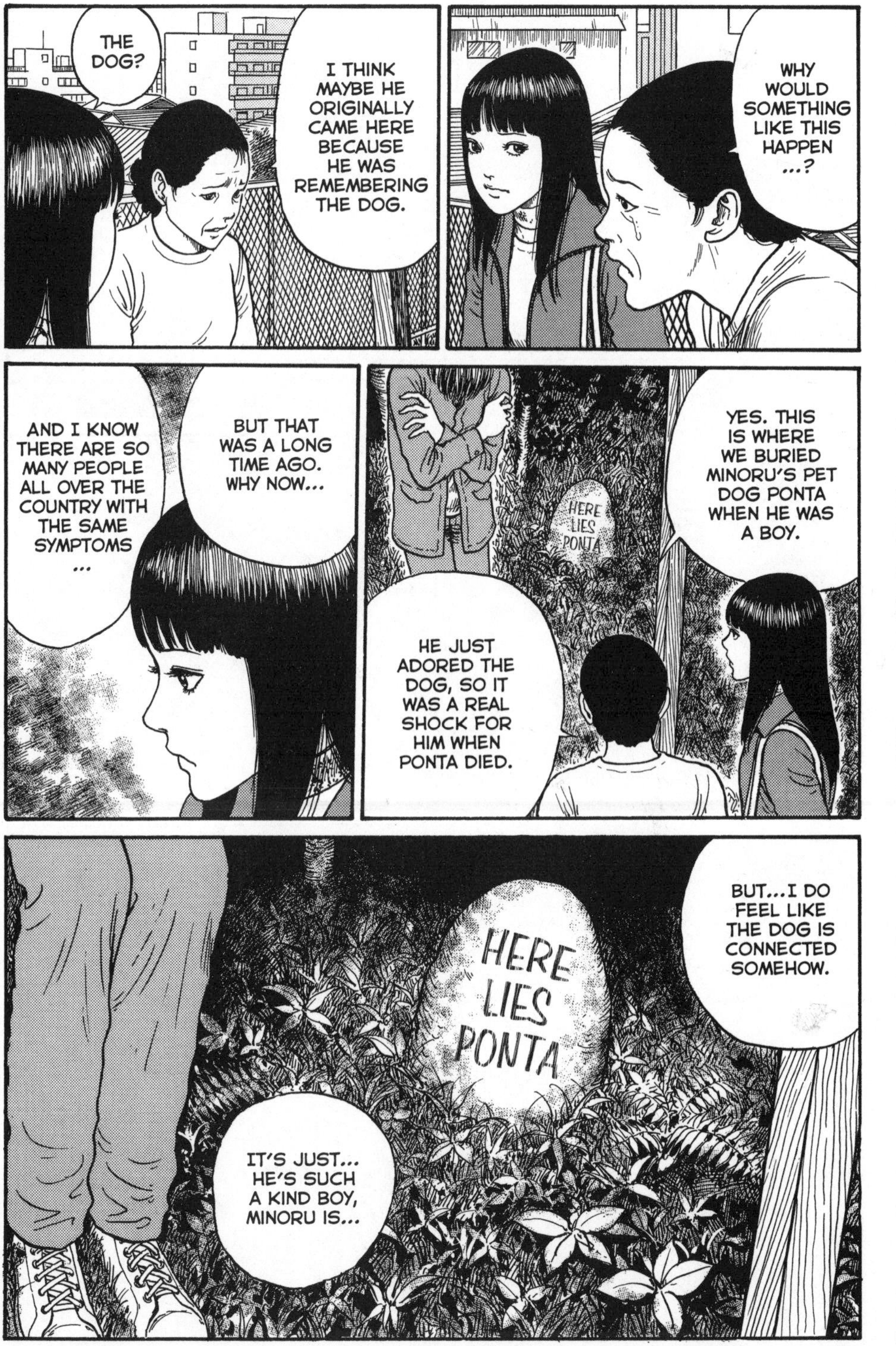
WHY WOULD SOMETHING LIKE THIS HAPPEN ...?
I THINK MAYBE HE ORIGINALLY CAME HERE BECAUSE HE WAS REMEMBERING THE DOG.
THE DOG?
YES. THIS IS WHERE WE BURIED MINORU'S PET DOG PONTA WHEN HE WAS A BOY.
HERE LIES PONTA
HE JUST ADORED THE DOG, SO IT WAS A REAL SHOCK FOR HIM WHEN PONTA DIED.
BUT THAT WAS A LONG TIME AGO. WHY NOW...
AND I KNOW THERE ARE SO MANY PEOPLE ALL OVER THE COUNTRY WITH THE SAME SYMPTOMS ...
BUT...I DO FEEL LIKE THE DOG IS CONNECTED SOMEHOW.
HERE LIES PONTA
IT'S JUST... HE'S SUCH A KIND BOY, MINORU IS...

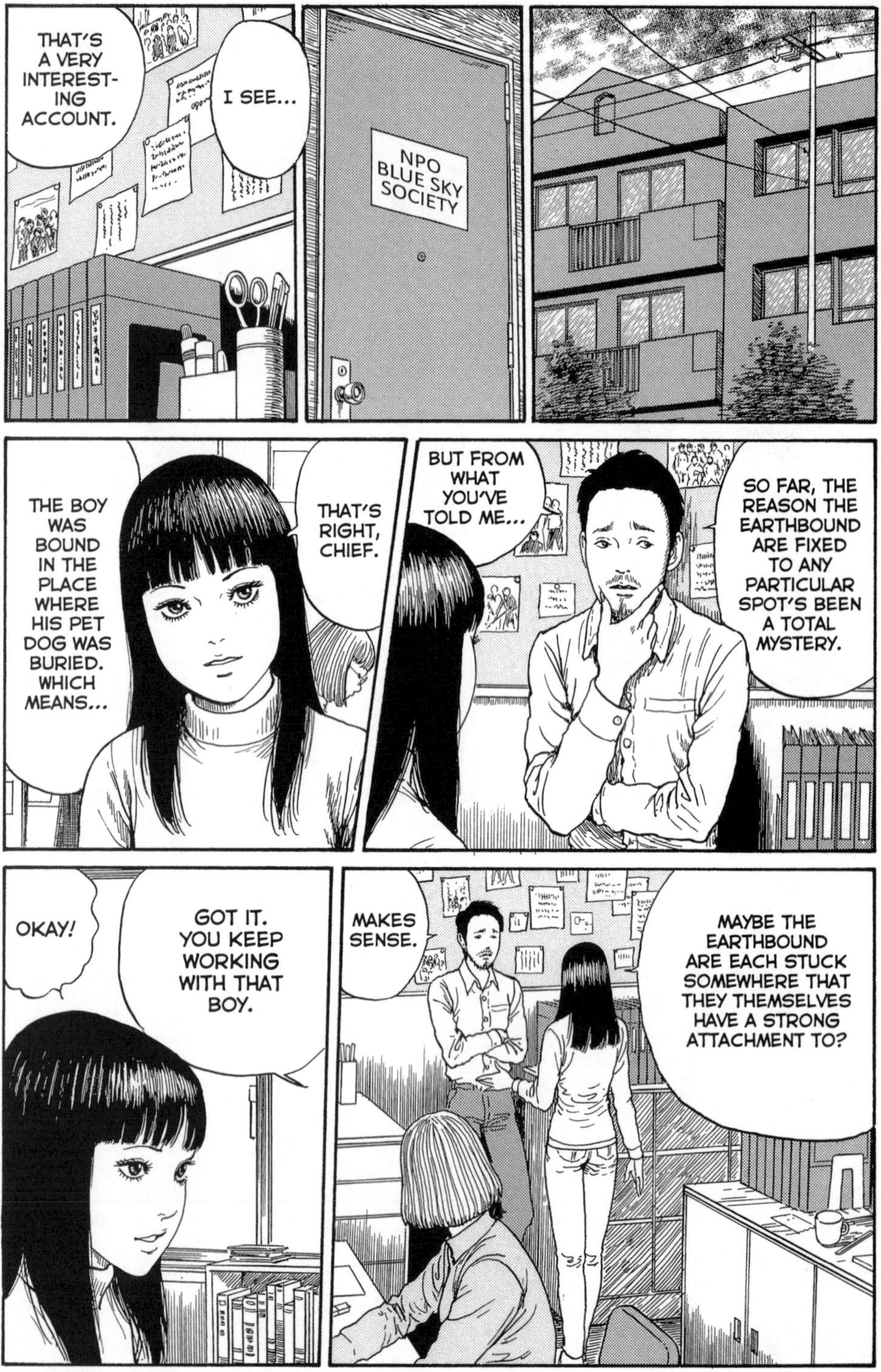
NPO BLUE SKY SOCIETY
I SEE...
THAT'S A VERY INTERESTING ACCOUNT.
SO FAR, THE REASON THE EARTHBOUND ARE FIXED TO ANY PARTICULAR SPOT'S BEEN A TOTAL MYSTERY.
BUT FROM WHAT YOU'VE TOLD ME...
THAT'S RIGHT, CHIEF.
THE BOY WAS BOUND IN THE PLACE WHERE HIS PET DOG WAS BURIED. WHICH MEANS...
MAYBE THE EARTHBOUND ARE EACH STUCK SOMEWHERE THAT THEY THEMSELVES HAVE A STRONG ATTACHMENT TO?
MAKES SENSE.
GOT IT. YOU KEEP WORKING WITH THAT BOY.
OKAY!

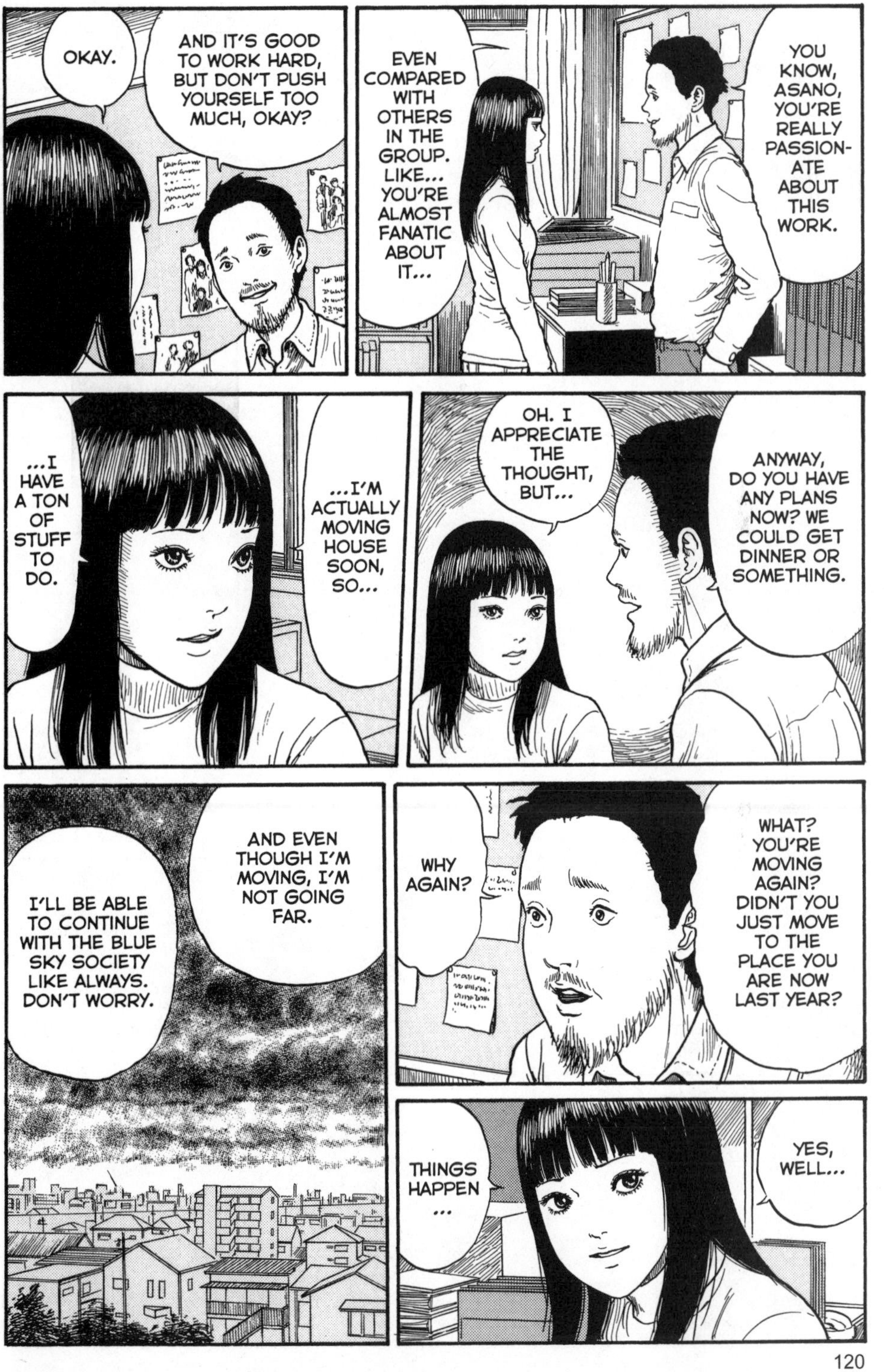
YOU KNOW, ASANO, YOU'RE REALLY PASSIONATE ABOUT THIS WORK.
EVEN COMPARED WITH OTHERS IN THE GROUP. LIKE... YOU'RE ALMOST FANATIC ABOUT IT...
AND IT'S GOOD TO WORK HARD, BUT DON'T PUSH YOURSELF TOO MUCH, OKAY?
OKAY.
ANYWAY, DO YOU HAVE ANY PLANS NOW? WE COULD GET DINNER OR SOMETHING.
OH. I APPRECIATE THE THOUGHT, BUT...
...I'M ACTUALLY MOVING HOUSE SOON, SO...
...I HAVE A TON OF STUFF TO DO.
WHAT? YOU'RE MOVING AGAIN? DIDN'T YOU JUST MOVE TO THE PLACE YOU ARE NOW LAST YEAR?
WHY AGAIN?
YES, WELL...
THINGS HAPPEN...
AND EVEN THOUGH I'M MOVING, I'M NOT GOING FAR.
I'LL BE ABLE TO CONTINUE WITH THE BLUE SKY SOCIETY LIKE ALWAYS. DON'T WORRY.

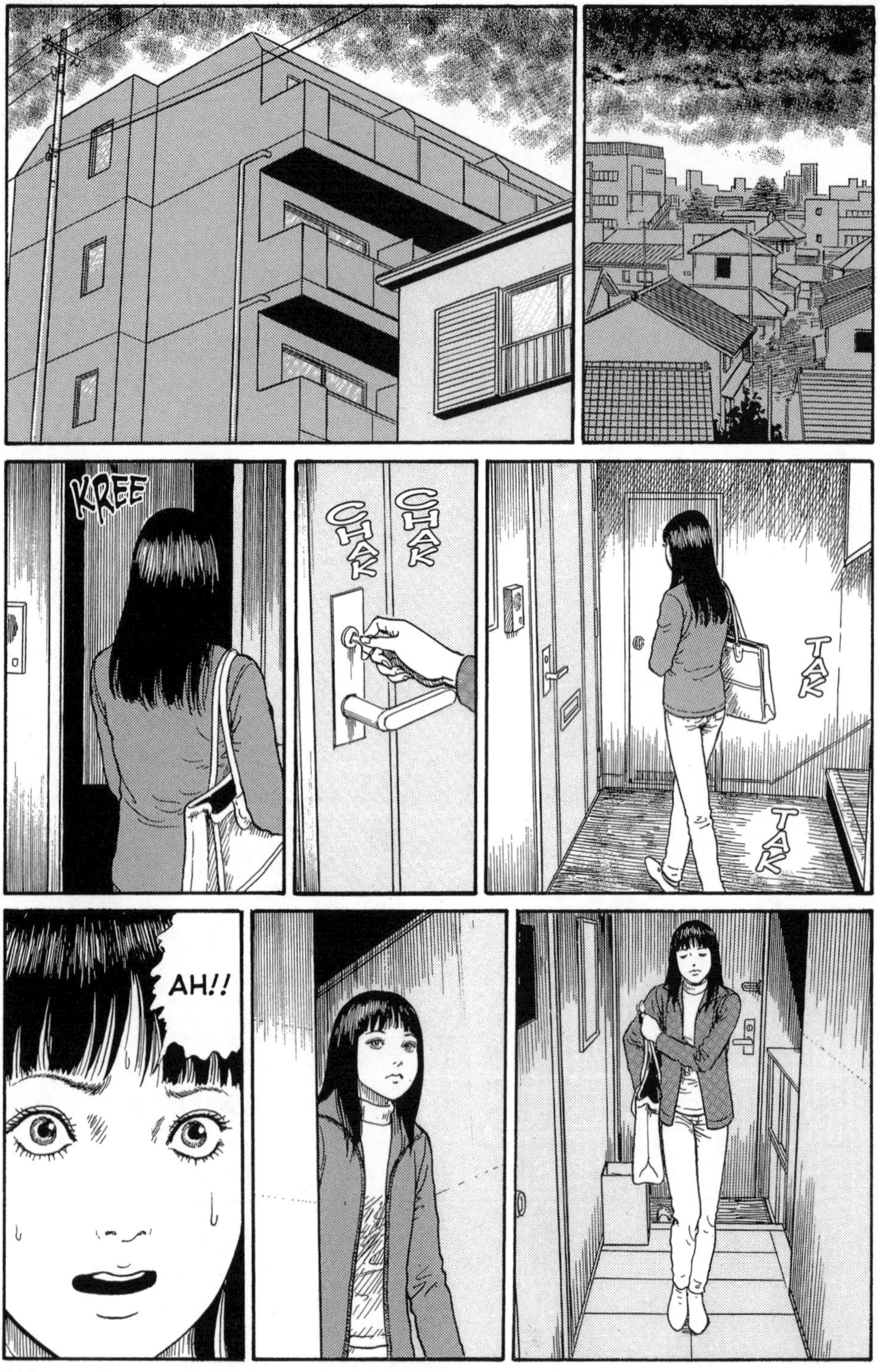
TAK
TAK
CHAK
CHAK
KREE
AH!!

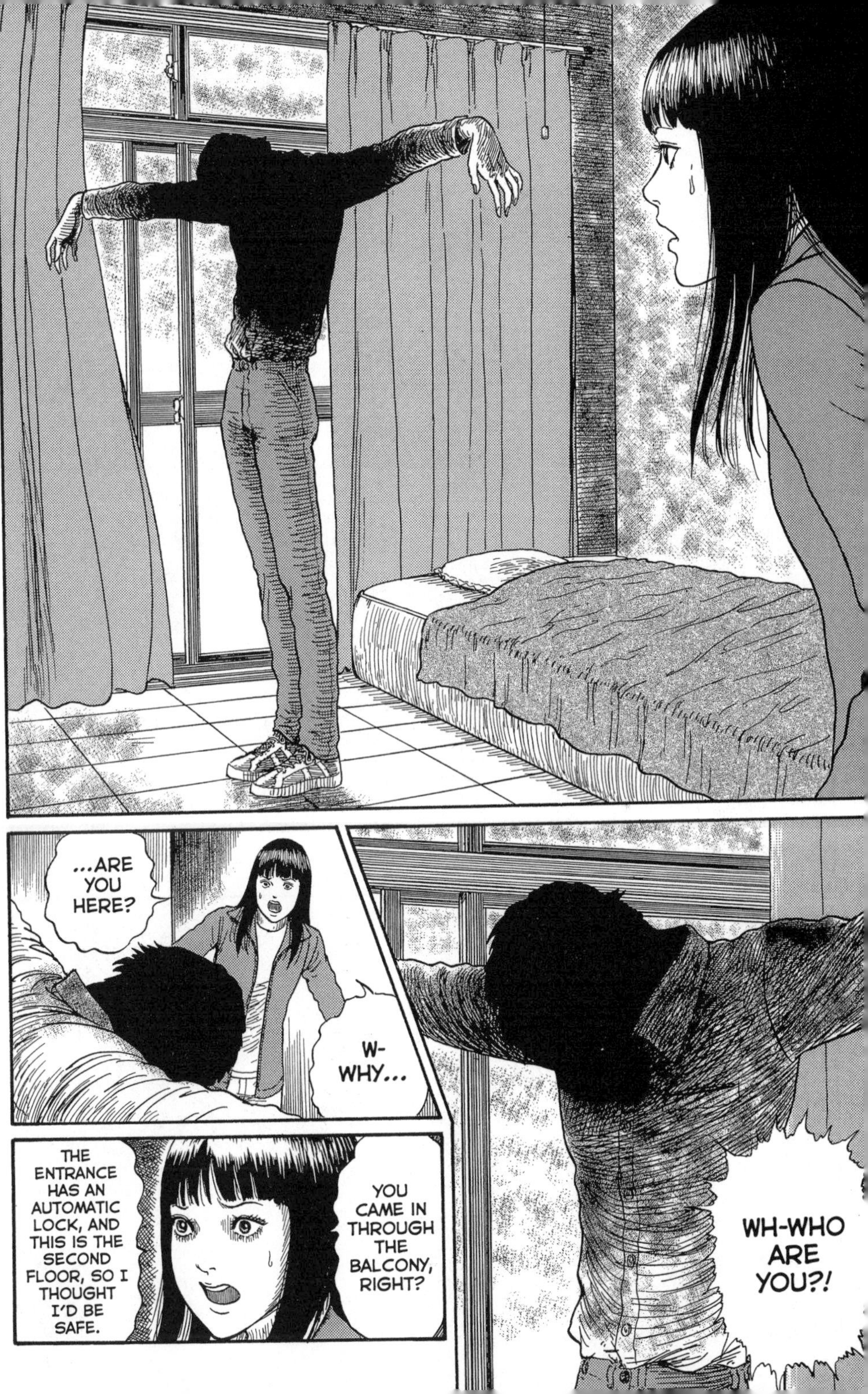
WH-WHO ARE YOU?!
W-WHY...
...ARE YOU HERE?
YOU CAME IN THROUGH THE BALCONY, RIGHT?
THE ENTRANCE HAS AN AUTOMATIC LOCK, AND THIS IS THE SECOND FLOOR, SO I THOUGHT I'D BE SAFE.

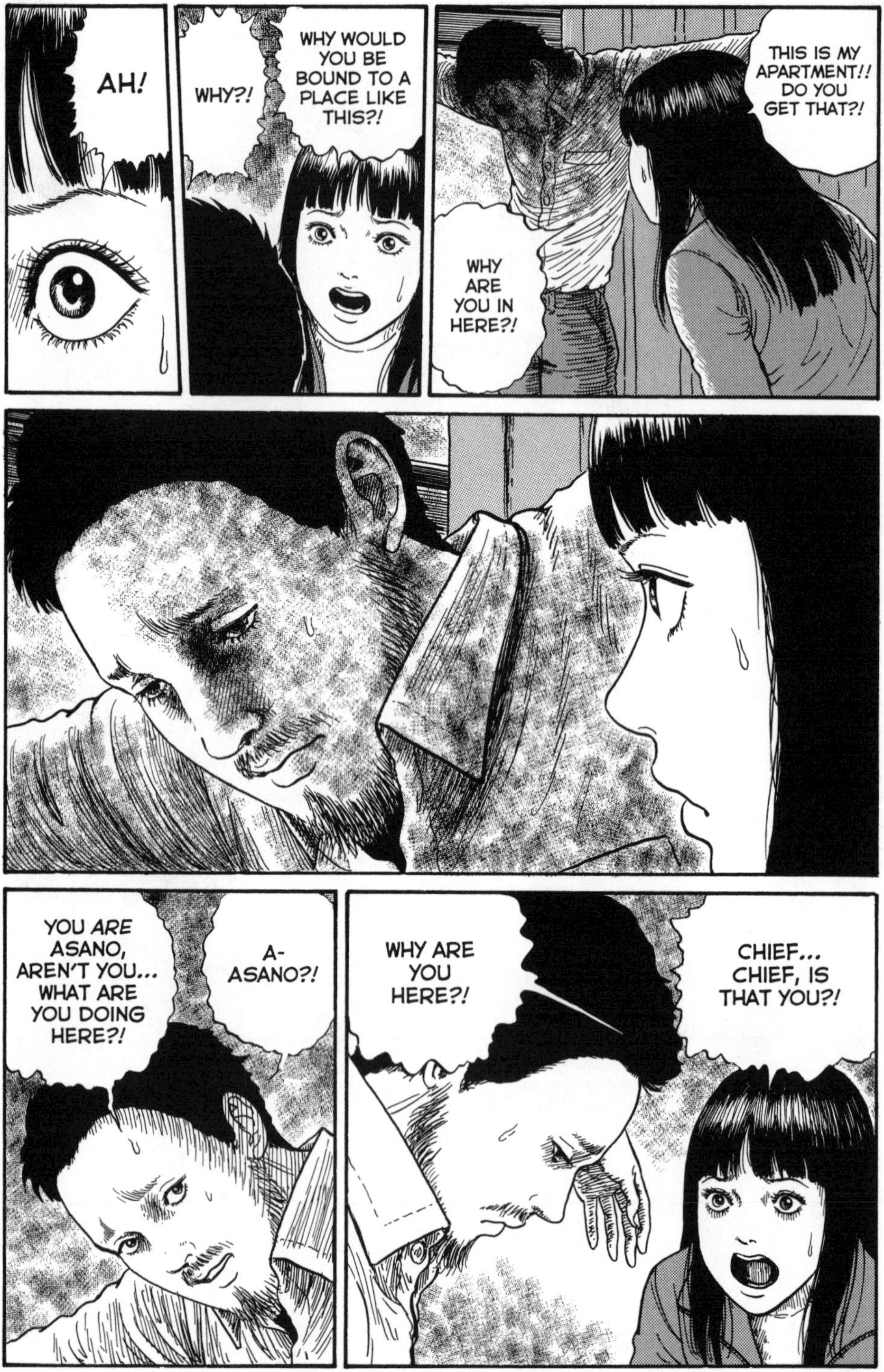
THIS IS MY APARTMENT!! DO YOU GET THAT?!
WHY ARE YOU IN HERE?!
WHY WOULD YOU BE BOUND TO A PLACE LIKE THIS?!
WHY?!
AH!
CHIEF... CHIEF, IS THAT YOU?!
WHY ARE YOU HERE?!
A- ASANO?!
YOU *ARE* ASANO, AREN'T YOU... WHAT ARE YOU DOING HERE?!

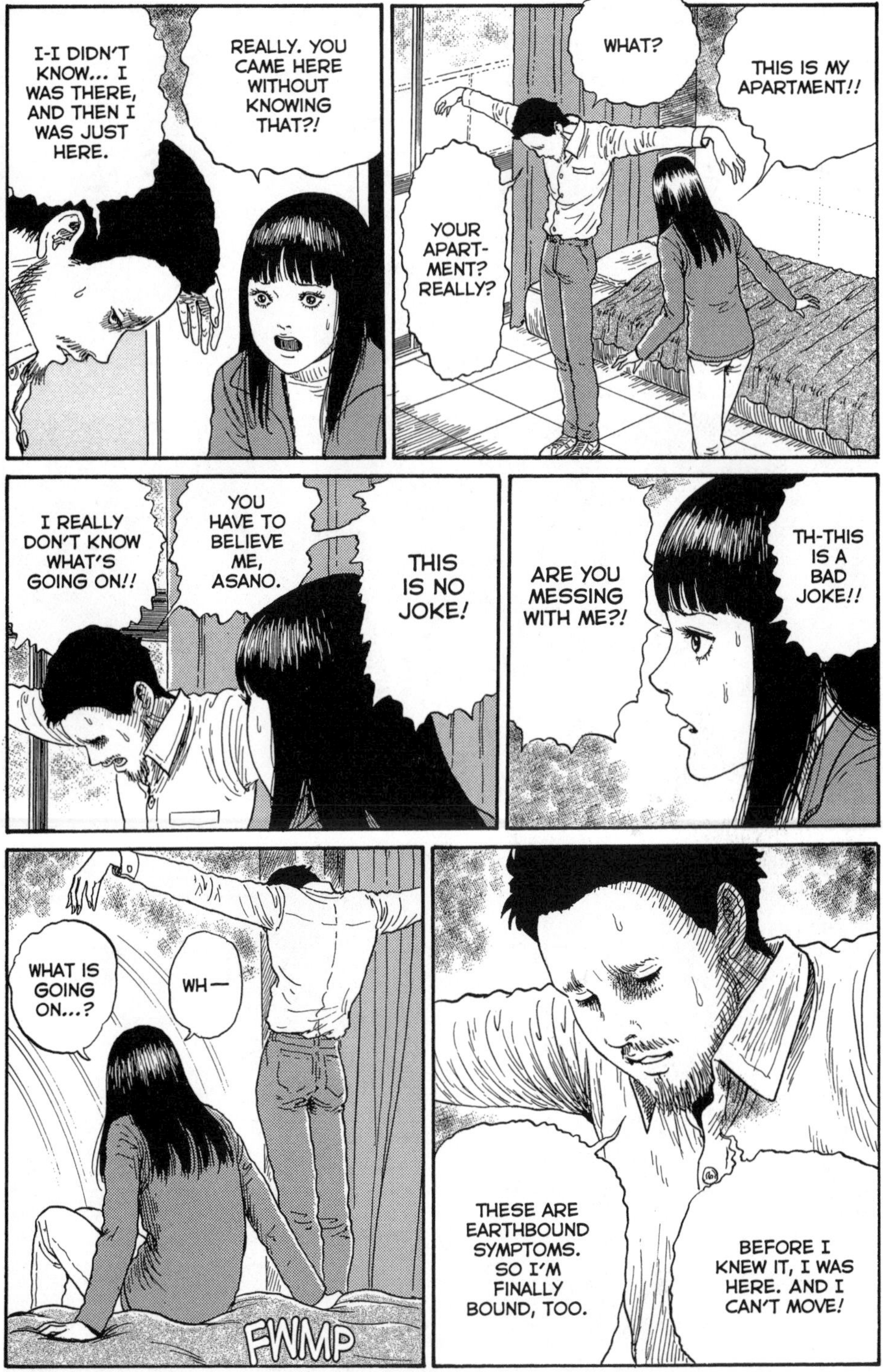
THIS IS MY APARTMENT!!
WHAT?
YOUR APARTMENT? REALLY?
REALLY. YOU CAME HERE WITHOUT KNOWING THAT?!
I-I DIDN'T KNOW... I WAS THERE, AND THEN I WAS JUST HERE.
TH-THIS IS A BAD JOKE!!
ARE YOU MESSING WITH ME?!
THIS IS NO JOKE!
YOU HAVE TO BELIEVE ME, ASANO.
I REALLY DON'T KNOW WHAT'S GOING ON!!
BEFORE I KNEW IT, I WAS HERE. AND I CAN'T MOVE!
THESE ARE EARTHBOUND SYMPTOMS. SO I'M FINALLY BOUND, TOO.
WH—
WHAT IS GOING ON...?
FWMP

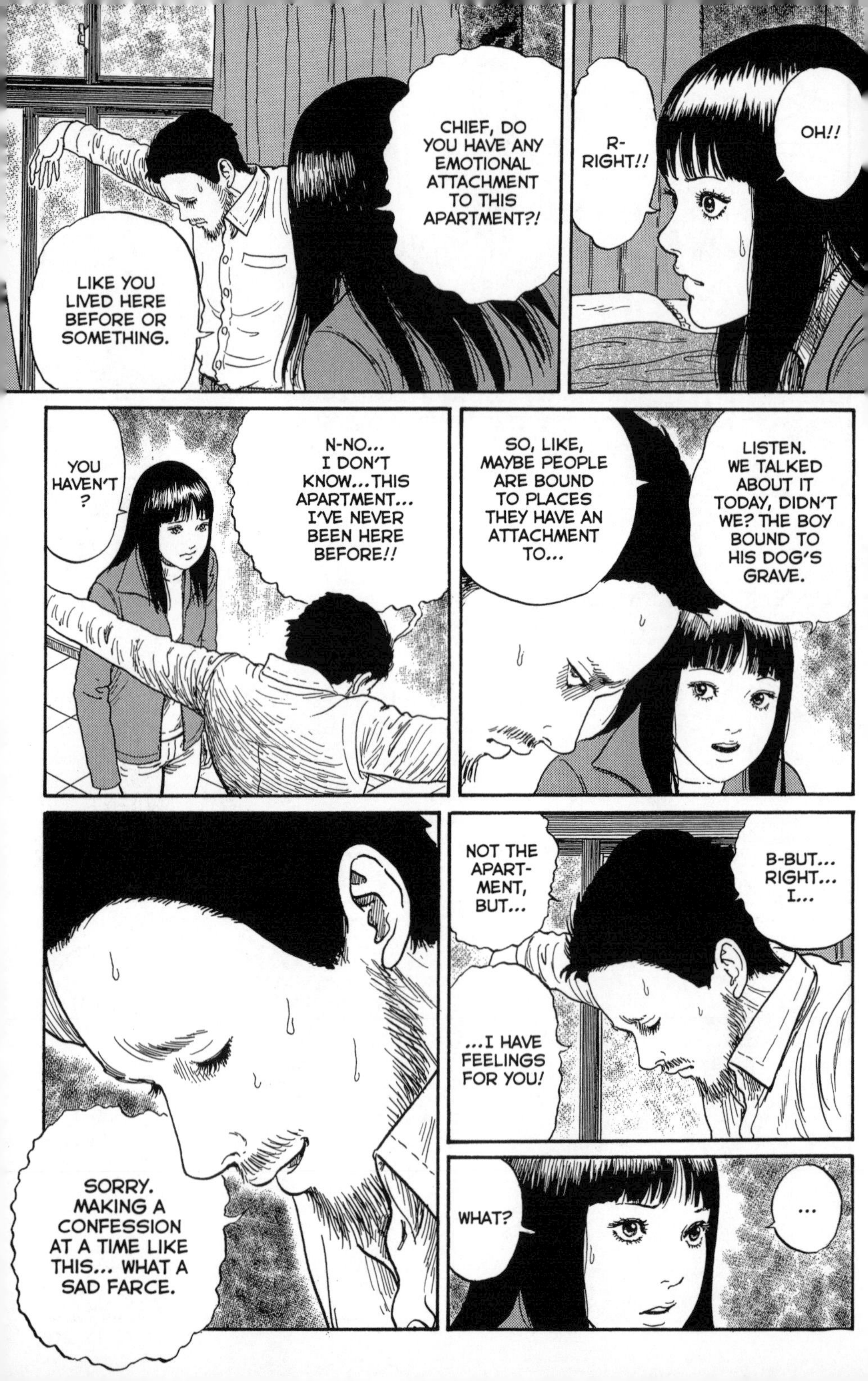
OH!!
R-RIGHT!!
CHIEF, DO YOU HAVE ANY EMOTIONAL ATTACHMENT TO THIS APARTMENT?!
LIKE YOU LIVED HERE BEFORE OR SOMETHING.
LISTEN. WE TALKED ABOUT IT TODAY, DIDN'T WE? THE BOY BOUND TO HIS DOG'S GRAVE.
SO, LIKE, MAYBE PEOPLE ARE BOUND TO PLACES THEY HAVE AN ATTACHMENT TO...
N-NO... I DON'T KNOW...THIS APARTMENT... I'VE NEVER BEEN HERE BEFORE!!
YOU HAVEN'T?
B-BUT... RIGHT... I...
NOT THE APART-MENT, BUT...
...I HAVE FEELINGS FOR YOU!
...
WHAT?
SORRY. MAKING A CONFESSION AT A TIME LIKE THIS... WHAT A SAD FARCE.

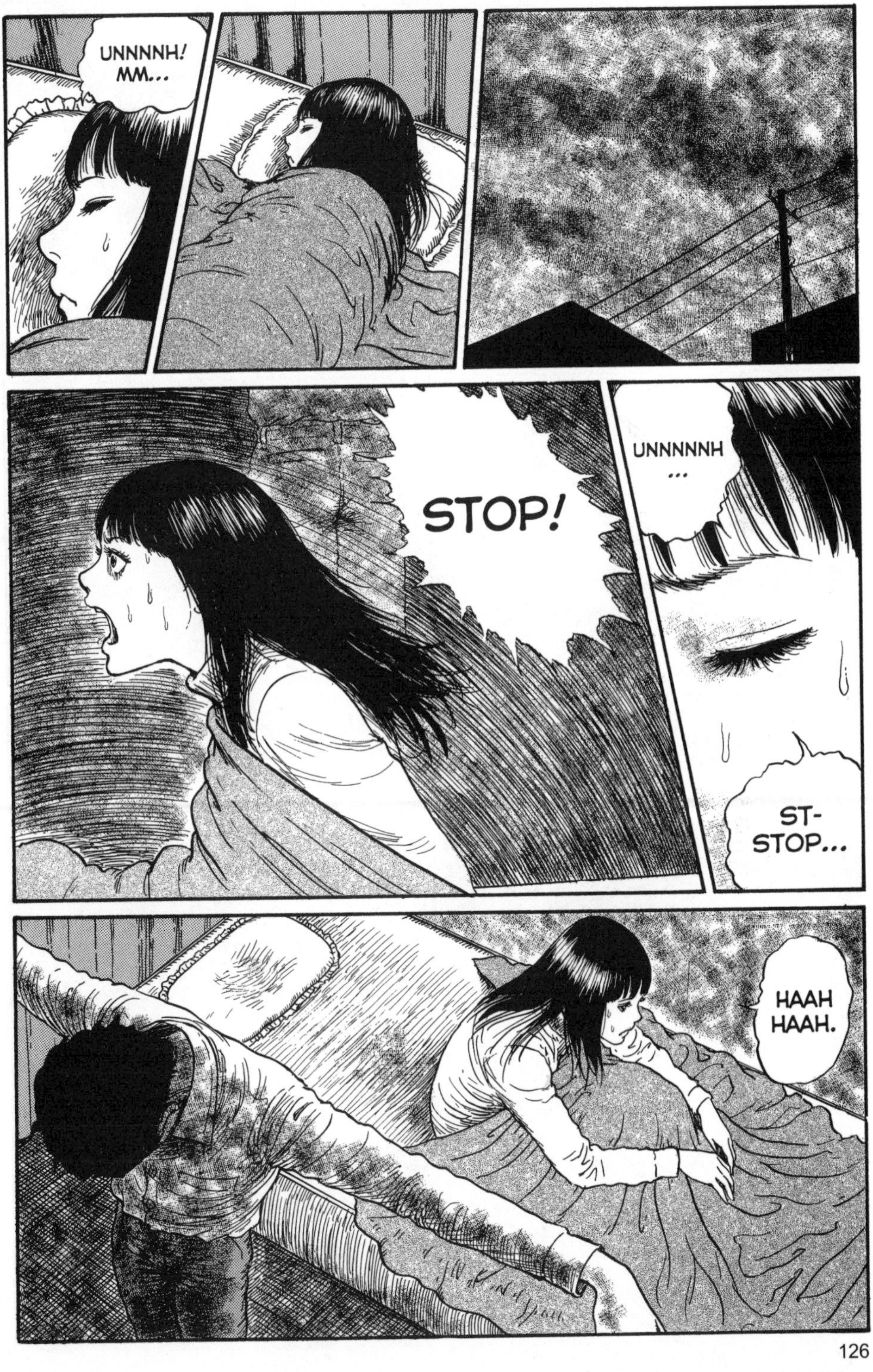
UNNNNH! MM...
UNNNNNH ...
ST- STOP...
STOP!
HAAH HAAH.

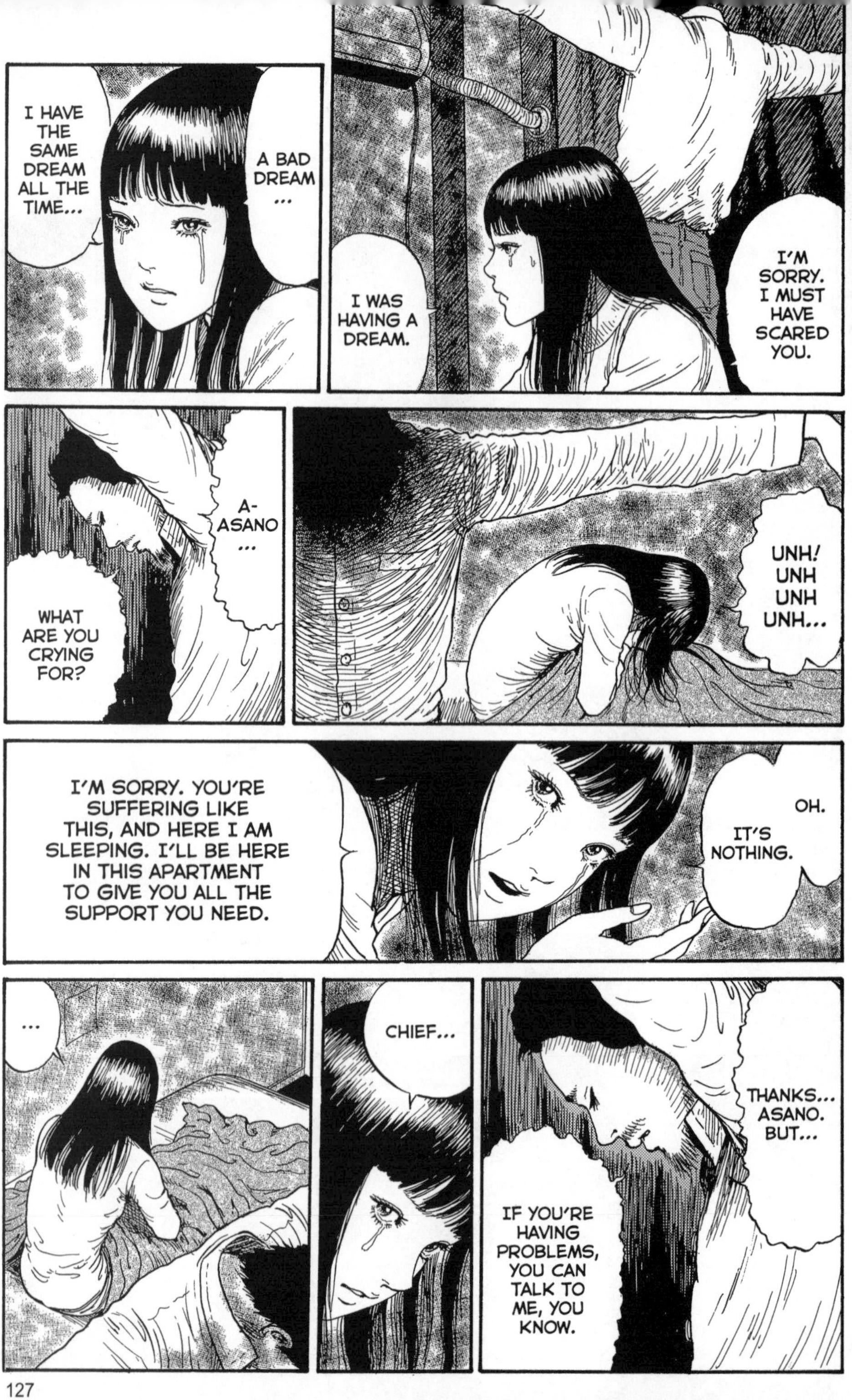
I'M SORRY. I MUST HAVE SCARED YOU.
I WAS HAVING A DREAM.
A BAD DREAM ...
I HAVE THE SAME DREAM ALL THE TIME...
UNH! UNH UNH UNH...
A- ASANO ...
WHAT ARE YOU CRYING FOR?
OH.
IT'S NOTHING.
I'M SORRY. YOU'RE SUFFERING LIKE THIS, AND HERE I AM SLEEPING. I'LL BE HERE IN THIS APARTMENT TO GIVE YOU ALL THE SUPPORT YOU NEED.
THANKS... ASANO. BUT...
IF YOU'RE HAVING PROBLEMS, YOU CAN TALK TO ME, YOU KNOW.
CHIEF...
...

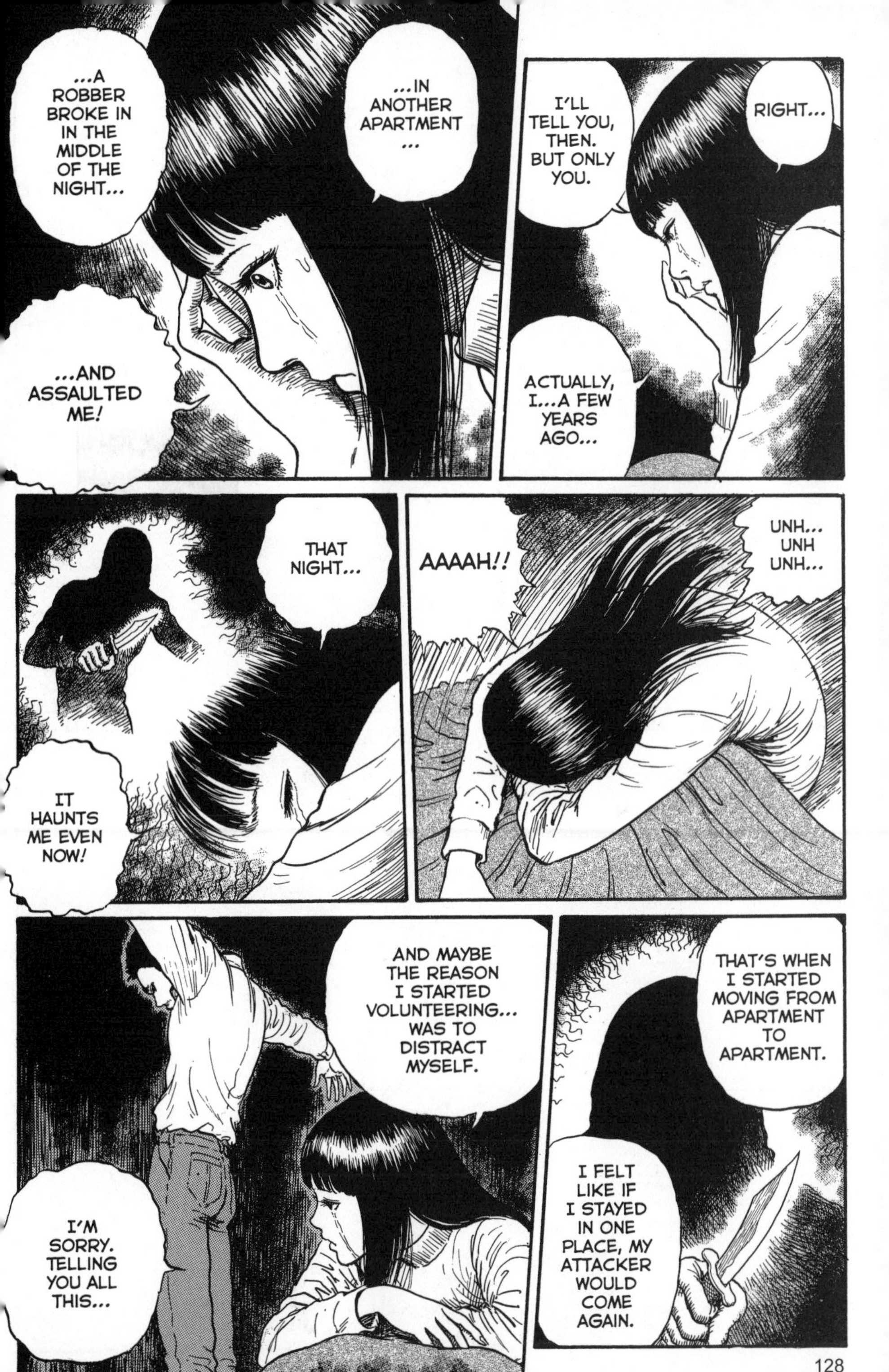
RIGHT...
I'LL TELL YOU, THEN. BUT ONLY YOU.
ACTUALLY, I...A FEW YEARS AGO...
...IN ANOTHER APARTMENT...
...A ROBBER BROKE IN IN THE MIDDLE OF THE NIGHT...
...AND ASSAULTED ME!
UNH... UNH UNH...
AAAAH!!
THAT NIGHT...
IT HAUNTS ME EVEN NOW!
THAT'S WHEN I STARTED MOVING FROM APARTMENT TO APARTMENT.
I FELT LIKE IF I STAYED IN ONE PLACE, MY ATTACKER WOULD COME AGAIN.
AND MAYBE THE REASON I STARTED VOLUNTEERING... WAS TO DISTRACT MYSELF.
I'M SORRY. TELLING YOU ALL THIS...

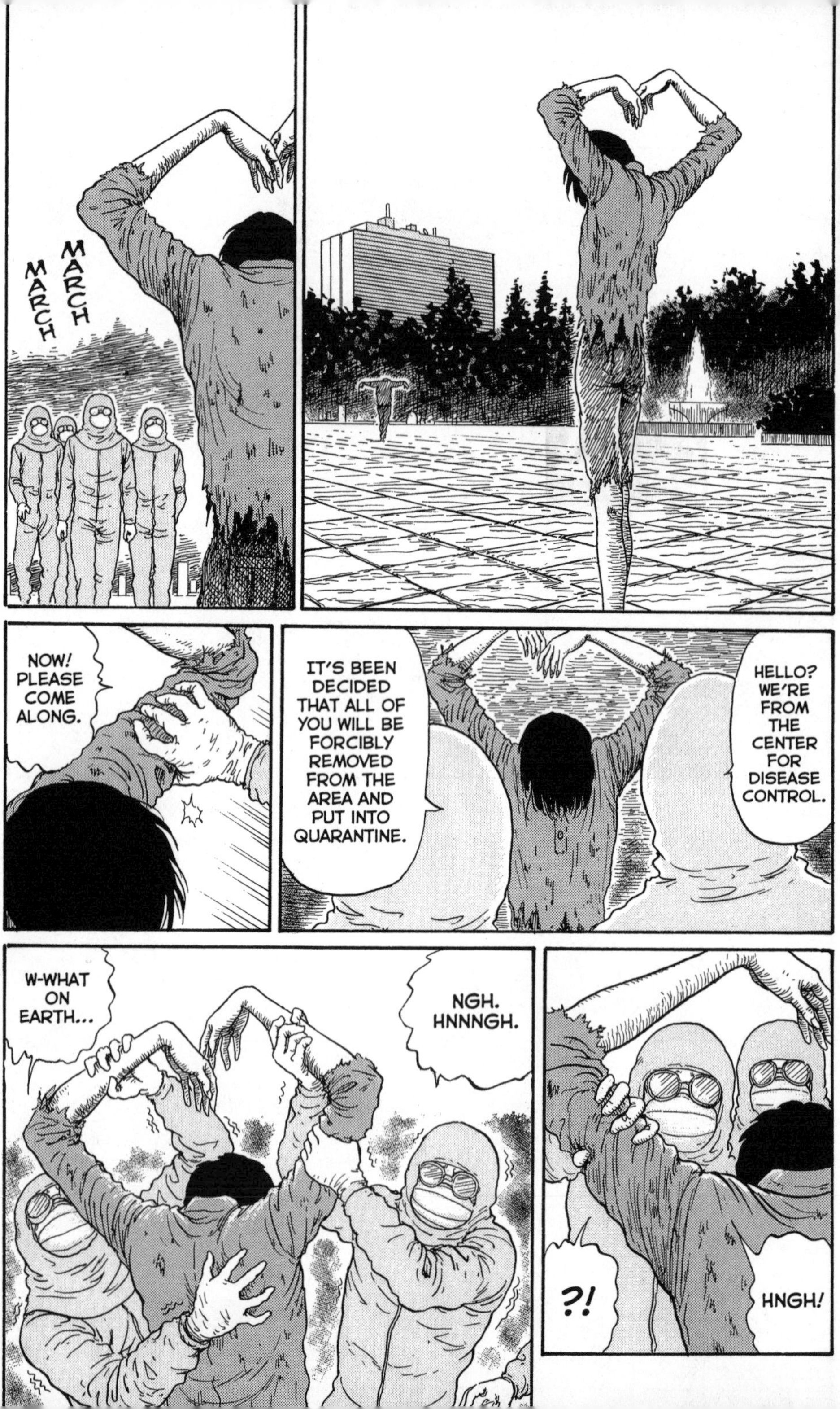
MARCH
MARCH
HELLO? WE'RE FROM THE CENTER FOR DISEASE CONTROL.
IT'S BEEN DECIDED THAT ALL OF YOU WILL BE FORCIBLY REMOVED FROM THE AREA AND PUT INTO QUARANTINE.
NOW! PLEASE COME ALONG.
HNGH!
?!
NGH. HNNNGH.
W-WHAT ON EARTH...

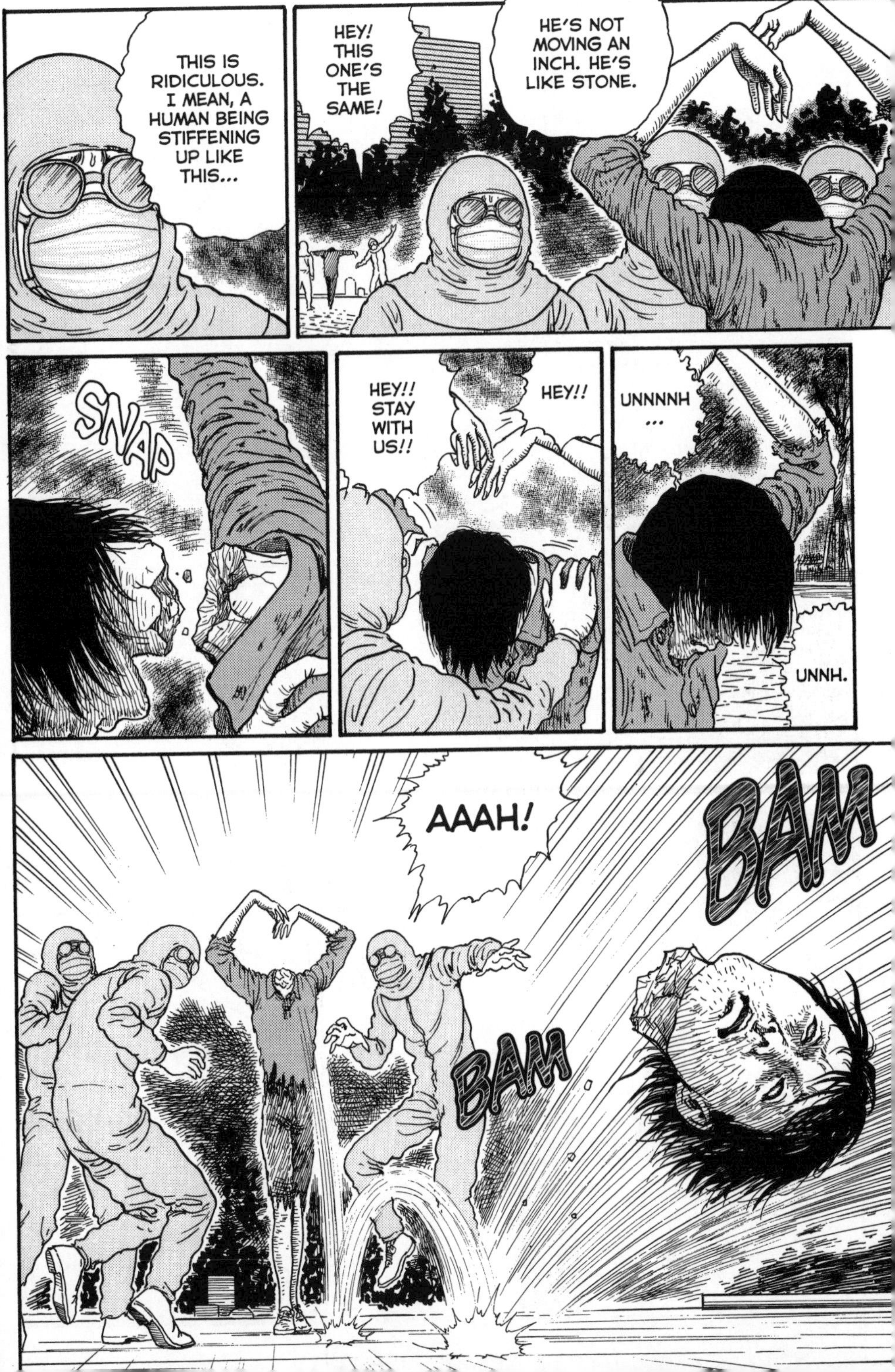
HE'S NOT MOVING AN INCH. HE'S LIKE STONE.
HEY! THIS ONE'S THE SAME!
THIS IS RIDICULOUS. I MEAN, A HUMAN BEING STIFFENING UP LIKE THIS...
UNNNNH ...
UNNH.
HEY!!
HEY!! STAY WITH US!!
SNAP
BAM
AAAH!
BAM

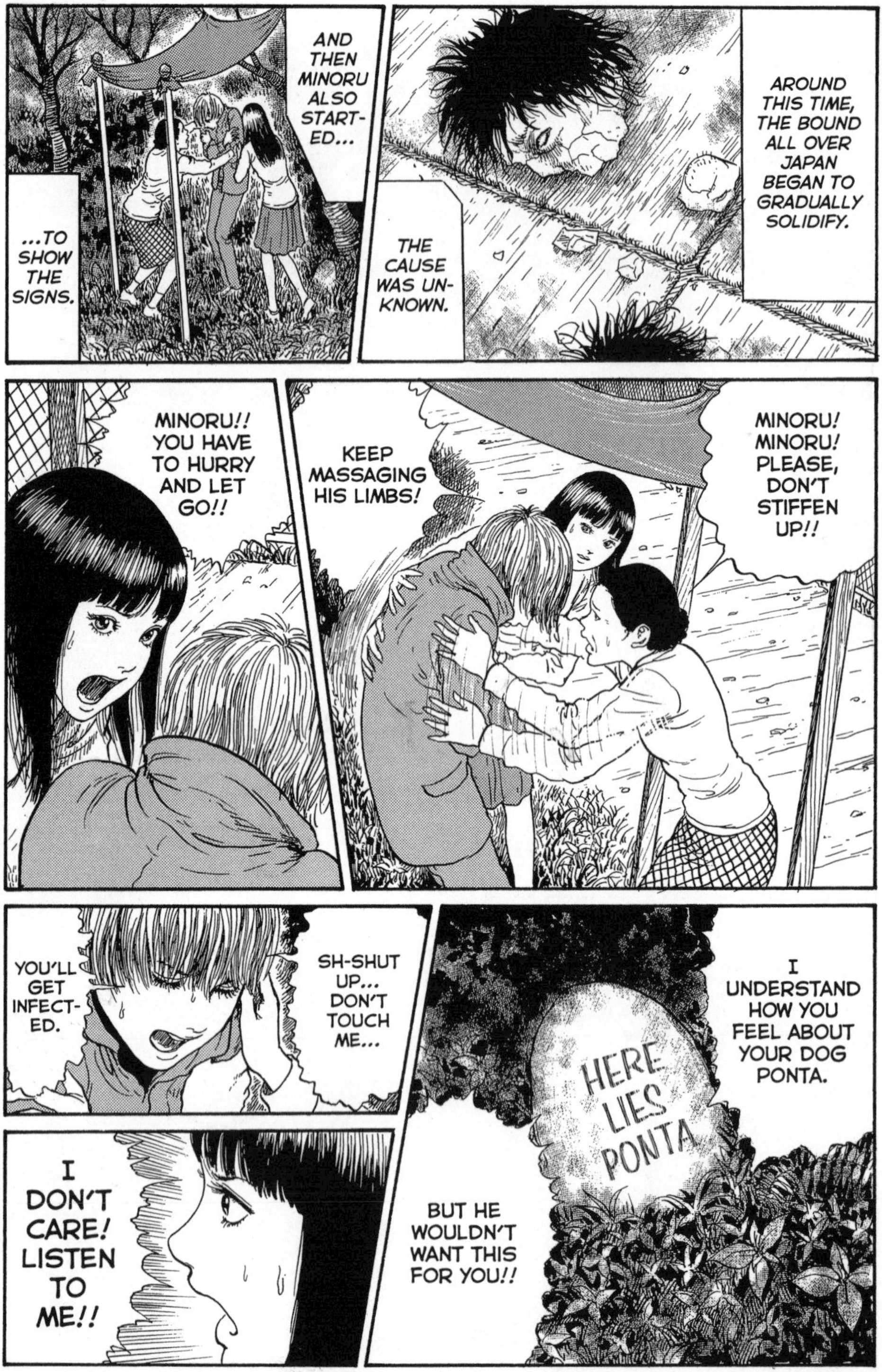
AROUND THIS TIME, THE BOUND ALL OVER JAPAN BEGAN TO GRADUALLY SOLIDIFY.
THE CAUSE WAS UNKNOWN.
AND THEN MINORU ALSO START-ED...
...TO SHOW THE SIGNS.
MINORU! MINORU! PLEASE, DON'T STIFFEN UP!!
KEEP MASSAGING HIS LIMBS!
MINORU!! YOU HAVE TO HURRY AND LET GO!!
I UNDERSTAND HOW YOU FEEL ABOUT YOUR DOG PONTA.
HERE LIES PONTA
BUT HE WOULDN'T WANT THIS FOR YOU!!
SH-SHUT UP... DON'T TOUCH ME...
YOU'LL GET INFECT-ED.
I DON'T CARE! LISTEN TO ME!!

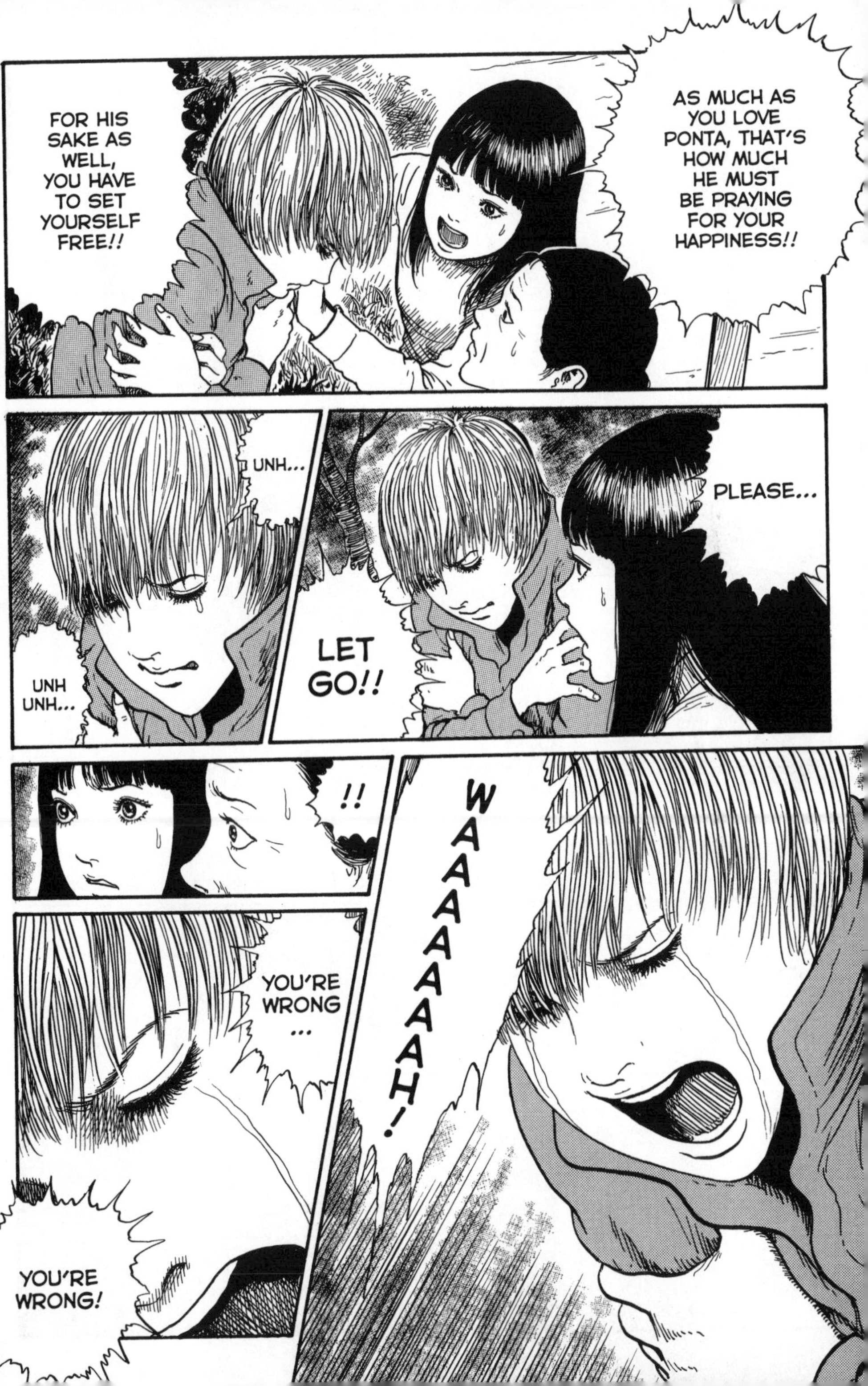
AS MUCH AS YOU LOVE PONTA, THAT'S HOW MUCH HE MUST BE PRAYING FOR YOUR HAPPINESS!!
FOR HIS SAKE AS WELL, YOU HAVE TO SET YOURSELF FREE!!
PLEASE...
LET GO!!
UNH...
UNH UNH...
WAAAAAAAAH!
!!
YOU'RE WRONG ...
YOU'RE WRONG!

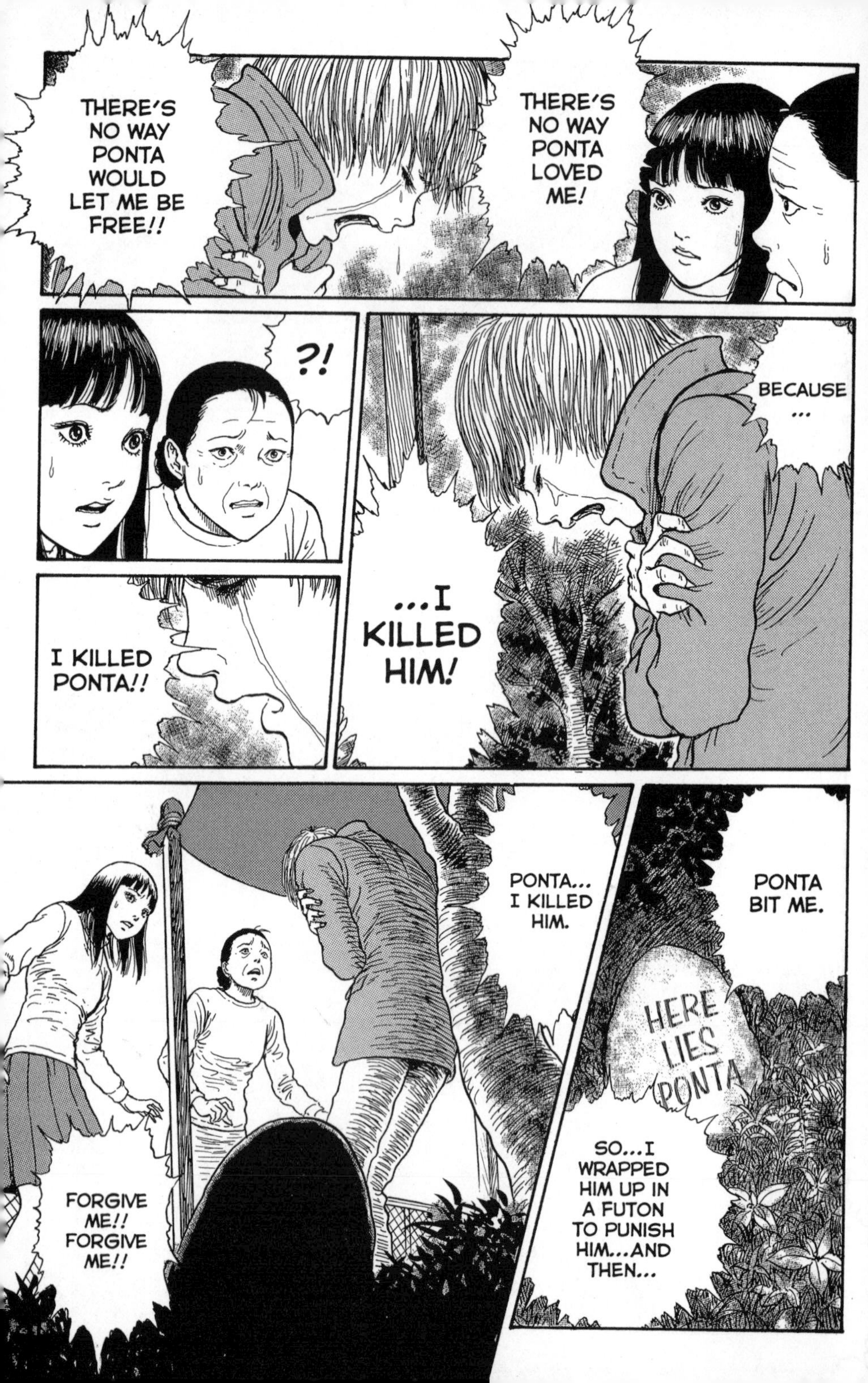
THERE'S NO WAY PONTA LOVED ME!
THERE'S NO WAY PONTA WOULD LET ME BE FREE!!
BECAUSE...
...I KILLED HIM!
?!
I KILLED PONTA!!
PONTA BIT ME.
HERE LIES PONTA
SO...I WRAPPED HIM UP IN A FUTON TO PUNISH HIM...AND THEN...
PONTA... I KILLED HIM.
FORGIVE ME!! FORGIVE ME!!

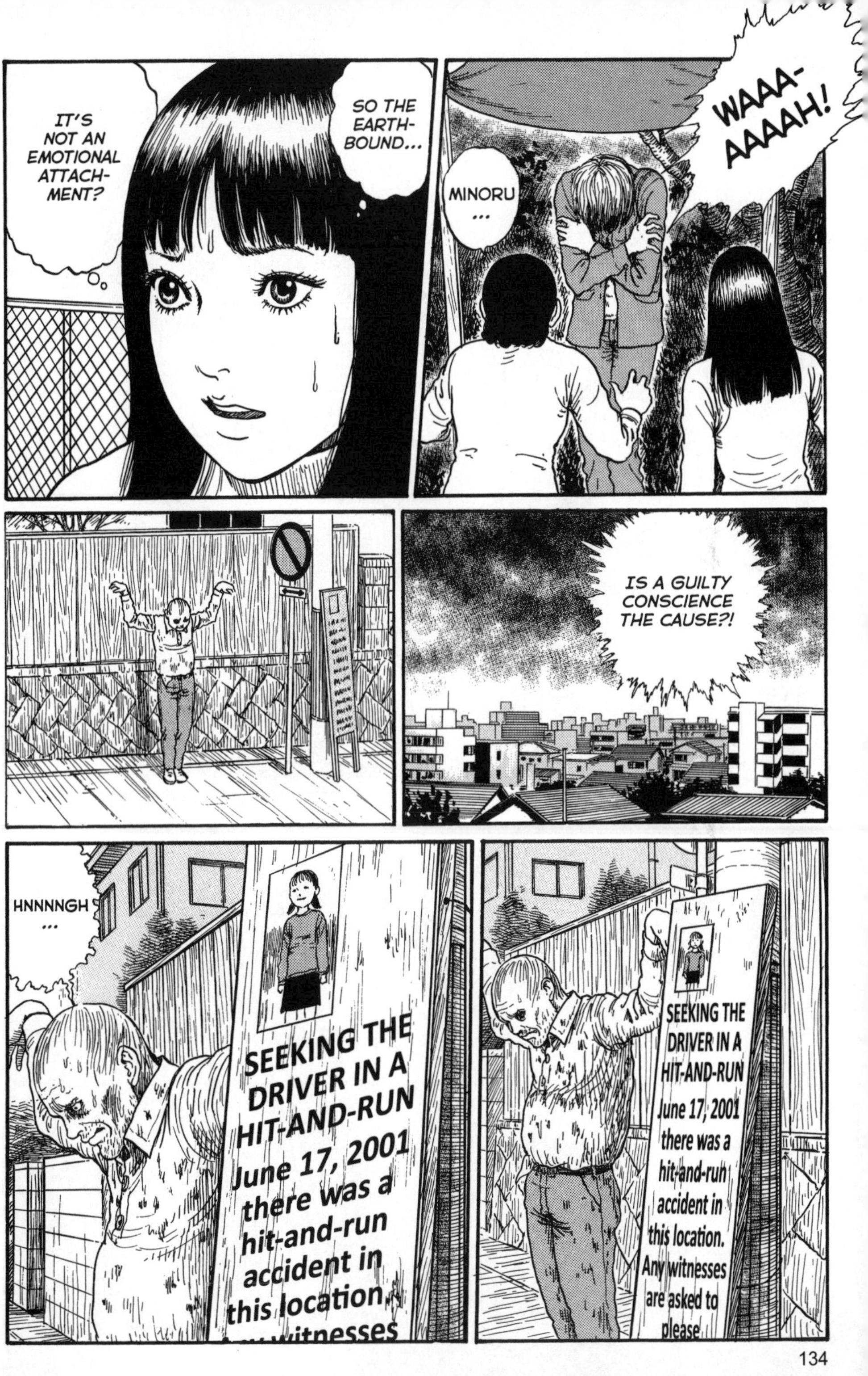
MINORU ...
WAAA-AAAAH!
SO THE EARTH-BOUND...
IT'S NOT AN EMOTIONAL ATTACH-MENT?
IS A GUILTY CONSCIENCE THE CAUSE?!
SEEKING THE DRIVER IN A HIT-AND-RUN
June 17, 2001 there was a hit-and-run accident in this location. Any witnesses are asked to please
HNNNNGH ...
SEEKING THE DRIVER IN A HIT-AND-RUN
June 17, 2001 there was a hit-and-run accident in this location.

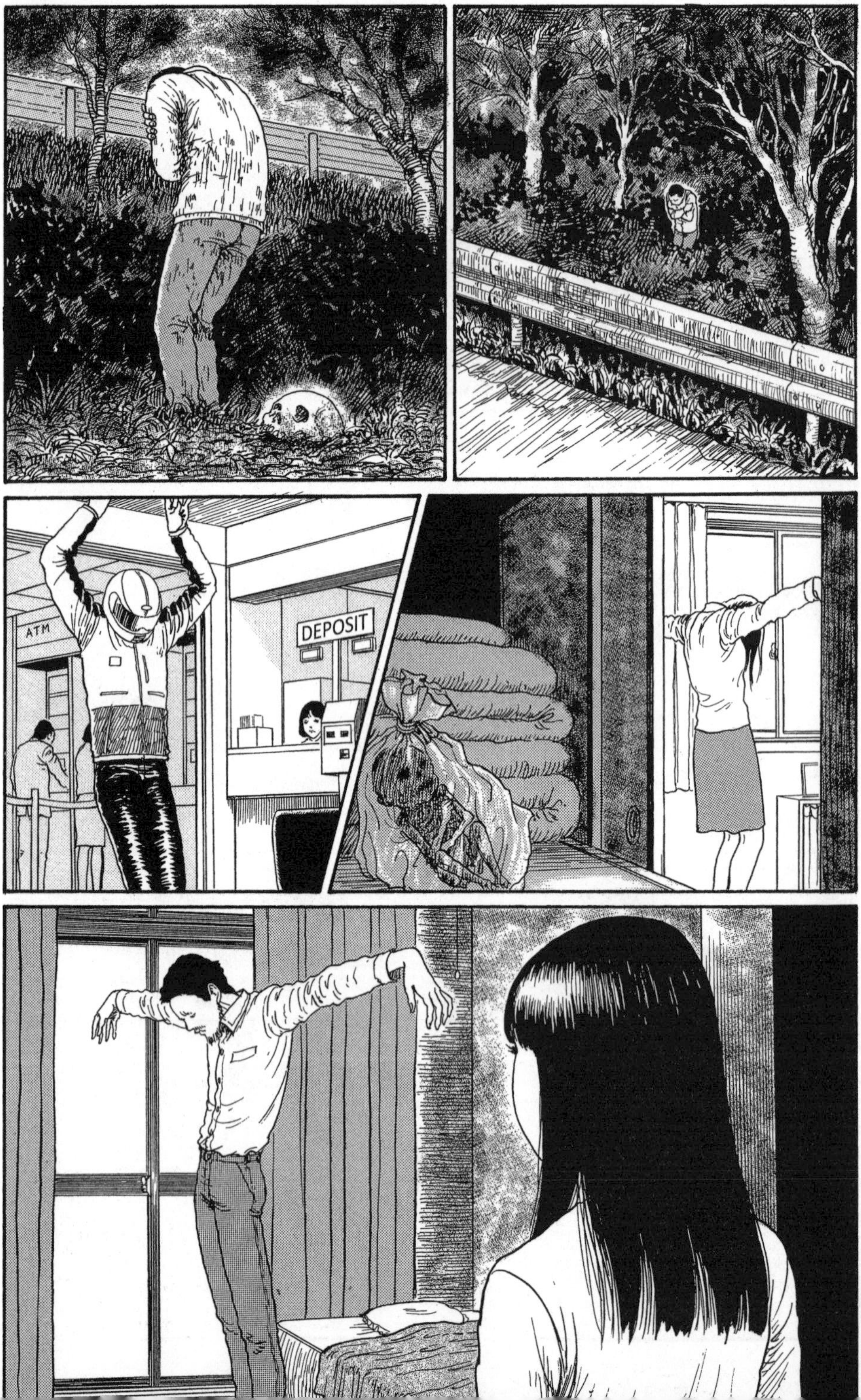
DEPOSIT
ATM

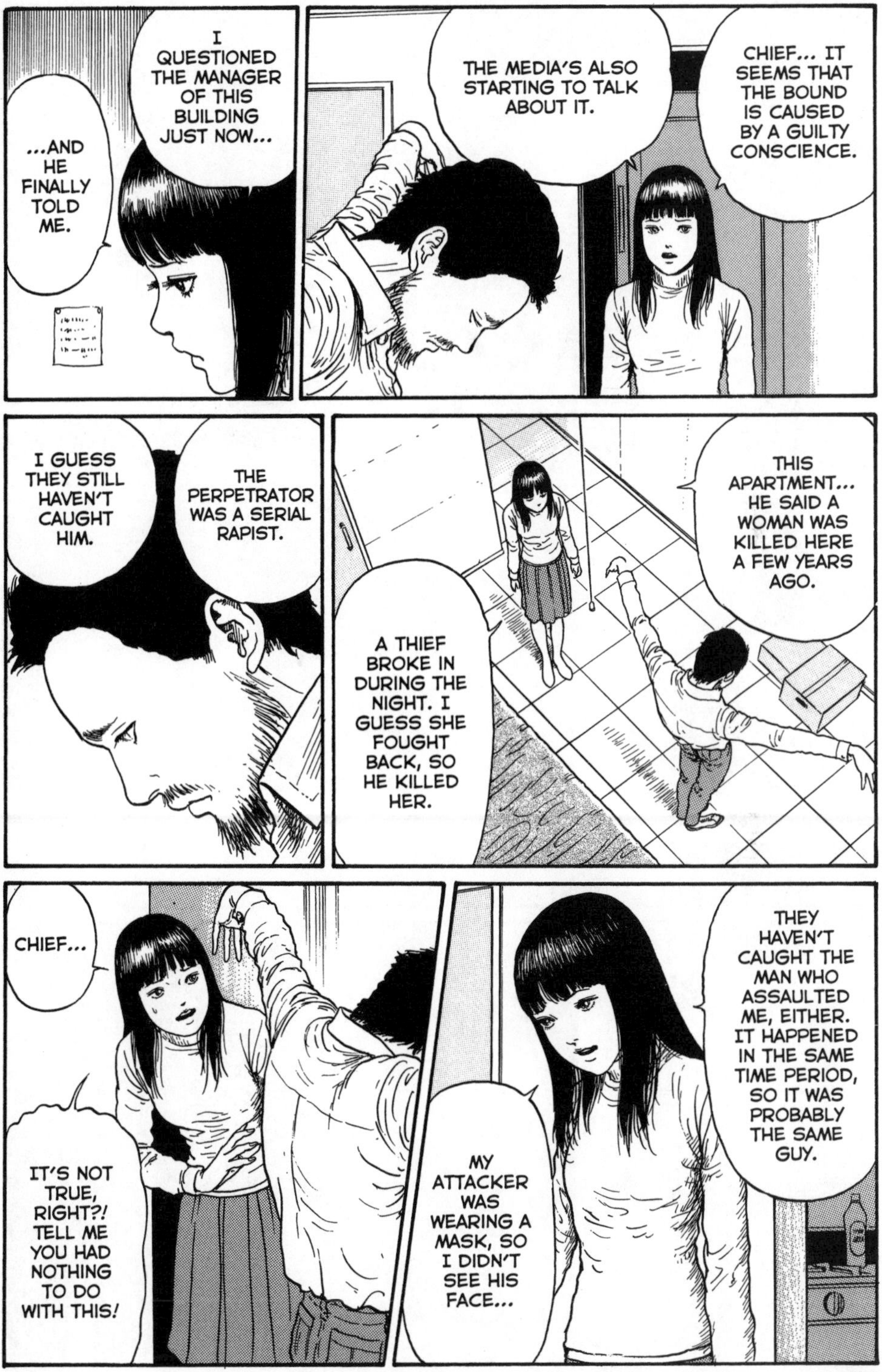
CHIEF... IT SEEMS THAT THE BOUND IS CAUSED BY A GUILTY CONSCIENCE.
THE MEDIA'S ALSO STARTING TO TALK ABOUT IT.
I QUESTIONED THE MANAGER OF THIS BUILDING JUST NOW...
...AND HE FINALLY TOLD ME.
THIS APARTMENT... HE SAID A WOMAN WAS KILLED HERE A FEW YEARS AGO.
A THIEF BROKE IN DURING THE NIGHT. I GUESS SHE FOUGHT BACK, SO HE KILLED HER.
THE PERPETRATOR WAS A SERIAL RAPIST.
I GUESS THEY STILL HAVEN'T CAUGHT HIM.
THEY HAVEN'T CAUGHT THE MAN WHO ASSAULTED ME, EITHER. IT HAPPENED IN THE SAME TIME PERIOD, SO IT WAS PROBABLY THE SAME GUY.
MY ATTACKER WAS WEARING A MASK, SO I DIDN'T SEE HIS FACE...
CHIEF...
IT'S NOT TRUE, RIGHT?! TELL ME YOU HAD NOTHING TO DO WITH THIS!

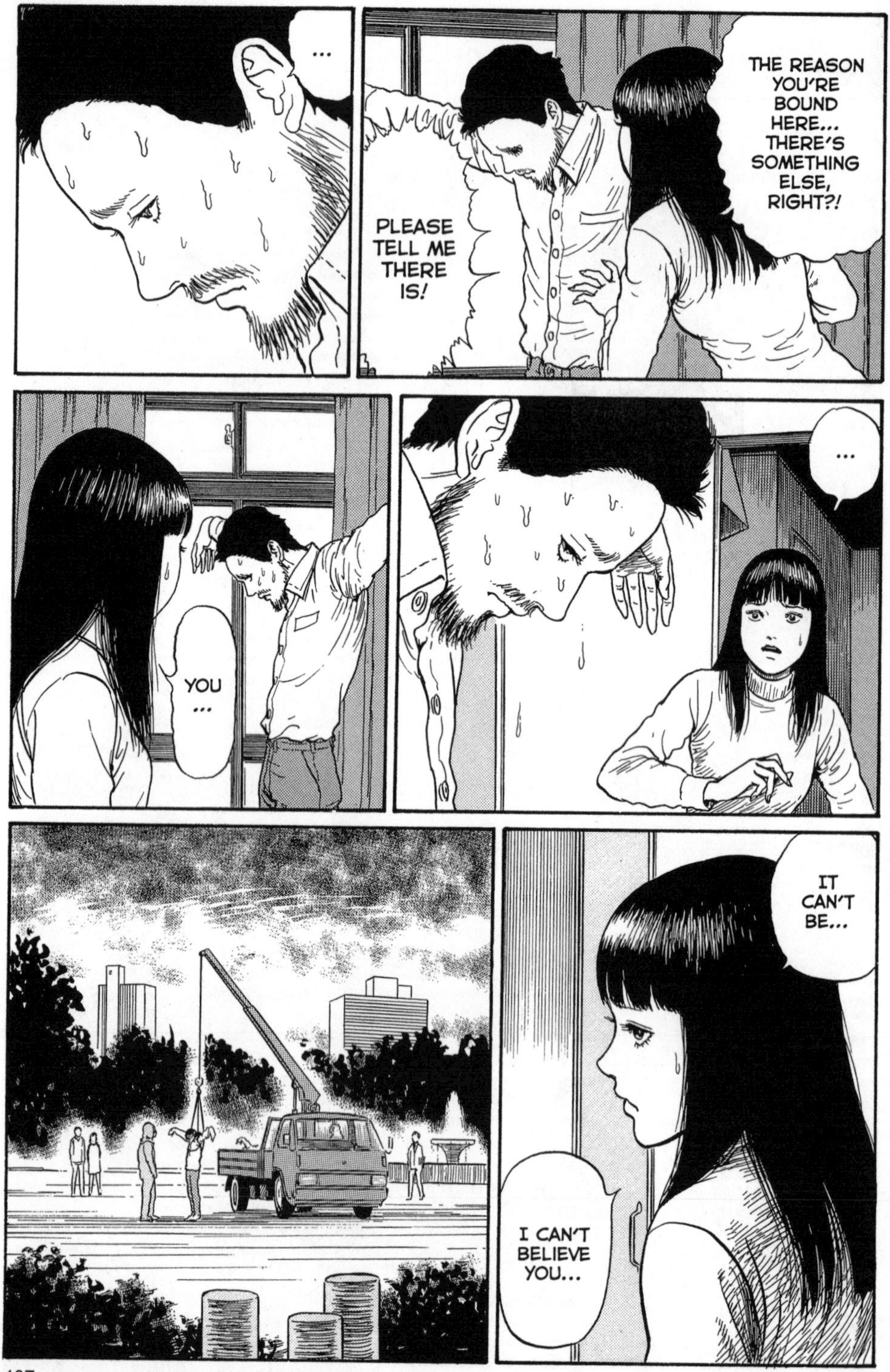
THE REASON YOU'RE BOUND HERE... THERE'S SOMETHING ELSE, RIGHT?!
PLEASE TELL ME THERE IS!
...
...
YOU ...
IT CAN'T BE...
I CAN'T BELIEVE YOU...

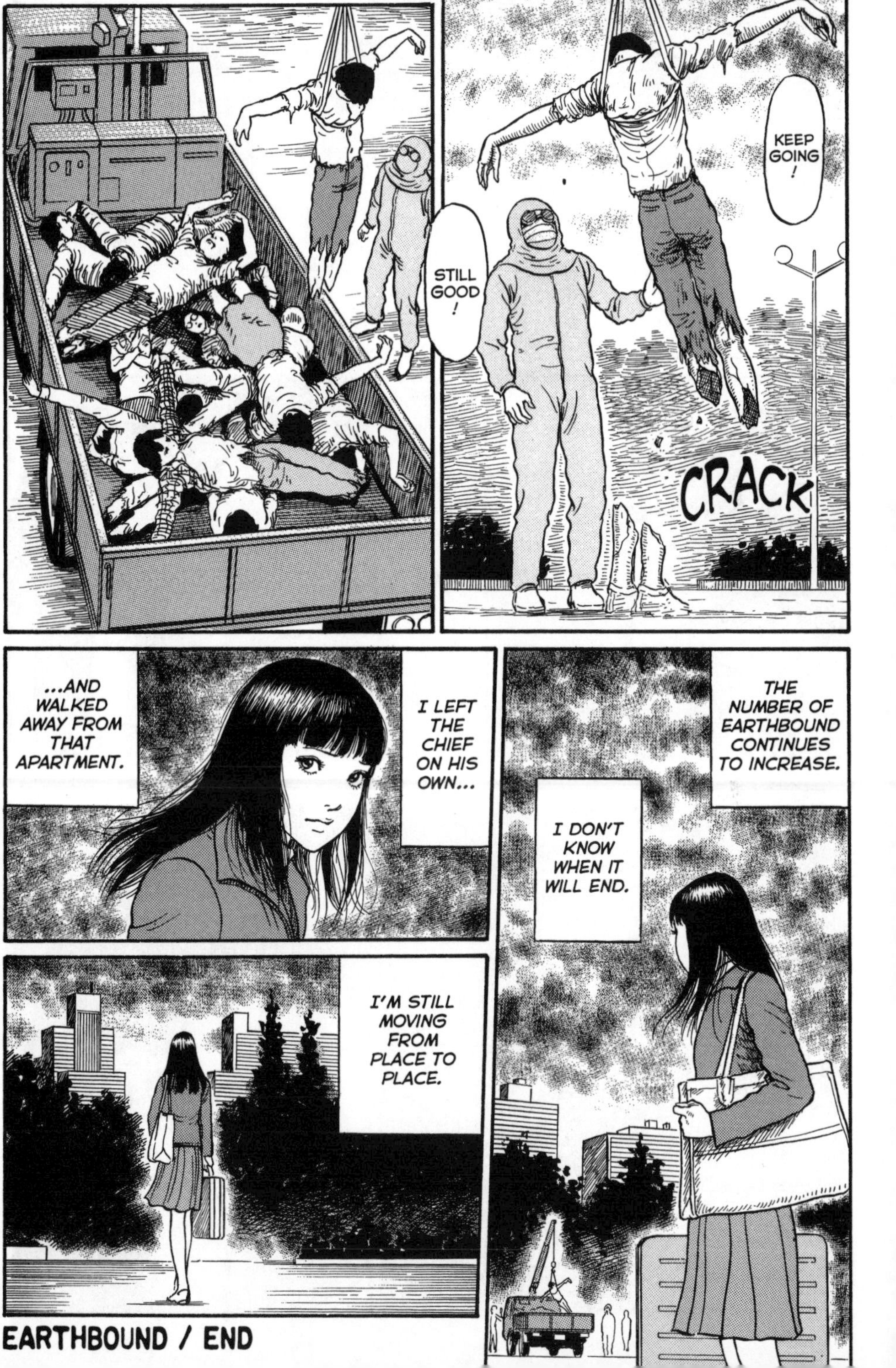
KEEP GOING!
STILL GOOD!
CRACK
THE NUMBER OF EARTHBOUND CONTINUES TO INCREASE.
I DON'T KNOW WHEN IT WILL END.
I LEFT THE CHIEF ON HIS OWN...
...AND WALKED AWAY FROM THAT APARTMENT.
I'M STILL MOVING FROM PLACE TO PLACE.

EARTHBOUND / END

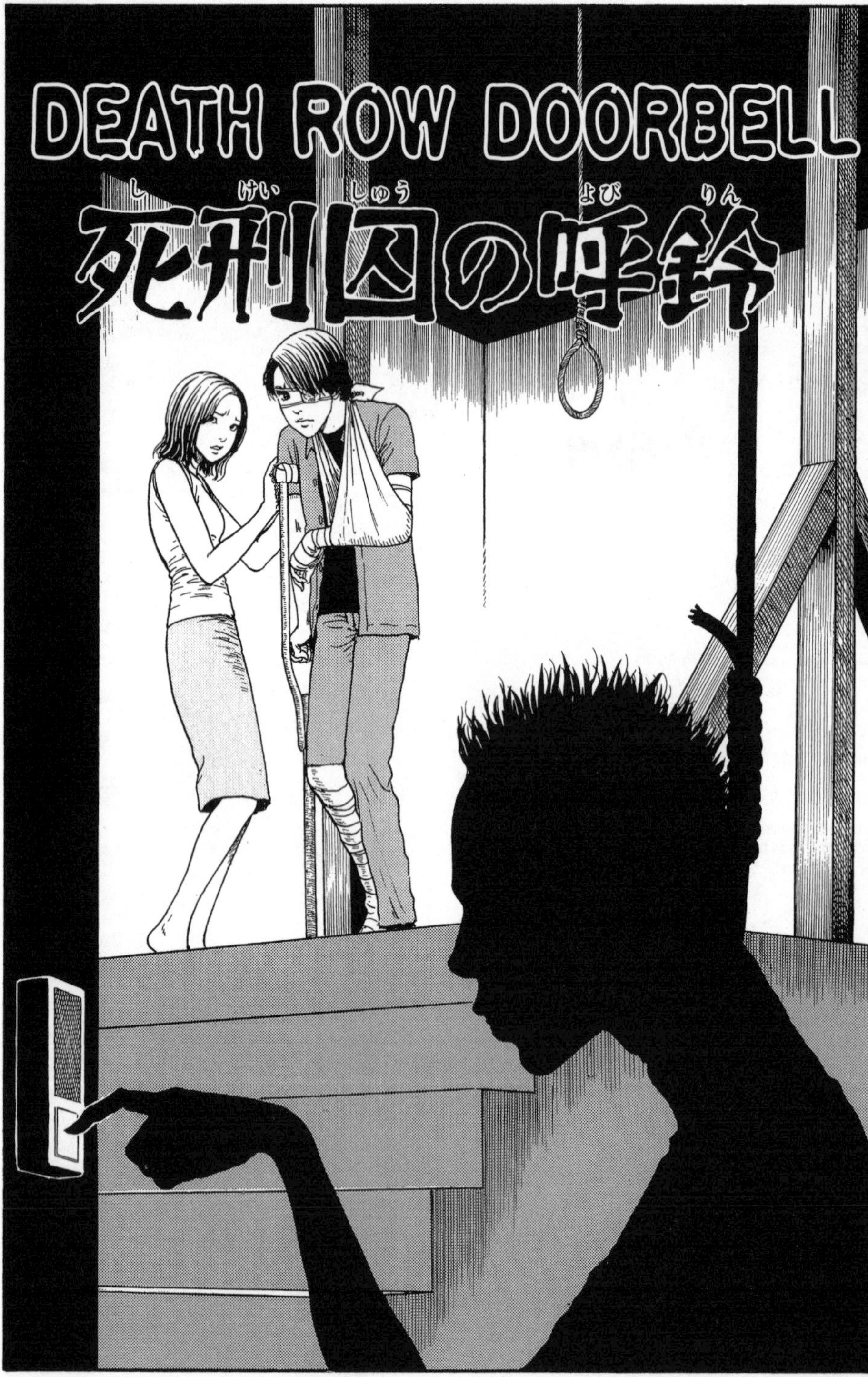
DEATH ROW DOORBELL
死刑囚(しけいしゅう)の呼鈴(よびりん)

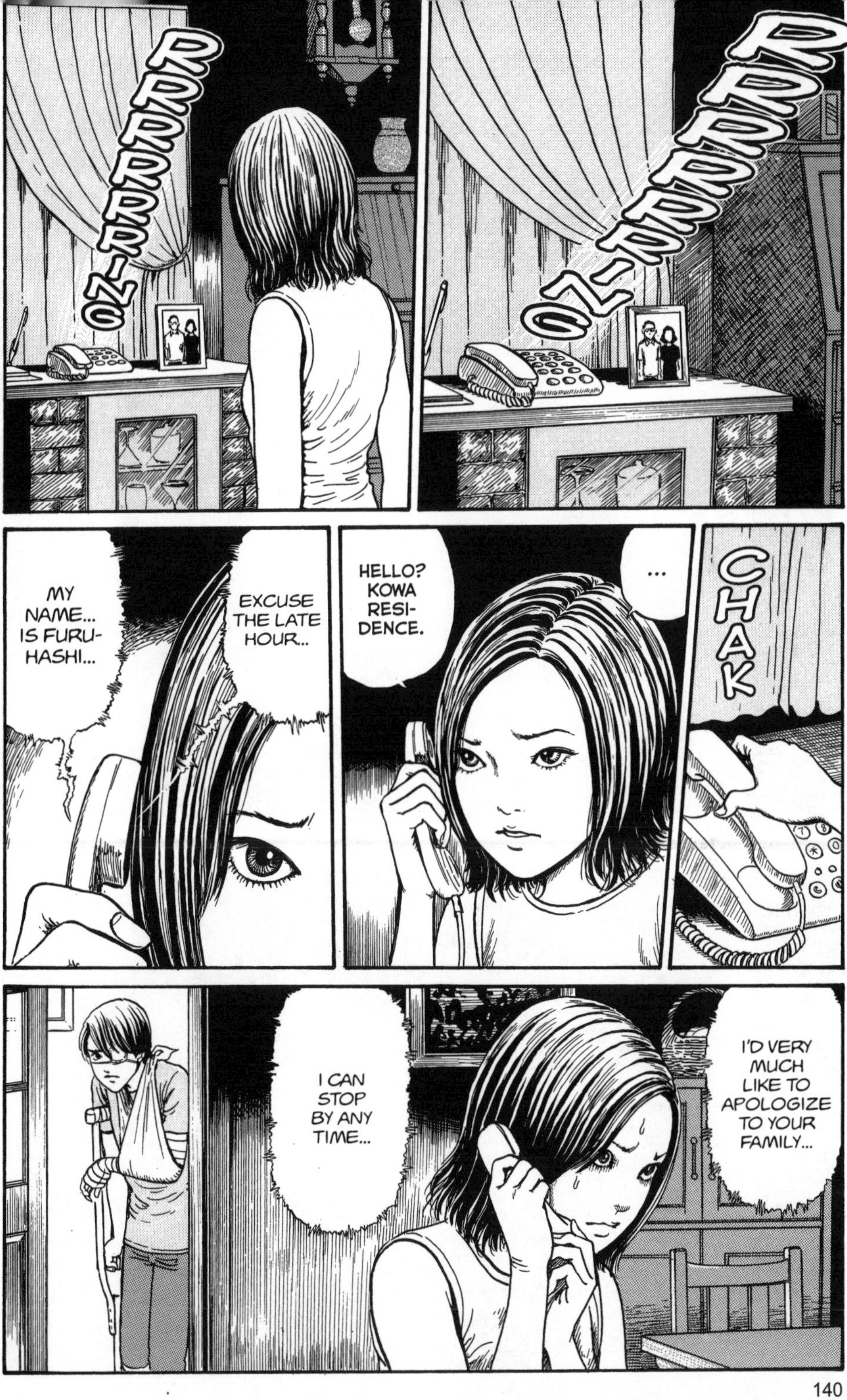
RRRRRRRING
RRRRRRRING
CHAK
...
HELLO? KOWA RESIDENCE.
EXCUSE THE LATE HOUR...
MY NAME... IS FURUHASHI...
I'D VERY MUCH LIKE TO APOLOGIZE TO YOUR FAMILY...
I CAN STOP BY ANY TIME...

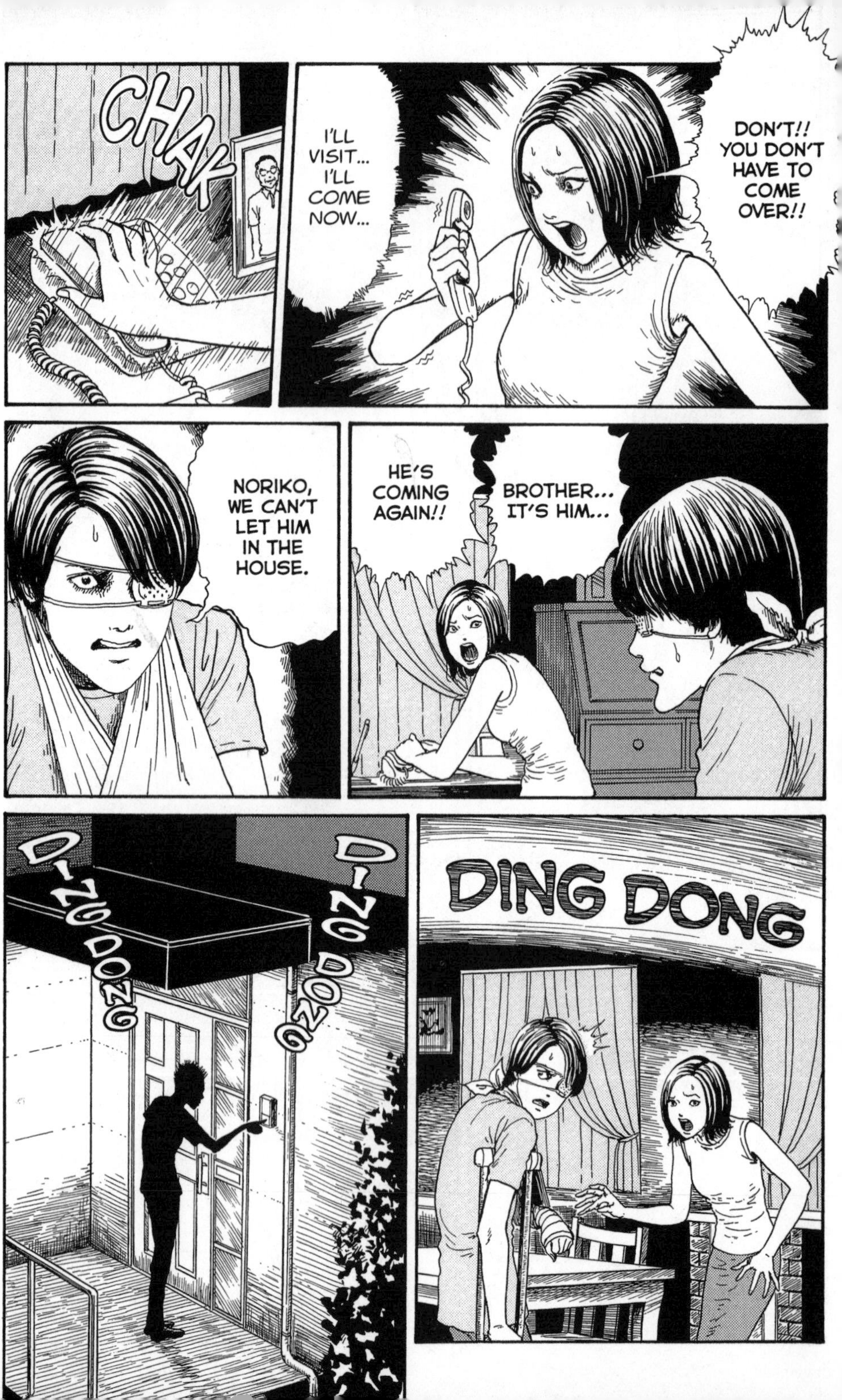
DON'T!! YOU DON'T HAVE TO COME OVER!!
I'LL VISIT... I'LL COME NOW...
CHAK
BROTHER... IT'S HIM...
HE'S COMING AGAIN!!
NORIKO, WE CAN'T LET HIM IN THE HOUSE.
DING DONG
DING DONG
DING DONG

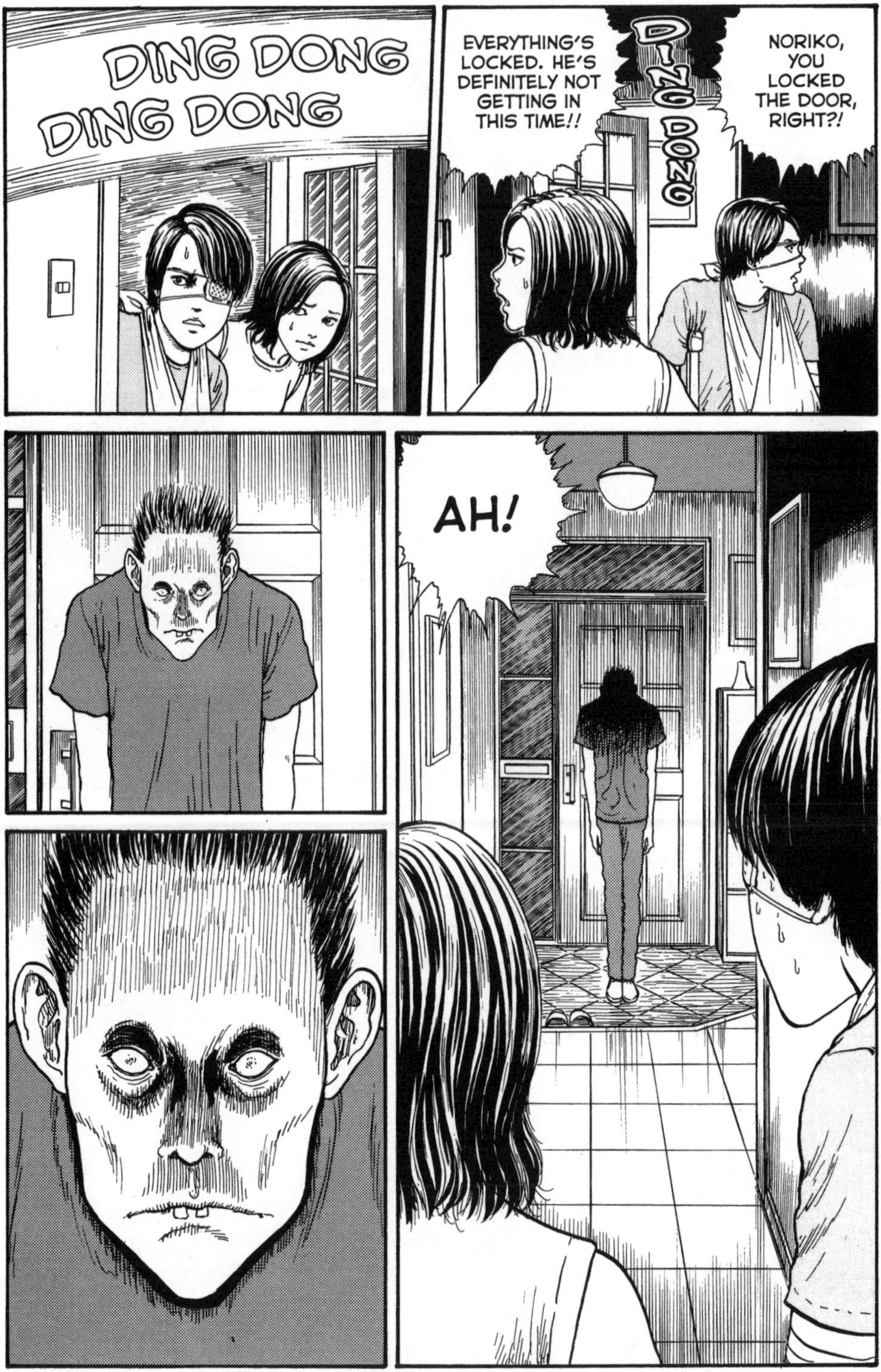
NORIKO, YOU LOCKED THE DOOR, RIGHT?!
DING DONG
EVERYTHING'S LOCKED. HE'S DEFINITELY NOT GETTING IN THIS TIME!!
DING DONG
DING DONG
AH!

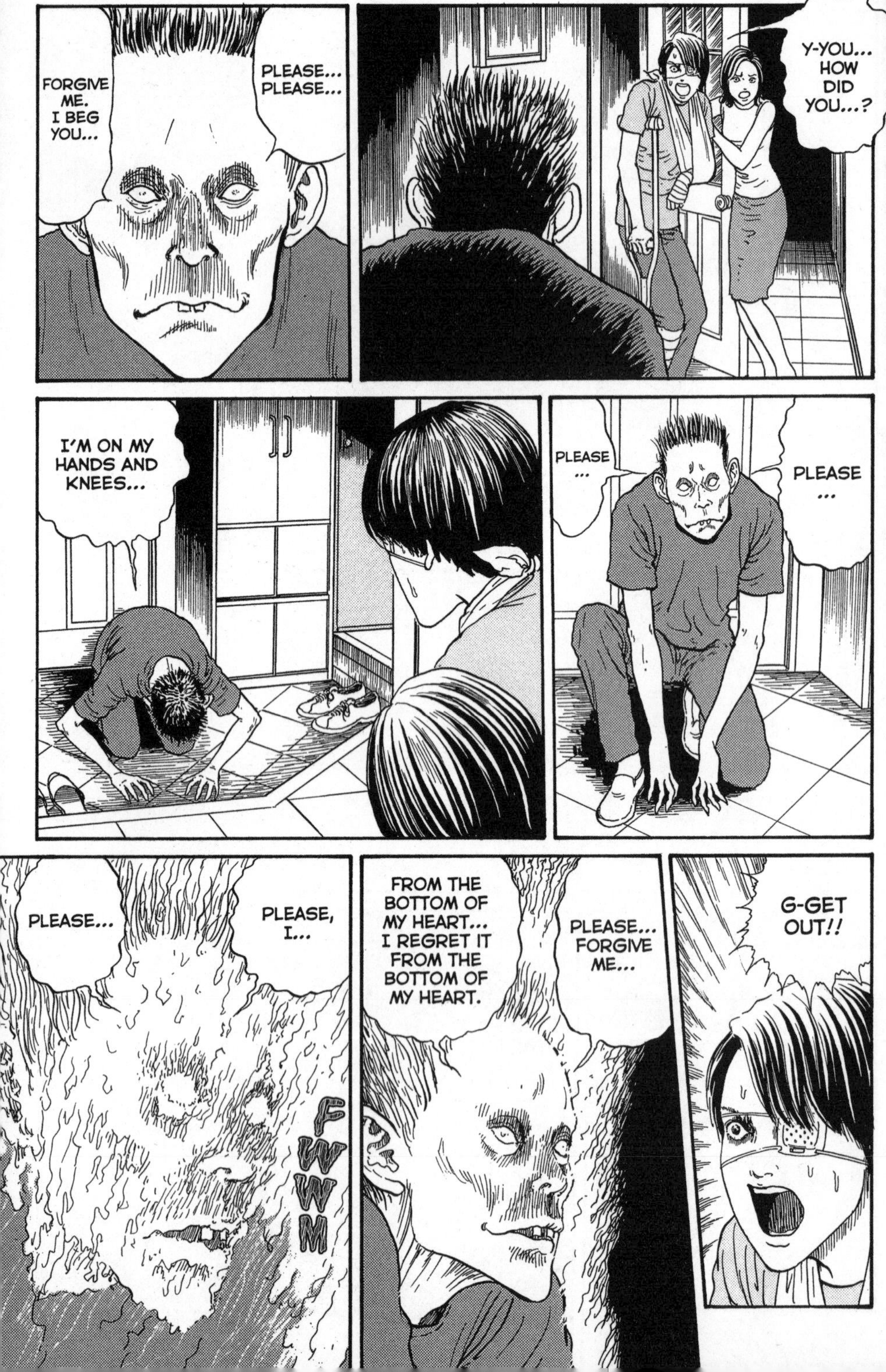
Y-YOU... HOW DID YOU...?
PLEASE... PLEASE...
FORGIVE ME. I BEG YOU...
PLEASE ...
PLEASE ...
I'M ON MY HANDS AND KNEES...
G-GET OUT!!
PLEASE... FORGIVE ME...
FROM THE BOTTOM OF MY HEART... I REGRET IT FROM THE BOTTOM OF MY HEART.
PLEASE, I...
PLEASE...
FWWM

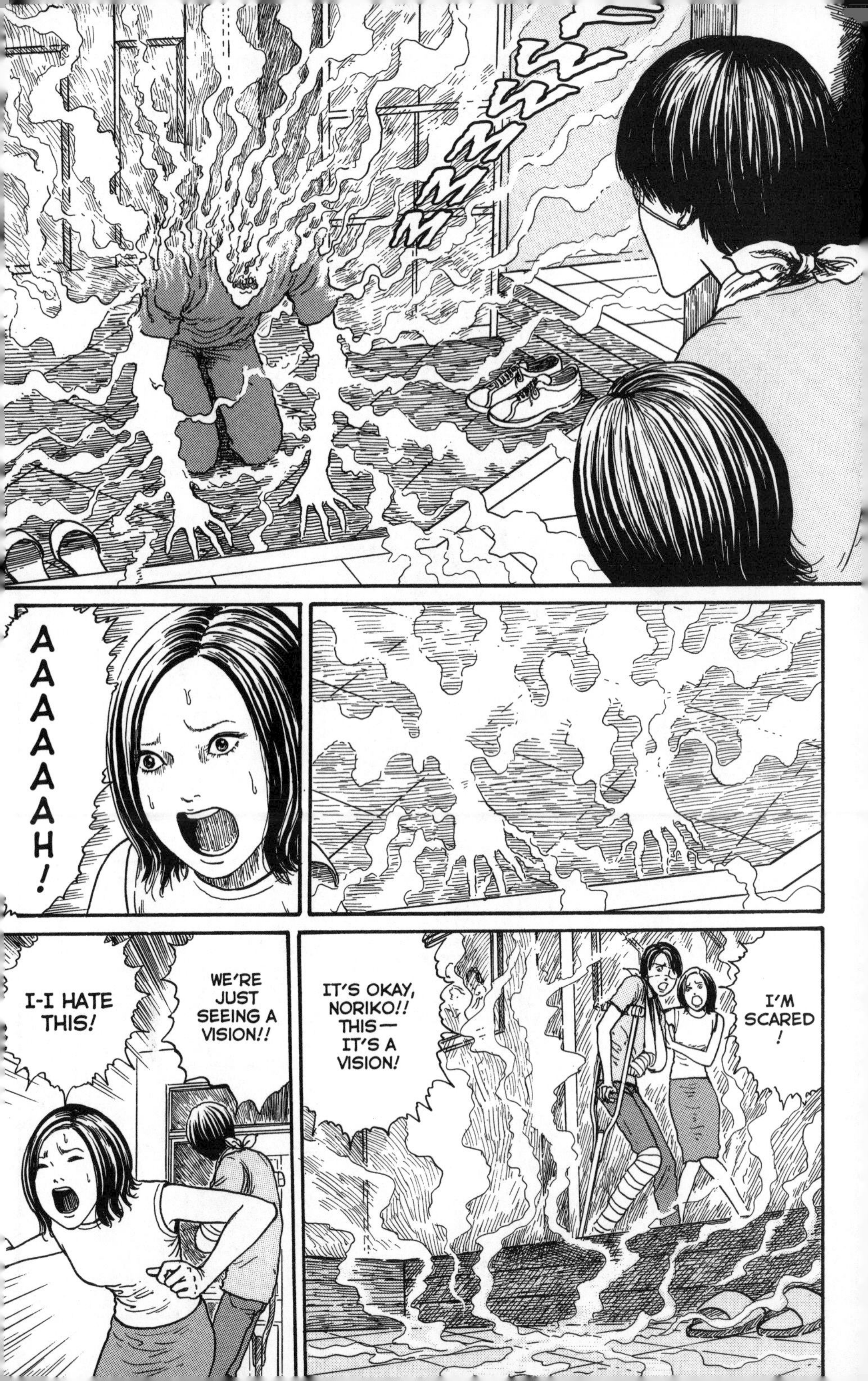
WWMMM
AAAAAAH!
I'M SCARED!
IT'S OKAY, NORIKO!! THIS— IT'S A VISION!
WE'RE JUST SEEING A VISION!!
I-I HATE THIS!

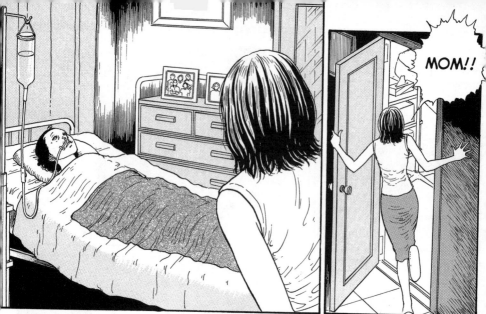

MOM!!

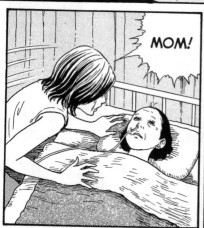

MOM!

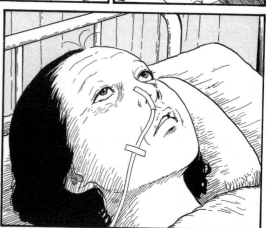

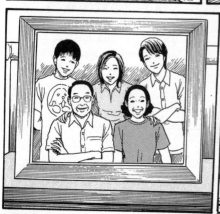

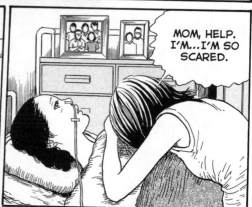

MOM, HELP. I'M...I'M SO SCARED.

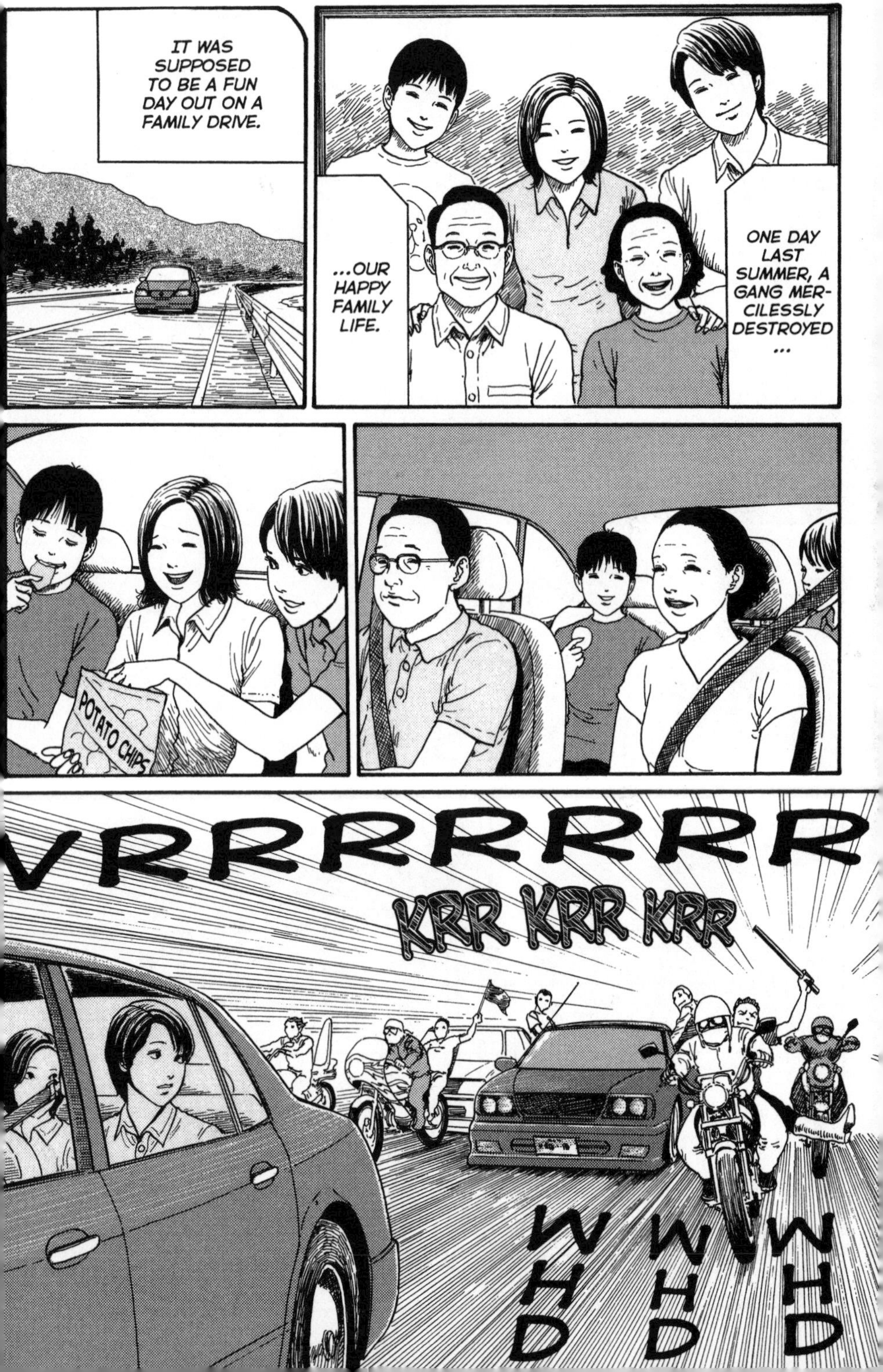
ONE DAY LAST SUMMER, A GANG MERCILESSLY DESTROYED ...
...OUR HAPPY FAMILY LIFE.
IT WAS SUPPOSED TO BE A FUN DAY OUT ON A FAMILY DRIVE.
POTATO CHIPS
VRRRRRRR
KRR KRR KRR
WHD
WHD
WHD

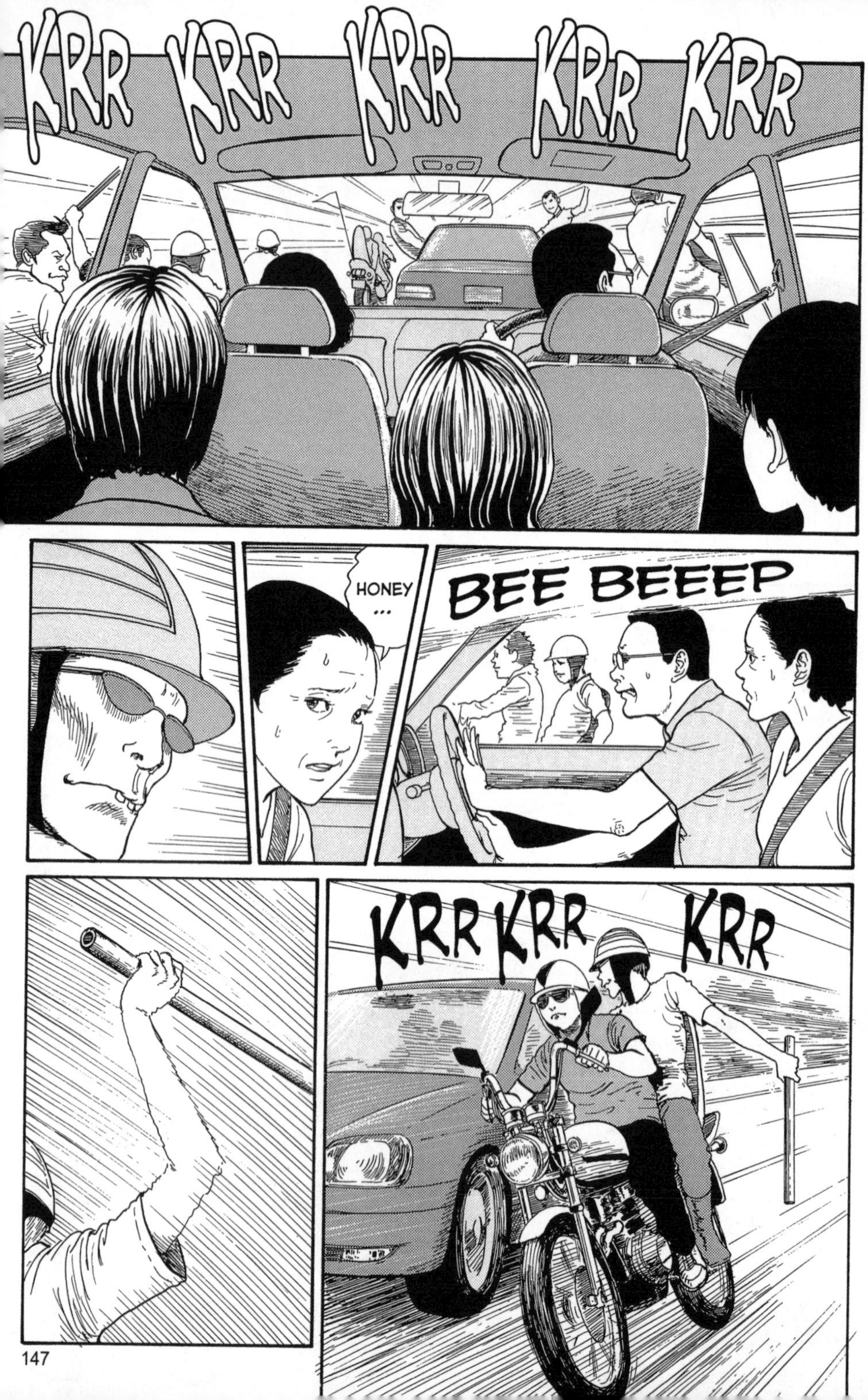
KRR KRR KRR KRR KRR
BEE BEEEP
HONEY ...
KRR KRR KRR

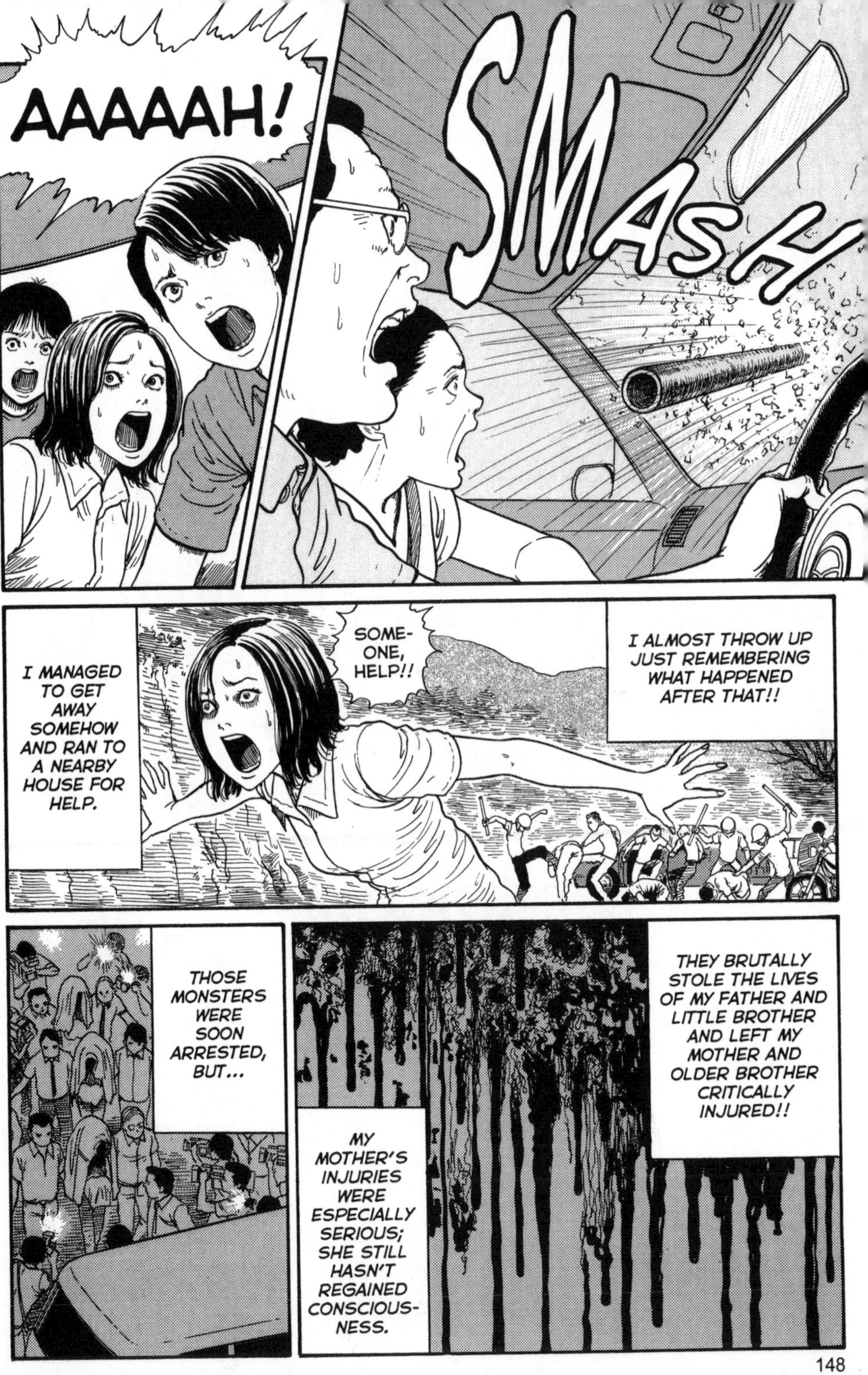
SMASH
AAAAAH!
I ALMOST THROW UP JUST REMEMBERING WHAT HAPPENED AFTER THAT!!
SOME-ONE, HELP!!
I MANAGED TO GET AWAY SOMEHOW AND RAN TO A NEARBY HOUSE FOR HELP.
THEY BRUTALLY STOLE THE LIVES OF MY FATHER AND LITTLE BROTHER AND LEFT MY MOTHER AND OLDER BROTHER CRITICALLY INJURED!!
MY MOTHER'S INJURIES WERE ESPECIALLY SERIOUS; SHE STILL HASN'T REGAINED CONSCIOUS-NESS.
THOSE MONSTERS WERE SOON ARRESTED, BUT...

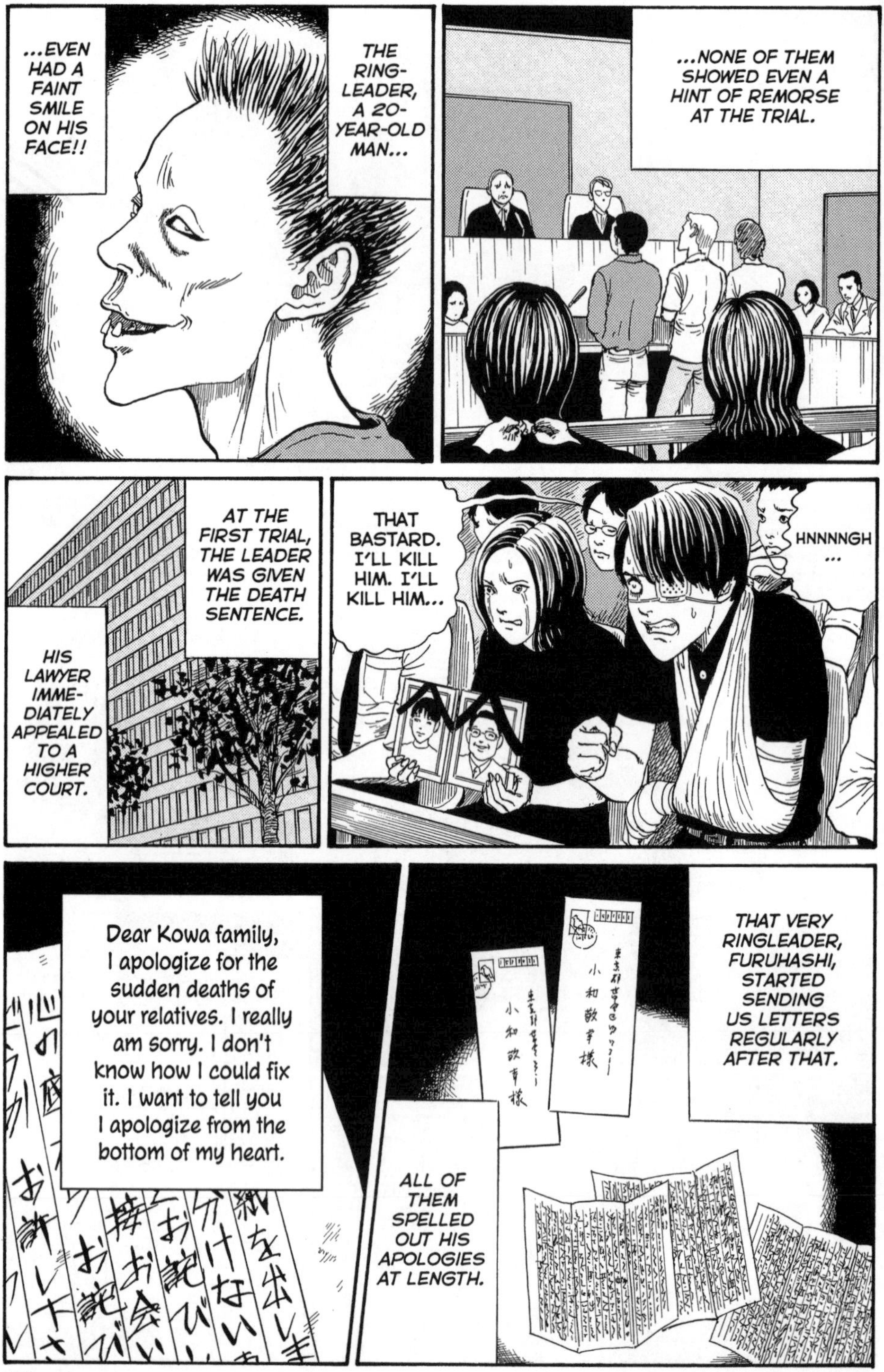
...NONE OF THEM SHOWED EVEN A HINT OF REMORSE AT THE TRIAL.
THE RING-LEADER, A 20-YEAR-OLD MAN...
...EVEN HAD A FAINT SMILE ON HIS FACE!!
HNNNNGH ...
THAT BASTARD. I'LL KILL HIM. I'LL KILL HIM...
AT THE FIRST TRIAL, THE LEADER WAS GIVEN THE DEATH SENTENCE.
HIS LAWYER IMMEDIATELY APPEALED TO A HIGHER COURT.
THAT VERY RINGLEADER, FURUHASHI, STARTED SENDING US LETTERS REGULARLY AFTER THAT.
ALL OF THEM SPELLED OUT HIS APOLOGIES AT LENGTH.
Dear Kowa family, I apologize for the sudden deaths of your relatives. I really am sorry. I don't know how I could fix it. I want to tell you I apologize from the bottom of my heart.

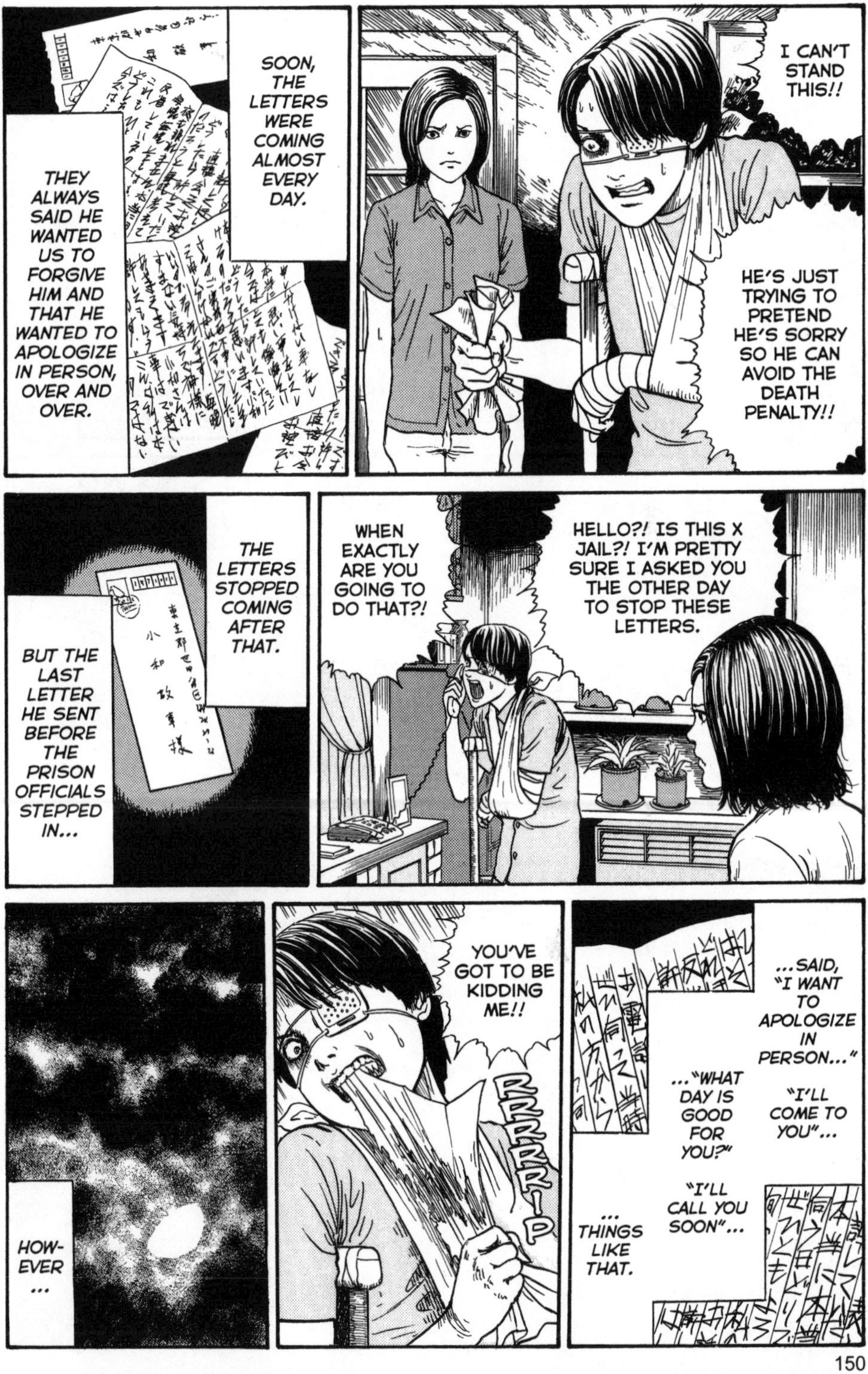
I CAN'T STAND THIS!!
HE'S JUST TRYING TO PRETEND HE'S SORRY SO HE CAN AVOID THE DEATH PENALTY!!
SOON, THE LETTERS WERE COMING ALMOST EVERY DAY.
THEY ALWAYS SAID HE WANTED US TO FORGIVE HIM AND THAT HE WANTED TO APOLOGIZE IN PERSON, OVER AND OVER.
HELLO?! IS THIS X JAIL?! I'M PRETTY SURE I ASKED YOU THE OTHER DAY TO STOP THESE LETTERS.
WHEN EXACTLY ARE YOU GOING TO DO THAT?!
THE LETTERS STOPPED COMING AFTER THAT.
BUT THE LAST LETTER HE SENT BEFORE THE PRISON OFFICIALS STEPPED IN...
...SAID, "I WANT TO APOLOGIZE IN PERSON..."
"I'LL COME TO YOU"...
..."WHAT DAY IS GOOD FOR YOU?"
"I'LL CALL YOU SOON"...
...THINGS LIKE THAT.
YOU'VE GOT TO BE KIDDING ME!!
RRRRRRIP
HOW-EVER...

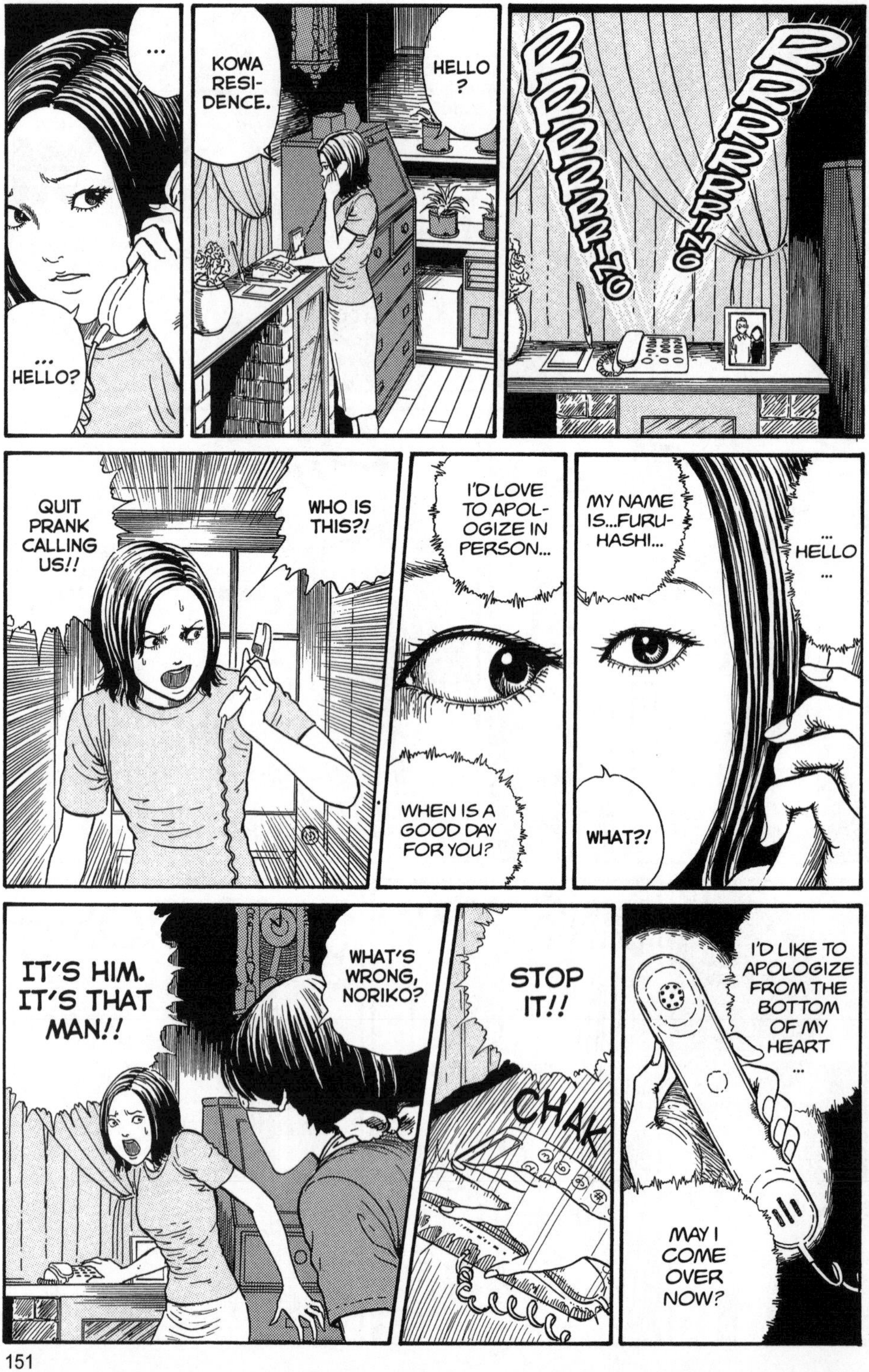
RRRRRRRING
RRRRRRRING
HELLO?
KOWA RESIDENCE.
...
...HELLO?
...HELLO...
MY NAME IS...FURUHASHI...
WHAT?!
I'D LOVE TO APOLOGIZE IN PERSON...
WHEN IS A GOOD DAY FOR YOU?
WHO IS THIS?!
QUIT PRANK CALLING US!!
I'D LIKE TO APOLOGIZE FROM THE BOTTOM OF MY HEART...
MAY I COME OVER NOW?
STOP IT!!
CHAK
WHAT'S WRONG, NORIKO?
IT'S HIM. IT'S THAT MAN!!

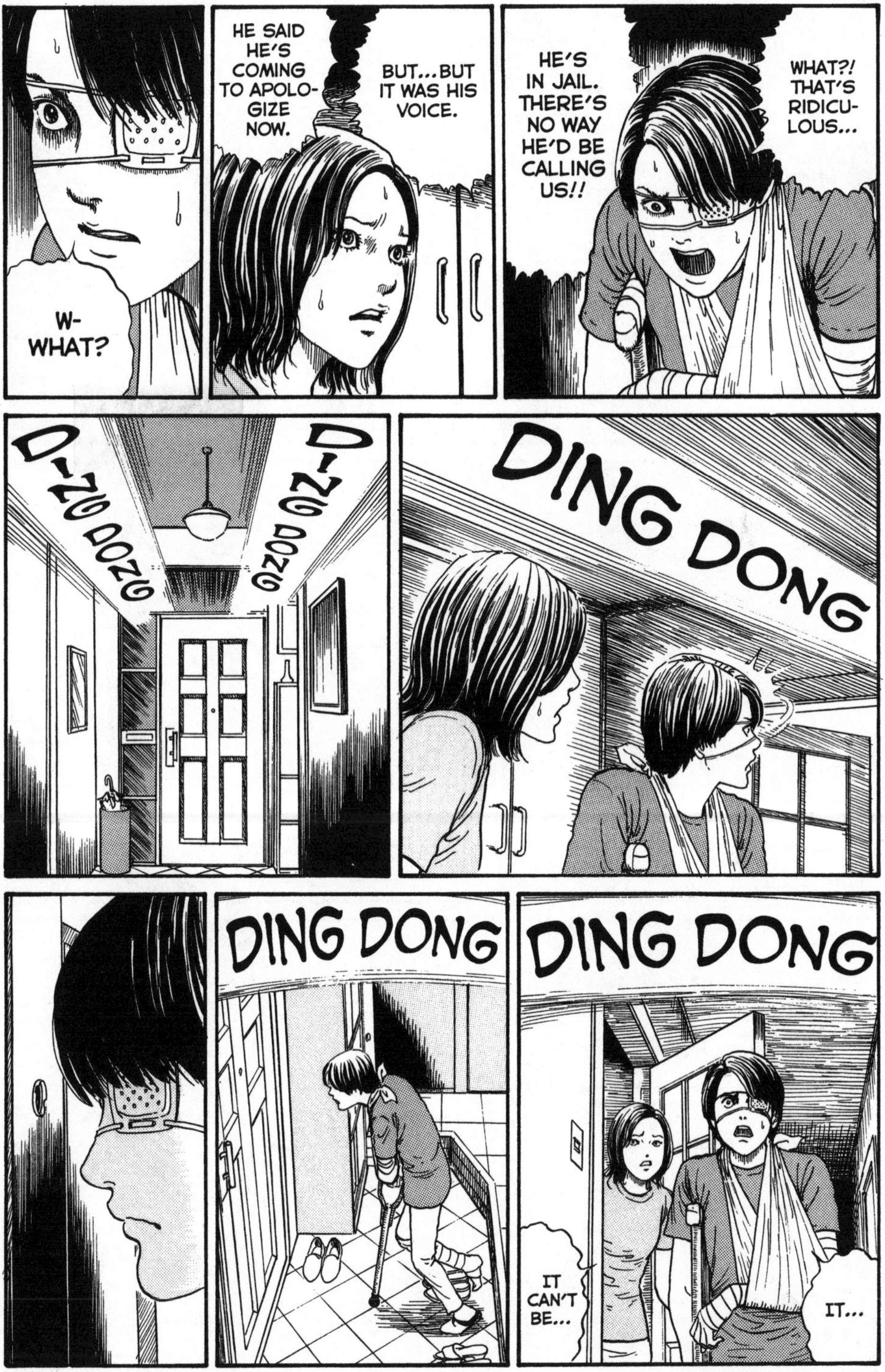
WHAT?! THAT'S RIDICU-LOUS...
HE'S IN JAIL. THERE'S NO WAY HE'D BE CALLING US!!
BUT...BUT IT WAS HIS VOICE.
HE SAID HE'S COMING TO APOLO-GIZE NOW.
W-WHAT?
DING DONG
DING DONG
DING DONG
DING DONG
IT...
IT CAN'T BE...
DING DONG

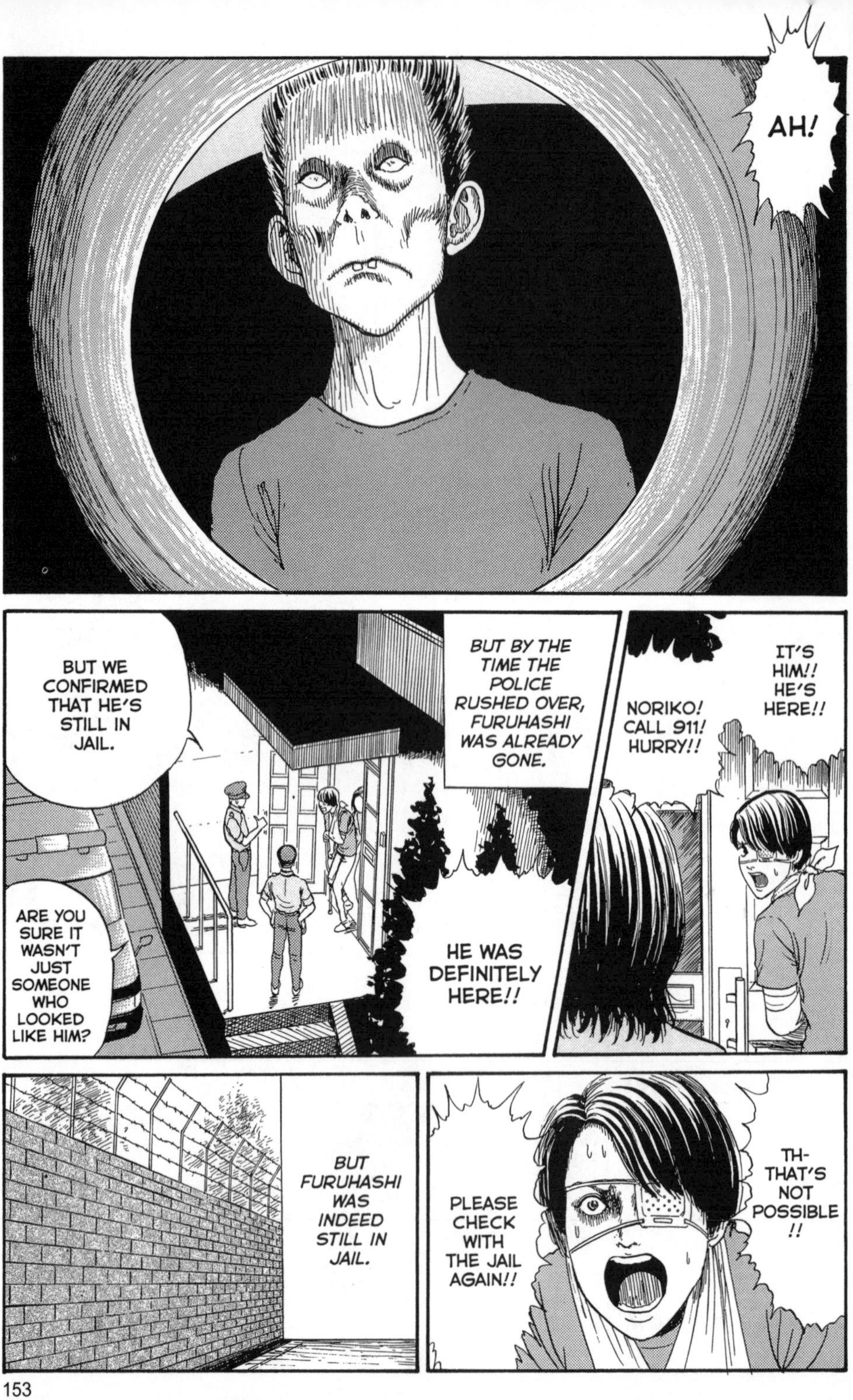
AH!
IT'S HIM!! HE'S HERE!!
NORIKO! CALL 911! HURRY!!
BUT BY THE TIME THE POLICE RUSHED OVER, FURUHASHI WAS ALREADY GONE.
BUT WE CONFIRMED THAT HE'S STILL IN JAIL.
ARE YOU SURE IT WASN'T JUST SOMEONE WHO LOOKED LIKE HIM?
HE WAS DEFINITELY HERE!!
TH- THAT'S NOT POSSIBLE!!
PLEASE CHECK WITH THE JAIL AGAIN!!
BUT FURUHASHI WAS INDEED STILL IN JAIL.

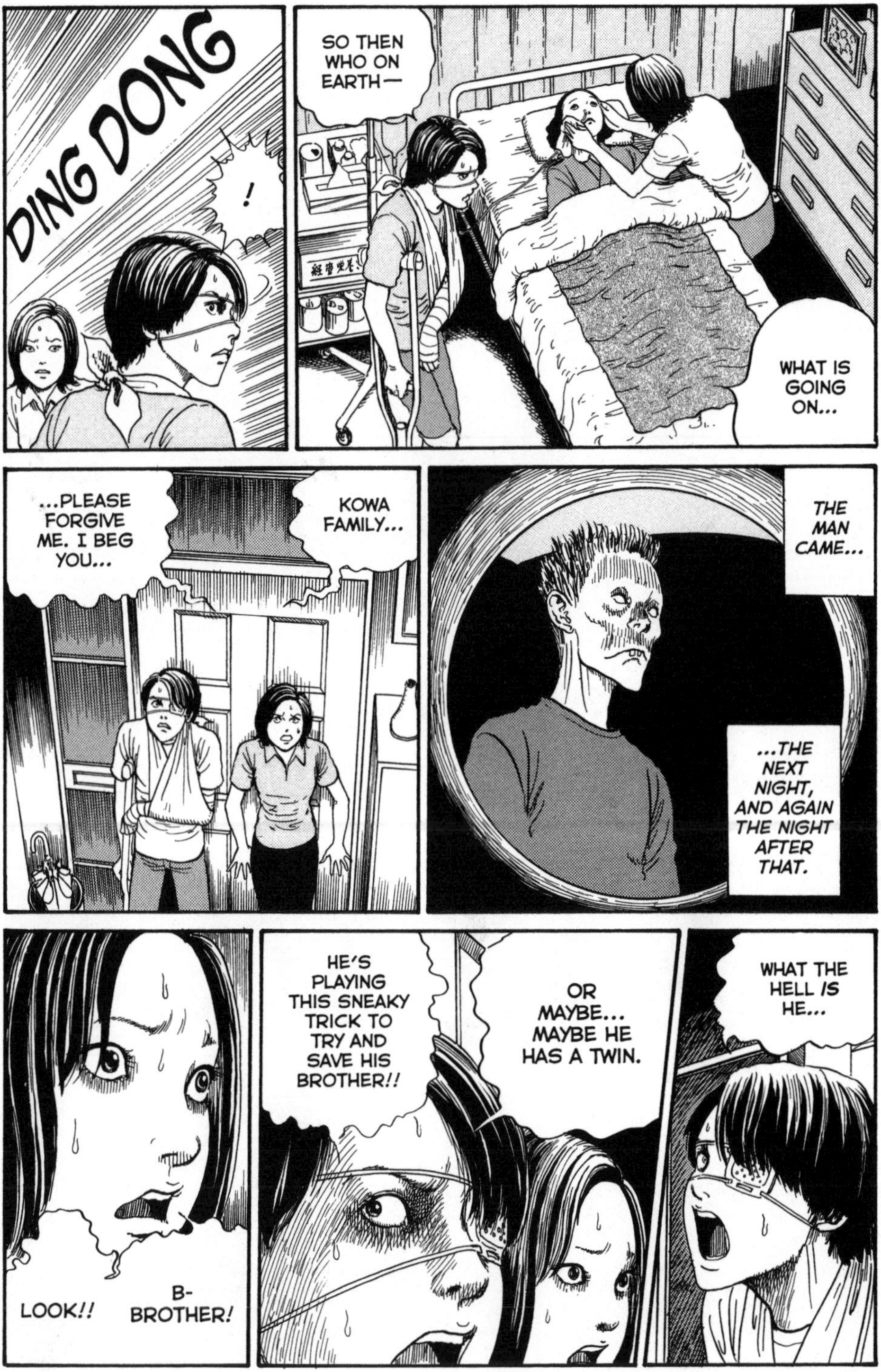
WHAT IS GOING ON...
SO THEN WHO ON EARTH—
DING DONG
!
THE MAN CAME...
...THE NEXT NIGHT, AND AGAIN THE NIGHT AFTER THAT.
KOWA FAMILY...
...PLEASE FORGIVE ME. I BEG YOU...
WHAT THE HELL *IS* HE...
OR MAYBE... MAYBE HE HAS A TWIN.
HE'S PLAYING THIS SNEAKY TRICK TO TRY AND SAVE HIS BROTHER!!
B-BROTHER!
LOOK!!

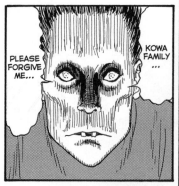

PLEASE FORGIVE ME...

KOWA FAMILY...

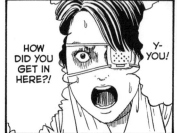

HOW DID YOU GET IN HERE?!

Y-YOU!

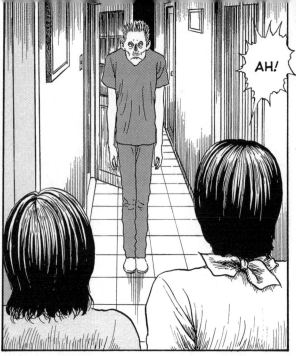

AH!

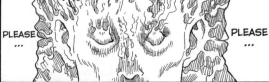

HE'S GONE...

PLEASE...

PLEASE...

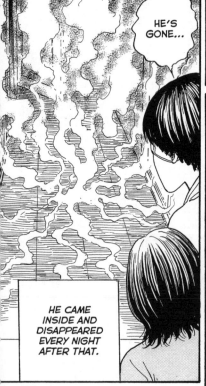

HE CAME INSIDE AND DISAPPEARED EVERY NIGHT AFTER THAT.

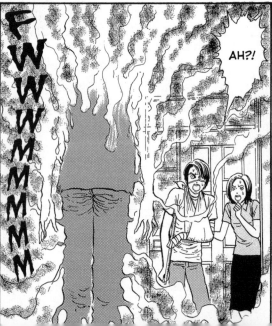

FWWWMMMMM

AH?!

155

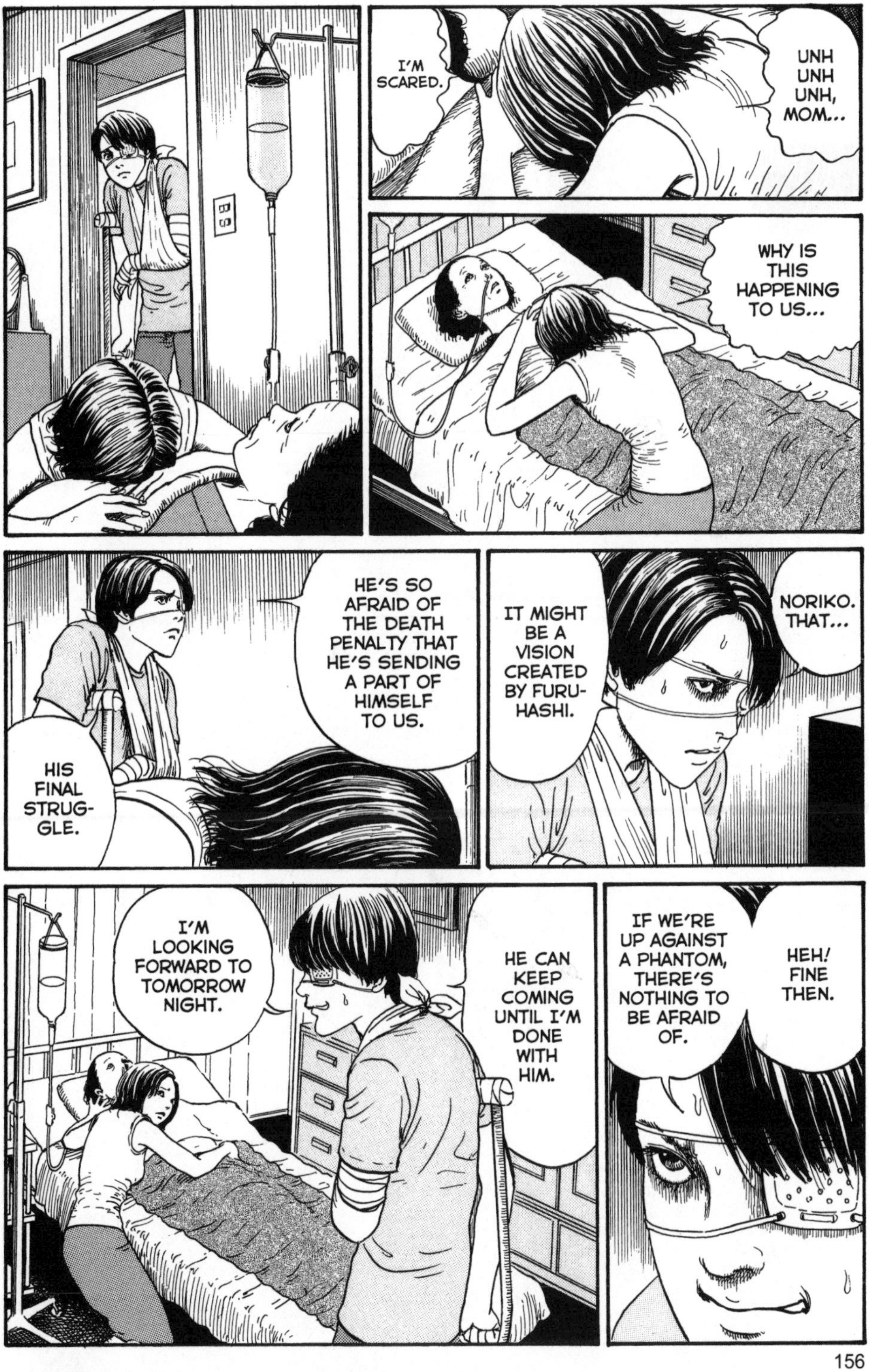
UNH UNH UNH, MOM...
I'M SCARED.
WHY IS THIS HAPPENING TO US...
NORIKO. THAT...
IT MIGHT BE A VISION CREATED BY FURU-HASHI.
HE'S SO AFRAID OF THE DEATH PENALTY THAT HE'S SENDING A PART OF HIMSELF TO US.
HIS FINAL STRUG-GLE.
HEH! FINE THEN.
IF WE'RE UP AGAINST A PHANTOM, THERE'S NOTHING TO BE AFRAID OF.
HE CAN KEEP COMING UNTIL I'M DONE WITH HIM.
I'M LOOKING FORWARD TO TOMORROW NIGHT.

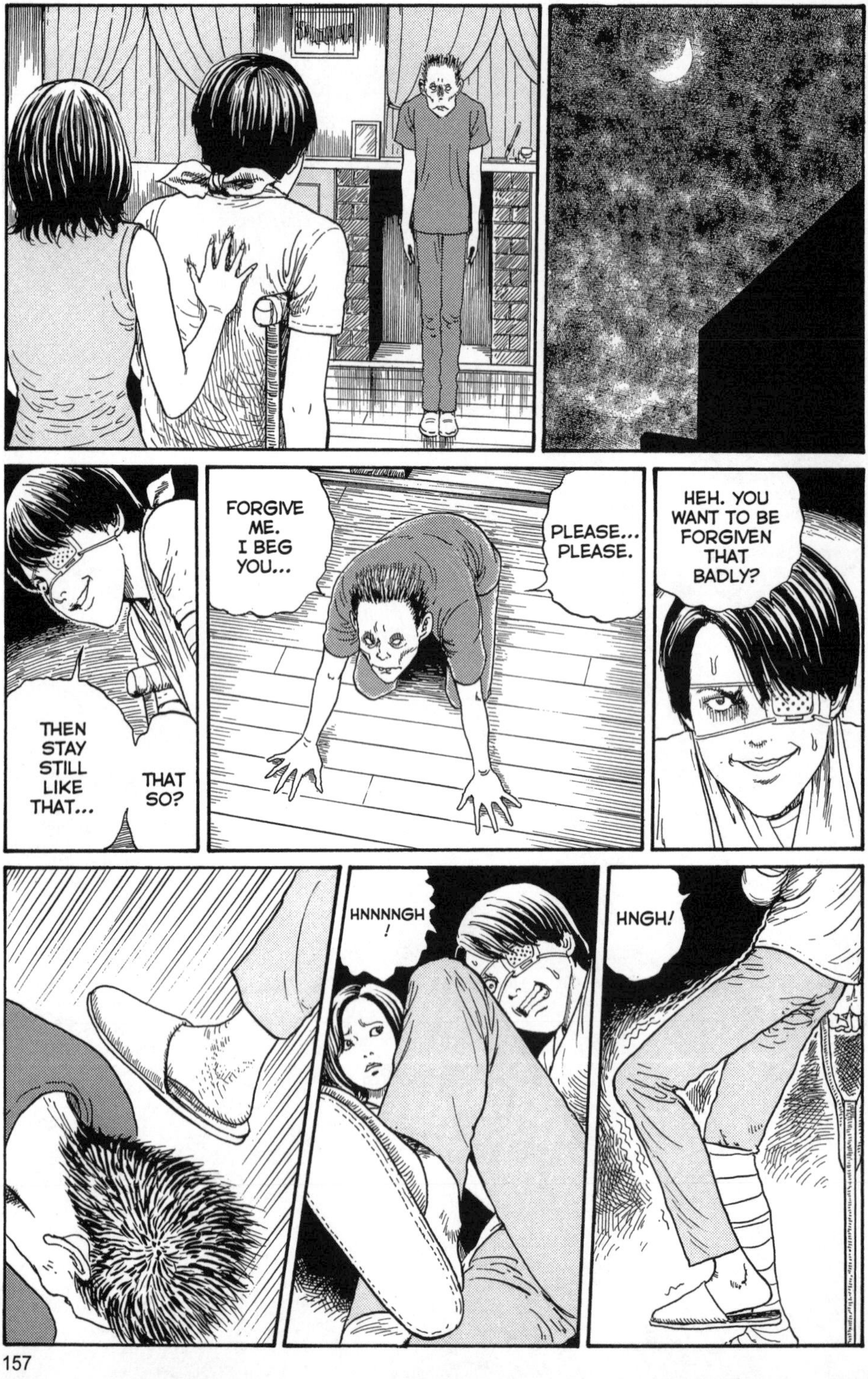
HEH. YOU WANT TO BE FORGIVEN THAT BADLY?
PLEASE... PLEASE.
FORGIVE ME. I BEG YOU...
THAT SO?
THEN STAY STILL LIKE THAT...
HNGH!
HNNNNGH!

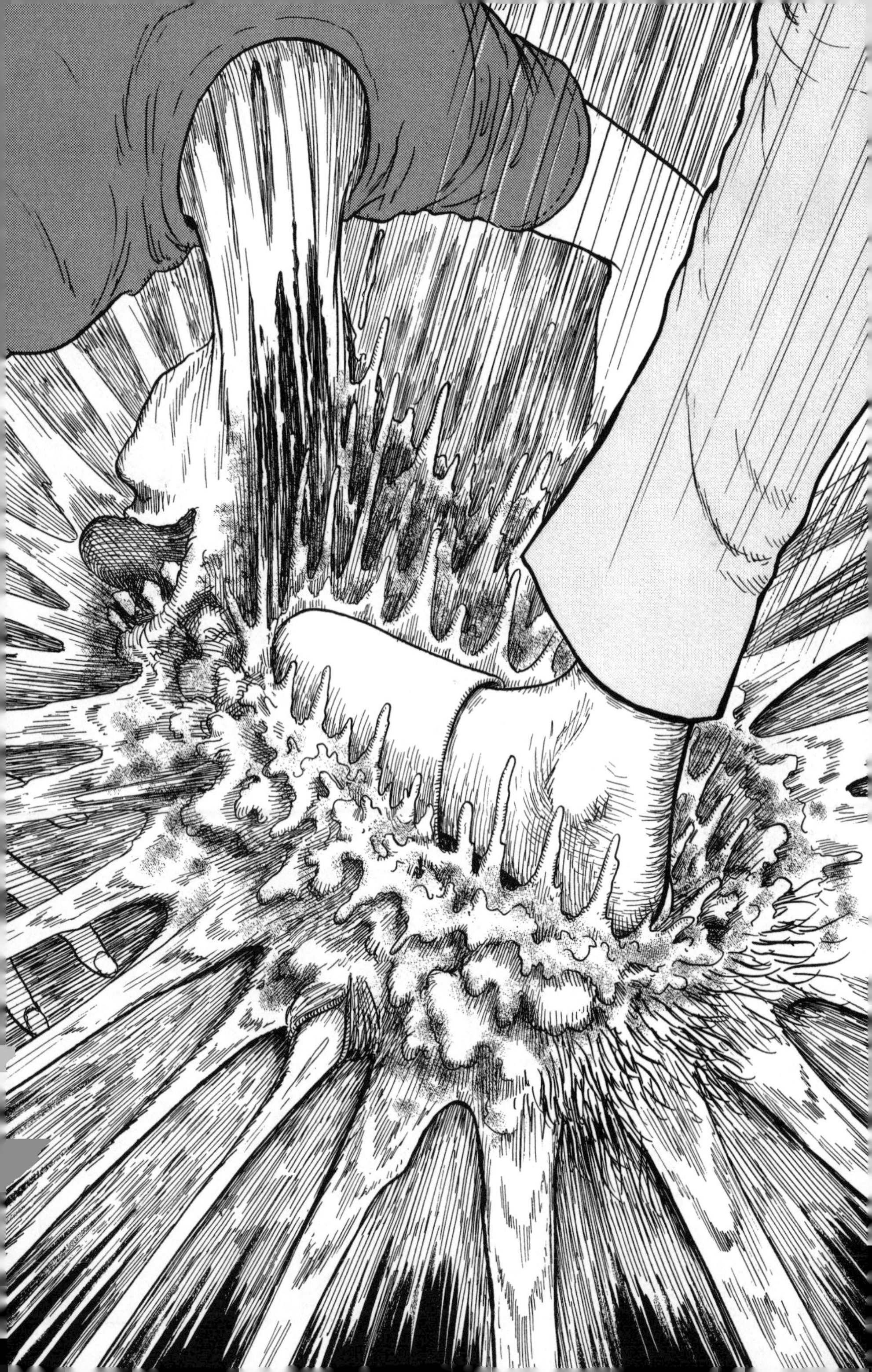

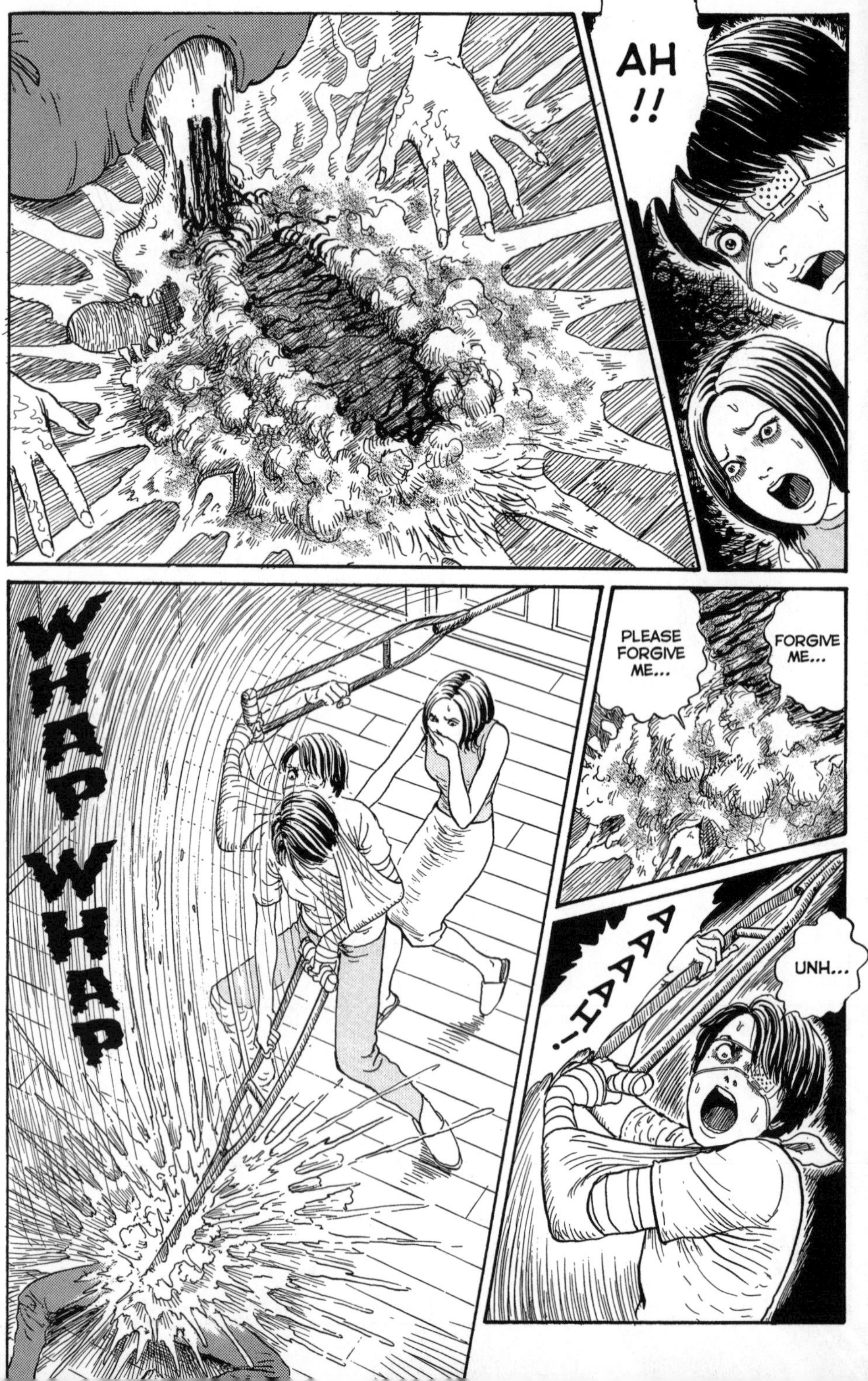
AH!!
FORGIVE ME...
PLEASE FORGIVE ME...
UNH...
AAAAH!!
WHAP WHAP WHAP

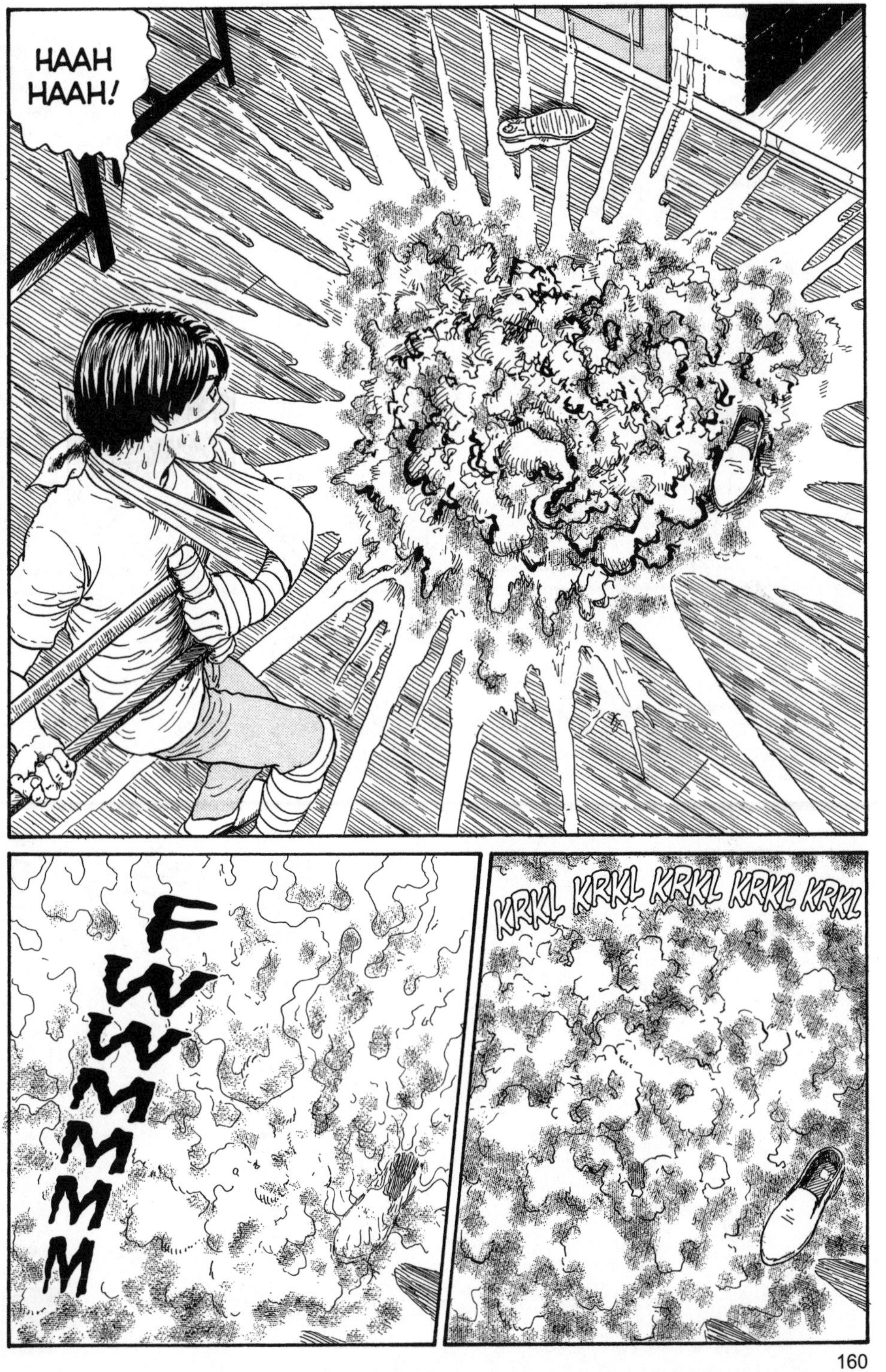
HAAH HAAH!
KRKL KRKL KRKL KRKL KRKL
FWWMMMM

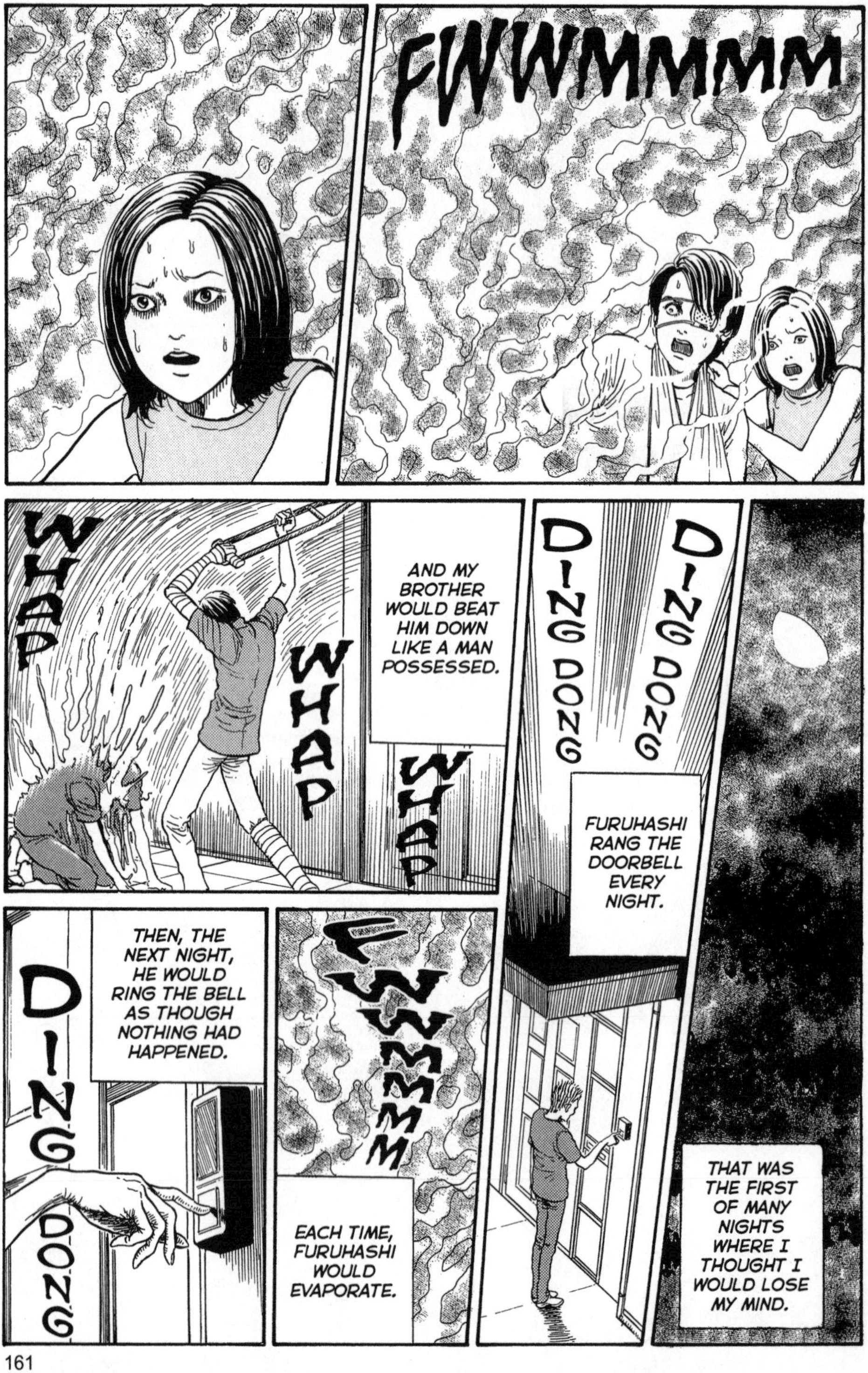
FWWMMMMM
THAT WAS THE FIRST OF MANY NIGHTS WHERE I THOUGHT I WOULD LOSE MY MIND.
DING DONG
DING DONG
FURUHASHI RANG THE DOORBELL EVERY NIGHT.
AND MY BROTHER WOULD BEAT HIM DOWN LIKE A MAN POSSESSED.
WHAP
WHAP
WHAP
FWWMMMM
EACH TIME, FURUHASHI WOULD EVAPORATE.
THEN, THE NEXT NIGHT, HE WOULD RING THE BELL AS THOUGH NOTHING HAD HAPPENED.
DING DONG

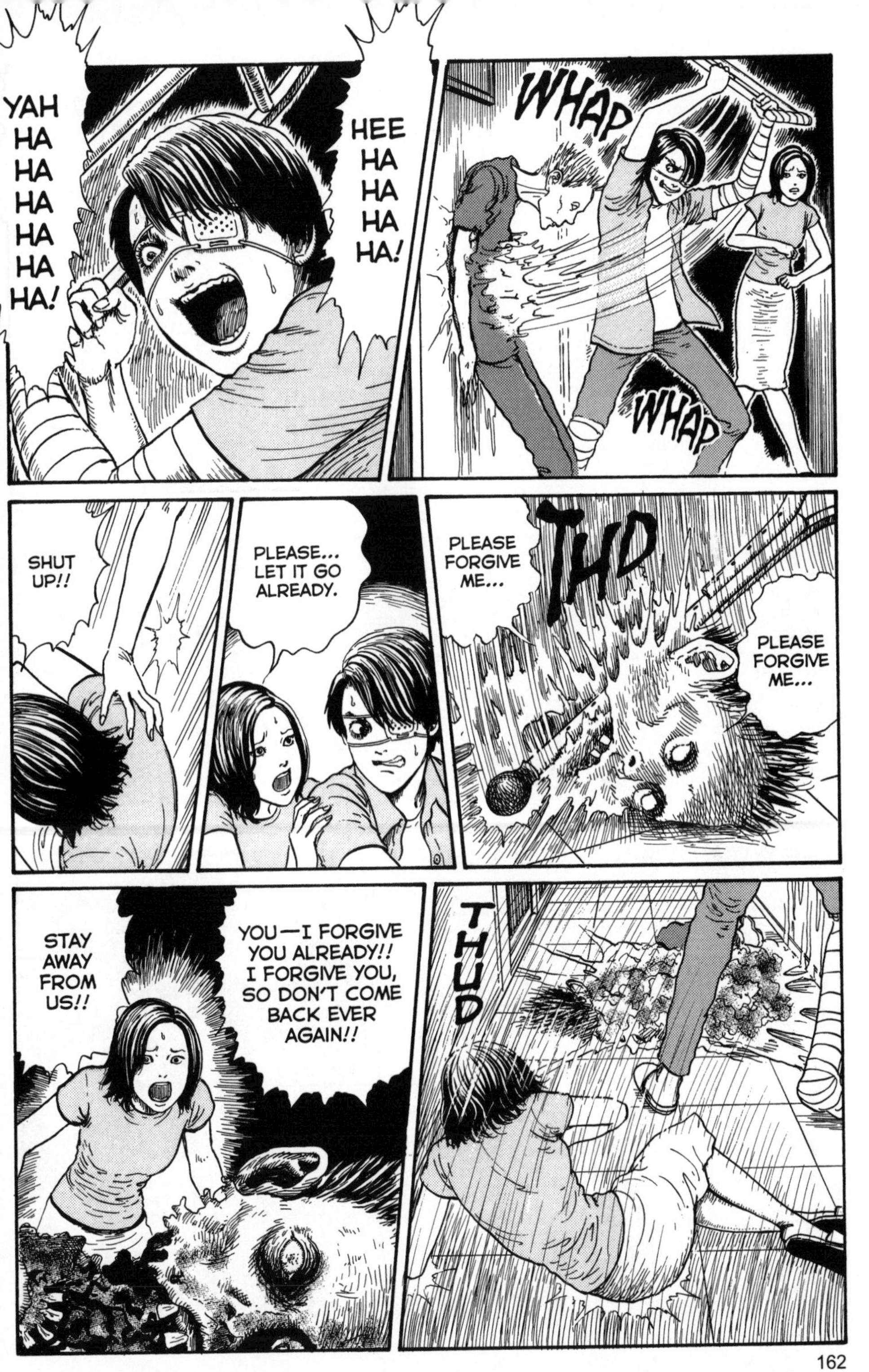
WHAP
WHAP
HEE HA HA HA HA!
YAH HA HA HA HA HA HA!
THD
PLEASE FORGIVE ME...
PLEASE FORGIVE ME...
PLEASE... LET IT GO ALREADY.
SHUT UP!!
THUD
YOU—I FORGIVE YOU ALREADY!! I FORGIVE YOU, SO DON'T COME BACK EVER AGAIN!!
STAY AWAY FROM US!!

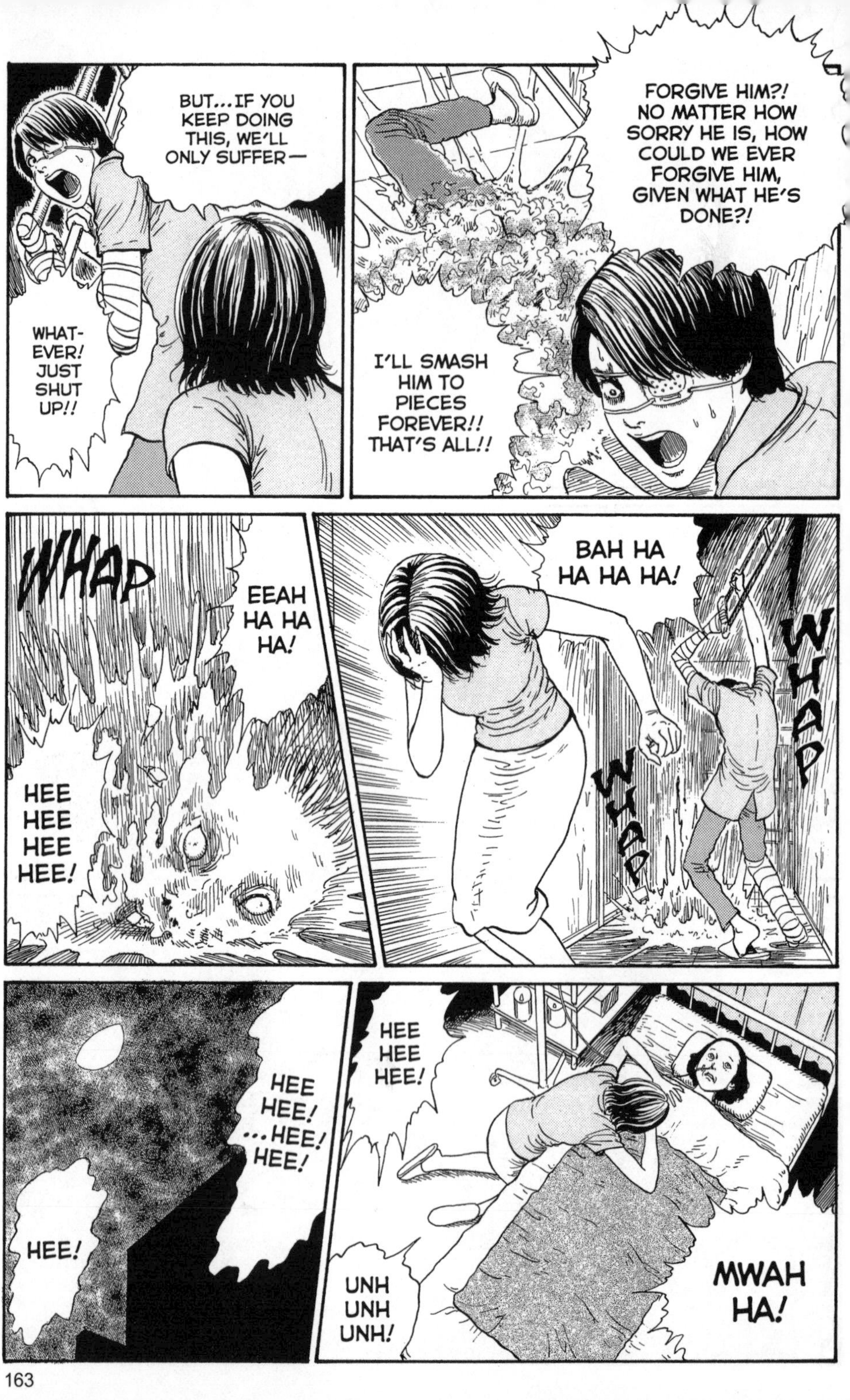
FORGIVE HIM?! NO MATTER HOW SORRY HE IS, HOW COULD WE EVER FORGIVE HIM, GIVEN WHAT HE'S DONE?!
I'LL SMASH HIM TO PIECES FOREVER!! THAT'S ALL!!
BUT...IF YOU KEEP DOING THIS, WE'LL ONLY SUFFER—
WHAT-EVER! JUST SHUT UP!!
BAH HA HA HA HA!
WHAP
WHAP
WHAP
EEAH HA HA HA!
HEE HEE HEE HEE!
HEE HEE HEE!
MWAH HA!
UNH UNH UNH!
HEE HEE! ...HEE! HEE!
HEE!

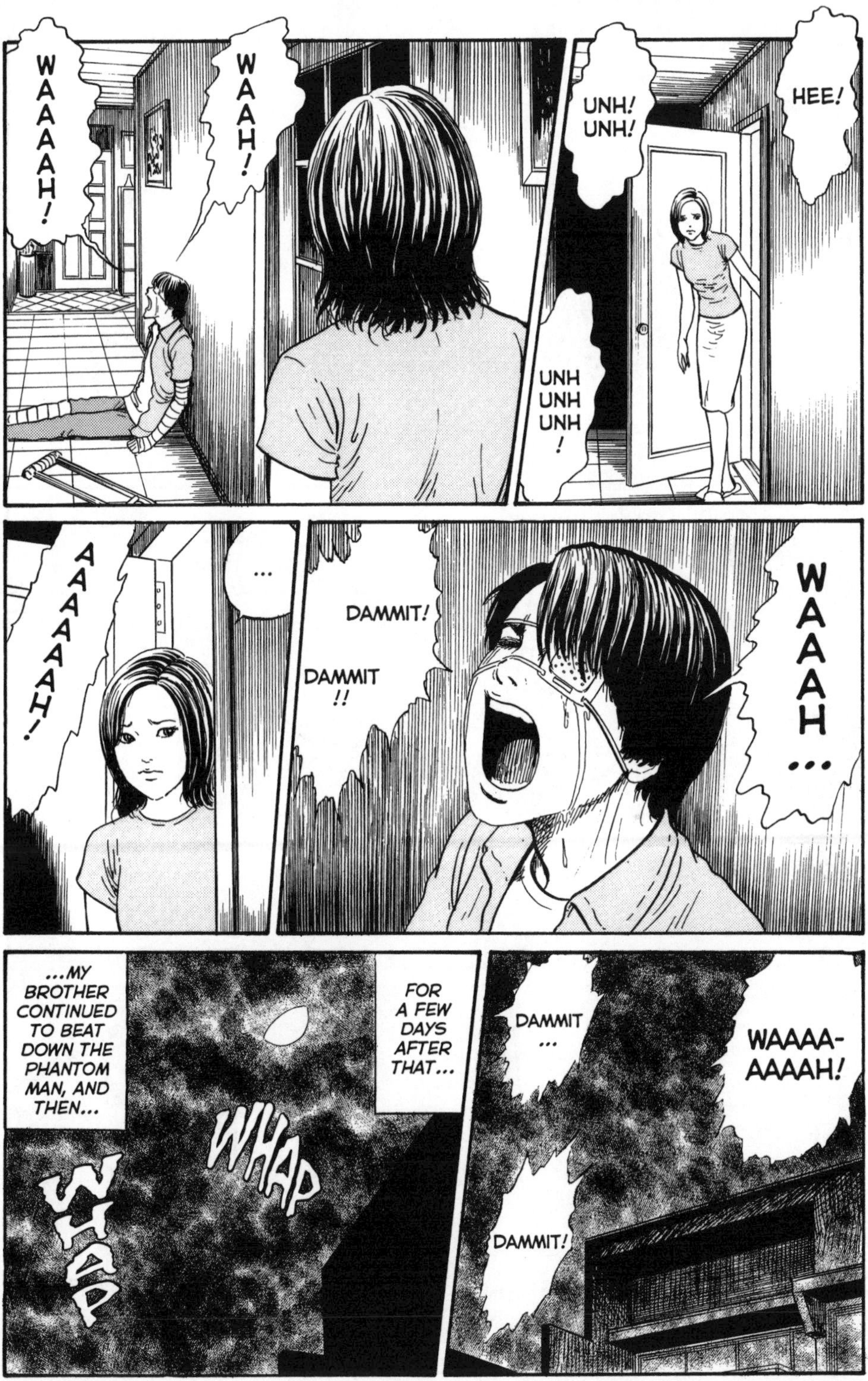
HEE!
UNH! UNH!
UNH UNH UNH!
WAAH!
WAAAAAH!
WAAAH...
DAMMIT!
DAMMIT!!
...
AAAAAAH!
WAAAA-AAAAH!
DAMMIT...
DAMMIT!
FOR A FEW DAYS AFTER THAT...
...MY BROTHER CONTINUED TO BEAT DOWN THE PHANTOM MAN, AND THEN...
WHAP
WHAP

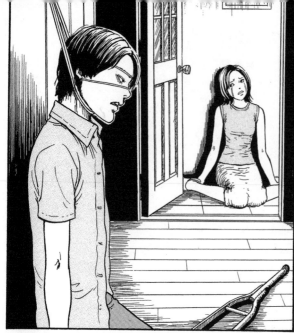

HE KILLED HIMSELF.

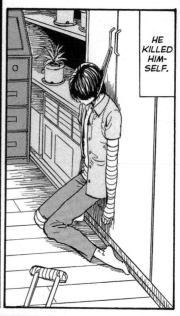

DING DONG

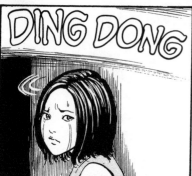

WHY...

WHY... WHY IS THIS HAPPENING TO US?

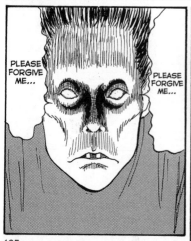

PLEASE FORGIVE ME...

PLEASE FORGIVE ME...

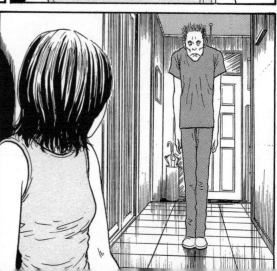

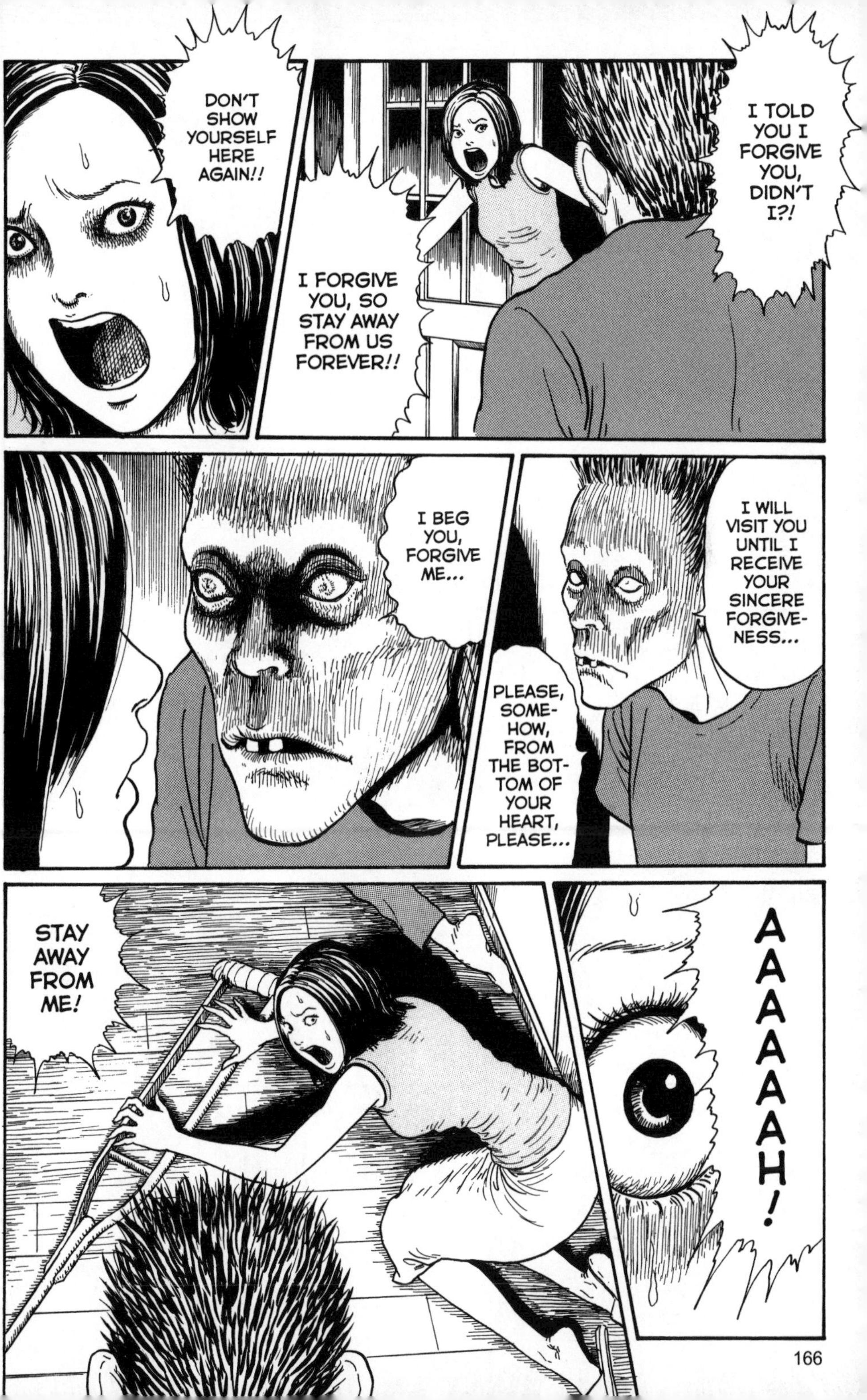
I TOLD YOU I FORGIVE YOU, DIDN'T I?!
I FORGIVE YOU, SO STAY AWAY FROM US FOREVER!!
DON'T SHOW YOURSELF HERE AGAIN!!
I WILL VISIT YOU UNTIL I RECEIVE YOUR SINCERE FORGIVE-NESS...
PLEASE, SOME-HOW, FROM THE BOT-TOM OF YOUR HEART, PLEASE...
I BEG YOU, FORGIVE ME...
AAAAAAH!
STAY AWAY FROM ME!

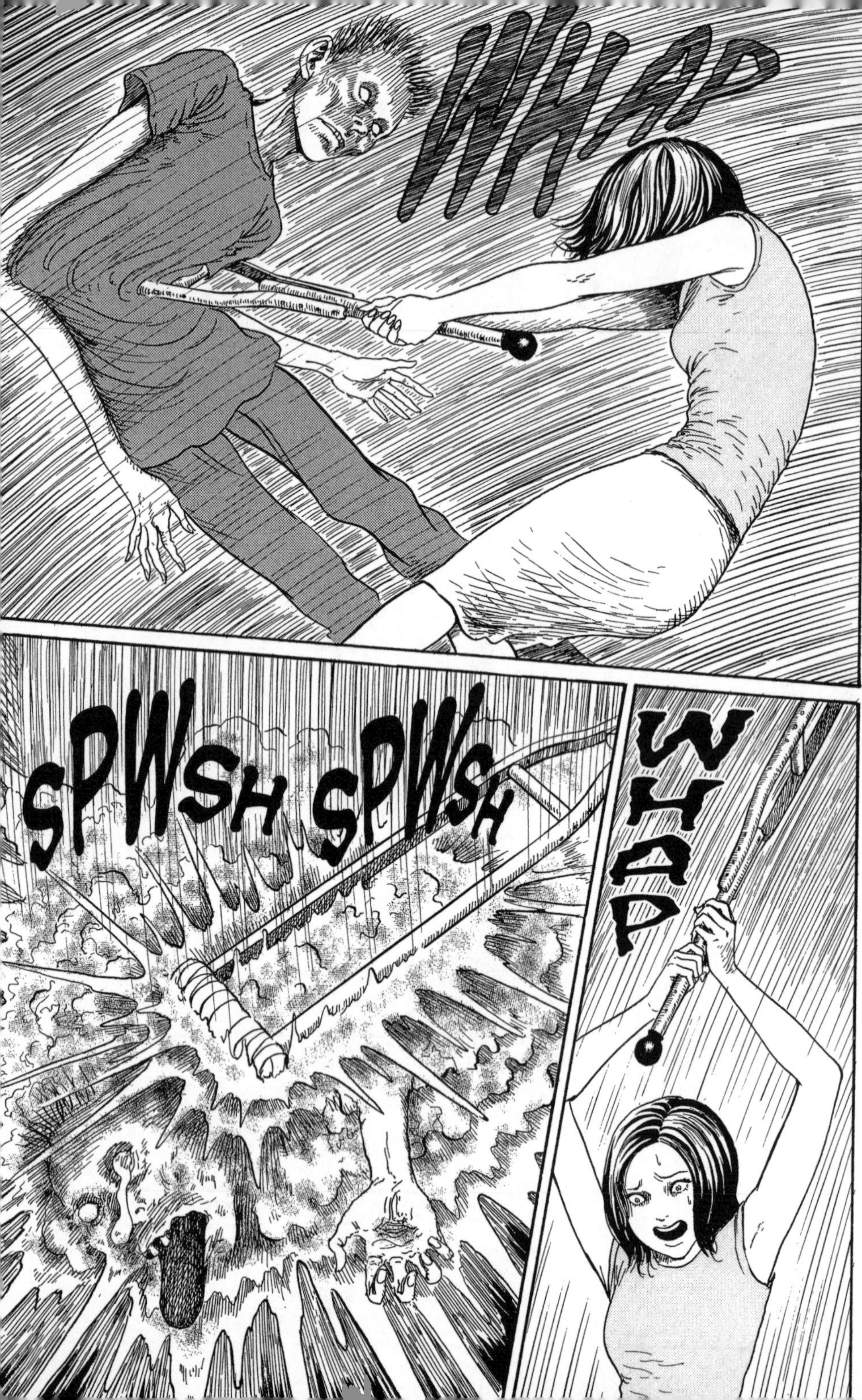
WHAP
WHAP
SPWSH SPWSH

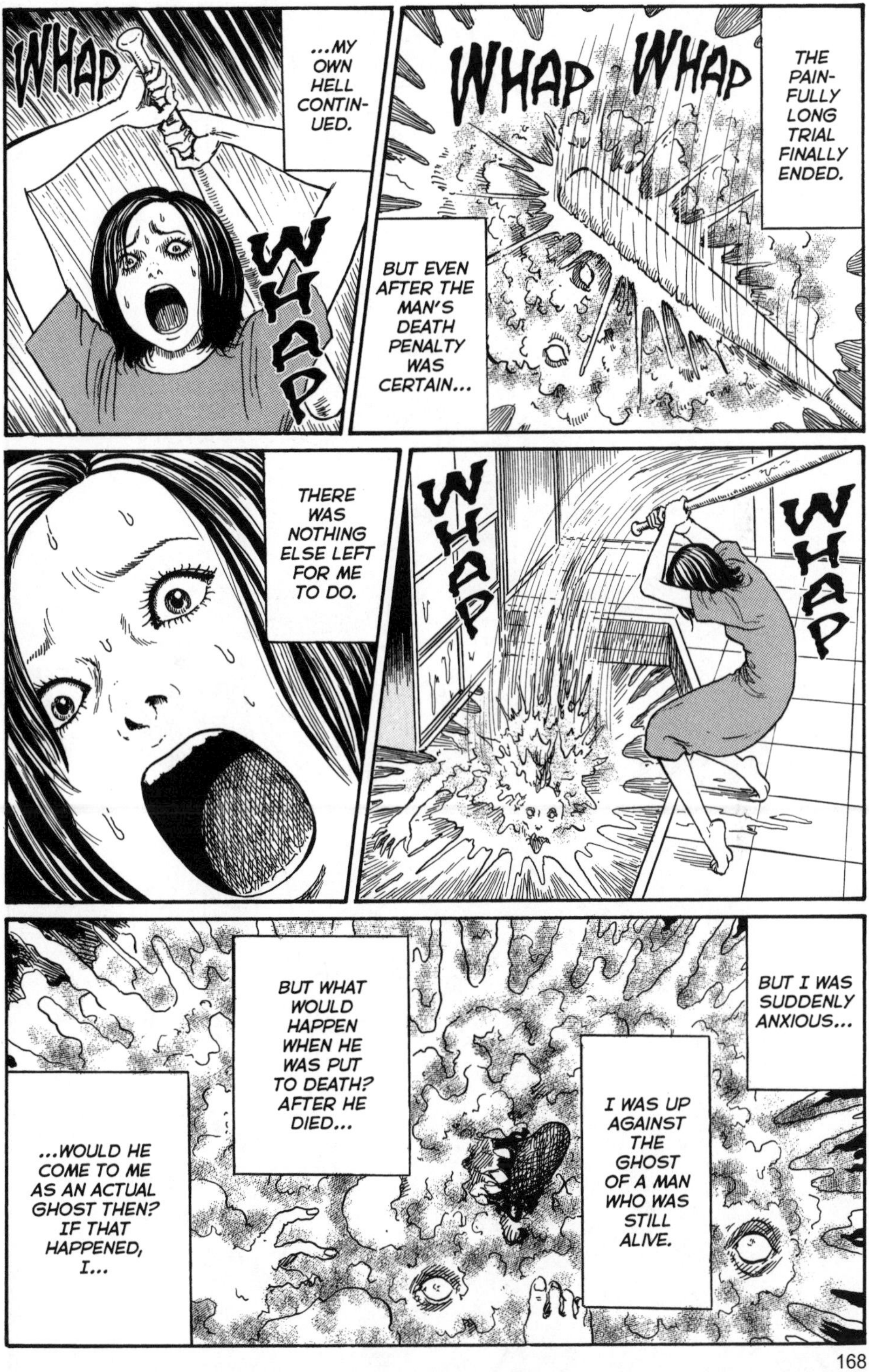

THE PAINFULLY LONG TRIAL FINALLY ENDED.
WHAP WHAP
BUT EVEN AFTER THE MAN'S DEATH PENALTY WAS CERTAIN...
...MY OWN HELL CONTINUED.
WHAP
WHAP
WHAP
WHAP
THERE WAS NOTHING ELSE LEFT FOR ME TO DO.
BUT I WAS SUDDENLY ANXIOUS...
I WAS UP AGAINST THE GHOST OF A MAN WHO WAS STILL ALIVE.
BUT WHAT WOULD HAPPEN WHEN HE WAS PUT TO DEATH? AFTER HE DIED...
...WOULD HE COME TO ME AS AN ACTUAL GHOST THEN? IF THAT HAPPENED, I...

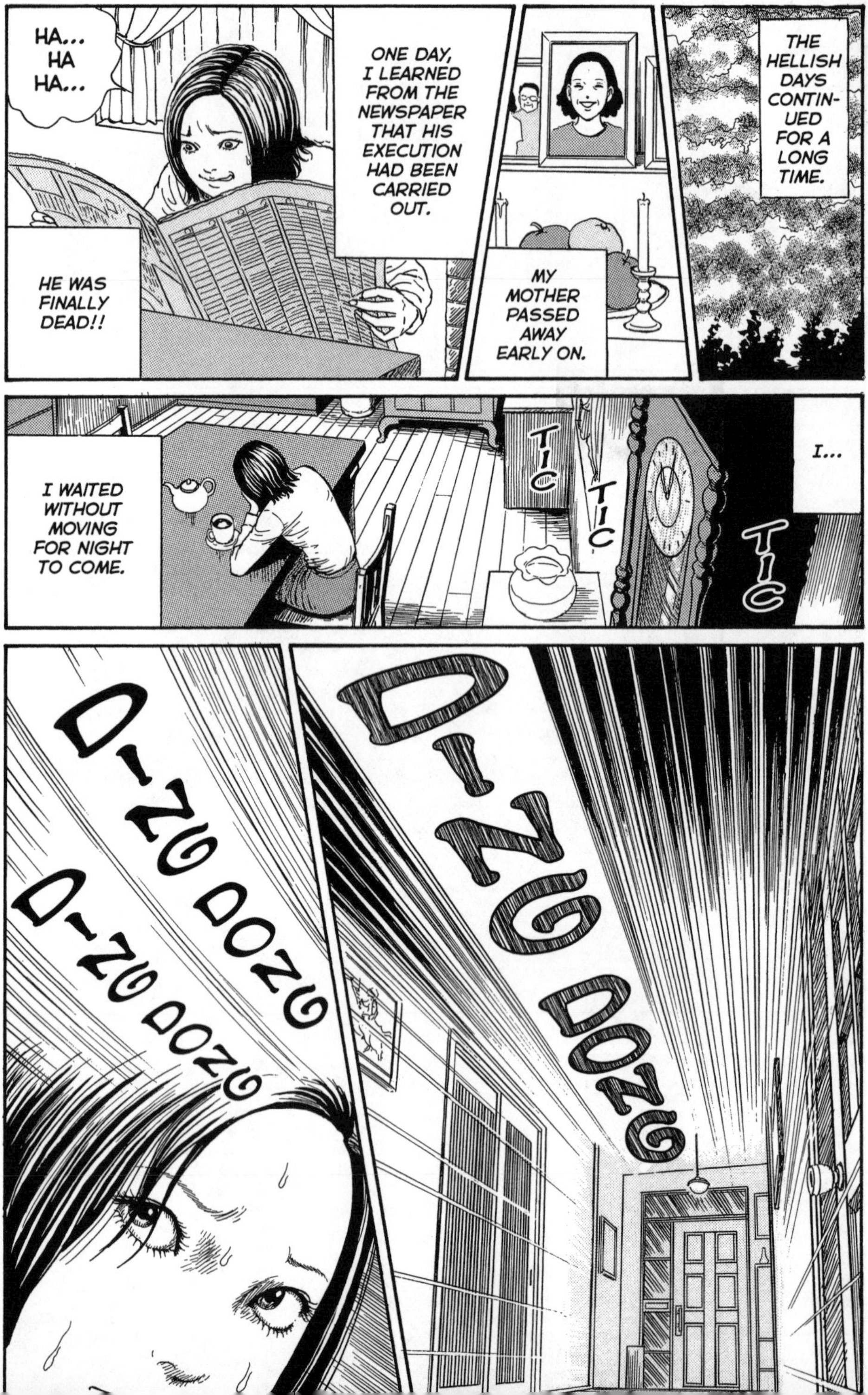
THE HELLISH DAYS CONTINUED FOR A LONG TIME.
MY MOTHER PASSED AWAY EARLY ON.
ONE DAY, I LEARNED FROM THE NEWSPAPER THAT HIS EXECUTION HAD BEEN CARRIED OUT.
HA... HA HA...
HE WAS FINALLY DEAD!!
I...
TIC
TIC
TIC
I WAITED WITHOUT MOVING FOR NIGHT TO COME.
DING DONG
DING DONG
DING DONG

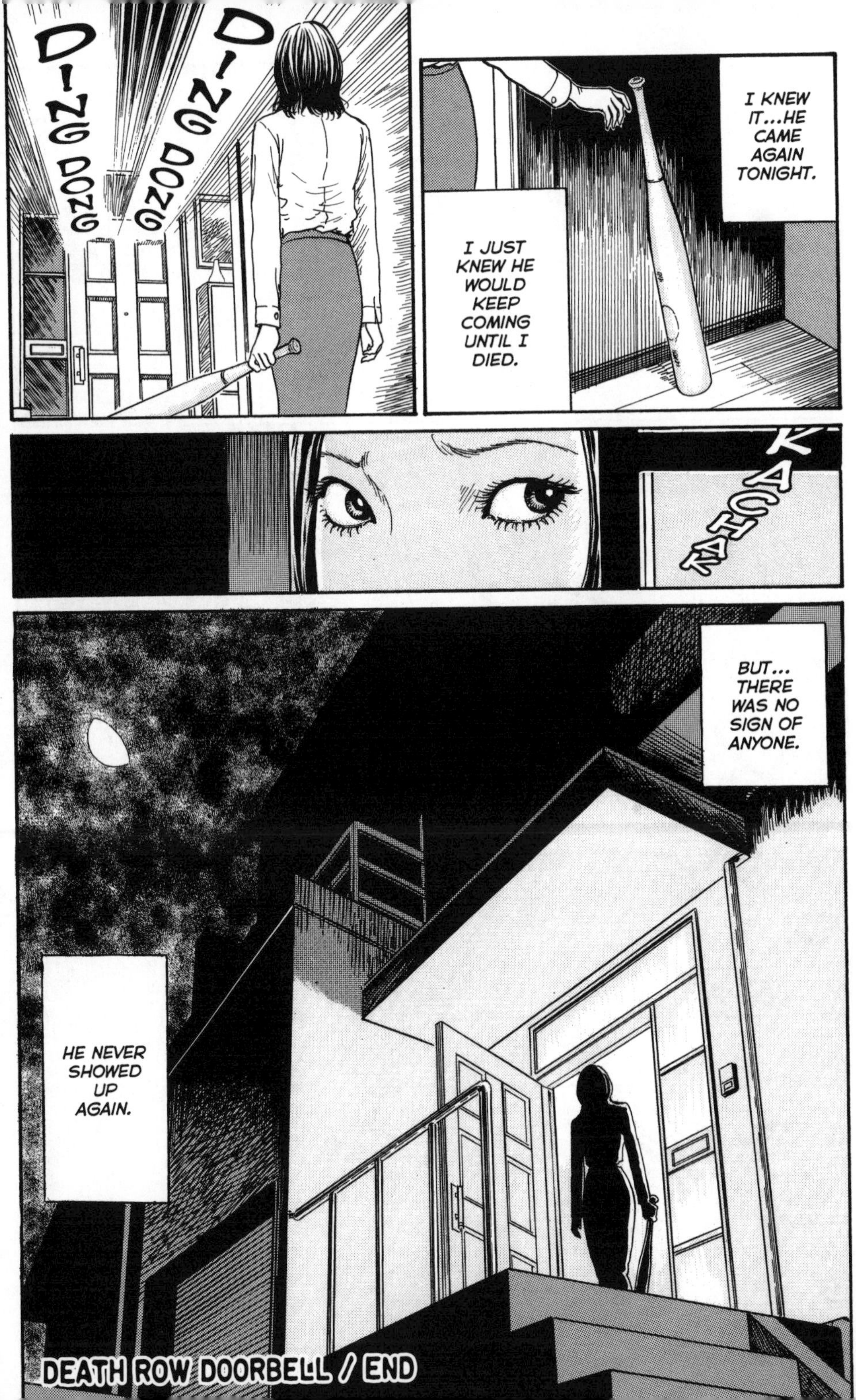
I KNEW IT...HE CAME AGAIN TONIGHT.
I JUST KNEW HE WOULD KEEP COMING UNTIL I DIED.
DING DONG
DING DONG
KACHAK
BUT... THERE WAS NO SIGN OF ANYONE.
HE NEVER SHOWED UP AGAIN.
DEATH ROW DOORBELL / END

THE MYSTERY OF THE HAUNTED HOUSE

お化け屋敷の謎

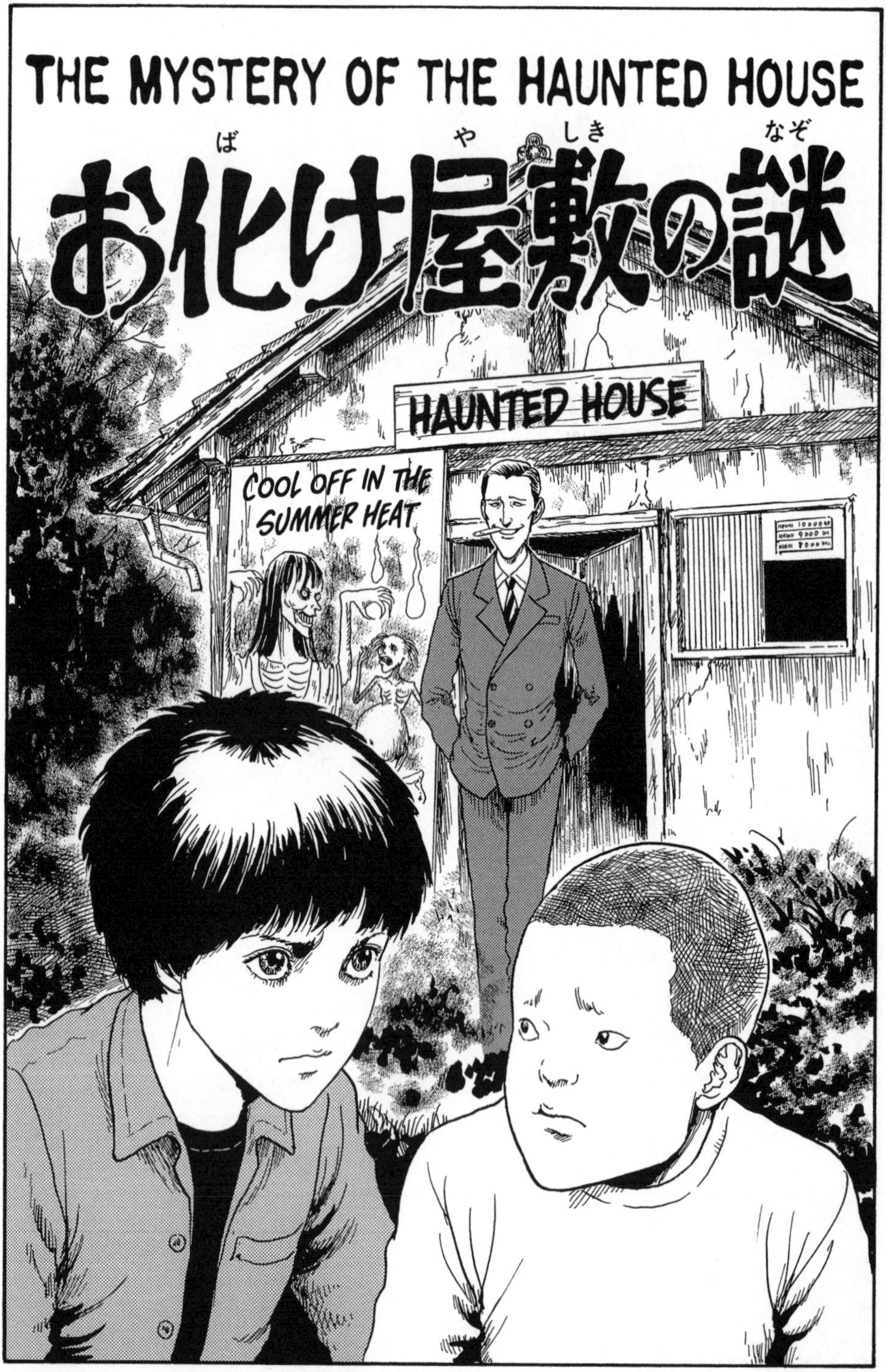

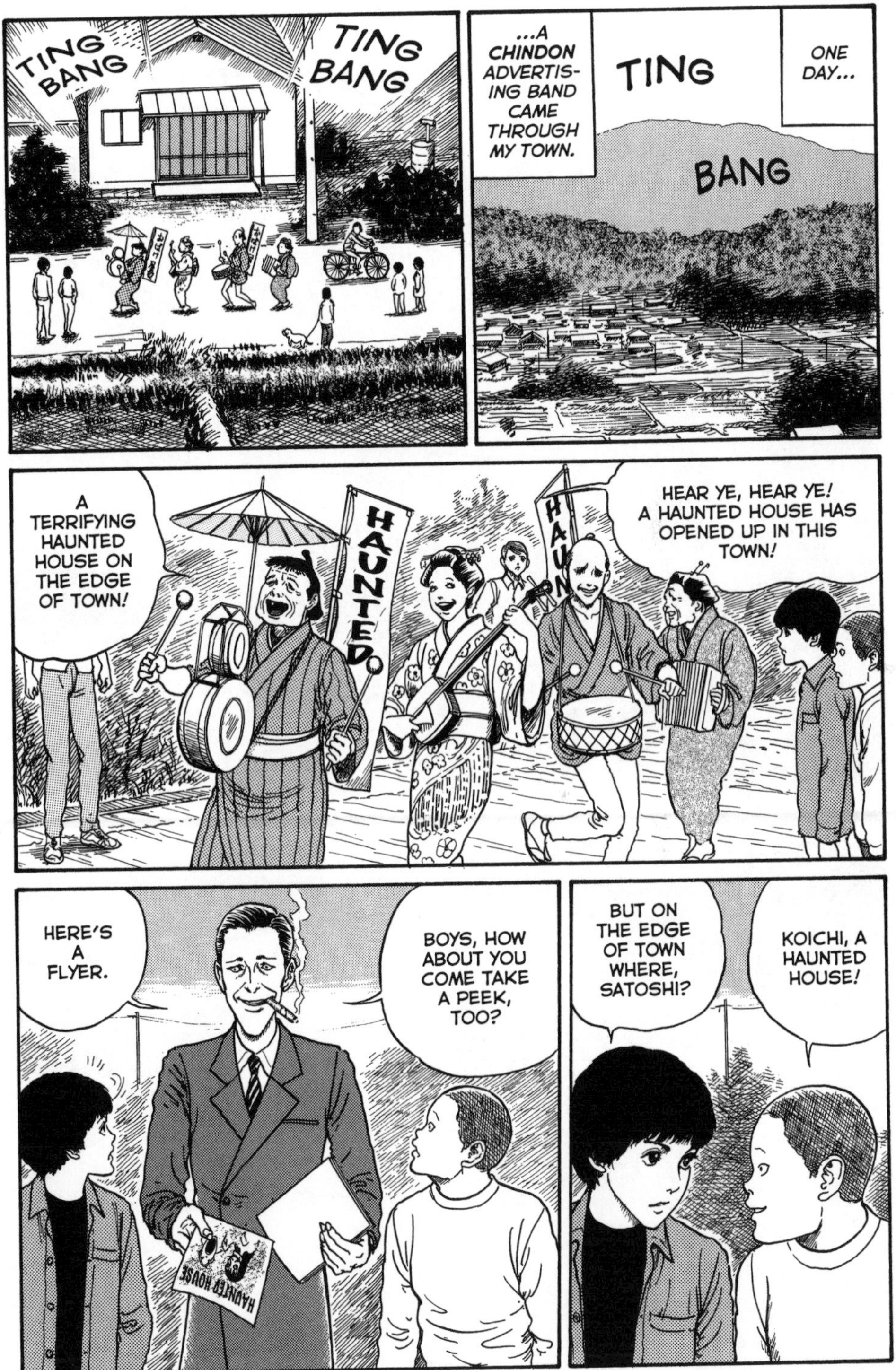
ONE DAY...
TING
...A CHINDON ADVERTIS-ING BAND CAME THROUGH MY TOWN.
BANG
TING BANG
TING BANG
HEAR YE, HEAR YE! A HAUNTED HOUSE HAS OPENED UP IN THIS TOWN!
HAUN
HAUNTED
A TERRIFYING HAUNTED HOUSE ON THE EDGE OF TOWN!
KOICHI, A HAUNTED HOUSE!
BUT ON THE EDGE OF TOWN WHERE, SATOSHI?
BOYS, HOW ABOUT YOU COME TAKE A PEEK, TOO?
HERE'S A FLYER.
HAUNTED HOUSE

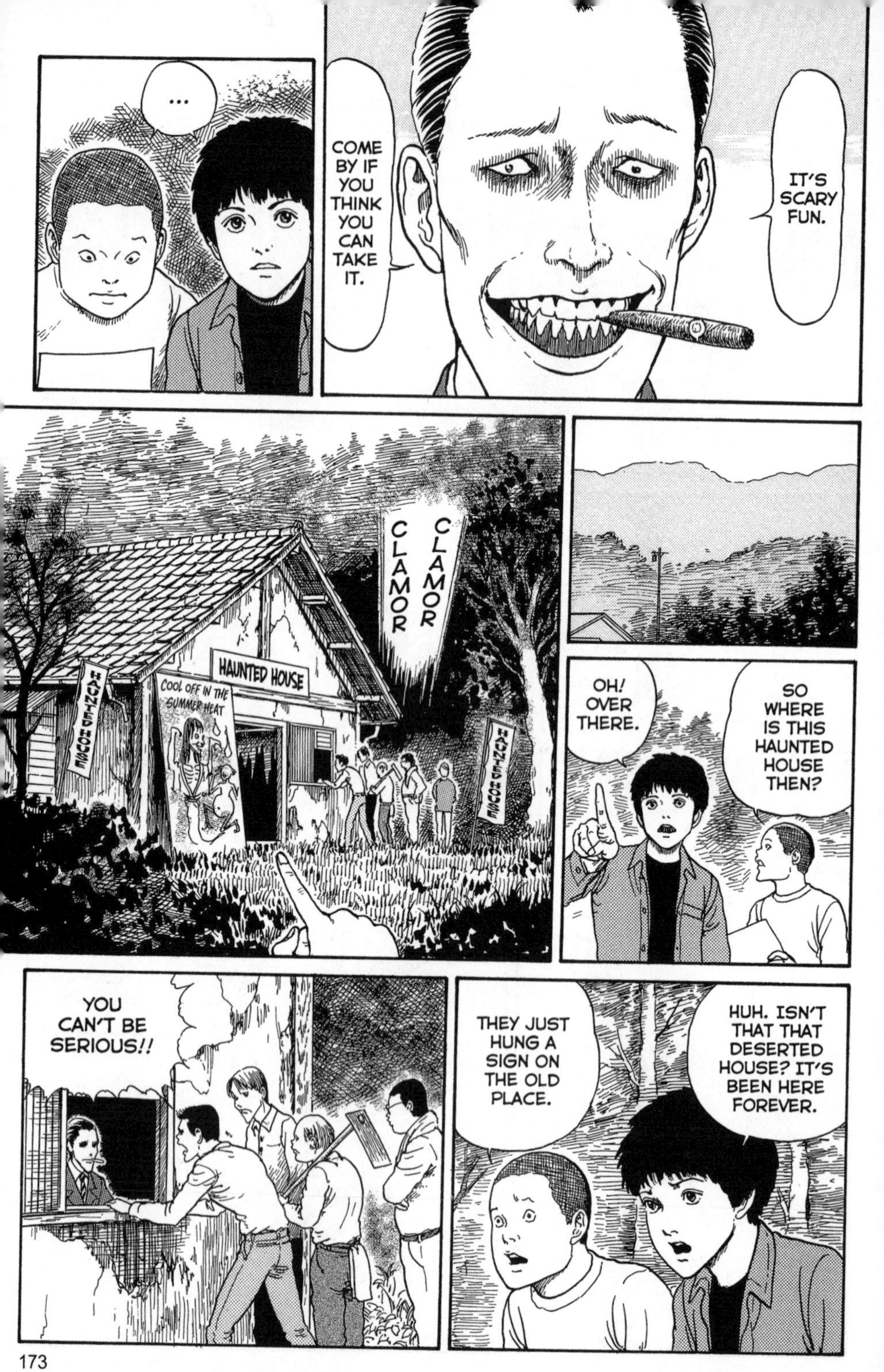
IT'S SCARY FUN.
COME BY IF YOU THINK YOU CAN TAKE IT.
...
SO WHERE IS THIS HAUNTED HOUSE THEN?
OH! OVER THERE.
CLAMOR CLAMOR
HAUNTED HOUSE
COOL OFF IN THE SUMMER HEAT
HAUNTED HOUSE
HAUNTED HOUSE
HUH. ISN'T THAT THAT DESERTED HOUSE? IT'S BEEN HERE FOREVER.
THEY JUST HUNG A SIGN ON THE OLD PLACE.
YOU CAN'T BE SERIOUS!!

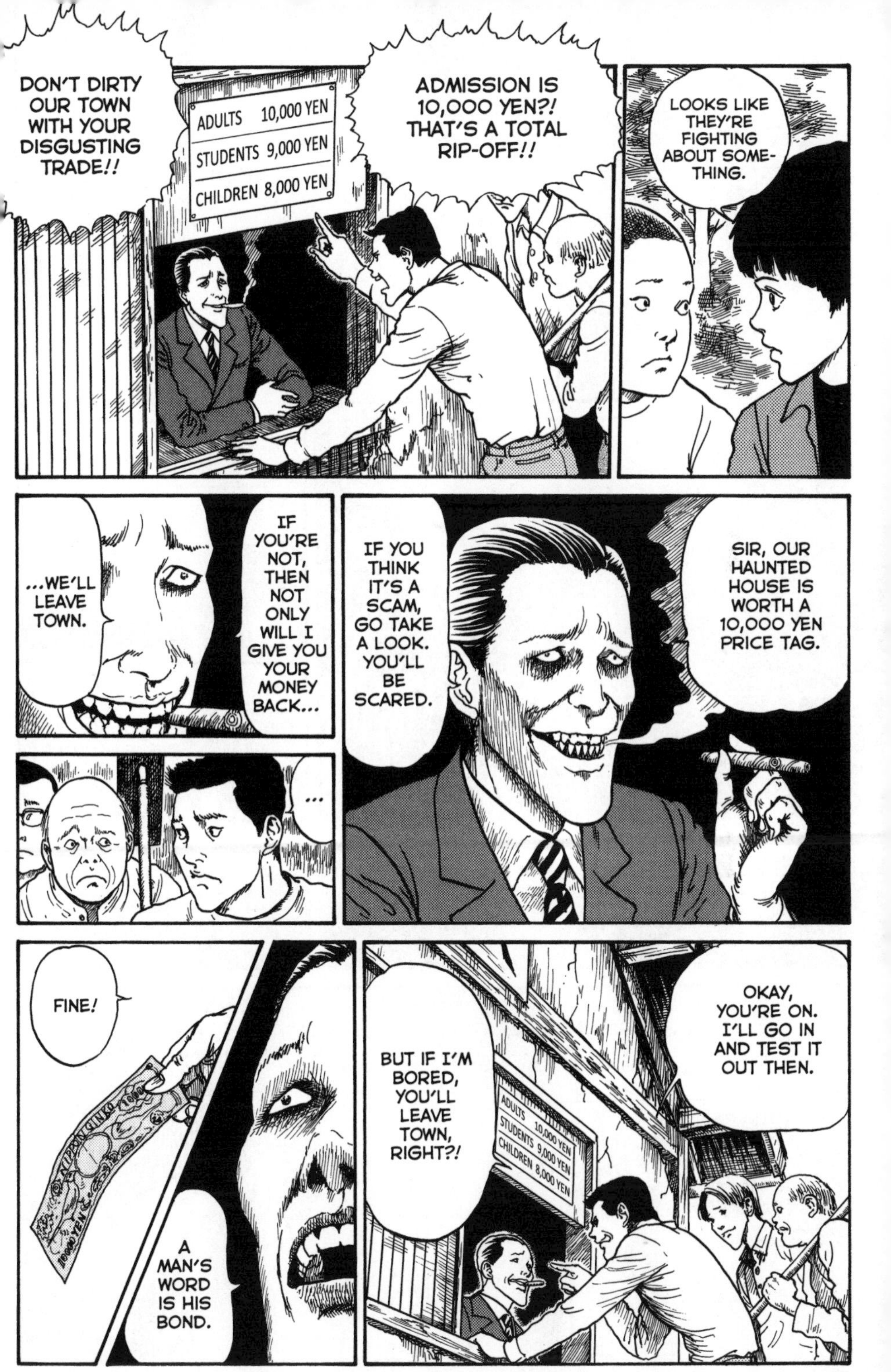
LOOKS LIKE THEY'RE FIGHTING ABOUT SOMETHING.
ADMISSION IS 10,000 YEN?! THAT'S A TOTAL RIP-OFF!!
ADULTS 10,000 YEN
STUDENTS 9,000 YEN
CHILDREN 8,000 YEN
DON'T DIRTY OUR TOWN WITH YOUR DISGUSTING TRADE!!
SIR, OUR HAUNTED HOUSE IS WORTH A 10,000 YEN PRICE TAG.
IF YOU THINK IT'S A SCAM, GO TAKE A LOOK. YOU'LL BE SCARED.
IF YOU'RE NOT, THEN NOT ONLY WILL I GIVE YOU YOUR MONEY BACK...
...WE'LL LEAVE TOWN.
...
OKAY, YOU'RE ON. I'LL GO IN AND TEST IT OUT THEN.
BUT IF I'M BORED, YOU'LL LEAVE TOWN, RIGHT?!
ADULTS 10,000 YEN
STUDENTS 9,000 YEN
CHILDREN 8,000 YEN
A MAN'S WORD IS HIS BOND.
FINE!

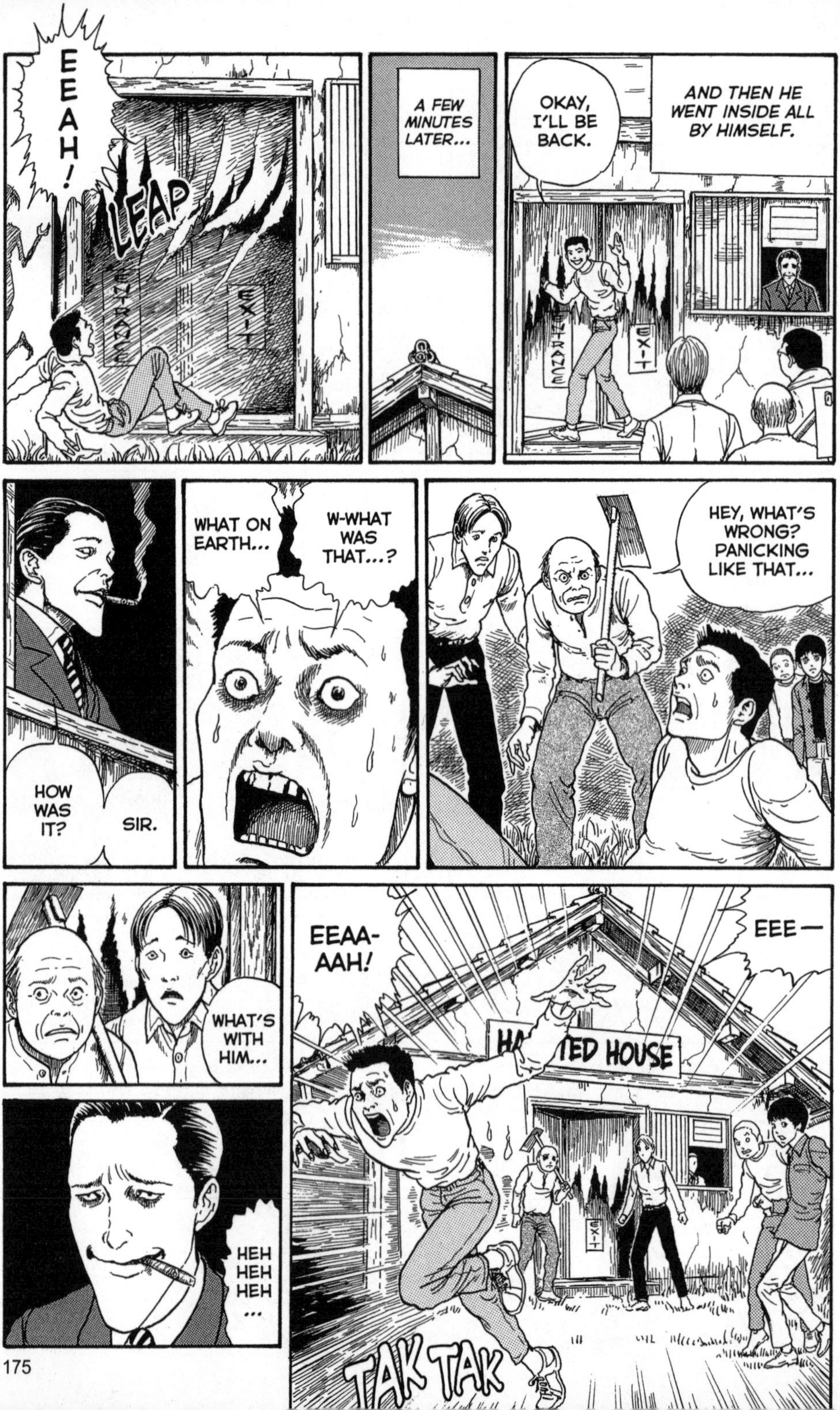
AND THEN HE WENT INSIDE ALL BY HIMSELF.
OKAY, I'LL BE BACK.
ENTRANCE
EXIT
A FEW MINUTES LATER...
EEEAH!
LEAP
ENTRANCE
EXIT
HEY, WHAT'S WRONG? PANICKING LIKE THAT...
W-WHAT WAS THAT...?
WHAT ON EARTH...
HOW WAS IT?
SIR.
EEE—
EEAA-AAH!
HA TED HOUSE
EXIT
TAK TAK
WHAT'S WITH HIM...
HEH HEH HEH ...

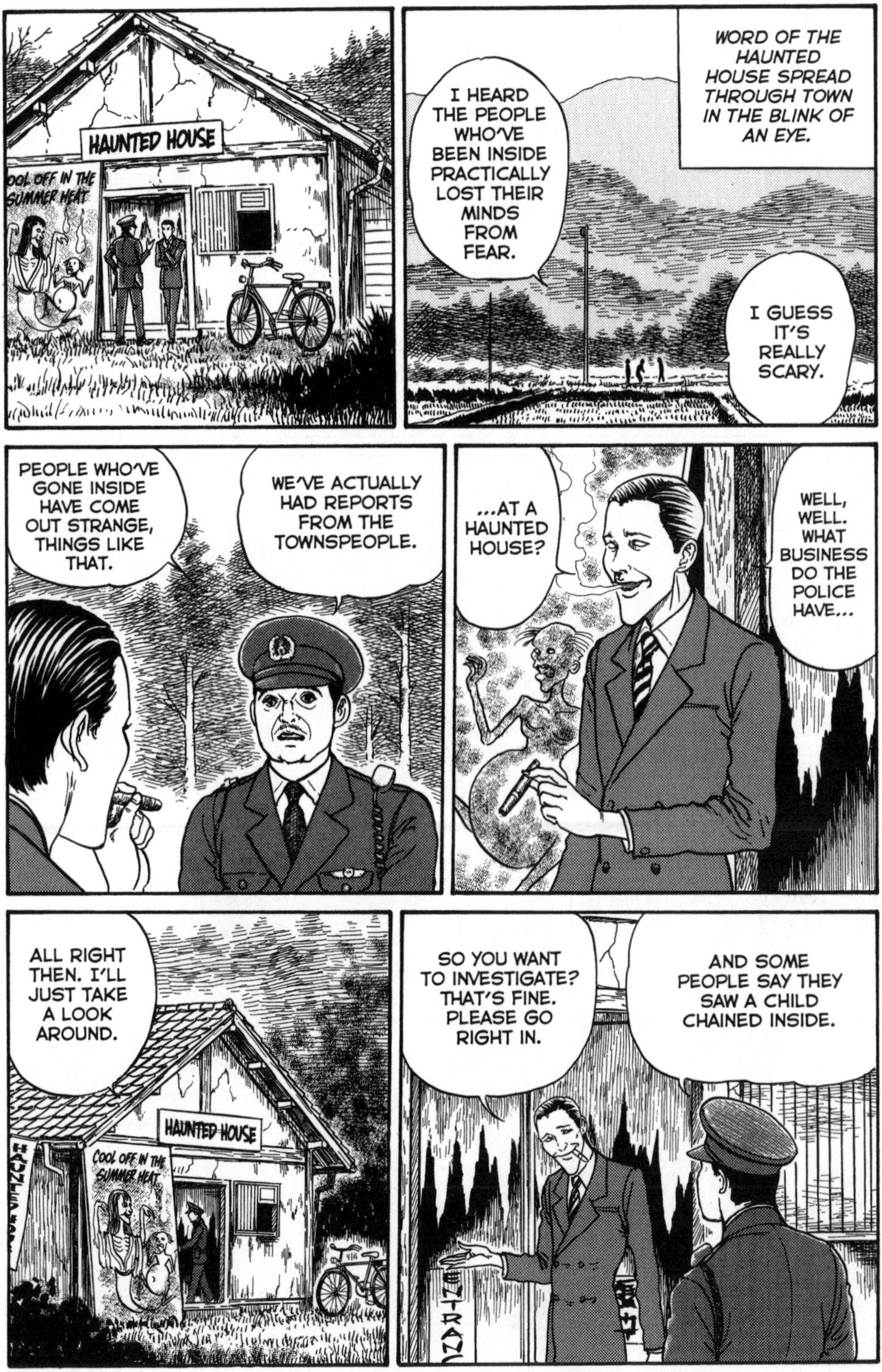
WORD OF THE HAUNTED HOUSE SPREAD THROUGH TOWN IN THE BLINK OF AN EYE.
I HEARD THE PEOPLE WHO'VE BEEN INSIDE PRACTICALLY LOST THEIR MINDS FROM FEAR.
I GUESS IT'S REALLY SCARY.
HAUNTED HOUSE
OOL OFF IN THE SUMMER HEAT
WELL, WELL. WHAT BUSINESS DO THE POLICE HAVE...
...AT A HAUNTED HOUSE?
WE'VE ACTUALLY HAD REPORTS FROM THE TOWNSPEOPLE.
PEOPLE WHO'VE GONE INSIDE HAVE COME OUT STRANGE, THINGS LIKE THAT.
AND SOME PEOPLE SAY THEY SAW A CHILD CHAINED INSIDE.
SO YOU WANT TO INVESTIGATE? THAT'S FINE. PLEASE GO RIGHT IN.
ALL RIGHT THEN. I'LL JUST TAKE A LOOK AROUND.
HAUNTED HOUSE
COOL OFF IN THE SUMMER HEAT

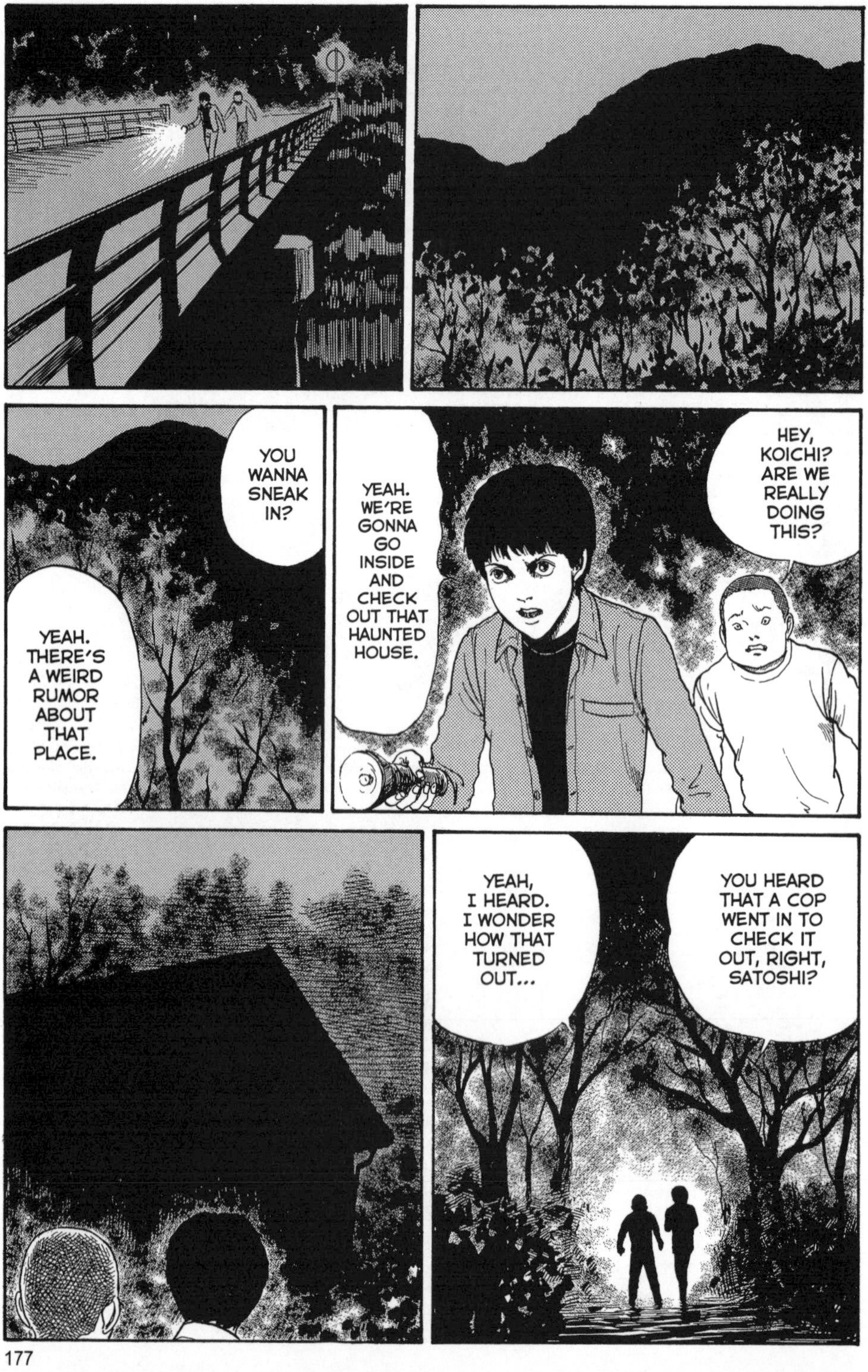
HEY, KOICHI? ARE WE REALLY DOING THIS?
YEAH. WE'RE GONNA GO INSIDE AND CHECK OUT THAT HAUNTED HOUSE.
YOU WANNA SNEAK IN?
YEAH. THERE'S A WEIRD RUMOR ABOUT THAT PLACE.
YOU HEARD THAT A COP WENT IN TO CHECK IT OUT, RIGHT, SATOSHI?
YEAH, I HEARD. I WONDER HOW THAT TURNED OUT...

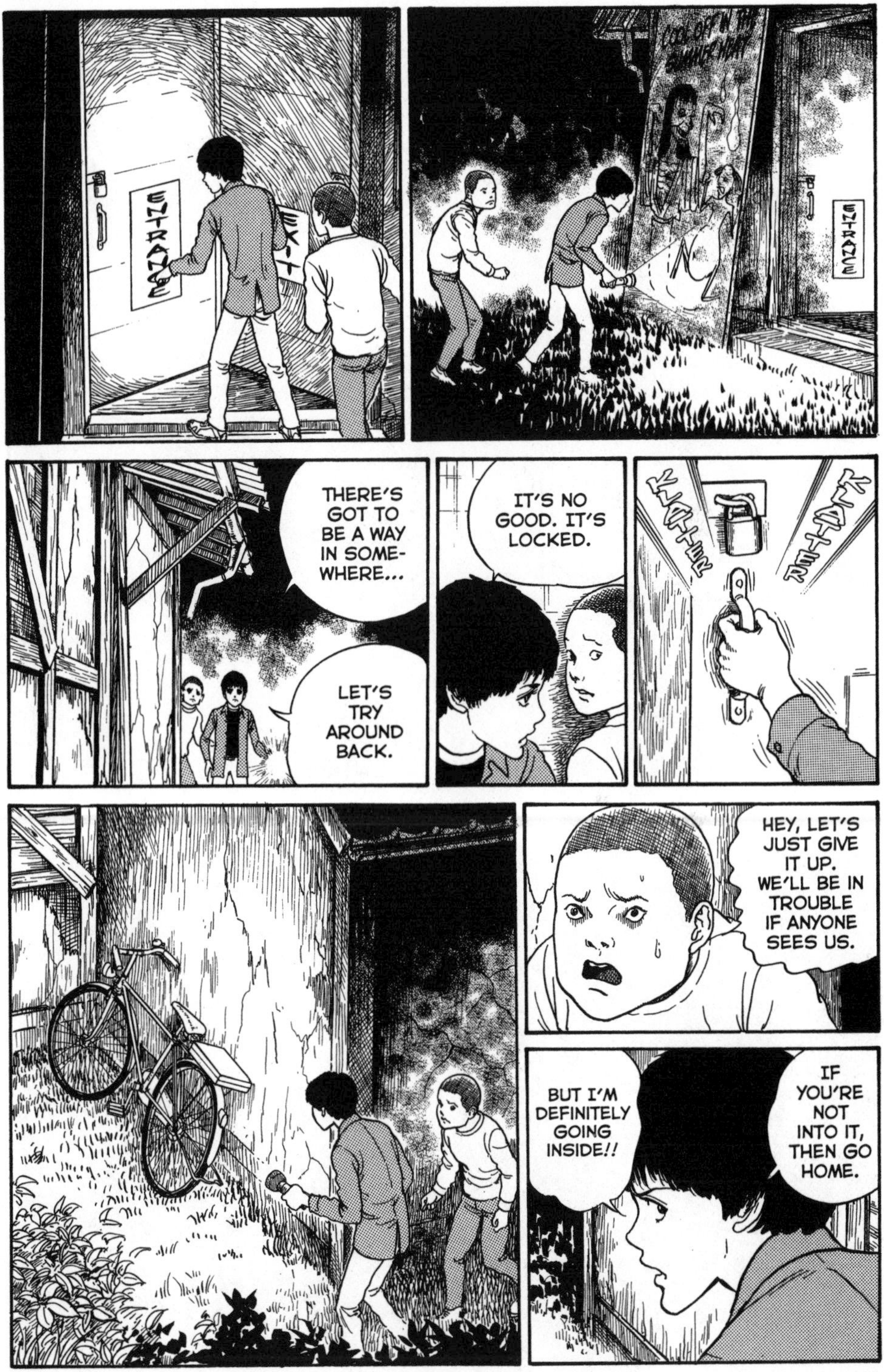
ENTRANCE
ENTRANCE
EXIT
KLATTER
KLATTER
IT'S NO GOOD. IT'S LOCKED.
THERE'S GOT TO BE A WAY IN SOME-WHERE...
LET'S TRY AROUND BACK.
HEY, LET'S JUST GIVE IT UP. WE'LL BE IN TROUBLE IF ANYONE SEES US.
IF YOU'RE NOT INTO IT, THEN GO HOME.
BUT I'M DEFINITELY GOING INSIDE!!

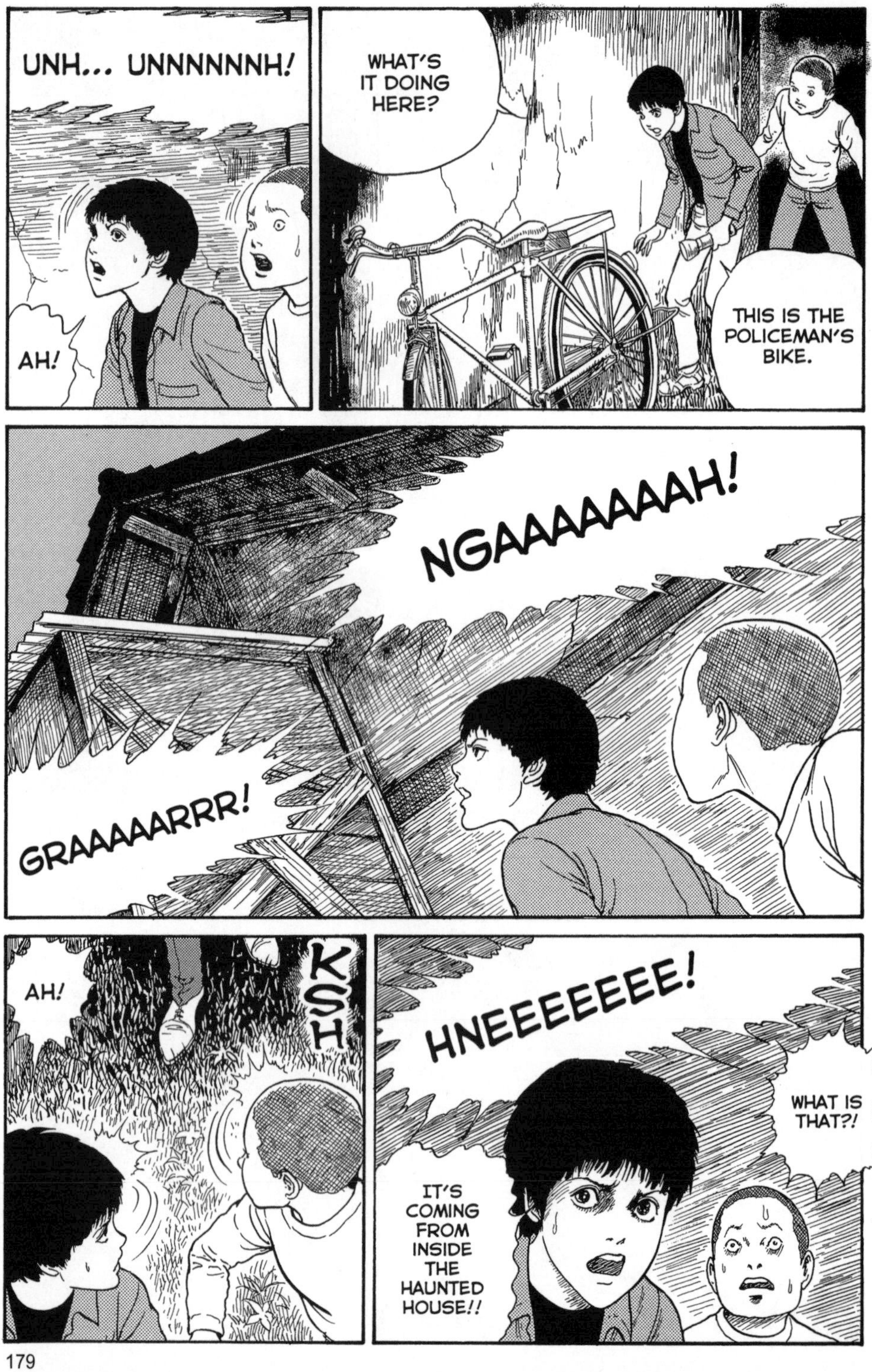
WHAT'S IT DOING HERE?
THIS IS THE POLICEMAN'S BIKE.
UNH... UNNNNNNH!
AH!
NGAAAAAAAH!
GRAAAAARRR!
HNEEEEEEEE!
WHAT IS THAT?!
IT'S COMING FROM INSIDE THE HAUNTED HOUSE!!
KSH
AH!

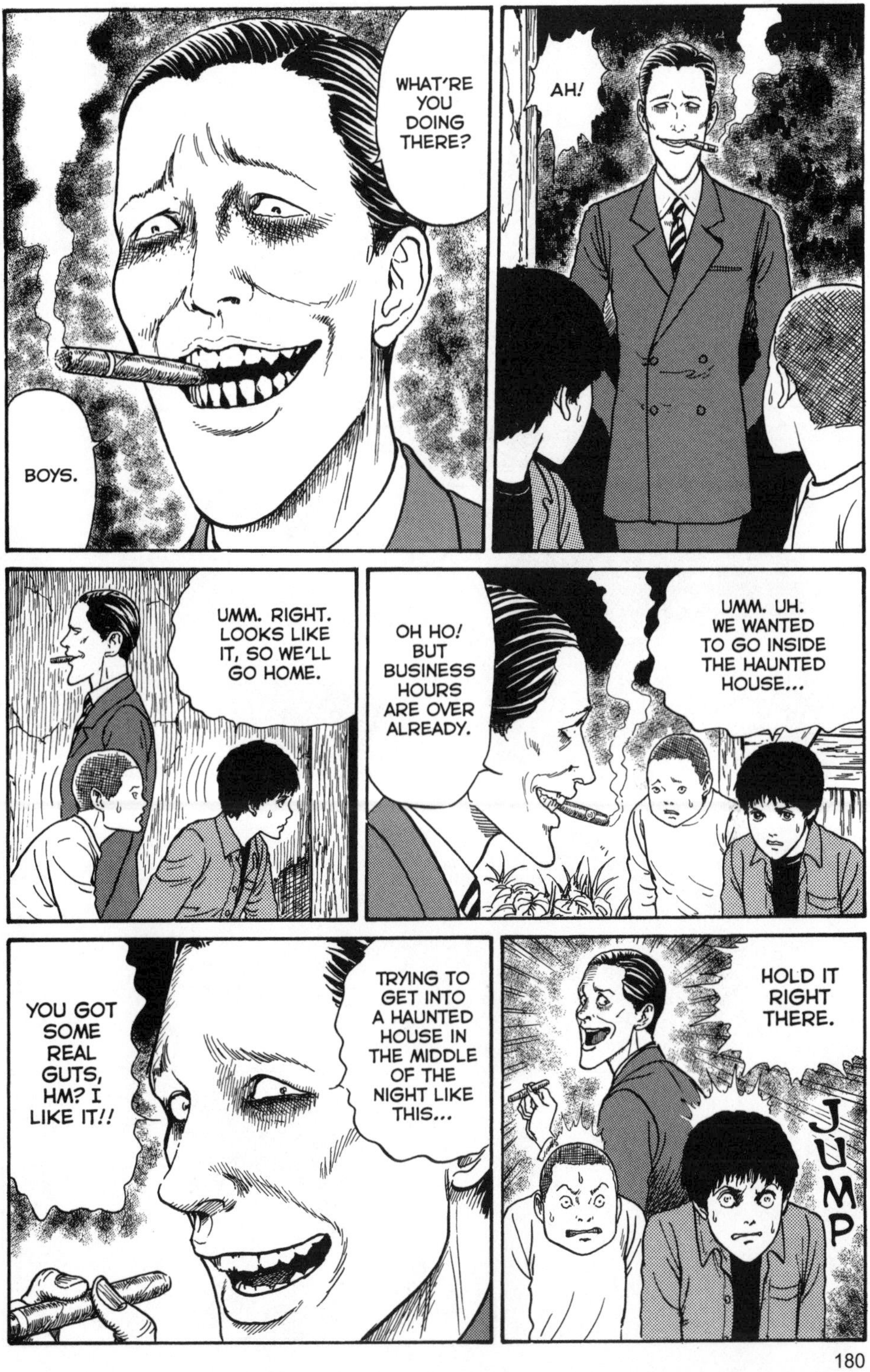
AH!
WHAT'RE YOU DOING THERE?
BOYS.
UMM. UH. WE WANTED TO GO INSIDE THE HAUNTED HOUSE...
OH HO! BUT BUSINESS HOURS ARE OVER ALREADY.
UMM. RIGHT. LOOKS LIKE IT, SO WE'LL GO HOME.
HOLD IT RIGHT THERE.
JUMP
TRYING TO GET INTO A HAUNTED HOUSE IN THE MIDDLE OF THE NIGHT LIKE THIS...
YOU GOT SOME REAL GUTS, HM? I LIKE IT!!

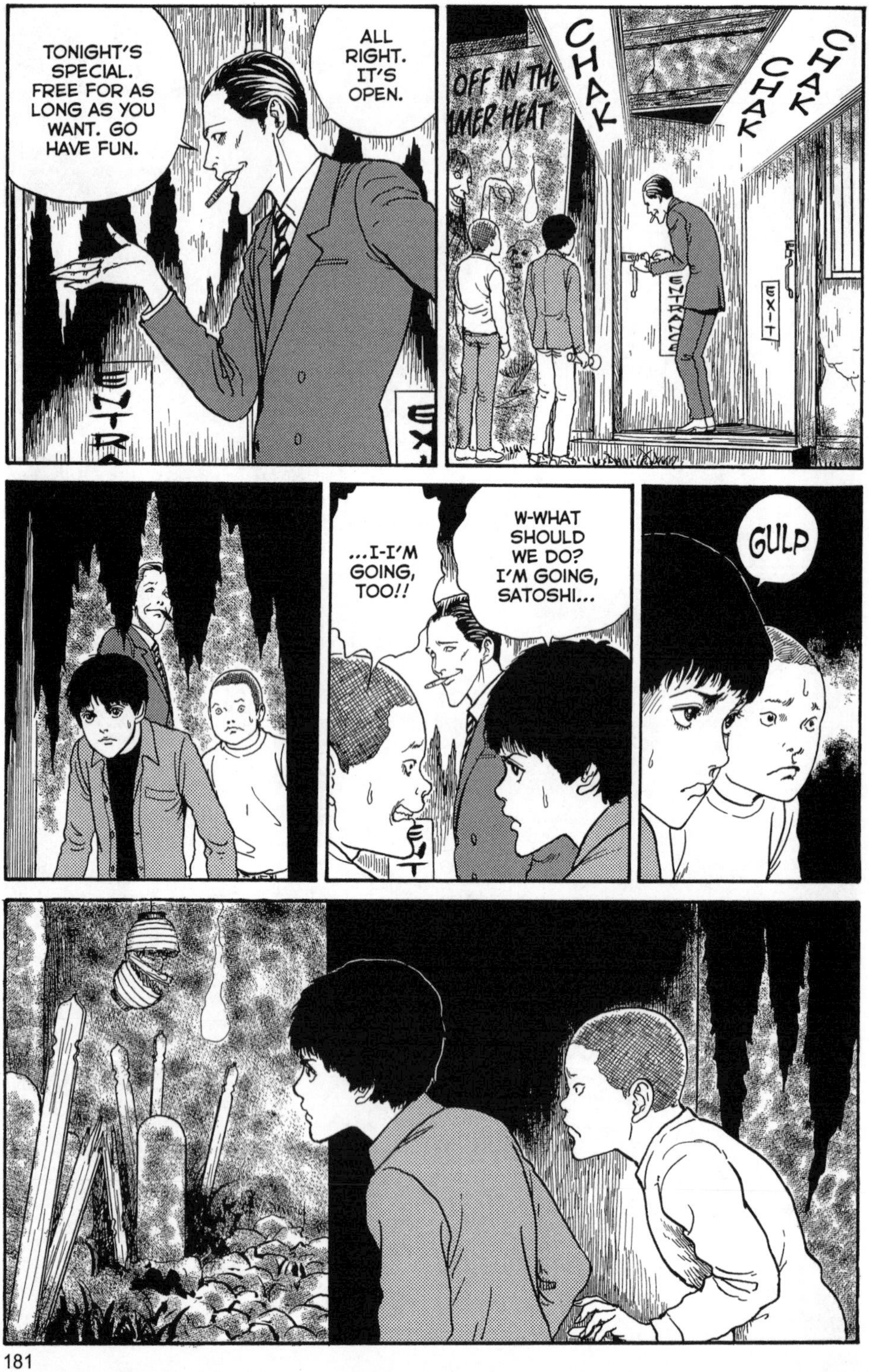
CHAK CHAK
CHAK
OFF IN THE
MER HEAT
ENTRANCE
EXIT
ALL RIGHT. IT'S OPEN.
TONIGHT'S SPECIAL. FREE FOR AS LONG AS YOU WANT. GO HAVE FUN.
GULP
W-WHAT SHOULD WE DO? I'M GOING, SATOSHI...
...I-I'M GOING, TOO!!
EXIT

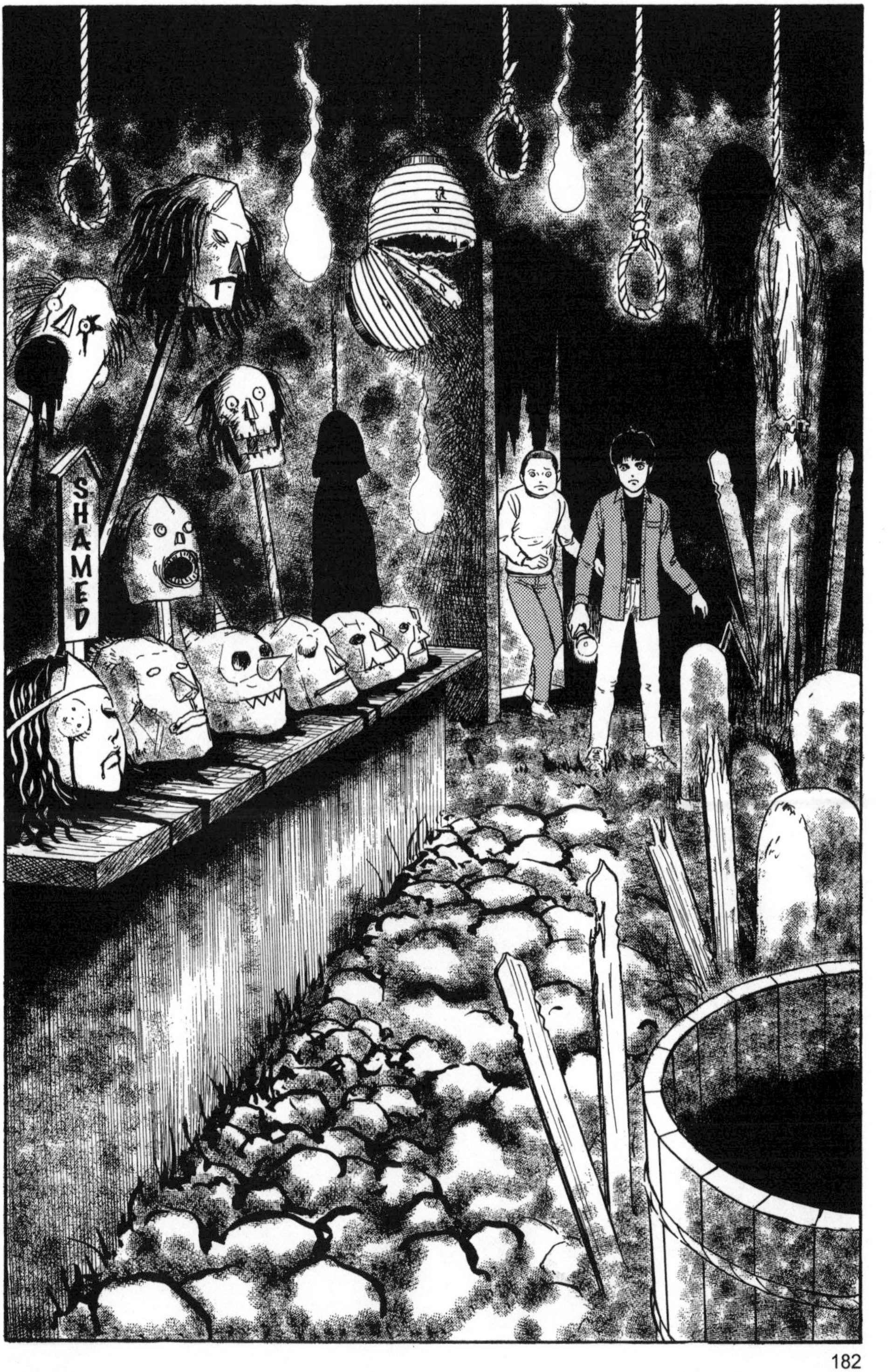
SHAMED

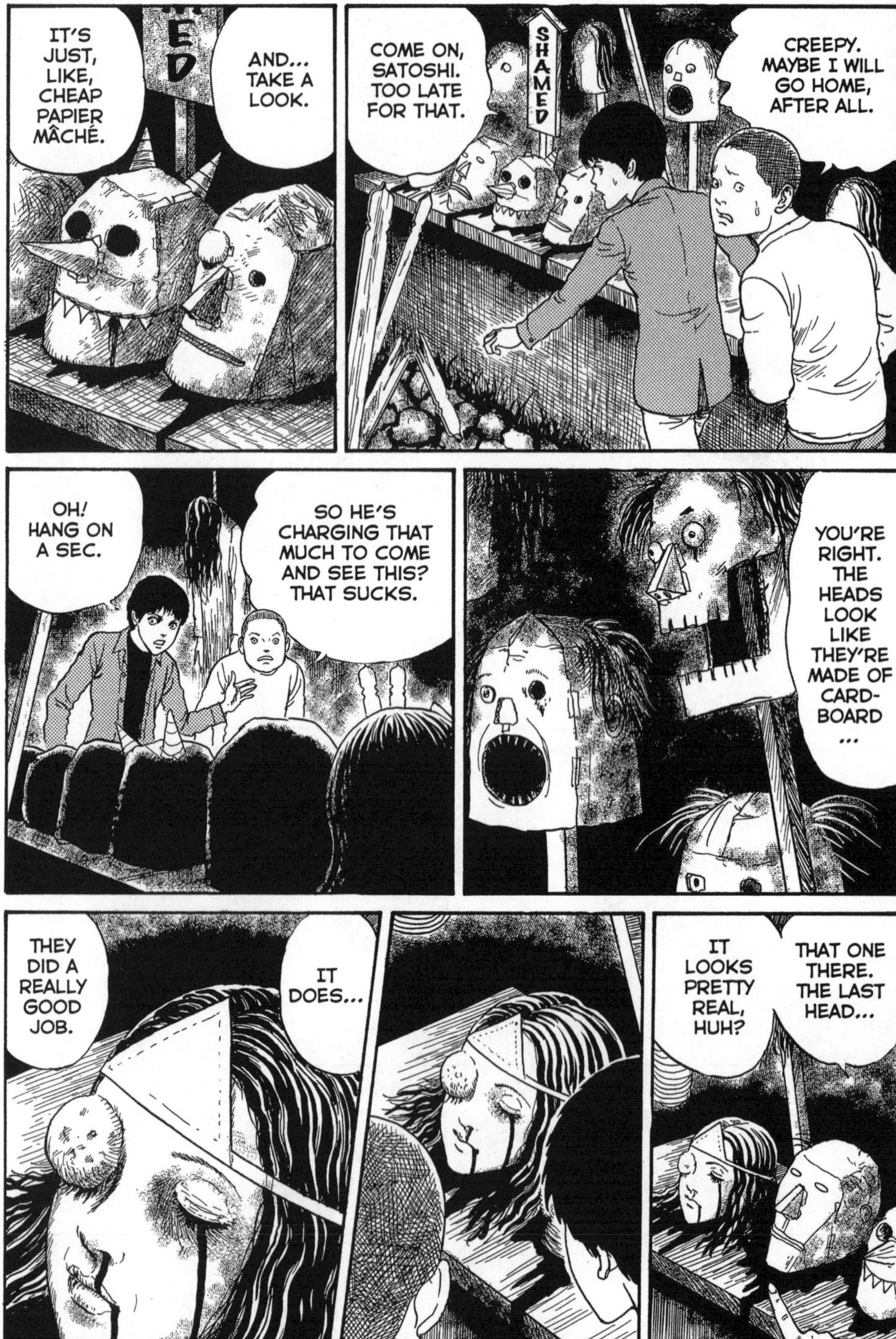
CREEPY. MAYBE I WILL GO HOME, AFTER ALL.
SHAMED
COME ON, SATOSHI. TOO LATE FOR THAT.
AND... TAKE A LOOK.
ED
IT'S JUST, LIKE, CHEAP PAPIER MÂCHÉ.
YOU'RE RIGHT. THE HEADS LOOK LIKE THEY'RE MADE OF CARD-BOARD ...
SO HE'S CHARGING THAT MUCH TO COME AND SEE THIS? THAT SUCKS.
OH! HANG ON A SEC.
THAT ONE THERE. THE LAST HEAD...
IT LOOKS PRETTY REAL, HUH?
IT DOES...
THEY DID A REALLY GOOD JOB.

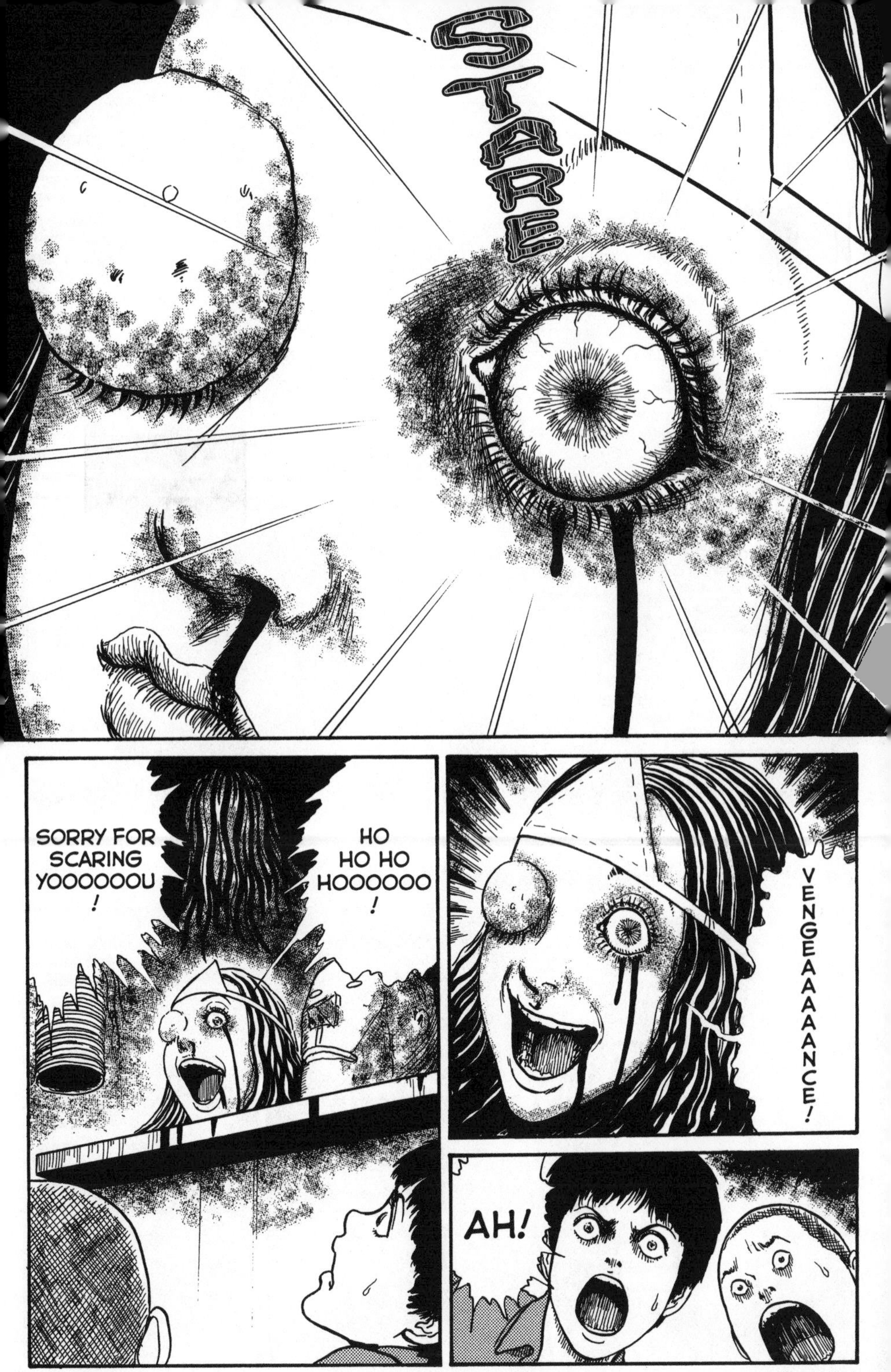
STARE
VENGEAAAAANCE!
AH!
HO HO HO HOOOOOO!
SORRY FOR SCARING YOOOOOOU!

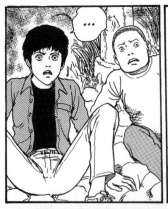

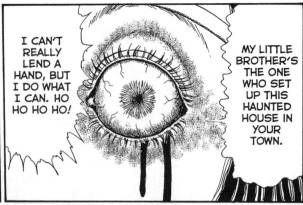

MY LITTLE BROTHER'S THE ONE WHO SET UP THIS HAUNTED HOUSE IN YOUR TOWN.
I CAN'T REALLY LEND A HAND, BUT I DO WHAT I CAN. HO HO HO HO!
...
HUH. SO IT'S JUST A HEAD COMING OUT OF THE TABLE.
I DON'T GET WHAT SHE'S TALKING ABOUT, EITHER.

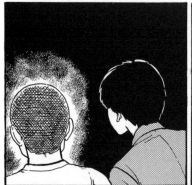

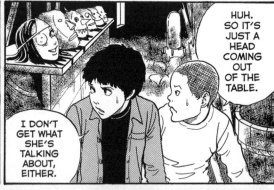

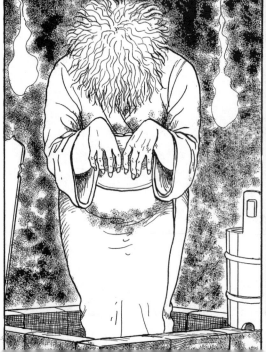

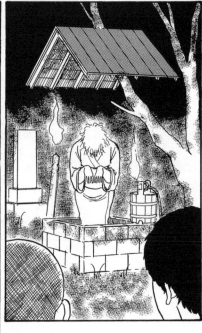

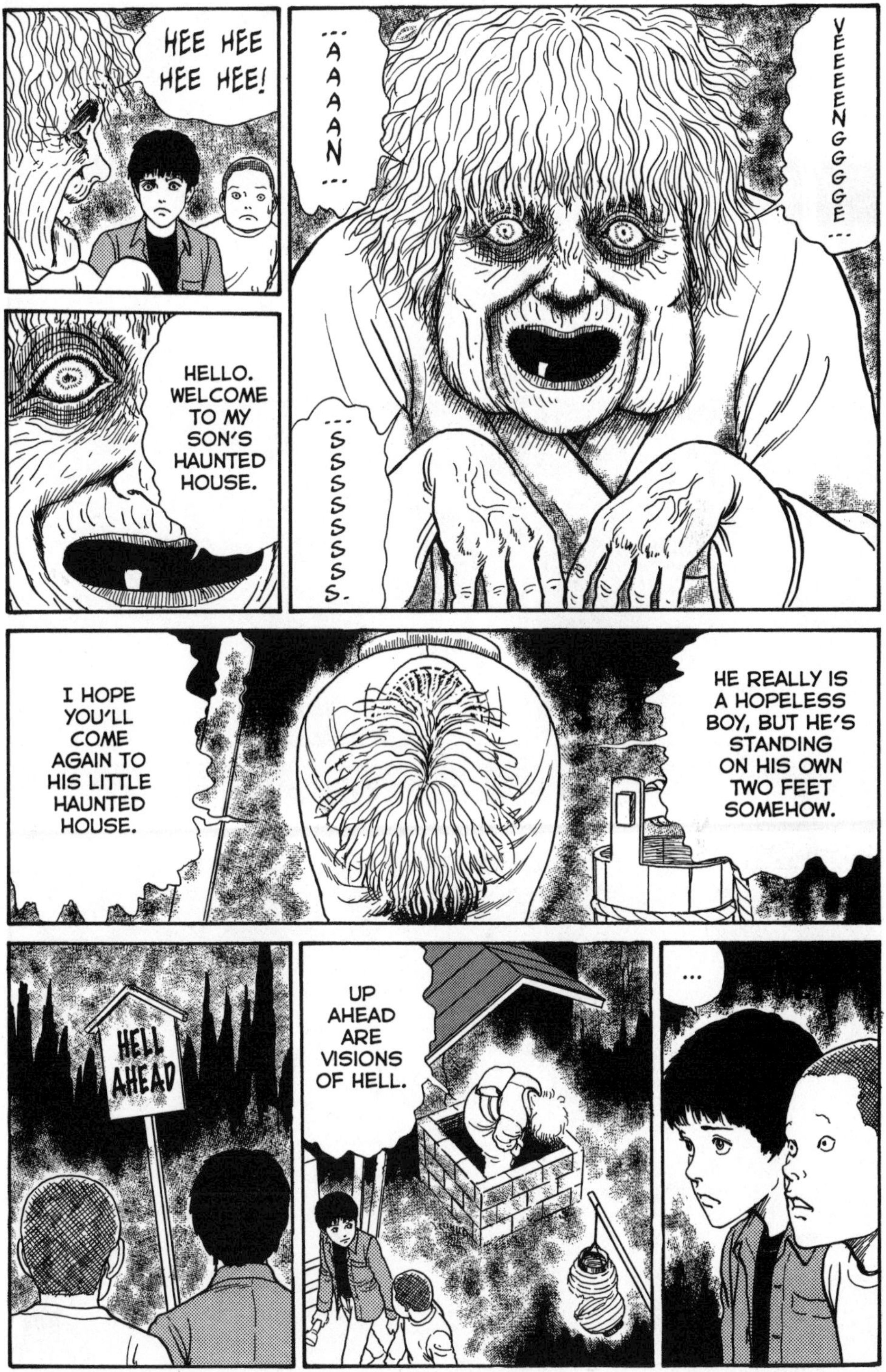

VEEEENGGGGE...
...AAAAN...
...SSSSSSSS.
HEE HEE HEE HEE!
HELLO. WELCOME TO MY SON'S HAUNTED HOUSE.
HE REALLY IS A HOPELESS BOY, BUT HE'S STANDING ON HIS OWN TWO FEET SOMEHOW.
I HOPE YOU'LL COME AGAIN TO HIS LITTLE HAUNTED HOUSE.
...
UP AHEAD ARE VISIONS OF HELL.
HELL AHEAD

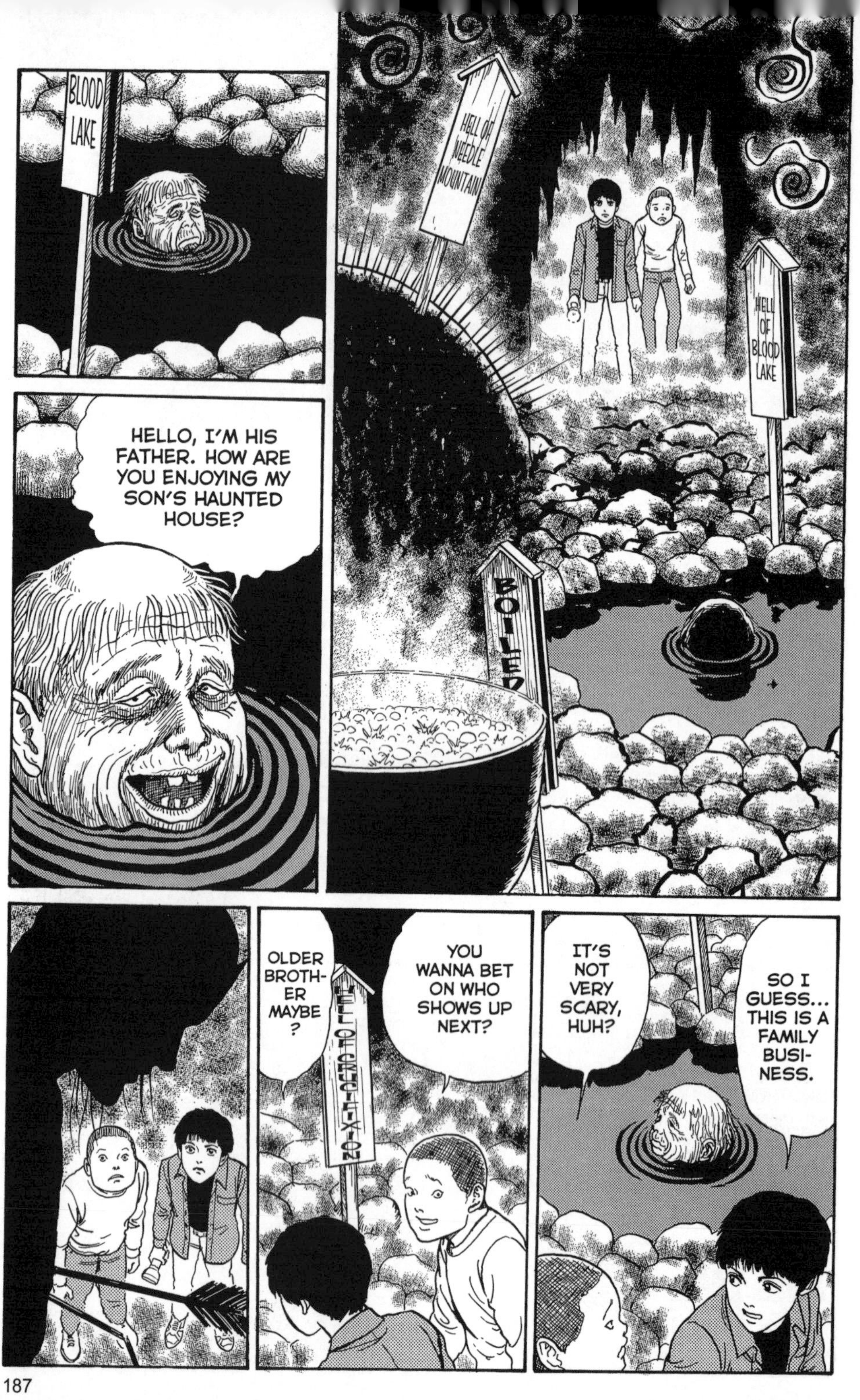
HELL OF NEEDLE MOUNTAIN
HELL OF BLOOD LAKE
BOILED
BLOOD LAKE
HELLO, I'M HIS FATHER. HOW ARE YOU ENJOYING MY SON'S HAUNTED HOUSE?
SO I GUESS... THIS IS A FAMILY BUSI-NESS.
IT'S NOT VERY SCARY, HUH?
YOU WANNA BET ON WHO SHOWS UP NEXT?
OLDER BROTH-ER MAYBE?
HELL OF CRUCIFIXION

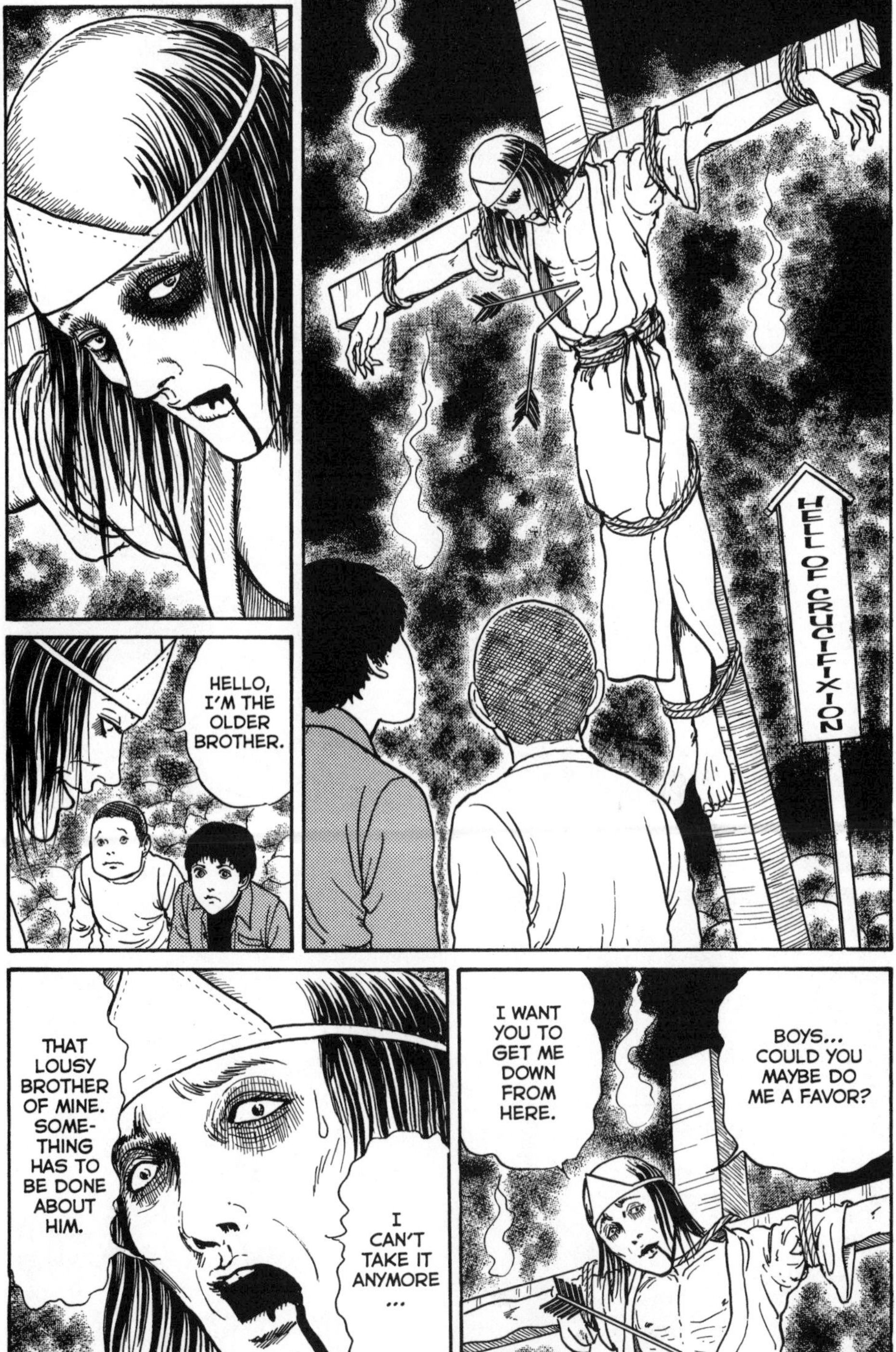
HELL OF CRUCIFIXION
HELLO, I'M THE OLDER BROTHER.
BOYS... COULD YOU MAYBE DO ME A FAVOR?
I WANT YOU TO GET ME DOWN FROM HERE.
THAT LOUSY BROTHER OF MINE. SOME-THING HAS TO BE DONE ABOUT HIM.
I CAN'T TAKE IT ANYMORE ...

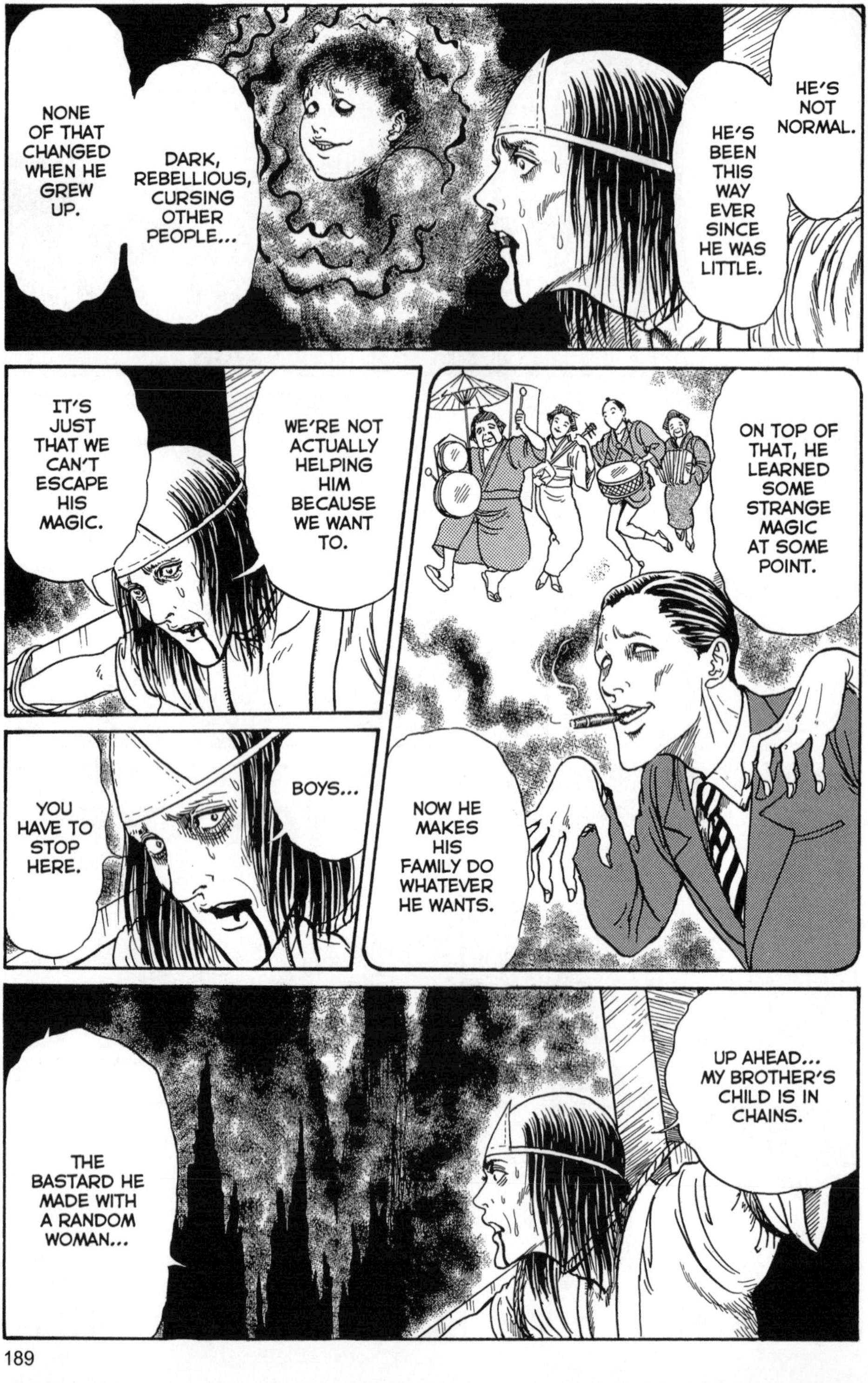
HE'S NOT NORMAL.
HE'S BEEN THIS WAY EVER SINCE HE WAS LITTLE.
DARK, REBELLIOUS, CURSING OTHER PEOPLE...
NONE OF THAT CHANGED WHEN HE GREW UP.
ON TOP OF THAT, HE LEARNED SOME STRANGE MAGIC AT SOME POINT.
NOW HE MAKES HIS FAMILY DO WHATEVER HE WANTS.
WE'RE NOT ACTUALLY HELPING HIM BECAUSE WE WANT TO.
IT'S JUST THAT WE CAN'T ESCAPE HIS MAGIC.
BOYS...
YOU HAVE TO STOP HERE.
UP AHEAD... MY BROTHER'S CHILD IS IN CHAINS.
THE BASTARD HE MADE WITH A RANDOM WOMAN...

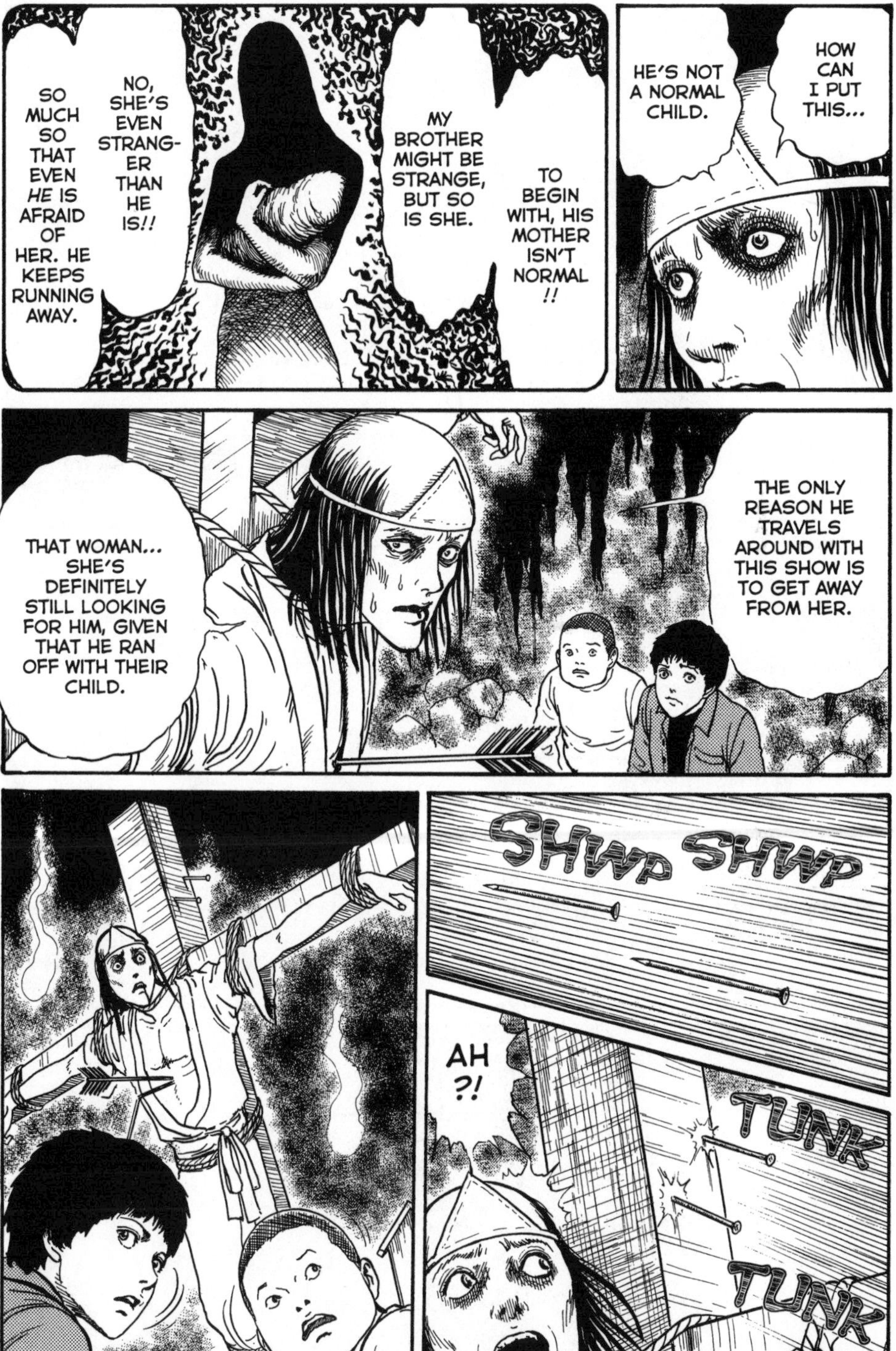
HOW CAN I PUT THIS...
HE'S NOT A NORMAL CHILD.
TO BEGIN WITH, HIS MOTHER ISN'T NORMAL!!
MY BROTHER MIGHT BE STRANGE, BUT SO IS SHE.
NO, SHE'S EVEN STRANGER THAN HE IS!!
SO MUCH SO THAT EVEN *HE* IS AFRAID OF HER. HE KEEPS RUNNING AWAY.
THE ONLY REASON HE TRAVELS AROUND WITH THIS SHOW IS TO GET AWAY FROM HER.
THAT WOMAN... SHE'S DEFINITELY STILL LOOKING FOR HIM, GIVEN THAT HE RAN OFF WITH THEIR CHILD.
SHWP SHWP
TUNK
AH ?!
TUNK

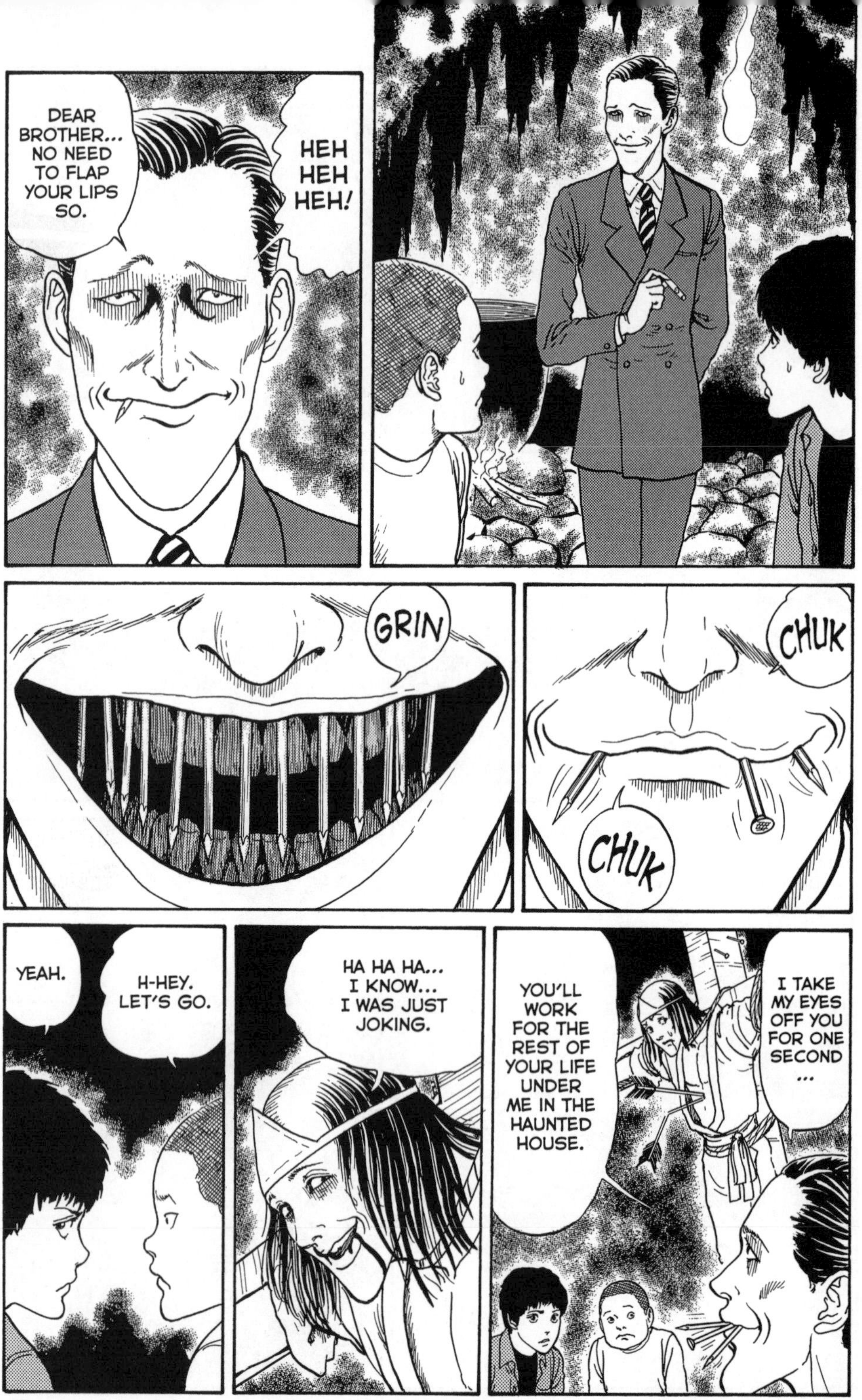
HEH HEH HEH!
DEAR BROTHER... NO NEED TO FLAP YOUR LIPS SO.
CHUK
CHUK
GRIN
I TAKE MY EYES OFF YOU FOR ONE SECOND ...
YOU'LL WORK FOR THE REST OF YOUR LIFE UNDER ME IN THE HAUNTED HOUSE.
HA HA HA... I KNOW... I WAS JUST JOKING.
H-HEY. LET'S GO.
YEAH.

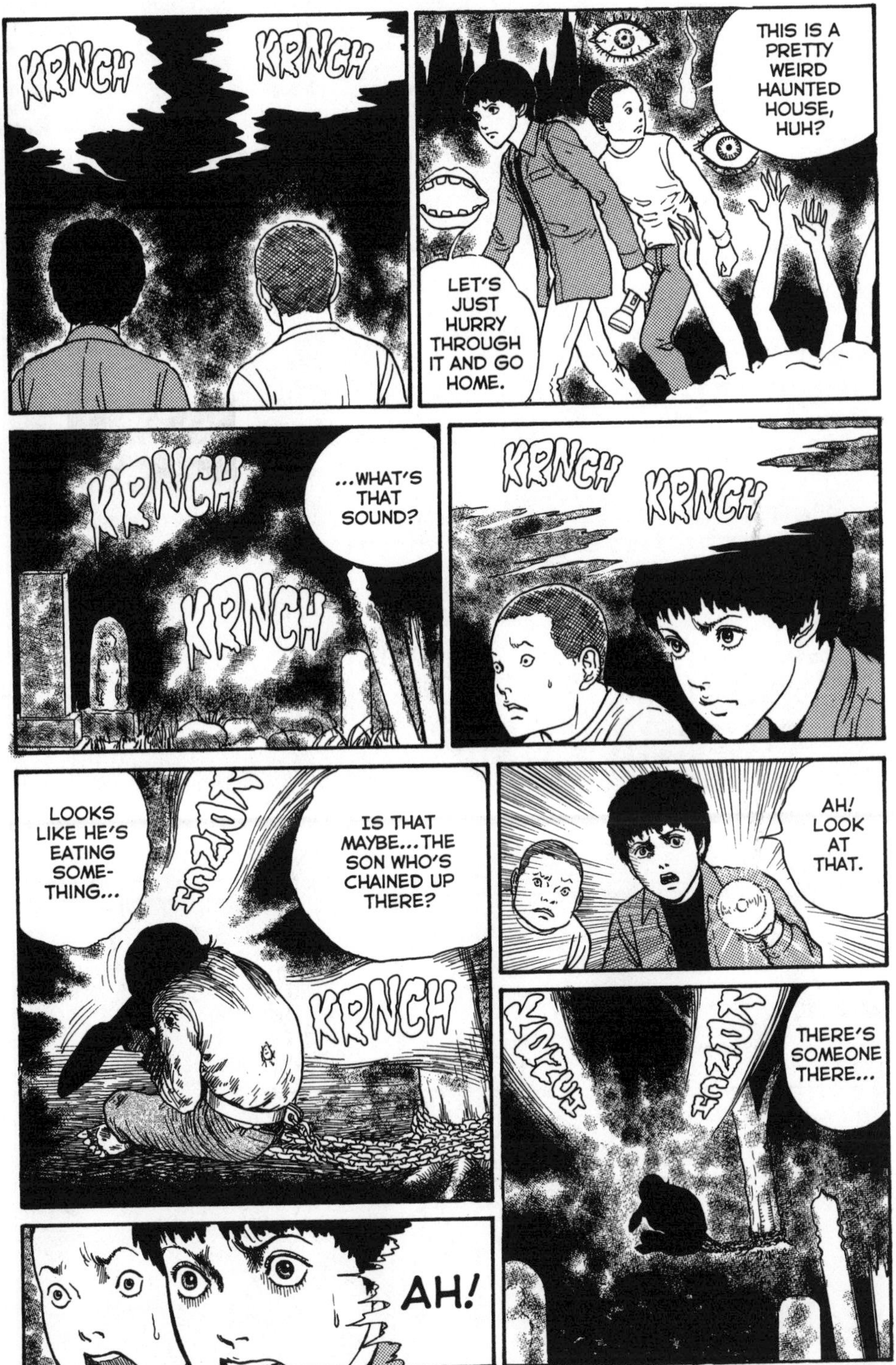
THIS IS A PRETTY WEIRD HAUNTED HOUSE, HUH?
LET'S JUST HURRY THROUGH IT AND GO HOME.
KRNCH
KRNCH
KRNCH
KRNCH
...WHAT'S THAT SOUND?
KRNCH
KRNCH
AH! LOOK AT THAT.
THERE'S SOMEONE THERE...
KRUNCH
KRUNCH
IS THAT MAYBE... THE SON WHO'S CHAINED UP THERE?
LOOKS LIKE HE'S EATING SOME-THING...
KRUNCH
KRNCH
AH!

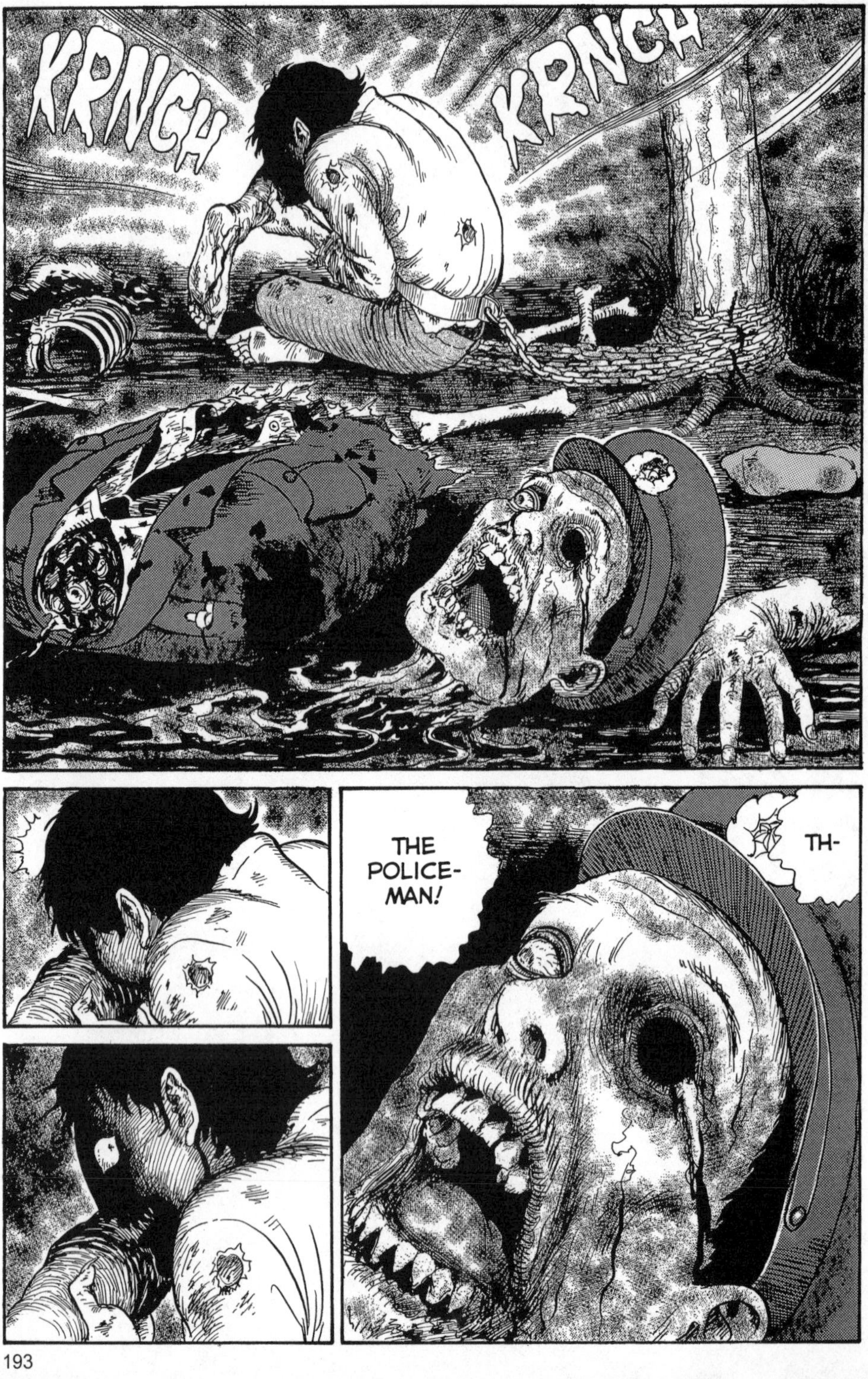
KRNCH
KRNCH
TH-
THE POLICE-MAN!

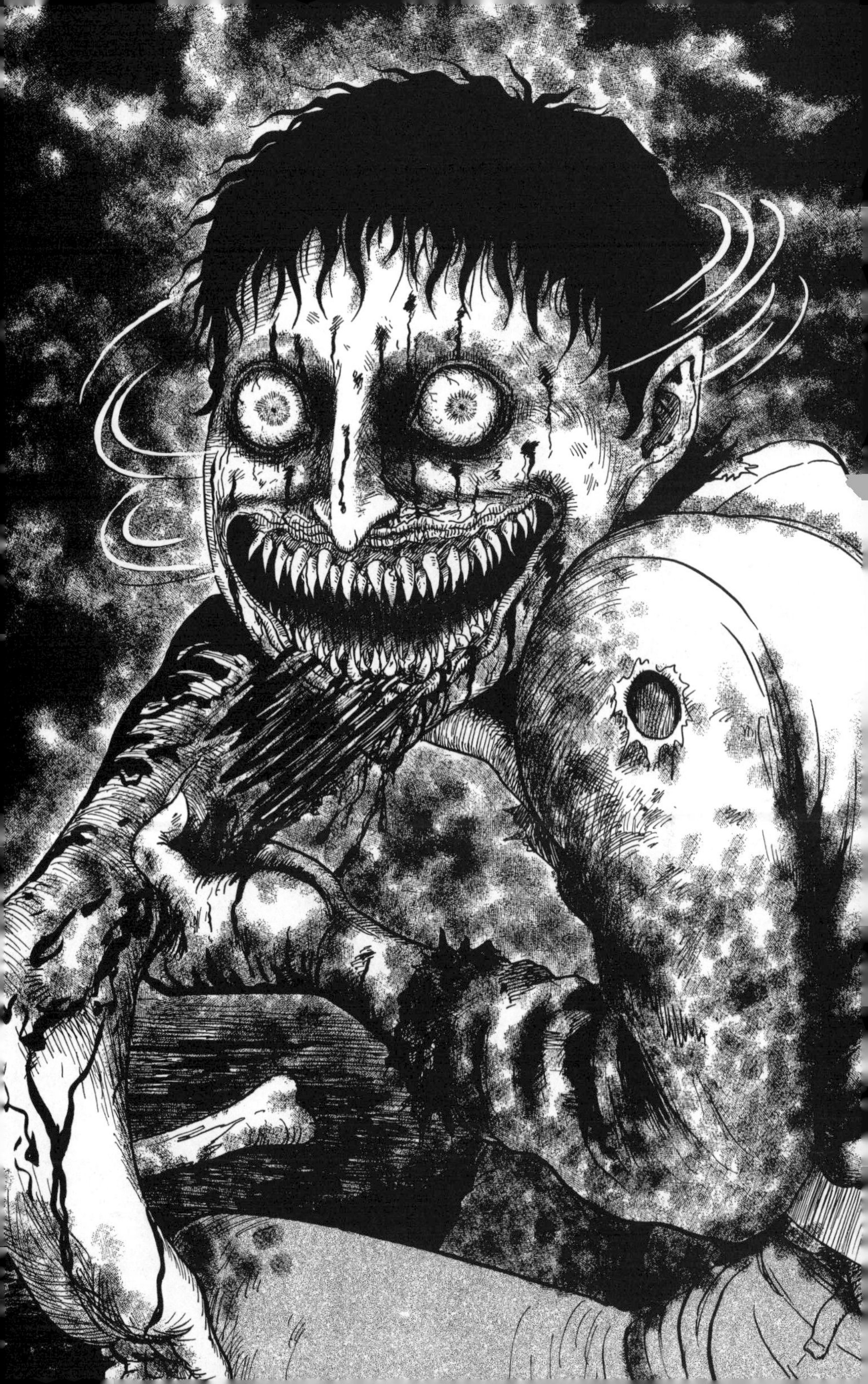

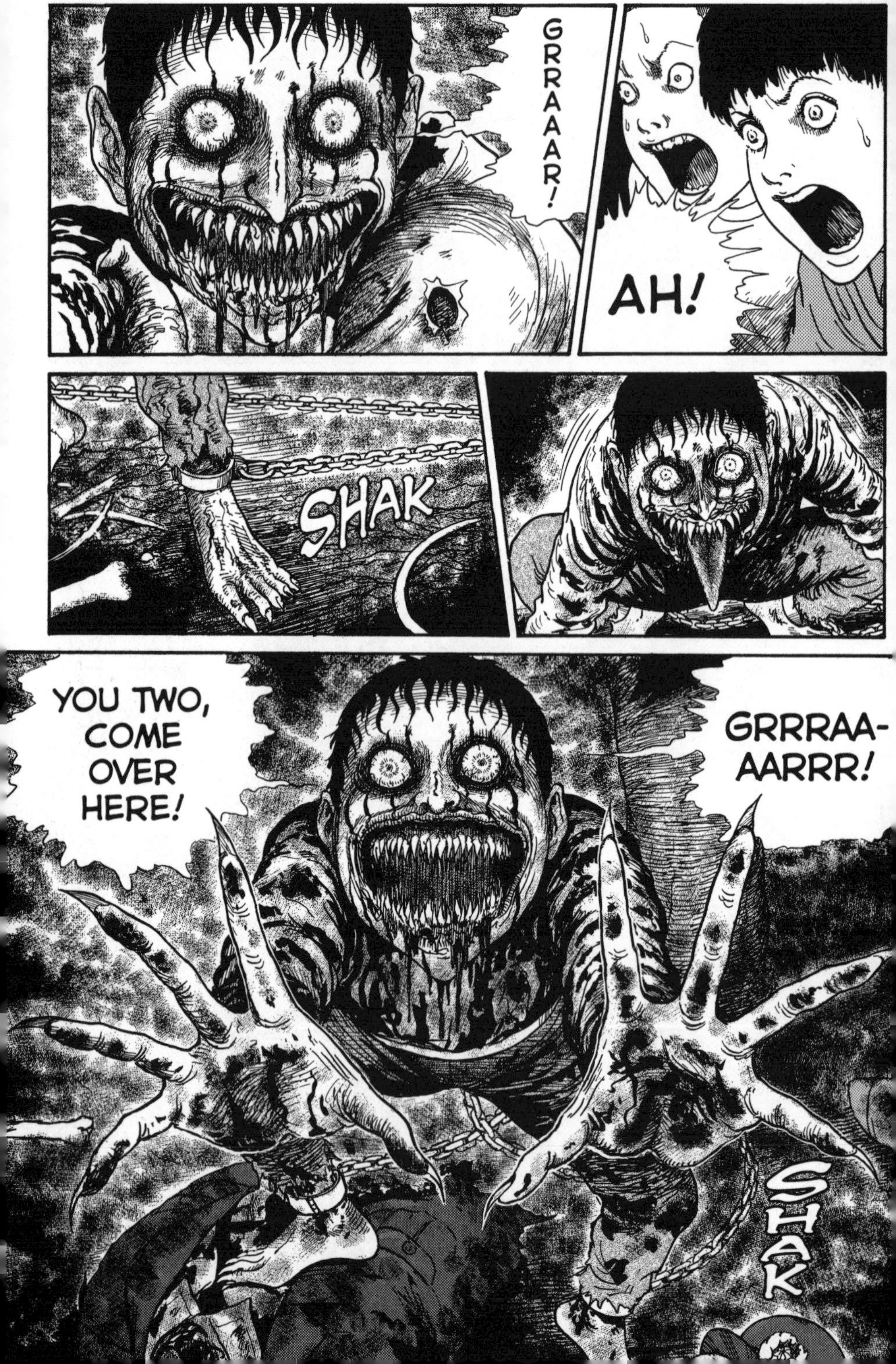
AH!
GRRAAAAR!
SHAK
GRRRAA-AARRR!
YOU TWO, COME OVER HERE!
SHAK

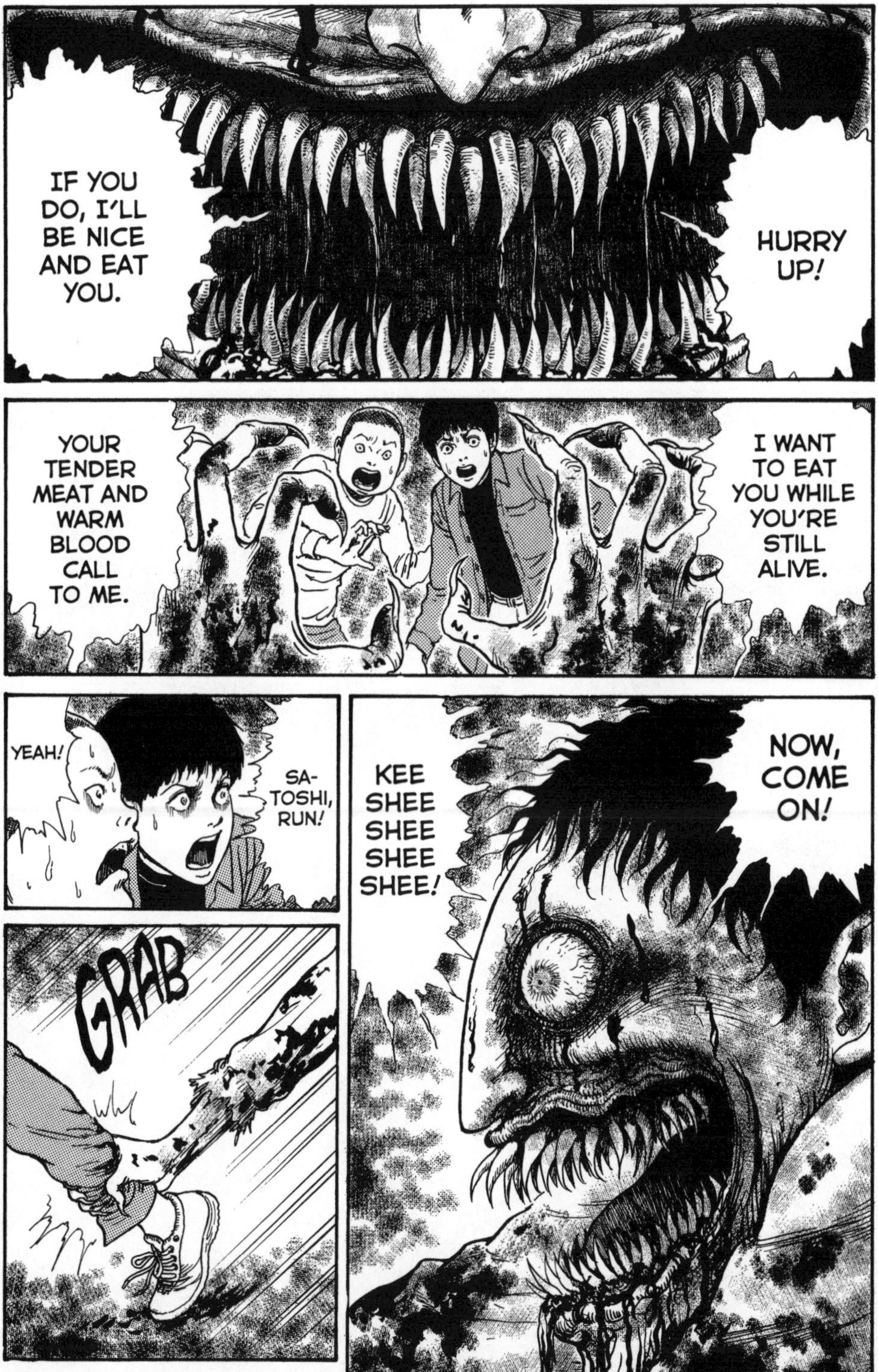
HURRY UP!
IF YOU DO, I'LL BE NICE AND EAT YOU.
I WANT TO EAT YOU WHILE YOU'RE STILL ALIVE.
YOUR TENDER MEAT AND WARM BLOOD CALL TO ME.
NOW, COME ON!
KEE SHEE SHEE SHEE SHEE!
SA-TOSHI, RUN!
YEAH!
GRAB

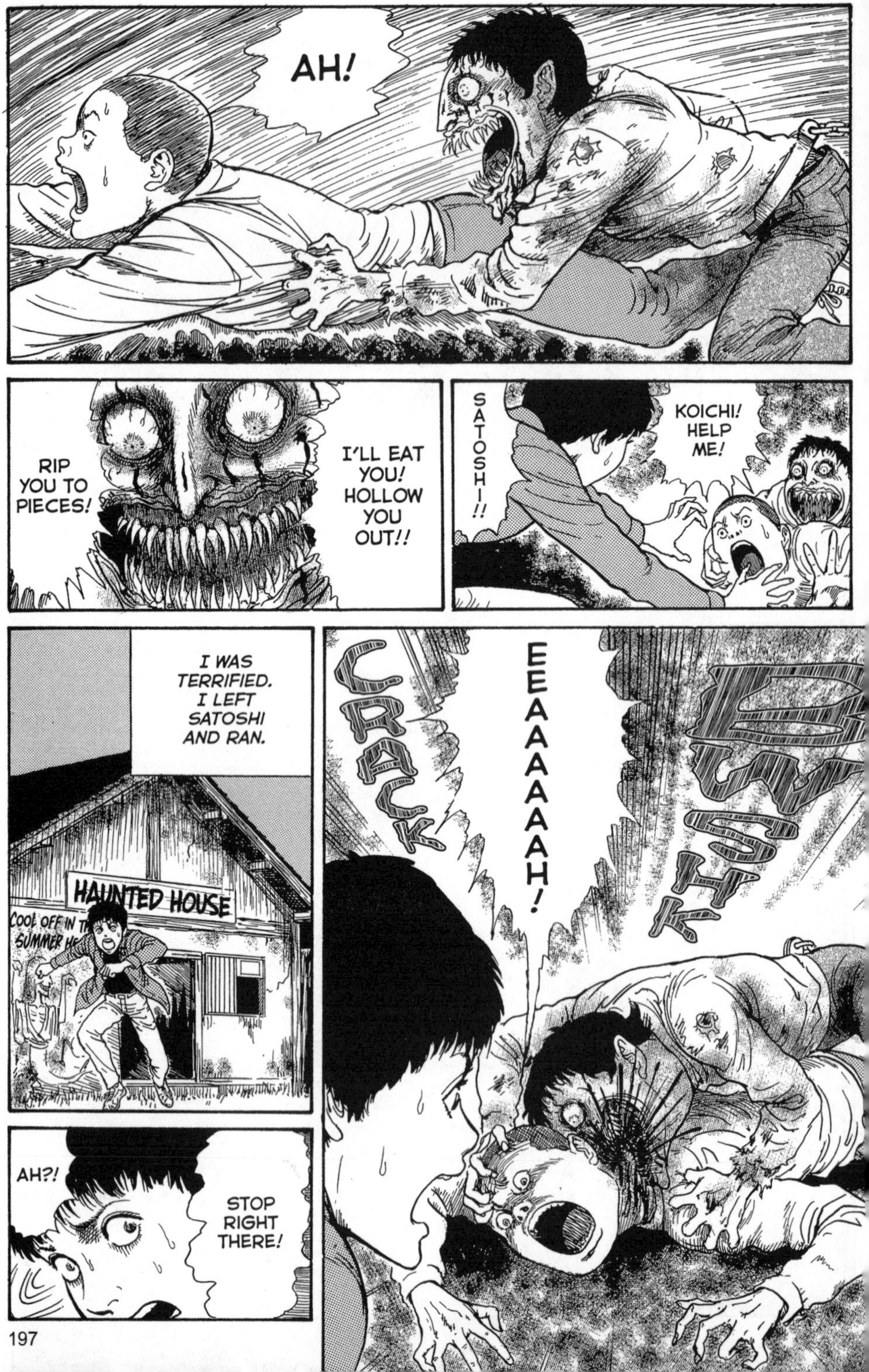
AH!
SATOSHI!!
KOICHI! HELP ME!
I'LL EAT YOU! HOLLOW YOU OUT!!
RIP YOU TO PIECES!
BWSHK
EEAAAAAAAH!
CRACK
I WAS TERRIFIED. I LEFT SATOSHI AND RAN.
HAUNTED HOUSE
STOP RIGHT THERE!
AH?!

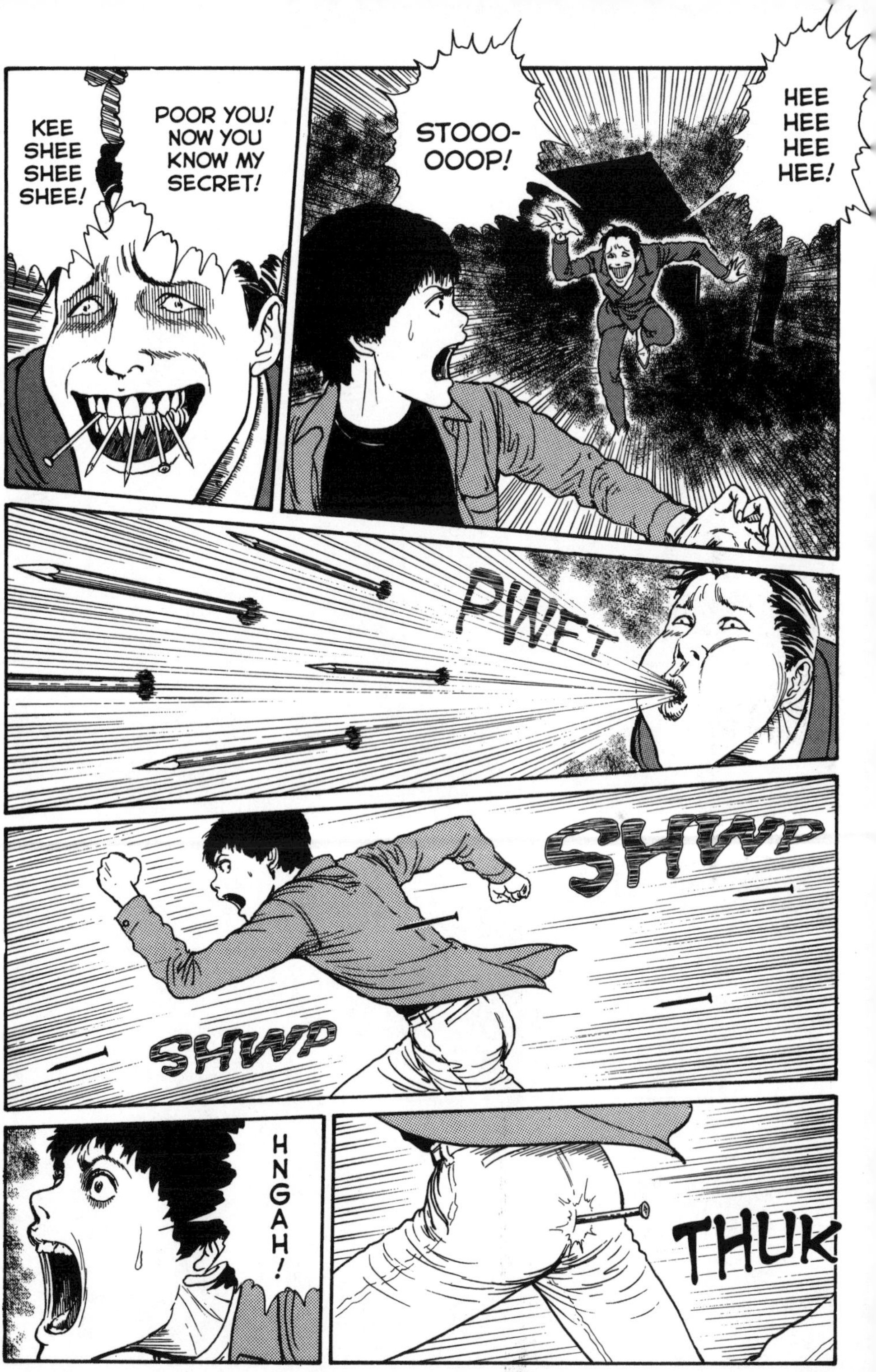
HEE HEE HEE HEE!
STOOO-OOOP!
POOR YOU! NOW YOU KNOW MY SECRET!
KEE SHEE SHEE SHEE!
PWFT
SHWP
SHWP
THUK
HNGAH!

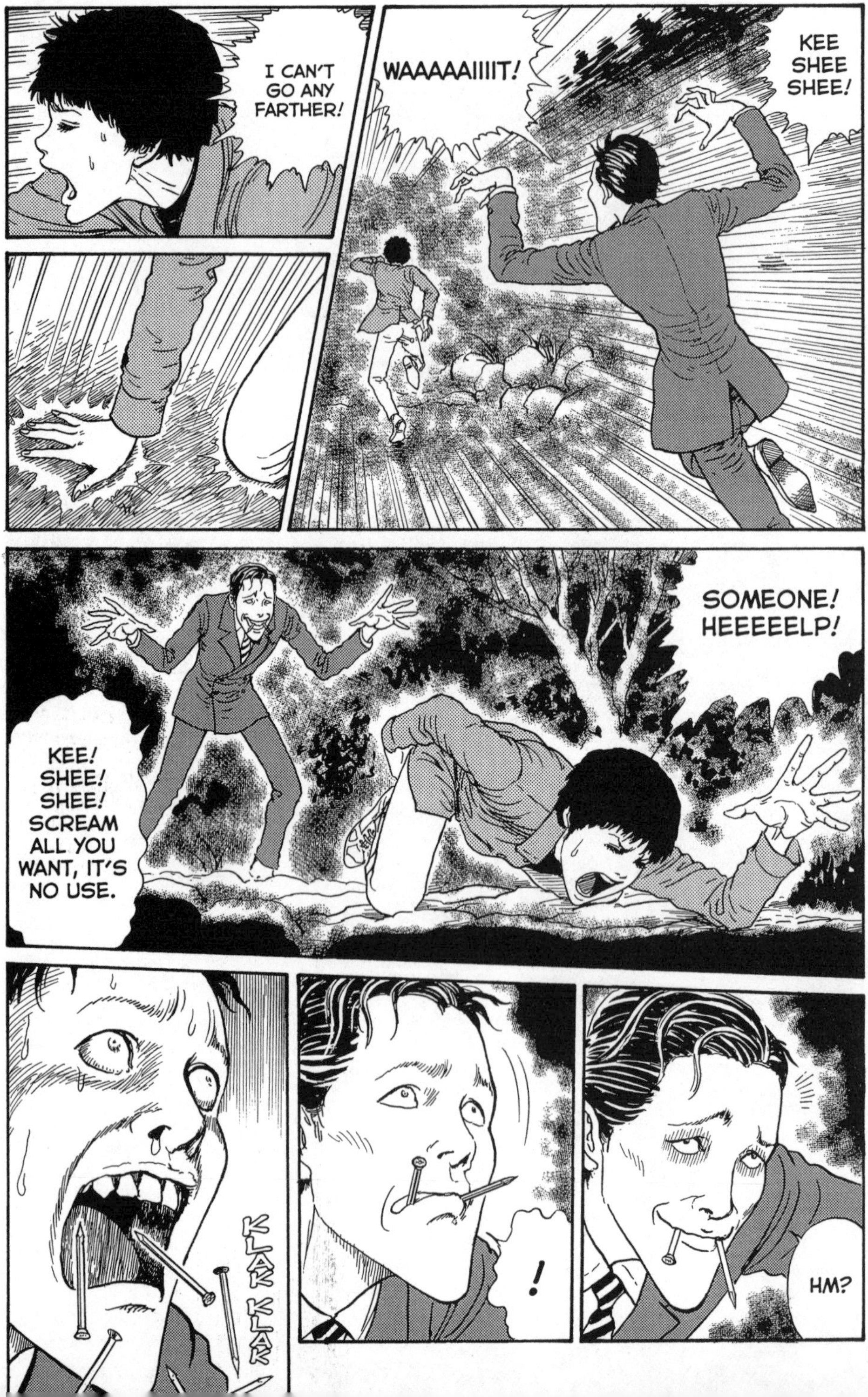
KEE SHEE SHEE!
WAAAAAIIIIT!
I CAN'T GO ANY FARTHER!
SOMEONE! HEEEEELP!
KEE! SHEE! SHEE! SCREAM ALL YOU WANT, IT'S NO USE.
HM?
!
KLAK KLAK

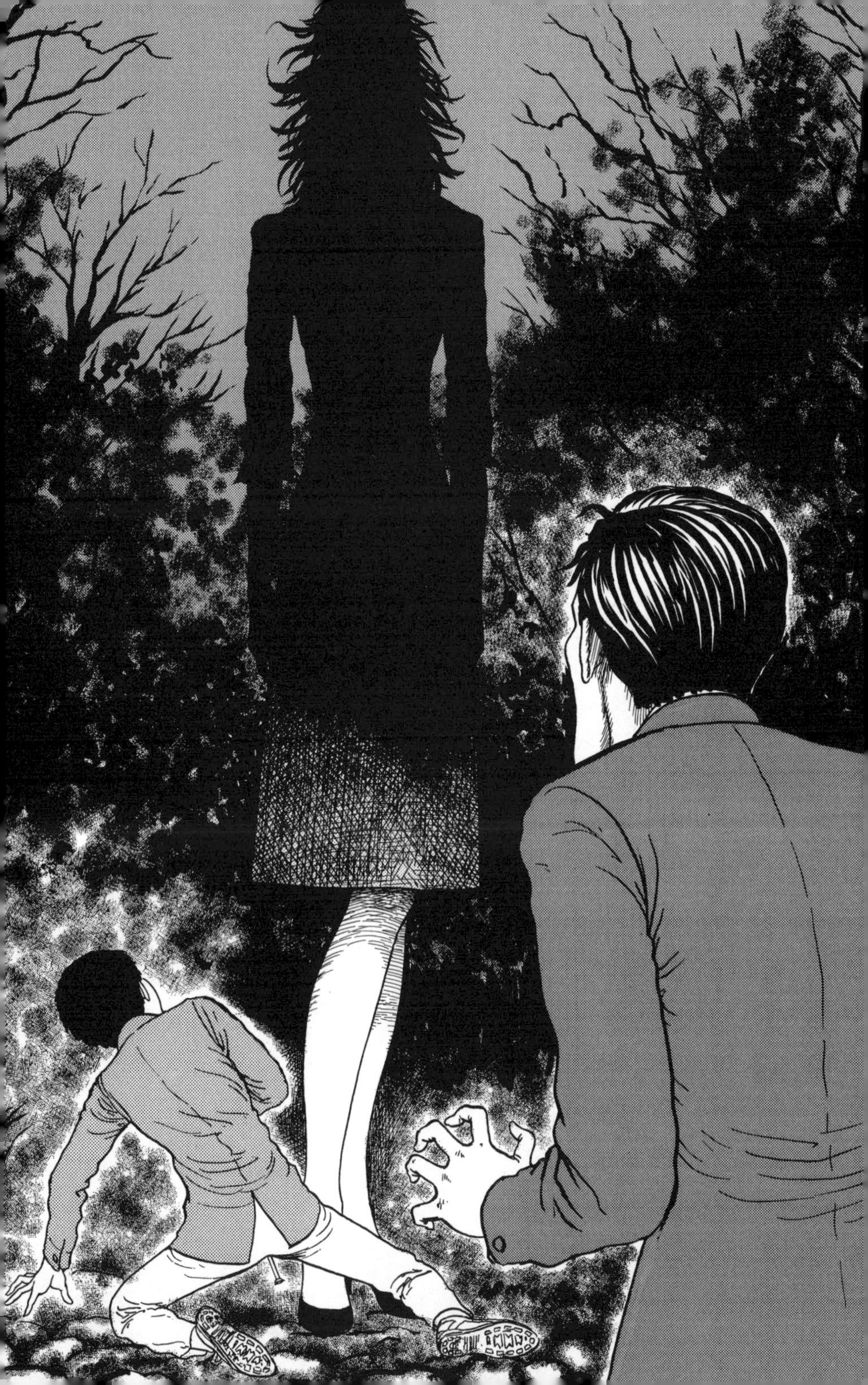

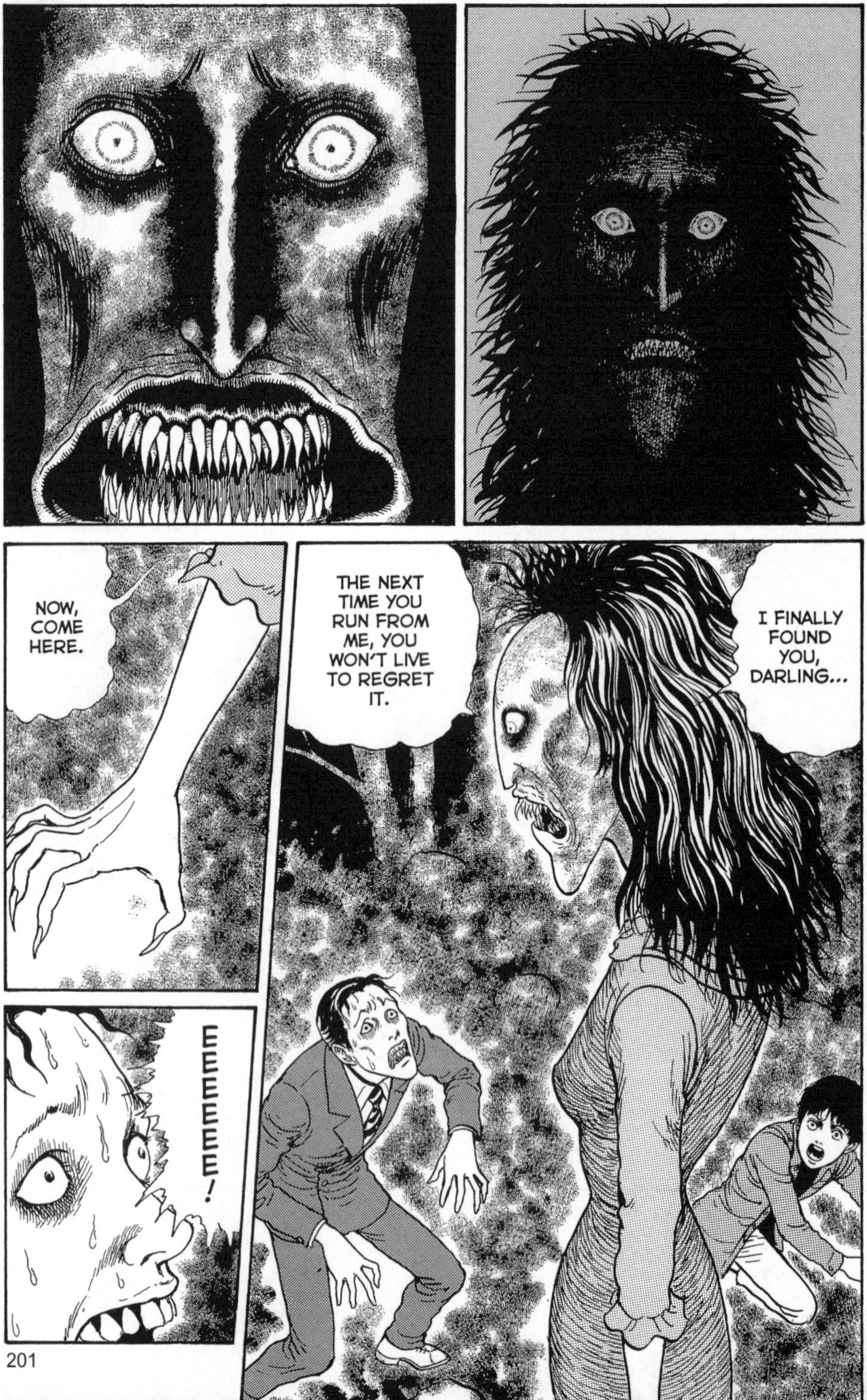
I FINALLY FOUND YOU, DARLING...
THE NEXT TIME YOU RUN FROM ME, YOU WON'T LIVE TO REGRET IT.
NOW, COME HERE.
EEEEEEE!

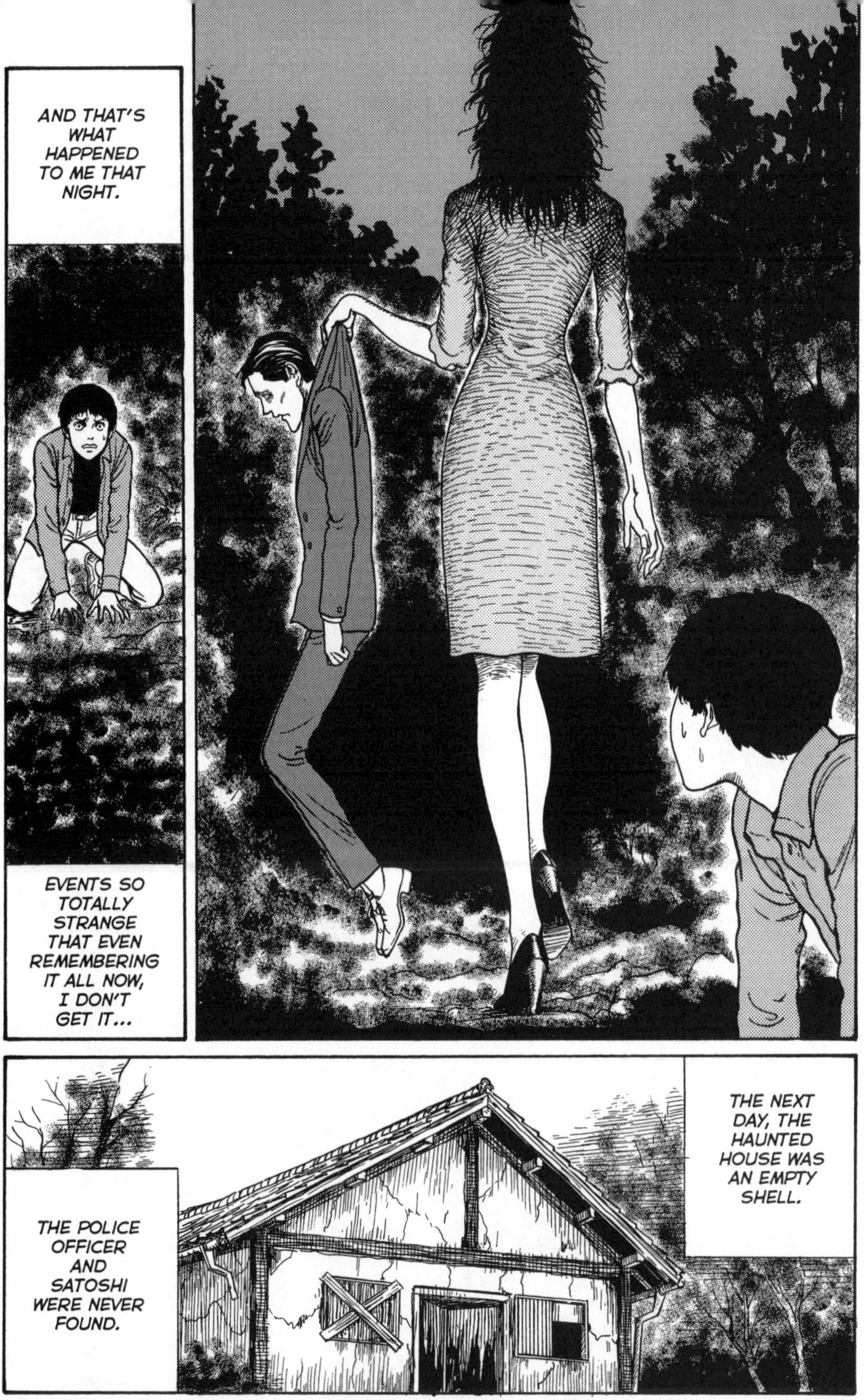
AND THAT'S WHAT HAPPENED TO ME THAT NIGHT.
EVENTS SO TOTALLY STRANGE THAT EVEN REMEMBERING IT ALL NOW, I DON'T GET IT...
THE NEXT DAY, THE HAUNTED HOUSE WAS AN EMPTY SHELL.
THE POLICE OFFICER AND SATOSHI WERE NEVER FOUND.

THE MYSTERY OF THE HAUNTED HOUSE / END

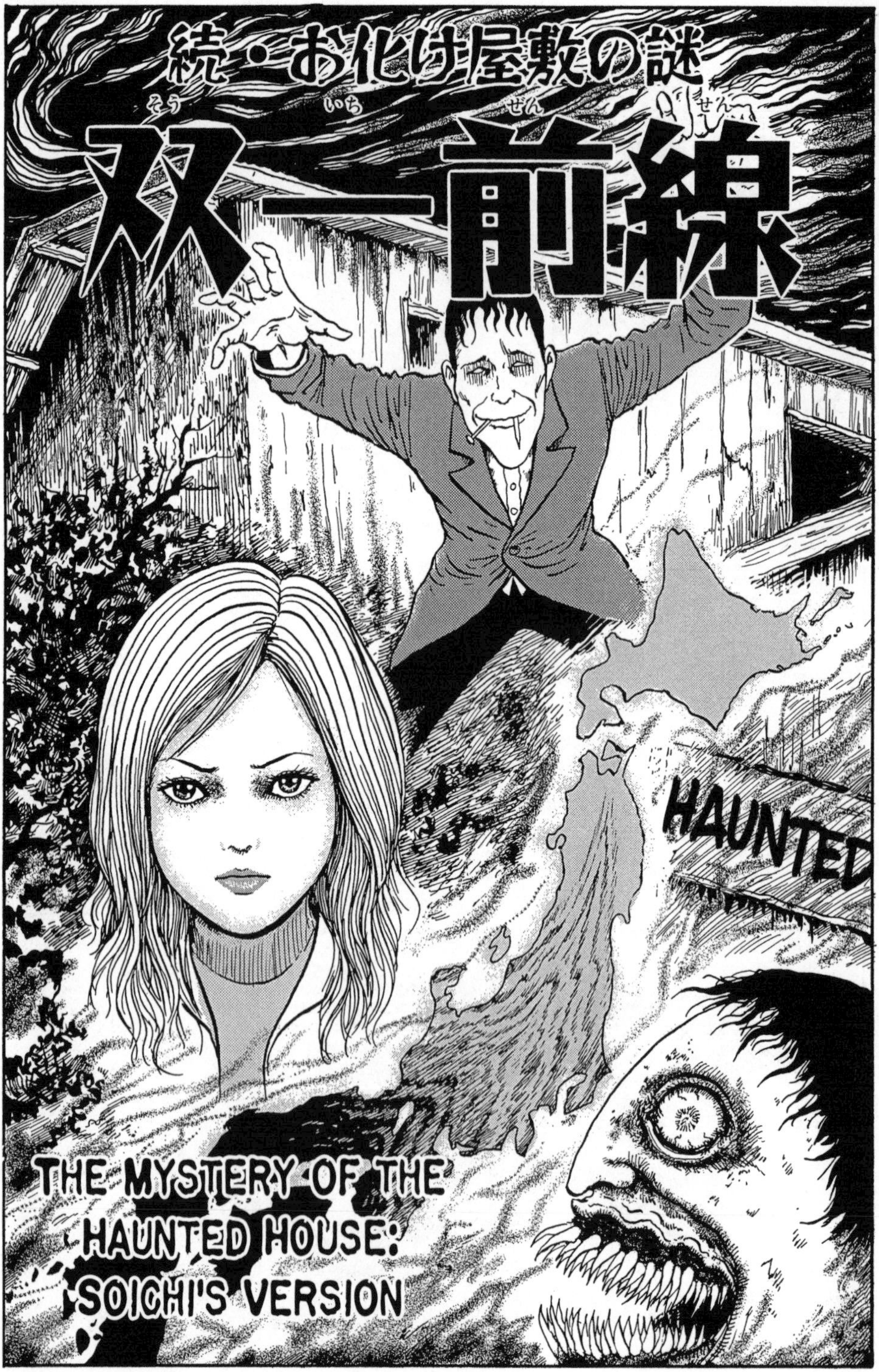
続・お化け屋敷の謎
そう いち ぜん せん
双一前線
HAUNTED
THE MYSTERY OF THE HAUNTED HOUSE: SOICHI'S VERSION

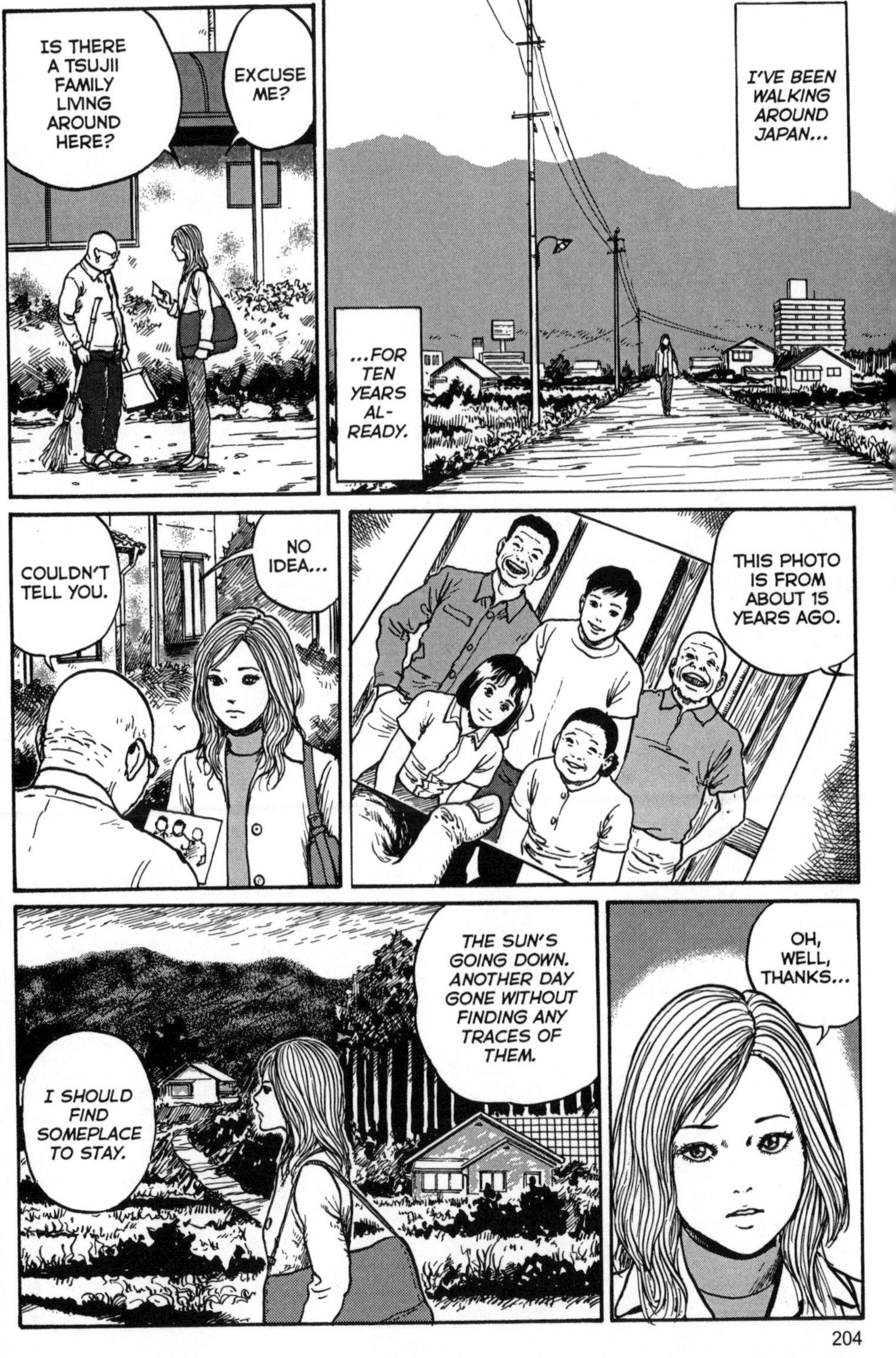
I'VE BEEN WALKING AROUND JAPAN...
...FOR TEN YEARS AL-READY.
EXCUSE ME?
IS THERE A TSUJII FAMILY LIVING AROUND HERE?
THIS PHOTO IS FROM ABOUT 15 YEARS AGO.
NO IDEA...
COULDN'T TELL YOU.
OH, WELL, THANKS...
THE SUN'S GOING DOWN. ANOTHER DAY GONE WITHOUT FINDING ANY TRACES OF THEM.
I SHOULD FIND SOMEPLACE TO STAY.

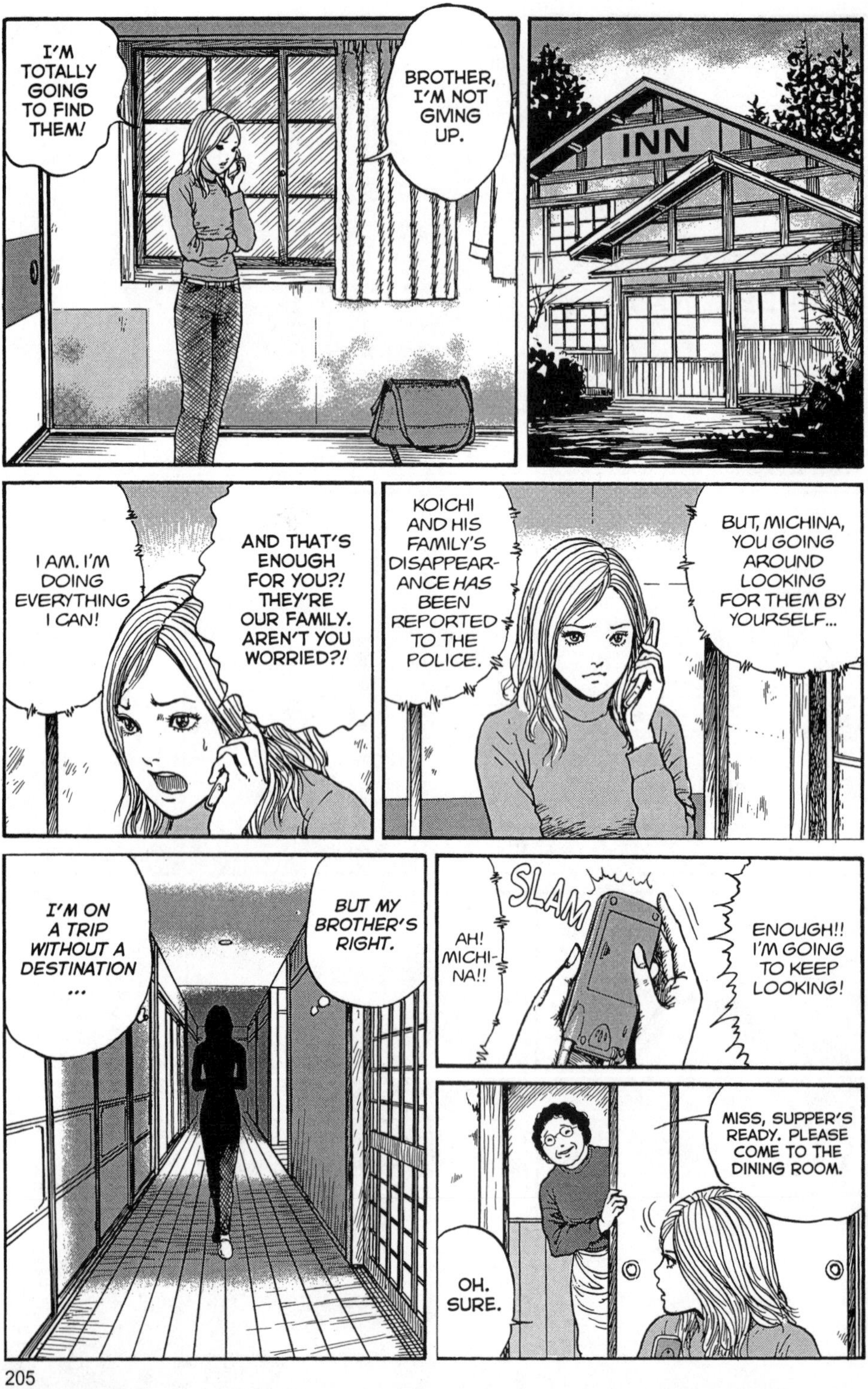
INN
BROTHER, I'M NOT GIVING UP.
I'M TOTALLY GOING TO FIND THEM!
BUT, MICHINA, YOU GOING AROUND LOOKING FOR THEM BY YOURSELF...
KOICHI AND HIS FAMILY'S DISAPPEARANCE *HAS* BEEN REPORTED TO THE POLICE.
AND THAT'S ENOUGH FOR YOU?! THEY'RE OUR FAMILY. AREN'T YOU WORRIED?!
I AM. I'M DOING EVERYTHING I CAN!
ENOUGH!! I'M GOING TO KEEP LOOKING!
SLAM
AH! MICHINA!!
MISS, SUPPER'S READY. PLEASE COME TO THE DINING ROOM.
OH. SURE.
BUT MY BROTHER'S RIGHT.
I'M ON A TRIP WITHOUT A DESTINATION ...

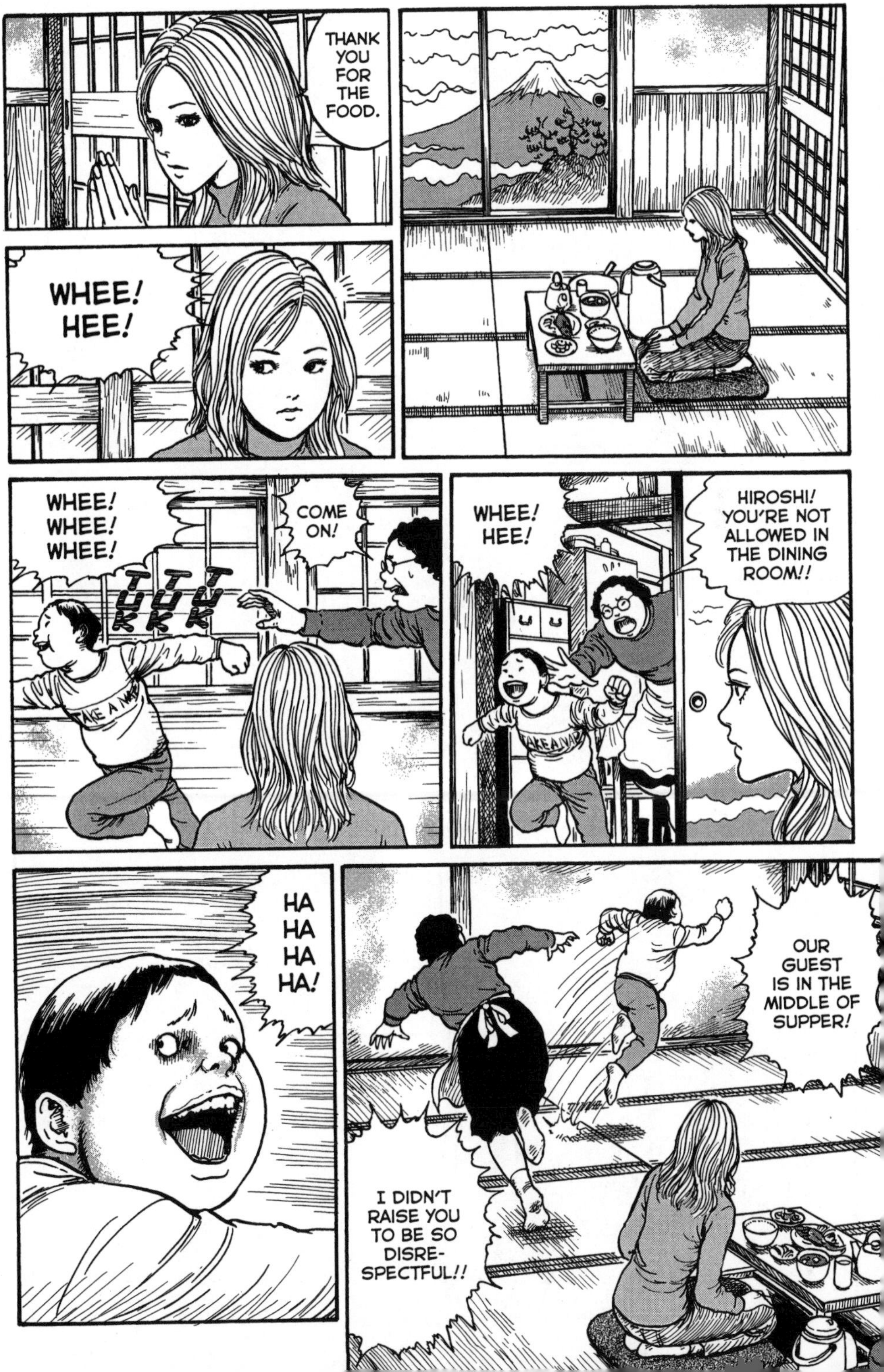
THANK YOU FOR THE FOOD.
WHEE! HEE!
HIROSHI! YOU'RE NOT ALLOWED IN THE DINING ROOM!!
WHEE! HEE!
COME ON!
WHEE! WHEE! WHEE!
TUK TUK TUK
OUR GUEST IS IN THE MIDDLE OF SUPPER!
I DIDN'T RAISE YOU TO BE SO DISRE-SPECTFUL!!
HA HA HA HA!

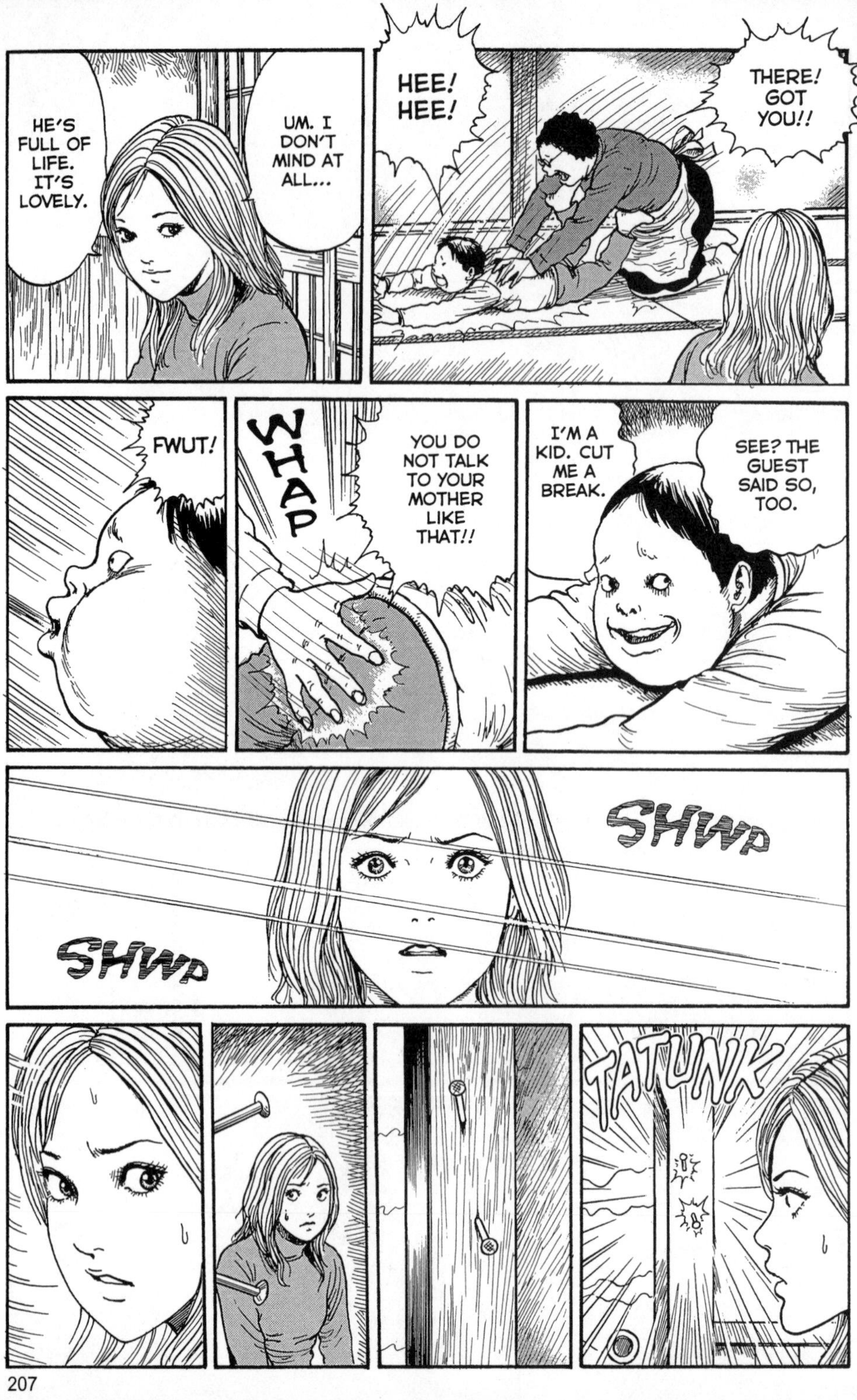
THERE! GOT YOU!!
HEE! HEE!
UM. I DON'T MIND AT ALL...
HE'S FULL OF LIFE. IT'S LOVELY.
SEE? THE GUEST SAID SO, TOO.
I'M A KID. CUT ME A BREAK.
YOU DO NOT TALK TO YOUR MOTHER LIKE THAT!!
WHAP
FWUT!
SHWP
SHWP
TATUNK

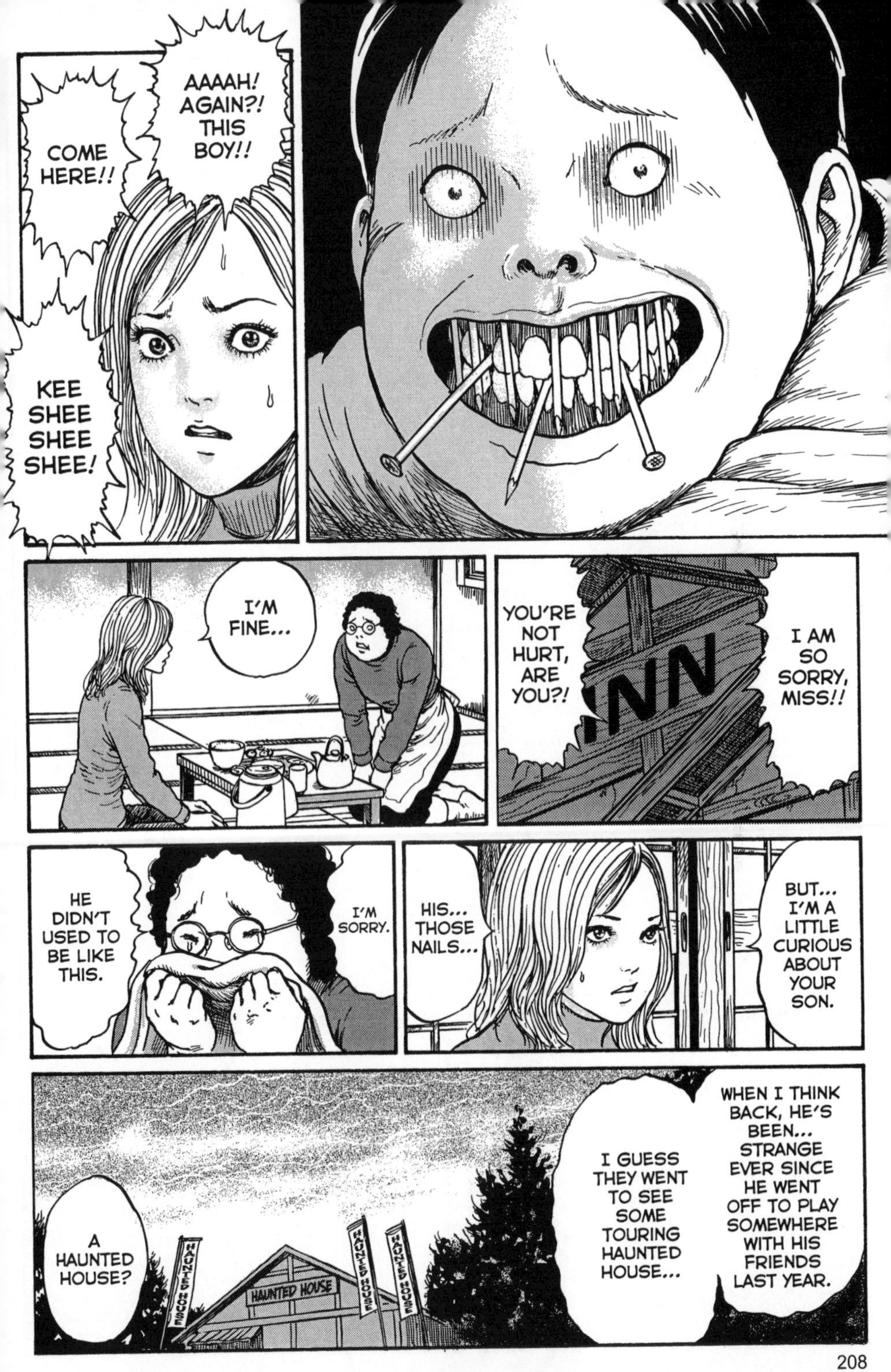
AAAAH! AGAIN?! THIS BOY!!
COME HERE!!
KEE SHEE SHEE SHEE!
INN
I AM SO SORRY, MISS!!
YOU'RE NOT HURT, ARE YOU?!
I'M FINE...
BUT... I'M A LITTLE CURIOUS ABOUT YOUR SON.
HIS... THOSE NAILS...
I'M SORRY.
HE DIDN'T USED TO BE LIKE THIS.
WHEN I THINK BACK, HE'S BEEN... STRANGE EVER SINCE HE WENT OFF TO PLAY SOMEWHERE WITH HIS FRIENDS LAST YEAR.
I GUESS THEY WENT TO SEE SOME TOURING HAUNTED HOUSE...
HAUNTED HOUSE
HAUNTED HOUSE
HAUNTED HOUSE
HAUNTED HOUSE
A HAUNTED HOUSE?

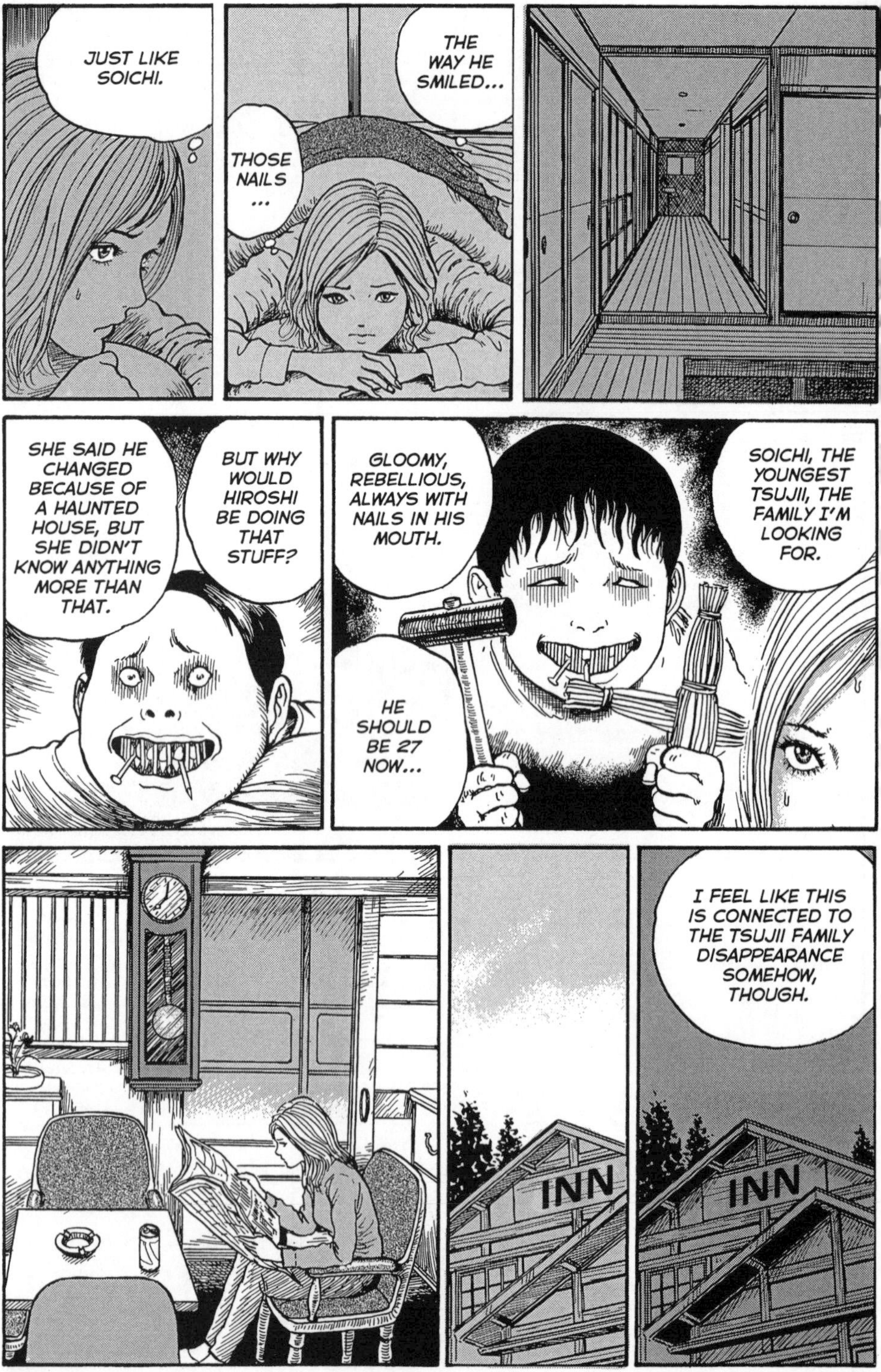
THE WAY HE SMILED...
THOSE NAILS ...
JUST LIKE SOICHI.
SOICHI, THE YOUNGEST TSUJII, THE FAMILY I'M LOOKING FOR.
GLOOMY, REBELLIOUS, ALWAYS WITH NAILS IN HIS MOUTH.
HE SHOULD BE 27 NOW...
BUT WHY WOULD HIROSHI BE DOING THAT STUFF?
SHE SAID HE CHANGED BECAUSE OF A HAUNTED HOUSE, BUT SHE DIDN'T KNOW ANYTHING MORE THAN THAT.
I FEEL LIKE THIS IS CONNECTED TO THE TSUJII FAMILY DISAPPEARANCE SOMEHOW, THOUGH.
INN
INN

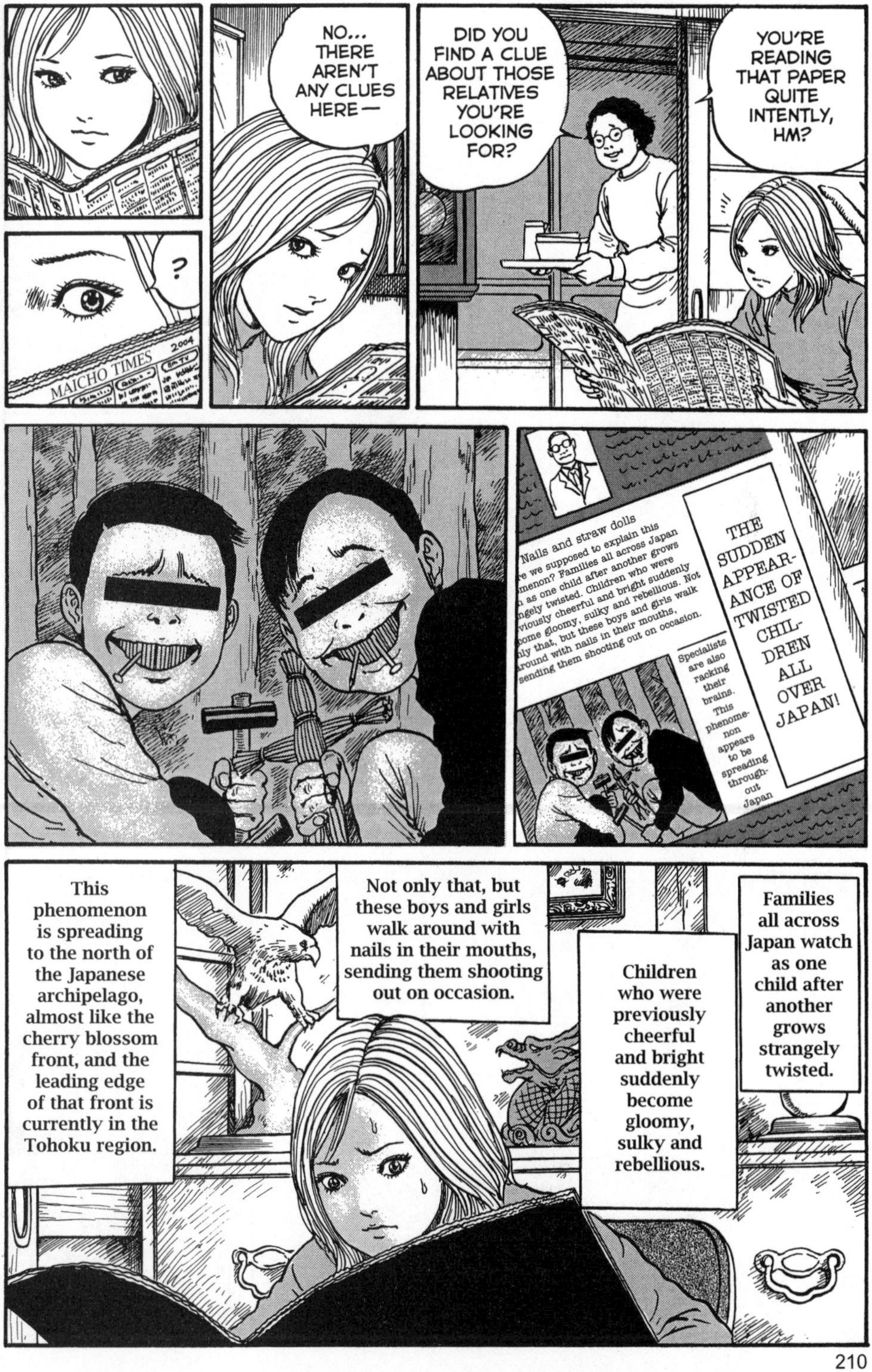
YOU'RE READING THAT PAPER QUITE INTENTLY, HM?
DID YOU FIND A CLUE ABOUT THOSE RELATIVES YOU'RE LOOKING FOR?
NO... THERE AREN'T ANY CLUES HERE—
?
2004
MAICHO TIMES
THE SUDDEN APPEAR-ANCE OF TWISTED CHIL-DREN ALL OVER JAPAN!
Nails and straw dolls
e we supposed to explain this
menon? Families all across Japan
n as one child after another grows
ngely twisted. Children who were
viously cheerful and bright suddenly
ome gloomy, sulky and rebellious. Not
ly that, but these boys and girls walk
around with nails in their mouths,
sending them shooting out on occasion.
Specialists are also racking their brains. This phenome-non appears to be spreading through-out Japan
Families all across Japan watch as one child after another grows strangely twisted.
Children who were previously cheerful and bright suddenly become gloomy, sulky and rebellious.
Not only that, but these boys and girls walk around with nails in their mouths, sending them shooting out on occasion.
This phenomenon is spreading to the north of the Japanese archipelago, almost like the cherry blossom front, and the leading edge of that front is currently in the Tohoku region.

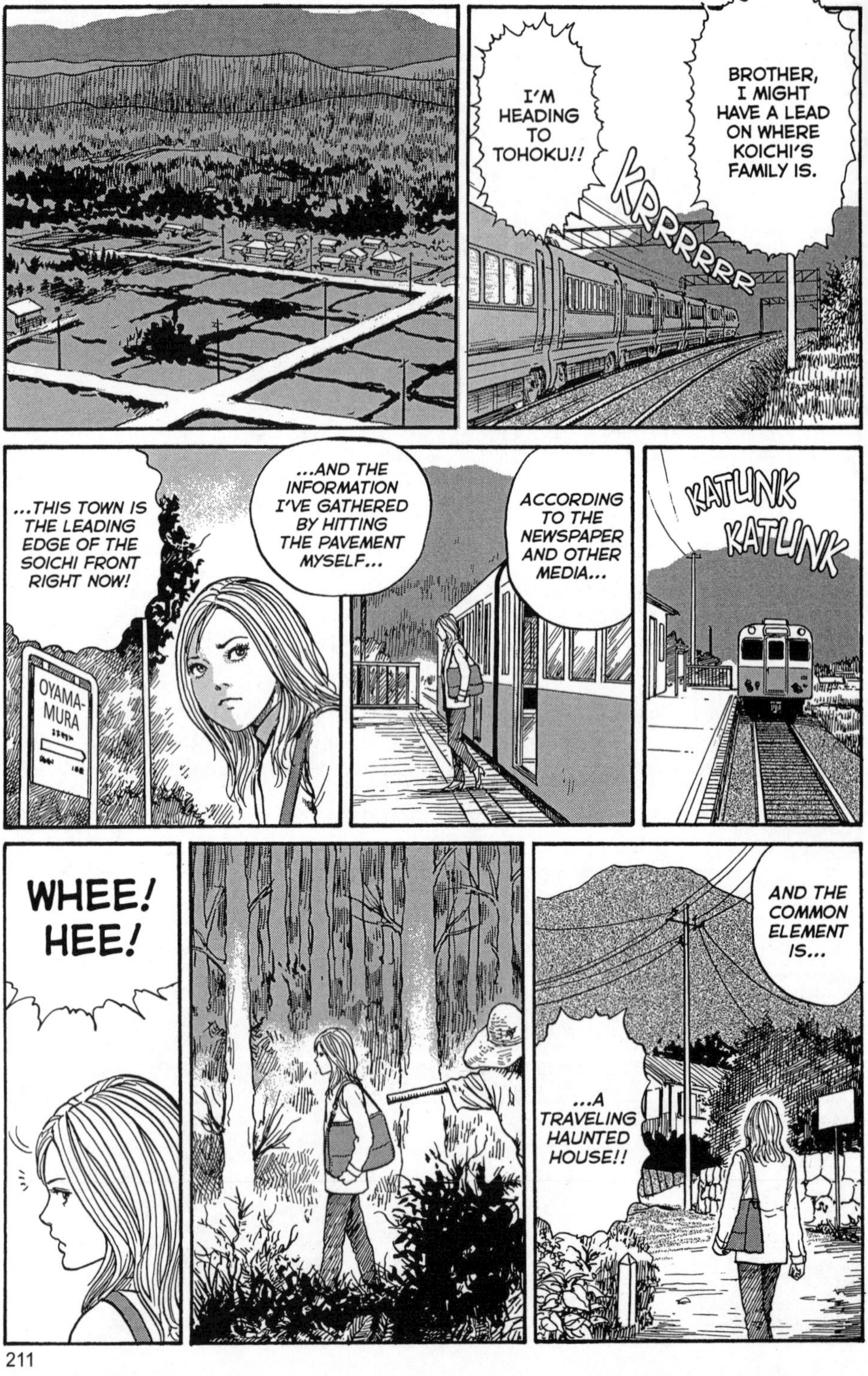
BROTHER, I MIGHT HAVE A LEAD ON WHERE KOICHI'S FAMILY IS.
I'M HEADING TO TOHOKU!!
KRRRRRRR
KATUNK
KATUNK
ACCORDING TO THE NEWSPAPER AND OTHER MEDIA...
...AND THE INFORMATION I'VE GATHERED BY HITTING THE PAVEMENT MYSELF...
...THIS TOWN IS THE LEADING EDGE OF THE SOICHI FRONT RIGHT NOW!
OYAMA-MURA
AND THE COMMON ELEMENT IS...
...A TRAVELING HAUNTED HOUSE!!
WHEE! HEE!

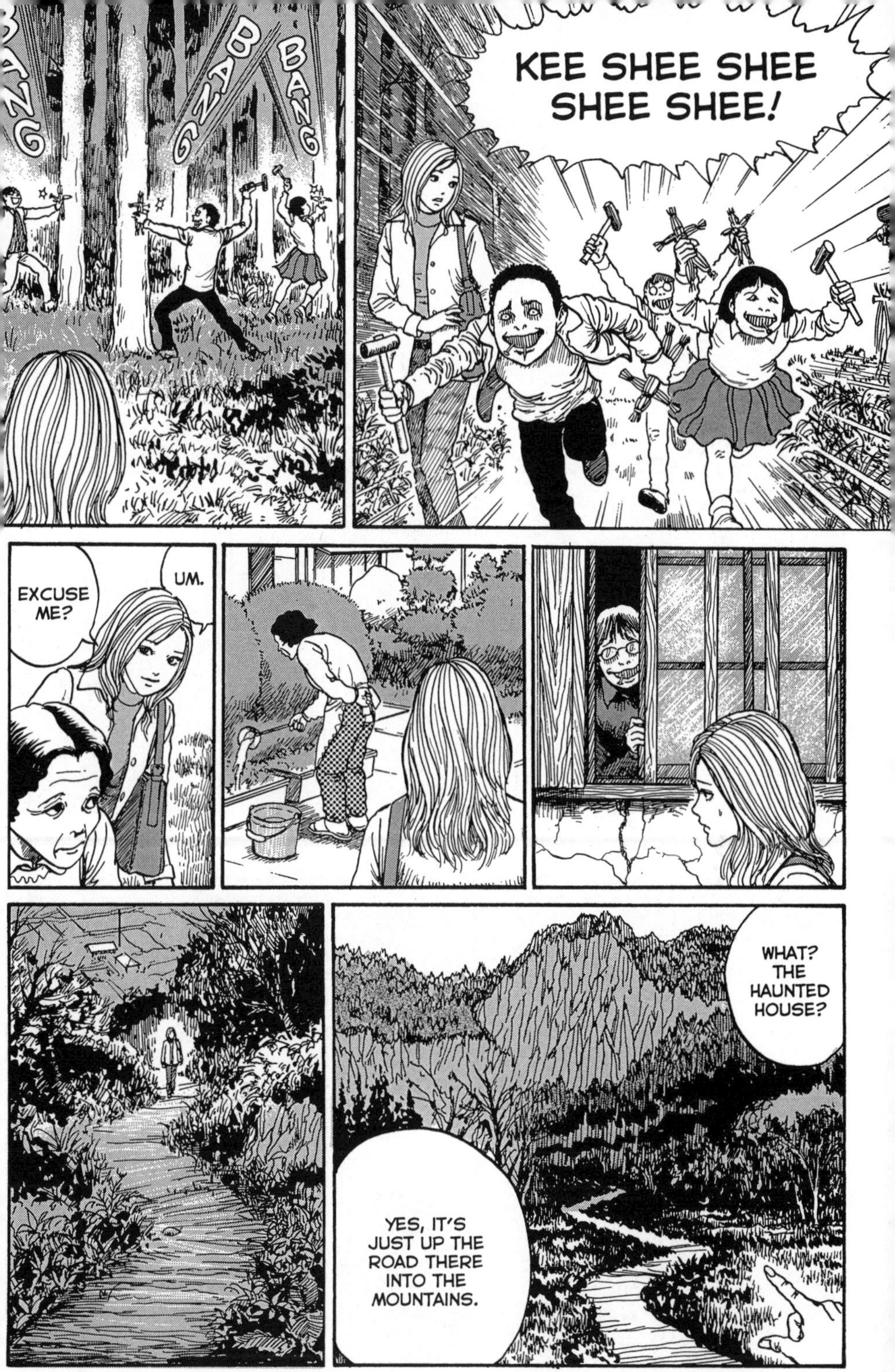
KEE SHEE SHEE SHEE SHEE!
BANG
BANG
BANG
UM.
EXCUSE ME?
WHAT? THE HAUNTED HOUSE?
YES, IT'S JUST UP THE ROAD THERE INTO THE MOUNTAINS.

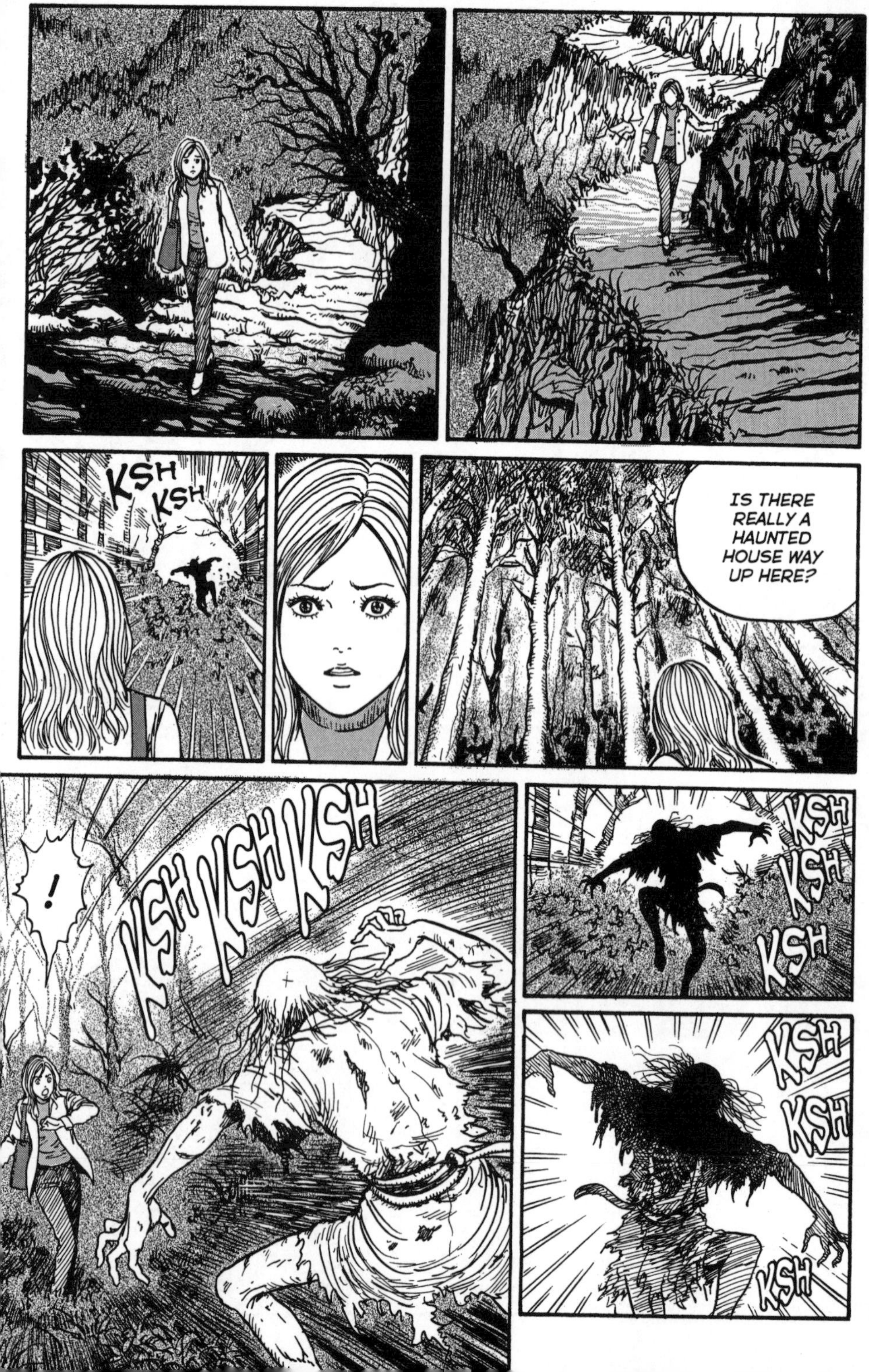
IS THERE REALLY A HAUNTED HOUSE WAY UP HERE?
KSH KSH
KSH KSH KSH
KSH KSH KSH
KSH KSH KSH
!

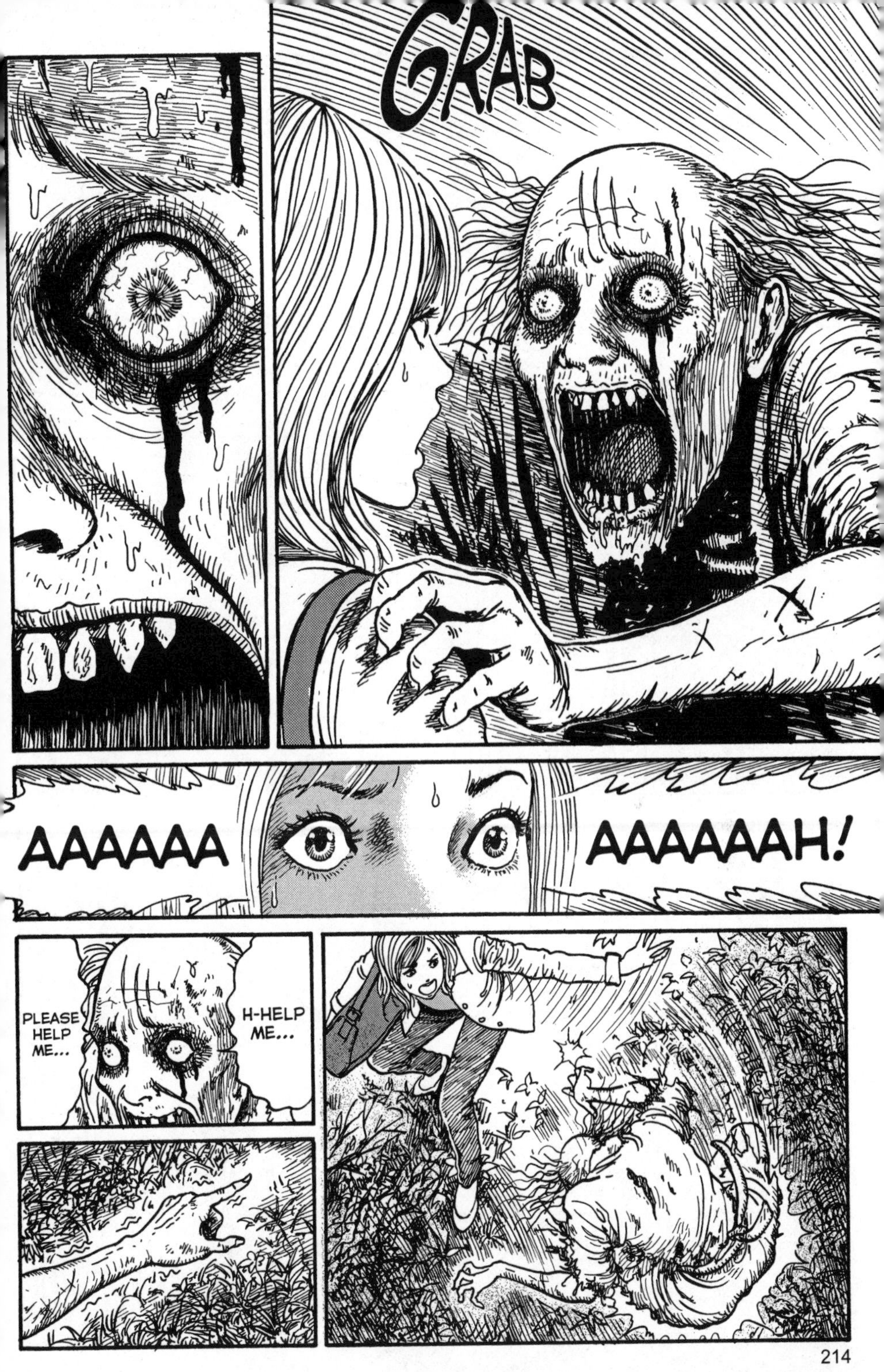
GRAB
AAAAAA
AAAAAAH!
H-HELP ME...
PLEASE HELP ME...

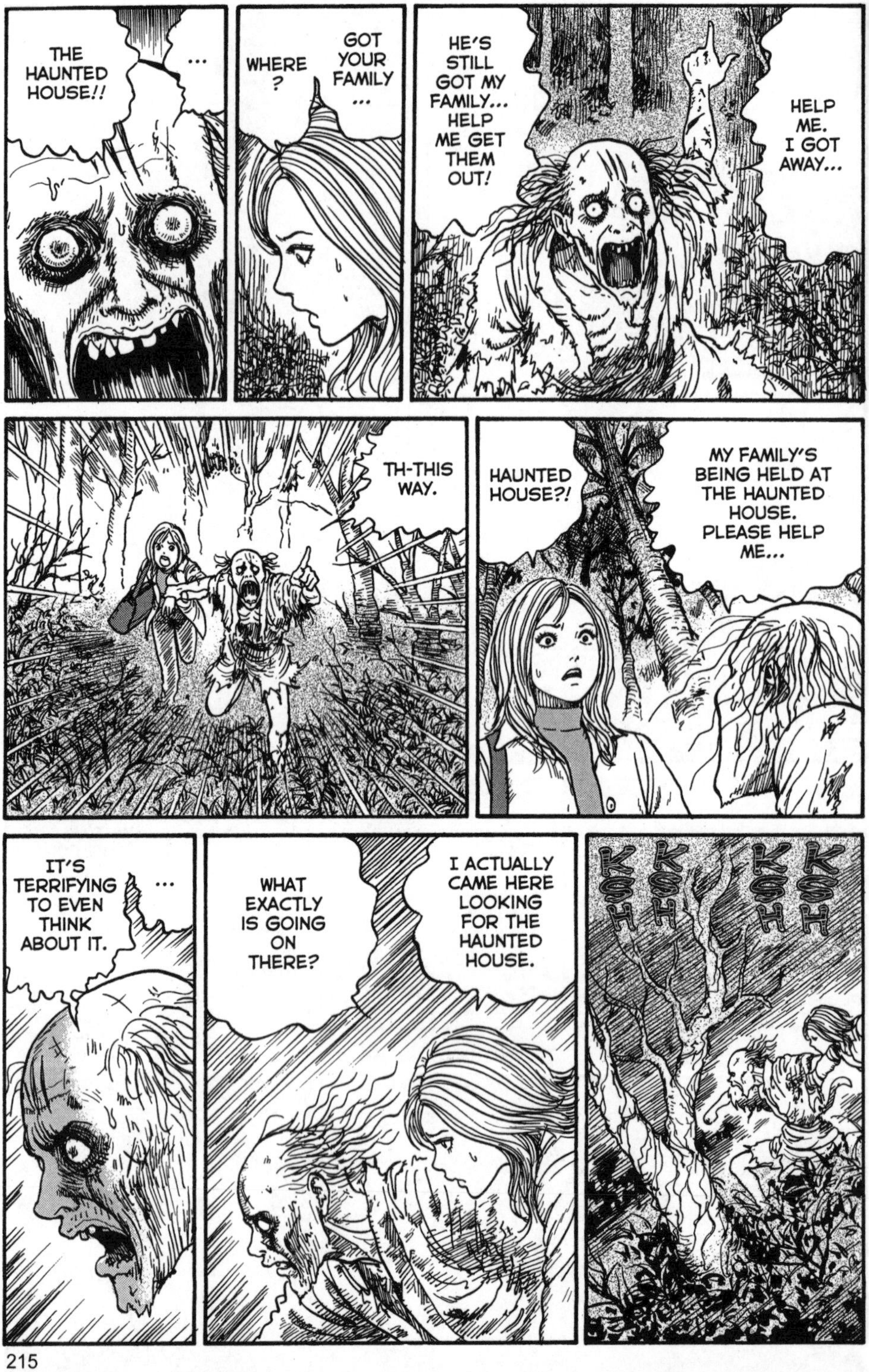
HELP ME. I GOT AWAY...
HE'S STILL GOT MY FAMILY... HELP ME GET THEM OUT!
GOT YOUR FAMILY...
WHERE?
...
THE HAUNTED HOUSE!!
MY FAMILY'S BEING HELD AT THE HAUNTED HOUSE. PLEASE HELP ME...
HAUNTED HOUSE?!
TH-THIS WAY.
KSH KSH KSH KSH
I ACTUALLY CAME HERE LOOKING FOR THE HAUNTED HOUSE.
WHAT EXACTLY IS GOING ON THERE?
...
IT'S TERRIFYING TO EVEN THINK ABOUT IT.

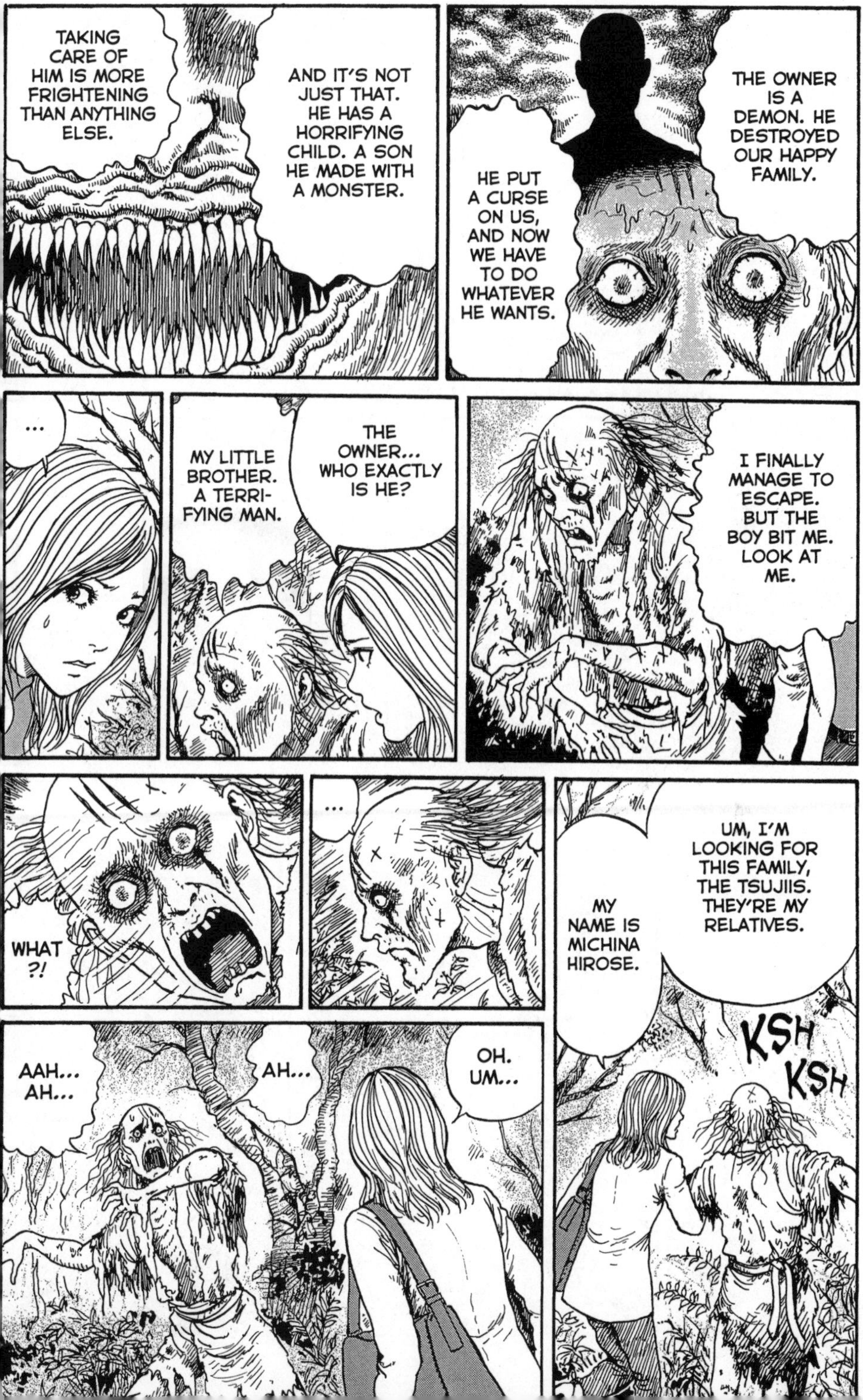
THE OWNER IS A DEMON. HE DESTROYED OUR HAPPY FAMILY.
HE PUT A CURSE ON US, AND NOW WE HAVE TO DO WHATEVER HE WANTS.
AND IT'S NOT JUST THAT. HE HAS A HORRIFYING CHILD. A SON HE MADE WITH A MONSTER.
TAKING CARE OF HIM IS MORE FRIGHTENING THAN ANYTHING ELSE.
I FINALLY MANAGE TO ESCAPE. BUT THE BOY BIT ME. LOOK AT ME.
THE OWNER... WHO EXACTLY IS HE?
MY LITTLE BROTHER. A TERRI- FYING MAN.
...
UM, I'M LOOKING FOR THIS FAMILY, THE TSUJIIS. THEY'RE MY RELATIVES.
MY NAME IS MICHINA HIROSE.
KSH KSH
...
WHAT ?!
OH. UM...
AH...
AAH... AH...

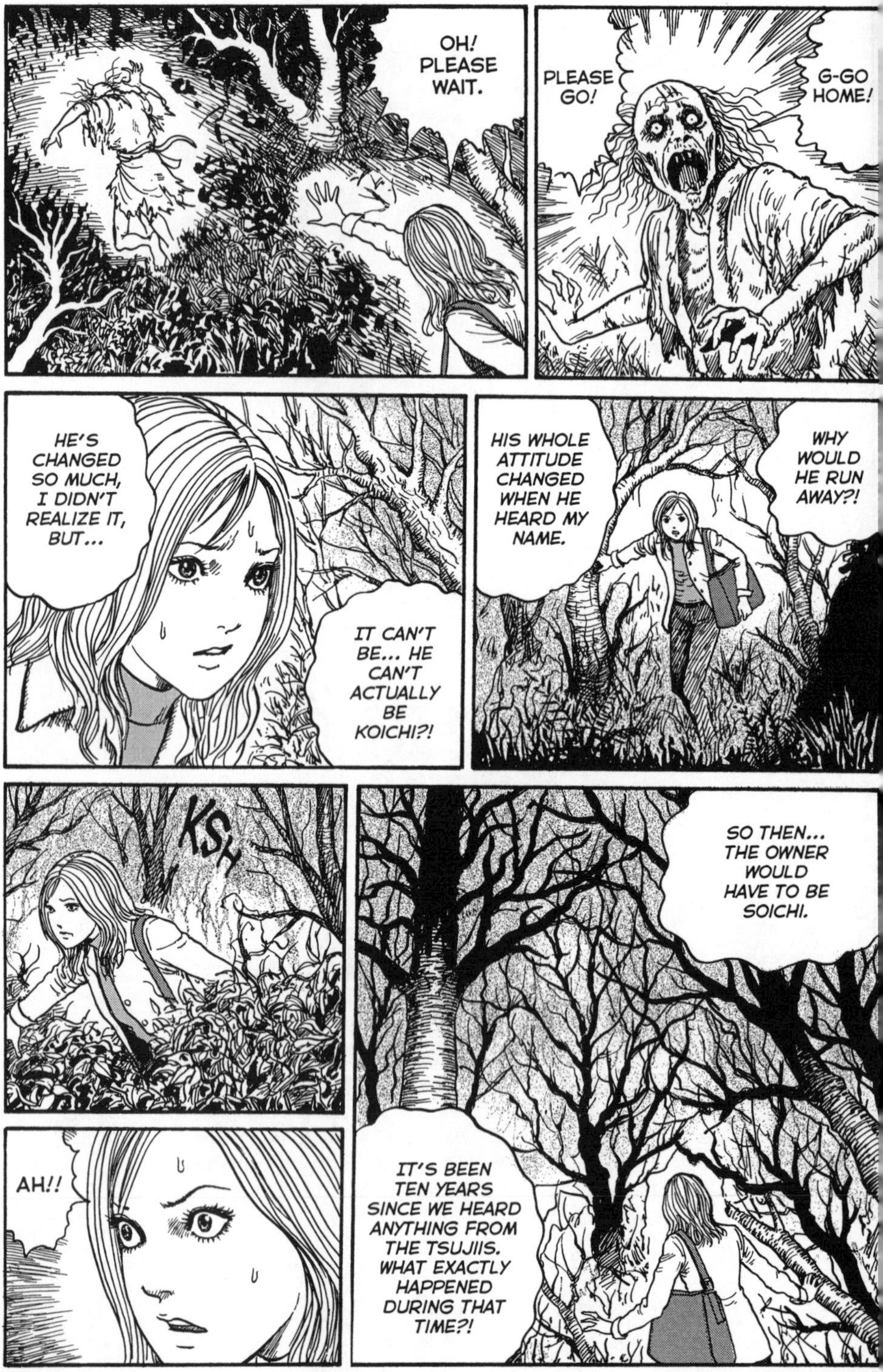
G-GO HOME!
PLEASE GO!
OH! PLEASE WAIT.
WHY WOULD HE RUN AWAY?!
HIS WHOLE ATTITUDE CHANGED WHEN HE HEARD MY NAME.
HE'S CHANGED SO MUCH, I DIDN'T REALIZE IT, BUT...
IT CAN'T BE... HE CAN'T ACTUALLY BE KOICHI?!
SO THEN... THE OWNER WOULD HAVE TO BE SOICHI.
IT'S BEEN TEN YEARS SINCE WE HEARD ANYTHING FROM THE TSUJIIS. WHAT EXACTLY HAPPENED DURING THAT TIME?!
KSH
AH!!

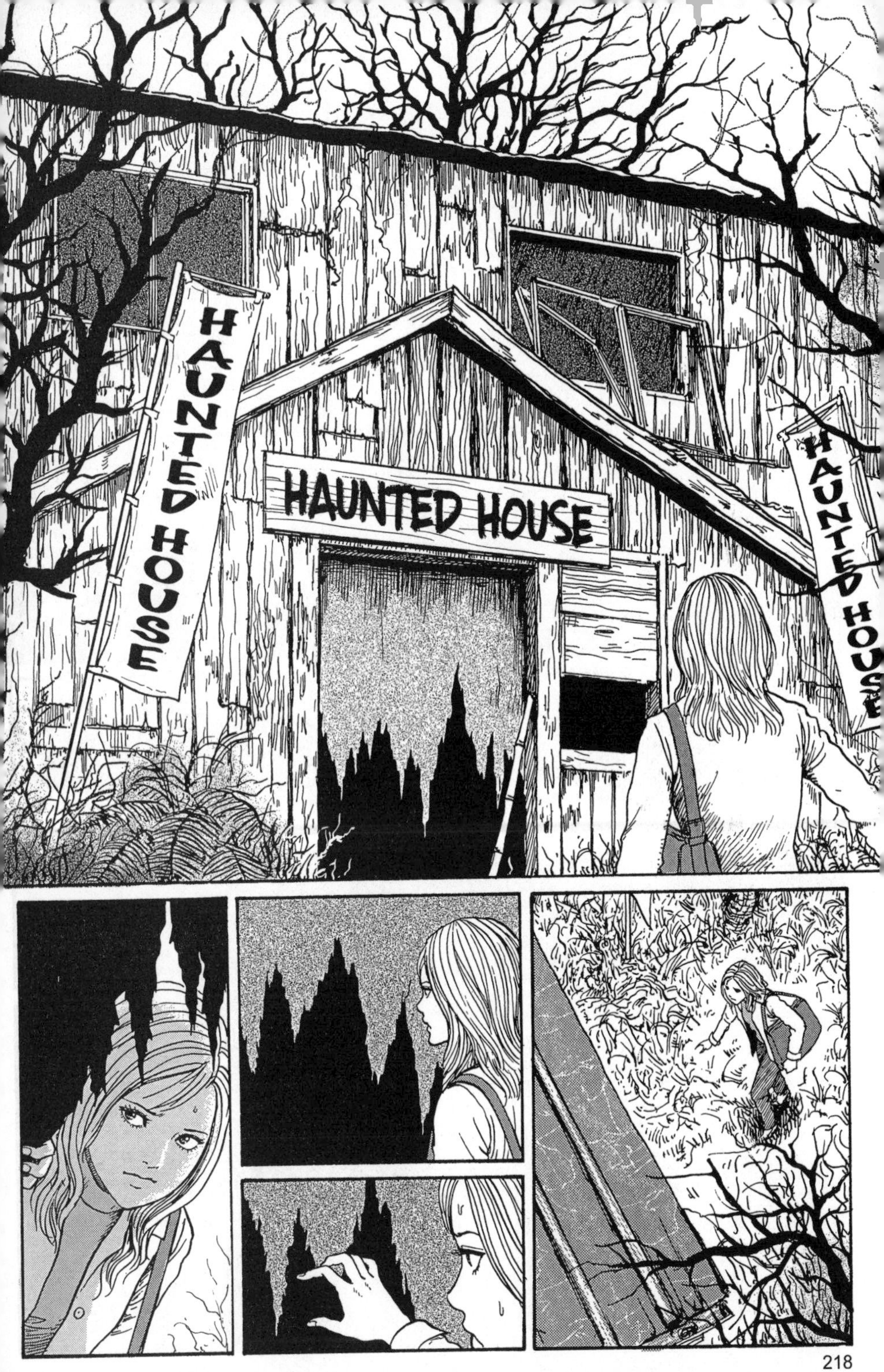
HAUNTED HOUSE
HAUNTED HOUSE
HAUNTED HOUSE

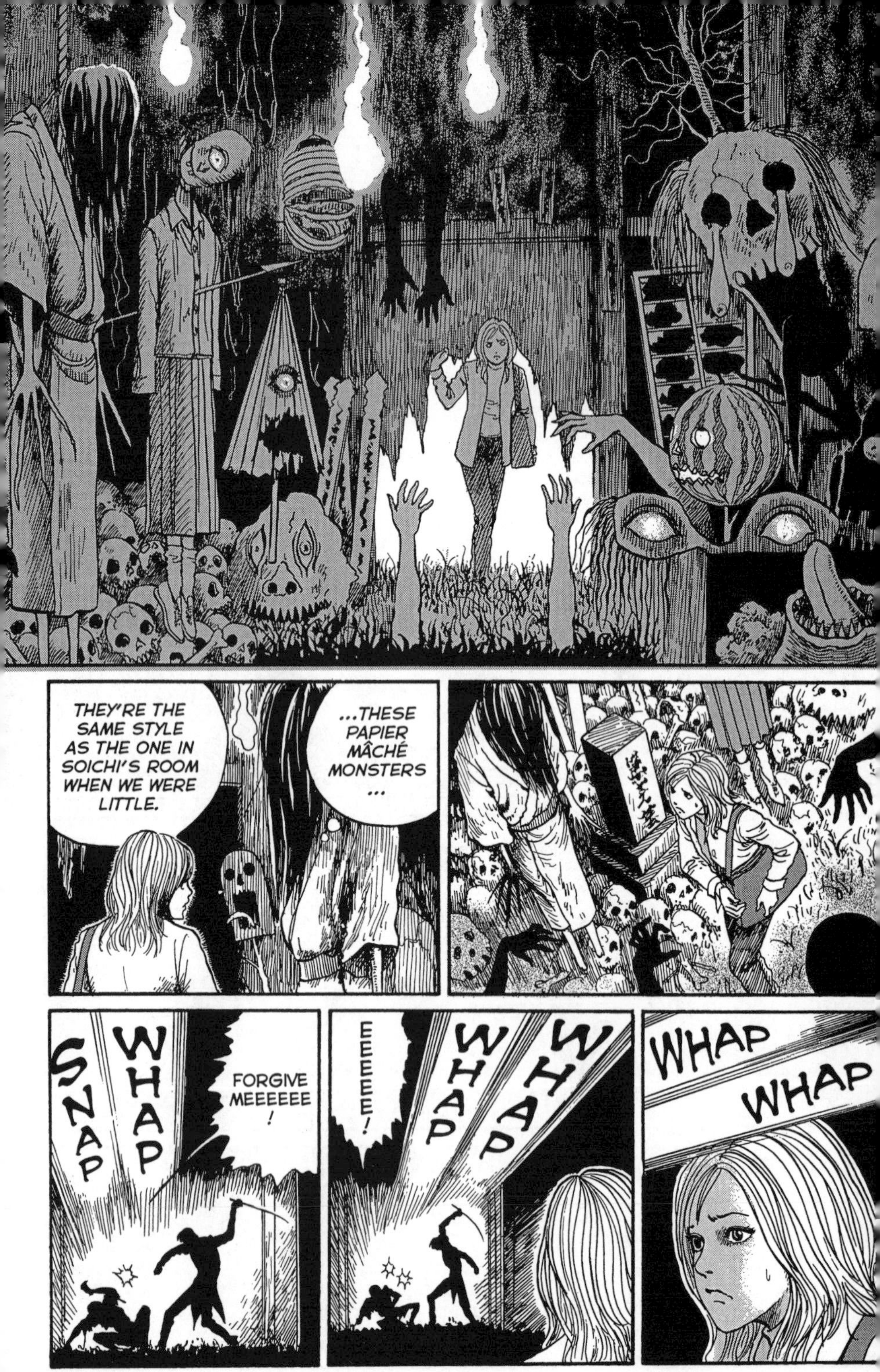

...THESE PAPIER MÂCHÉ MONSTERS ...
THEY'RE THE SAME STYLE AS THE ONE IN SOICHI'S ROOM WHEN WE WERE LITTLE.
WHAP
WHAP
WHAP
WHAP
EEEEE!
FORGIVE MEEEEEE!
WHAP
SNAP

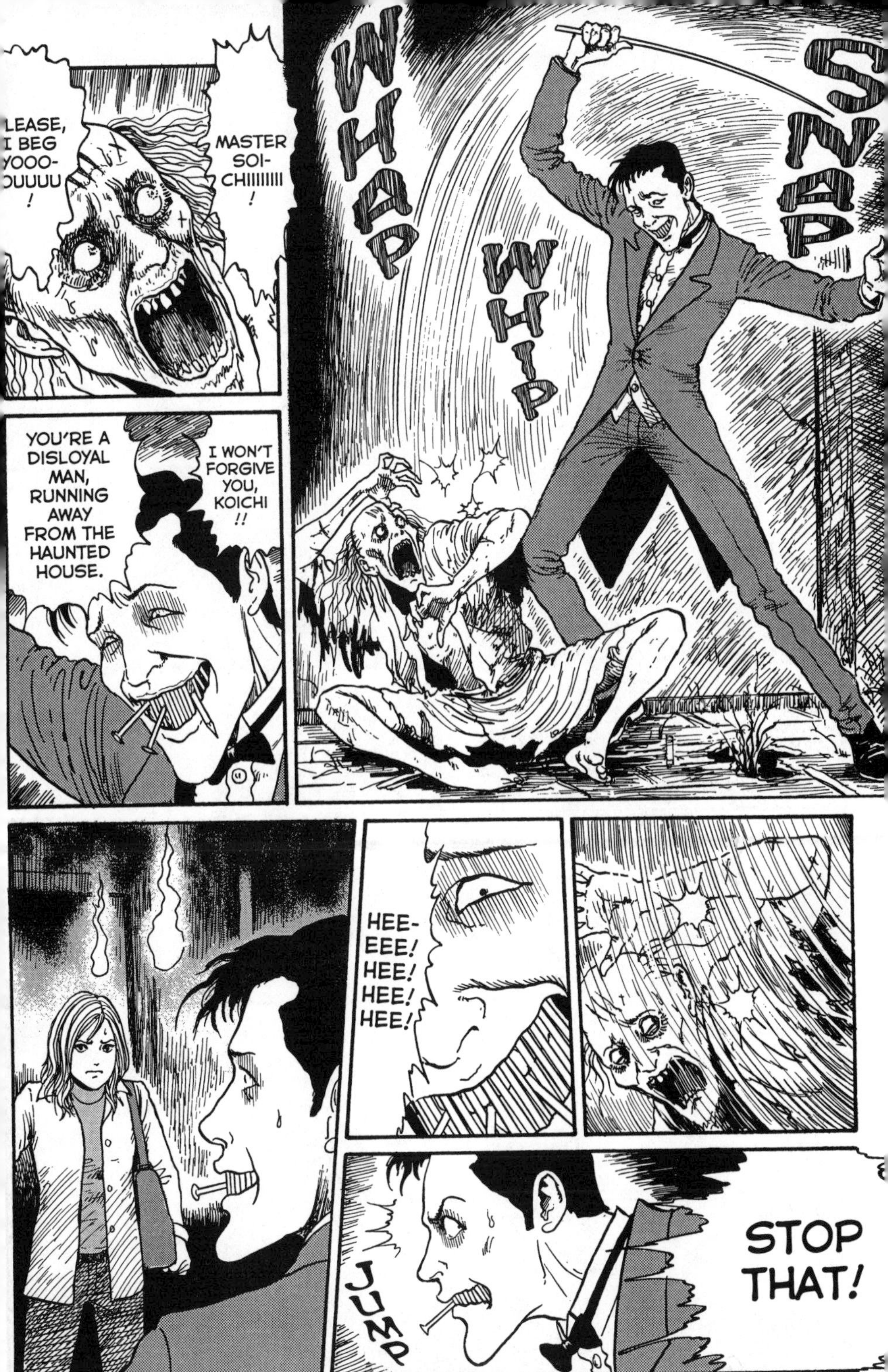

SNAP
WHAP
WHIP
MASTER SOI-CHIIIIIIII!
LEASE, I BEG YOOO-OUUUU!
I WON'T FORGIVE YOU, KOICHI!!
YOU'RE A DISLOYAL MAN, RUNNING AWAY FROM THE HAUNTED HOUSE.
HEE-EEE! HEE! HEE! HEE!
STOP THAT!
JUMP

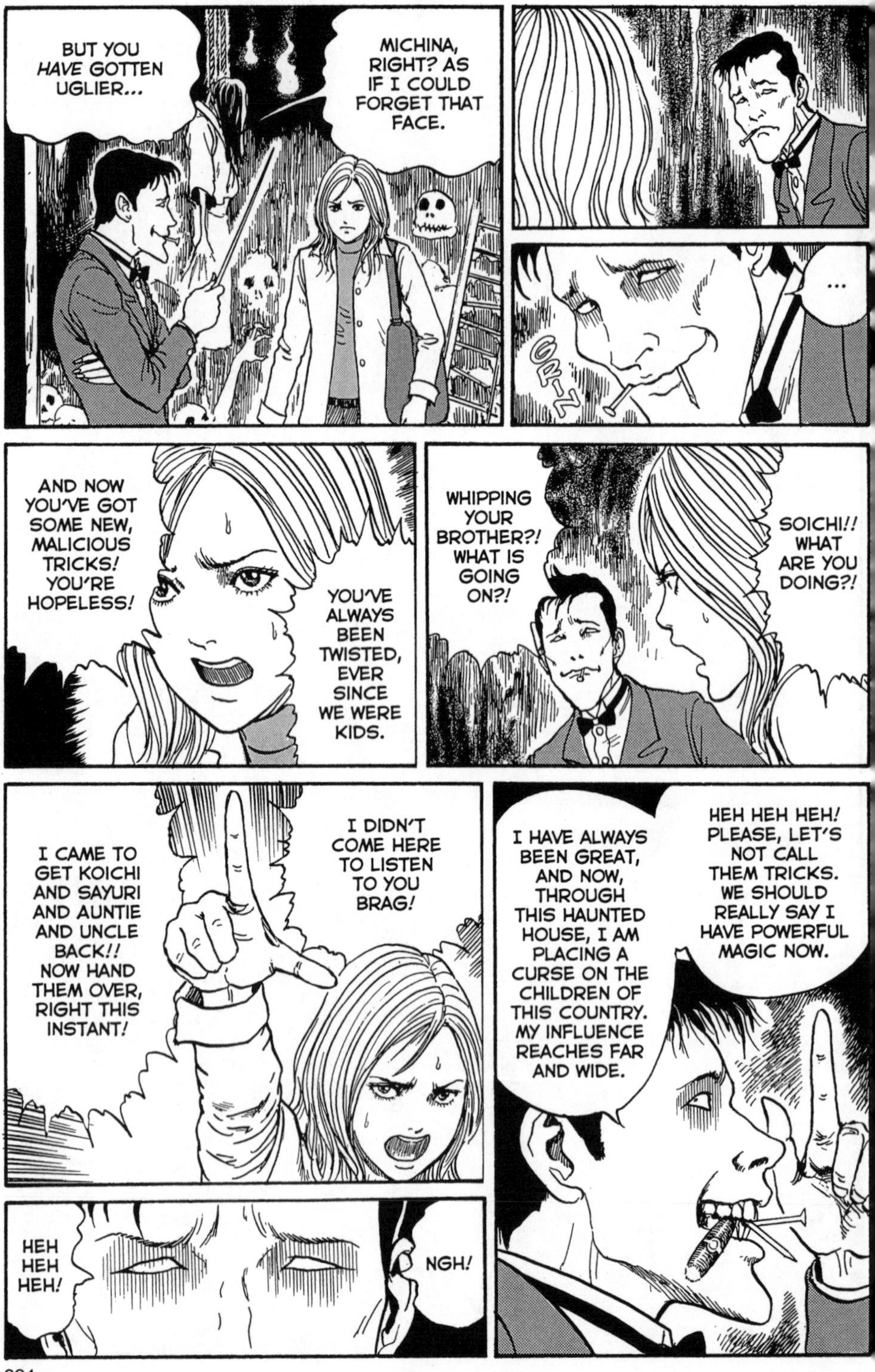
...
GRIN
MICHINA, RIGHT? AS IF I COULD FORGET THAT FACE.
BUT YOU *HAVE* GOTTEN UGLIER...
SOICHI!! WHAT ARE YOU DOING?!
WHIPPING YOUR BROTHER?! WHAT IS GOING ON?!
YOU'VE ALWAYS BEEN TWISTED, EVER SINCE WE WERE KIDS.
AND NOW YOU'VE GOT SOME NEW, MALICIOUS TRICKS! YOU'RE HOPELESS!
HEH HEH HEH! PLEASE, LET'S NOT CALL THEM TRICKS. WE SHOULD REALLY SAY I HAVE POWERFUL MAGIC NOW.
I HAVE ALWAYS BEEN GREAT, AND NOW, THROUGH THIS HAUNTED HOUSE, I AM PLACING A CURSE ON THE CHILDREN OF THIS COUNTRY. MY INFLUENCE REACHES FAR AND WIDE.
I DIDN'T COME HERE TO LISTEN TO YOU BRAG!
I CAME TO GET KOICHI AND SAYURI AND AUNTIE AND UNCLE BACK!! NOW HAND THEM OVER, RIGHT THIS INSTANT!
NGH!
HEH HEH HEH!

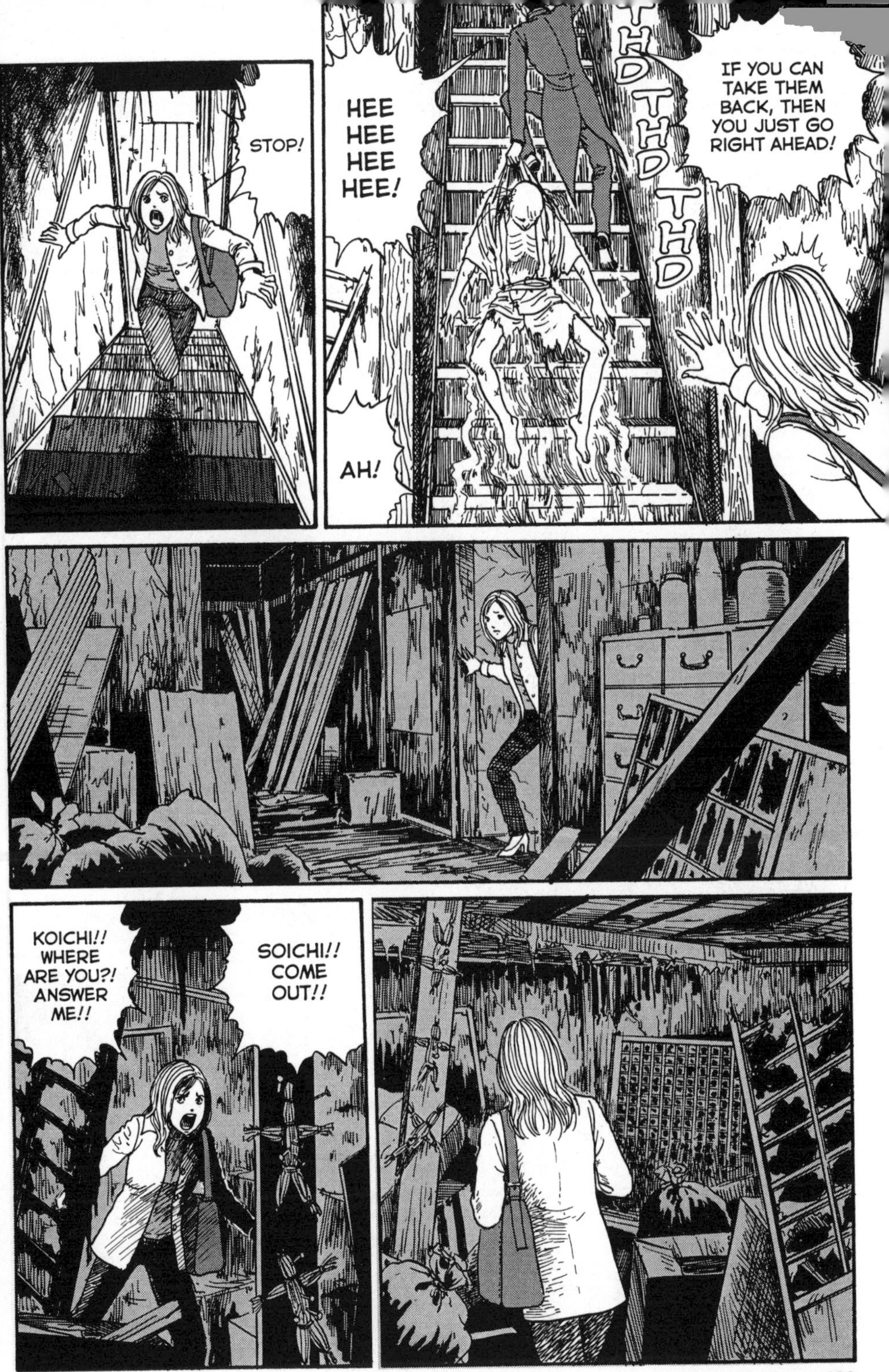
IF YOU CAN TAKE THEM BACK, THEN YOU JUST GO RIGHT AHEAD!
THD THD THD
HEE HEE HEE HEE!
AH!
STOP!
SOICHI!! COME OUT!!
KOICHI!! WHERE ARE YOU?! ANSWER ME!!

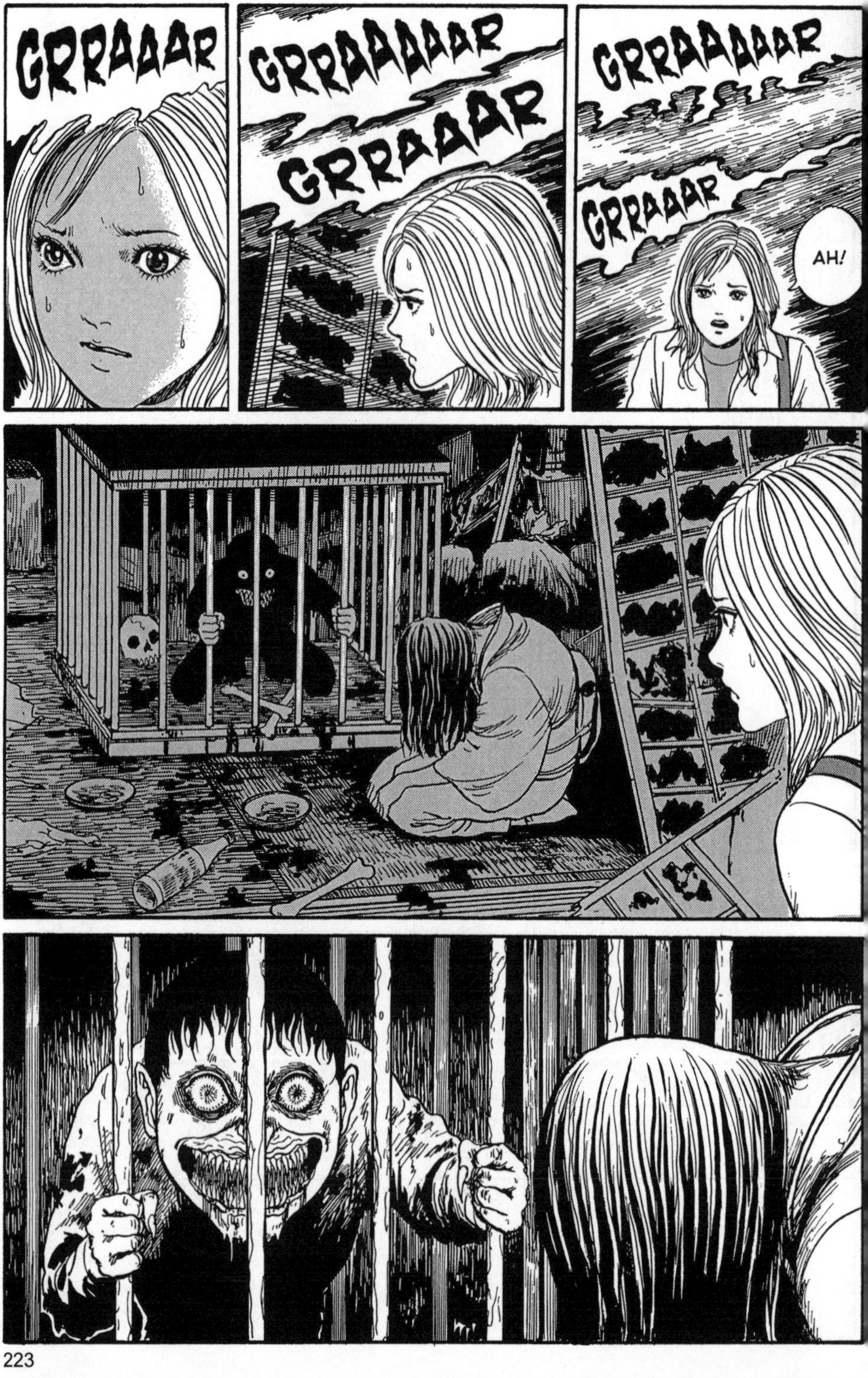
GRRAAAAAR
GRRAAAR
AH!
GRRAAAAAR
GRRAAAR
GRRAAAR

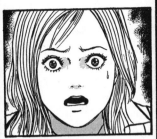

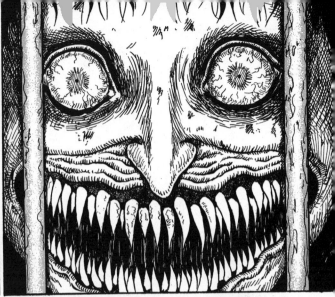

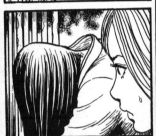

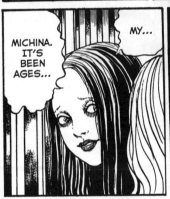

... SAYURI ?!
IT'S YOU, ISN'T IT?! IT'S ME, MICHINA!!
MY...
MICHINA. IT'S BEEN AGES...
SAYURI, WE HAVE TO HURRY AND GET OUT OF HERE!! AND KOICHI...
AND WHERE ARE AUNTIE AND UNCLE?! ARE THEY OKAY?!
MOM AND DAD....
THEY PASSED AWAY.
WHAT ?!
HOW ?!

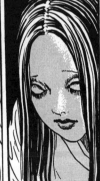

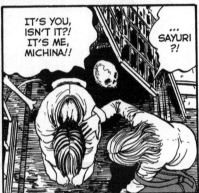

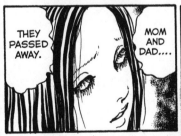

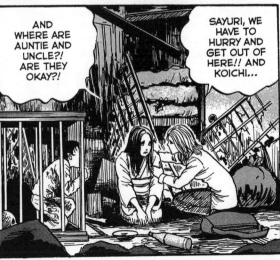

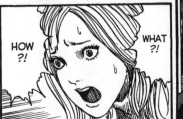

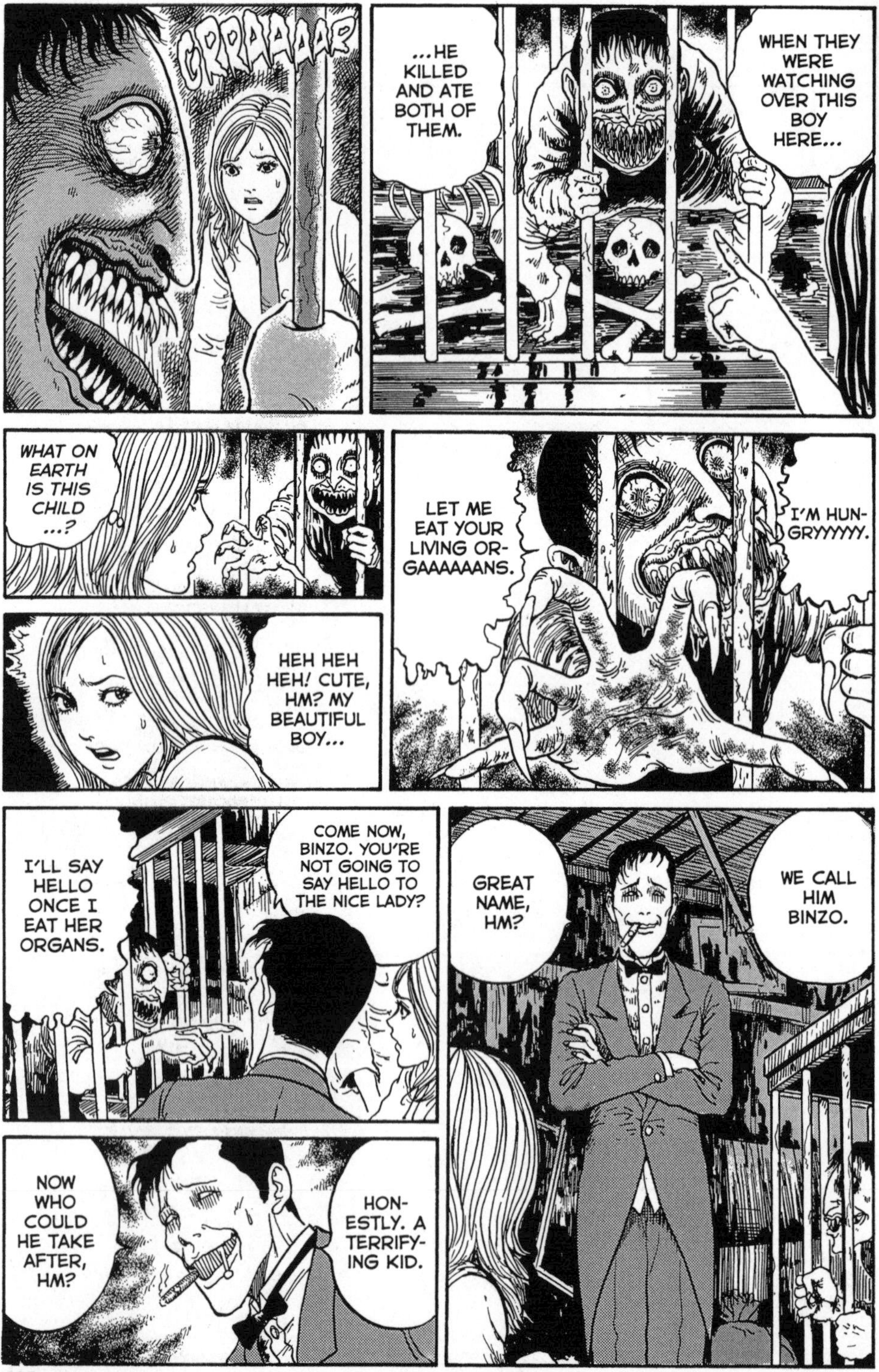
WHEN THEY WERE WATCHING OVER THIS BOY HERE...
...HE KILLED AND ATE BOTH OF THEM.
CRRAAAAR
I'M HUN-GRYYYYYY.
LET ME EAT YOUR LIVING OR-GAAAAAANS.
WHAT ON EARTH IS THIS CHILD ...?
HEH HEH HEH! CUTE, HM? MY BEAUTIFUL BOY...
WE CALL HIM BINZO.
GREAT NAME, HM?
COME NOW, BINZO. YOU'RE NOT GOING TO SAY HELLO TO THE NICE LADY?
I'LL SAY HELLO ONCE I EAT HER ORGANS.
HON-ESTLY. A TERRIFY-ING KID.
NOW WHO COULD HE TAKE AFTER, HM?

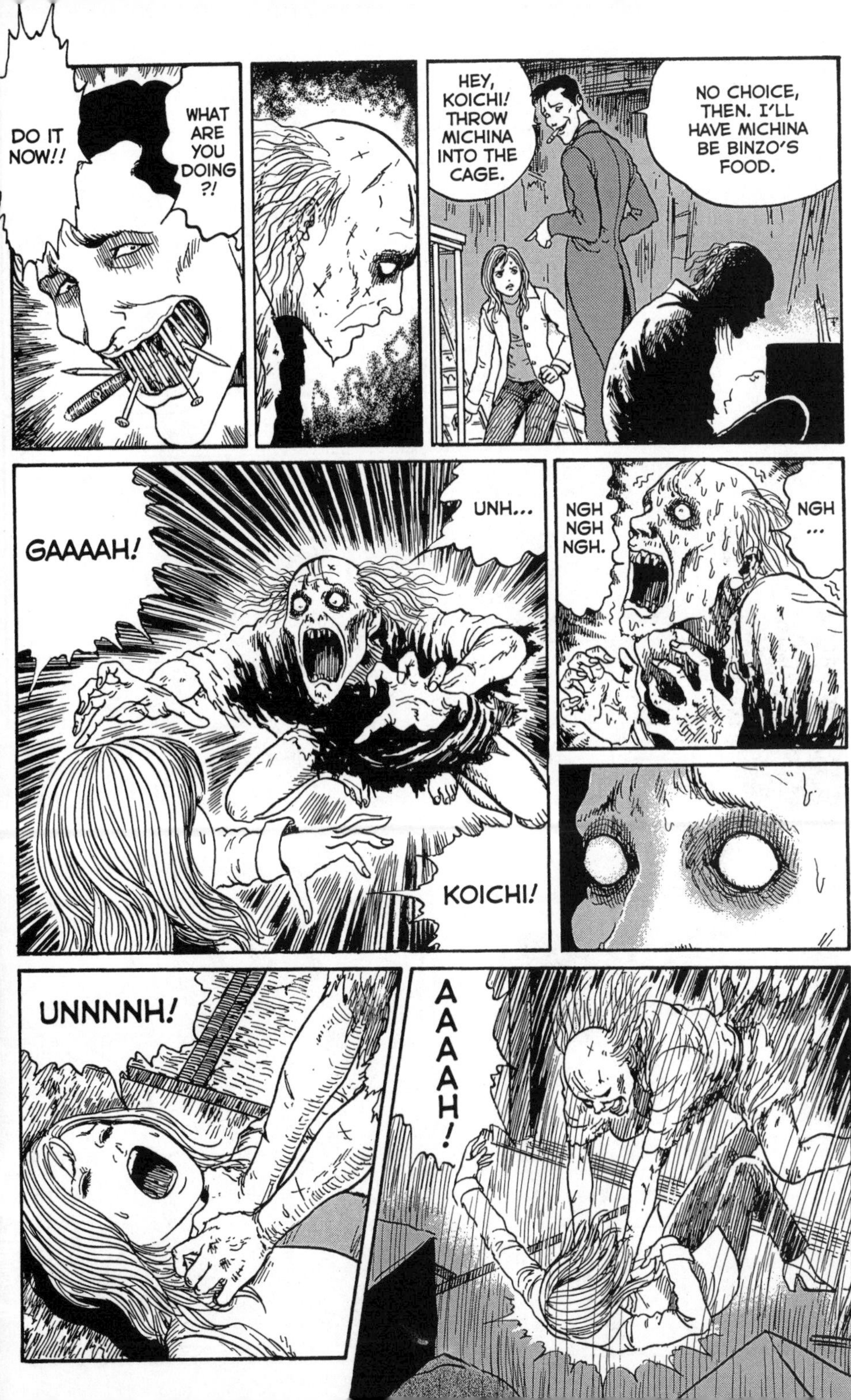
NO CHOICE, THEN. I'LL HAVE MICHINA BE BINZO'S FOOD.
HEY, KOICHI! THROW MICHINA INTO THE CAGE.
WHAT ARE YOU DOING ?!
DO IT NOW!!
NGH ...
NGH NGH NGH.
UNH...
GAAAAH!
KOICHI!
AAAAAH!
UNNNNH!

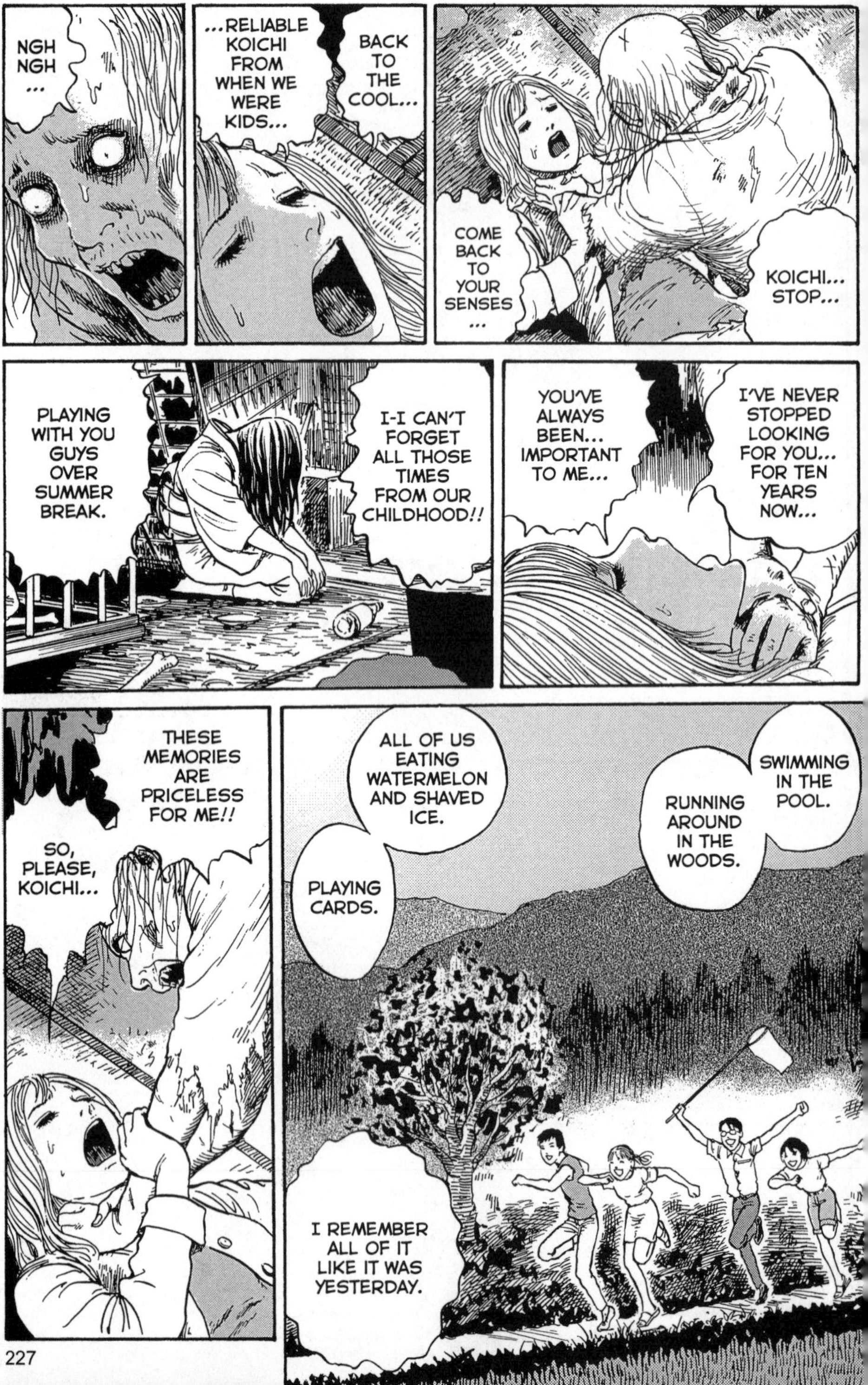
KOICHI... STOP...
COME BACK TO YOUR SENSES...
BACK TO THE COOL...
...RELIABLE KOICHI FROM WHEN WE WERE KIDS...
NGH NGH...
I'VE NEVER STOPPED LOOKING FOR YOU... FOR TEN YEARS NOW...
YOU'VE ALWAYS BEEN... IMPORTANT TO ME...
I-I CAN'T FORGET ALL THOSE TIMES FROM OUR CHILDHOOD!!
PLAYING WITH YOU GUYS OVER SUMMER BREAK.
SWIMMING IN THE POOL.
RUNNING AROUND IN THE WOODS.
ALL OF US EATING WATERMELON AND SHAVED ICE.
PLAYING CARDS.
I REMEMBER ALL OF IT LIKE IT WAS YESTERDAY.
THESE MEMORIES ARE PRICELESS FOR ME!!
SO, PLEASE, KOICHI...

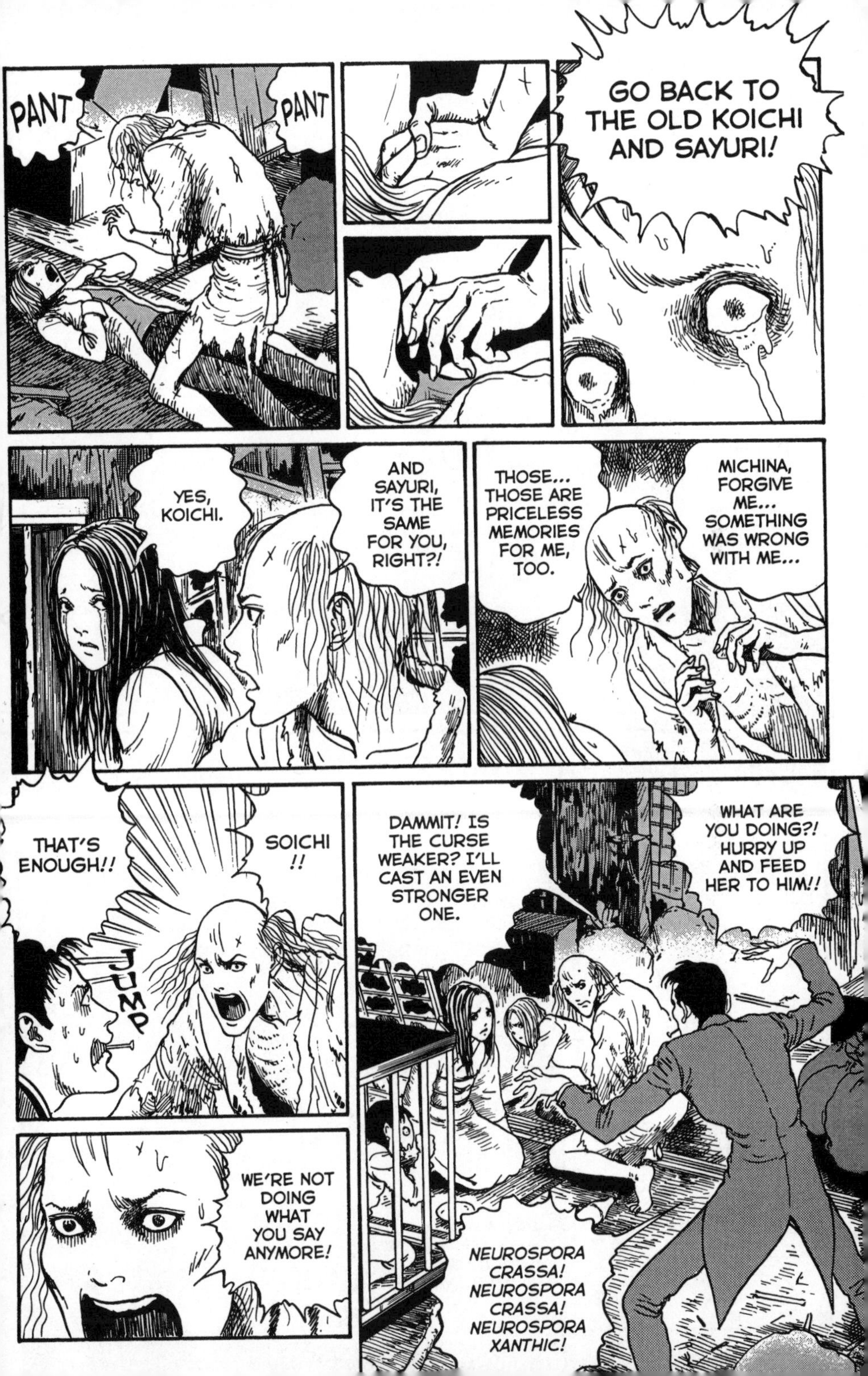
GO BACK TO THE OLD KOICHI AND SAYURI!
PANT
PANT
MICHINA, FORGIVE ME... SOMETHING WAS WRONG WITH ME...
THOSE... THOSE ARE PRICELESS MEMORIES FOR ME, TOO.
AND SAYURI, IT'S THE SAME FOR YOU, RIGHT?!
YES, KOICHI.
WHAT ARE YOU DOING?! HURRY UP AND FEED HER TO HIM!!
DAMMIT! IS THE CURSE WEAKER? I'LL CAST AN EVEN STRONGER ONE.
NEUROSPORA CRASSA! NEUROSPORA CRASSA! NEUROSPORA XANTHIC!
SOICHI!!
THAT'S ENOUGH!!
JUMP
WE'RE NOT DOING WHAT YOU SAY ANYMORE!

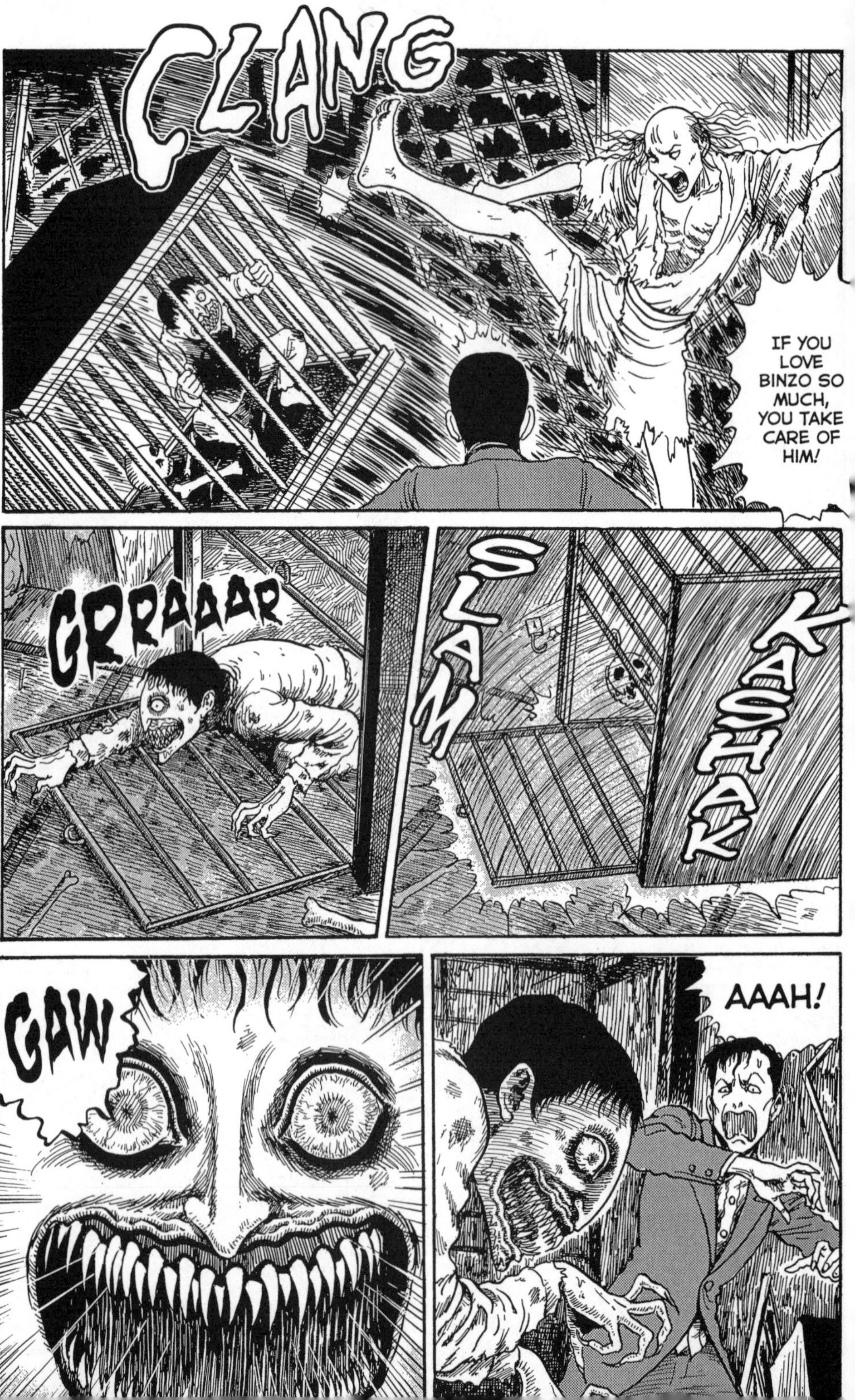
CLANG
IF YOU LOVE BINZO SO MUCH, YOU TAKE CARE OF HIM!
KASHAK
SLAM
GRRAAAR
AAAH!
GAW

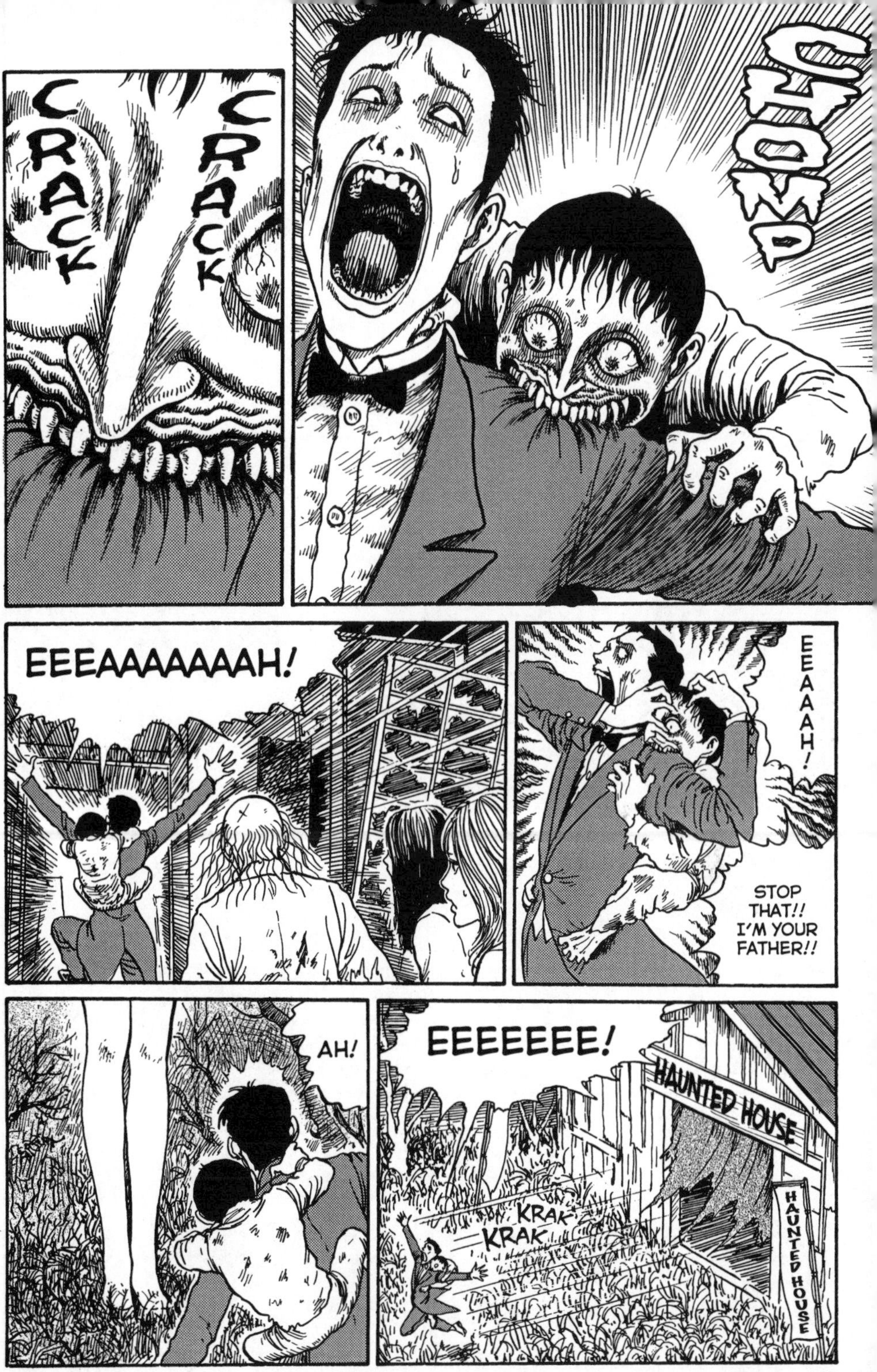
CHOMP
CRACK
CRACK
EEAAAH!
STOP THAT!! I'M YOUR FATHER!!
EEEAAAAAAAH!
EEEEEEE!
HAUNTED HOUSE
KRAK
KRAK
HAUNTED HOUSE
AH!

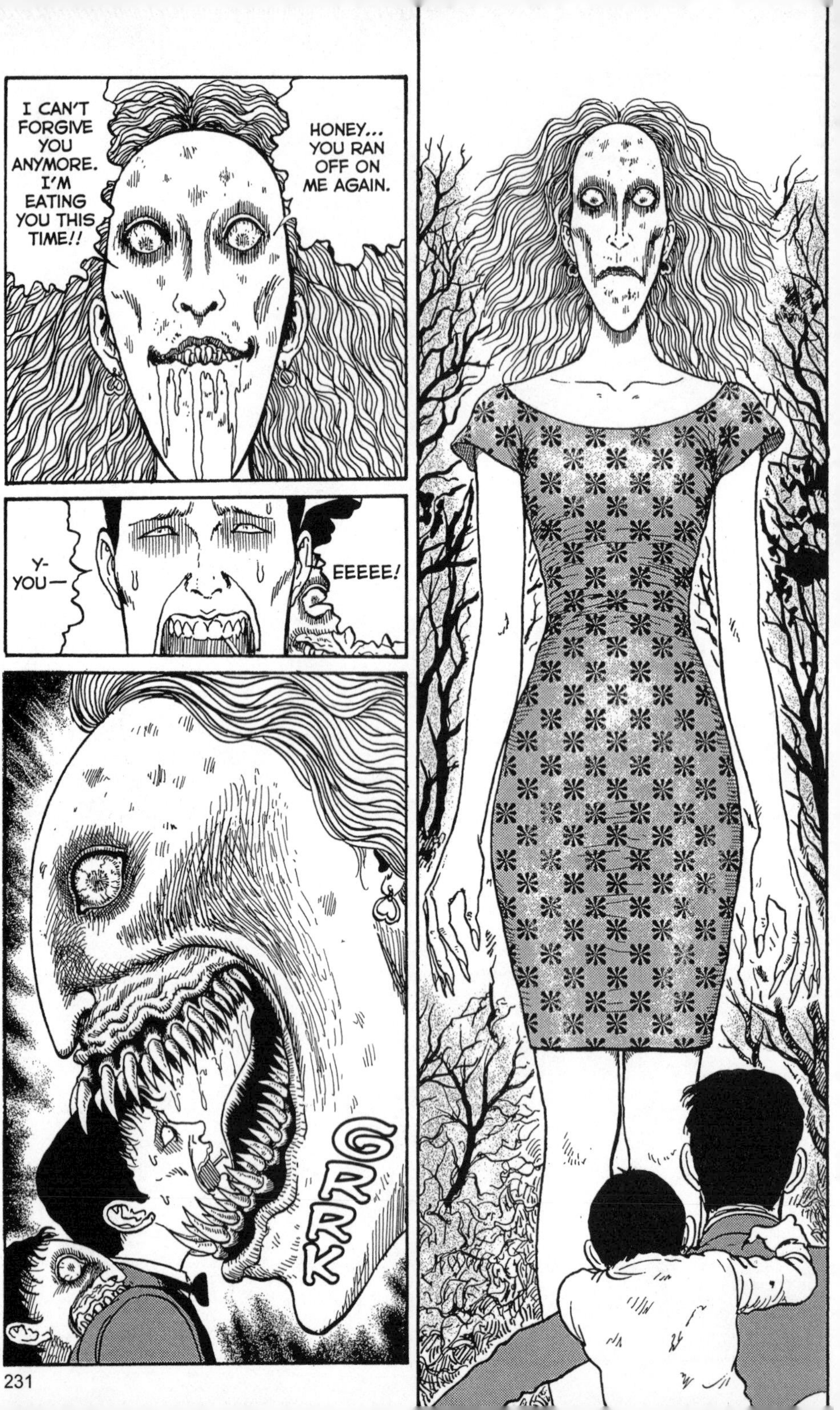
HONEY... YOU RAN OFF ON ME AGAIN.
I CAN'T FORGIVE YOU ANYMORE. I'M EATING YOU THIS TIME!!
EEEEE!
Y-YOU—
GRRK

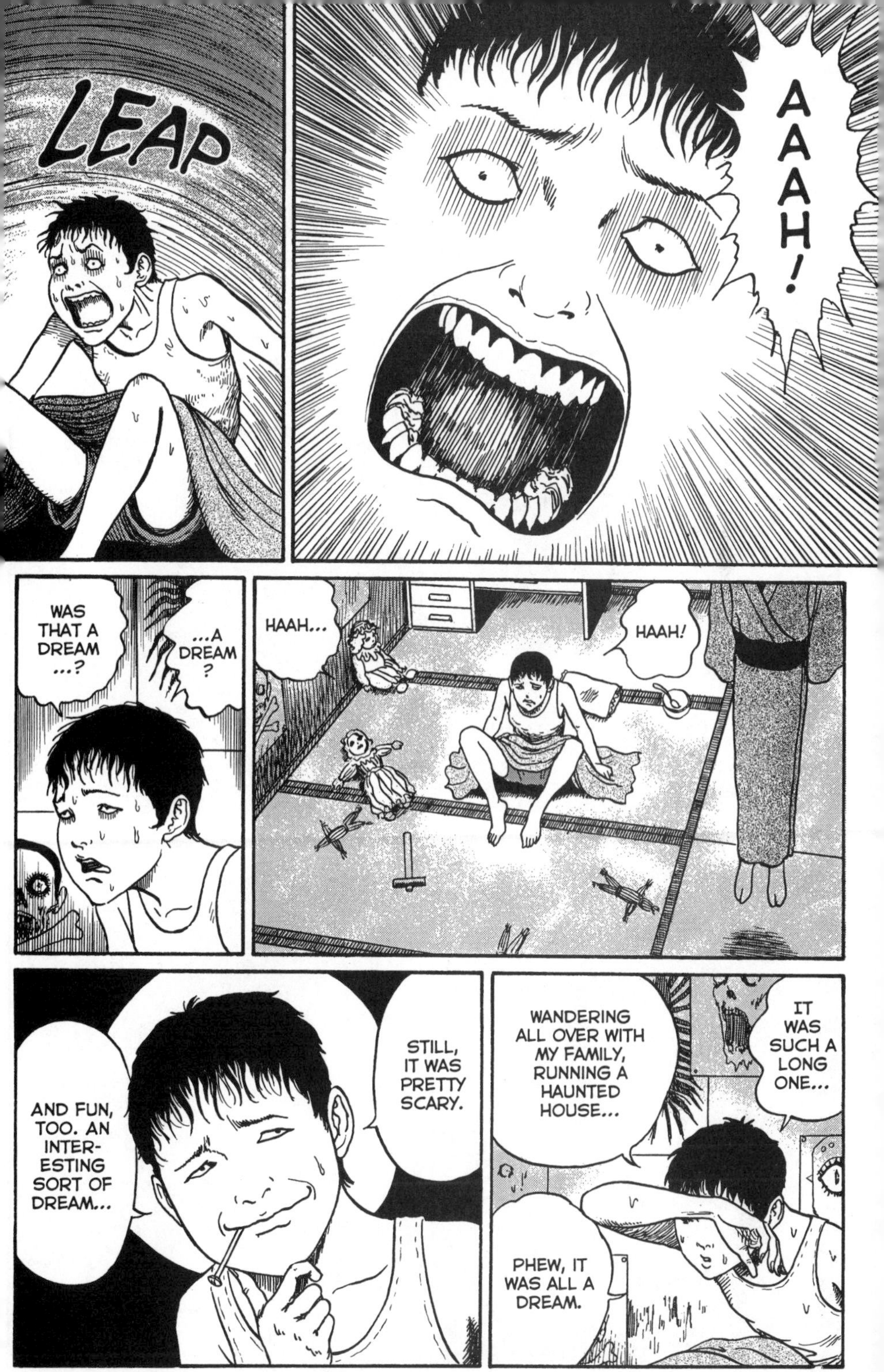
AAAH!
LEAP
HAAH!
HAAH...
...A DREAM?
WAS THAT A DREAM...?
IT WAS SUCH A LONG ONE...
WANDERING ALL OVER WITH MY FAMILY, RUNNING A HAUNTED HOUSE...
PHEW, IT WAS ALL A DREAM.
STILL, IT WAS PRETTY SCARY.
AND FUN, TOO. AN INTER-ESTING SORT OF DREAM...

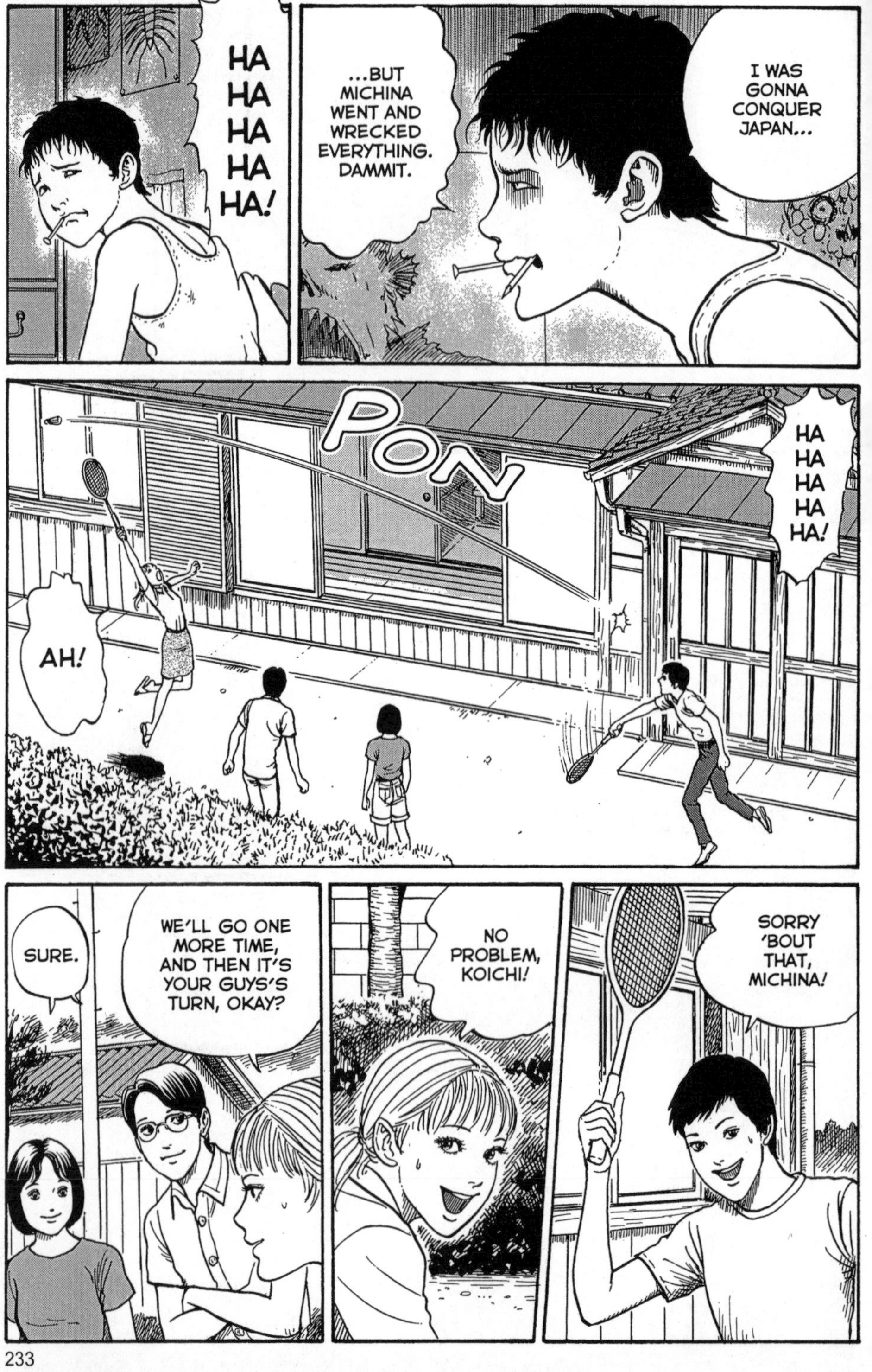
I WAS GONNA CONQUER JAPAN...
...BUT MICHINA WENT AND WRECKED EVERYTHING. DAMMIT.
HA HA HA HA HA!
HA HA HA HA HA!
PON
AH!
SORRY 'BOUT THAT, MICHINA!
NO PROBLEM, KOICHI!
WE'LL GO ONE MORE TIME, AND THEN IT'S YOUR GUYS'S TURN, OKAY?
SURE.

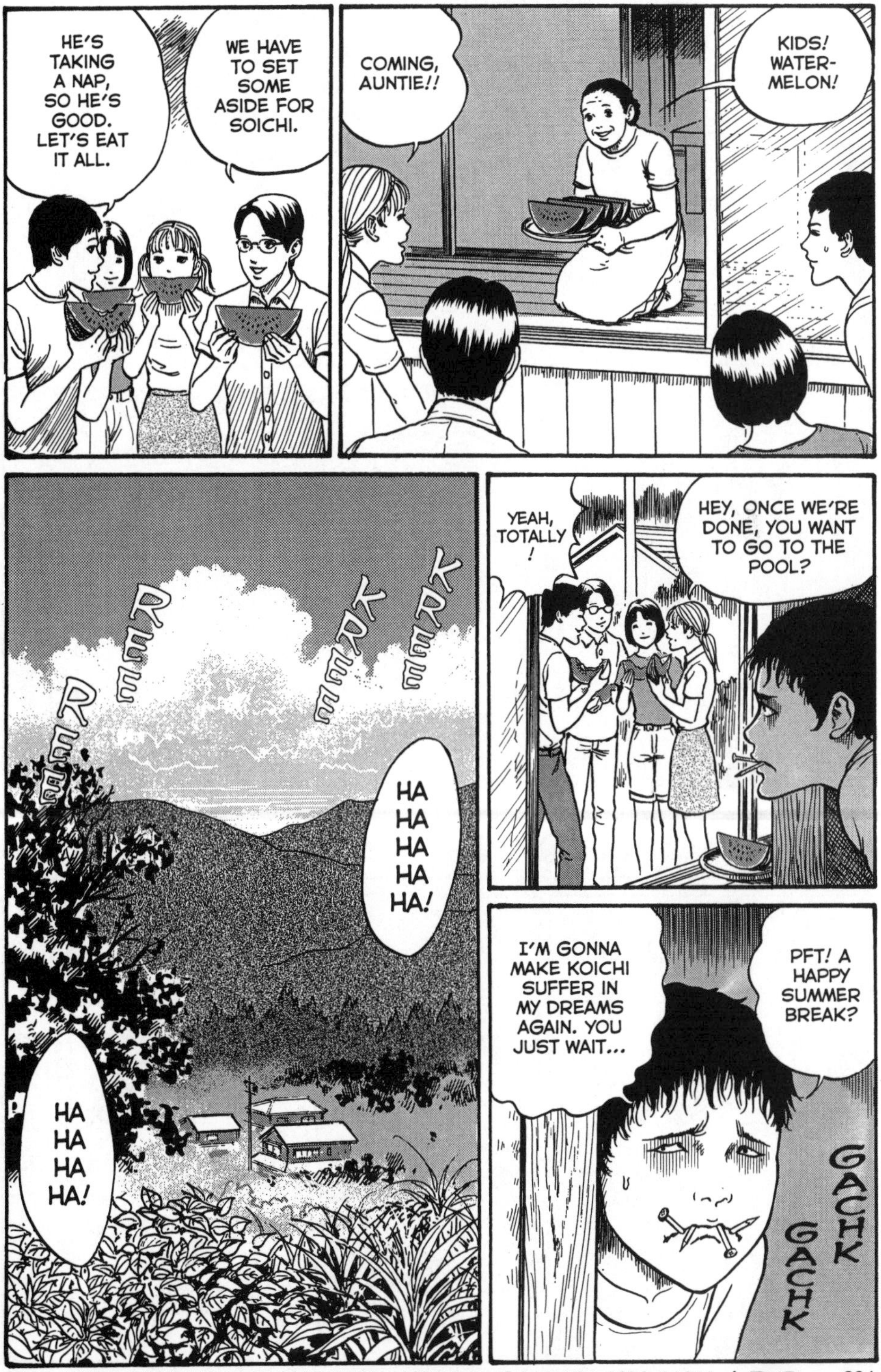
KIDS! WATER-MELON!
COMING, AUNTIE!!
WE HAVE TO SET SOME ASIDE FOR SOICHI.
HE'S TAKING A NAP, SO HE'S GOOD. LET'S EAT IT ALL.
HEY, ONCE WE'RE DONE, YOU WANT TO GO TO THE POOL?
YEAH, TOTALLY!
PFT! A HAPPY SUMMER BREAK?
I'M GONNA MAKE KOICHI SUFFER IN MY DREAMS AGAIN. YOU JUST WAIT...
GACHK
GACHK
KREE
KREE
REE
REE
HA HA HA HA HA!
HA HA HA HA!

THE MYSTERY OF THE HAUNTED HOUSE: SOICHI'S VERSION / END

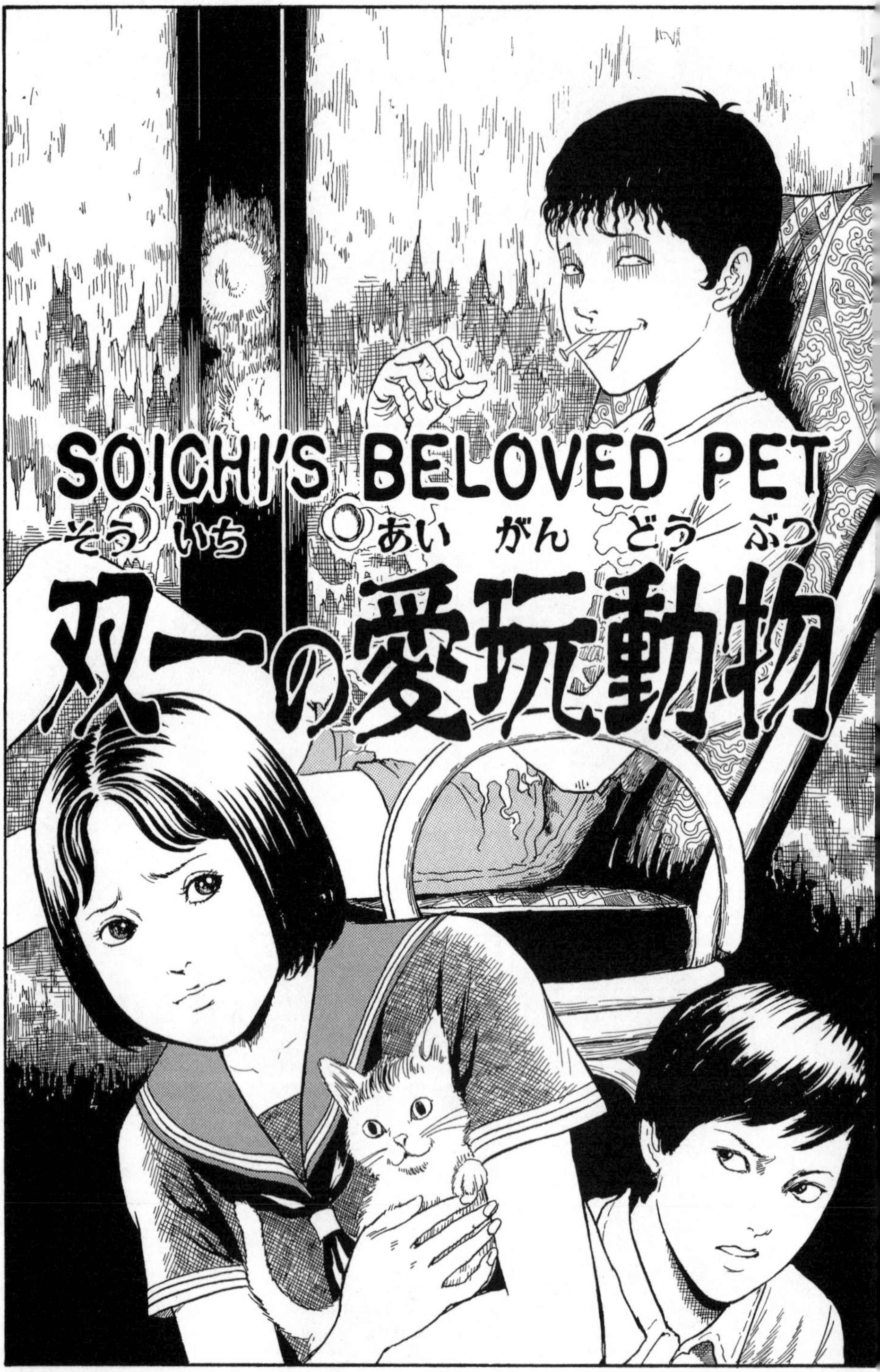
SOICHI'S BELOVED PET
双一の愛玩動物
そういち あいがんどうぶつ

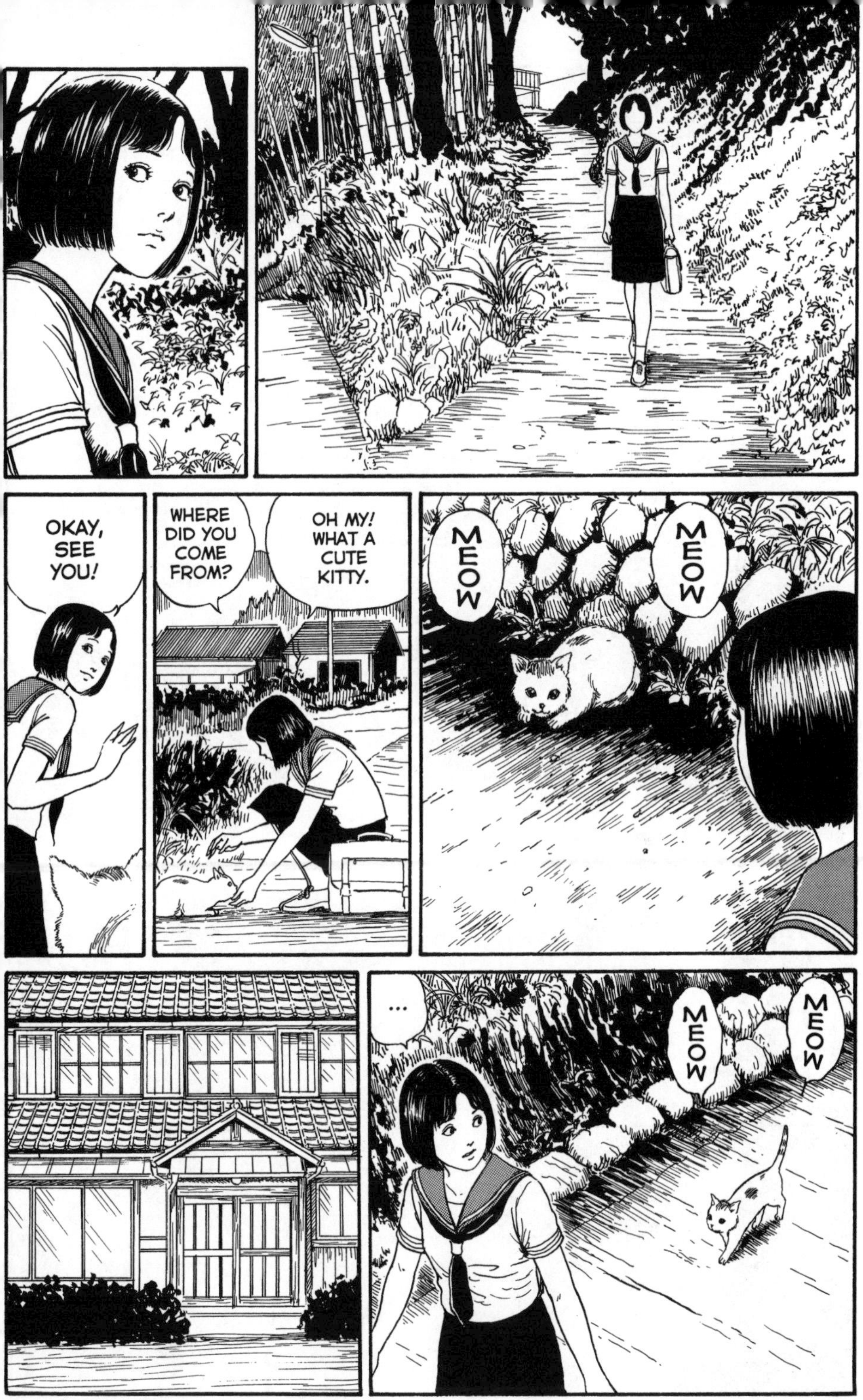
MEOW
MEOW
OH MY! WHAT A CUTE KITTY.
WHERE DID YOU COME FROM?
OKAY, SEE YOU!
MEOW
MEOW
...

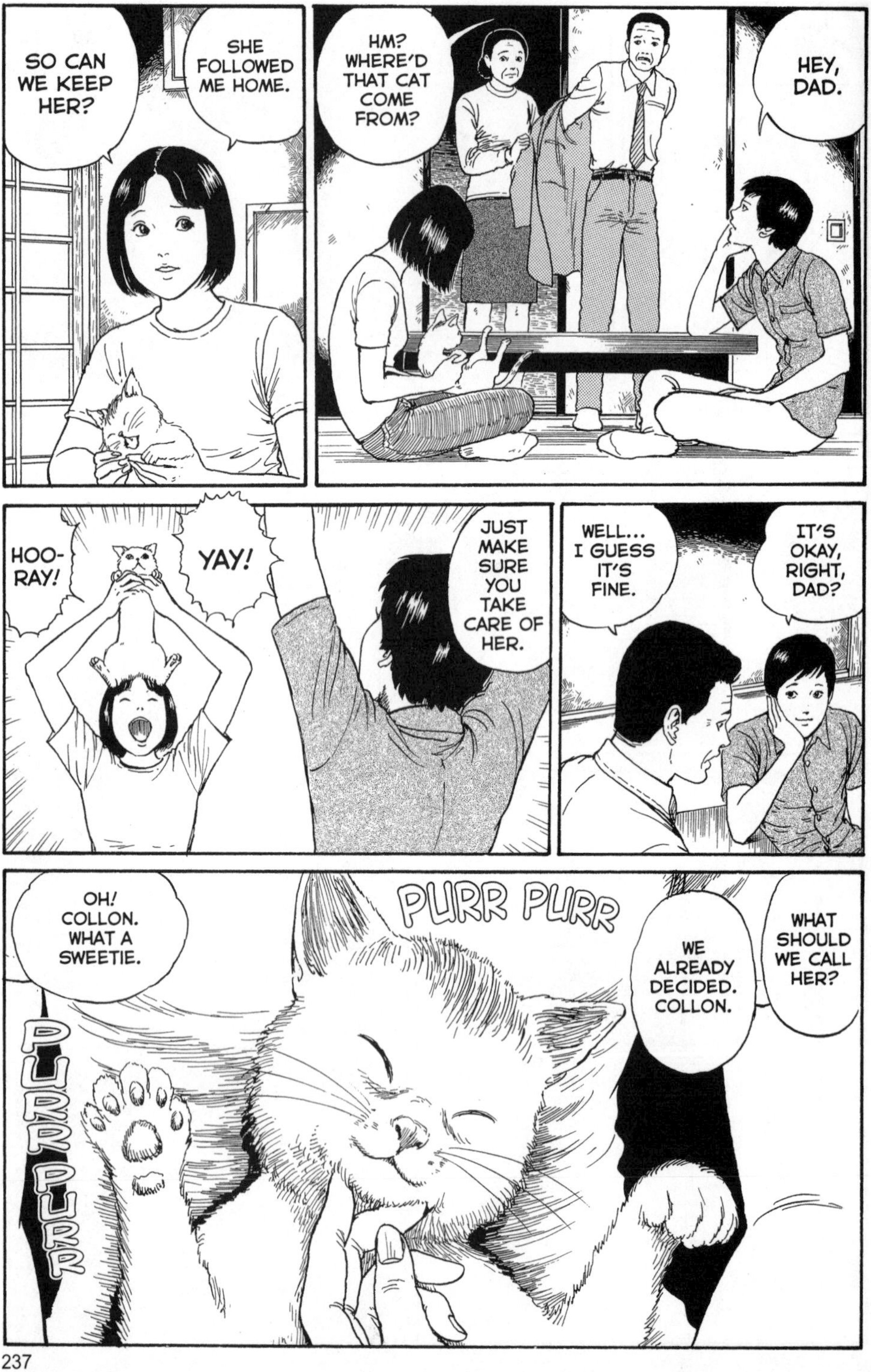
HEY, DAD.
HM? WHERE'D THAT CAT COME FROM?
SHE FOLLOWED ME HOME.
SO CAN WE KEEP HER?
IT'S OKAY, RIGHT, DAD?
WELL... I GUESS IT'S FINE.
JUST MAKE SURE YOU TAKE CARE OF HER.
YAY!
HOO-RAY!
WHAT SHOULD WE CALL HER?
WE ALREADY DECIDED. COLLON.
PURR PURR
OH! COLLON. WHAT A SWEETIE.
PURR PURR

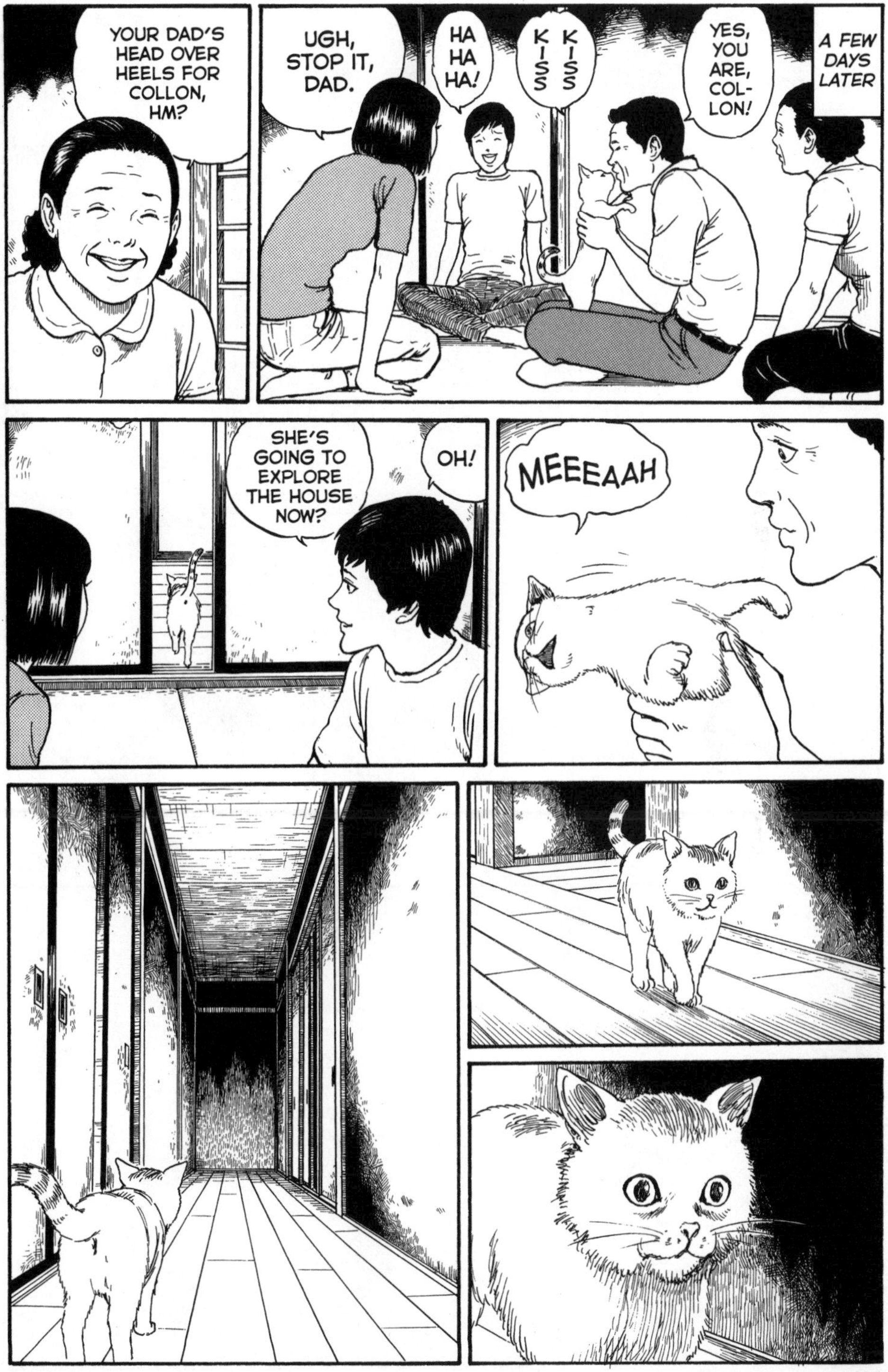
A FEW DAYS LATER
YES, YOU ARE, COL-LON!
KISS KISS
HA HA HA!
UGH, STOP IT, DAD.
YOUR DAD'S HEAD OVER HEELS FOR COLLON, HM?
MEEEAAH
OH!
SHE'S GOING TO EXPLORE THE HOUSE NOW?

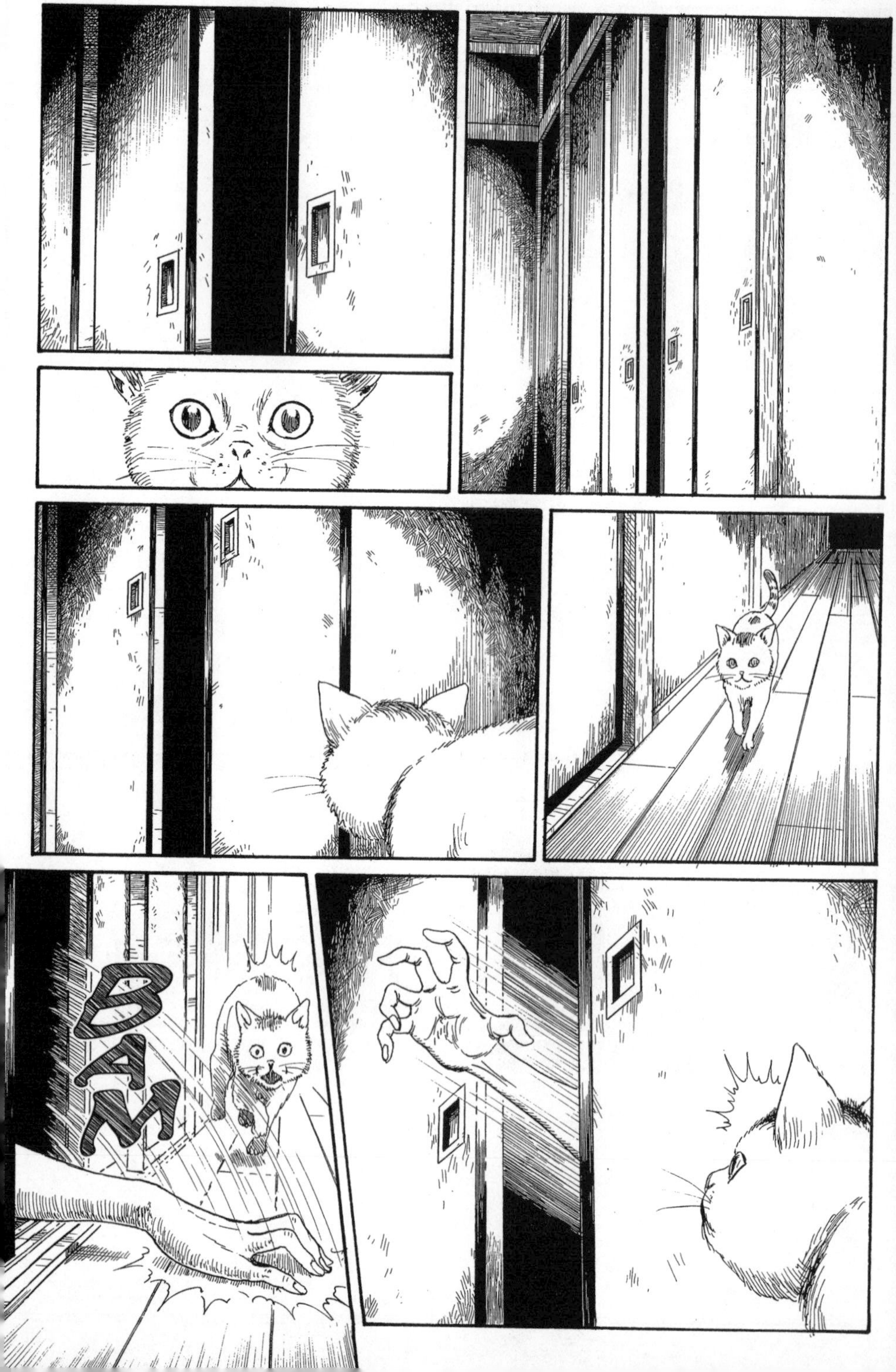
BAM

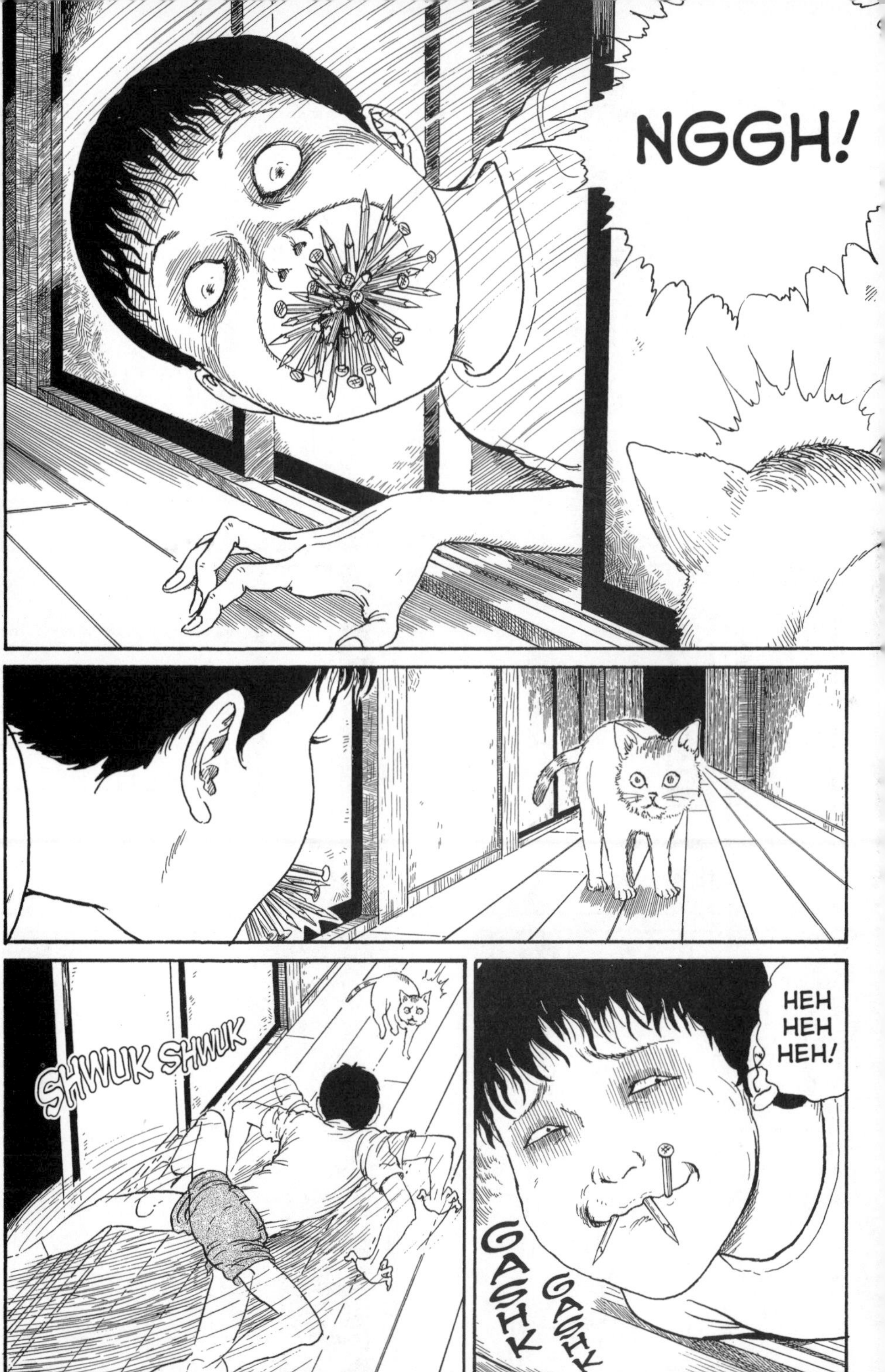
NGGH!
HEH HEH HEH!
GASHK GASHK
SHWUK SHWUK

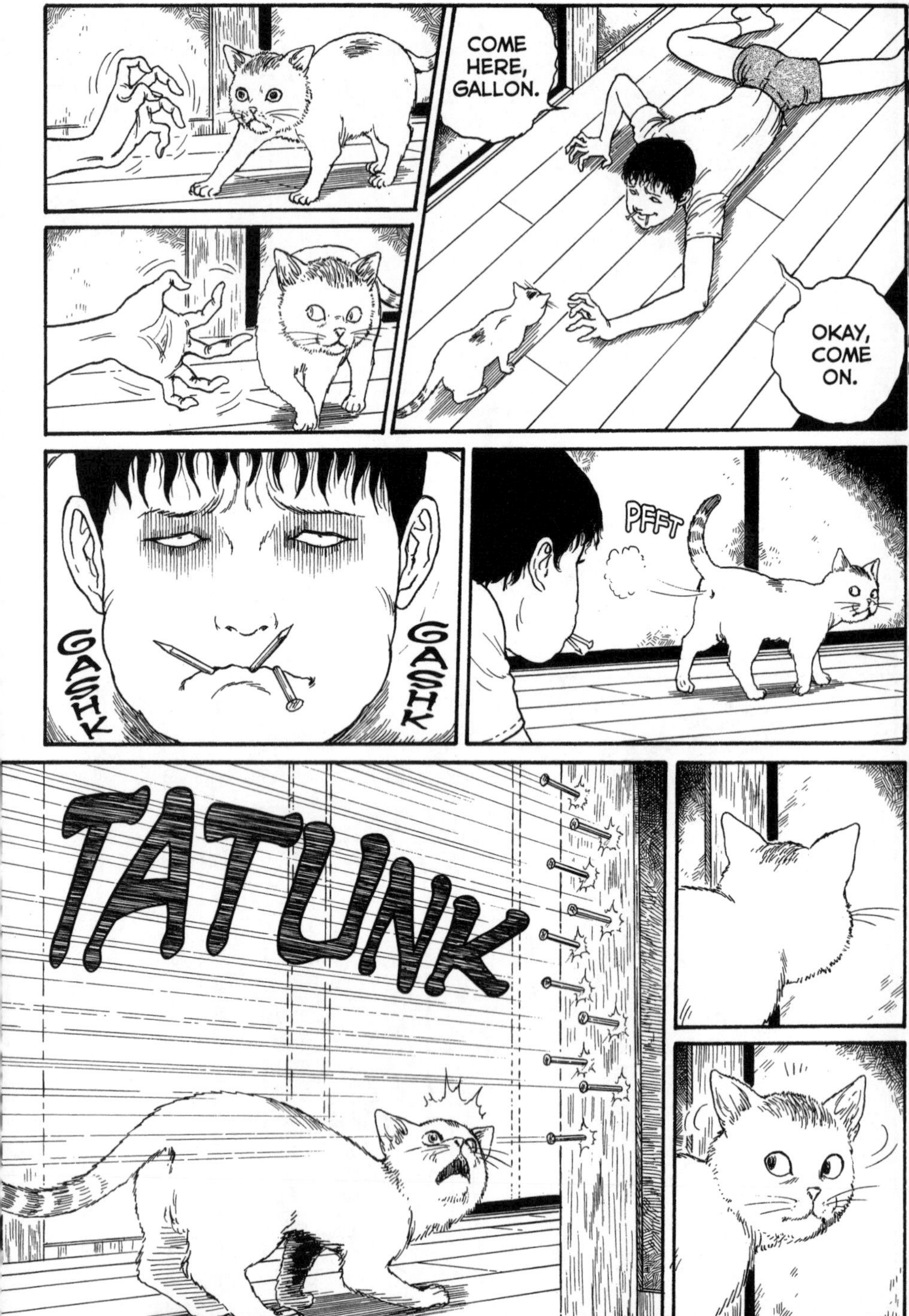
COME HERE, GALLON.
OKAY, COME ON.
PFFT
GASHK
GASHK
TATUNK

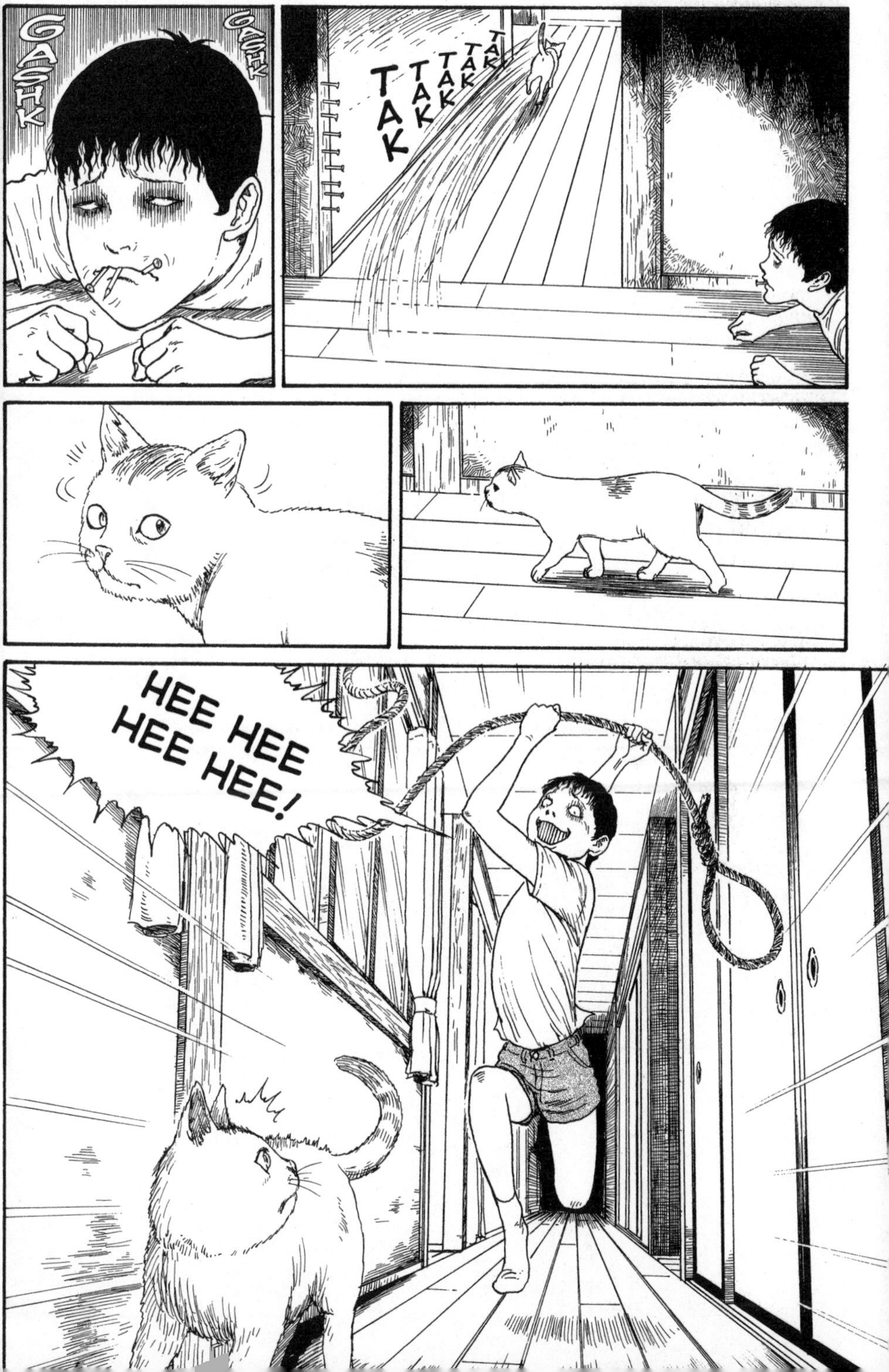
TAK TAK TAK TAK TAK
GASHK
GASHK
HEE HEE HEE HEE!

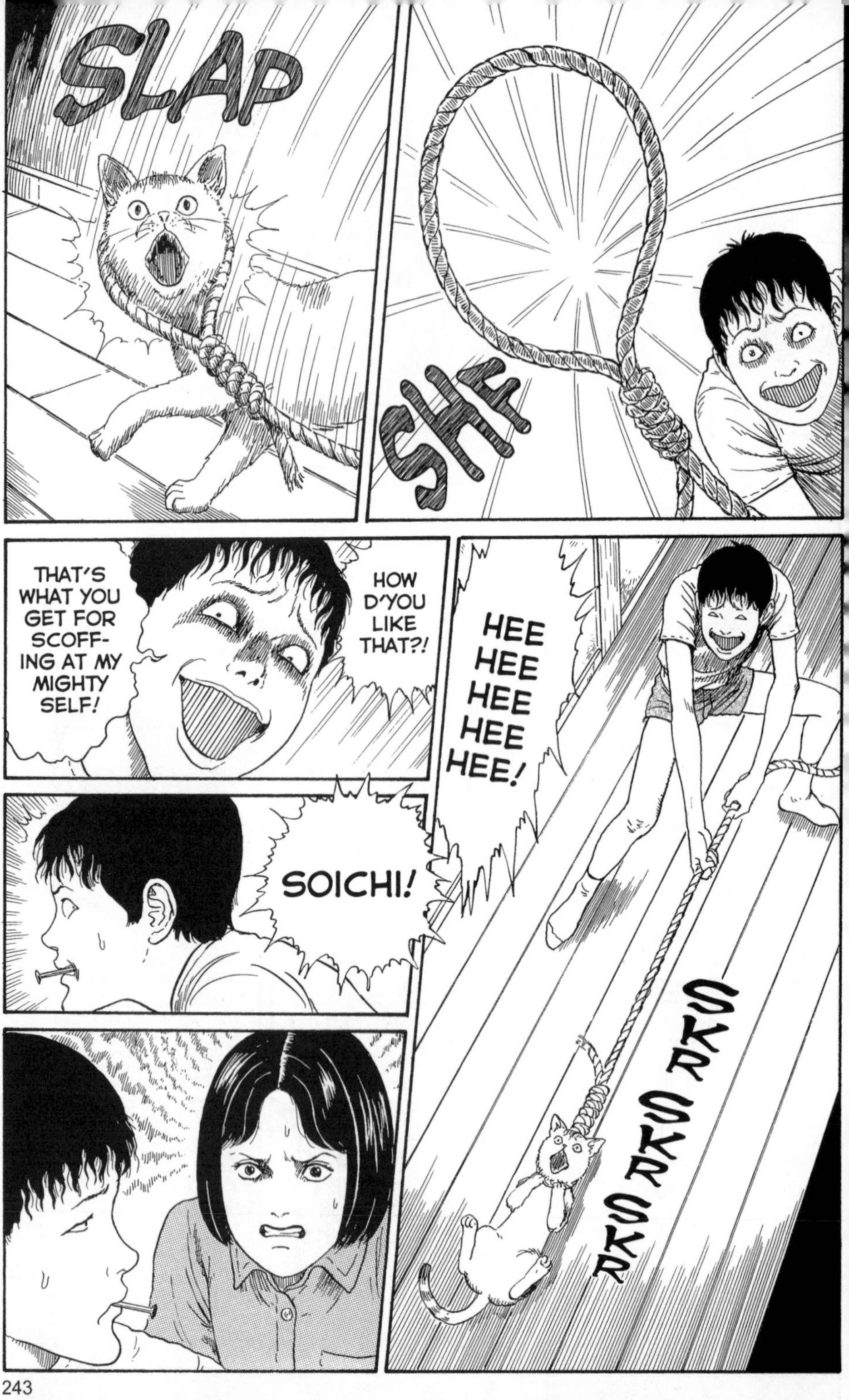
SHF
SLAP
HEE HEE HEE HEE HEE!
SKR SKR SKR SKR
HOW D'YOU LIKE THAT?!
THAT'S WHAT YOU GET FOR SCOFF-ING AT MY MIGHTY SELF!
SOICHI!

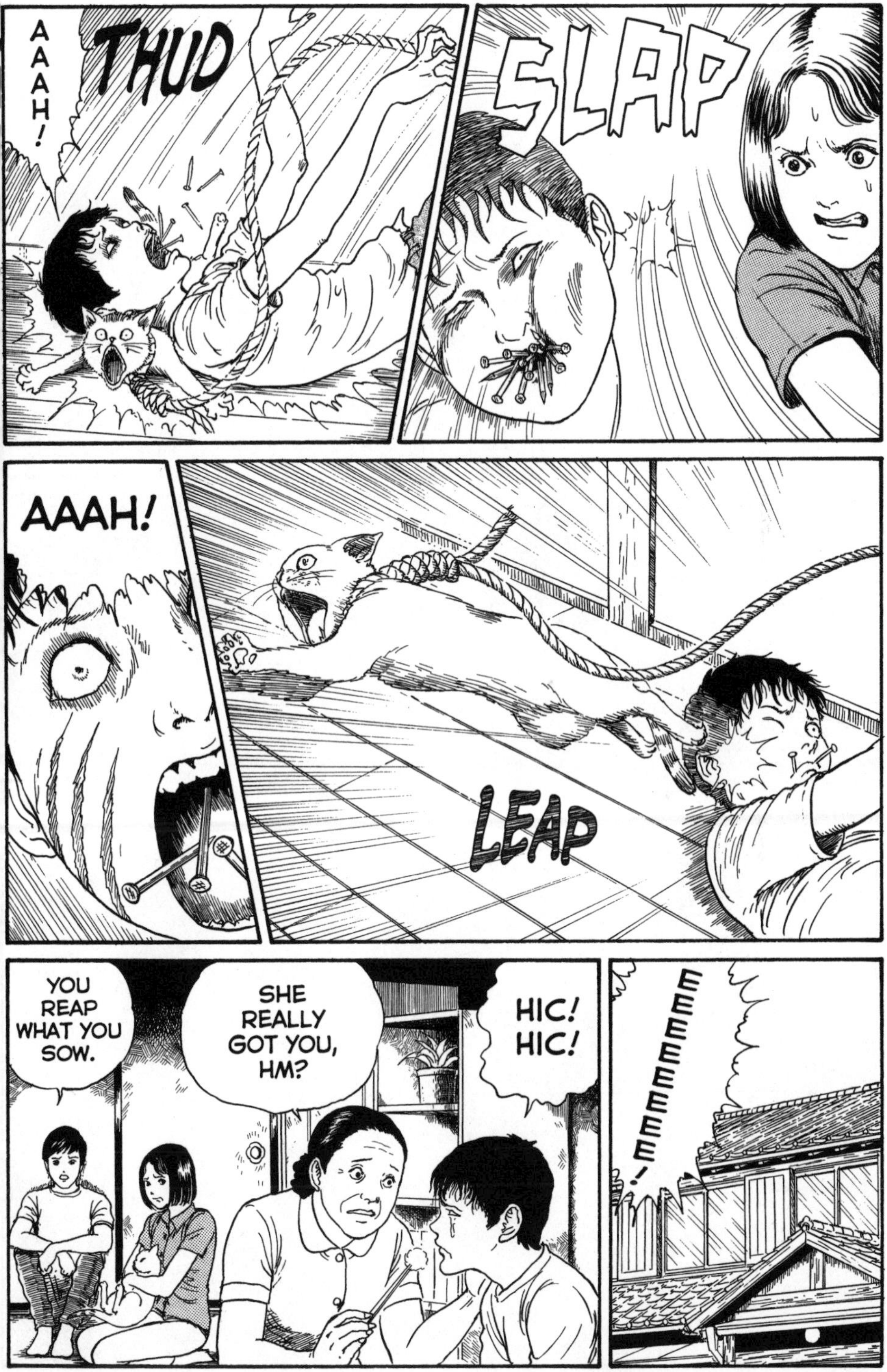
SLAP
THUD
AAAAH!
LEAP
AAAH!
EEEEEEEE!
HIC! HIC!
SHE REALLY GOT YOU, HM?
YOU REAP WHAT YOU SOW.

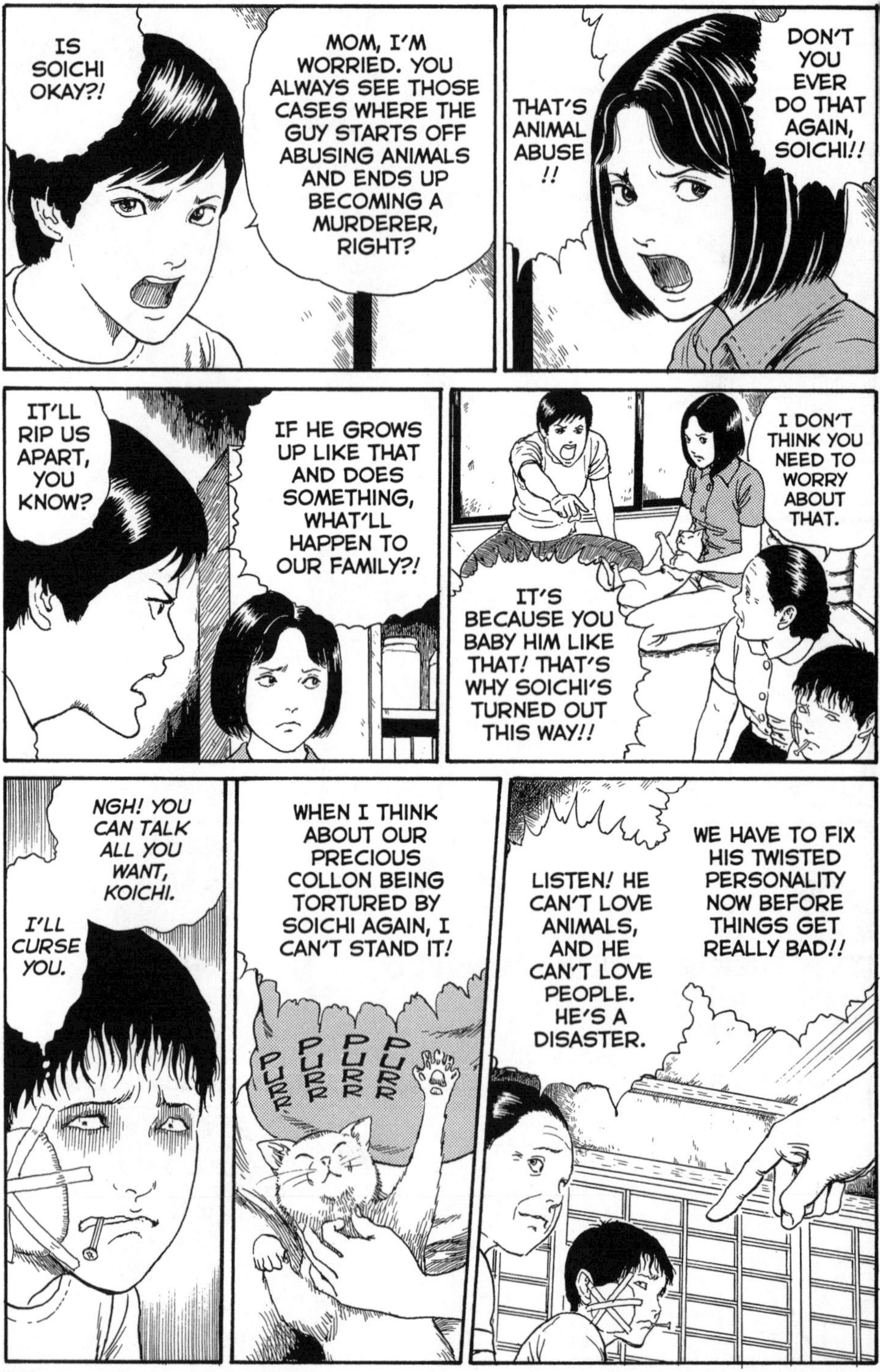
DON'T YOU EVER DO THAT AGAIN, SOICHI!!
THAT'S ANIMAL ABUSE!!
MOM, I'M WORRIED. YOU ALWAYS SEE THOSE CASES WHERE THE GUY STARTS OFF ABUSING ANIMALS AND ENDS UP BECOMING A MURDERER, RIGHT?
IS SOICHI OKAY?!
I DON'T THINK YOU NEED TO WORRY ABOUT THAT.
IT'S BECAUSE YOU BABY HIM LIKE THAT! THAT'S WHY SOICHI'S TURNED OUT THIS WAY!!
IF HE GROWS UP LIKE THAT AND DOES SOMETHING, WHAT'LL HAPPEN TO OUR FAMILY?!
IT'LL RIP US APART, YOU KNOW?
WE HAVE TO FIX HIS TWISTED PERSONALITY NOW BEFORE THINGS GET REALLY BAD!!
LISTEN! HE CAN'T LOVE ANIMALS, AND HE CAN'T LOVE PEOPLE. HE'S A DISASTER.
WHEN I THINK ABOUT OUR PRECIOUS COLLON BEING TORTURED BY SOICHI AGAIN, I CAN'T STAND IT!
PURR PURR PURR PURR
NGH! YOU CAN TALK ALL YOU WANT, KOICHI.
I'LL CURSE YOU.

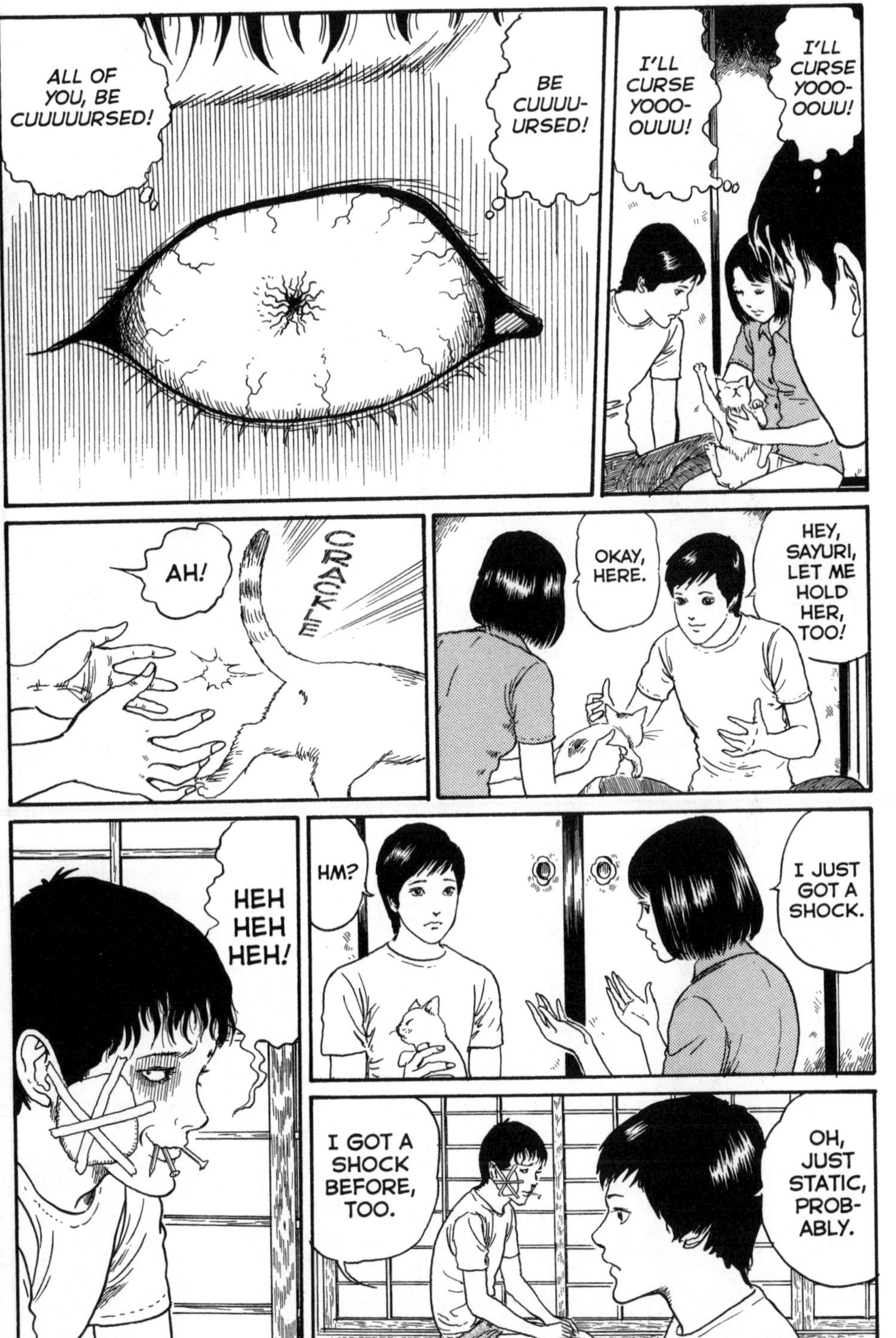
I'LL CURSE YOOO-OUUU!
I'LL CURSE YOOO-OUUU!
BE CUUUU-URSED!
ALL OF YOU, BE CUUUUURSED!
HEY, SAYURI, LET ME HOLD HER, TOO!
OKAY, HERE.
CRACKLE
AH!
I JUST GOT A SHOCK.
HM?
OH, JUST STATIC, PROBABLY.
I GOT A SHOCK BEFORE, TOO.
HEH HEH HEH!

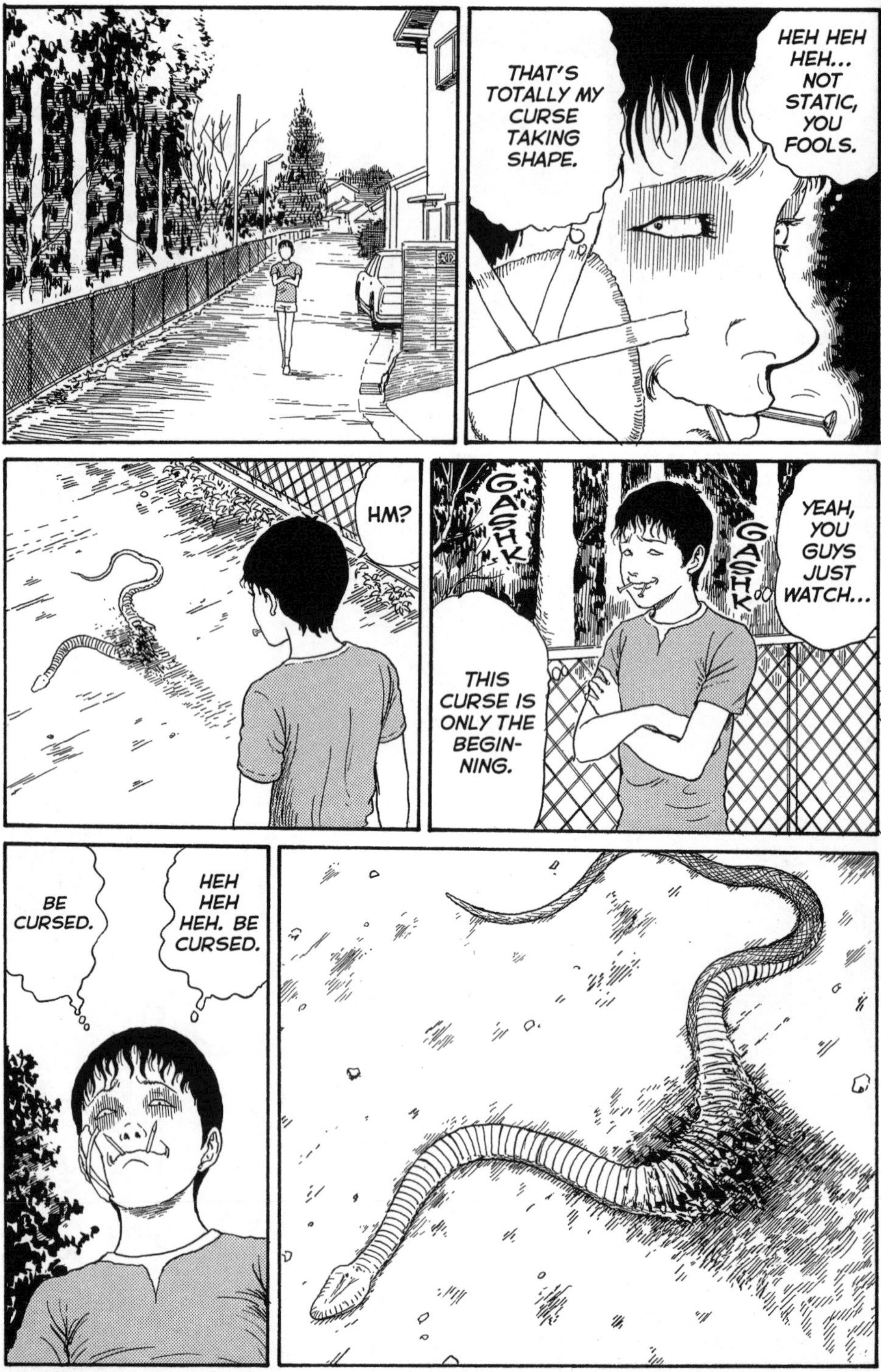
HEH HEH HEH... NOT STATIC, YOU FOOLS.
THAT'S TOTALLY MY CURSE TAKING SHAPE.
GASHK
GASHK
YEAH, YOU GUYS JUST WATCH...
THIS CURSE IS ONLY THE BEGIN-NING.
HM?
HEH HEH HEH. BE CURSED.
BE CURSED.

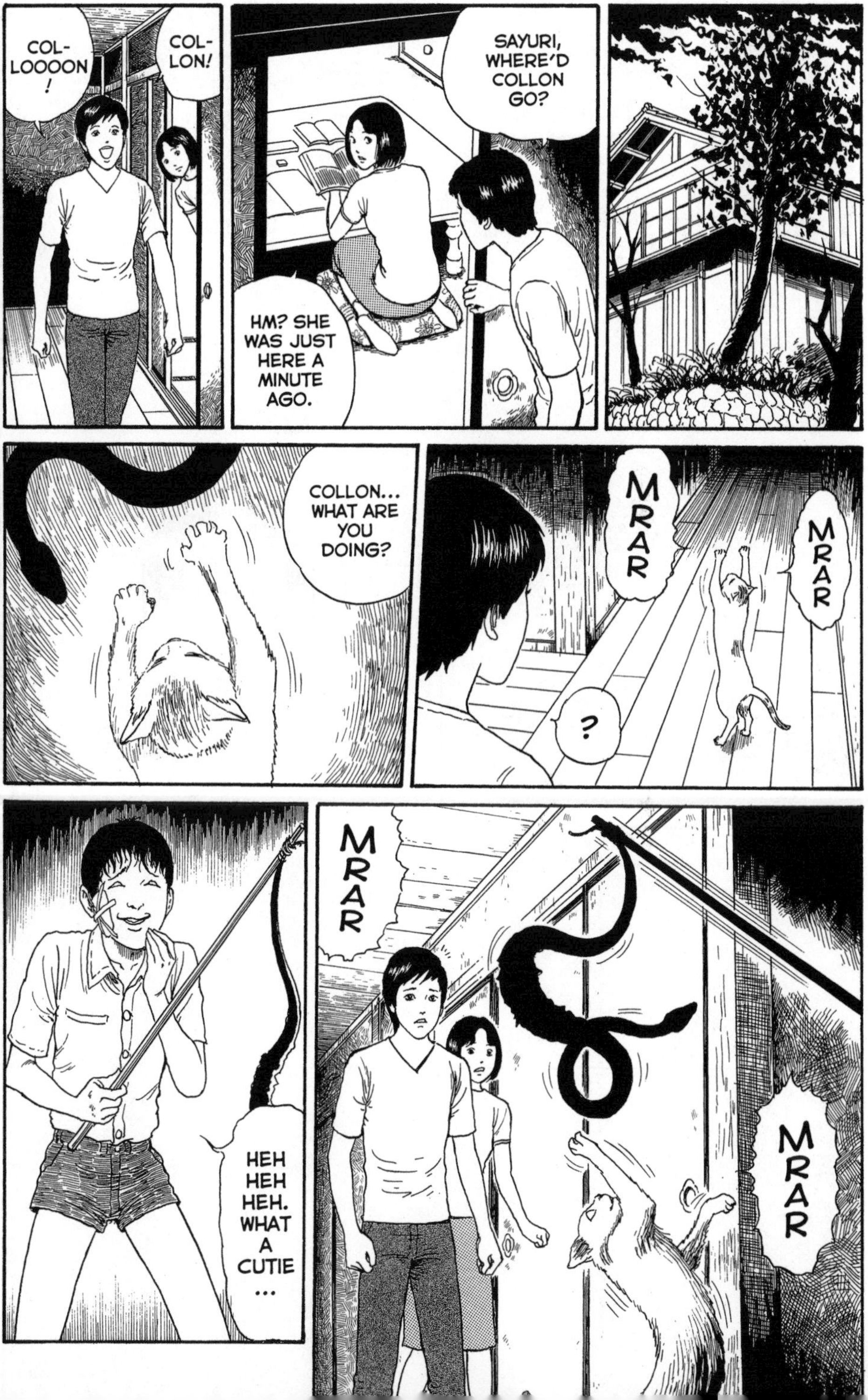
SAYURI, WHERE'D COLLON GO?
HM? SHE WAS JUST HERE A MINUTE AGO.
COL-LON!
COL-LOOOON!
MRAR
MRAR
?
COLLON... WHAT ARE YOU DOING?
MRAR
MRAR
HEH HEH HEH. WHAT A CUTIE...

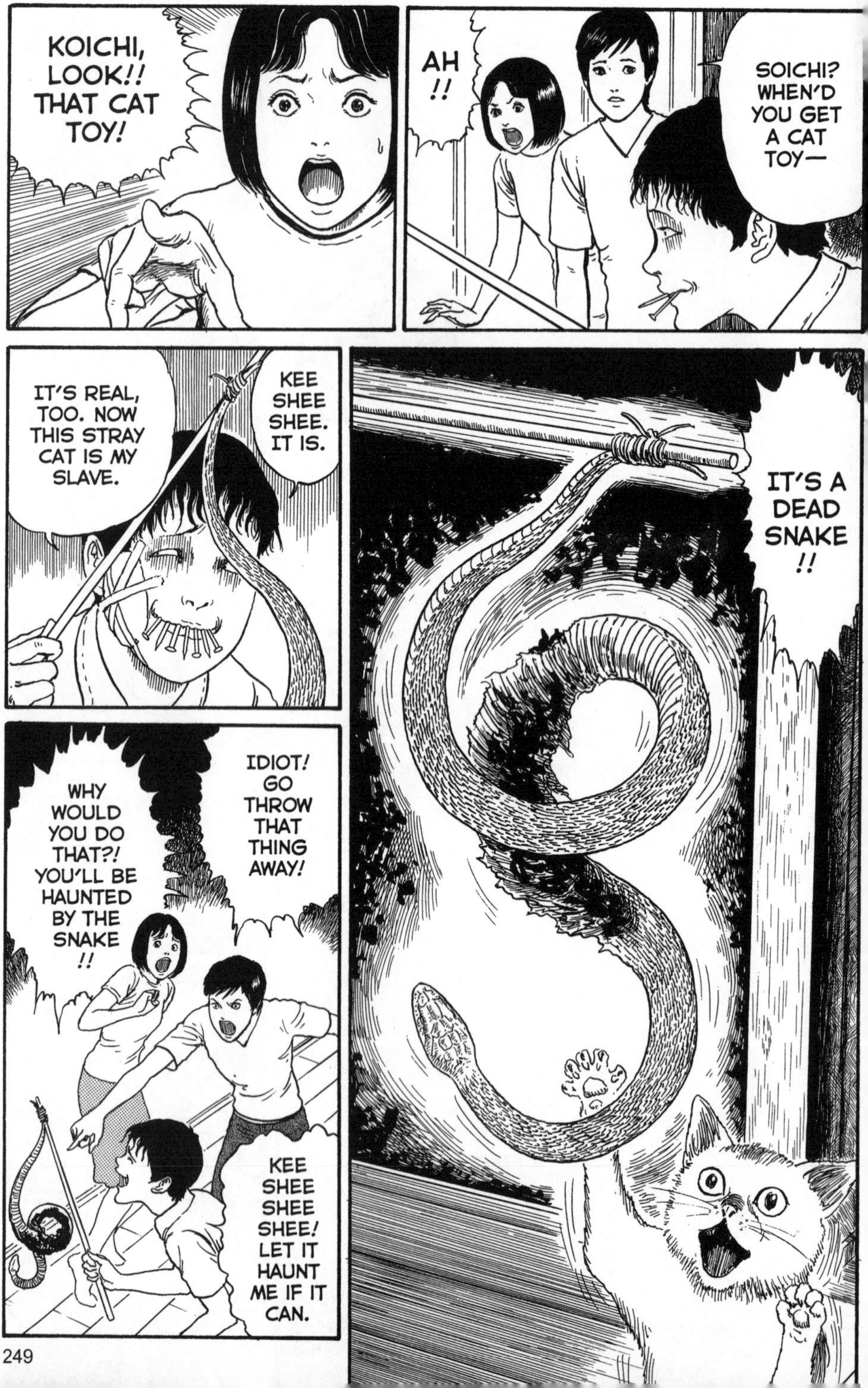
SOICHI? WHEN'D YOU GET A CAT TOY—
AH!!
KOICHI, LOOK!! THAT CAT TOY!
IT'S A DEAD SNAKE!!
KEE SHEE SHEE. IT IS.
IT'S REAL, TOO. NOW THIS STRAY CAT IS MY SLAVE.
IDIOT! GO THROW THAT THING AWAY!
WHY WOULD YOU DO THAT?! YOU'LL BE HAUNTED BY THE SNAKE!!
KEE SHEE SHEE SHEE! LET IT HAUNT ME IF IT CAN.

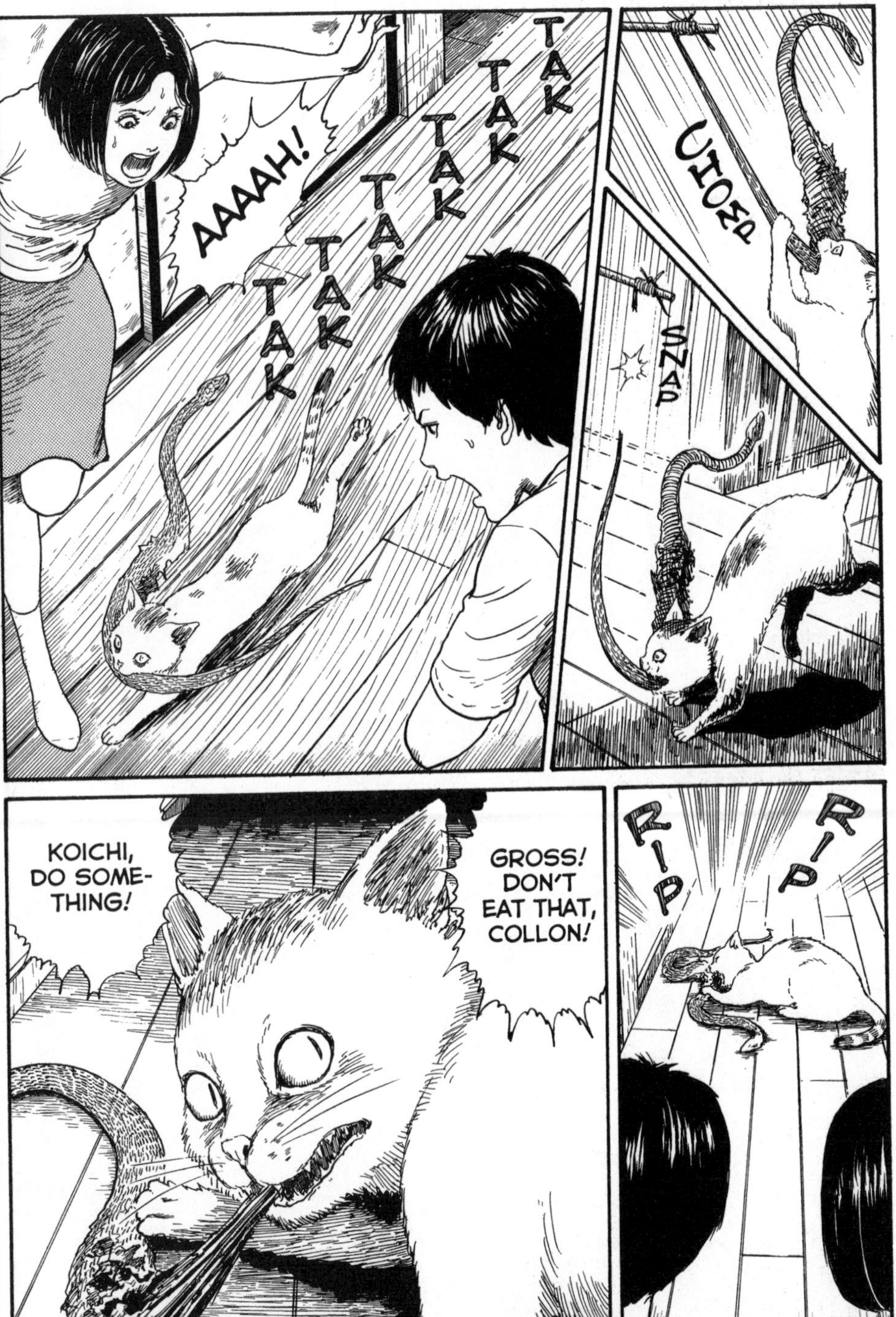
CHOMP
SNAP
AAAAH!
TAK TAK TAK TAK TAK TAK
RIP RIP
GROSS! DON'T EAT THAT, COLLON!
KOICHI, DO SOME-THING!

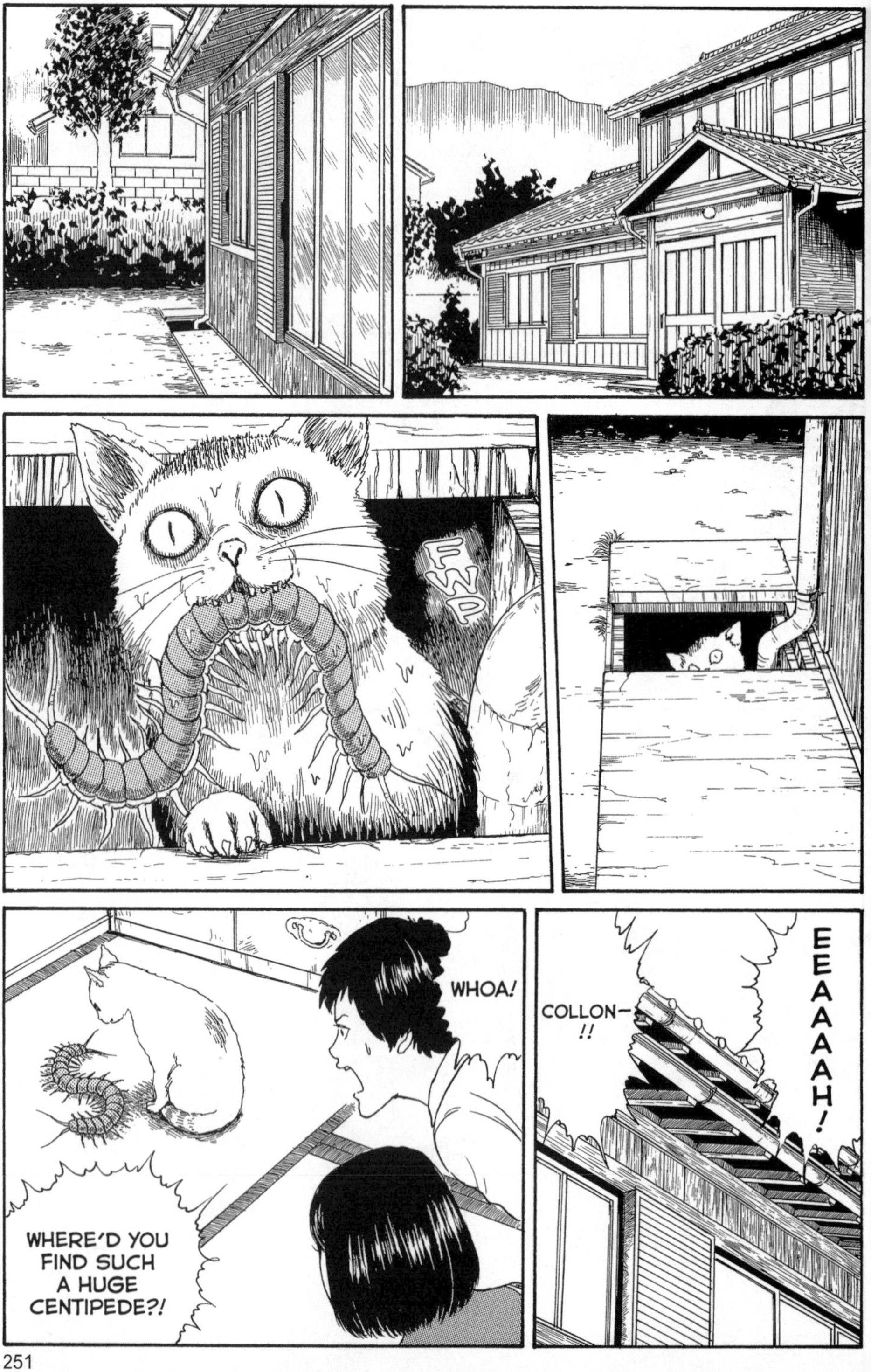
FWP
EEAAAAAH!
COLLON—!!
WHOA!
WHERE'D YOU FIND SUCH A HUGE CENTIPEDE?!

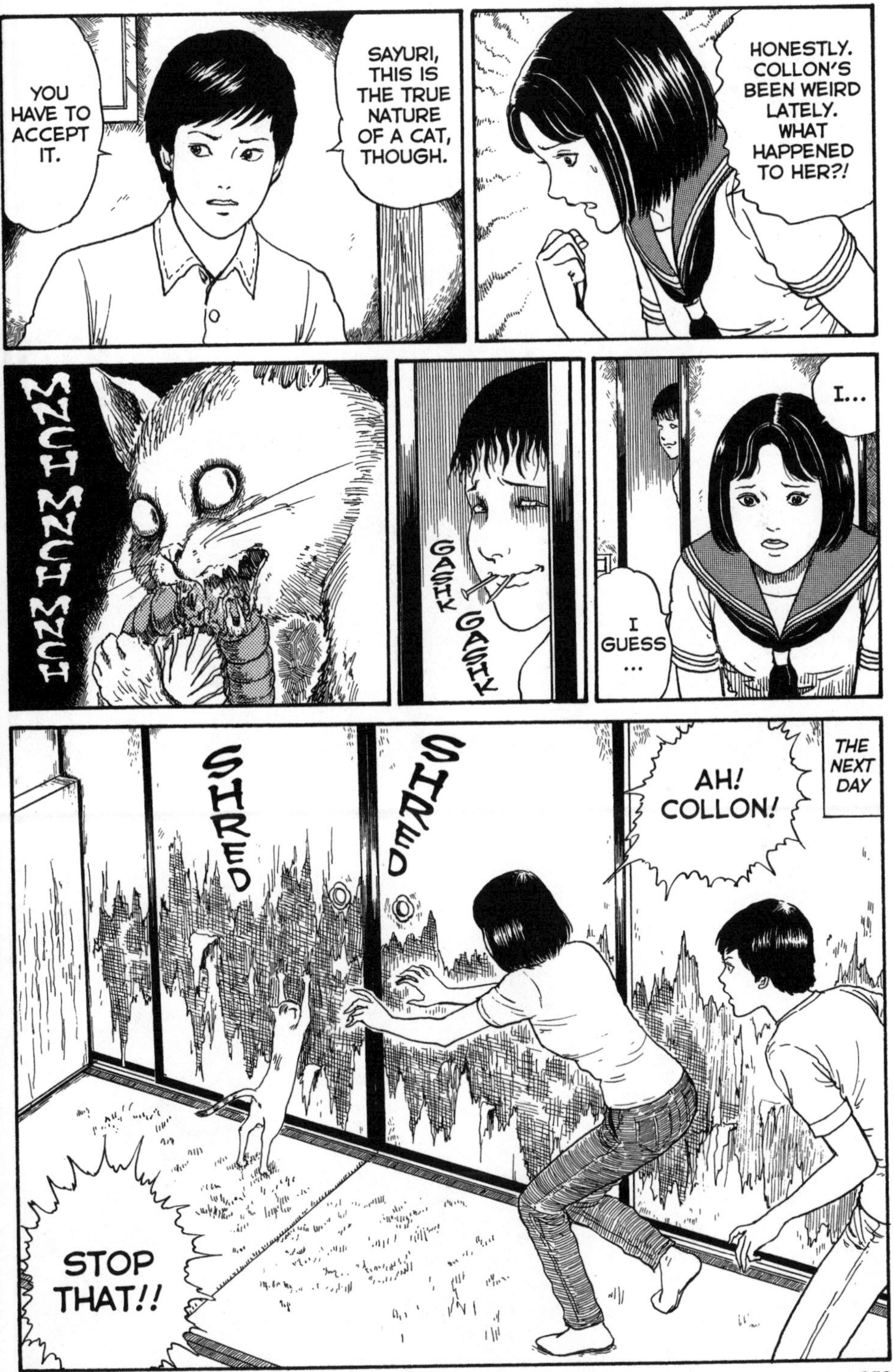

HONESTLY. COLLON'S BEEN WEIRD LATELY. WHAT HAPPENED TO HER?!
SAYURI, THIS IS THE TRUE NATURE OF A CAT, THOUGH.
YOU HAVE TO ACCEPT IT.
I...
I GUESS ...
GASHK GASHK
MNCH MNCH MNCH
THE NEXT DAY
AH! COLLON!
SHRED SHRED
STOP THAT!!

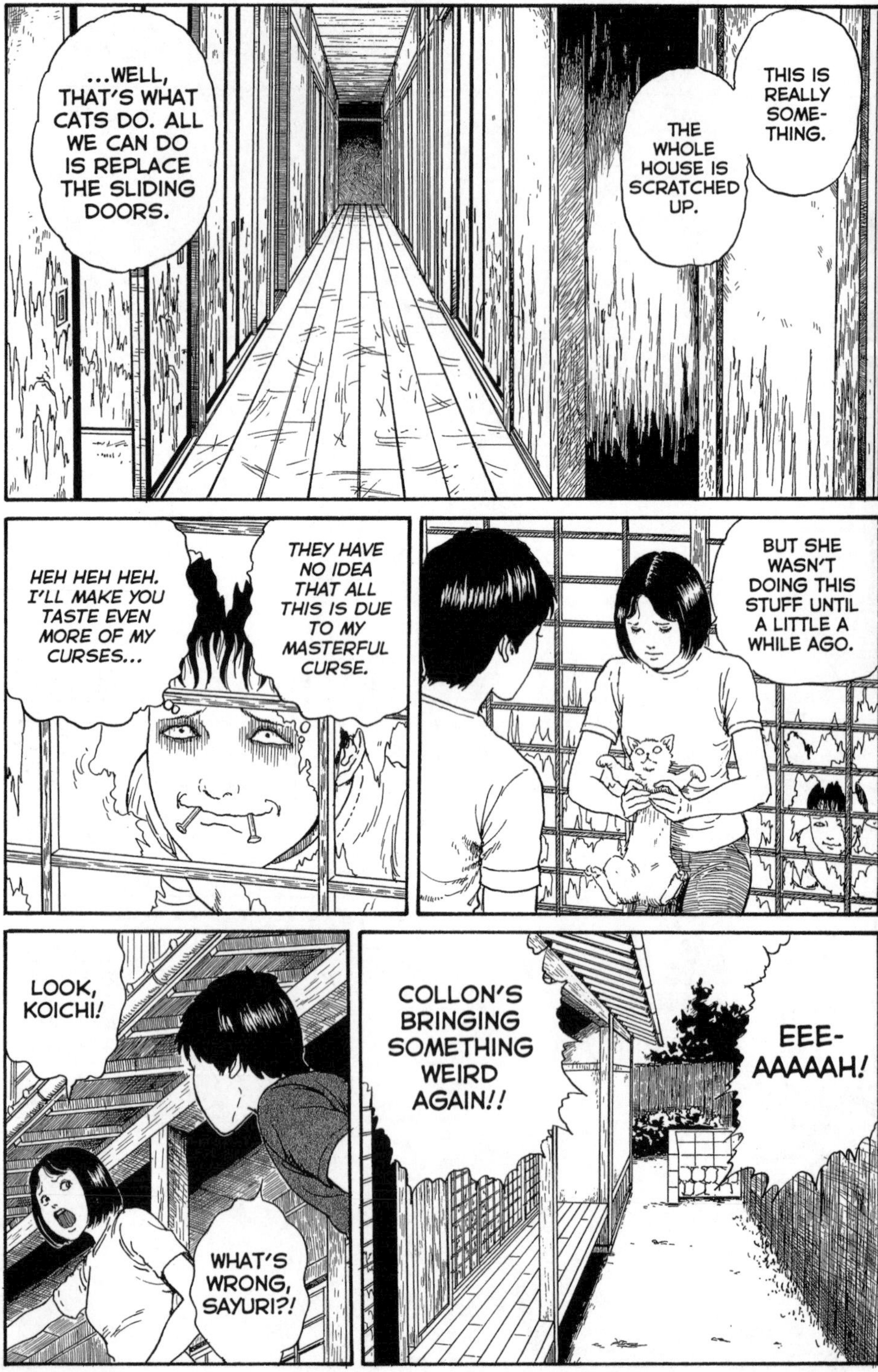
THIS IS REALLY SOME-THING.
THE WHOLE HOUSE IS SCRATCHED UP.
...WELL, THAT'S WHAT CATS DO. ALL WE CAN DO IS REPLACE THE SLIDING DOORS.
BUT SHE WASN'T DOING THIS STUFF UNTIL A LITTLE A WHILE AGO.
THEY HAVE NO IDEA THAT ALL THIS IS DUE TO MY MASTERFUL CURSE.
HEH HEH HEH. I'LL MAKE YOU TASTE EVEN MORE OF MY CURSES...
EEE-AAAAAH!
COLLON'S BRINGING SOMETHING WEIRD AGAIN!!
LOOK, KOICHI!
WHAT'S WRONG, SAYURI?!

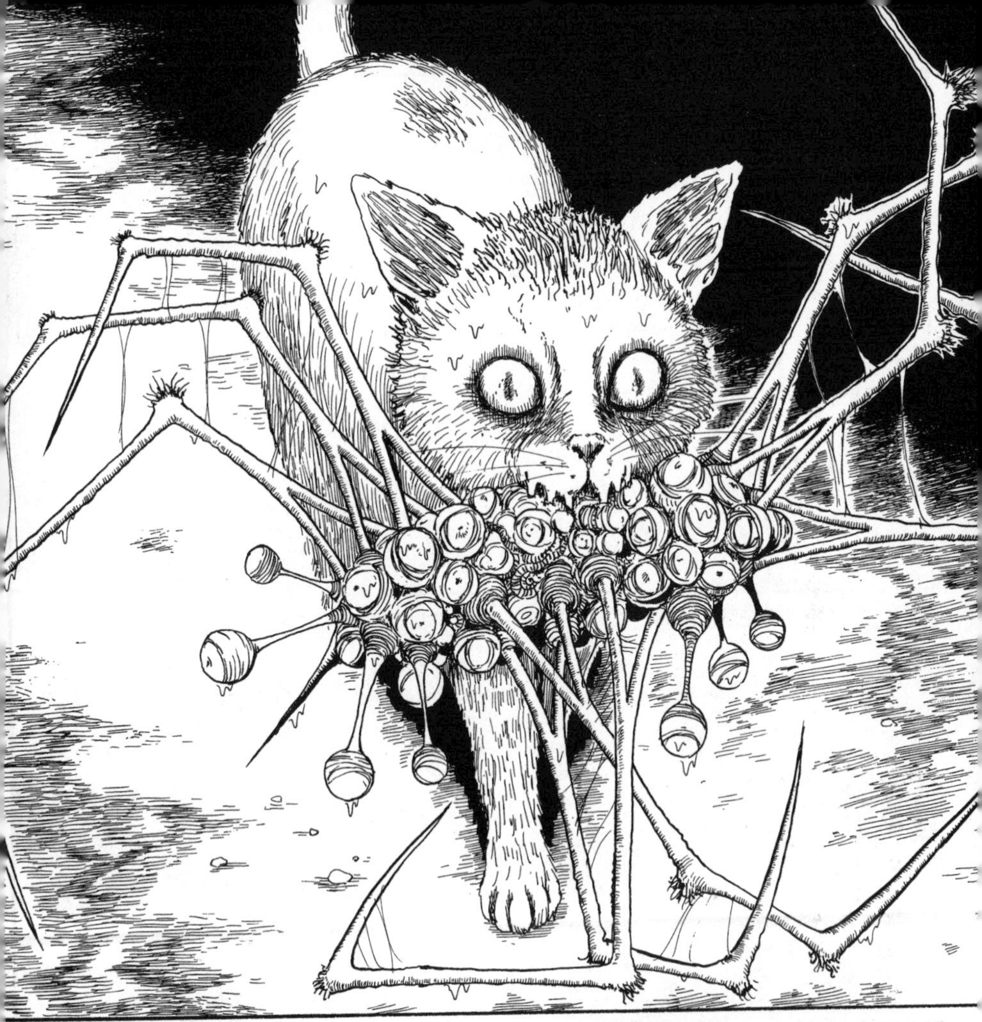

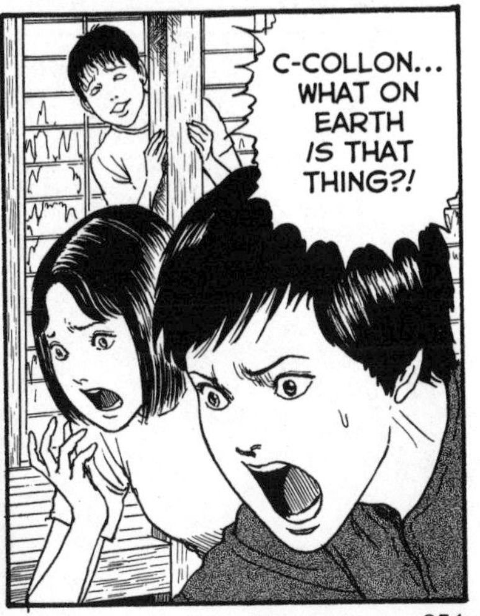
C-COLLON... WHAT ON EARTH IS THAT THING?!

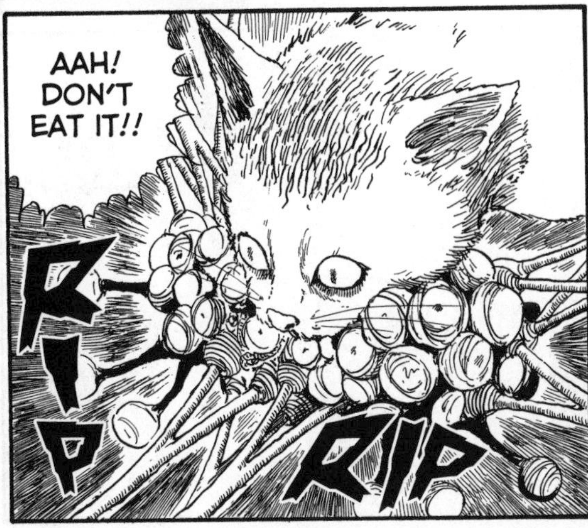
AAH! DON'T EAT IT!!
RIP
RIP

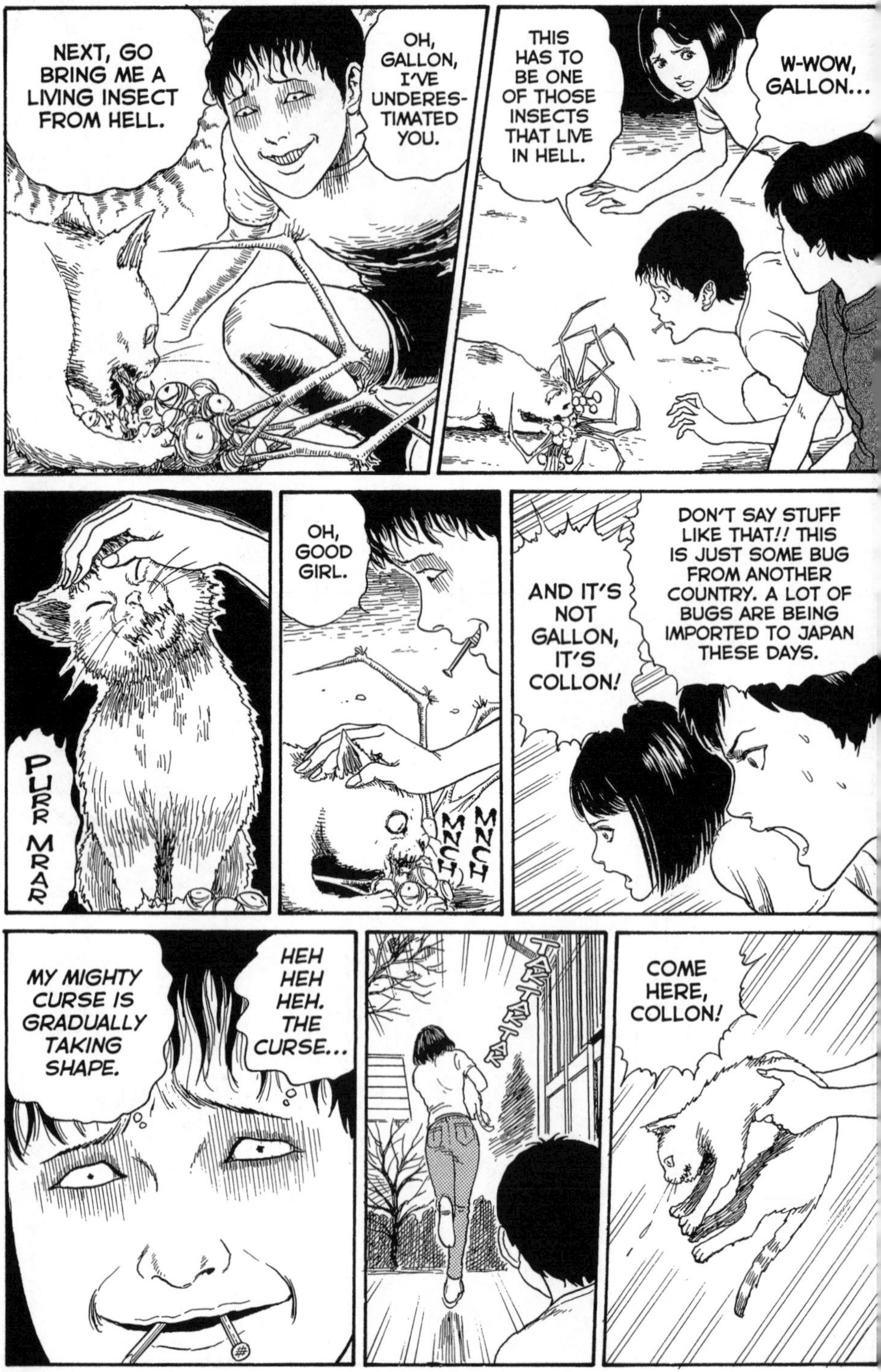
W-WOW, GALLON...
THIS HAS TO BE ONE OF THOSE INSECTS THAT LIVE IN HELL.
OH, GALLON, I'VE UNDERES-TIMATED YOU.
NEXT, GO BRING ME A LIVING INSECT FROM HELL.
DON'T SAY STUFF LIKE THAT!! THIS IS JUST SOME BUG FROM ANOTHER COUNTRY. A LOT OF BUGS ARE BEING IMPORTED TO JAPAN THESE DAYS.
AND IT'S NOT GALLON, IT'S COLLON!
OH, GOOD GIRL.
MNCH MNCH
PURR MRAR
COME HERE, COLLON!
TATATAT
HEH HEH HEH. THE CURSE...
MY MIGHTY CURSE IS GRADUALLY TAKING SHAPE.

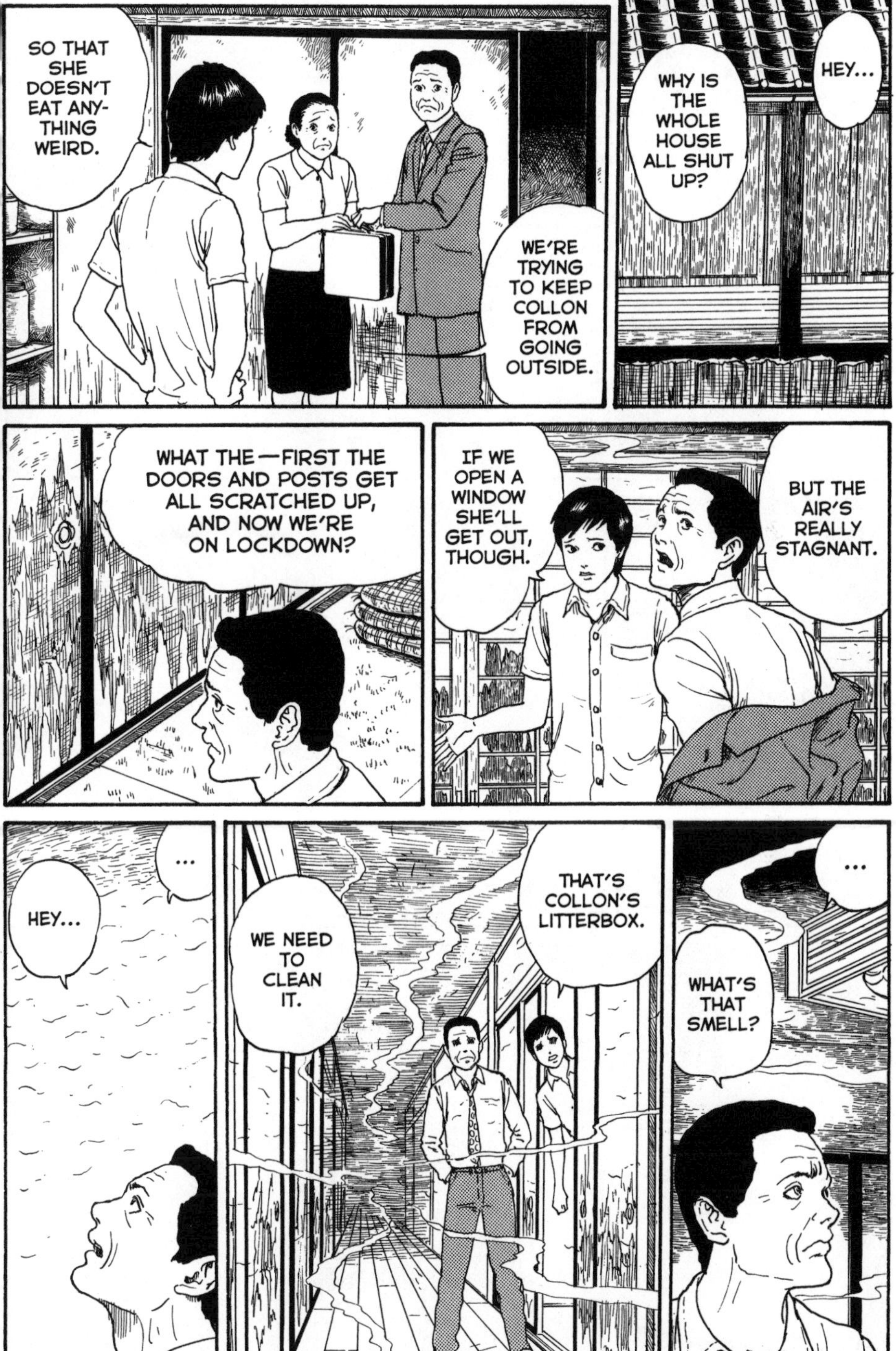
HEY...
WHY IS THE WHOLE HOUSE ALL SHUT UP?
WE'RE TRYING TO KEEP COLLON FROM GOING OUTSIDE.
SO THAT SHE DOESN'T EAT ANY-THING WEIRD.
BUT THE AIR'S REALLY STAGNANT.
IF WE OPEN A WINDOW SHE'LL GET OUT, THOUGH.
WHAT THE—FIRST THE DOORS AND POSTS GET ALL SCRATCHED UP, AND NOW WE'RE ON LOCKDOWN?
...
WHAT'S THAT SMELL?
THAT'S COLLON'S LITTERBOX.
WE NEED TO CLEAN IT.
...
HEY...

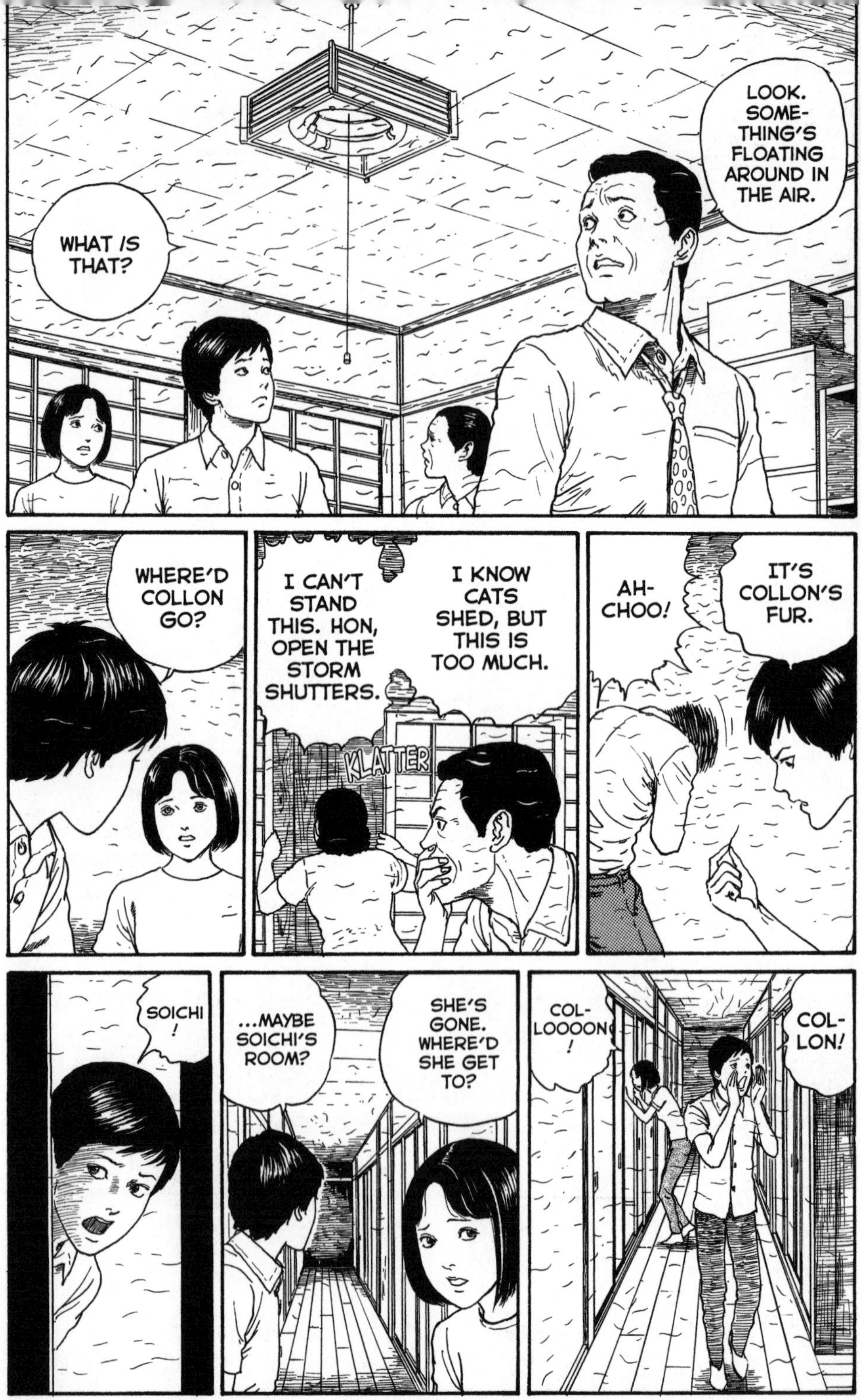
LOOK. SOME-THING'S FLOATING AROUND IN THE AIR.
WHAT IS THAT?
IT'S COLLON'S FUR.
AH-CHOO!
I KNOW CATS SHED, BUT THIS IS TOO MUCH.
I CAN'T STAND THIS. HON, OPEN THE STORM SHUTTERS.
KLATTER
WHERE'D COLLON GO?
COL-LON!
COL-LOOOON!
SHE'S GONE. WHERE'D SHE GET TO?
...MAYBE SOICHI'S ROOM?
SOICHI!

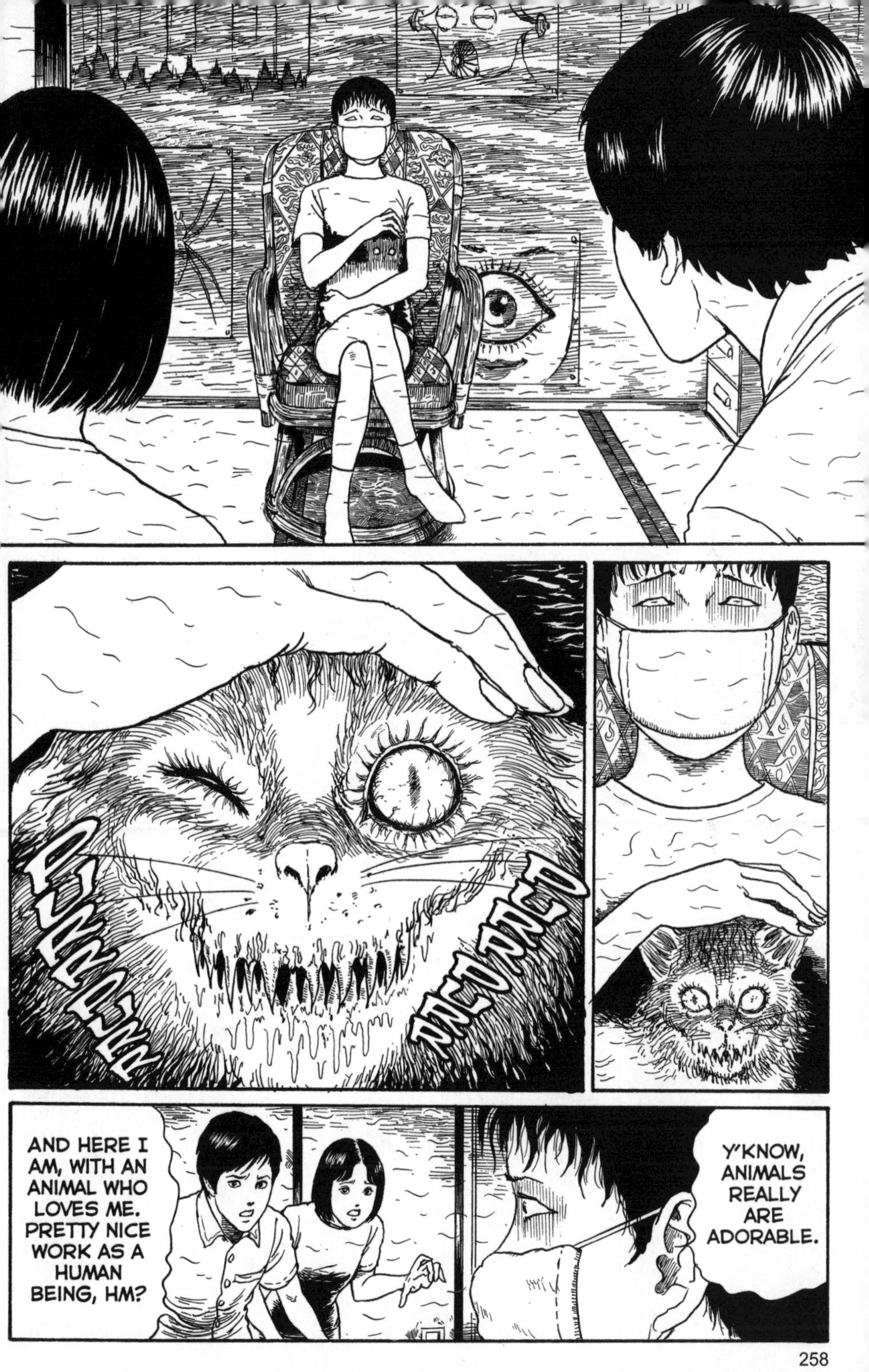
Y'KNOW, ANIMALS REALLY ARE ADORABLE.
AND HERE I AM, WITH AN ANIMAL WHO LOVES ME. PRETTY NICE WORK AS A HUMAN BEING, HM?

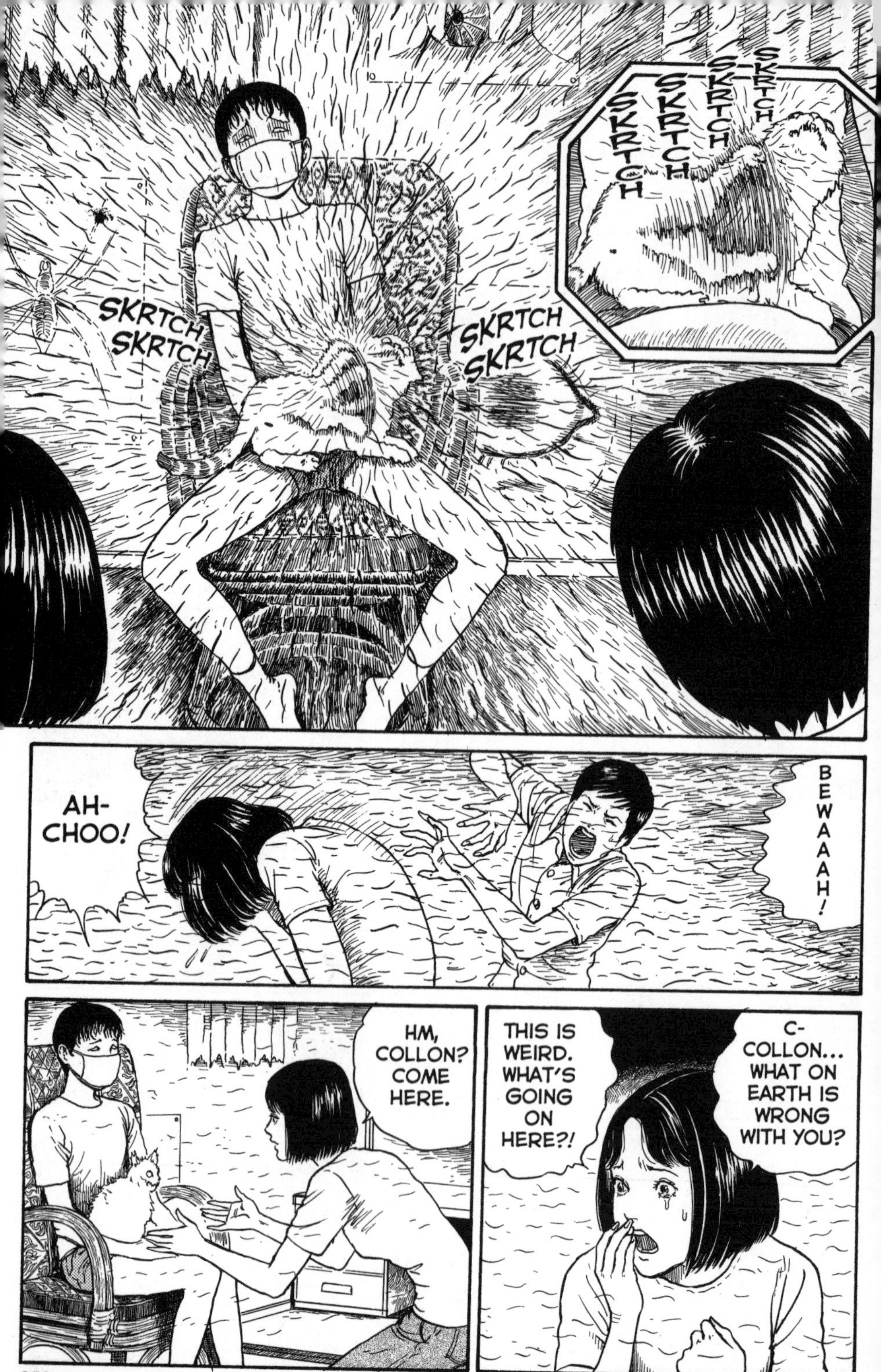
SKRTCH
SKRTCH
SKRTCH
SKRTCH
SKRTCH SKRTCH
SKRTCH SKRTCH
BEWAAAAH!
AH-CHOO!
C-COLLON... WHAT ON EARTH IS WRONG WITH YOU?
THIS IS WEIRD. WHAT'S GOING ON HERE?!
HM, COLLON? COME HERE.

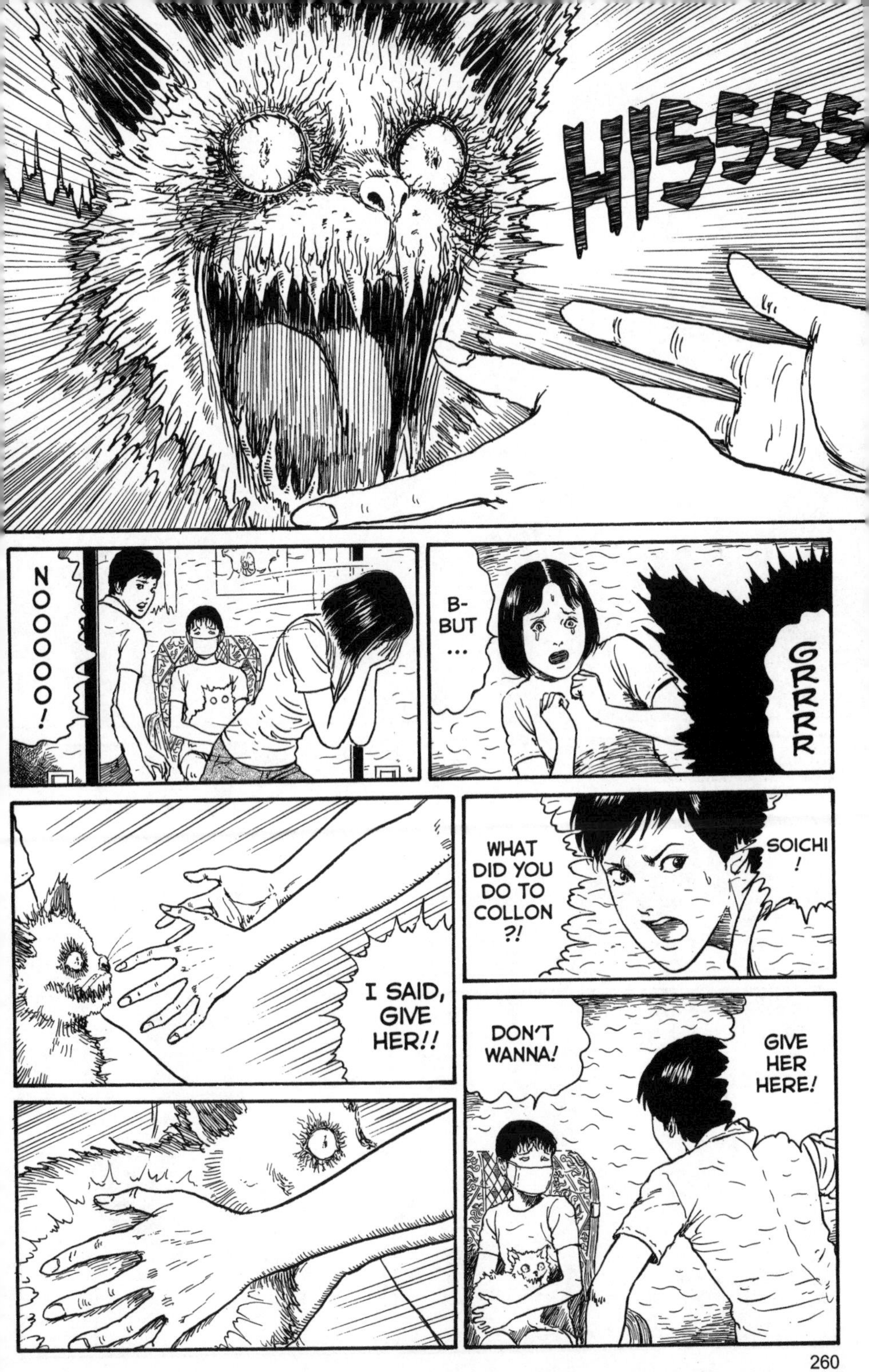
HISSSSS
B-BUT ...
GRRRR
NOOOOOO!
SOICHI!
WHAT DID YOU DO TO COLLON?!
I SAID, GIVE HER!!
GIVE HER HERE!
DON'T WANNA!

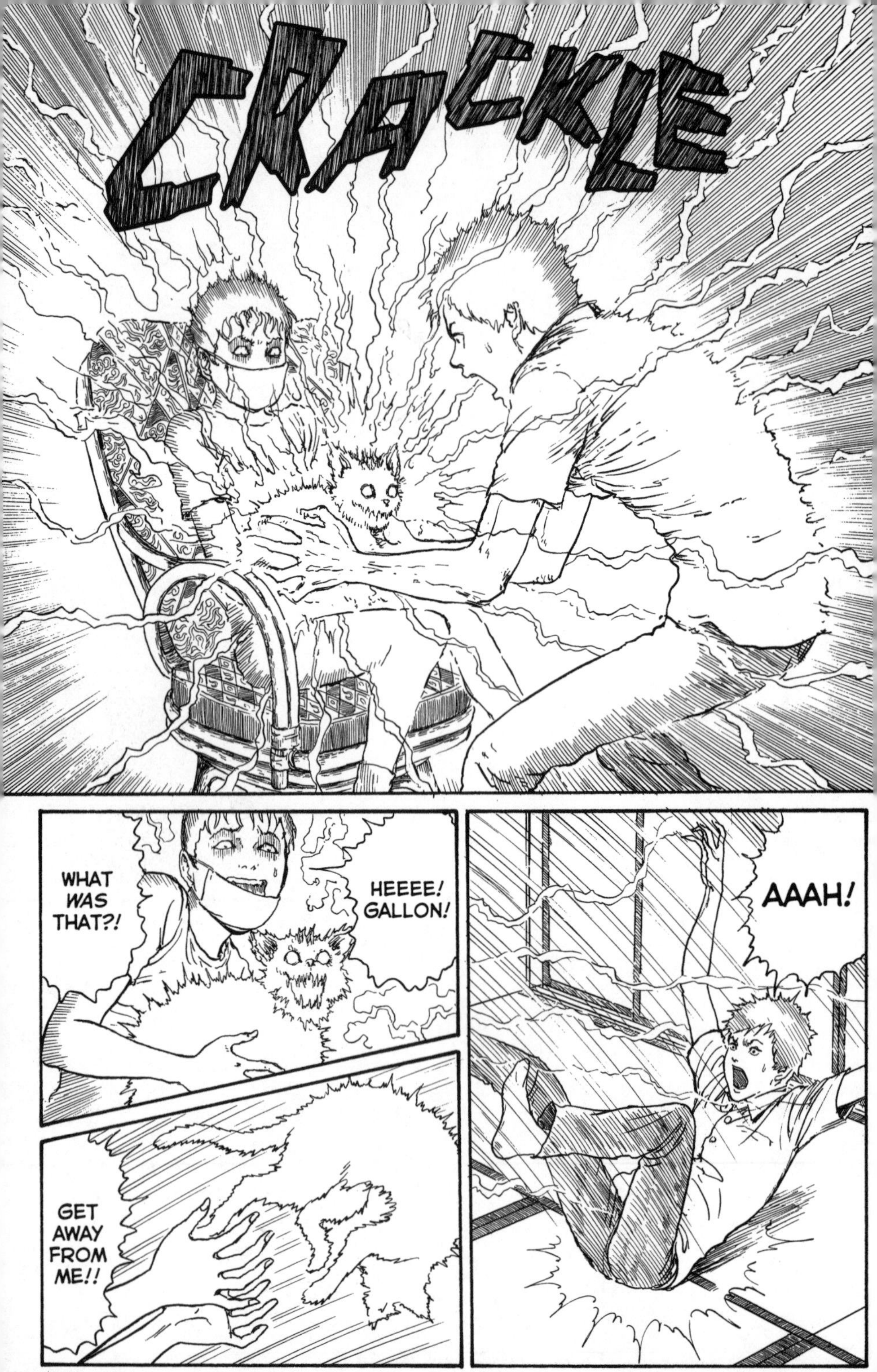
CRACKLE
AAAH!
HEEEE! GALLON!
WHAT *WAS* THAT?!
GET AWAY FROM ME!!

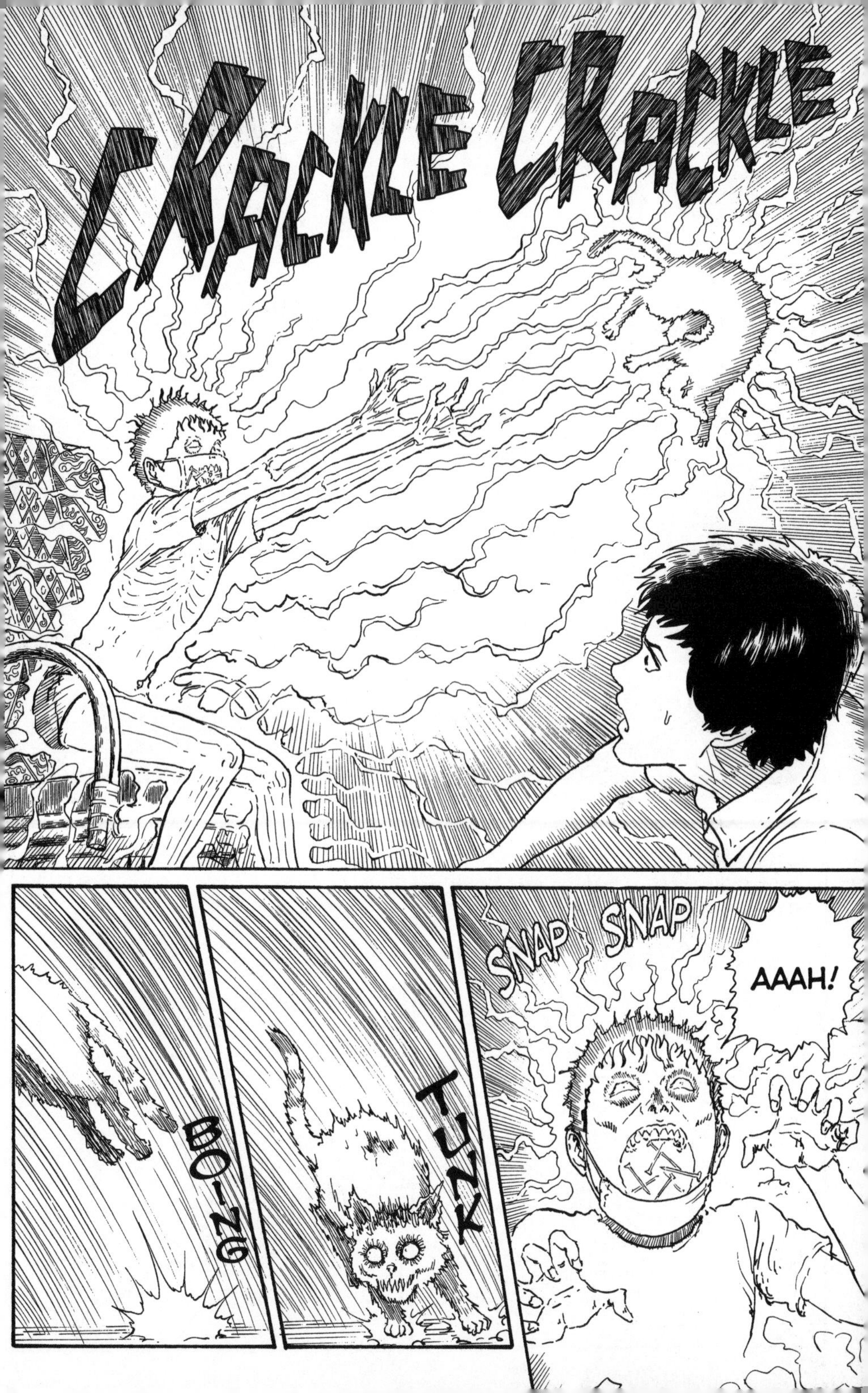
CRACKLE CRACKLE
SNAP SNAP
AAAH!
TUNK
BOING

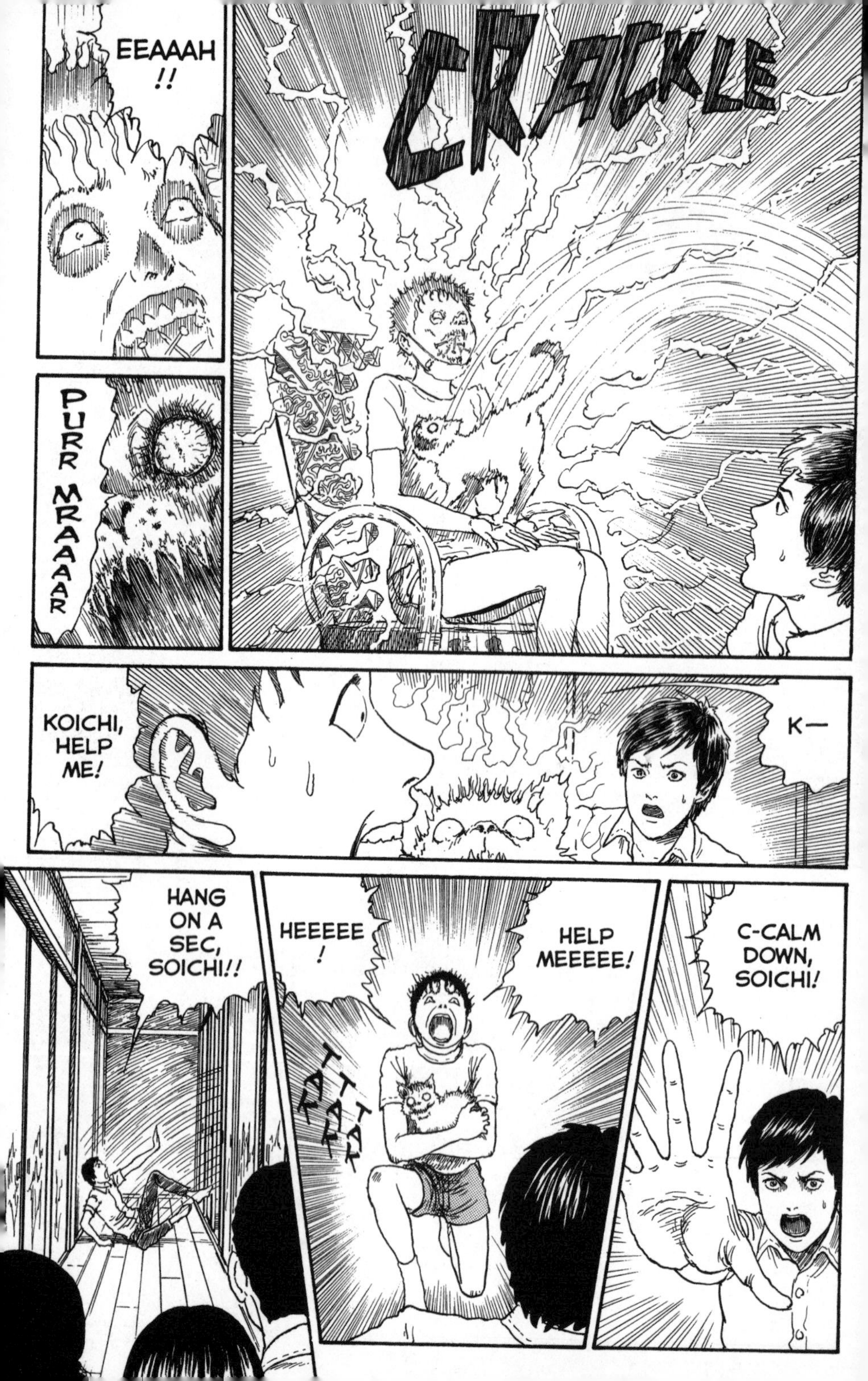
CRACKLE
EEAAAH!!
PURR MRAAAAR
K—
KOICHI, HELP ME!
C-CALM DOWN, SOICHI!
HELP MEEEEE!
HEEEEE!
TAK TAK TAK
HANG ON A SEC, SOICHI!!

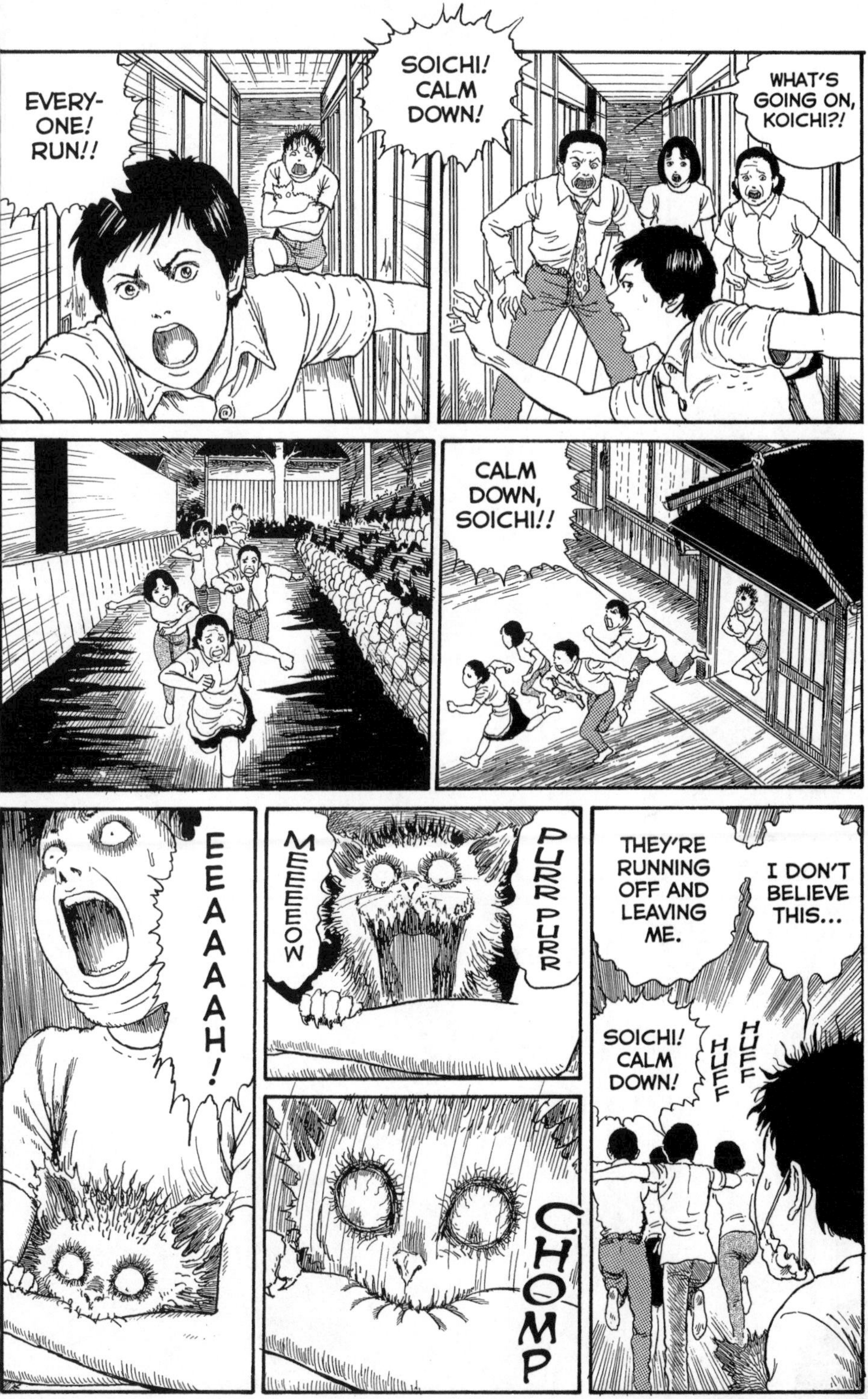
WHAT'S GOING ON, KOICHI?!
SOICHI! CALM DOWN!
EVERY-ONE! RUN!!
CALM DOWN, SOICHI!!
I DON'T BELIEVE THIS...
THEY'RE RUNNING OFF AND LEAVING ME.
HUFF HUFF
SOICHI! CALM DOWN!
PURR PURR
MEEEEOW
CHOMP
EEEAAAAAH!

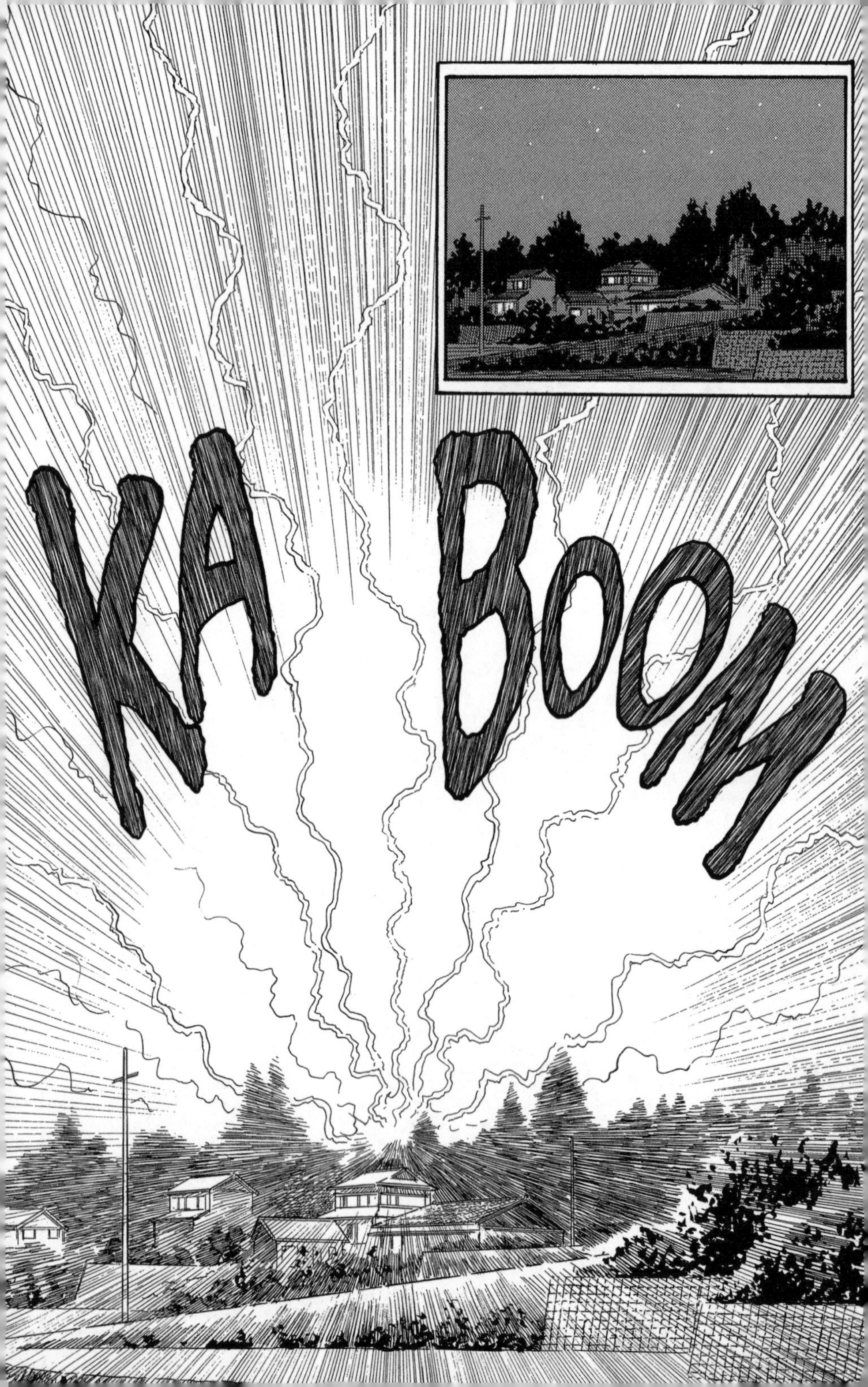
KA BOOM

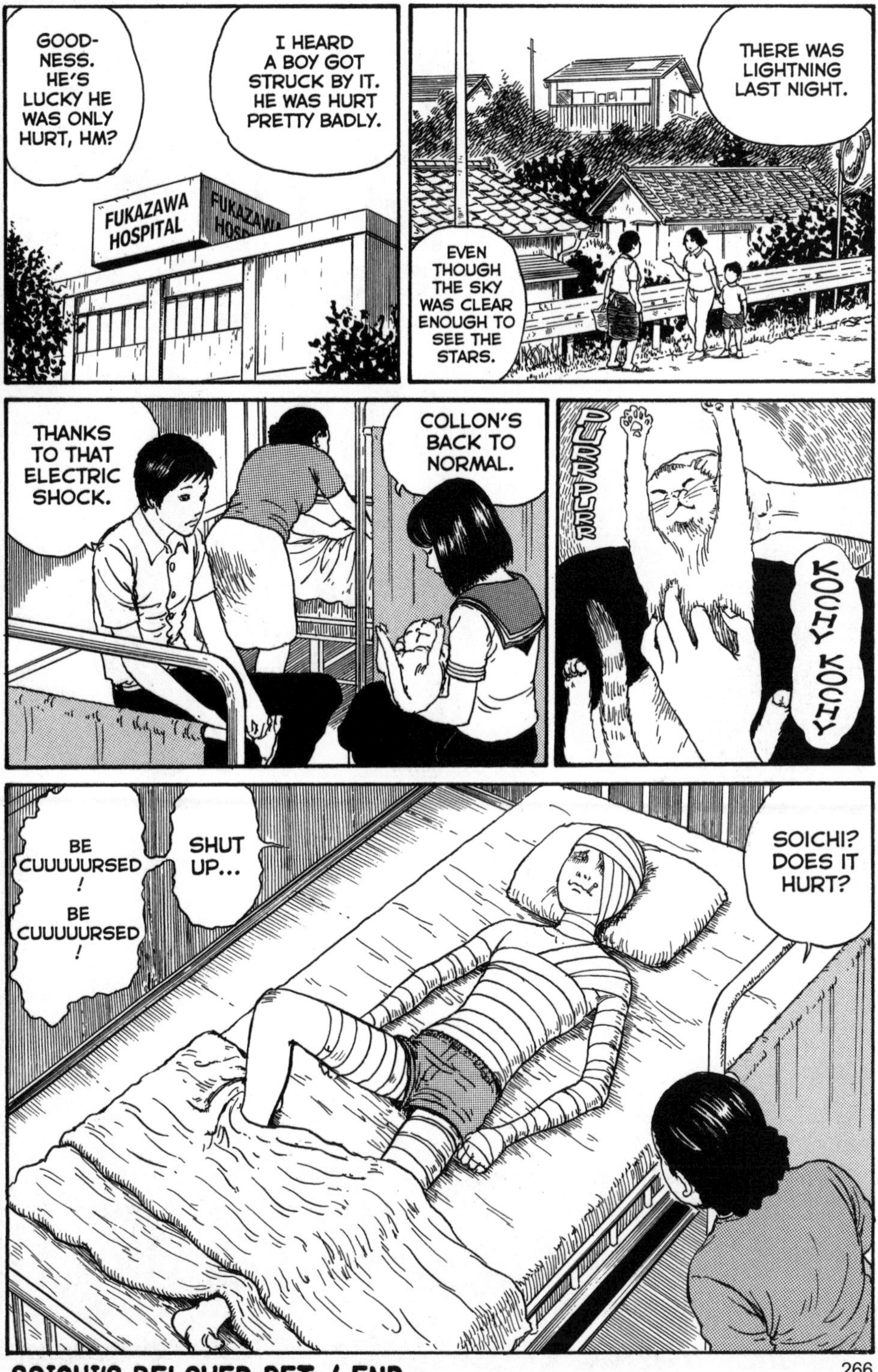
THERE WAS LIGHTNING LAST NIGHT.
EVEN THOUGH THE SKY WAS CLEAR ENOUGH TO SEE THE STARS.
I HEARD A BOY GOT STRUCK BY IT. HE WAS HURT PRETTY BADLY.
GOODNESS. HE'S LUCKY HE WAS ONLY HURT, HM?
FUKAZAWA HOSPITAL
PURR PURR
KOCHY KOCHY
COLLON'S BACK TO NORMAL.
THANKS TO THAT ELECTRIC SHOCK.
SOICHI? DOES IT HURT?
SHUT UP...
BE CUUUUURSED! BE CUUUUURSED!

SOICHI'S BELOVED PET / END

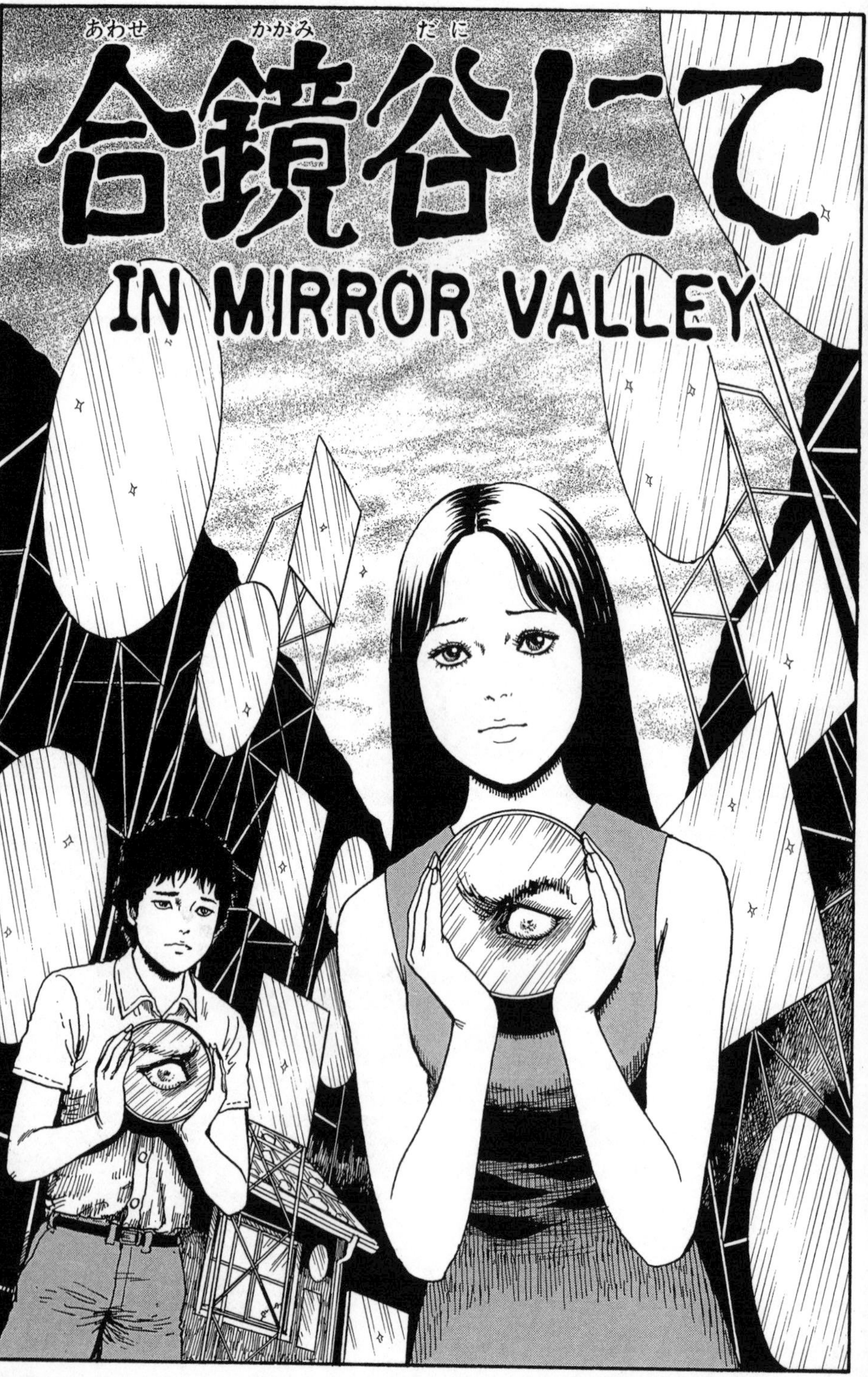
あわせかがみだに
合鏡谷にて
IN MIRROR VALLEY

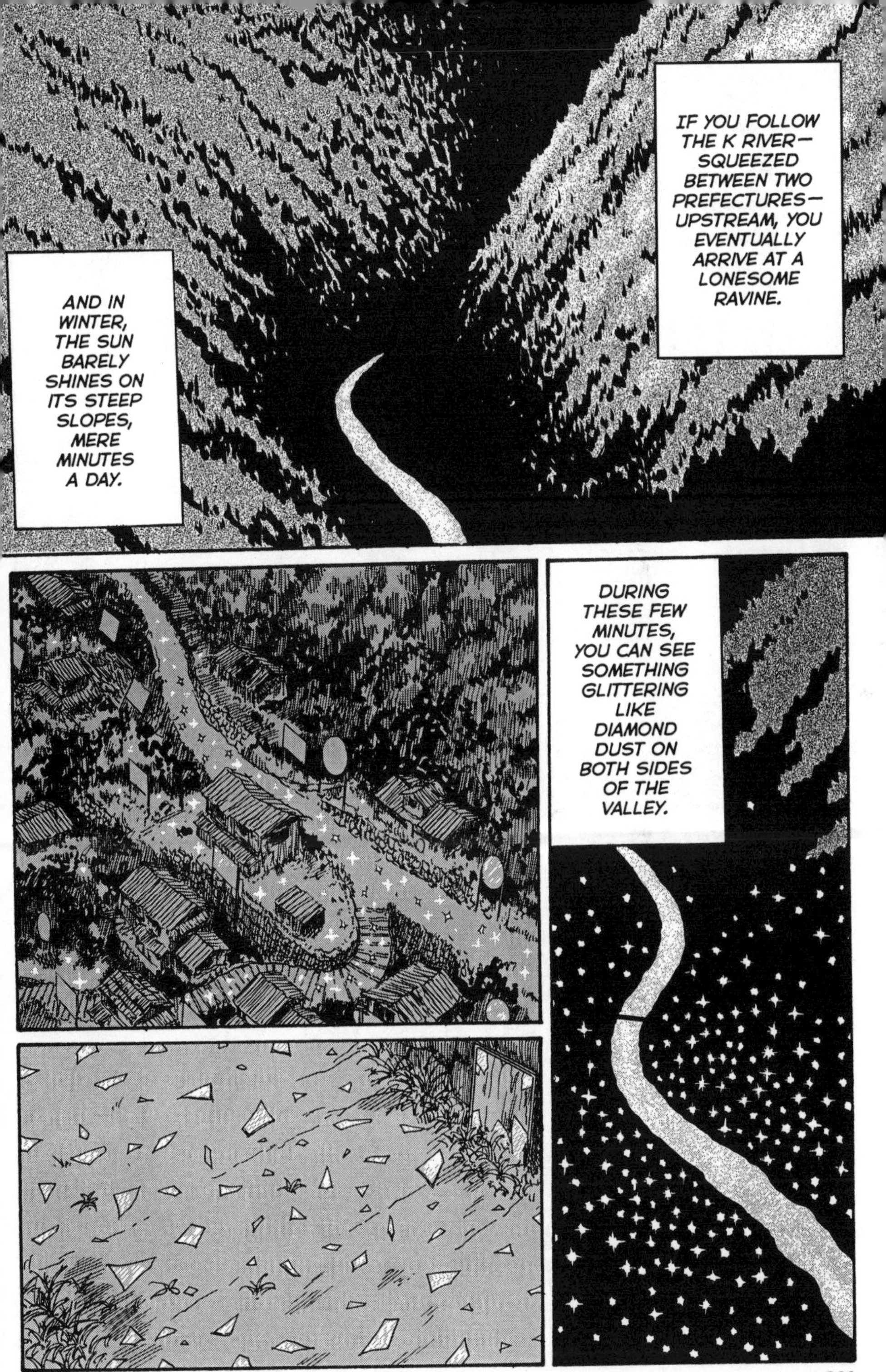
IF YOU FOLLOW THE K RIVER—SQUEEZED BETWEEN TWO PREFECTURES—UPSTREAM, YOU EVENTUALLY ARRIVE AT A LONESOME RAVINE.
AND IN WINTER, THE SUN BARELY SHINES ON ITS STEEP SLOPES, MERE MINUTES A DAY.
DURING THESE FEW MINUTES, YOU CAN SEE SOMETHING GLITTERING LIKE DIAMOND DUST ON BOTH SIDES OF THE VALLEY.

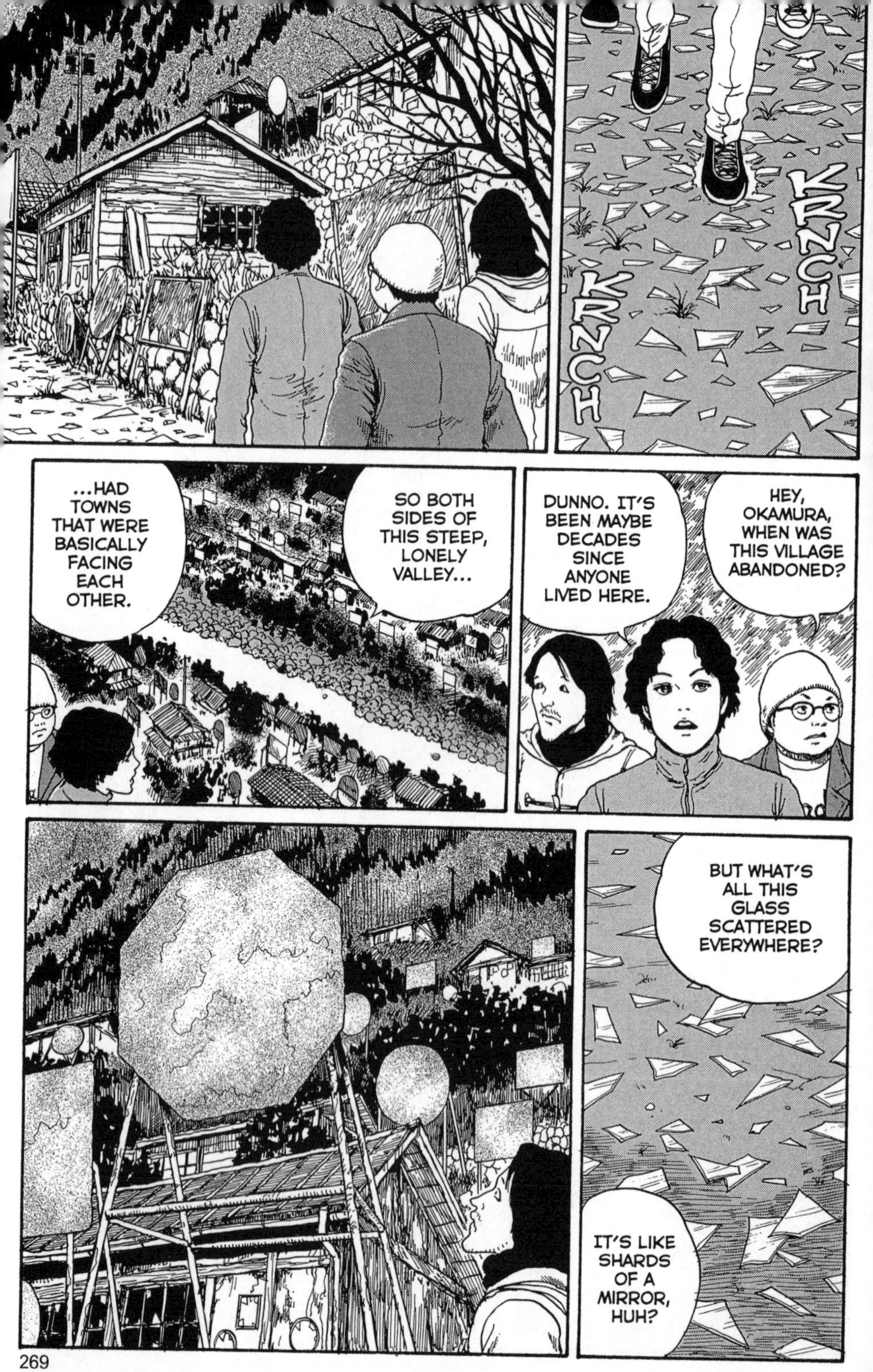
KRNCH
KRNCH
HEY, OKAMURA, WHEN WAS THIS VILLAGE ABANDONED?
DUNNO. IT'S BEEN MAYBE DECADES SINCE ANYONE LIVED HERE.
SO BOTH SIDES OF THIS STEEP, LONELY VALLEY...
...HAD TOWNS THAT WERE BASICALLY FACING EACH OTHER.
BUT WHAT'S ALL THIS GLASS SCATTERED EVERYWHERE?
IT'S LIKE SHARDS OF A MIRROR, HUH?

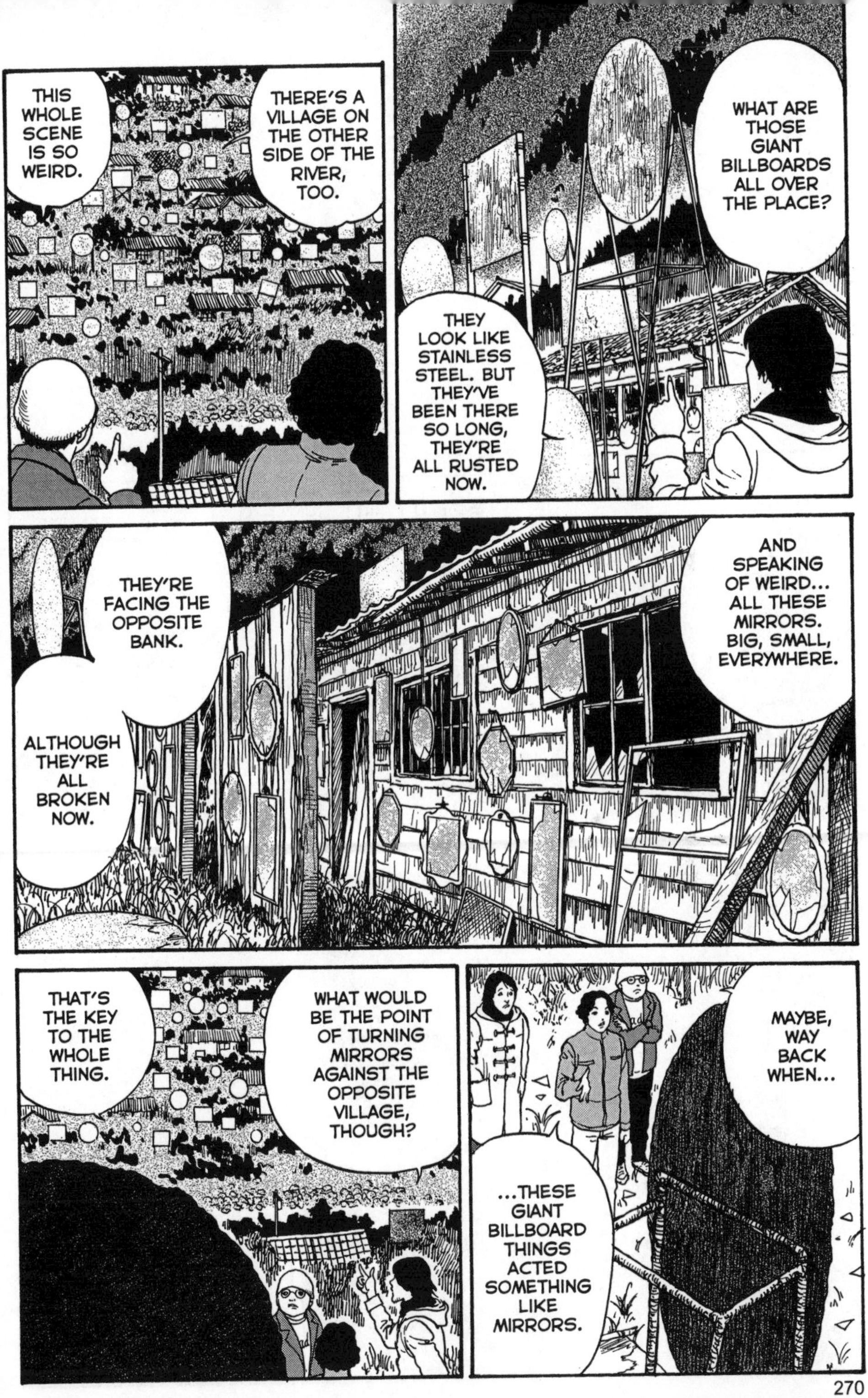
WHAT ARE THOSE GIANT BILLBOARDS ALL OVER THE PLACE?
THEY LOOK LIKE STAINLESS STEEL. BUT THEY'VE BEEN THERE SO LONG, THEY'RE ALL RUSTED NOW.
THERE'S A VILLAGE ON THE OTHER SIDE OF THE RIVER, TOO.
THIS WHOLE SCENE IS SO WEIRD.
AND SPEAKING OF WEIRD... ALL THESE MIRRORS. BIG, SMALL, EVERYWHERE.
THEY'RE FACING THE OPPOSITE BANK.
ALTHOUGH THEY'RE ALL BROKEN NOW.
MAYBE, WAY BACK WHEN...
...THESE GIANT BILLBOARD THINGS ACTED SOMETHING LIKE MIRRORS.
WHAT WOULD BE THE POINT OF TURNING MIRRORS AGAINST THE OPPOSITE VILLAGE, THOUGH?
THAT'S THE KEY TO THE WHOLE THING.

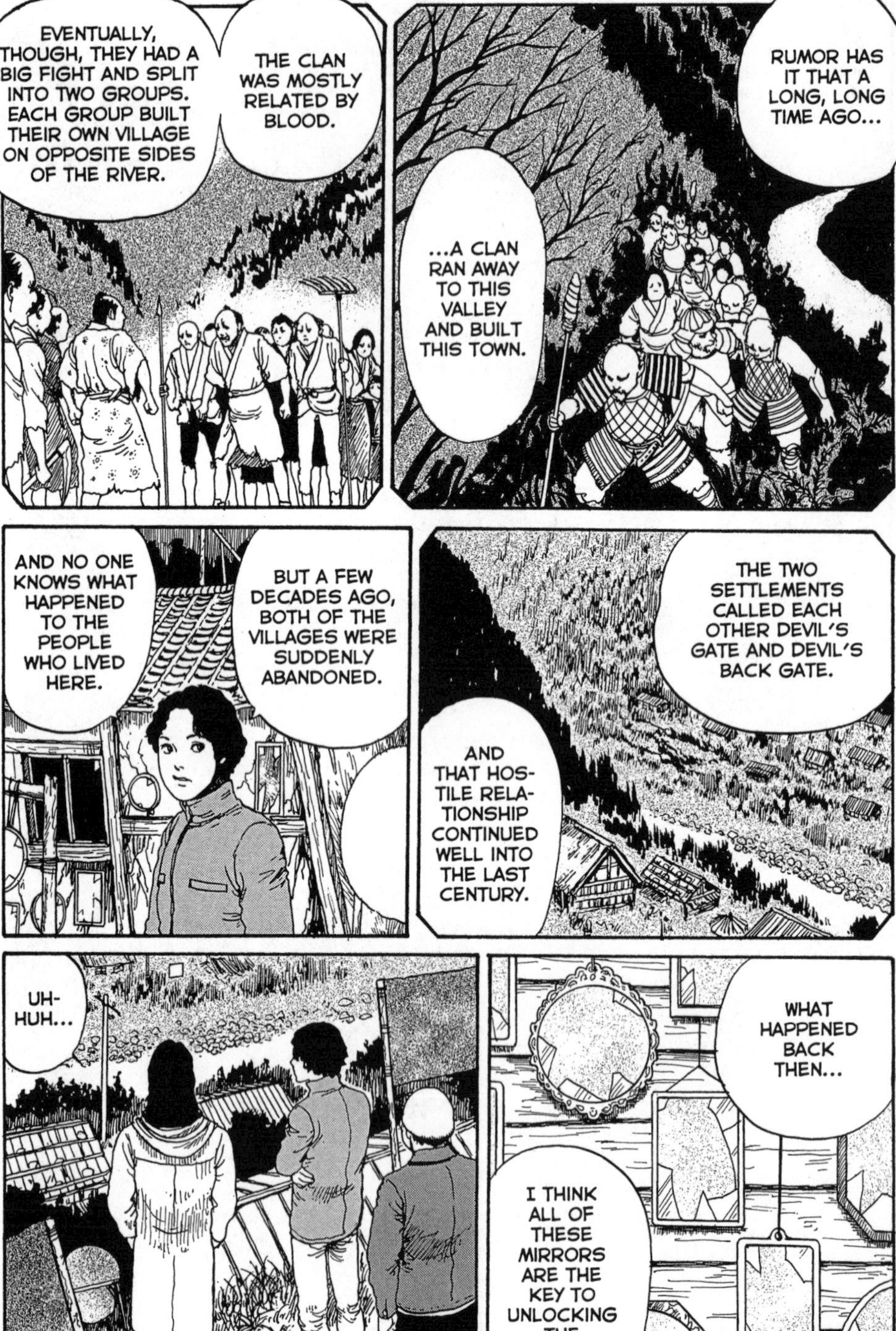
RUMOR HAS IT THAT A LONG, LONG TIME AGO...
...A CLAN RAN AWAY TO THIS VALLEY AND BUILT THIS TOWN.
THE CLAN WAS MOSTLY RELATED BY BLOOD.
EVENTUALLY, THOUGH, THEY HAD A BIG FIGHT AND SPLIT INTO TWO GROUPS. EACH GROUP BUILT THEIR OWN VILLAGE ON OPPOSITE SIDES OF THE RIVER.
THE TWO SETTLEMENTS CALLED EACH OTHER DEVIL'S GATE AND DEVIL'S BACK GATE.
AND THAT HOS-TILE RELA-TIONSHIP CONTINUED WELL INTO THE LAST CENTURY.
BUT A FEW DECADES AGO, BOTH OF THE VILLAGES WERE SUDDENLY ABANDONED.
AND NO ONE KNOWS WHAT HAPPENED TO THE PEOPLE WHO LIVED HERE.
WHAT HAPPENED BACK THEN...
I THINK ALL OF THESE MIRRORS ARE THE KEY TO UNLOCKING THE MYSTERY.
UH-HUH...

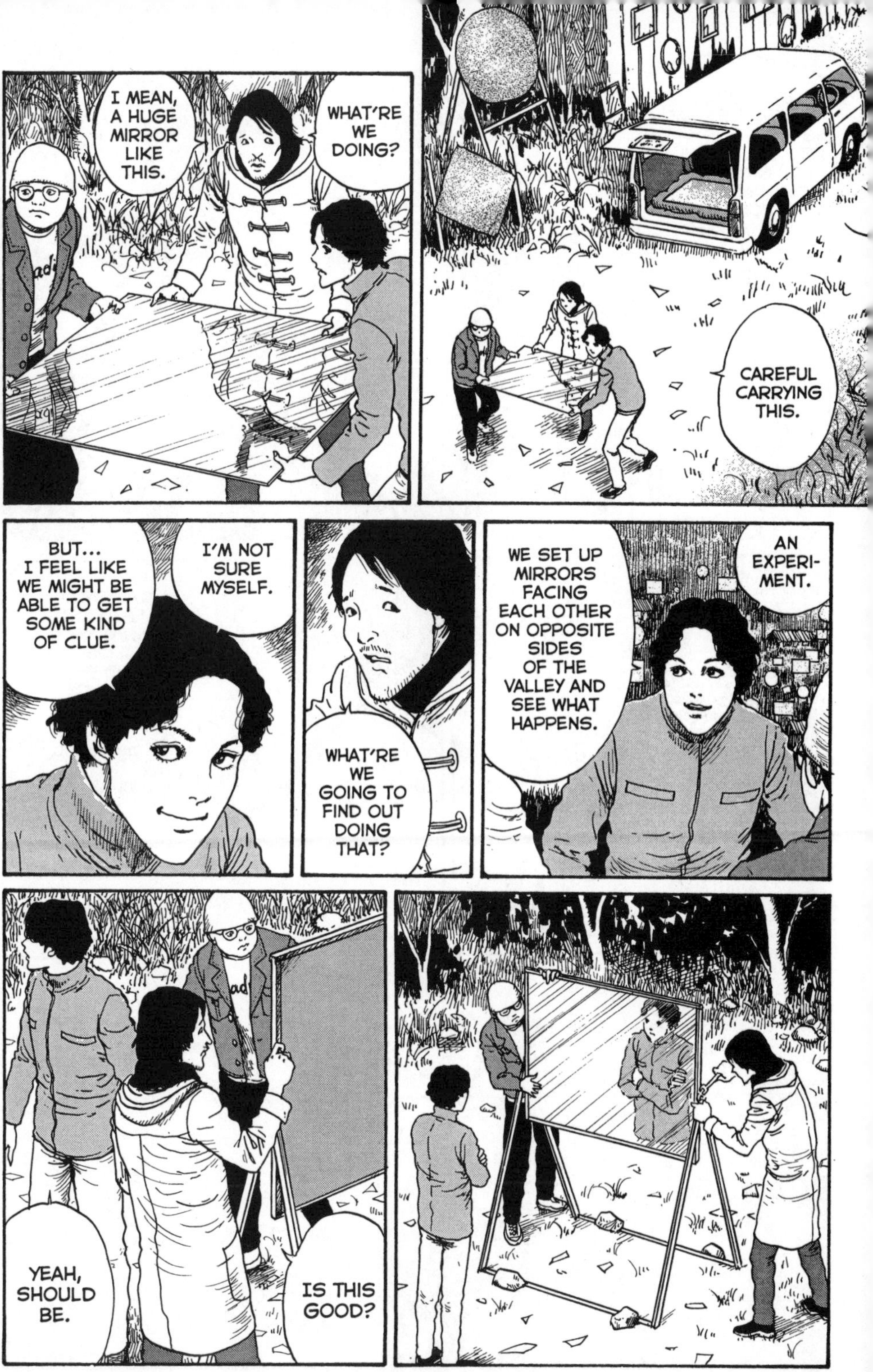
CAREFUL CARRYING THIS.
WHAT'RE WE DOING?
I MEAN, A HUGE MIRROR LIKE THIS.
AN EXPERIMENT.
WE SET UP MIRRORS FACING EACH OTHER ON OPPOSITE SIDES OF THE VALLEY AND SEE WHAT HAPPENS.
WHAT'RE WE GOING TO FIND OUT DOING THAT?
I'M NOT SURE MYSELF.
BUT... I FEEL LIKE WE MIGHT BE ABLE TO GET SOME KIND OF CLUE.
IS THIS GOOD?
YEAH, SHOULD BE.

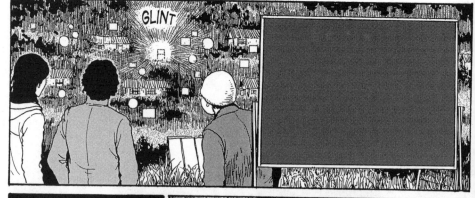

GLINT

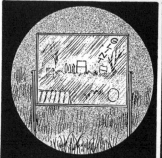

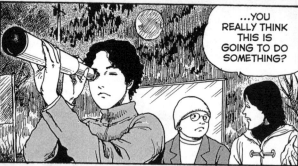

...YOU REALLY THINK THIS IS GOING TO DO SOMETHING?

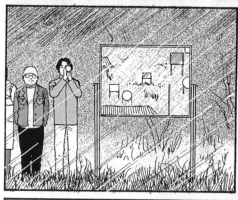

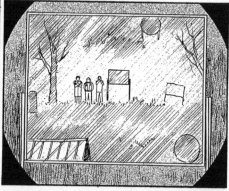

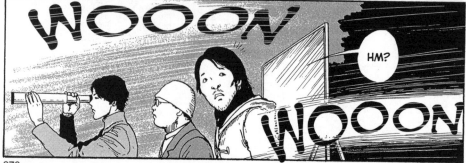

WOOON

HM?

WOOON

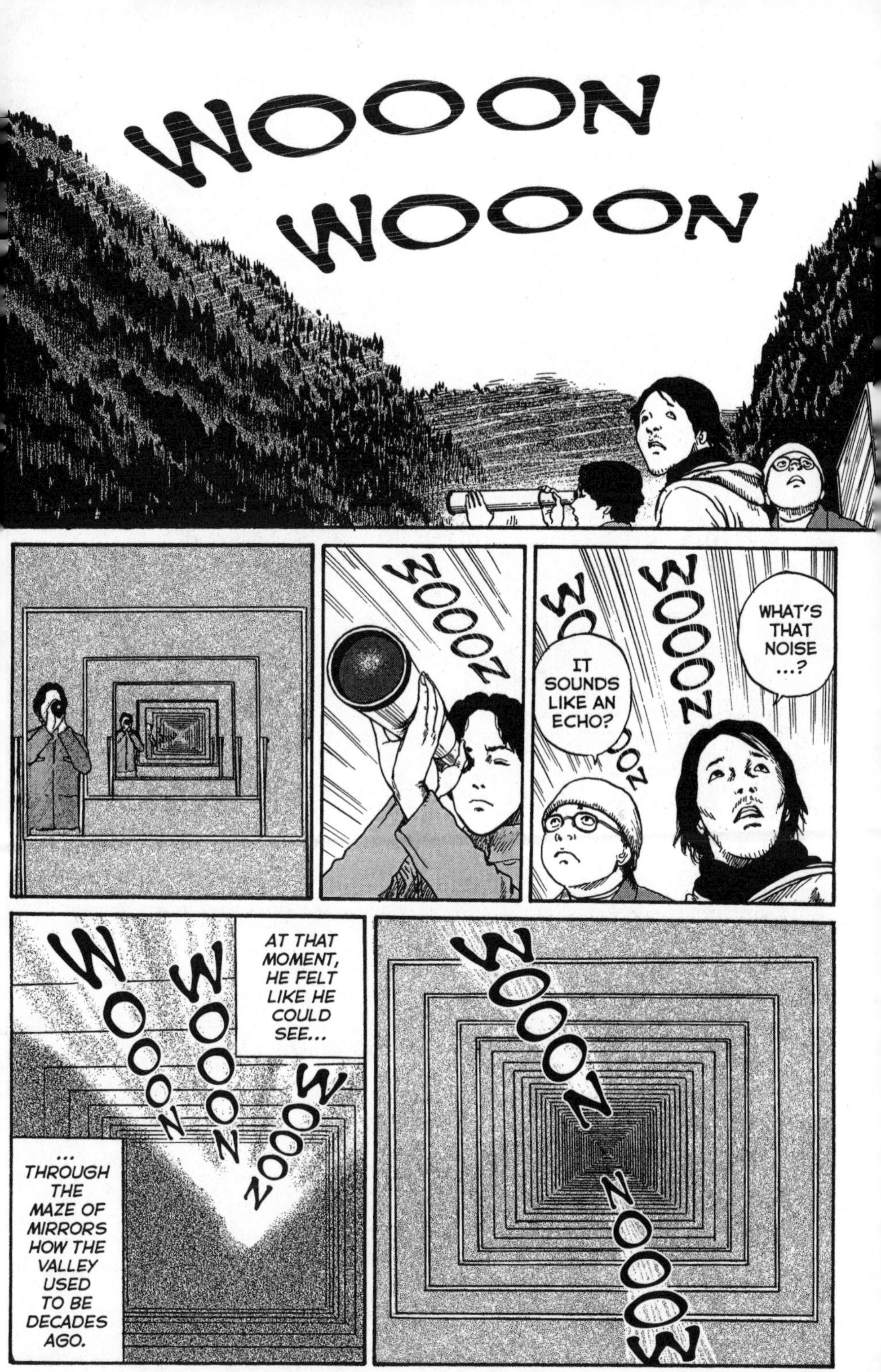
WOOON
WOOON
WOOON
WHAT'S THAT NOISE ...?
IT SOUNDS LIKE AN ECHO?
WOOON
WOOON
WOOON
AT THAT MOMENT, HE FELT LIKE HE COULD SEE...
WOOON
WOOON
WOOON
... THROUGH THE MAZE OF MIRRORS HOW THE VALLEY USED TO BE DECADES AGO.

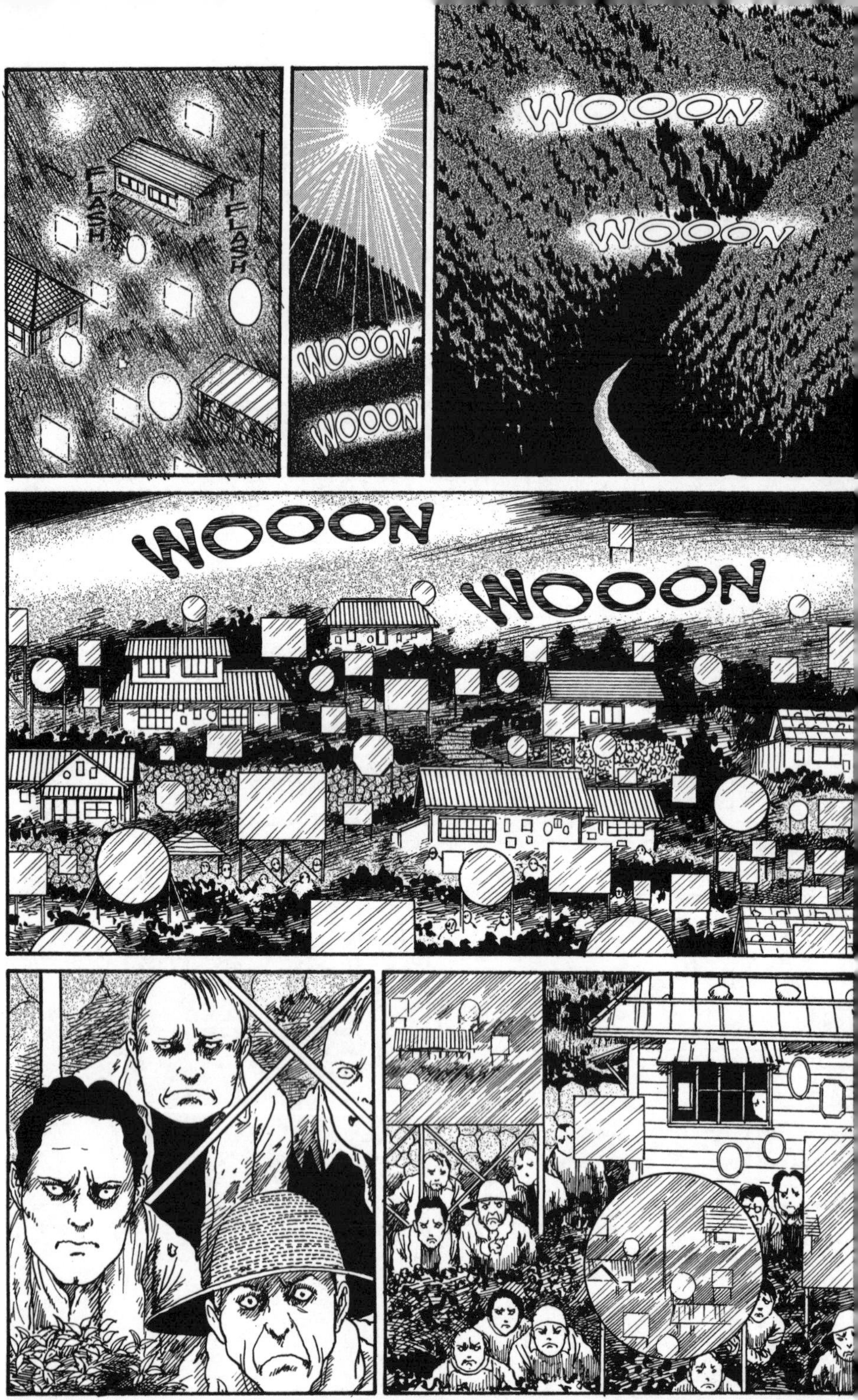
WOOON
WOOON
WOOON
WOOON
FLASH
FLASH
WOOON
WOOON

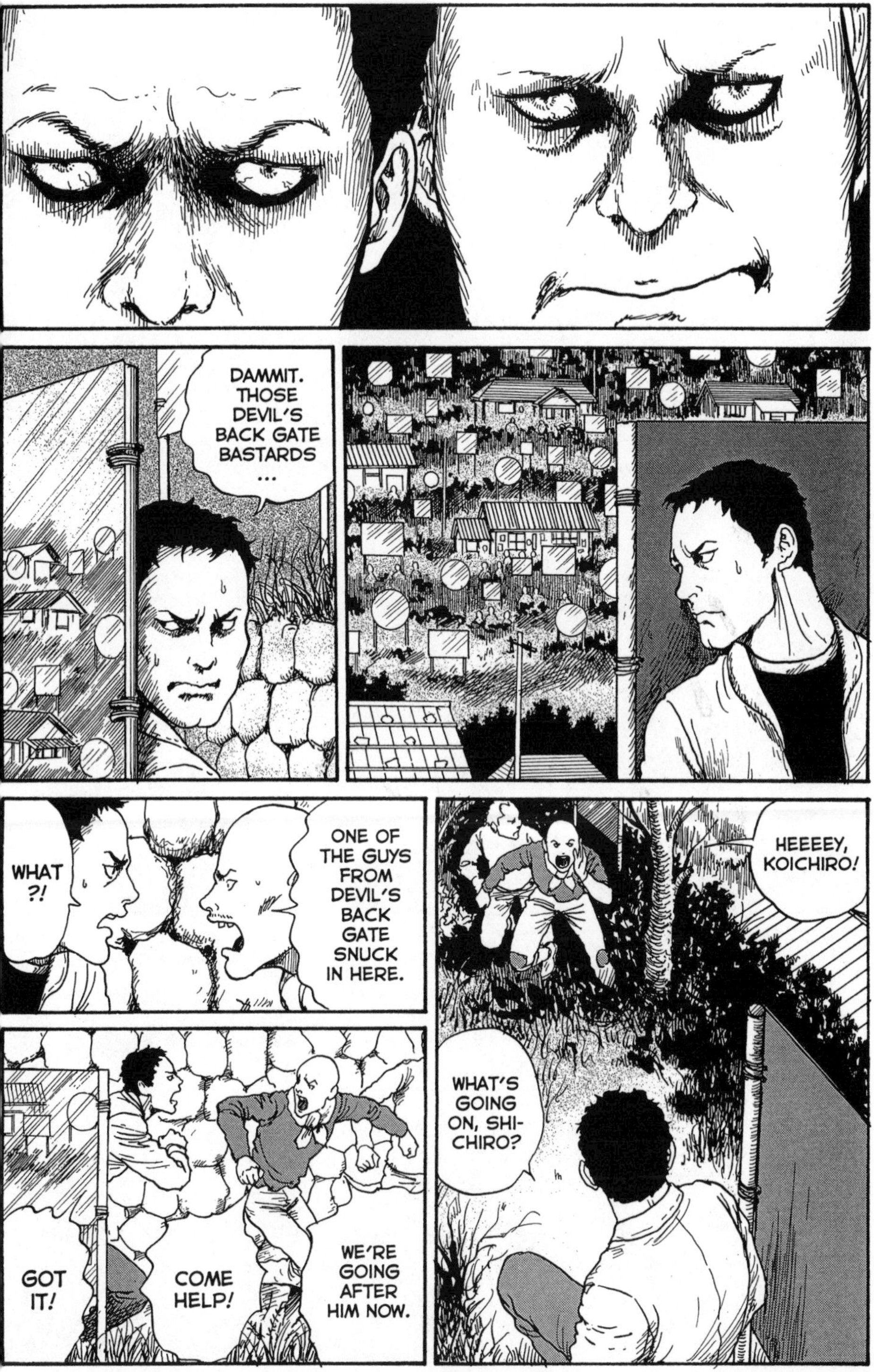
DAMMIT. THOSE DEVIL'S BACK GATE BASTARDS ...
HEEEEY, KOICHIRO!
WHAT'S GOING ON, SHICHIRO?
ONE OF THE GUYS FROM DEVIL'S BACK GATE SNUCK IN HERE.
WHAT ?!
WE'RE GOING AFTER HIM NOW.
COME HELP!
GOT IT!

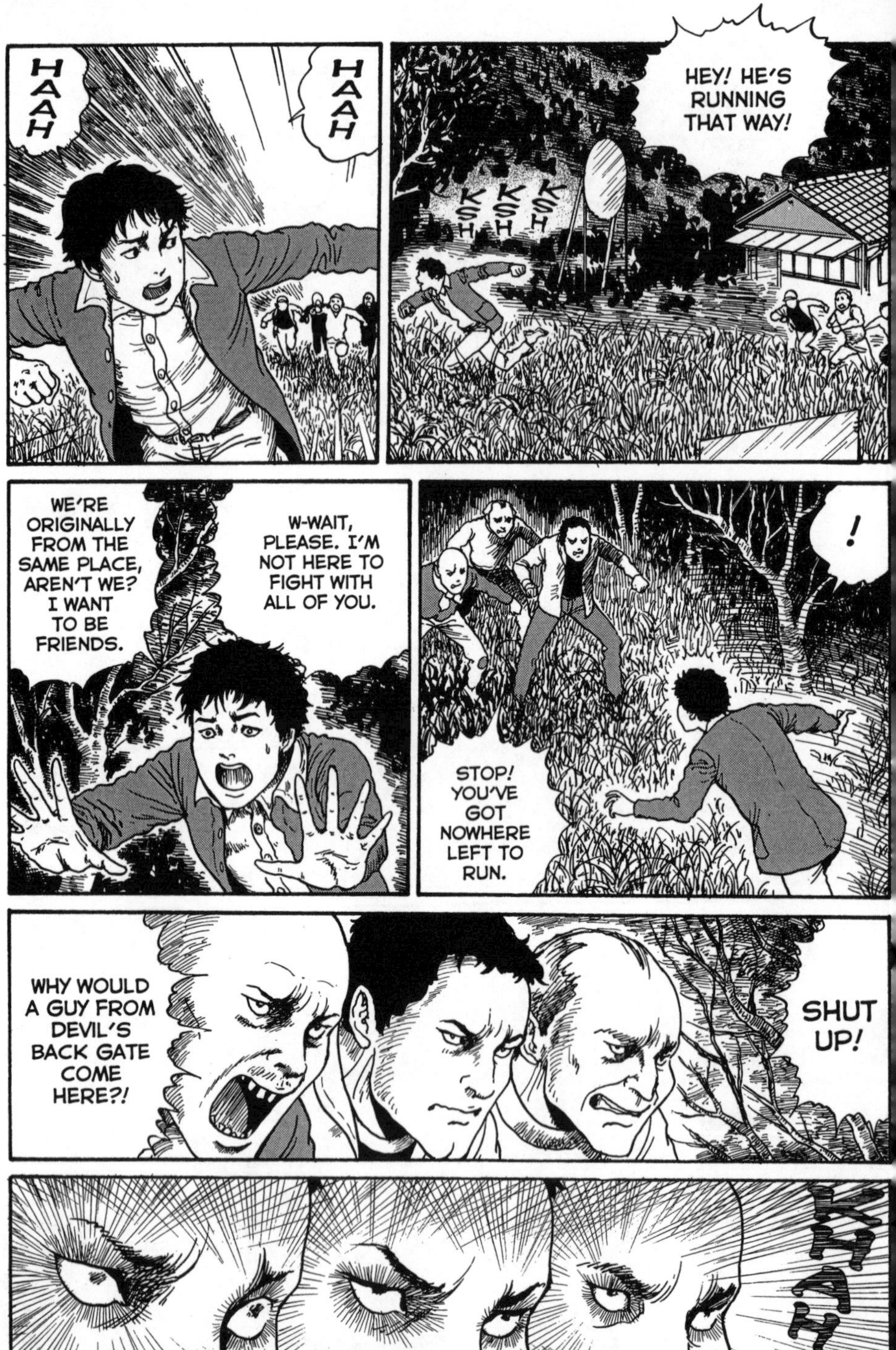
HEY! HE'S RUNNING THAT WAY!
KSH KSH KSH
HAAH
HAAH
!
STOP! YOU'VE GOT NOWHERE LEFT TO RUN.
W-WAIT, PLEASE. I'M NOT HERE TO FIGHT WITH ALL OF YOU.
WE'RE ORIGINALLY FROM THE SAME PLACE, AREN'T WE? I WANT TO BE FRIENDS.
SHUT UP!
WHY WOULD A GUY FROM DEVIL'S BACK GATE COME HERE?!

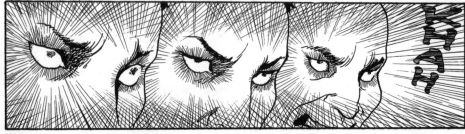

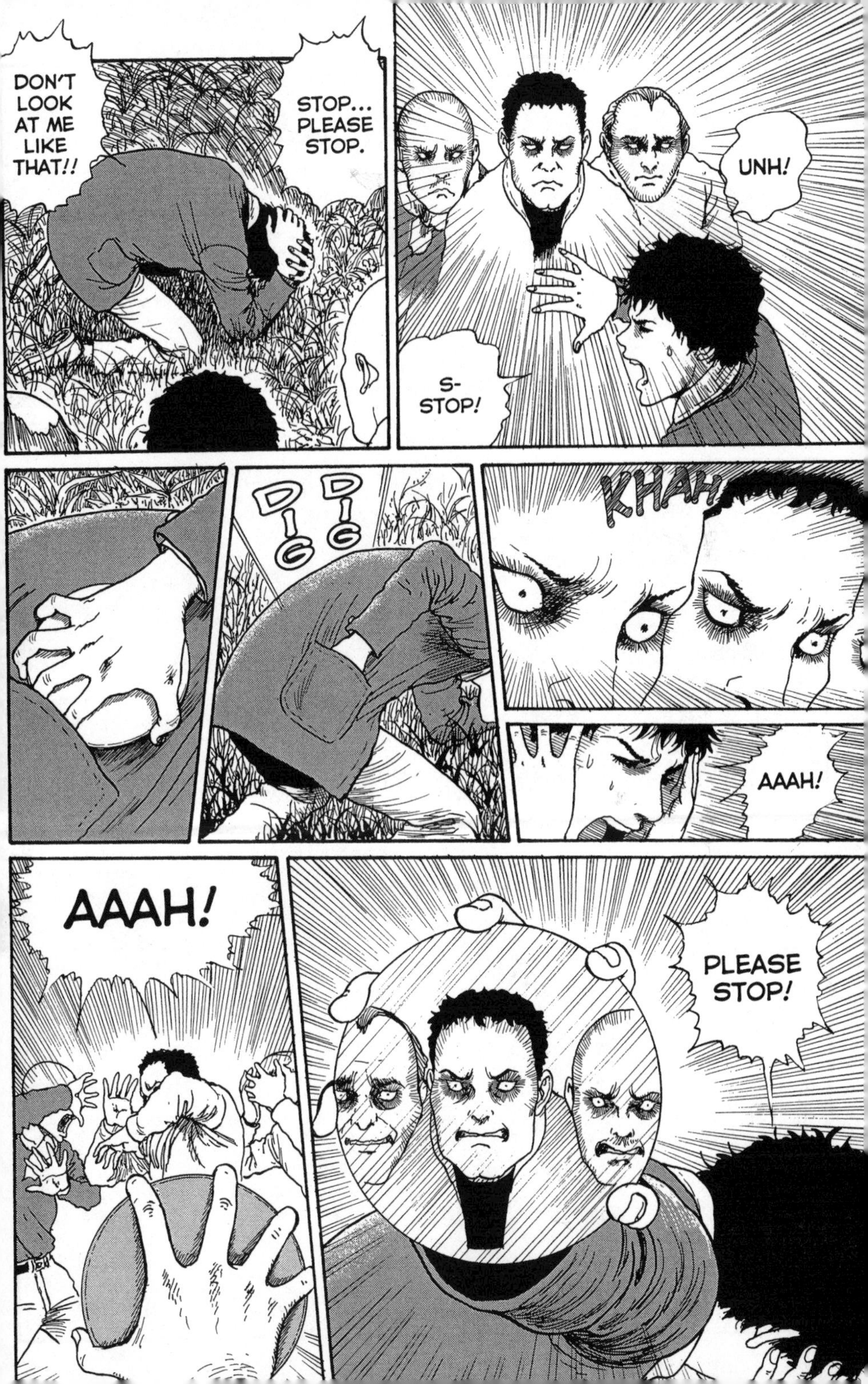
UNH!
S-STOP!
STOP... PLEASE STOP.
DON'T LOOK AT ME LIKE THAT!!
KHAH
AAAH!
DIG DIG
PLEASE STOP!
AAAH!

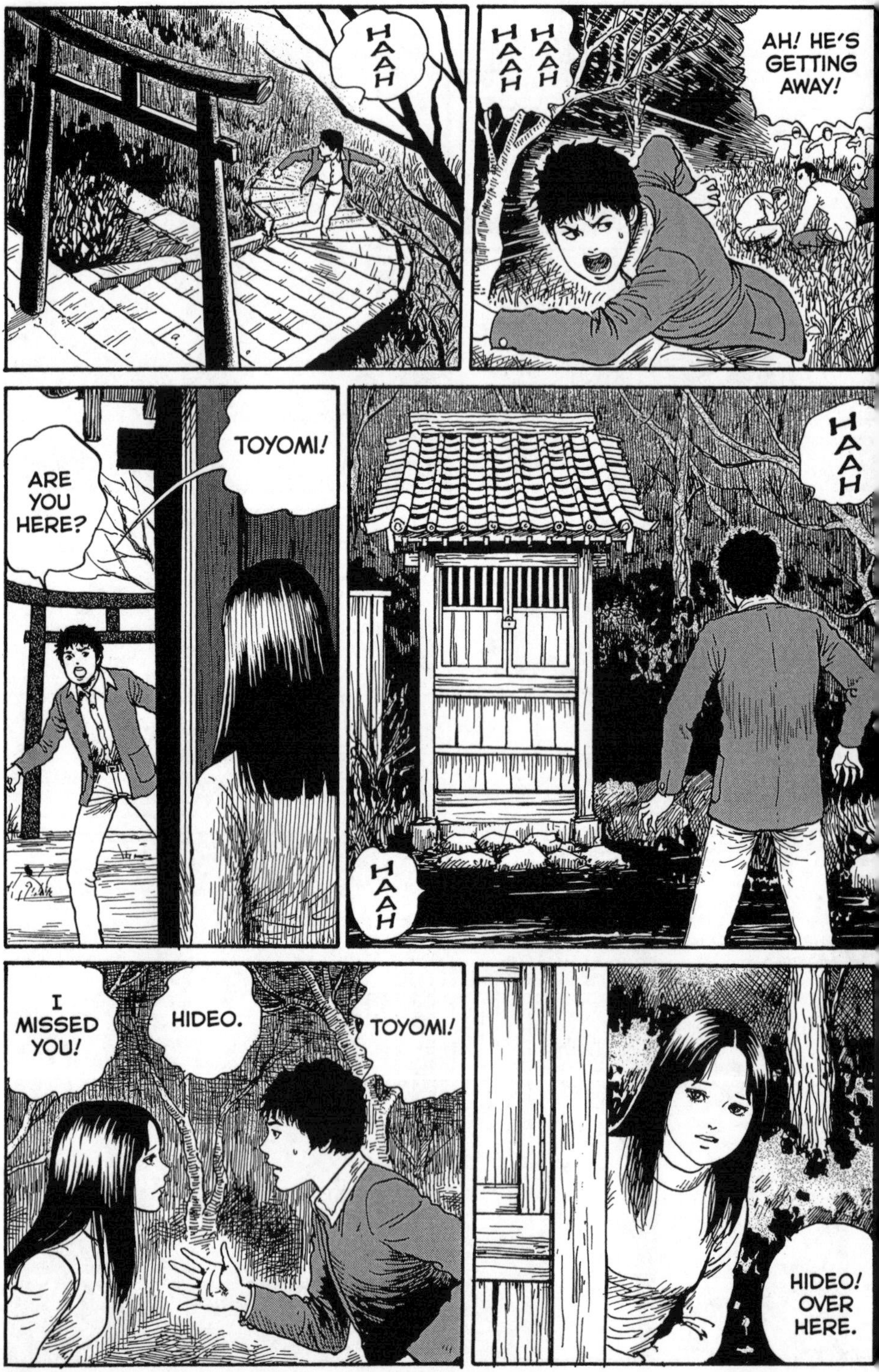
AH! HE'S GETTING AWAY!
HAAH
HAAH
HAAH
HAAH
HAAH
TOYOMI!
ARE YOU HERE?
HIDEO! OVER HERE.
TOYOMI!
HIDEO.
I MISSED YOU!

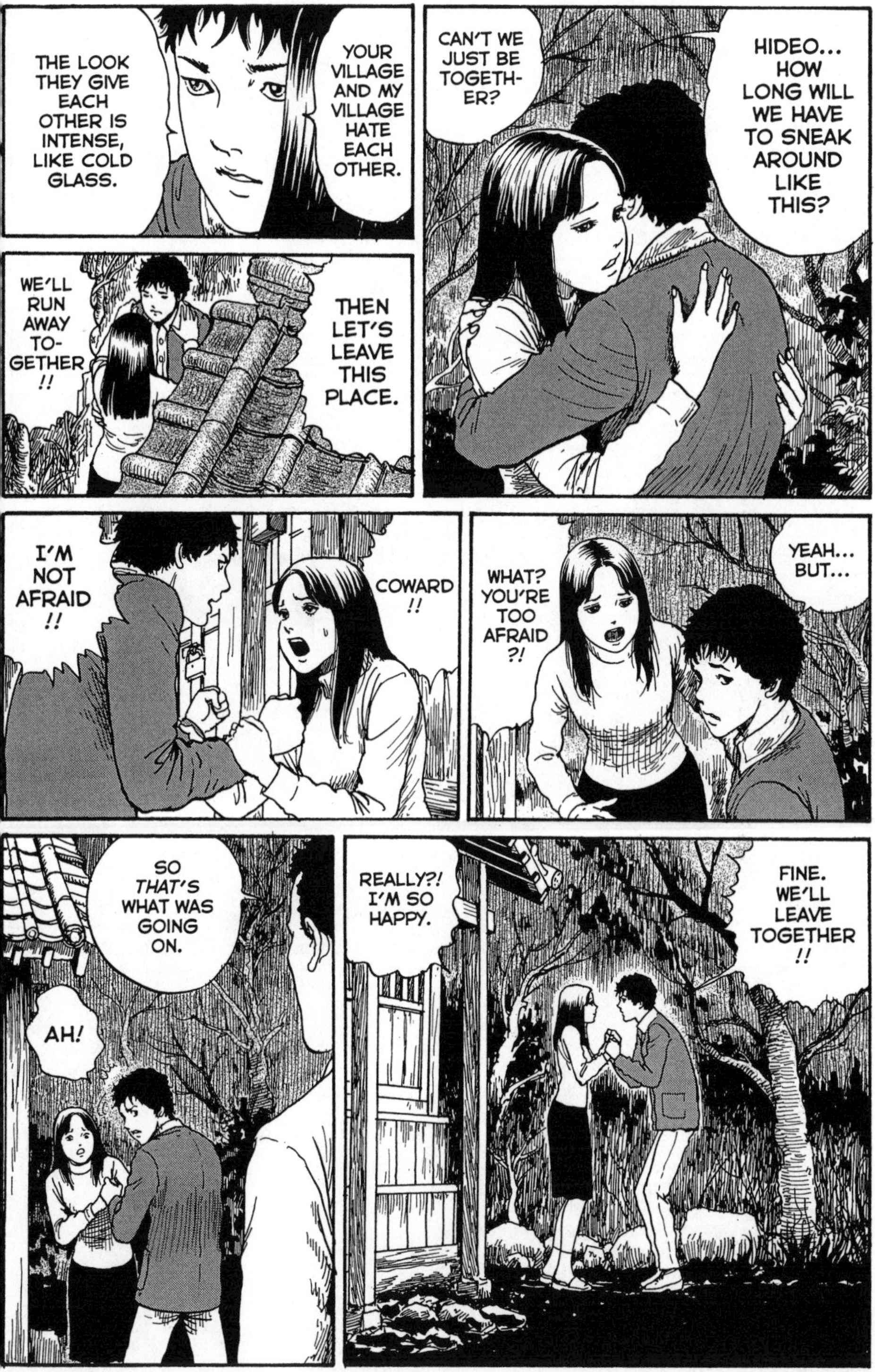
HIDEO... HOW LONG WILL WE HAVE TO SNEAK AROUND LIKE THIS?
CAN'T WE JUST BE TOGETH-ER?
YOUR VILLAGE AND MY VILLAGE HATE EACH OTHER.
THE LOOK THEY GIVE EACH OTHER IS INTENSE, LIKE COLD GLASS.
THEN LET'S LEAVE THIS PLACE.
WE'LL RUN AWAY TO-GETHER!!
YEAH... BUT...
WHAT? YOU'RE TOO AFRAID?!
COWARD!!
I'M NOT AFRAID!!
FINE. WE'LL LEAVE TOGETHER!!
REALLY?! I'M SO HAPPY.
SO *THAT'S* WHAT WAS GOING ON.
AH!

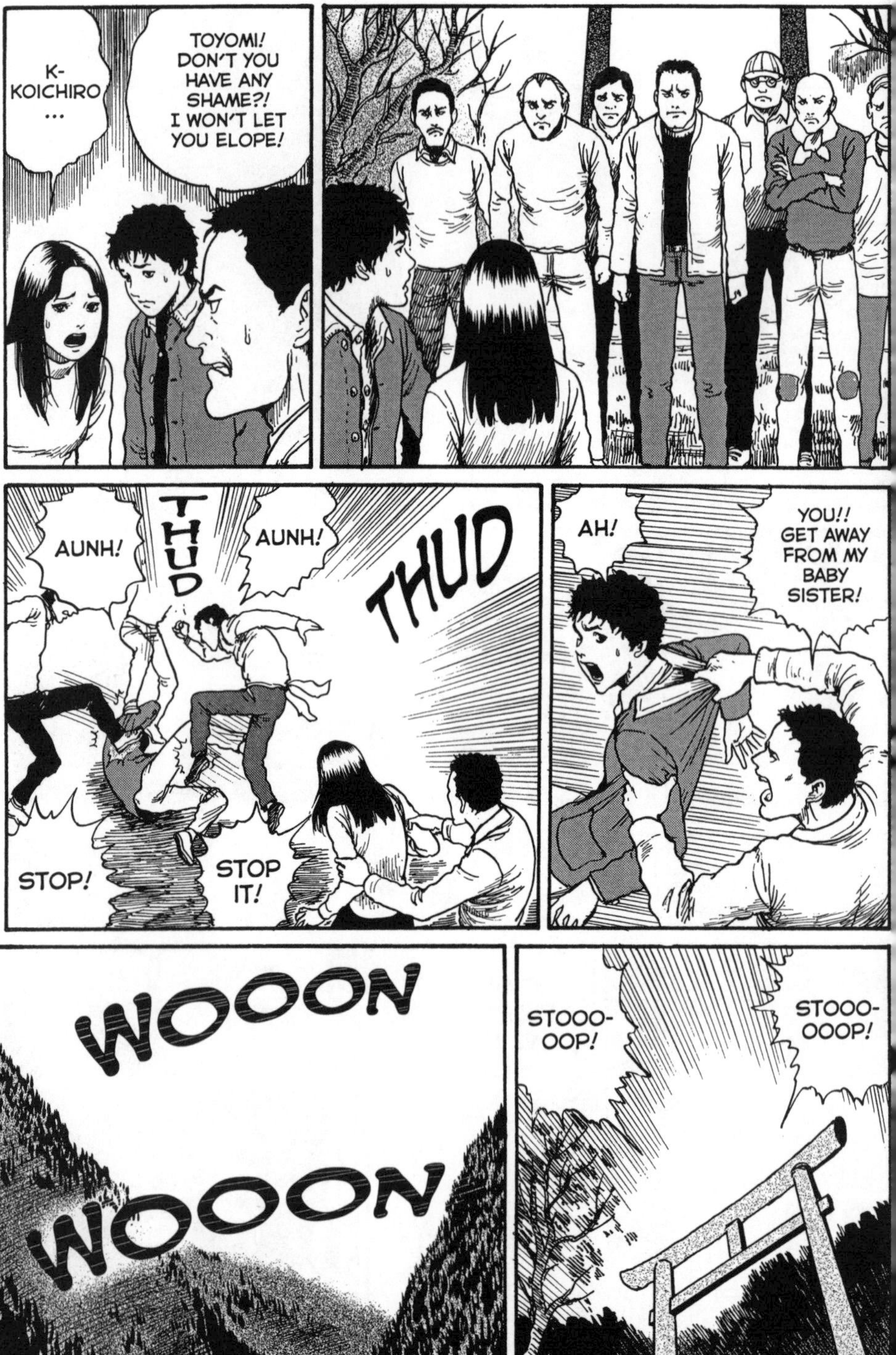
TOYOMI! DON'T YOU HAVE ANY SHAME?! I WON'T LET YOU ELOPE!
K-KOICHIRO ...
YOU!! GET AWAY FROM MY BABY SISTER!
AH!
THUD
AUNH!
THUD
AUNH!
STOP IT!
STOP!
STOOO-OOOP!
STOOO-OOP!
WOOON
WOOON

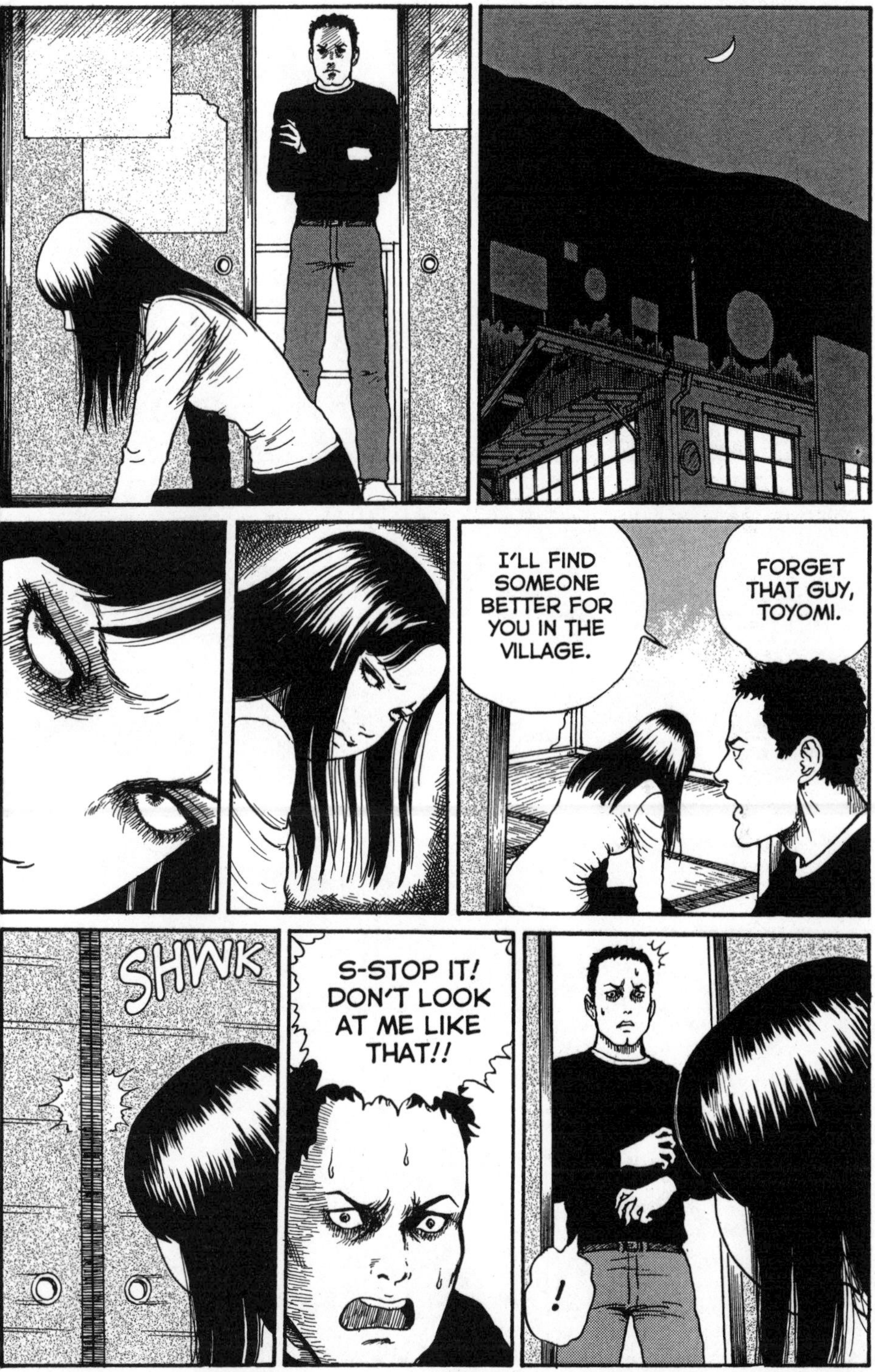
FORGET THAT GUY, TOYOMI.
I'LL FIND SOMEONE BETTER FOR YOU IN THE VILLAGE.
!
S-STOP IT! DON'T LOOK AT ME LIKE THAT!!
SHWK

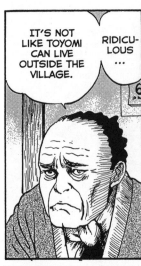

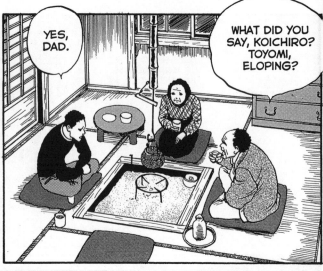

WHAT DID YOU SAY, KOICHIRO? TOYOMI, ELOPING?
YES, DAD.
RIDICU-LOUS...
IT'S NOT LIKE TOYOMI CAN LIVE OUTSIDE THE VILLAGE.
OUR CLAN'S NOT LIKE OTHER PEOPLE.
WE'RE INEVITABLY SEEN AS HERETICS ELSEWHERE. WE ALWAYS COME CRAWLING BACK.
OUR PEOPLE...
OUR EYES HAVE A DISTINCT FEATURE.
WHEN WE HATE ANOTHER PERSON, OUR GAZE MAKES THEM FEEL A STRONG PHYSICAL DISCOMFORT.
BECAUSE OF THIS PECULIAR NATURE, OUR ANCESTORS WERE NOT ACCEPTED BY THE REST OF SOCIETY.
THEY WERE PERSE-CUTED...
...AND CHASED TO THIS PLACE.

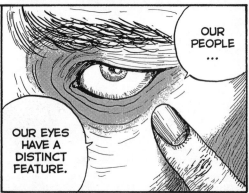

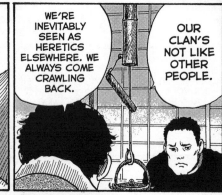

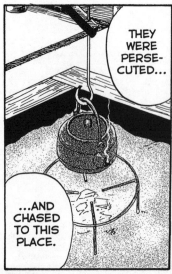

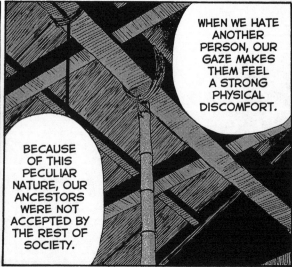

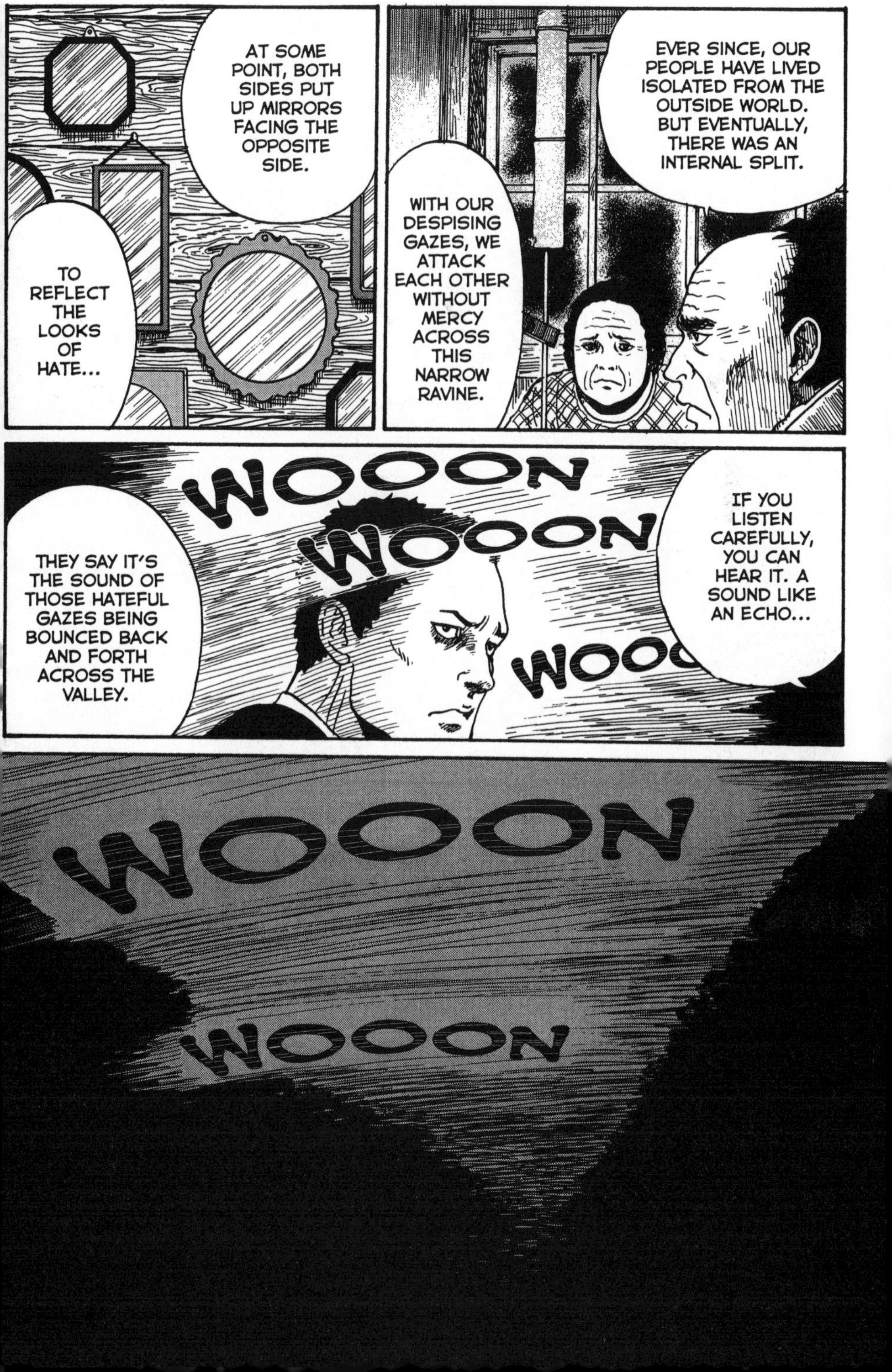
EVER SINCE, OUR PEOPLE HAVE LIVED ISOLATED FROM THE OUTSIDE WORLD. BUT EVENTUALLY, THERE WAS AN INTERNAL SPLIT.
WITH OUR DESPISING GAZES, WE ATTACK EACH OTHER WITHOUT MERCY ACROSS THIS NARROW RAVINE.
AT SOME POINT, BOTH SIDES PUT UP MIRRORS FACING THE OPPOSITE SIDE.
TO REFLECT THE LOOKS OF HATE...
IF YOU LISTEN CAREFULLY, YOU CAN HEAR IT. A SOUND LIKE AN ECHO...
WOOON
WOOON
THEY SAY IT'S THE SOUND OF THOSE HATEFUL GAZES BEING BOUNCED BACK AND FORTH ACROSS THE VALLEY.
WOOO
WOOON
WOOON

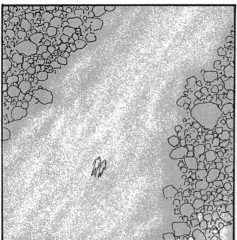

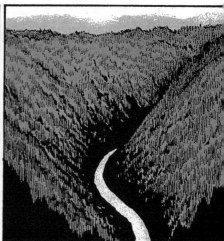

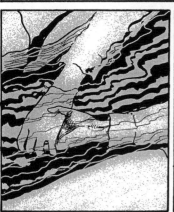

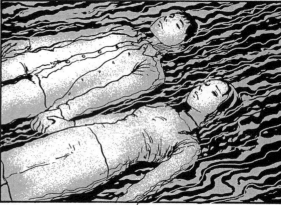

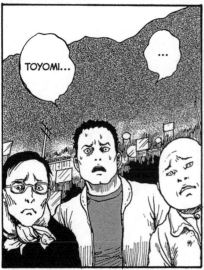

TOYOMI...

...

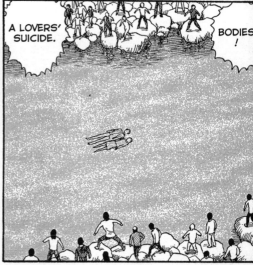

A LOVERS' SUICIDE.

BODIES!

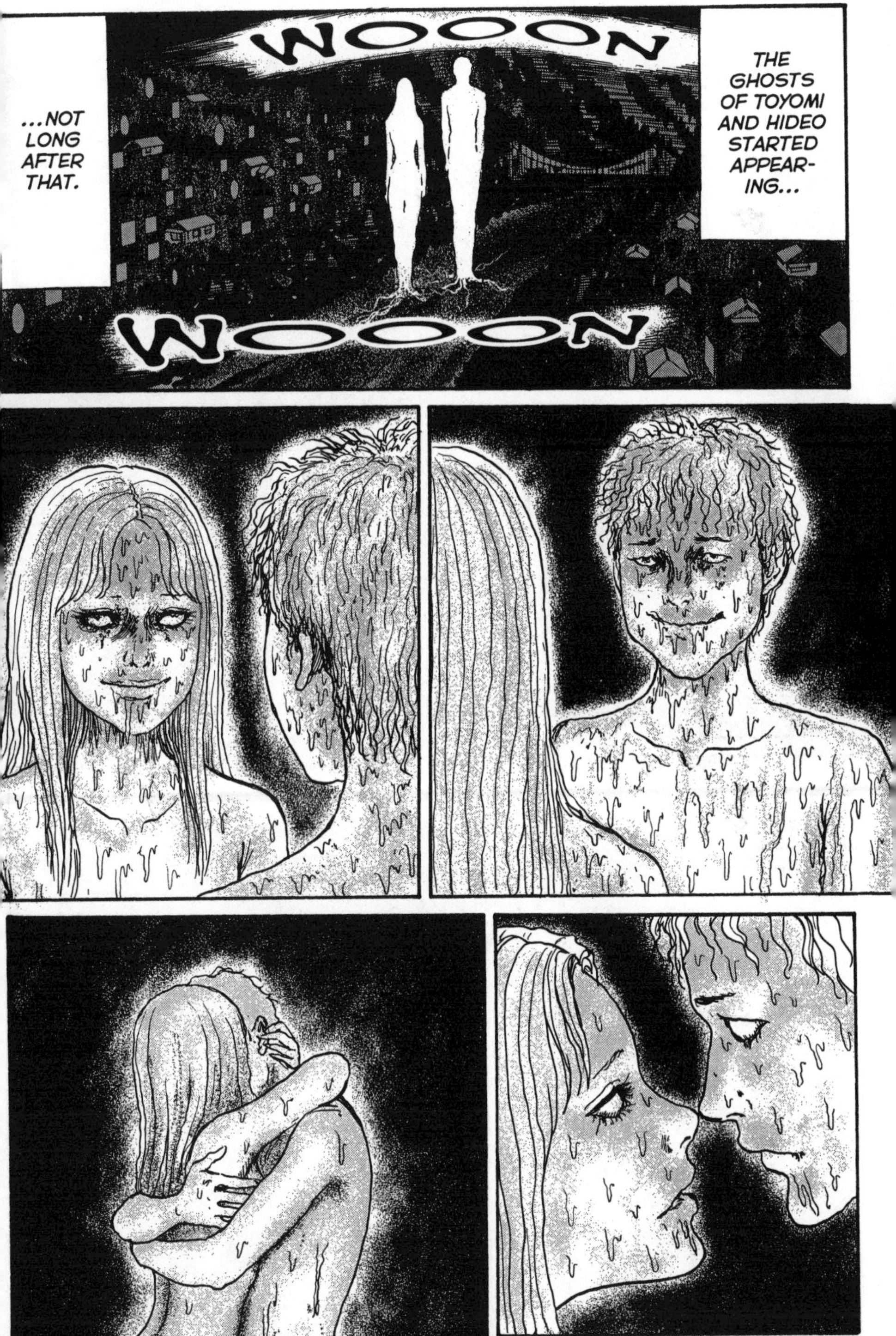
THE GHOSTS OF TOYOMI AND HIDEO STARTED APPEAR-ING...
WOOON
...NOT LONG AFTER THAT.
WOOON

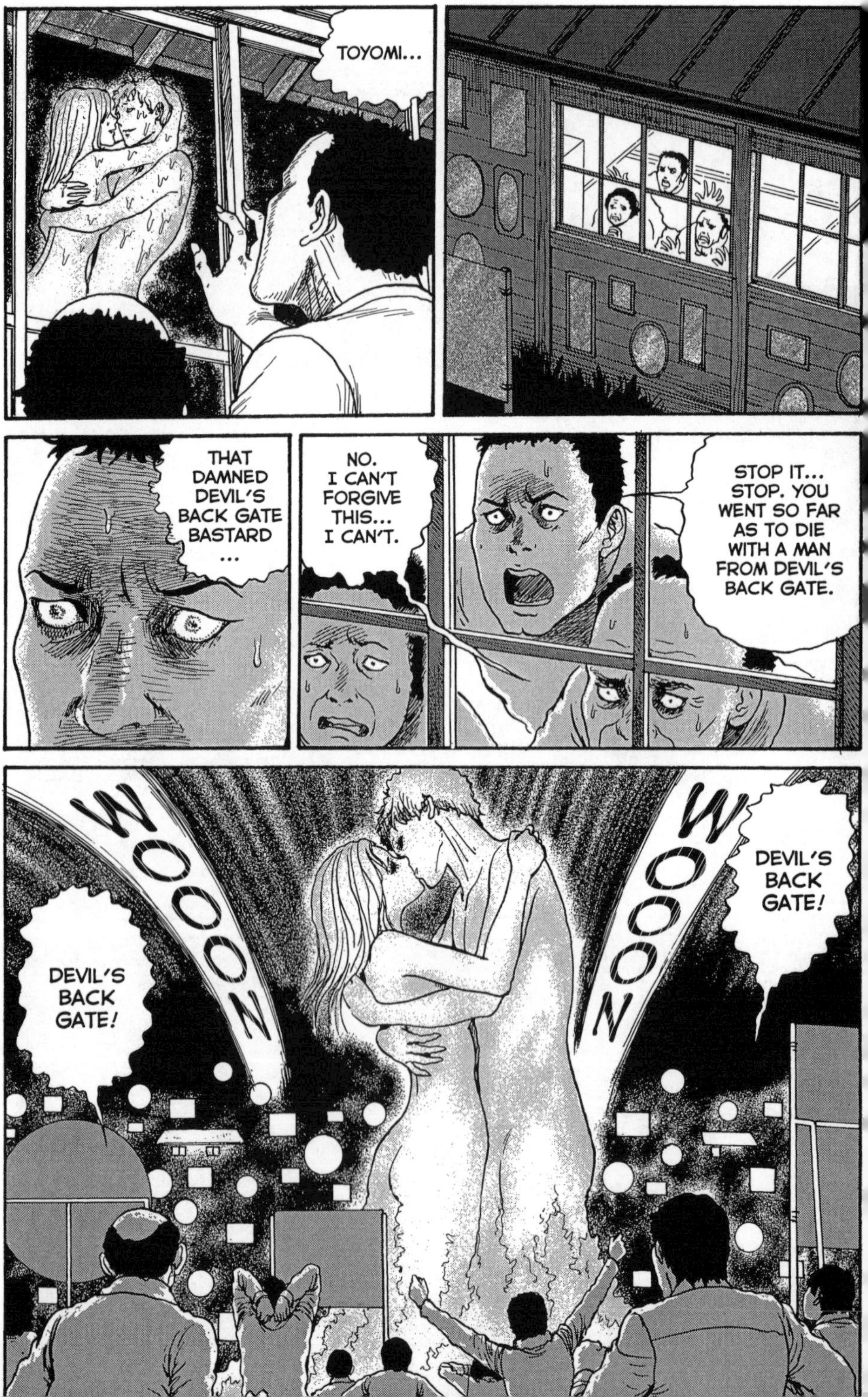
TOYOMI...
STOP IT... STOP. YOU WENT SO FAR AS TO DIE WITH A MAN FROM DEVIL'S BACK GATE.
NO. I CAN'T FORGIVE THIS... I CAN'T.
THAT DAMNED DEVIL'S BACK GATE BASTARD ...
WOOOON
DEVIL'S BACK GATE!
WOOOON
DEVIL'S BACK GATE!

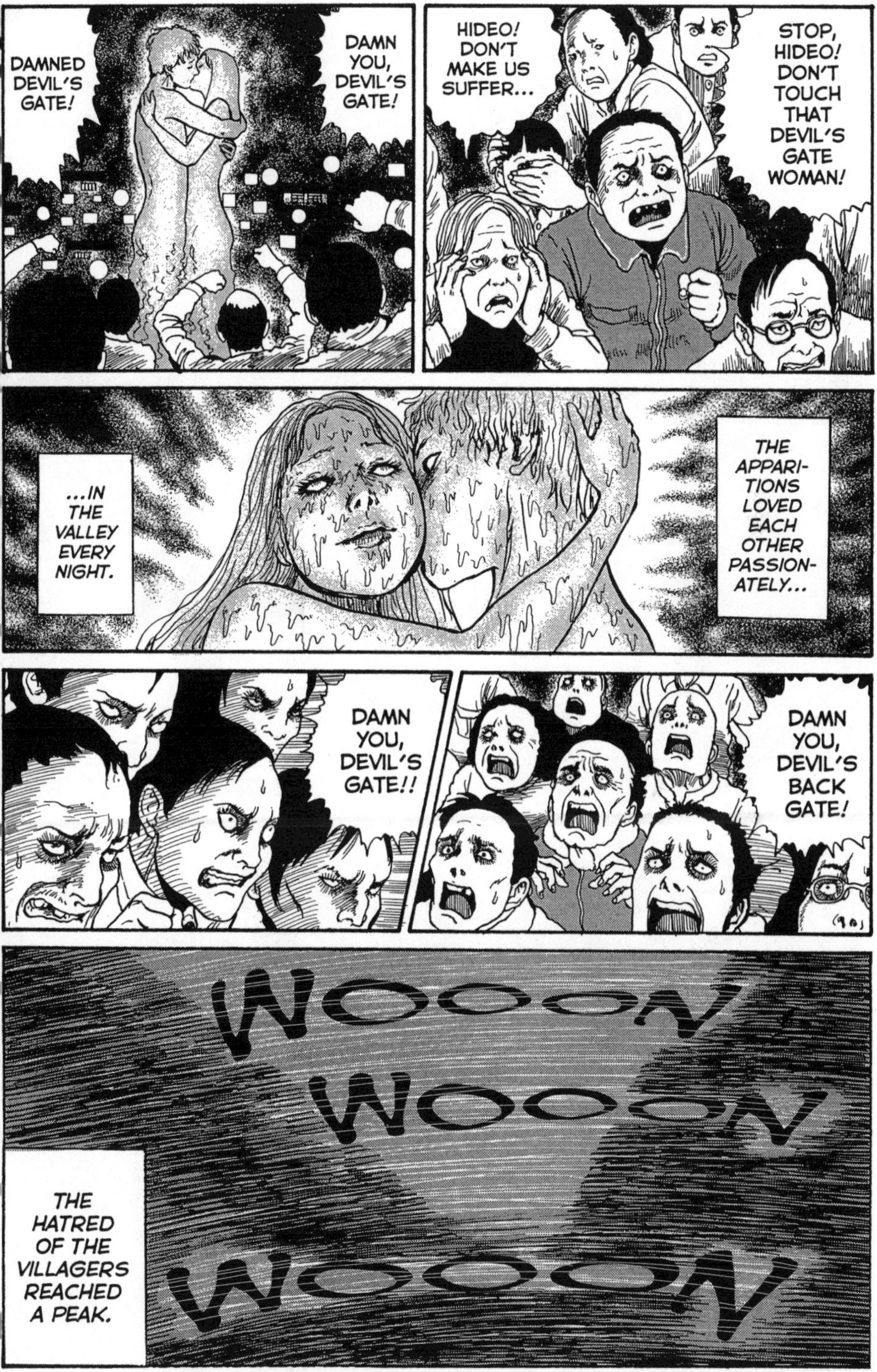
STOP, HIDEO! DON'T TOUCH THAT DEVIL'S GATE WOMAN!
HIDEO! DON'T MAKE US SUFFER...
DAMN YOU, DEVIL'S GATE!
DAMNED DEVIL'S GATE!
THE APPARITIONS LOVED EACH OTHER PASSIONATELY...
...IN THE VALLEY EVERY NIGHT.
DAMN YOU, DEVIL'S BACK GATE!
DAMN YOU, DEVIL'S GATE!!
WOOON
WOOON
WOOON
THE HATRED OF THE VILLAGERS REACHED A PEAK.

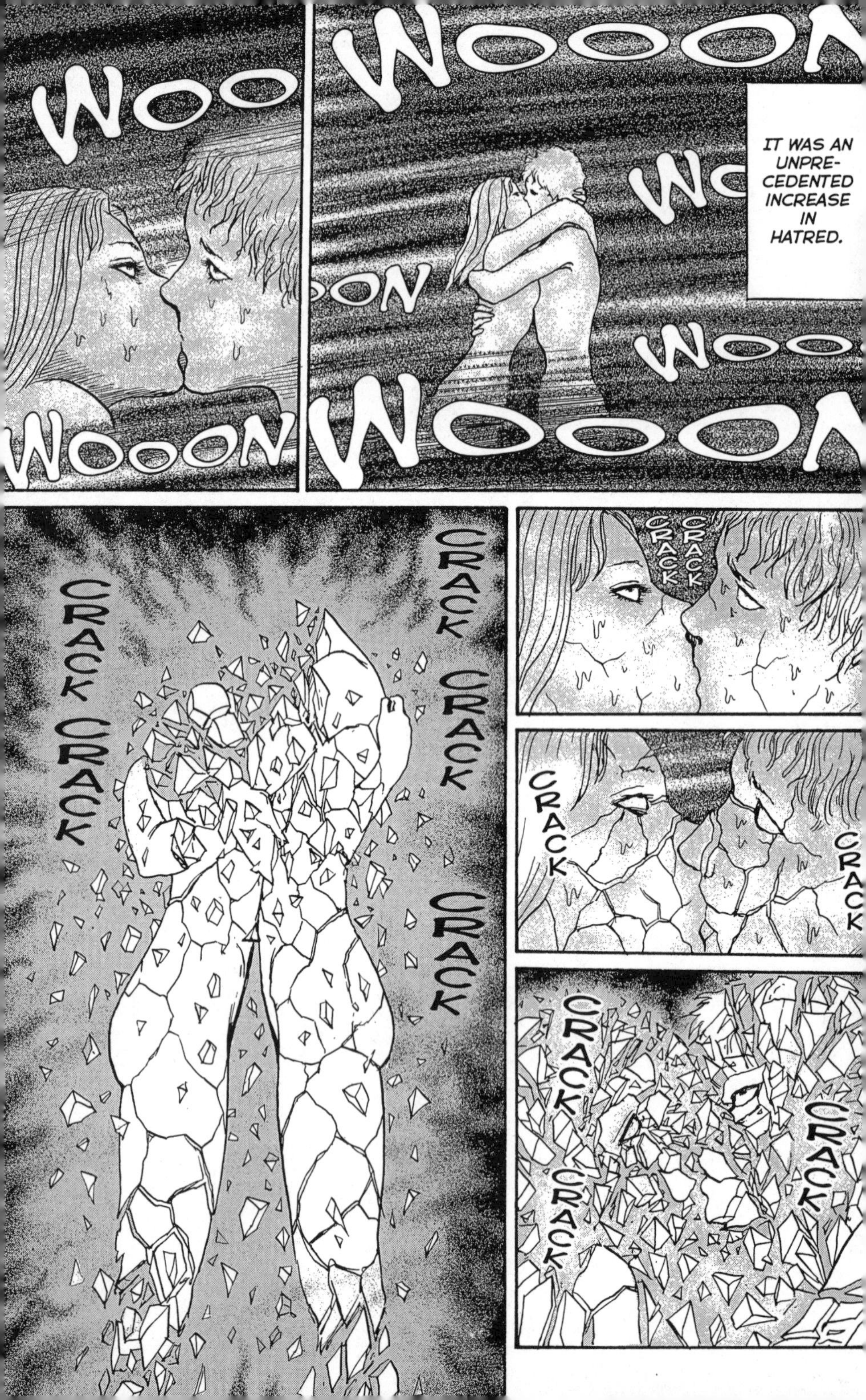
WOOO
IT WAS AN UNPRECEDENTED INCREASE IN HATRED.
WO
OON
WOO
WOOON
WOO
WOOON
CRACK CRACK
CRACK
CRACK
CRACK
CRACK
CRACK
CRACK CRACK
CRACK CRACK CRACK

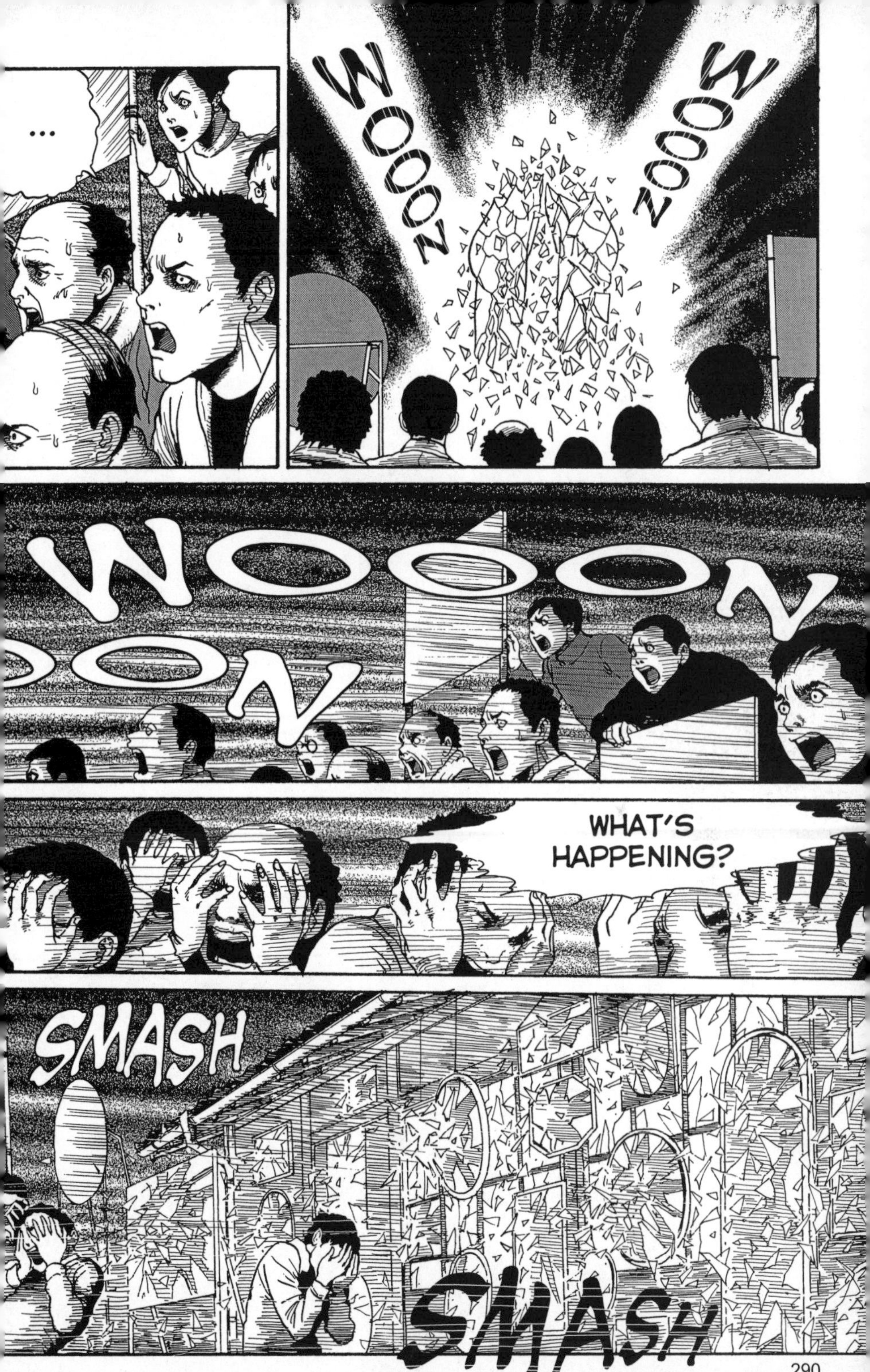
WOOOON
WOOOON
...
WOOOON
OOON
WHAT'S HAPPENING?
SMASH
SMASH

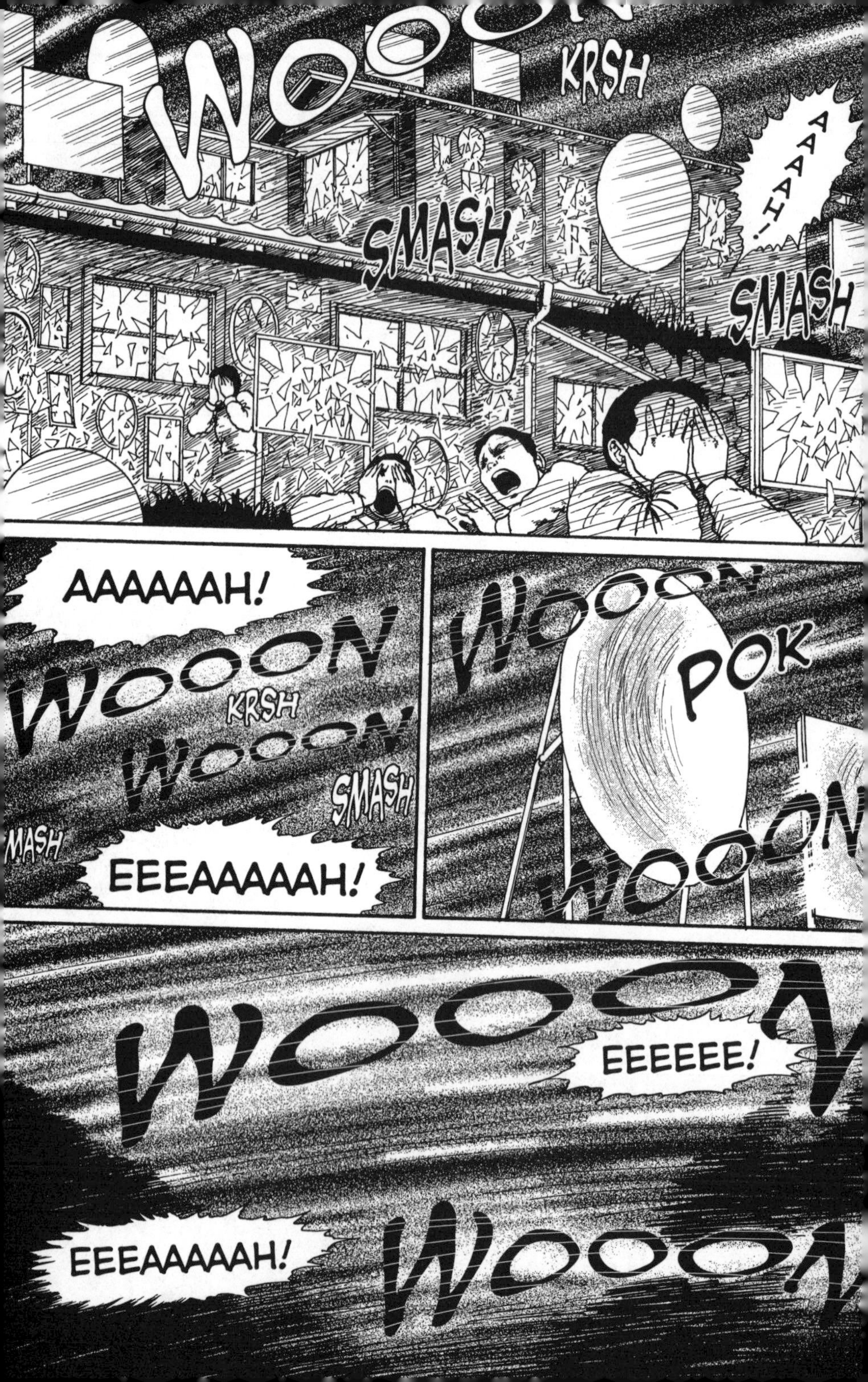
AAAAAH!
KRSH
WOOO
SMASH
SMASH
WOOOON
POK
WOOOON
AAAAAAH!
WOOON
KRSH
WOOOON
SMASH
MASH
EEEAAAAAH!
WOOO
EEEEEE!
EEEAAAAAH!
WOOO

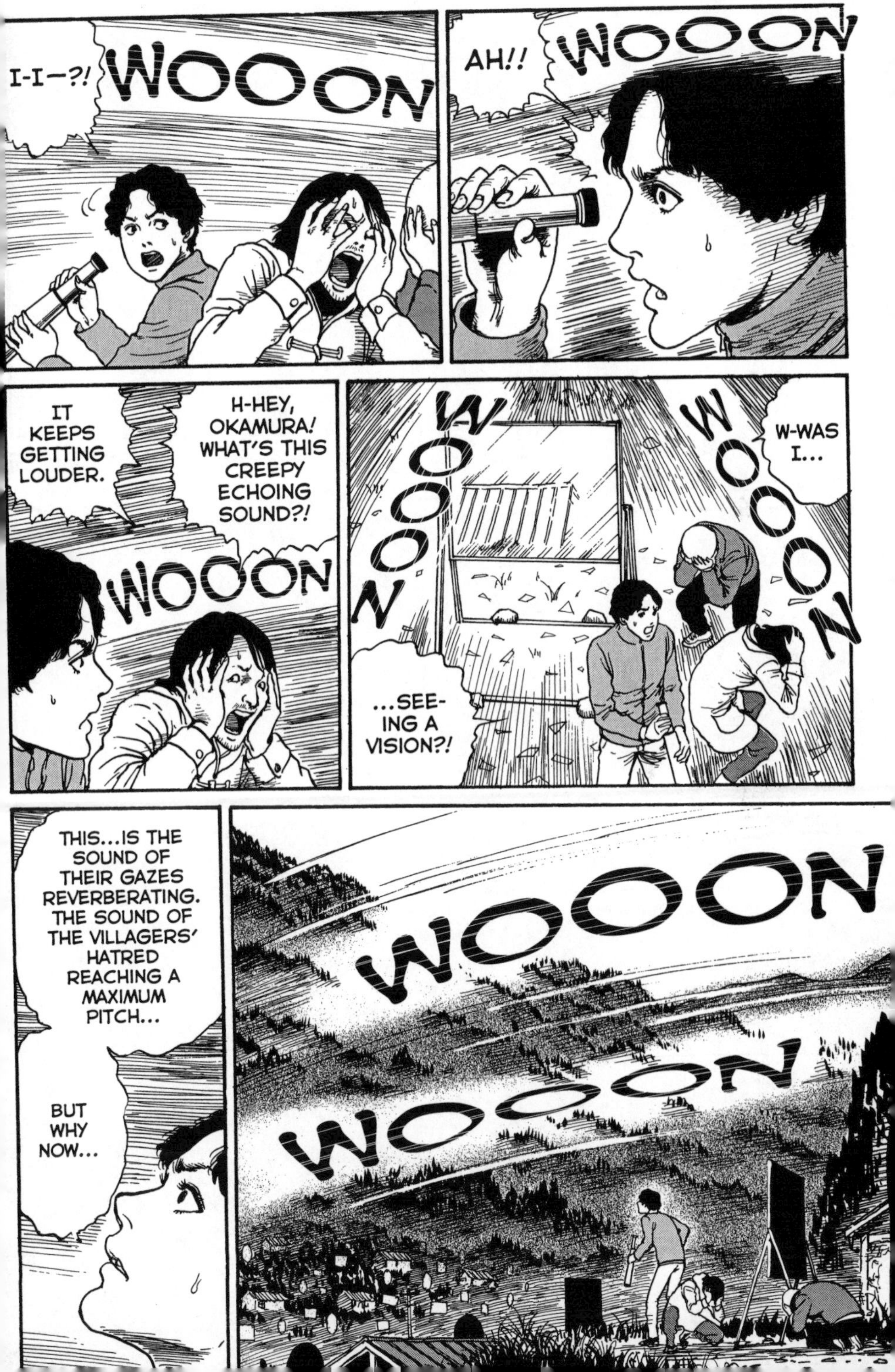
AH!!
WOOOON
I-I—?!
WOOOON
W-WAS I...
WOOOON
WOOOON
...SEE-ING A VISION?!
H-HEY, OKAMURA! WHAT'S THIS CREEPY ECHOING SOUND?!
IT KEEPS GETTING LOUDER.
WOOON
WOOOON
WOOOON
THIS...IS THE SOUND OF THEIR GAZES REVERBERATING. THE SOUND OF THE VILLAGERS' HATRED REACHING A MAXIMUM PITCH...
BUT WHY NOW...

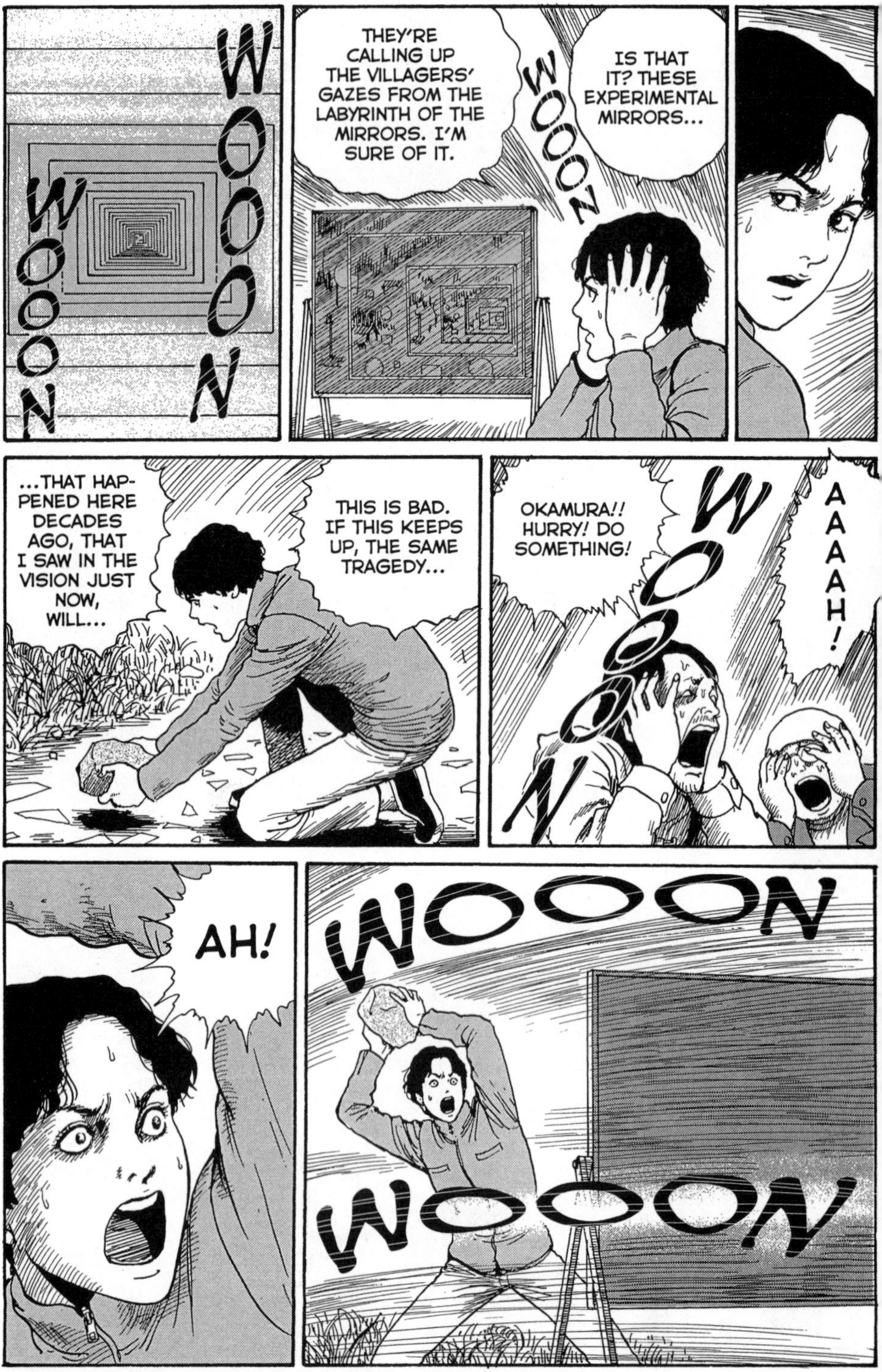
IS THAT IT? THESE EXPERIMENTAL MIRRORS...
WOOOON
THEY'RE CALLING UP THE VILLAGERS' GAZES FROM THE LABYRINTH OF THE MIRRORS. I'M SURE OF IT.
WOOOON
WOOOON
AAAAH!
WOOOON
OKAMURA!! HURRY! DO SOMETHING!
THIS IS BAD. IF THIS KEEPS UP, THE SAME TRAGEDY...
...THAT HAPPENED HERE DECADES AGO, THAT I SAW IN THE VISION JUST NOW, WILL...
WOOOON
WOOOON
AH!

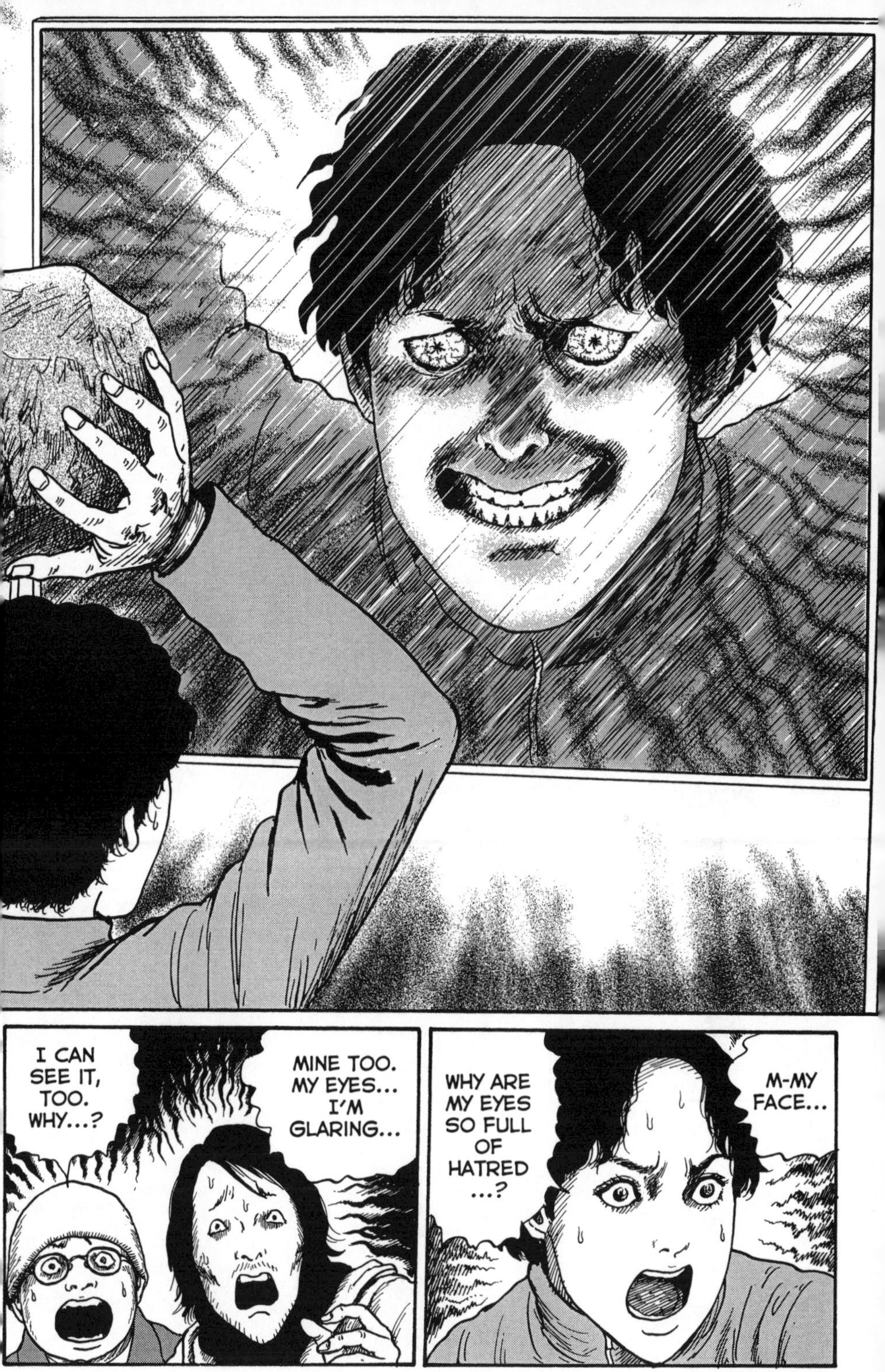
M-MY FACE...
WHY ARE MY EYES SO FULL OF HATRED ...?
MINE TOO. MY EYES... I'M GLARING...
I CAN SEE IT, TOO. WHY...?

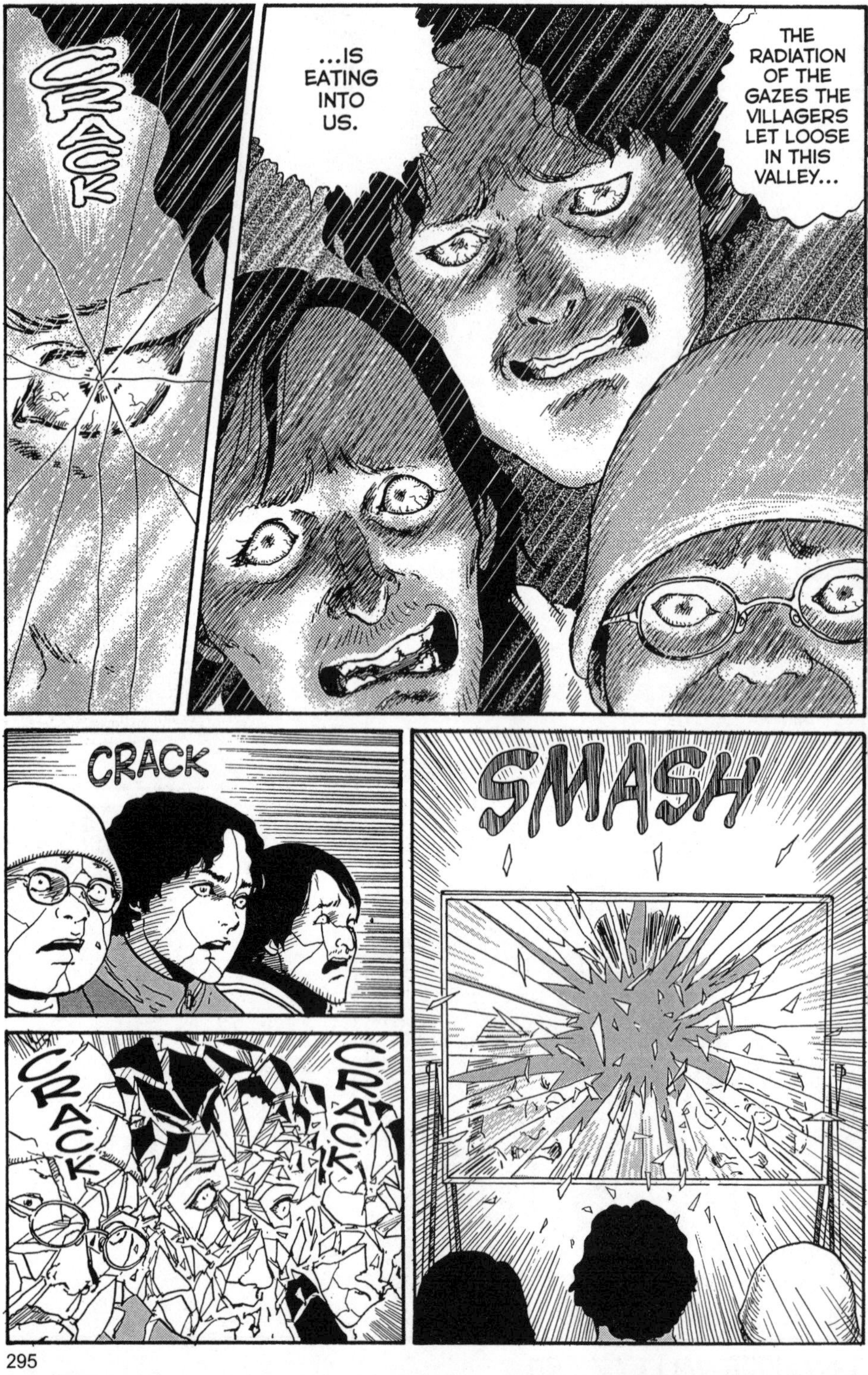
THE RADIATION OF THE GAZES THE VILLAGERS LET LOOSE IN THIS VALLEY...
...IS EATING INTO US.
CRACK
SMASH
CRACK
CRACK
CRACK

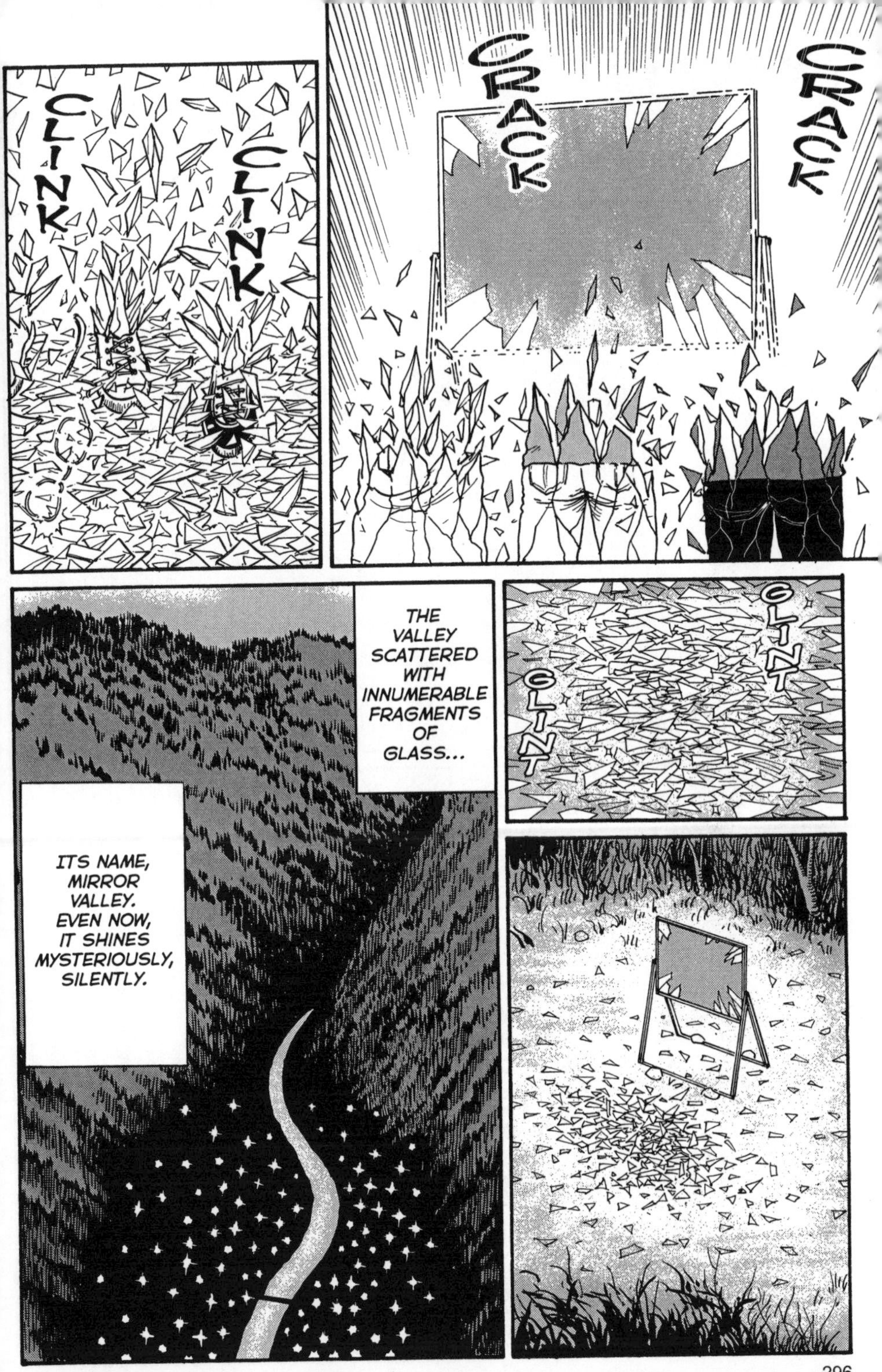
CRACK
CRACK
CLINK
CLINK
GLINT
GLINT
THE VALLEY SCATTERED WITH INNUMERABLE FRAGMENTS OF GLASS...
ITS NAME, MIRROR VALLEY. EVEN NOW, IT SHINES MYSTERIOUSLY, SILENTLY.

IN MIRROR VALLEY / END

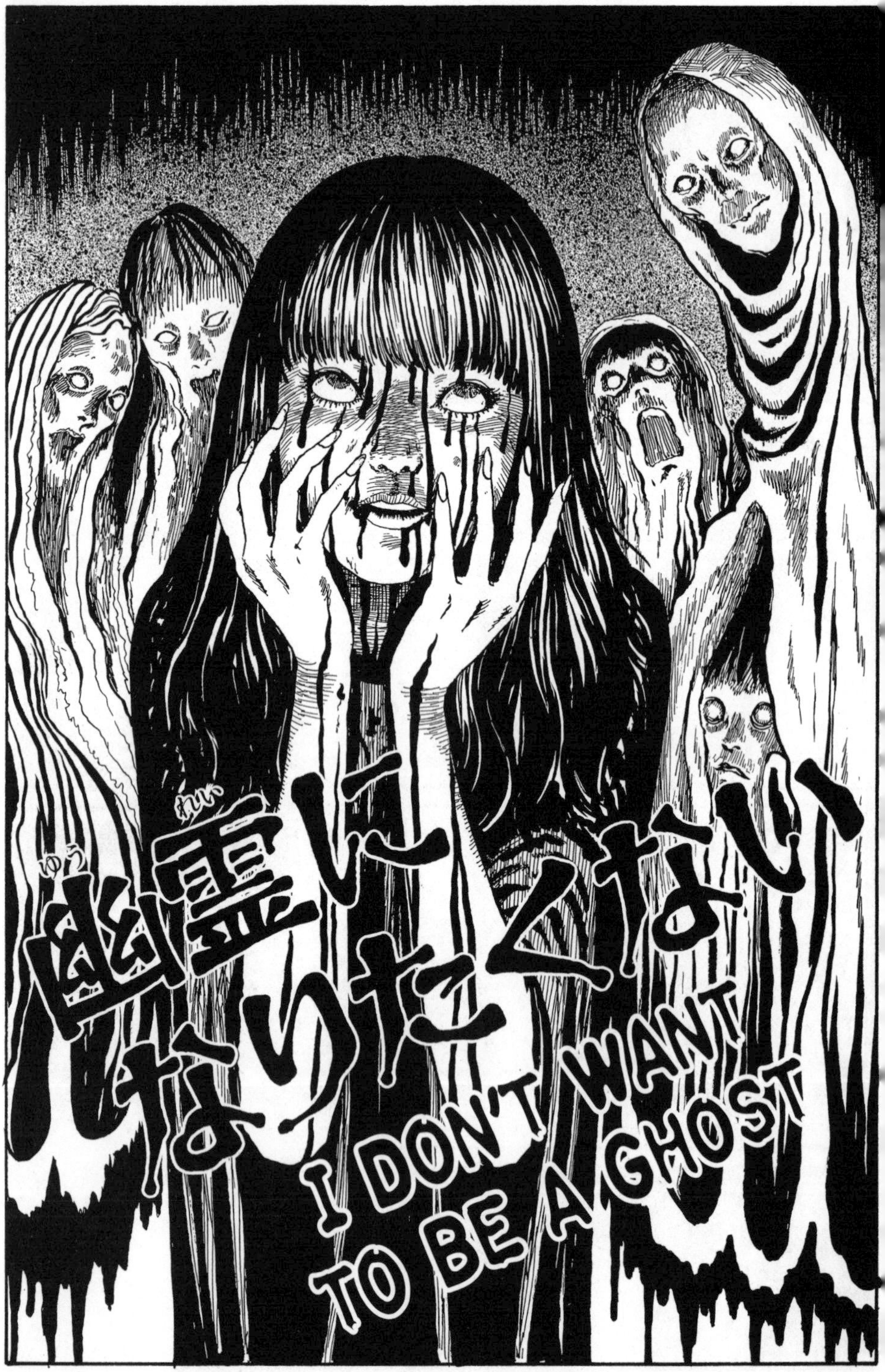
幽霊になりたくない
I DON'T WANT TO BE A GHOST

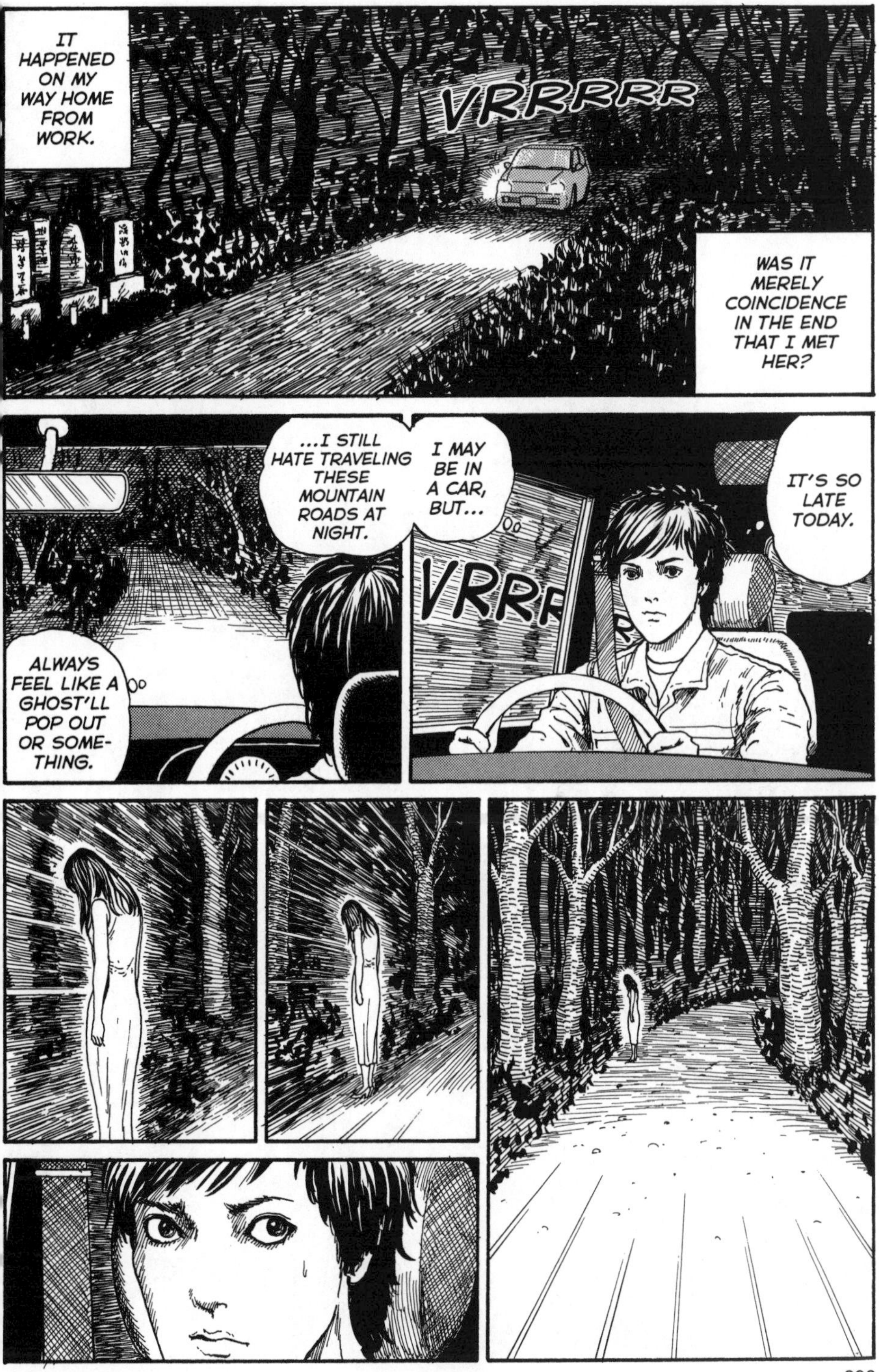
IT HAPPENED ON MY WAY HOME FROM WORK.
VRRRRRR
WAS IT MERELY COINCIDENCE IN THE END THAT I MET HER?
IT'S SO LATE TODAY.
I MAY BE IN A CAR, BUT...
VRRRR
...I STILL HATE TRAVELING THESE MOUNTAIN ROADS AT NIGHT.
ALWAYS FEEL LIKE A GHOST'LL POP OUT OR SOME-THING.

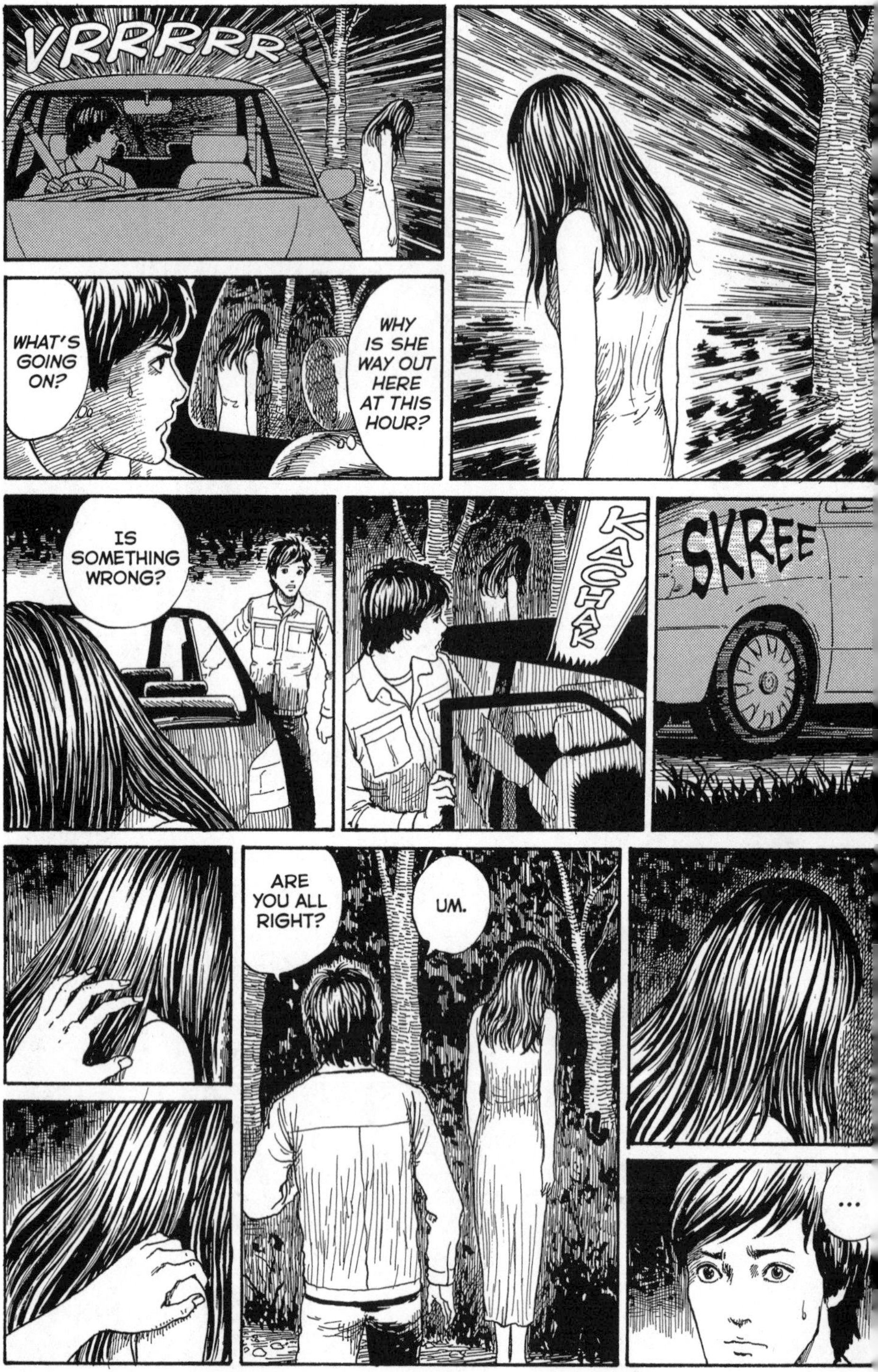
VRRRRR
WHY IS SHE WAY OUT HERE AT THIS HOUR?
WHAT'S GOING ON?
SKREE
KACHAK
IS SOMETHING WRONG?
...
UM.
ARE YOU ALL RIGHT?

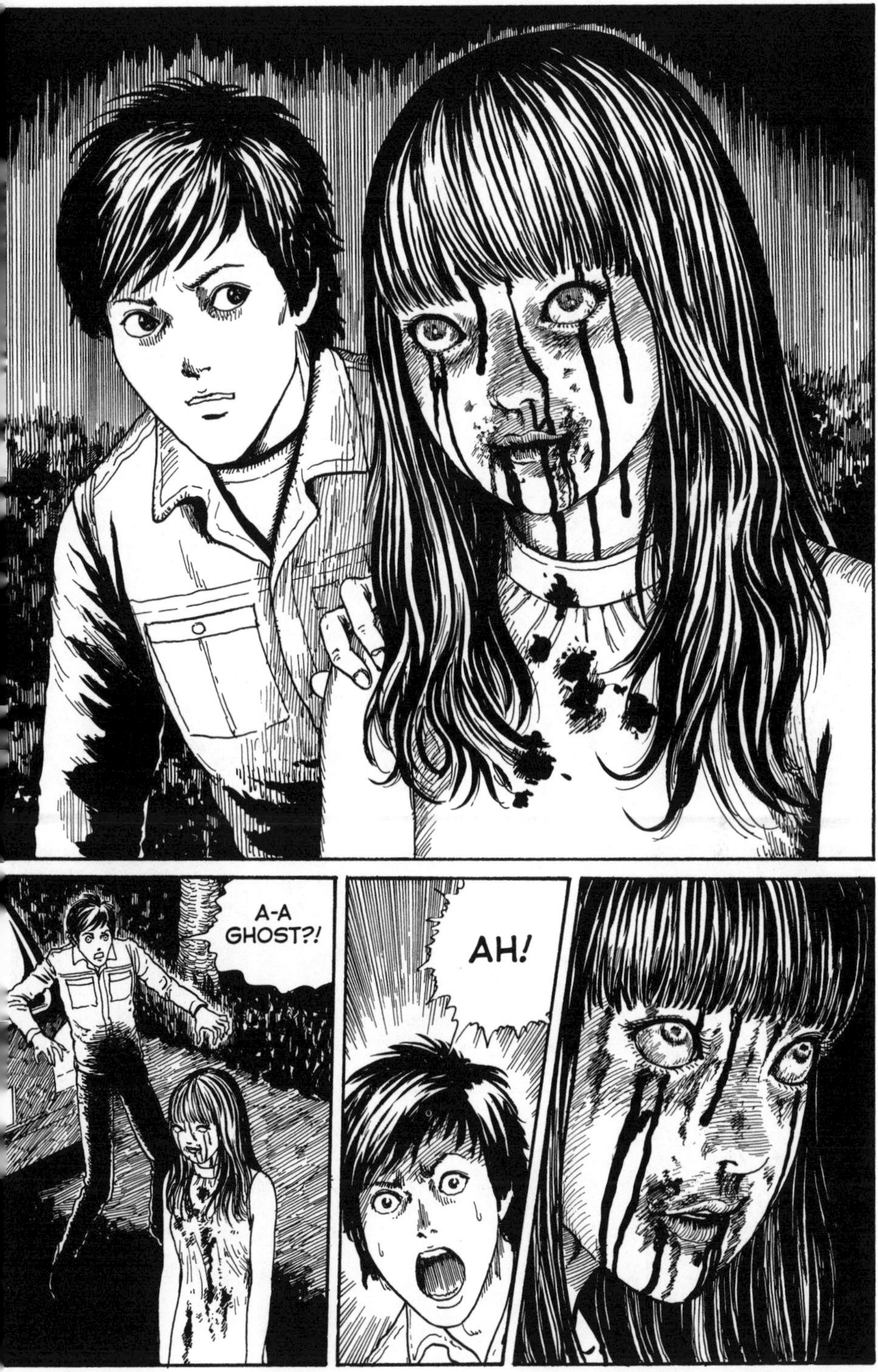
AH!
A-A GHOST?!

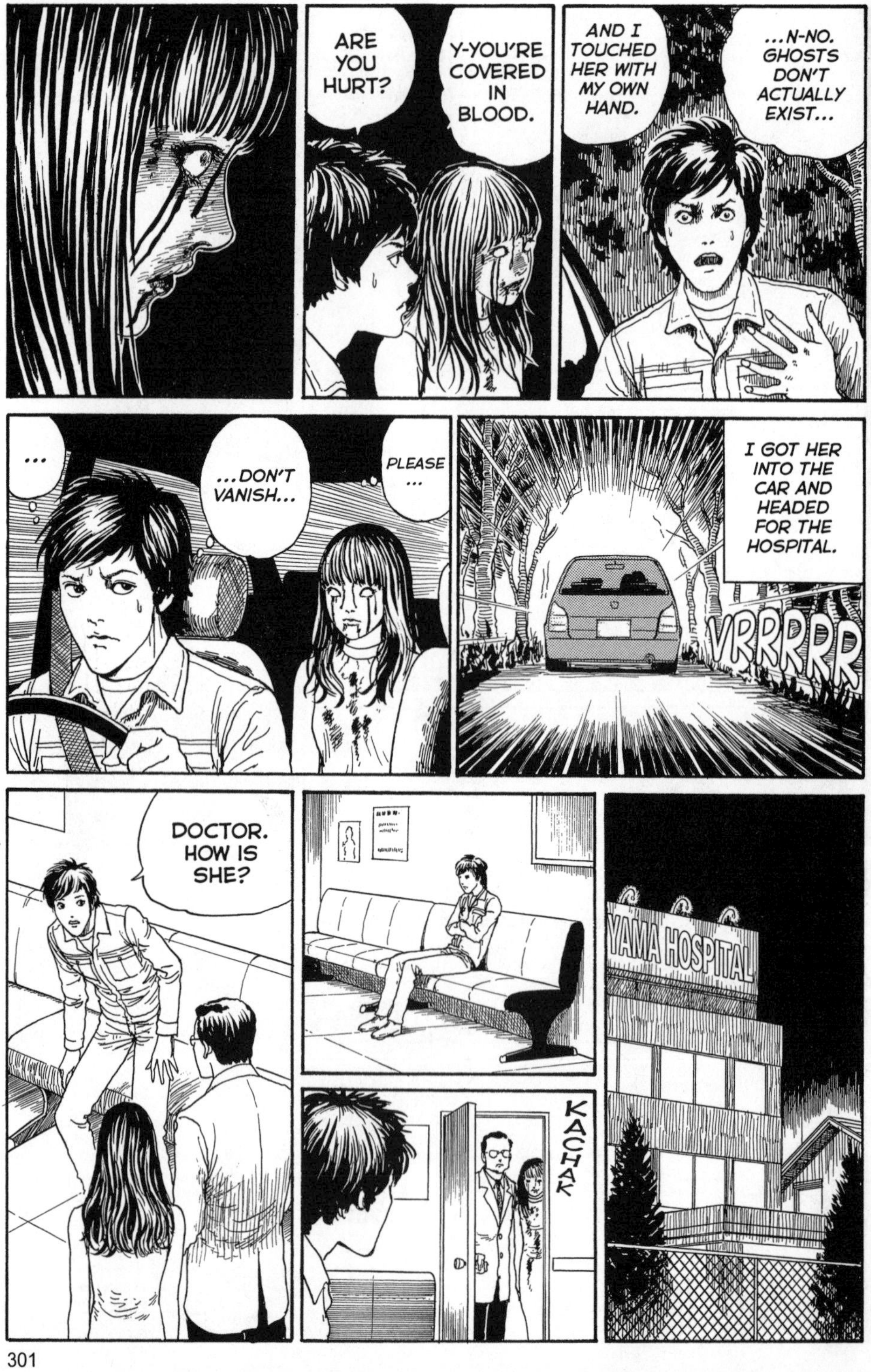
...N-NO. GHOSTS DON'T ACTUALLY EXIST...
AND I TOUCHED HER WITH MY OWN HAND.
Y-YOU'RE COVERED IN BLOOD.
ARE YOU HURT?
I GOT HER INTO THE CAR AND HEADED FOR THE HOSPITAL.
VRRRRR
PLEASE ...
...DON'T VANISH...
...
YAMA HOSPITAL
KACHAK
DOCTOR. HOW IS SHE?

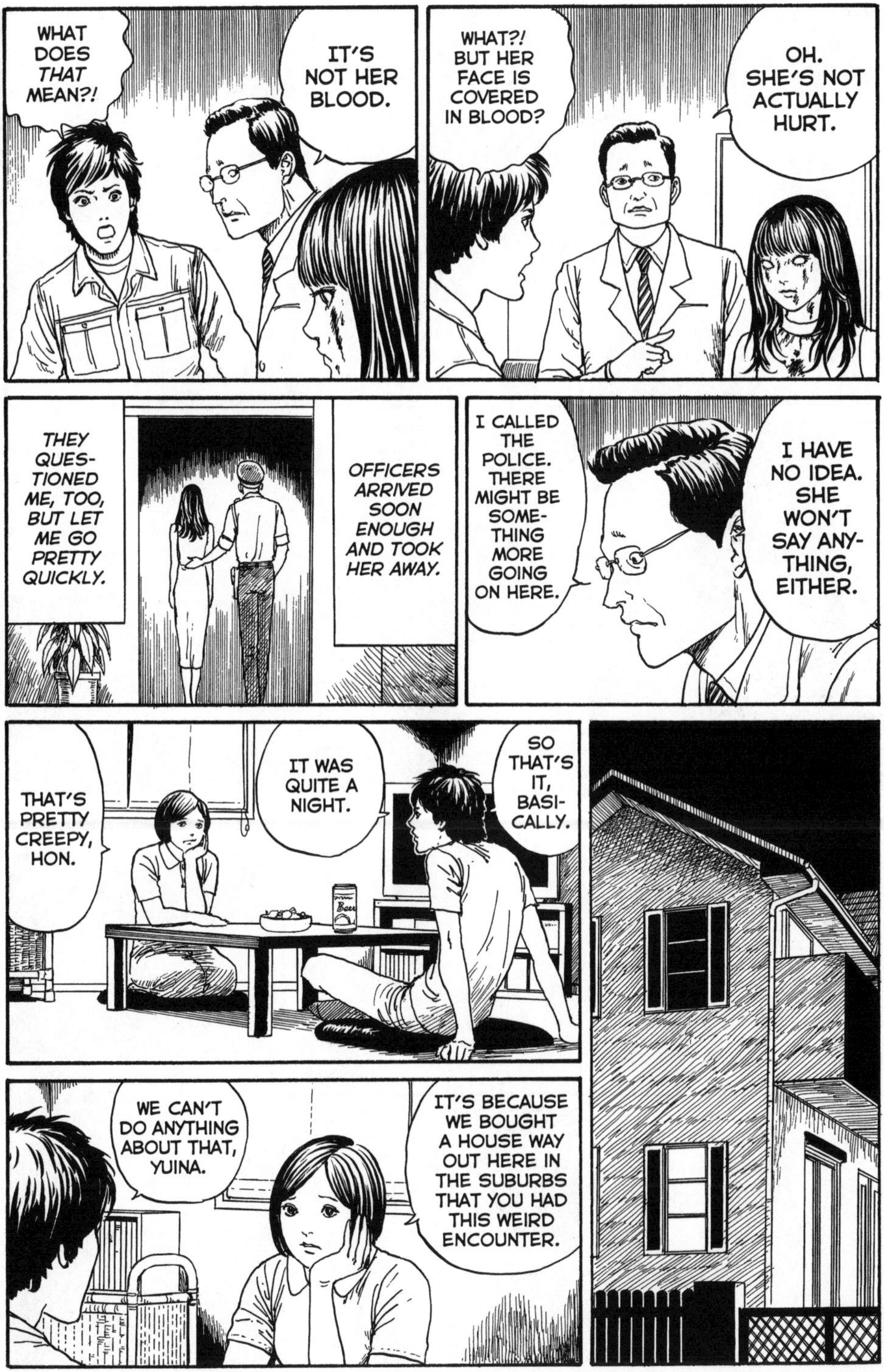
OH. SHE'S NOT ACTUALLY HURT.
WHAT?! BUT HER FACE IS COVERED IN BLOOD?
IT'S NOT HER BLOOD.
WHAT DOES *THAT* MEAN?!
I HAVE NO IDEA. SHE WON'T SAY ANYTHING, EITHER.
I CALLED THE POLICE. THERE MIGHT BE SOMETHING MORE GOING ON HERE.
OFFICERS ARRIVED SOON ENOUGH AND TOOK HER AWAY.
THEY QUESTIONED ME, TOO, BUT LET ME GO PRETTY QUICKLY.
SO THAT'S IT, BASICALLY.
IT WAS QUITE A NIGHT.
THAT'S PRETTY CREEPY, HON.
IT'S BECAUSE WE BOUGHT A HOUSE WAY OUT HERE IN THE SUBURBS THAT YOU HAD THIS WEIRD ENCOUNTER.
WE CAN'T DO ANYTHING ABOUT THAT, YUINA.

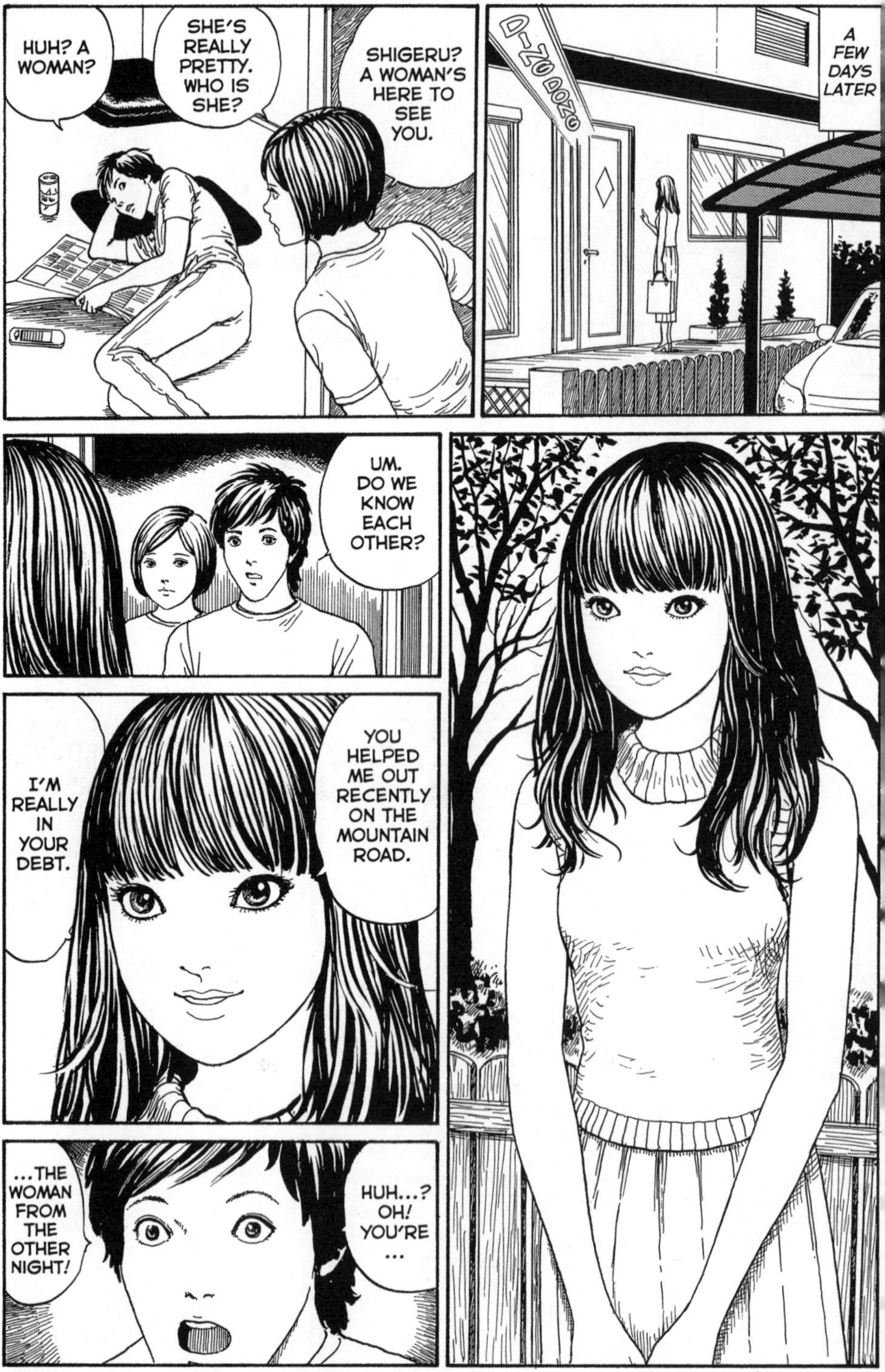
A FEW DAYS LATER
SHIGERU? A WOMAN'S HERE TO SEE YOU.
SHE'S REALLY PRETTY. WHO IS SHE?
HUH? A WOMAN?
UM. DO WE KNOW EACH OTHER?
YOU HELPED ME OUT RECENTLY ON THE MOUNTAIN ROAD.
I'M REALLY IN YOUR DEBT.
HUH...? OH! YOU'RE ...
...THE WOMAN FROM THE OTHER NIGHT!

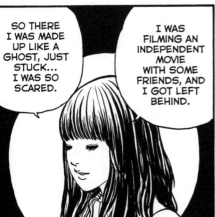

I WAS FILMING AN INDEPENDENT MOVIE WITH SOME FRIENDS, AND I GOT LEFT BEHIND.
SO THERE I WAS MADE UP LIKE A GHOST, JUST STUCK... I WAS SO SCARED.
WHAT? WAS THAT WHAT HAPPENED? HA HA HA!
BUT YOU REALLY GAVE ME A SHOCK THERE.
WHEN THIS BEAUTIFUL WOMAN—MISAKI—WAS LEAVING...
...SHE SECRETLY HANDED ME A SCRAP OF PAPER.
I'd like to see you again.
My cell:
090-1
0107
SHIGERU? WHAT'S WRONG?
OH... IT'S NOTH-ING.

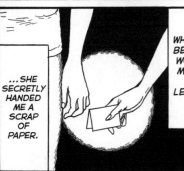

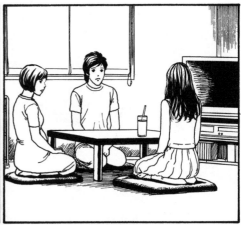

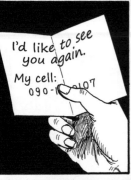

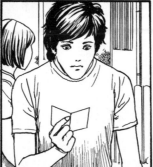

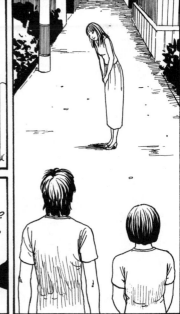

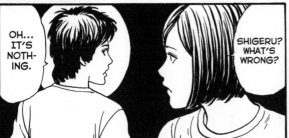

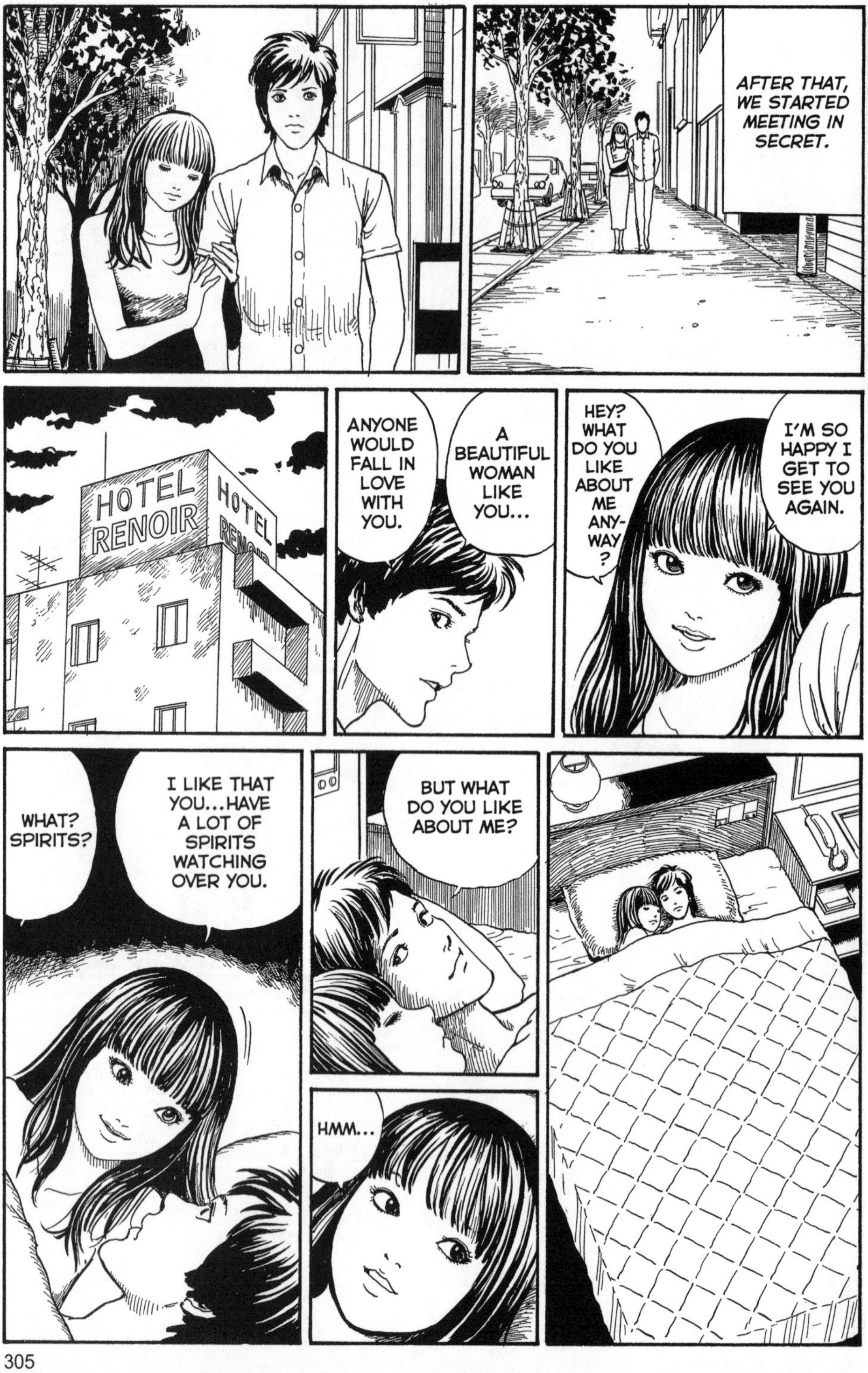
AFTER THAT, WE STARTED MEETING IN SECRET.
I'M SO HAPPY I GET TO SEE YOU AGAIN.
HEY? WHAT DO YOU LIKE ABOUT ME ANYWAY?
A BEAUTIFUL WOMAN LIKE YOU...
ANYONE WOULD FALL IN LOVE WITH YOU.
HOTEL RENOIR
HOTEL RENOIR
BUT WHAT DO YOU LIKE ABOUT ME?
HMM...
I LIKE THAT YOU...HAVE A LOT OF SPIRITS WATCHING OVER YOU.
WHAT? SPIRITS?

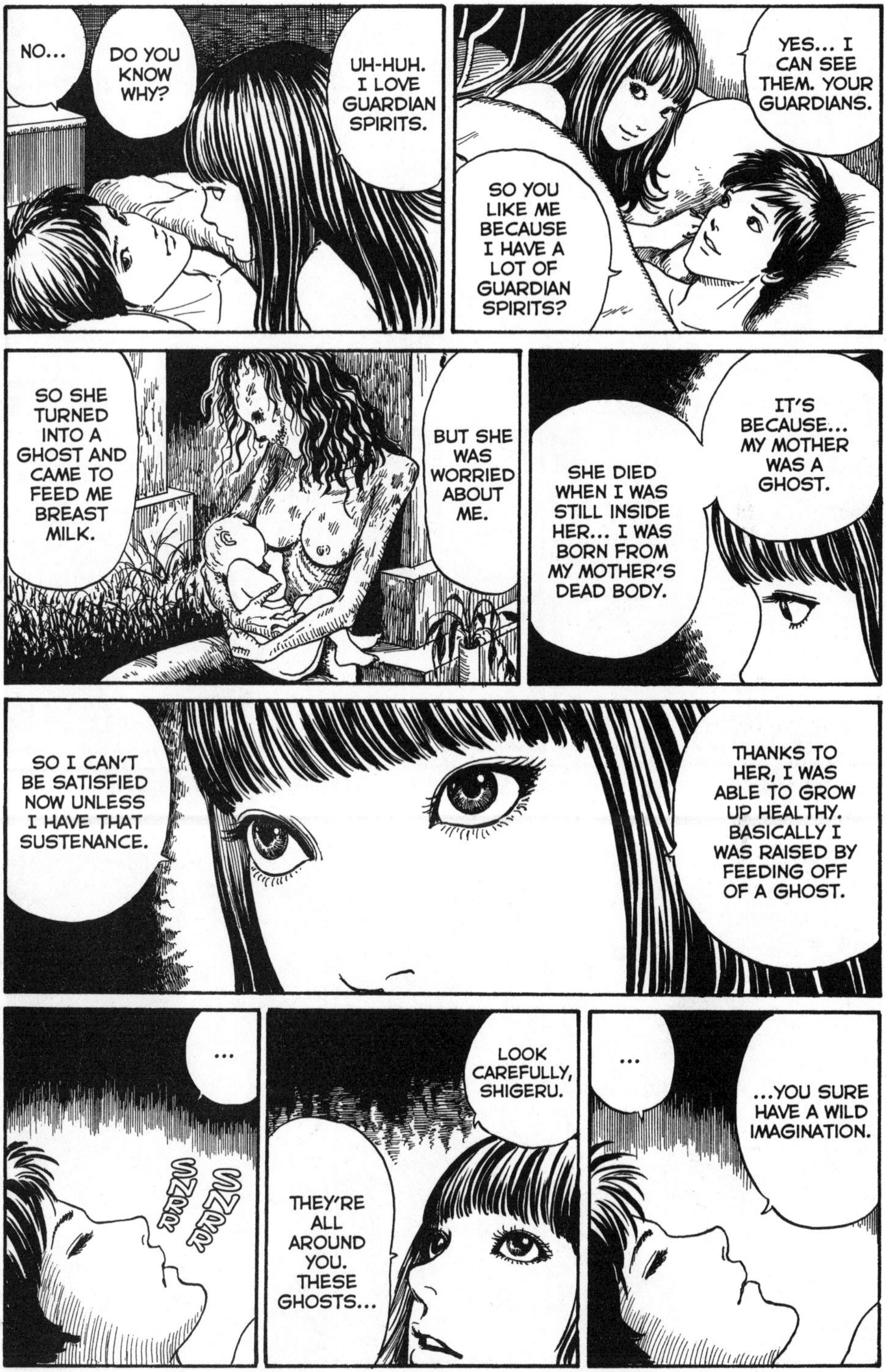
YES... I CAN SEE THEM. YOUR GUARDIANS.
SO YOU LIKE ME BECAUSE I HAVE A LOT OF GUARDIAN SPIRITS?
UH-HUH. I LOVE GUARDIAN SPIRITS.
DO YOU KNOW WHY?
NO...
IT'S BECAUSE... MY MOTHER WAS A GHOST.
SHE DIED WHEN I WAS STILL INSIDE HER... I WAS BORN FROM MY MOTHER'S DEAD BODY.
BUT SHE WAS WORRIED ABOUT ME.
SO SHE TURNED INTO A GHOST AND CAME TO FEED ME BREAST MILK.
THANKS TO HER, I WAS ABLE TO GROW UP HEALTHY. BASICALLY I WAS RAISED BY FEEDING OFF OF A GHOST.
SO I CAN'T BE SATISFIED NOW UNLESS I HAVE THAT SUSTENANCE.
...YOU SURE HAVE A WILD IMAGINATION.
...
LOOK CAREFULLY, SHIGERU.
THEY'RE ALL AROUND YOU. THESE GHOSTS...
...
SNRR
SNRR

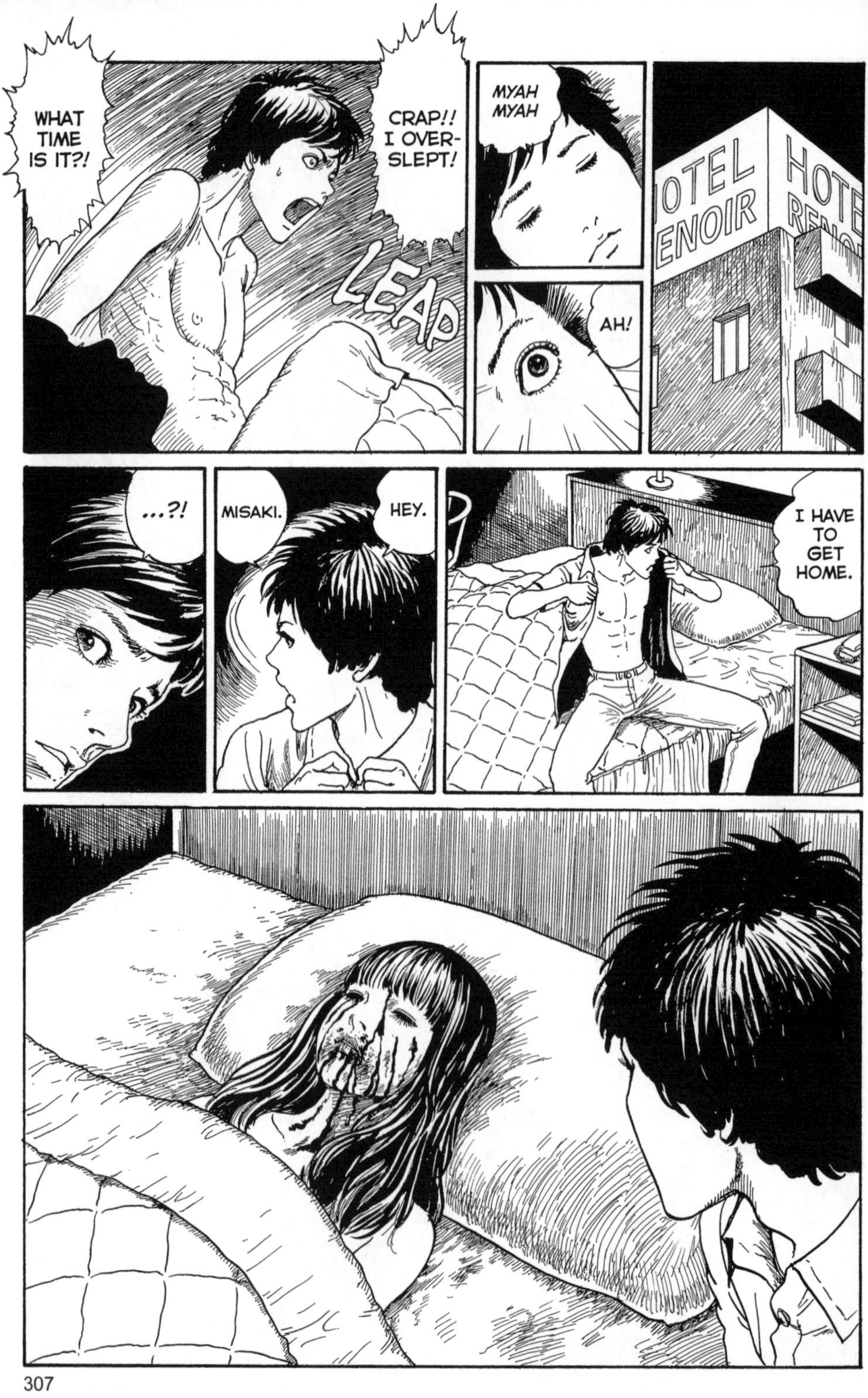
OTEL
ENOIR
MYAH MYAH
AH!
CRAP!! I OVER-SLEPT!
WHAT TIME IS IT?!
LEAP
I HAVE TO GET HOME.
HEY.
MISAKI.
...?!

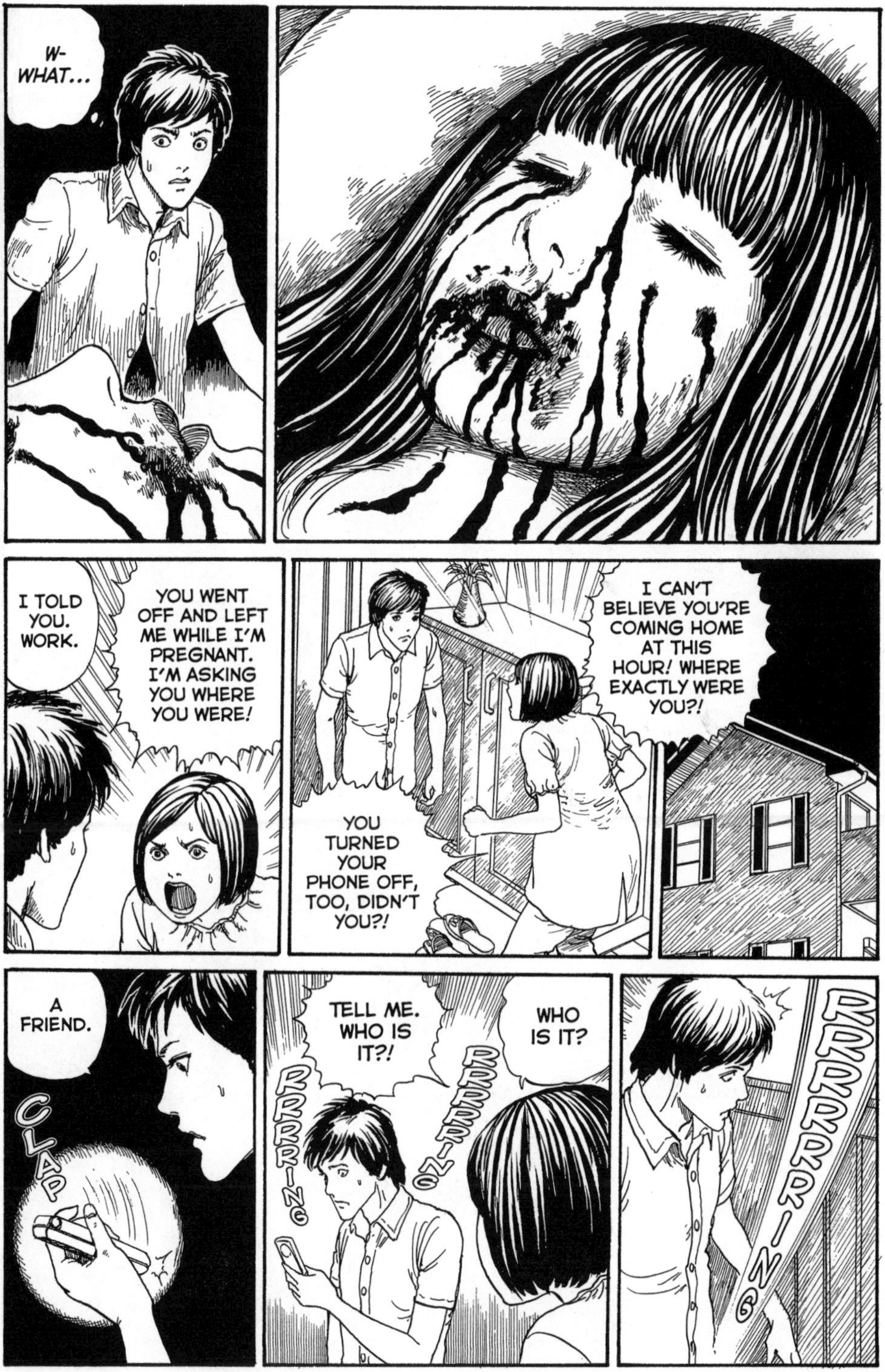
W-
WHAT...
I CAN'T BELIEVE YOU'RE COMING HOME AT THIS HOUR! WHERE EXACTLY WERE YOU?!
YOU TURNED YOUR PHONE OFF, TOO, DIDN'T YOU?!
YOU WENT OFF AND LEFT ME WHILE I'M PREGNANT. I'M ASKING YOU WHERE YOU WERE!
I TOLD YOU. WORK.
RRRRRRRRRING
WHO IS IT?
TELL ME. WHO IS IT?!
RRRRRING
RRRRING
A FRIEND.
CLAP

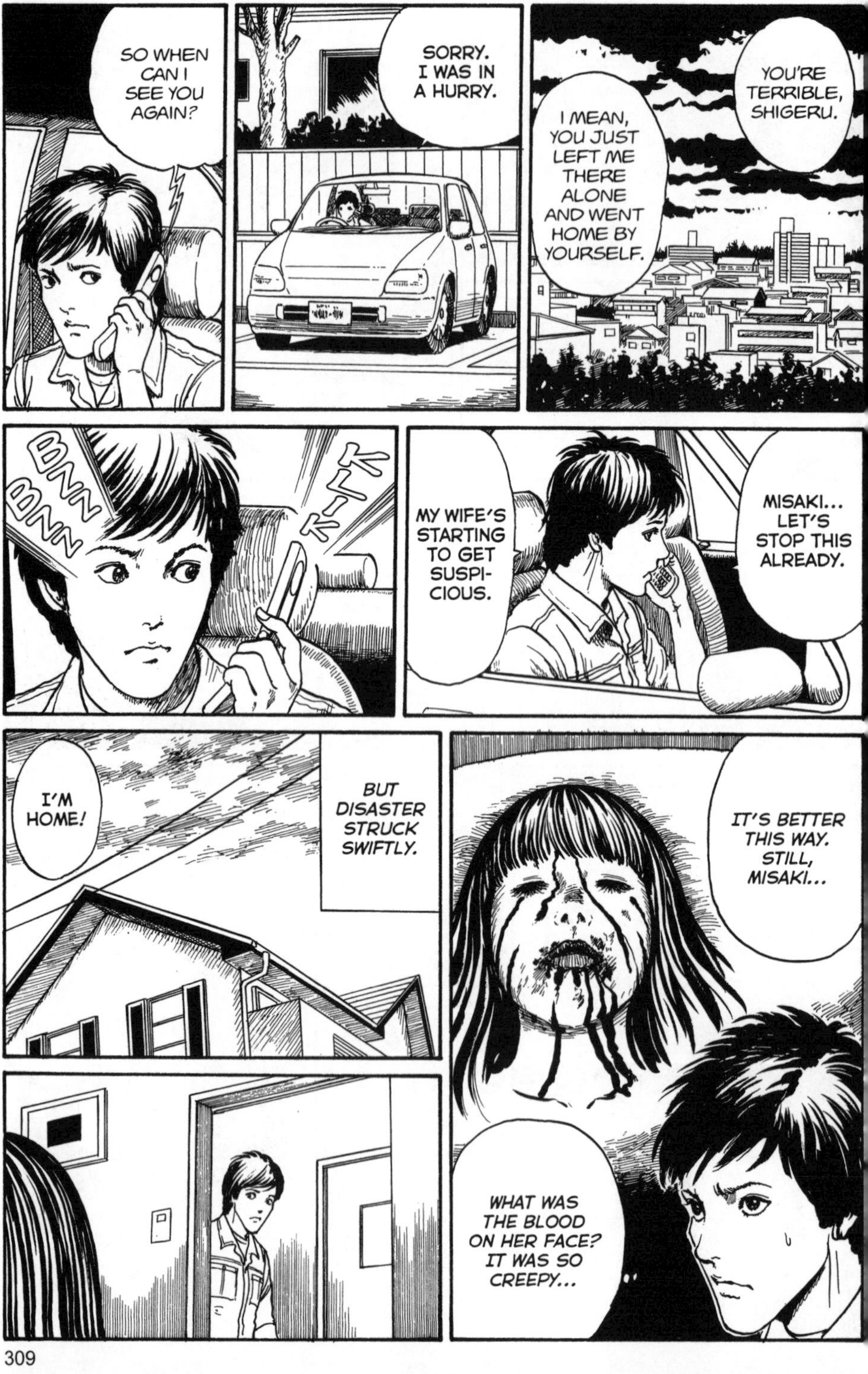
YOU'RE TERRIBLE, SHIGERU.
I MEAN, YOU JUST LEFT ME THERE ALONE AND WENT HOME BY YOURSELF.
SORRY. I WAS IN A HURRY.
SO WHEN CAN I SEE YOU AGAIN?
MISAKI... LET'S STOP THIS ALREADY.
MY WIFE'S STARTING TO GET SUSPICIOUS.
KLIK
BNN BNN
IT'S BETTER THIS WAY. STILL, MISAKI...
WHAT WAS THE BLOOD ON HER FACE? IT WAS SO CREEPY...
BUT DISASTER STRUCK SWIFTLY.
I'M HOME!

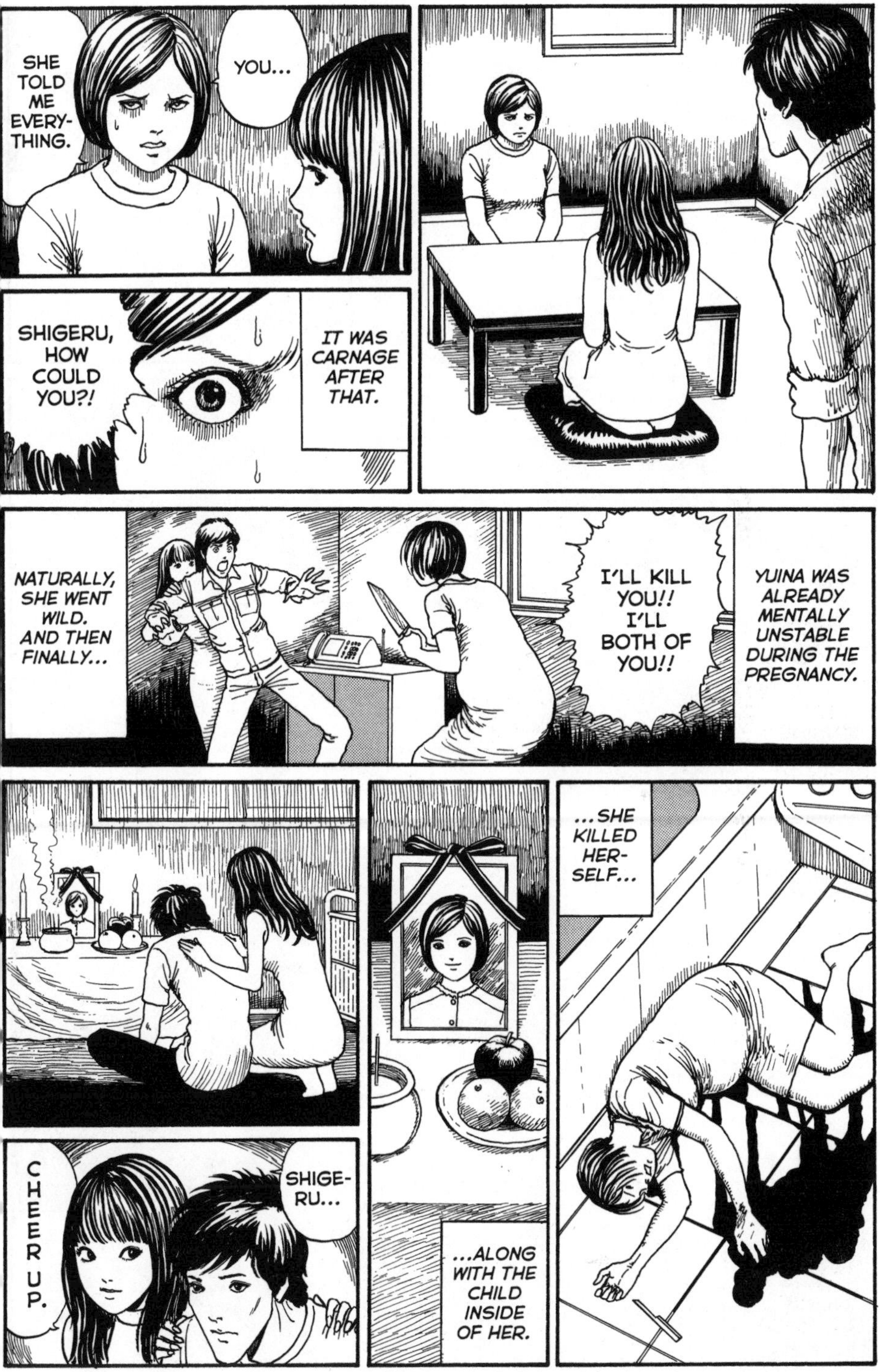
YOU...
SHE TOLD ME EVERY-THING.
IT WAS CARNAGE AFTER THAT.
SHIGERU, HOW COULD YOU?!
YUINA WAS ALREADY MENTALLY UNSTABLE DURING THE PREGNANCY.
I'LL KILL YOU!! I'LL BOTH OF YOU!!
NATURALLY, SHE WENT WILD. AND THEN FINALLY...
...SHE KILLED HER-SELF...
...ALONG WITH THE CHILD INSIDE OF HER.
SHIGE-RU...
CHEER UP.

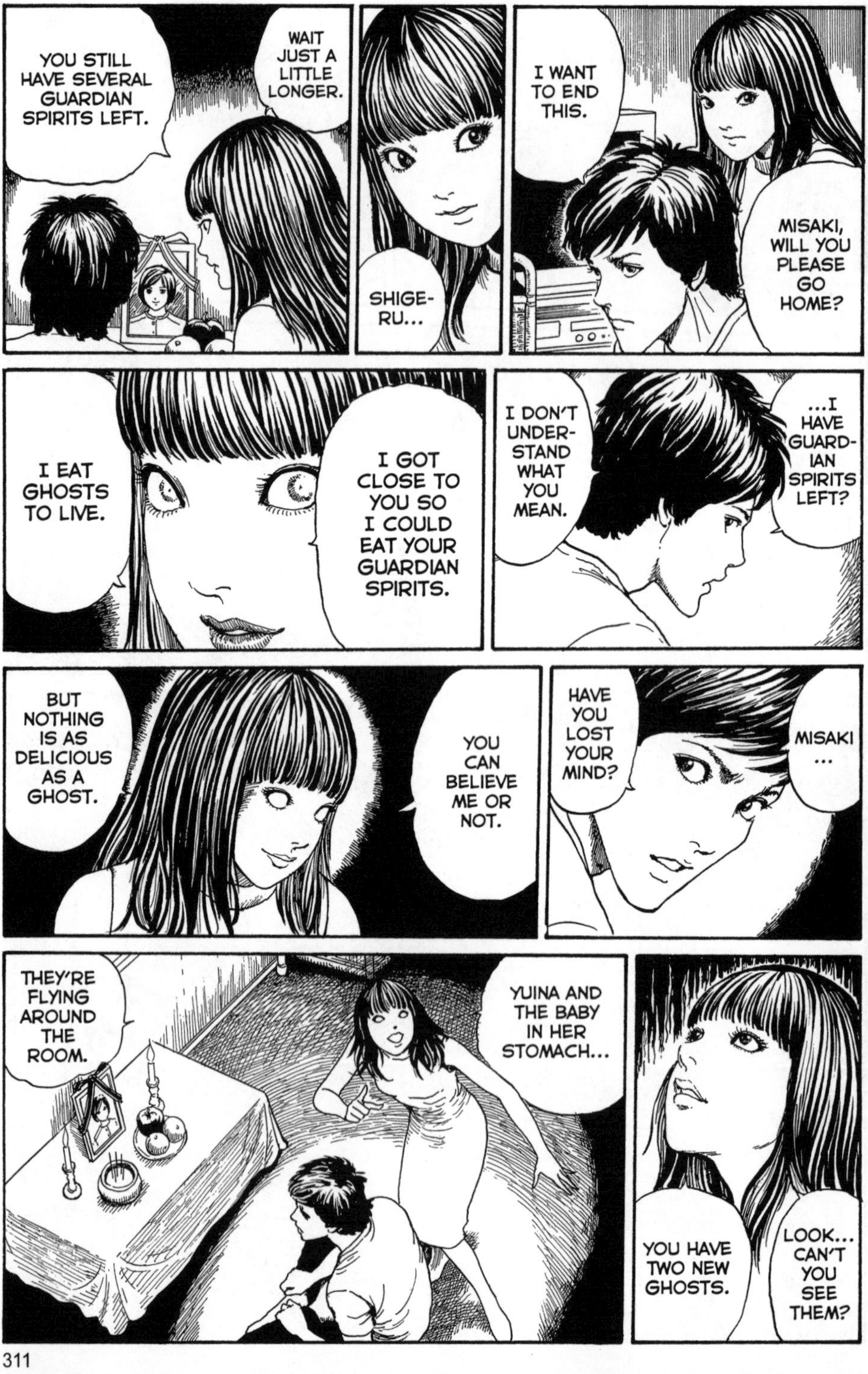
MISAKI, WILL YOU PLEASE GO HOME?
I WANT TO END THIS.
SHIGE-RU...
WAIT JUST A LITTLE LONGER.
YOU STILL HAVE SEVERAL GUARDIAN SPIRITS LEFT.
...I HAVE GUARDIAN SPIRITS LEFT?
I DON'T UNDERSTAND WHAT YOU MEAN.
I GOT CLOSE TO YOU SO I COULD EAT YOUR GUARDIAN SPIRITS.
I EAT GHOSTS TO LIVE.
MISAKI ...
HAVE YOU LOST YOUR MIND?
YOU CAN BELIEVE ME OR NOT.
BUT NOTHING IS AS DELICIOUS AS A GHOST.
LOOK... CAN'T YOU SEE THEM?
YOU HAVE TWO NEW GHOSTS.
YUINA AND THE BABY IN HER STOMACH...
THEY'RE FLYING AROUND THE ROOM.

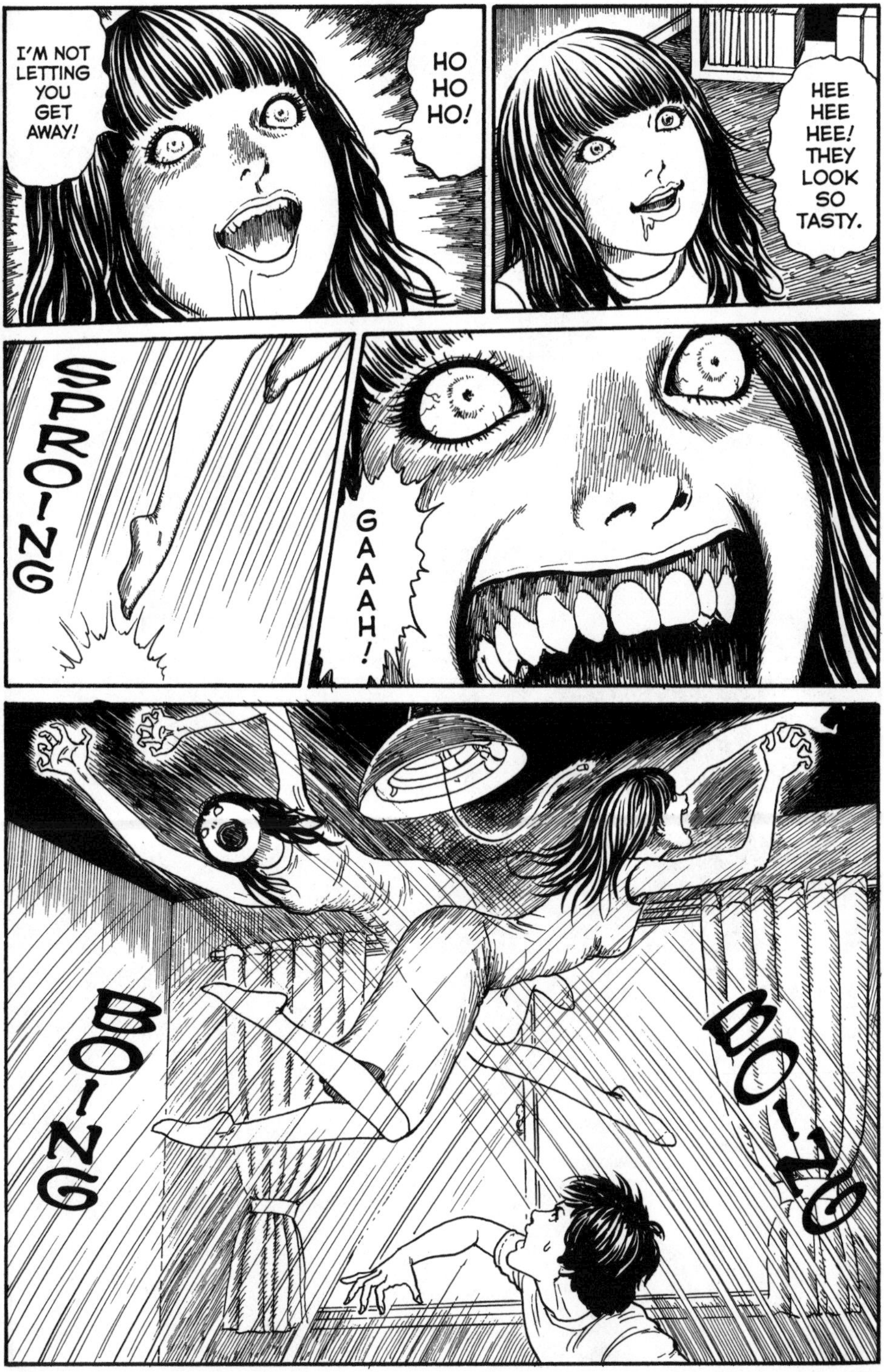
HEE HEE HEE! THEY LOOK SO TASTY.
HO HO HO!
I'M NOT LETTING YOU GET AWAY!
GAAAAH!
SPROING
BOING
BOING

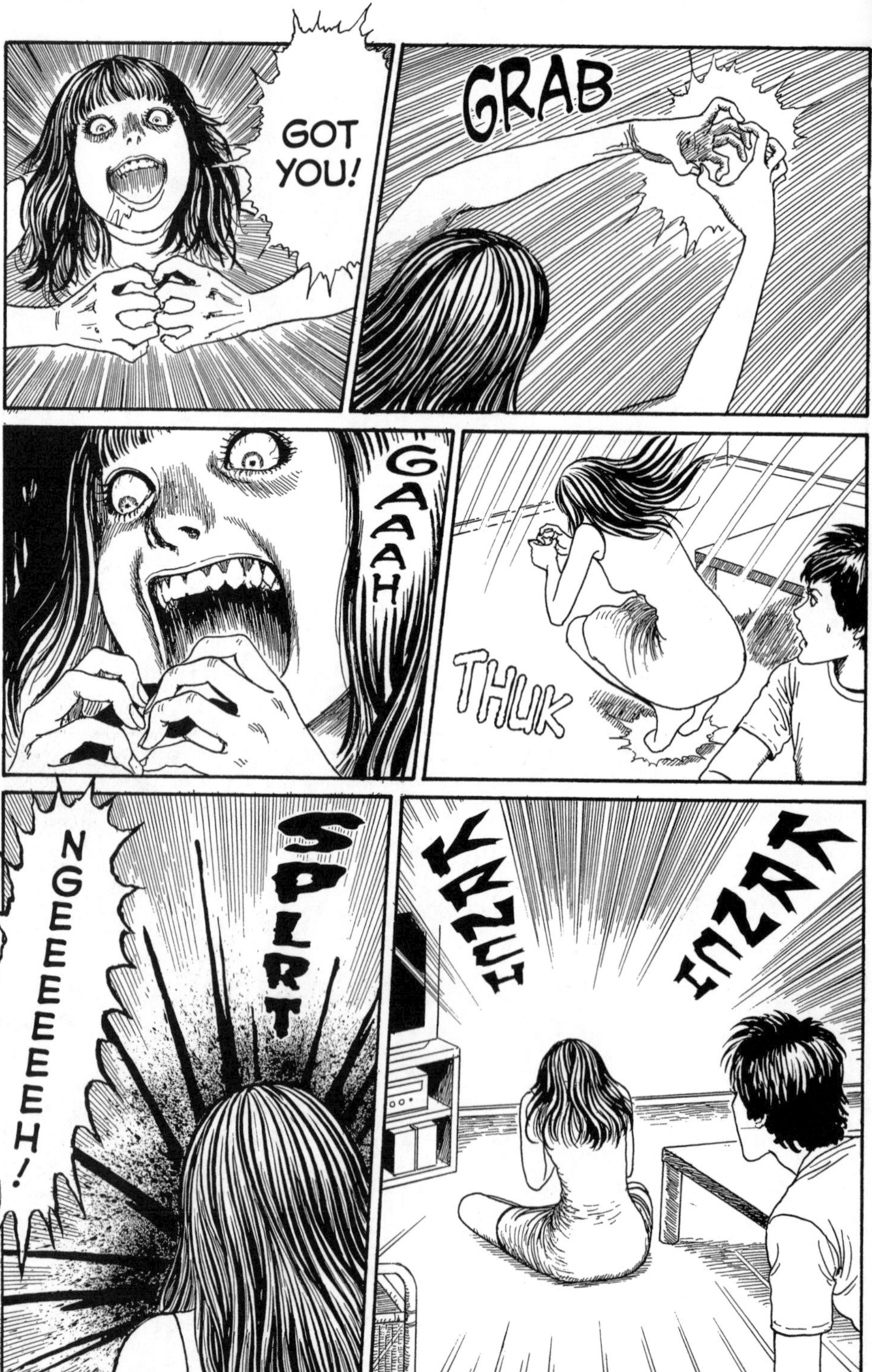
GRAB
GOT YOU!
THUK
GAAAH
KRNCH
KRNCH
SPLRT
NGEEEEEEEH!

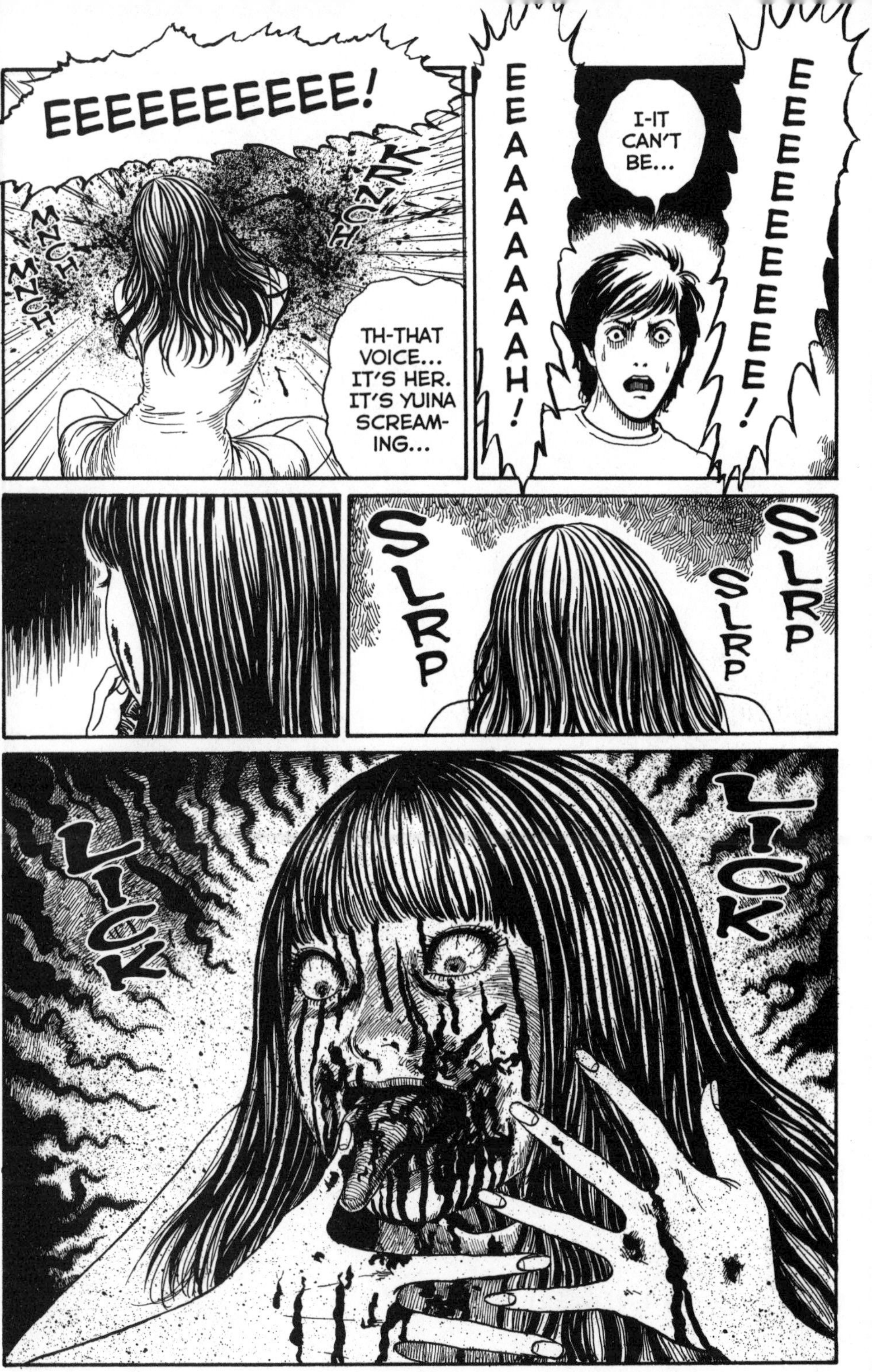
EEEEEEEEE!
I-IT CAN'T BE...
EEAAAAAAH!
EEEEEEEEEE!
KRNCH
MNCH MNCH
TH-THAT VOICE... IT'S HER. IT'S YUINA SCREAMING...
SLRP
SLRP
SLRP
LICK
LICK

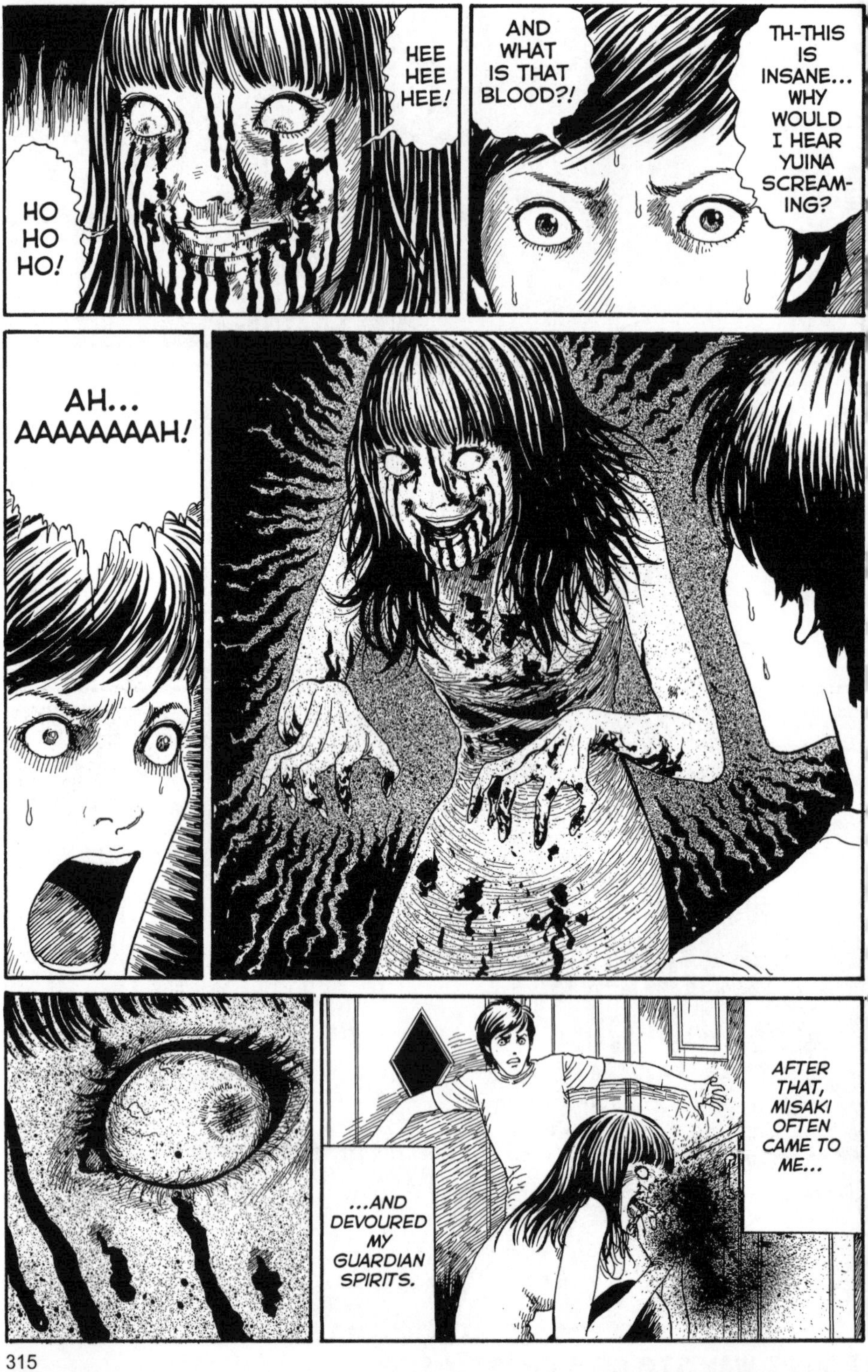
TH-THIS IS INSANE... WHY WOULD I HEAR YUINA SCREAMING?
AND WHAT IS THAT BLOOD?!
HEE HEE HEE!
HO HO HO!
AH... AAAAAAAAH!
AFTER THAT, MISAKI OFTEN CAME TO ME...
...AND DEVOURED MY GUARDIAN SPIRITS.

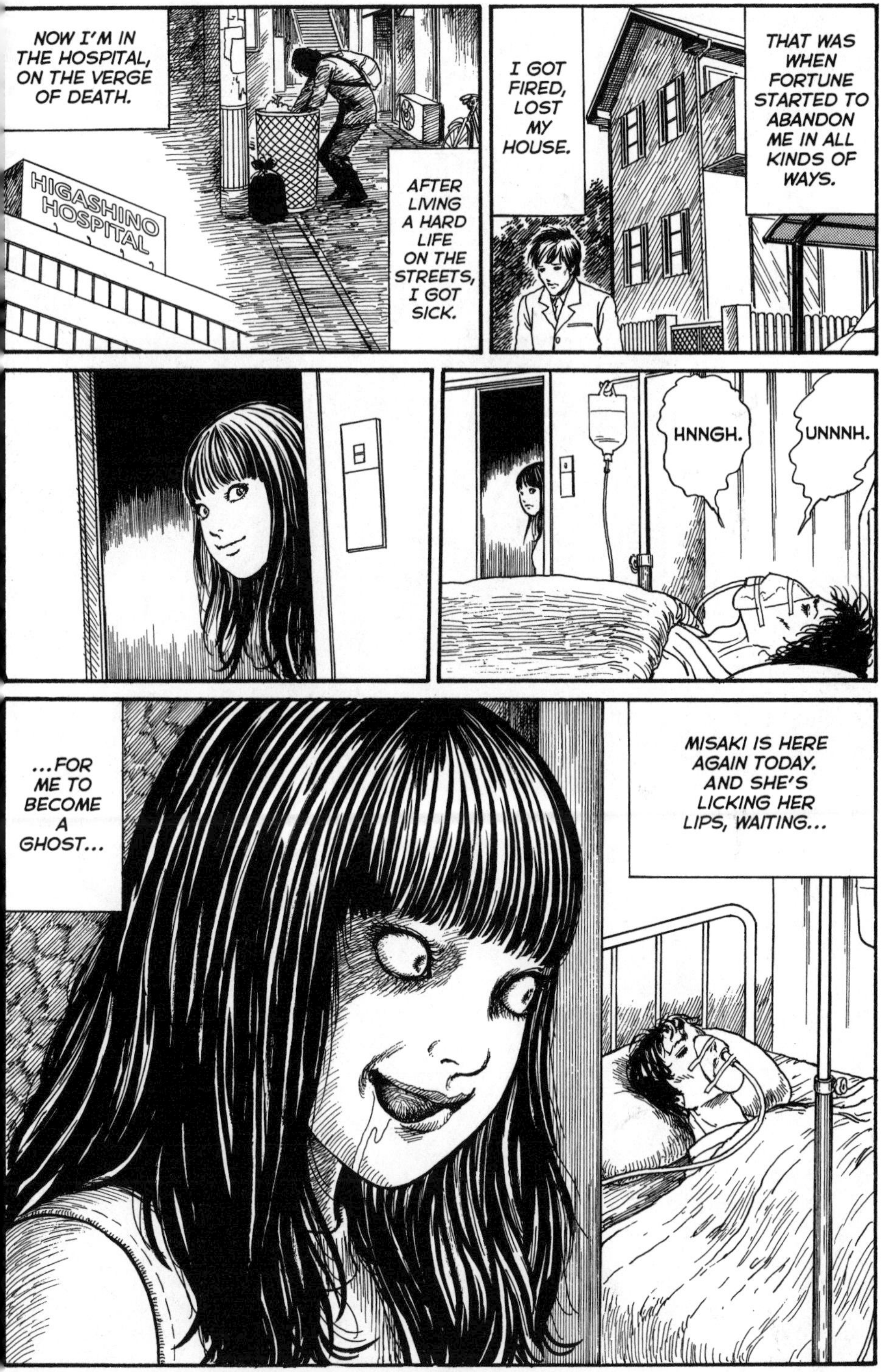
THAT WAS WHEN FORTUNE STARTED TO ABANDON ME IN ALL KINDS OF WAYS.
I GOT FIRED, LOST MY HOUSE.
AFTER LIVING A HARD LIFE ON THE STREETS, I GOT SICK.
NOW I'M IN THE HOSPITAL, ON THE VERGE OF DEATH.
HIGASHINO HOSPITAL
UNNNH.
HNNGH.
MISAKI IS HERE AGAIN TODAY. AND SHE'S LICKING HER LIPS, WAITING...
...FOR ME TO BECOME A GHOST...

I DON'T WANT TO BE A GHOST / END

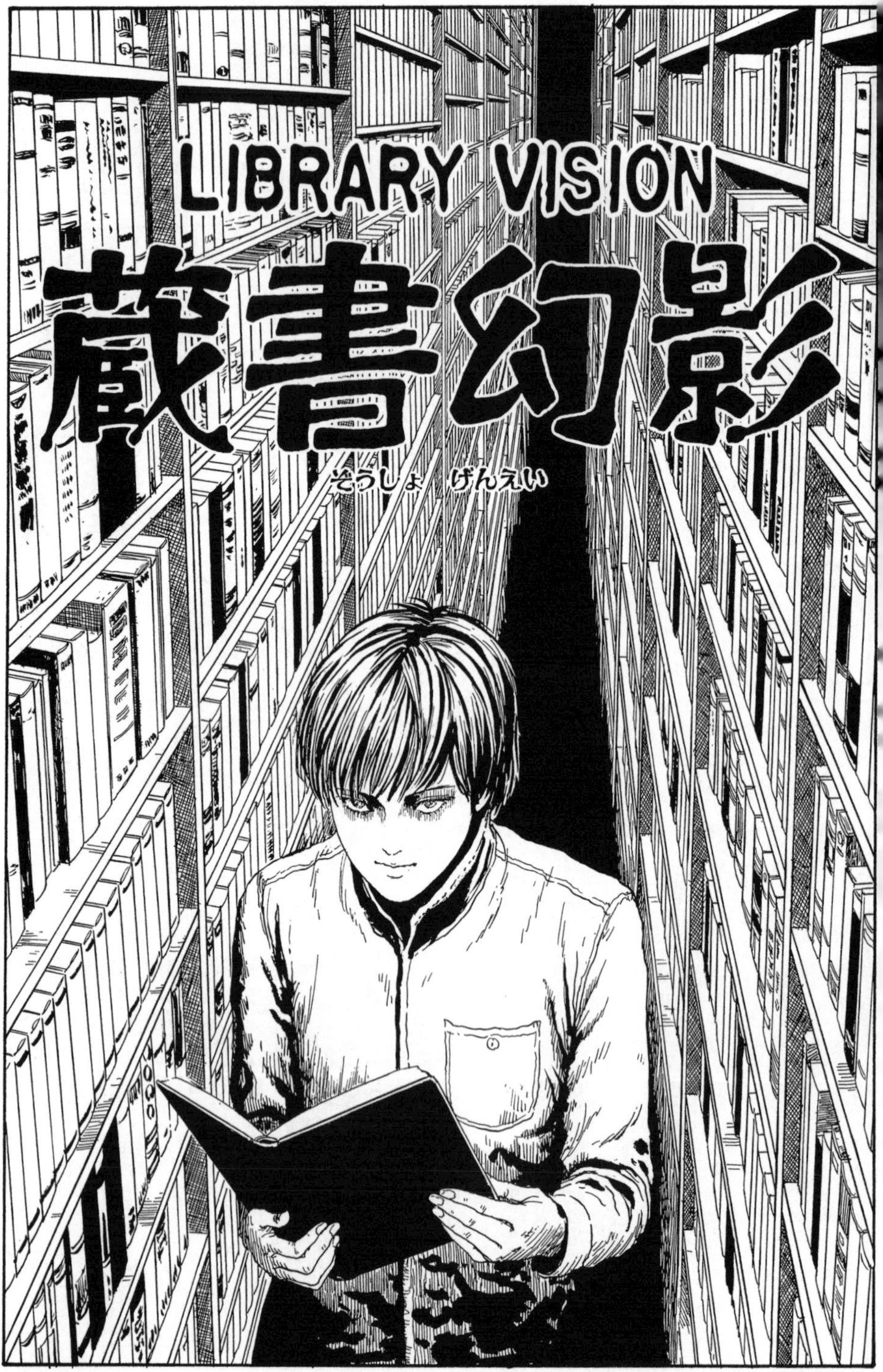
LIBRARY VISION
蔵書幻影
ぞうしょ げんえい

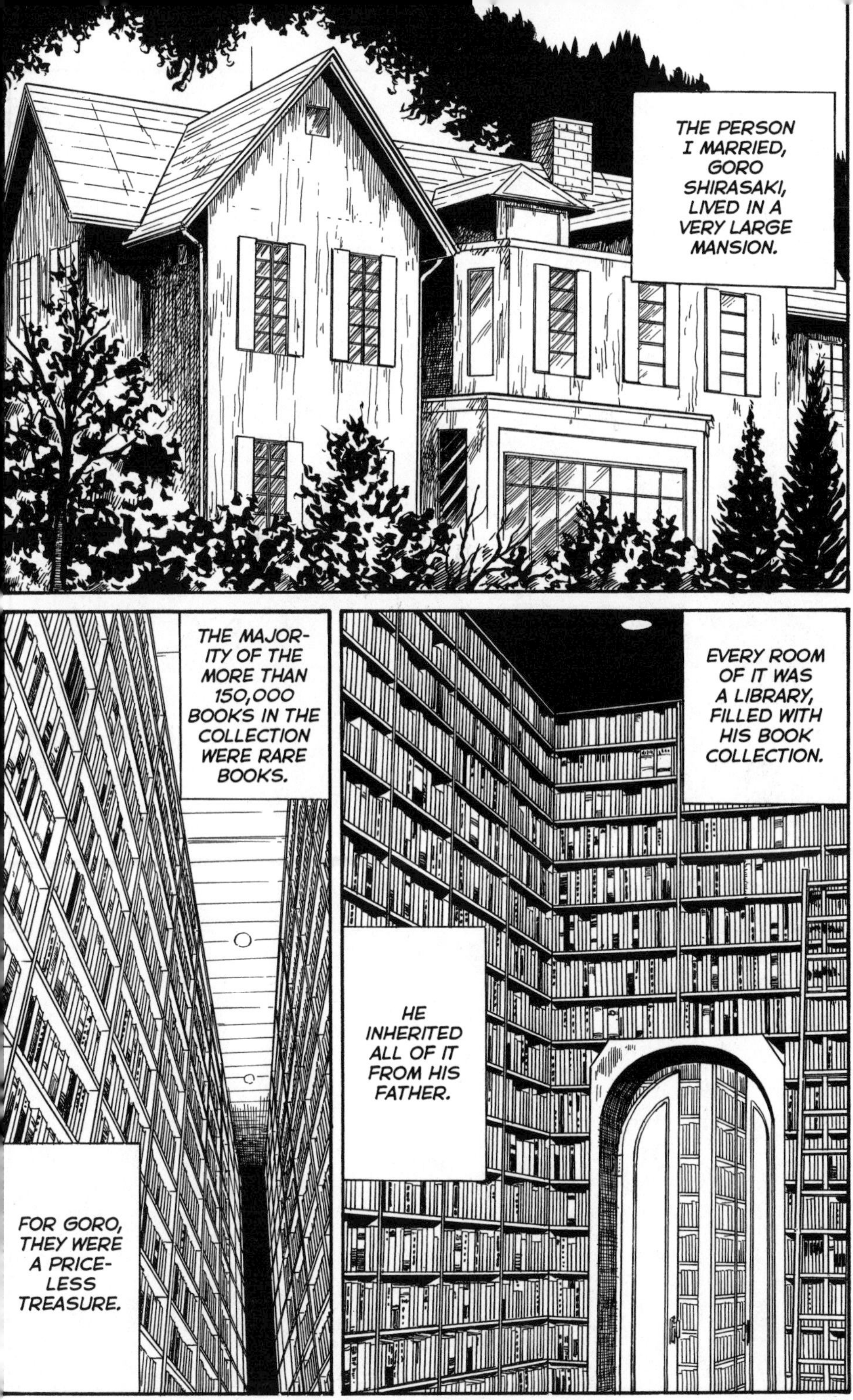
THE PERSON I MARRIED, GORO SHIRASAKI, LIVED IN A VERY LARGE MANSION.
EVERY ROOM OF IT WAS A LIBRARY, FILLED WITH HIS BOOK COLLECTION.
HE INHERITED ALL OF IT FROM HIS FATHER.
THE MAJORITY OF THE MORE THAN 150,000 BOOKS IN THE COLLECTION WERE RARE BOOKS.
FOR GORO, THEY WERE A PRICELESS TREASURE.

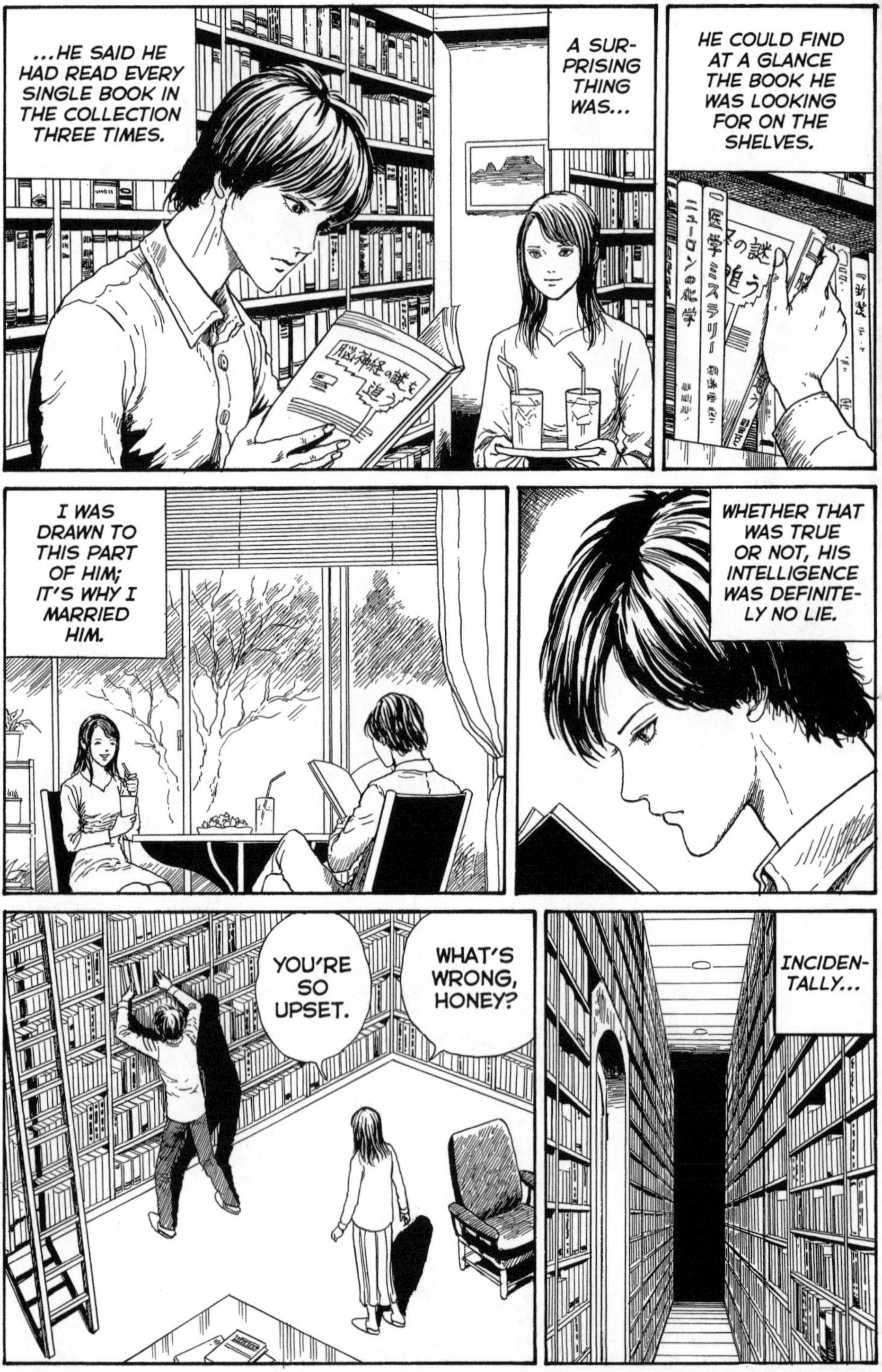
...HE SAID HE HAD READ EVERY SINGLE BOOK IN THE COLLECTION THREE TIMES.
A SUR-PRISING THING WAS...
HE COULD FIND AT A GLANCE THE BOOK HE WAS LOOKING FOR ON THE SHELVES.
I WAS DRAWN TO THIS PART OF HIM; IT'S WHY I MARRIED HIM.
WHETHER THAT WAS TRUE OR NOT, HIS INTELLIGENCE WAS DEFINITE-LY NO LIE.
WHAT'S WRONG, HONEY?
YOU'RE SO UPSET.
INCIDEN-TALLY...

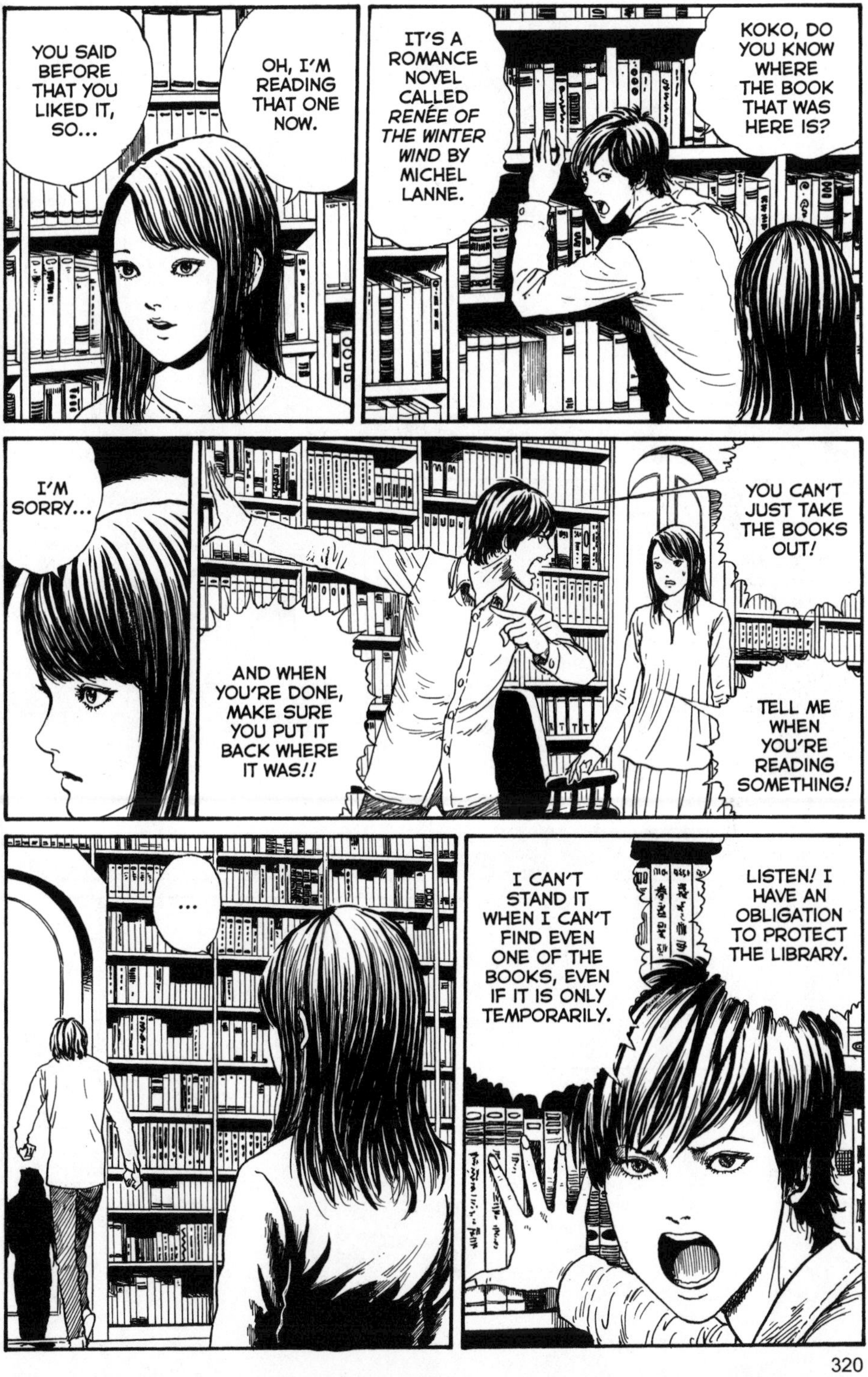
KOKO, DO YOU KNOW WHERE THE BOOK THAT WAS HERE IS?
IT'S A ROMANCE NOVEL CALLED *RENÉE OF THE WINTER WIND* BY MICHEL LANNE.
OH, I'M READING THAT ONE NOW.
YOU SAID BEFORE THAT YOU LIKED IT, SO...
YOU CAN'T JUST TAKE THE BOOKS OUT!
TELL ME WHEN YOU'RE READING SOMETHING!
AND WHEN YOU'RE DONE, MAKE SURE YOU PUT IT BACK WHERE IT WAS!!
I'M SORRY...
LISTEN! I HAVE AN OBLIGATION TO PROTECT THE LIBRARY.
I CAN'T STAND IT WHEN I CAN'T FIND EVEN ONE OF THE BOOKS, EVEN IF IT IS ONLY TEMPORARILY.
...

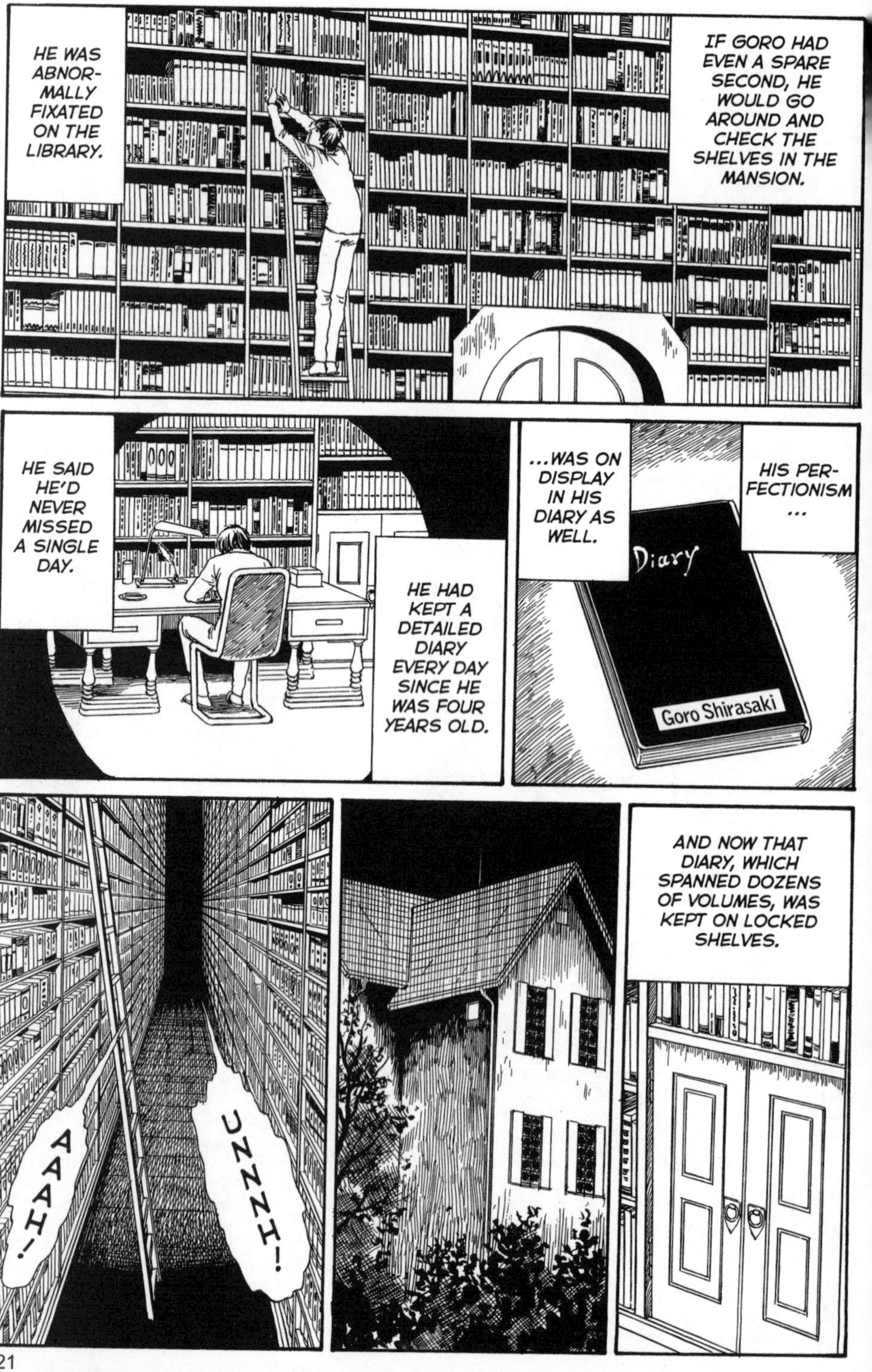
IF GORO HAD EVEN A SPARE SECOND, HE WOULD GO AROUND AND CHECK THE SHELVES IN THE MANSION.
HE WAS ABNORMALLY FIXATED ON THE LIBRARY.
HIS PERFECTIONISM...
...WAS ON DISPLAY IN HIS DIARY AS WELL.
Diary
Goro Shirasaki
HE HAD KEPT A DETAILED DIARY EVERY DAY SINCE HE WAS FOUR YEARS OLD.
HE SAID HE'D NEVER MISSED A SINGLE DAY.
AND NOW THAT DIARY, WHICH SPANNED DOZENS OF VOLUMES, WAS KEPT ON LOCKED SHELVES.
UNNNH!
AAAAH!

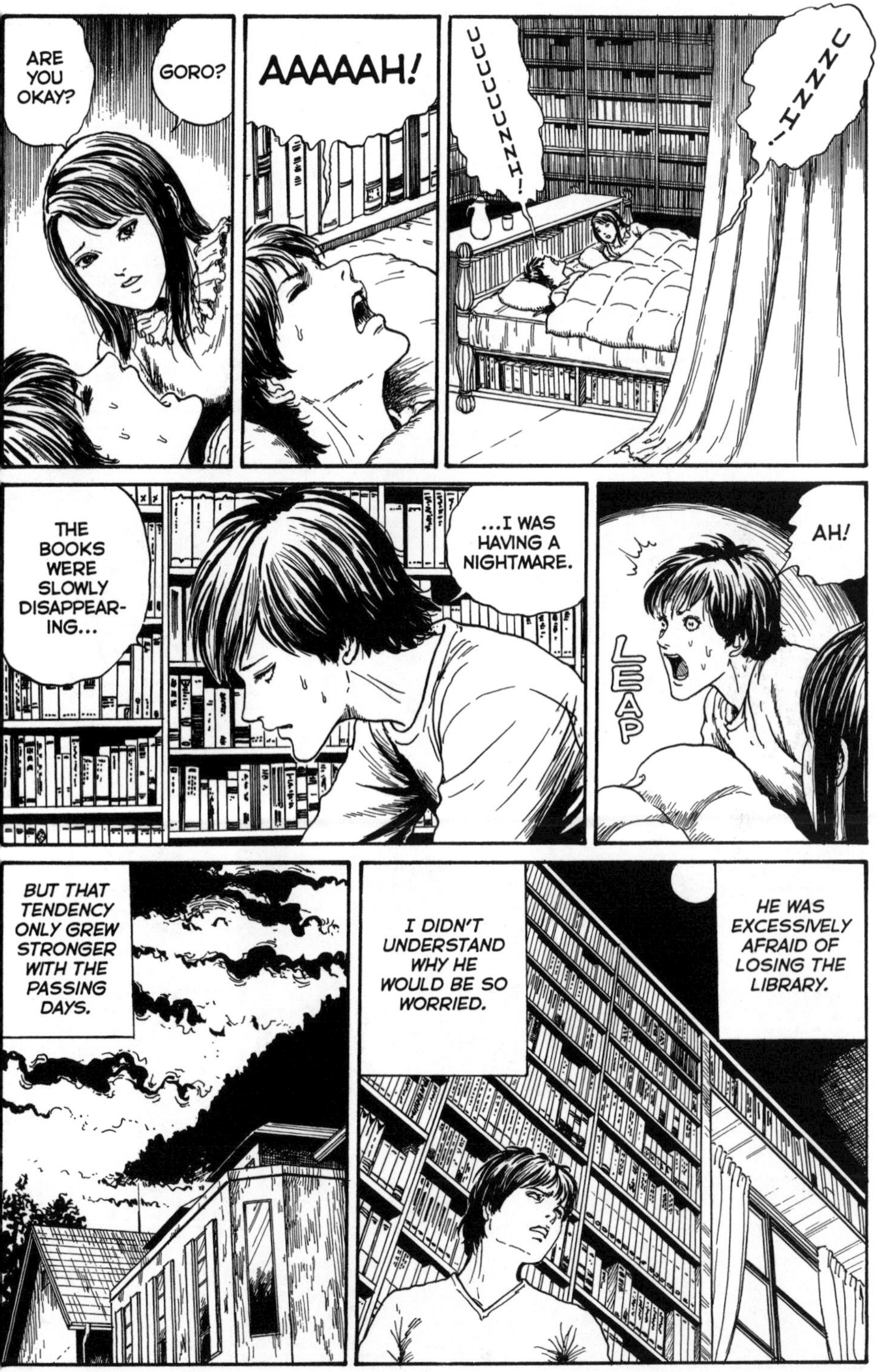
UUUUUUNNH!
.-IZZZC
AAAAAH!
GORO?
ARE YOU OKAY?
AH!
LEAP
...I WAS HAVING A NIGHTMARE.
THE BOOKS WERE SLOWLY DISAPPEAR-ING...
HE WAS EXCESSIVELY AFRAID OF LOSING THE LIBRARY.
I DIDN'T UNDERSTAND WHY HE WOULD BE SO WORRIED.
BUT THAT TENDENCY ONLY GREW STRONGER WITH THE PASSING DAYS.

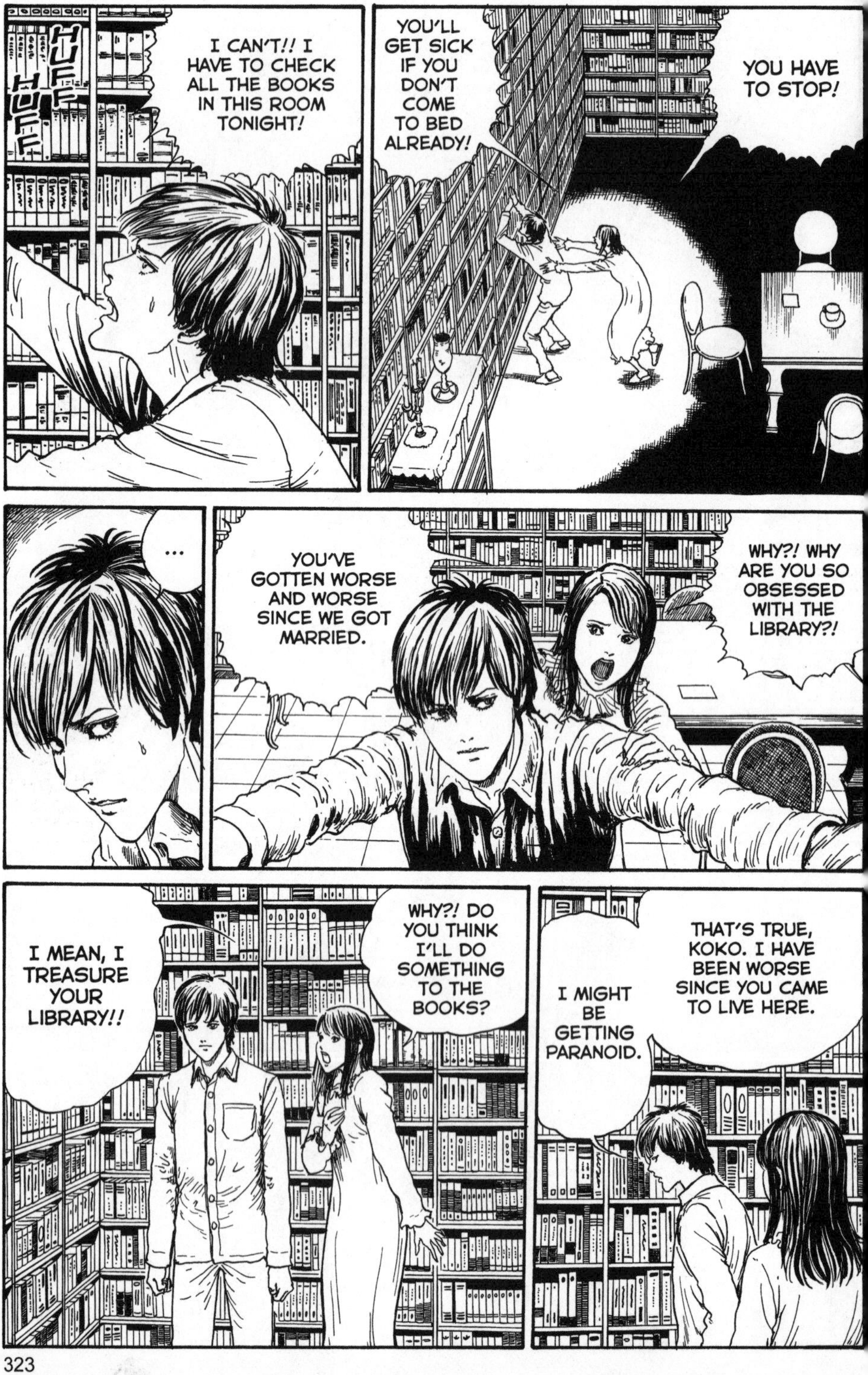
YOU HAVE TO STOP!
YOU'LL GET SICK IF YOU DON'T COME TO BED ALREADY!
I CAN'T!! I HAVE TO CHECK ALL THE BOOKS IN THIS ROOM TONIGHT!
HUFF HUFF
WHY?! WHY ARE YOU SO OBSESSED WITH THE LIBRARY?!
YOU'VE GOTTEN WORSE AND WORSE SINCE WE GOT MARRIED.
...
THAT'S TRUE, KOKO. I HAVE BEEN WORSE SINCE YOU CAME TO LIVE HERE.
I MIGHT BE GETTING PARANOID.
WHY?! DO YOU THINK I'LL DO SOMETHING TO THE BOOKS?
I MEAN, I TREASURE YOUR LIBRARY!!

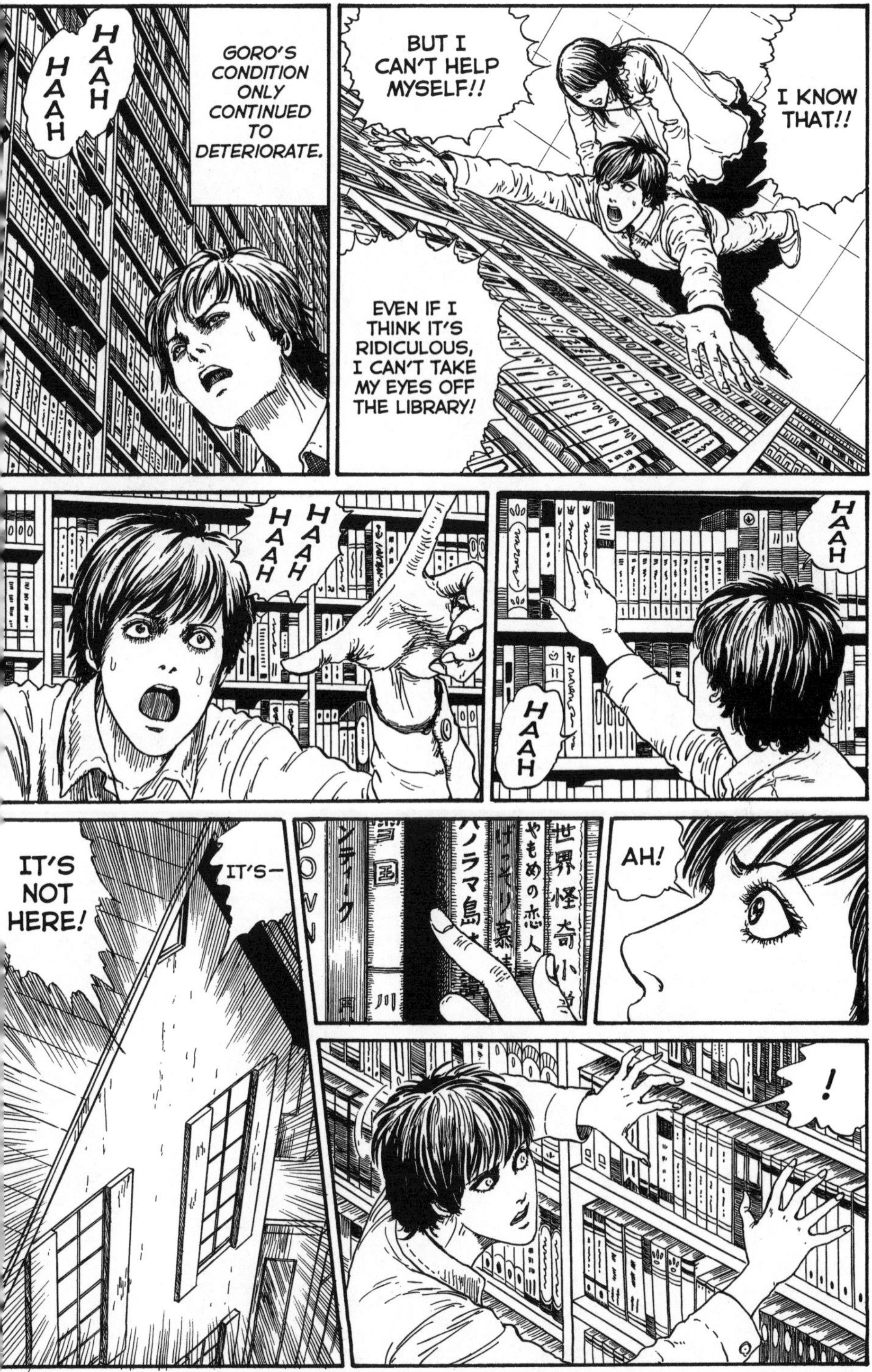
BUT I CAN'T HELP MYSELF!!
I KNOW THAT!!
EVEN IF I THINK IT'S RIDICULOUS, I CAN'T TAKE MY EYES OFF THE LIBRARY!
GORO'S CONDITION ONLY CONTINUED TO DETERIORATE.
HAAH HAAH
HAAH
HAAH
HAAH HAAH
AH!
!
IT'S—
IT'S NOT HERE!

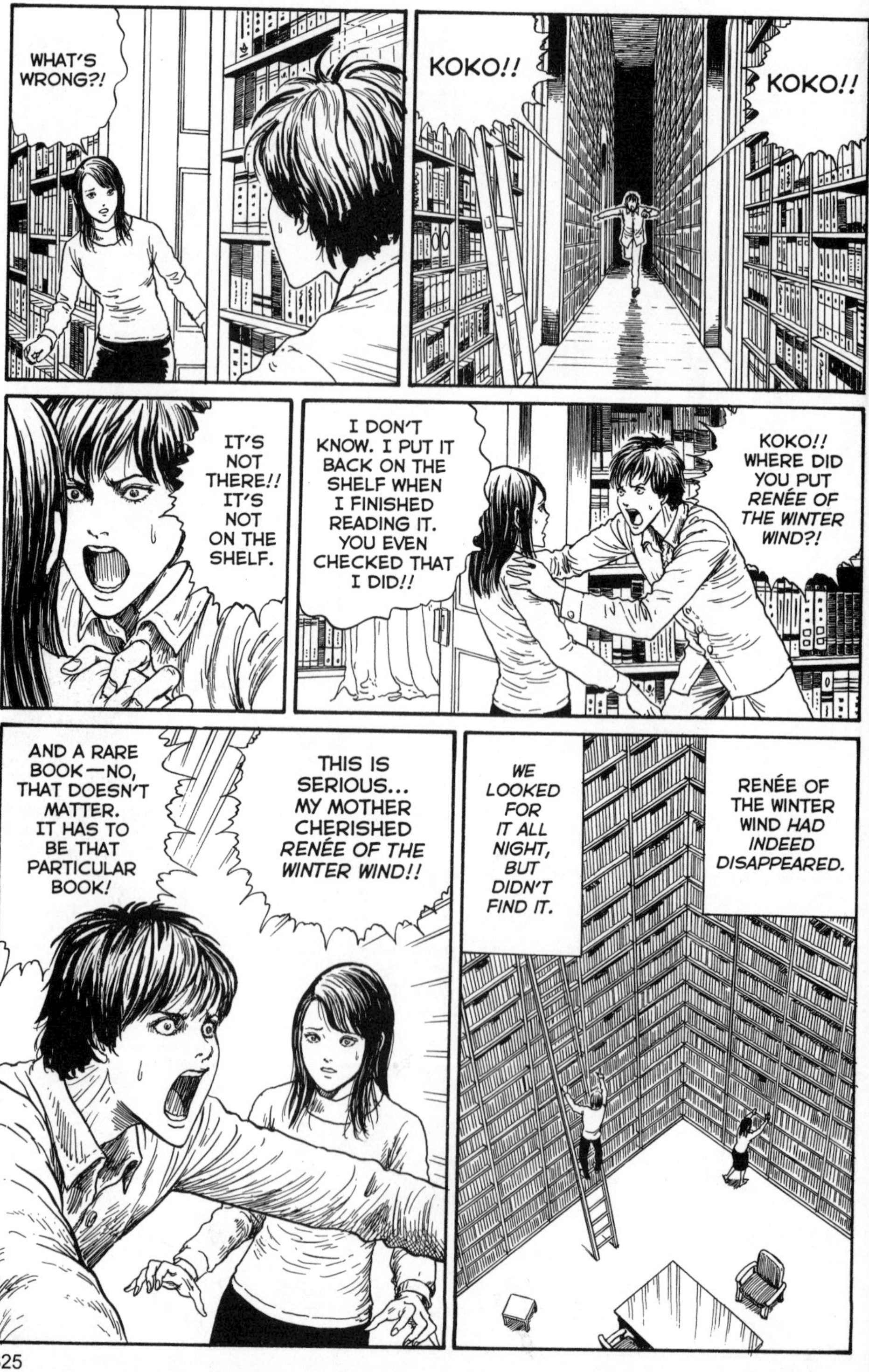
KOKO!!
KOKO!!
WHAT'S WRONG?!
KOKO!! WHERE DID YOU PUT *RENÉE OF THE WINTER WIND?!*
I DON'T KNOW. I PUT IT BACK ON THE SHELF WHEN I FINISHED READING IT. YOU EVEN CHECKED THAT I DID!!
IT'S NOT THERE!! IT'S NOT ON THE SHELF.
RENÉE OF THE WINTER WIND HAD INDEED DISAPPEARED.
WE LOOKED FOR IT ALL NIGHT, BUT DIDN'T FIND IT.
THIS IS SERIOUS... MY MOTHER CHERISHED *RENÉE OF THE WINTER WIND!!*
AND A RARE BOOK—NO, THAT DOESN'T MATTER. IT HAS TO BE THAT PARTICULAR BOOK!

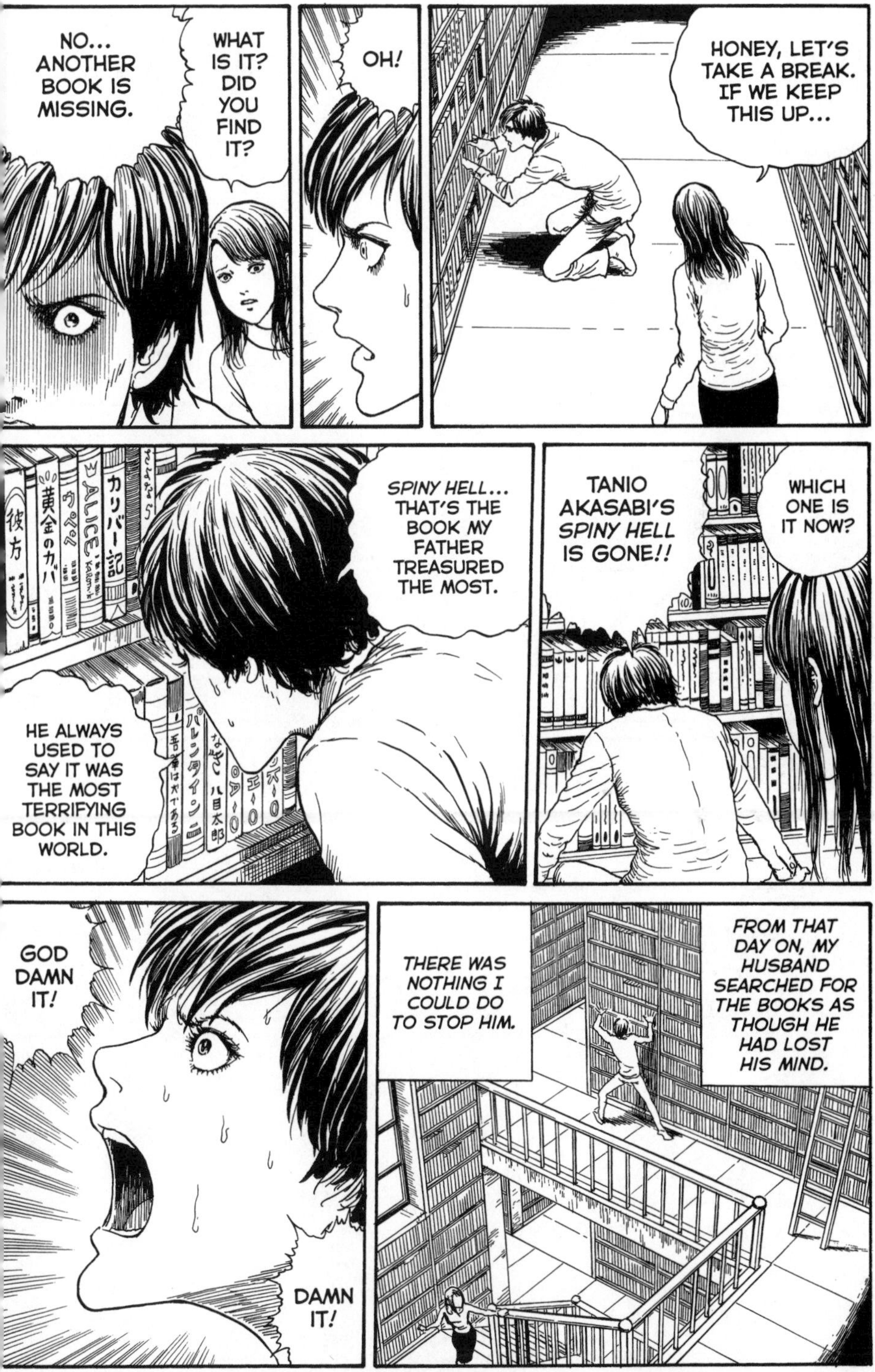
HONEY, LET'S TAKE A BREAK. IF WE KEEP THIS UP...
OH!
WHAT IS IT? DID YOU FIND IT?
NO... ANOTHER BOOK IS MISSING.
WHICH ONE IS IT NOW?
TANIO AKASABI'S *SPINY HELL* IS GONE!!
SPINY HELL... THAT'S THE BOOK MY FATHER TREASURED THE MOST.
HE ALWAYS USED TO SAY IT WAS THE MOST TERRIFYING BOOK IN THIS WORLD.
FROM THAT DAY ON, MY HUSBAND SEARCHED FOR THE BOOKS AS THOUGH HE HAD LOST HIS MIND.
THERE WAS NOTHING I COULD DO TO STOP HIM.
GOD DAMN IT!
DAMN IT!

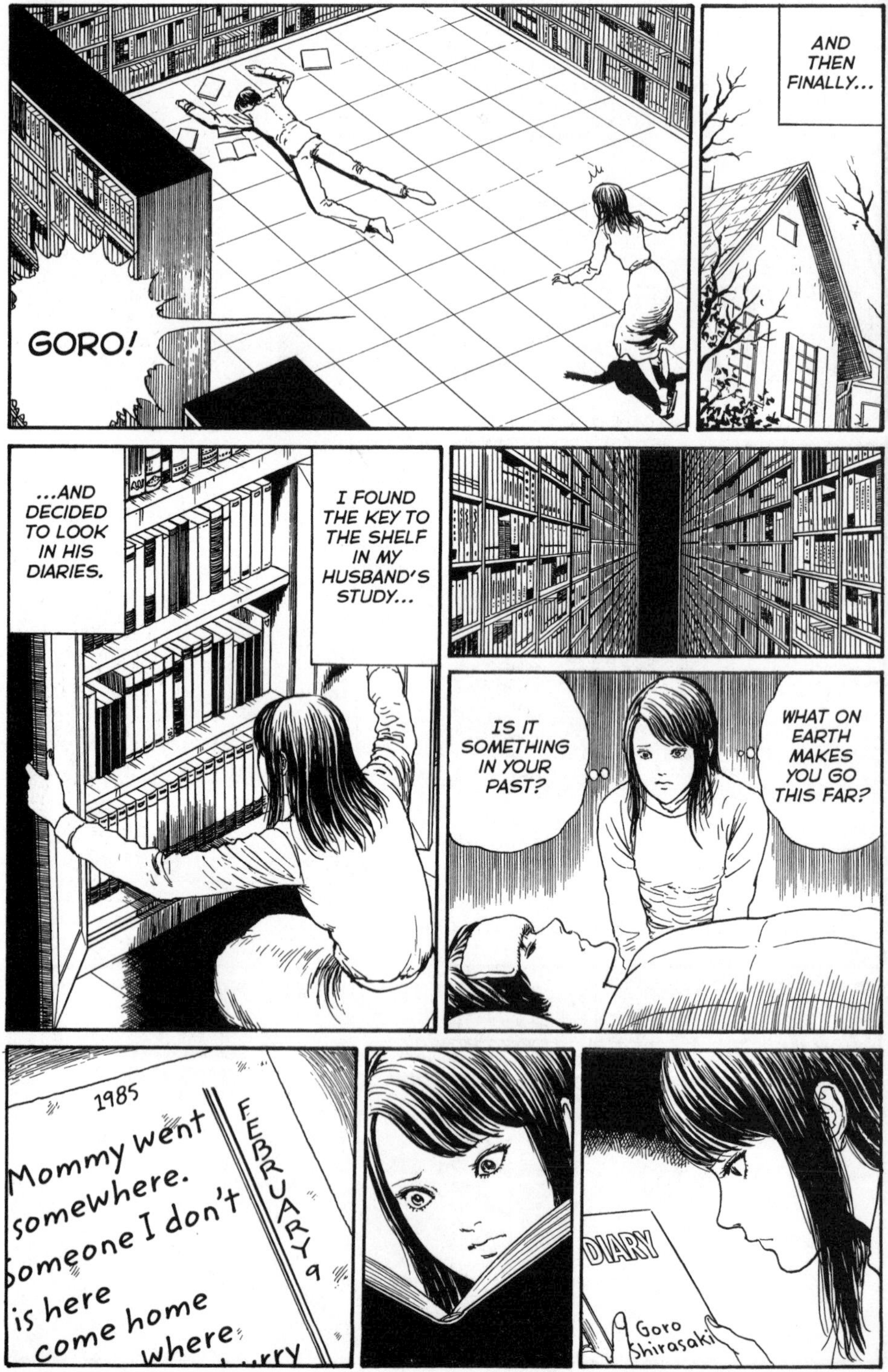
AND THEN FINALLY...
GORO!
WHAT ON EARTH MAKES YOU GO THIS FAR?
IS IT SOMETHING IN YOUR PAST?
I FOUND THE KEY TO THE SHELF IN MY HUSBAND'S STUDY...
...AND DECIDED TO LOOK IN HIS DIARIES.
DIARY
Goro Shirasaki
1985
FEBRUARY 9
Mommy went
somewhere.
Someone I don't
is here
come home
where

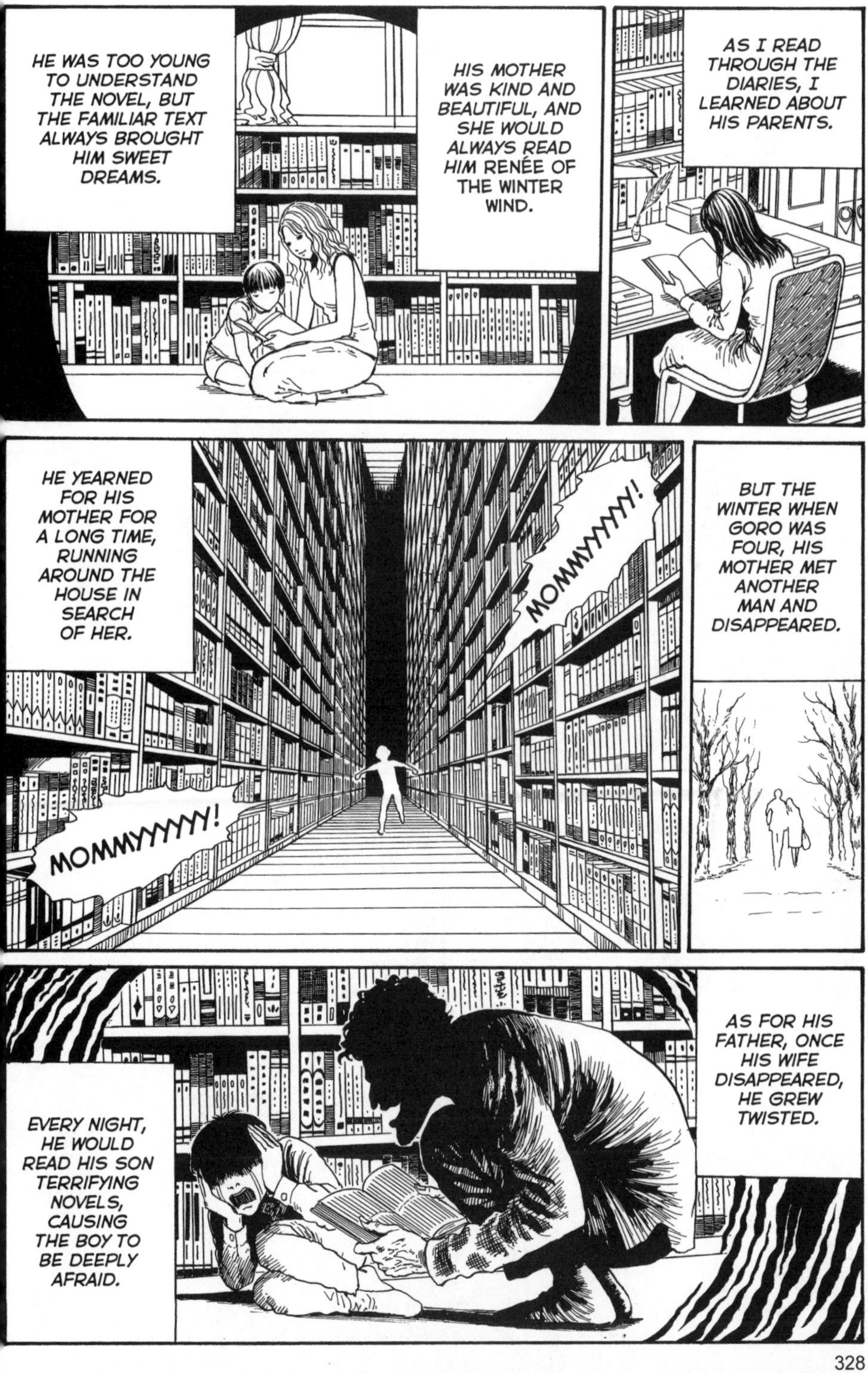
AS I READ THROUGH THE DIARIES, I LEARNED ABOUT HIS PARENTS.
HIS MOTHER WAS KIND AND BEAUTIFUL, AND SHE WOULD ALWAYS READ HIM RENÉE OF THE WINTER WIND.
HE WAS TOO YOUNG TO UNDERSTAND THE NOVEL, BUT THE FAMILIAR TEXT ALWAYS BROUGHT HIM SWEET DREAMS.
BUT THE WINTER WHEN GORO WAS FOUR, HIS MOTHER MET ANOTHER MAN AND DISAPPEARED.
MOMMYYYYY!
HE YEARNED FOR HIS MOTHER FOR A LONG TIME, RUNNING AROUND THE HOUSE IN SEARCH OF HER.
MOMMYYYYY!
AS FOR HIS FATHER, ONCE HIS WIFE DISAPPEARED, HE GREW TWISTED.
EVERY NIGHT, HE WOULD READ HIS SON TERRIFYING NOVELS, CAUSING THE BOY TO BE DEEPLY AFRAID.

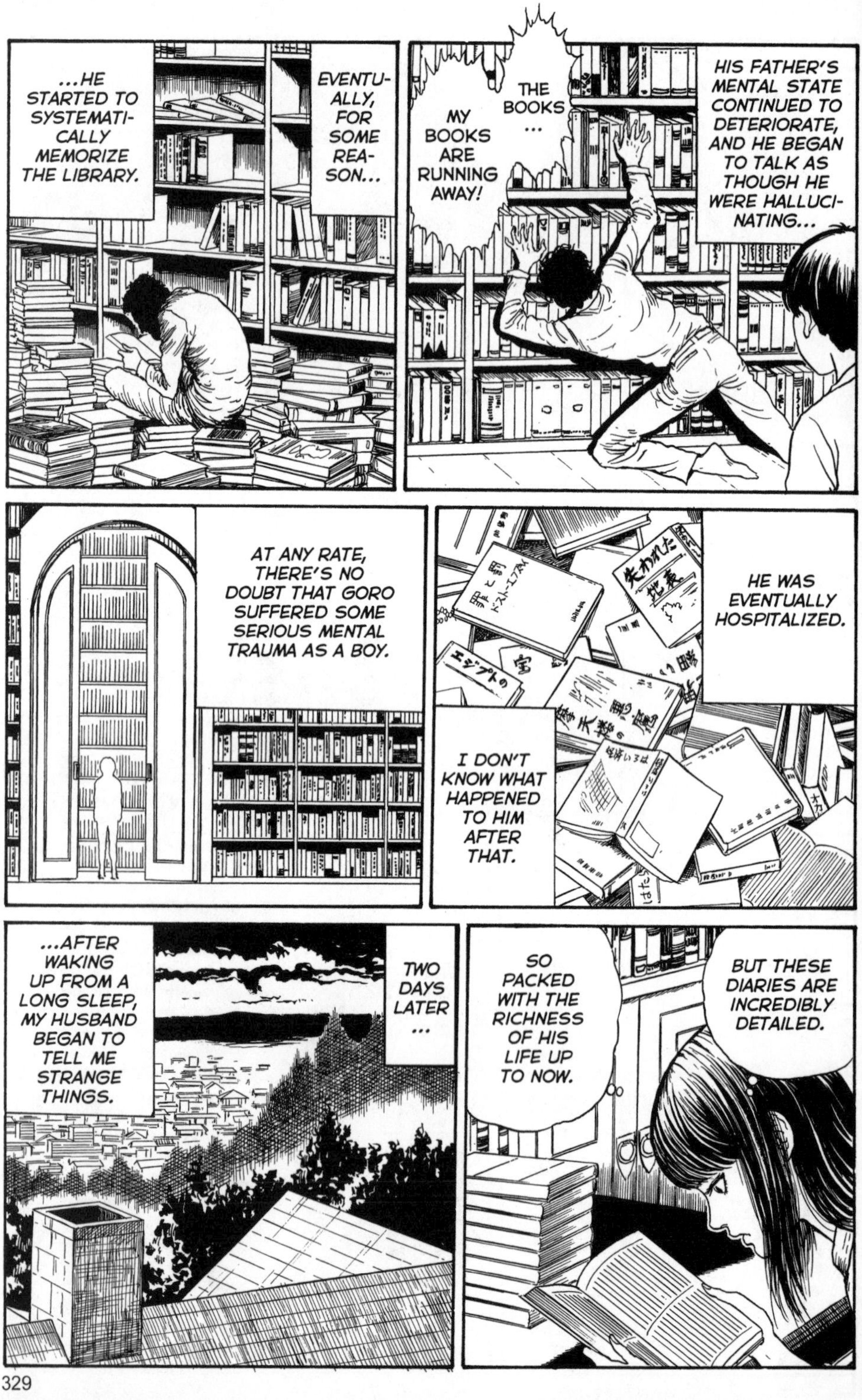
HIS FATHER'S MENTAL STATE CONTINUED TO DETERIORATE, AND HE BEGAN TO TALK AS THOUGH HE WERE HALLUCINATING...
THE BOOKS ...
MY BOOKS ARE RUNNING AWAY!
EVENTUALLY, FOR SOME REASON...
...HE STARTED TO SYSTEMATICALLY MEMORIZE THE LIBRARY.
HE WAS EVENTUALLY HOSPITALIZED.
I DON'T KNOW WHAT HAPPENED TO HIM AFTER THAT.
AT ANY RATE, THERE'S NO DOUBT THAT GORO SUFFERED SOME SERIOUS MENTAL TRAUMA AS A BOY.
BUT THESE DIARIES ARE INCREDIBLY DETAILED.
SO PACKED WITH THE RICHNESS OF HIS LIFE UP TO NOW.
TWO DAYS LATER ...
...AFTER WAKING UP FROM A LONG SLEEP, MY HUSBAND BEGAN TO TELL ME STRANGE THINGS.

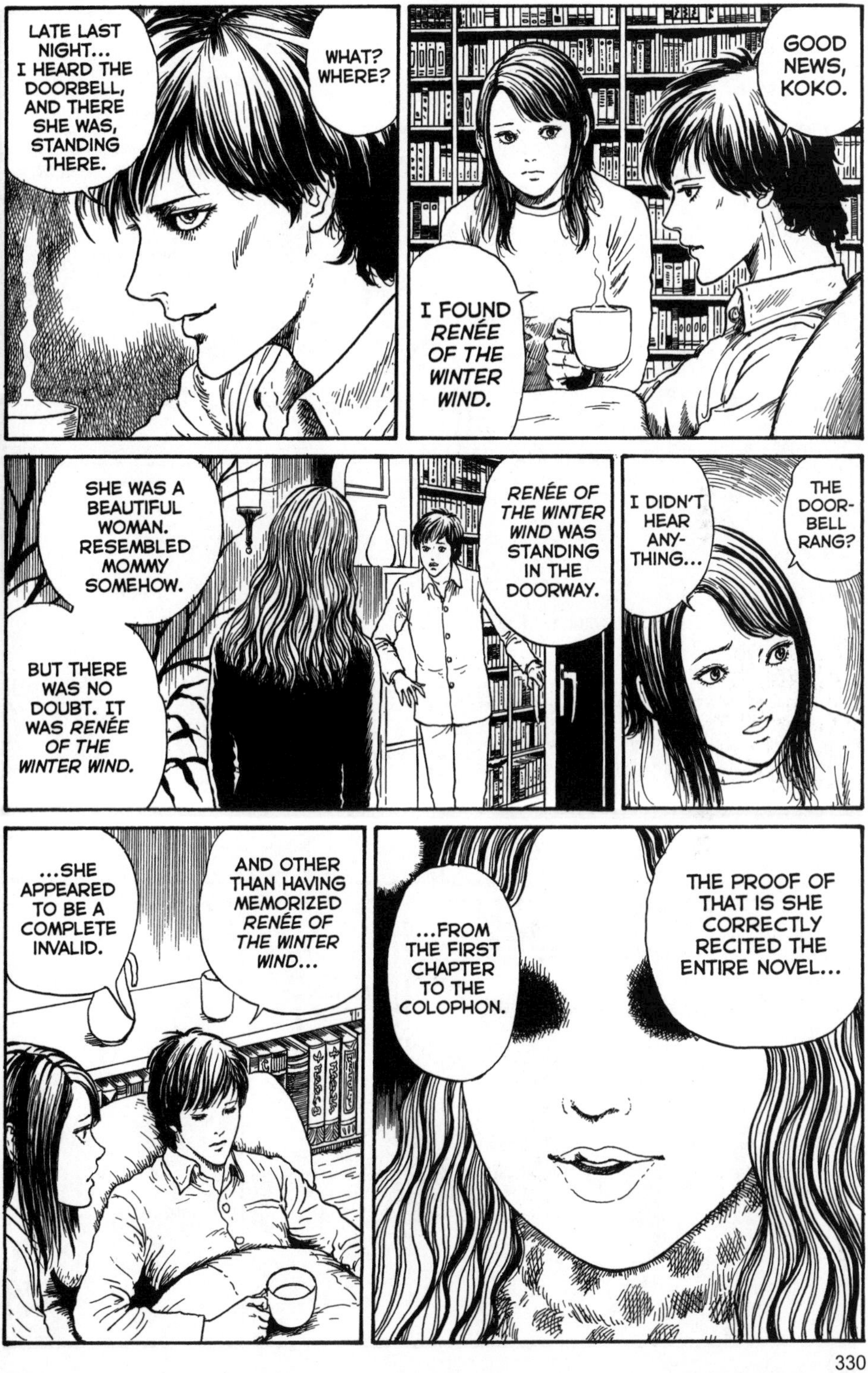
GOOD NEWS, KOKO.
I FOUND *RENÉE OF THE WINTER WIND.*
WHAT? WHERE?
LATE LAST NIGHT... I HEARD THE DOORBELL, AND THERE SHE WAS, STANDING THERE.
THE DOOR-BELL RANG?
I DIDN'T HEAR ANY-THING...
RENÉE OF THE WINTER WIND WAS STANDING IN THE DOORWAY.
SHE WAS A BEAUTIFUL WOMAN. RESEMBLED MOMMY SOMEHOW.
BUT THERE WAS NO DOUBT. IT WAS *RENÉE OF THE WINTER WIND.*
THE PROOF OF THAT IS SHE CORRECTLY RECITED THE ENTIRE NOVEL...
...FROM THE FIRST CHAPTER TO THE COLOPHON.
AND OTHER THAN HAVING MEMORIZED *RENÉE OF THE WINTER WIND*...
...SHE APPEARED TO BE A COMPLETE INVALID.

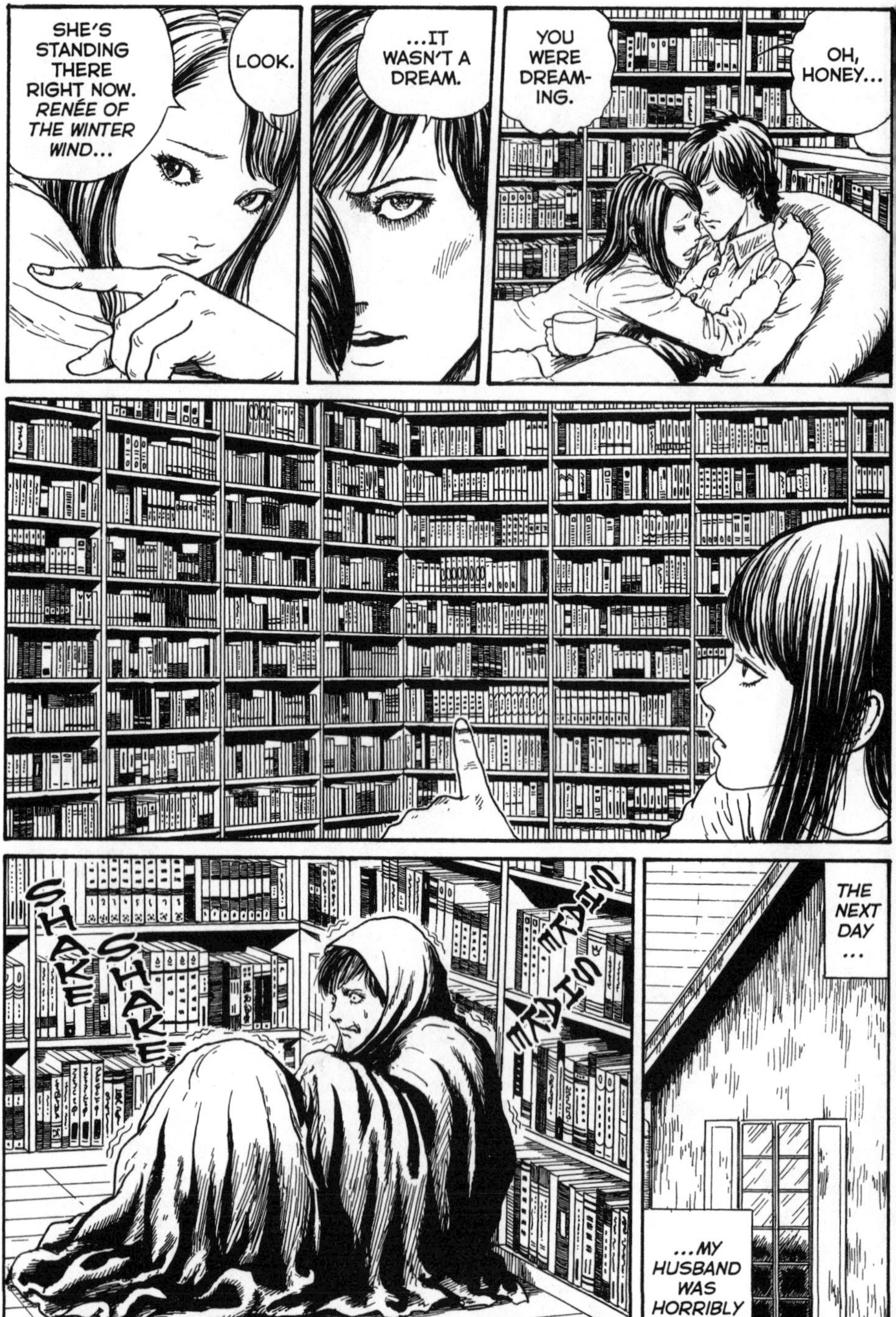
OH, HONEY...
YOU WERE DREAM-ING.
...IT WASN'T A DREAM.
LOOK.
SHE'S STANDING THERE RIGHT NOW. *RENÉE OF THE WINTER WIND*...
THE NEXT DAY...
...MY HUSBAND WAS HORRIBLY FRIGHT-ENED.
SHIVER SHIVER
SHAKE SHAKE

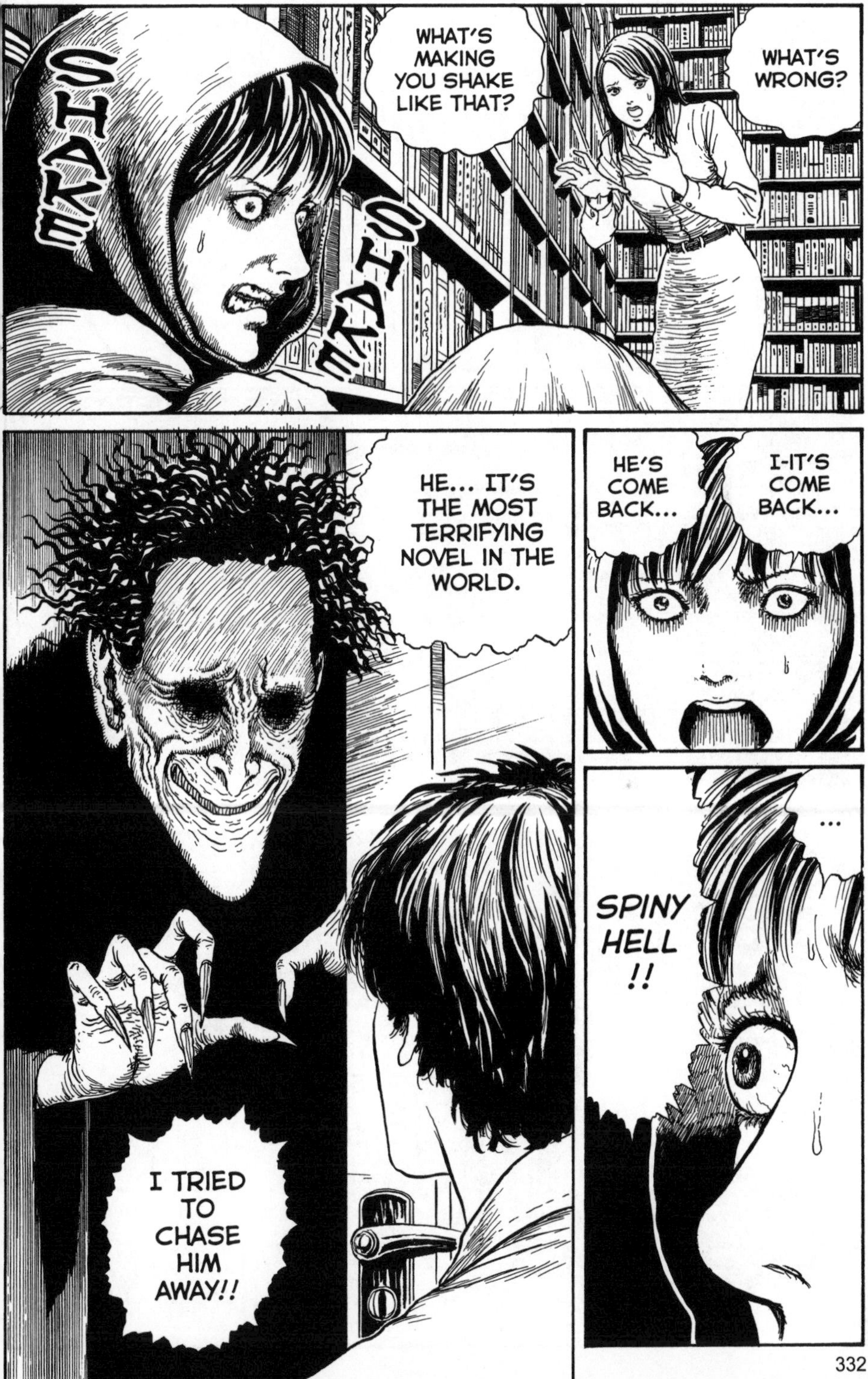
WHAT'S WRONG?
WHAT'S MAKING YOU SHAKE LIKE THAT?
SHAKE
SHAKE
I-IT'S COME BACK...
HE'S COME BACK...
...
SPINY HELL!!
HE... IT'S THE MOST TERRIFYING NOVEL IN THE WORLD.
I TRIED TO CHASE HIM AWAY!!

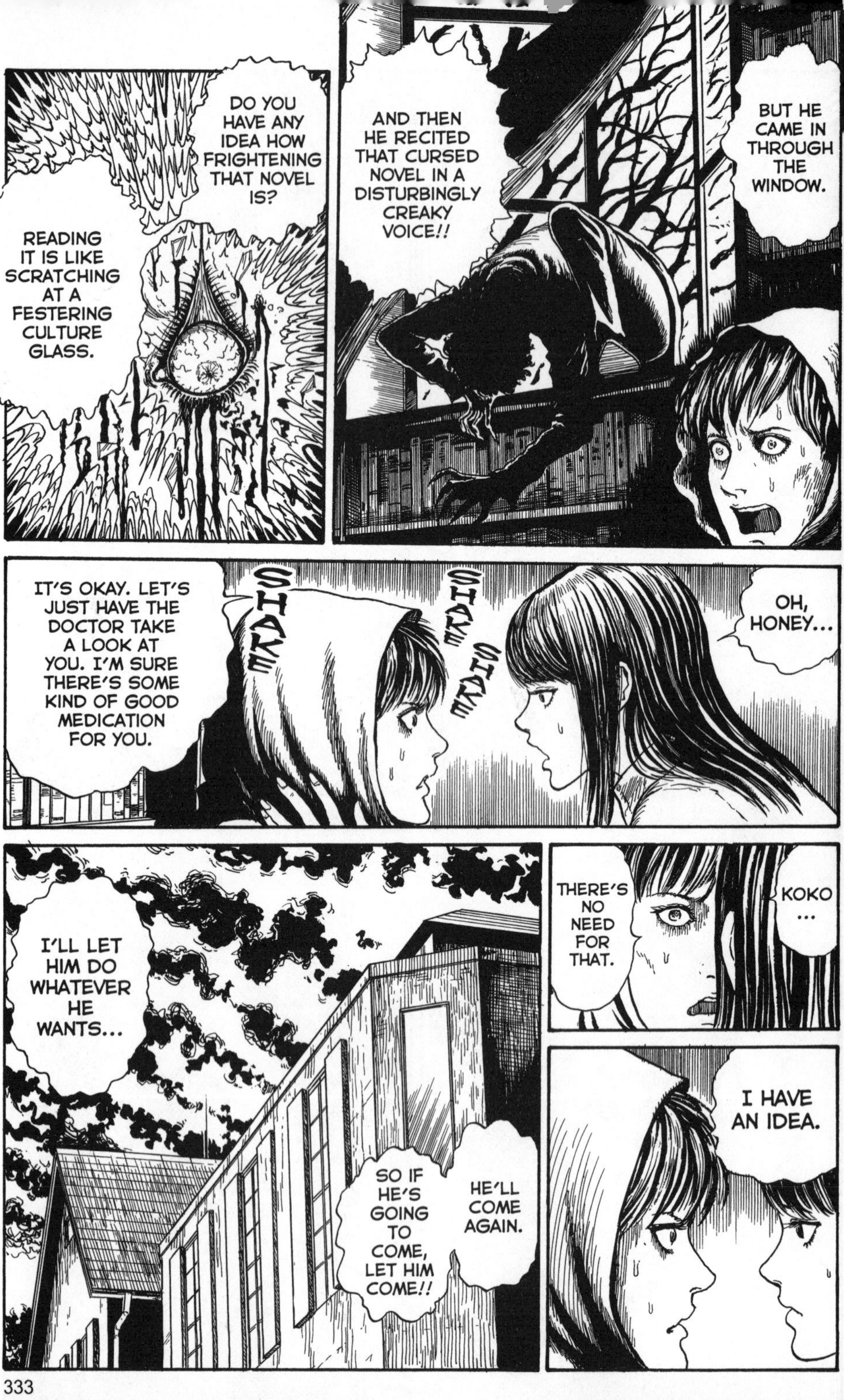

BUT HE CAME IN THROUGH THE WINDOW.
AND THEN HE RECITED THAT CURSED NOVEL IN A DISTURBINGLY CREAKY VOICE!!
DO YOU HAVE ANY IDEA HOW FRIGHTENING THAT NOVEL IS?
READING IT IS LIKE SCRATCHING AT A FESTERING CULTURE GLASS.
OH, HONEY...
SHAKE
SHAKE
SHAKE
IT'S OKAY. LET'S JUST HAVE THE DOCTOR TAKE A LOOK AT YOU. I'M SURE THERE'S SOME KIND OF GOOD MEDICATION FOR YOU.
KOKO ...
THERE'S NO NEED FOR THAT.
I HAVE AN IDEA.
HE'LL COME AGAIN.
SO IF HE'S GOING TO COME, LET HIM COME!!
I'LL LET HIM DO WHATEVER HE WANTS...

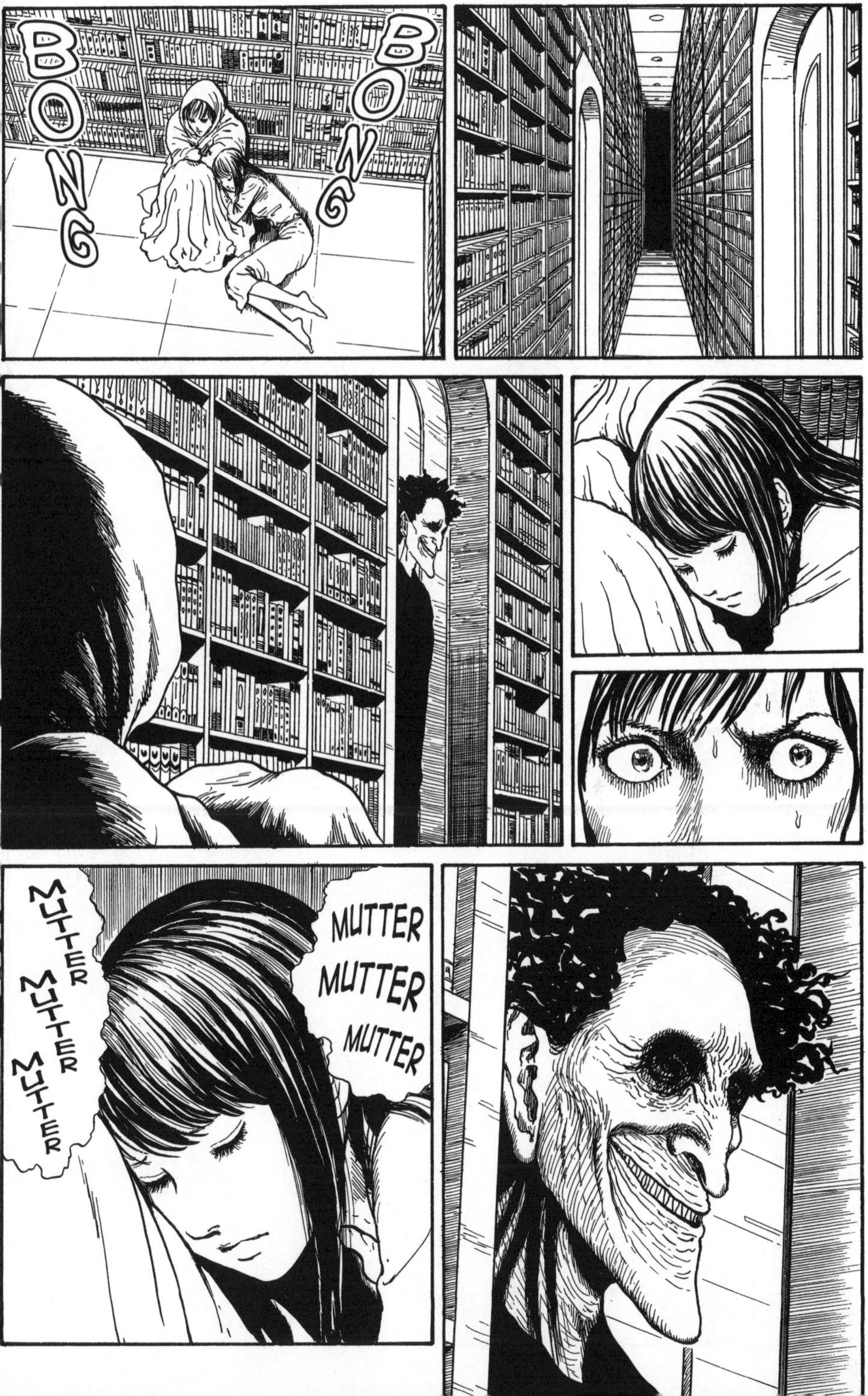
BONG
BONG
MUTTER
MUTTER
MUTTER
MUTTER
MUTTER
MUTTER

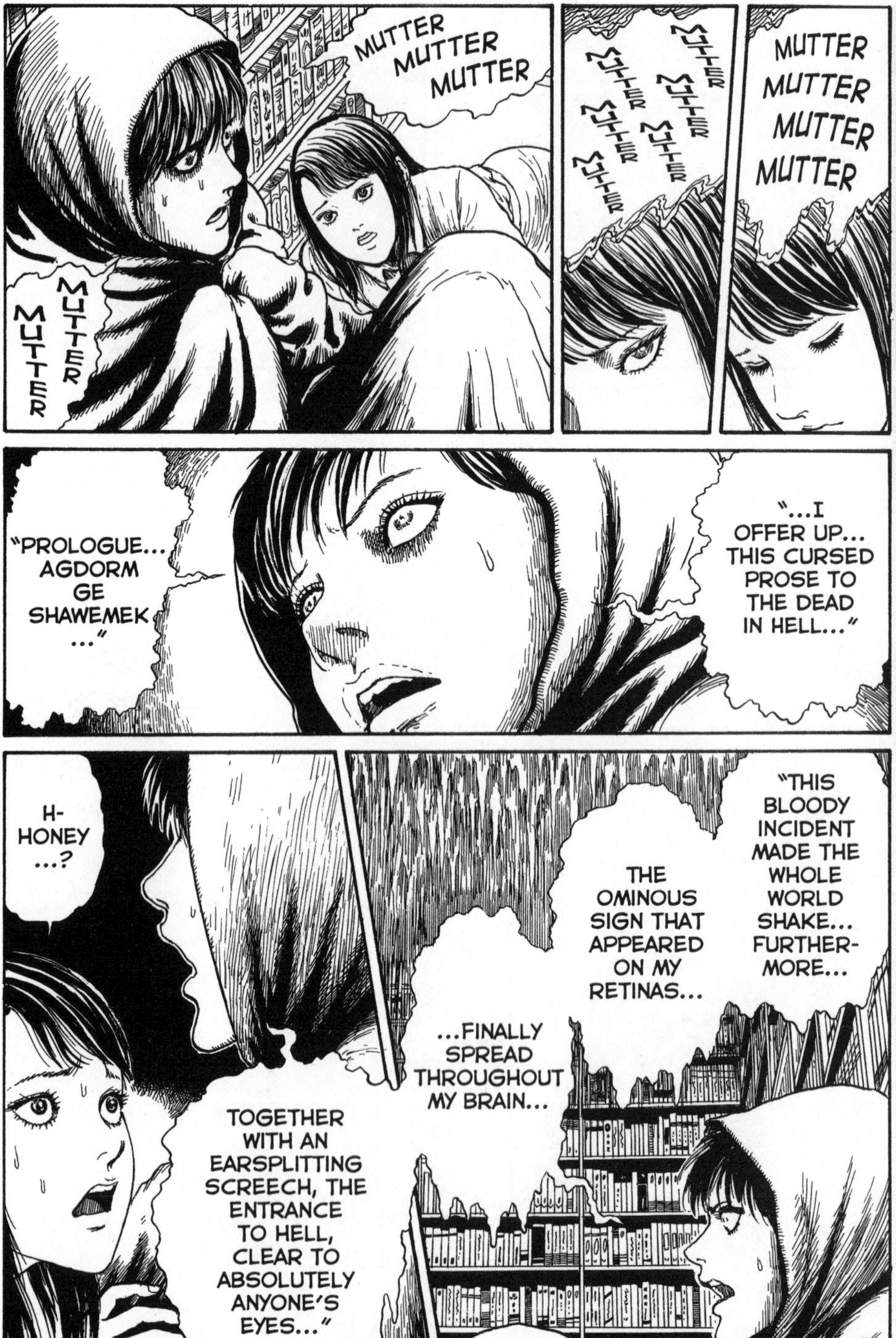

MUTTER MUTTER MUTTER MUTTER
MUTTER MUTTER MUTTER MUTTER MUTTER
MUTTER MUTTER MUTTER
MUTTER MUTTER
"...I OFFER UP... THIS CURSED PROSE TO THE DEAD IN HELL..."
"PROLOGUE... AGDORM GE SHAWEMEK ..."
"THIS BLOODY INCIDENT MADE THE WHOLE WORLD SHAKE... FURTHER-MORE...
THE OMINOUS SIGN THAT APPEARED ON MY RETINAS...
...FINALLY SPREAD THROUGHOUT MY BRAIN...
TOGETHER WITH AN EARSPLITTING SCREECH, THE ENTRANCE TO HELL, CLEAR TO ABSOLUTELY ANYONE'S EYES..."
H-HONEY ...?

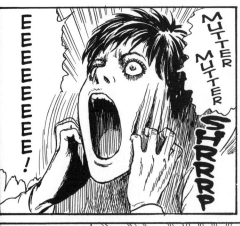

GORO CONTINUED TO MUTTER FOR SEVERAL HOURS.
MUTTER MUTTER
MUTTER MUTTER MUTTER
EEEEEEEEE!
MUTTER MUTTER
SHRRRP
FROM TIME TO TIME HE WOULD INJURE HIMSELF, AS THOUGH HE WERE UNABLE TO WITHSTAND THE FEAR.
EEEEE!
MUTTER MUTTER
IT WAS ALMOST LIKE HE WAS FIGHTING WITH SOMEONE.
MUTTER MUTTER MUTTER MUTTER
MUTTER MUTTER
"...TO BEGIN WITH, THAT INCIDENT HAS DEVOURED MY SPIRIT TO THIS EXTENT..."
G-GORO!
"...WHAT HAS BROUGHT ABOUT THESE ABHORRENT CHANGES IN MY FLESH IS WITHOUT A DOUBT THE SIDE EFFECTS OF HELL."
"THE EERIE CURETTAGE THAT THIS CURSED SURGEON PERFORMED IN 1955 TOOK ME TO AN EVEN MORE ABNORMAL CONDITION..."
NO! STOP IT!

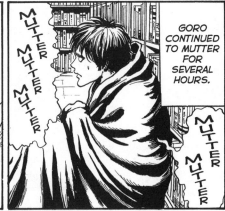

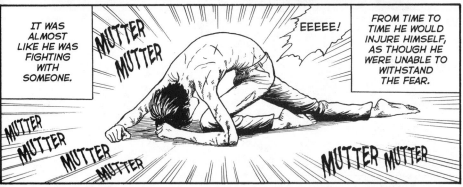

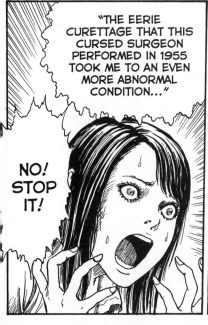

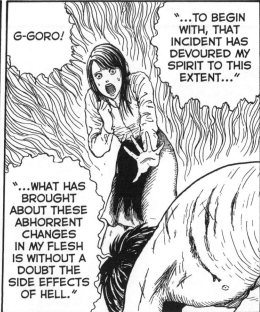

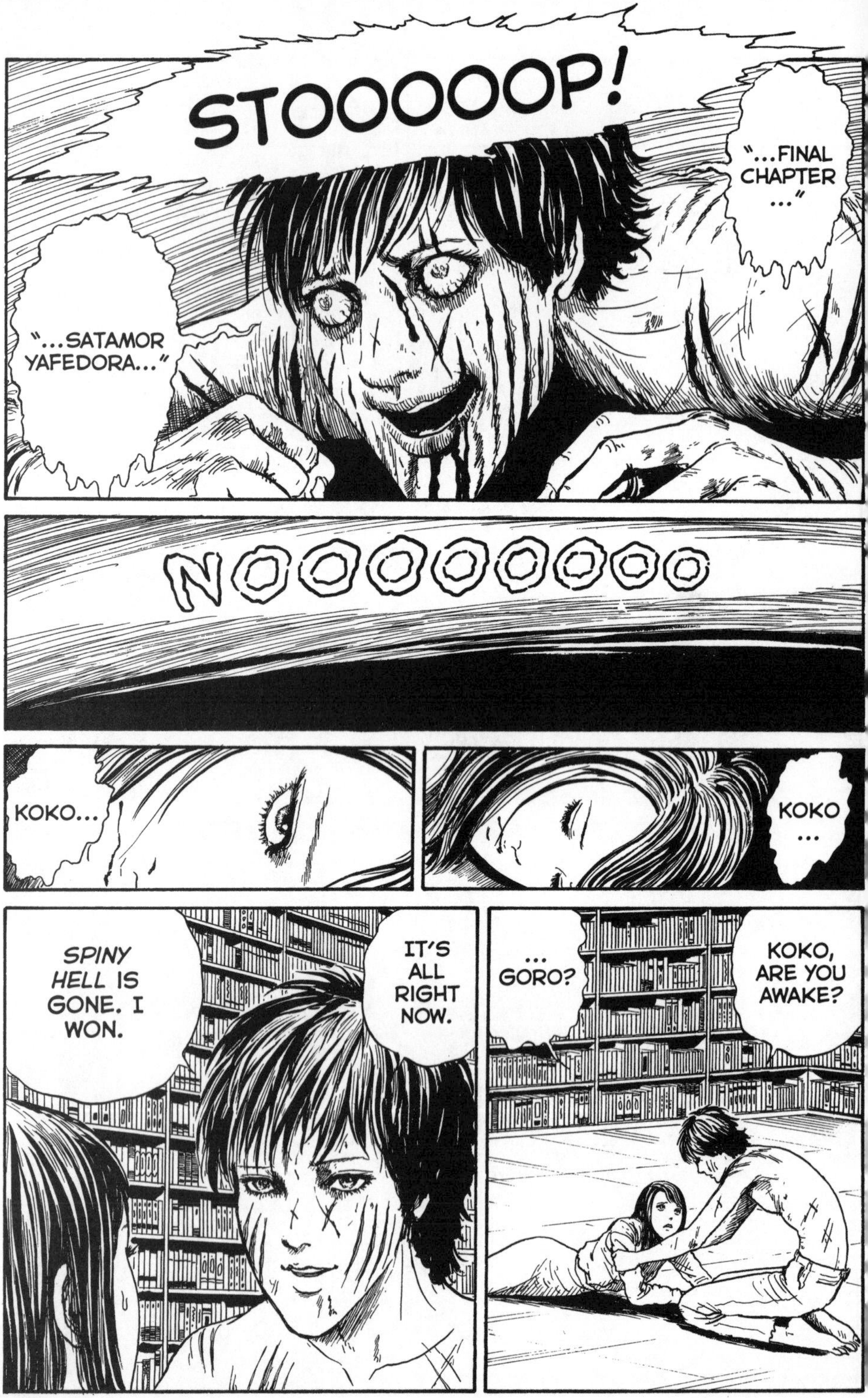
STOOOOOP!
"...FINAL CHAPTER..."
"...SATAMOR YAFEDORA..."
NOOOOOOOO
KOKO ...
KOKO...
KOKO, ARE YOU AWAKE?
... GORO?
IT'S ALL RIGHT NOW.
SPINY HELL IS GONE. I WON.

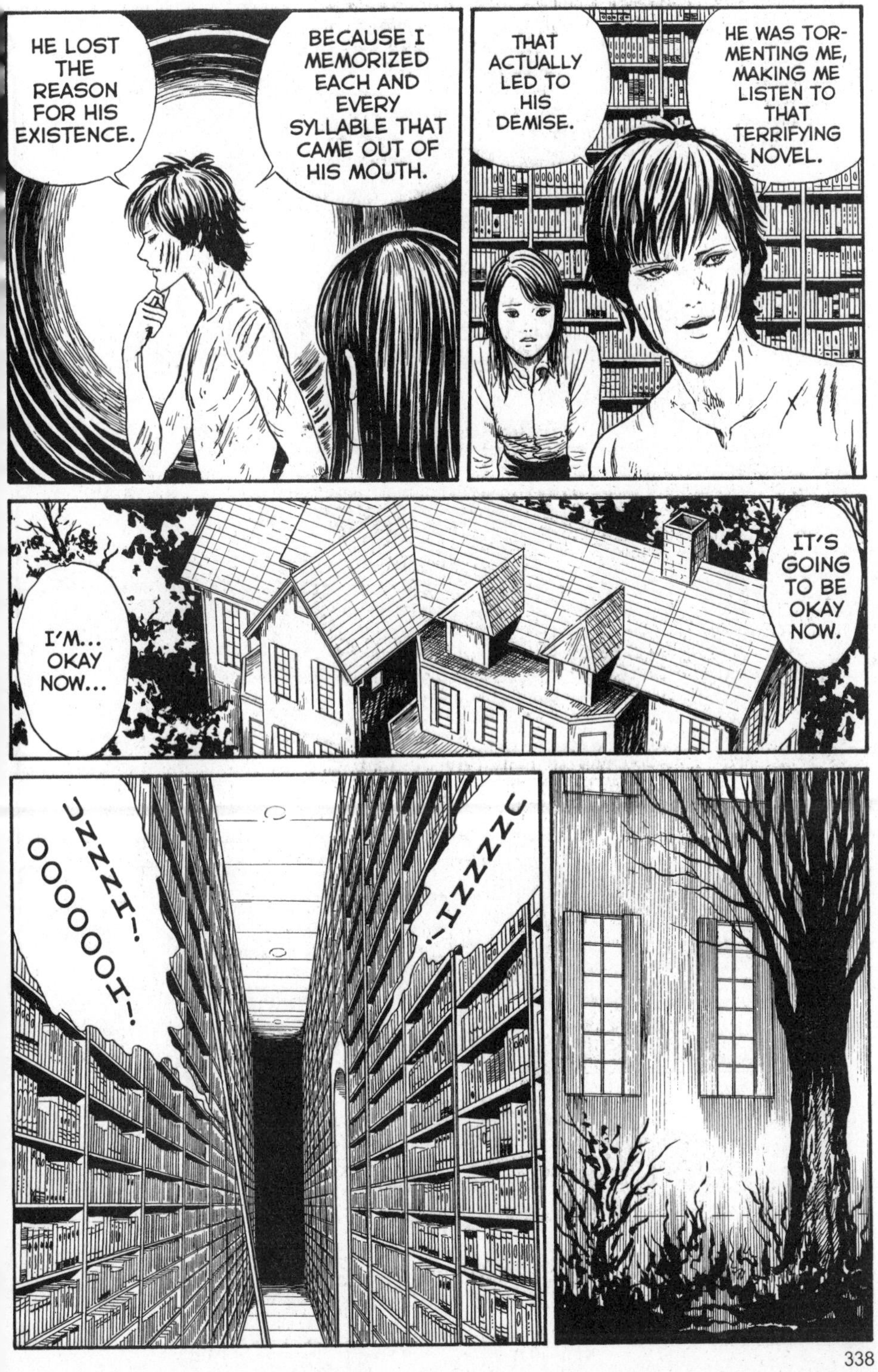
HE WAS TOR-MENTING ME, MAKING ME LISTEN TO THAT TERRIFYING NOVEL.
THAT ACTUALLY LED TO HIS DEMISE.
BECAUSE I MEMORIZED EACH AND EVERY SYLLABLE THAT CAME OUT OF HIS MOUTH.
HE LOST THE REASON FOR HIS EXISTENCE.
IT'S GOING TO BE OKAY NOW.
I'M... OKAY NOW...
IZZZZU!
UNZZZI!!
OOOOOOH!!

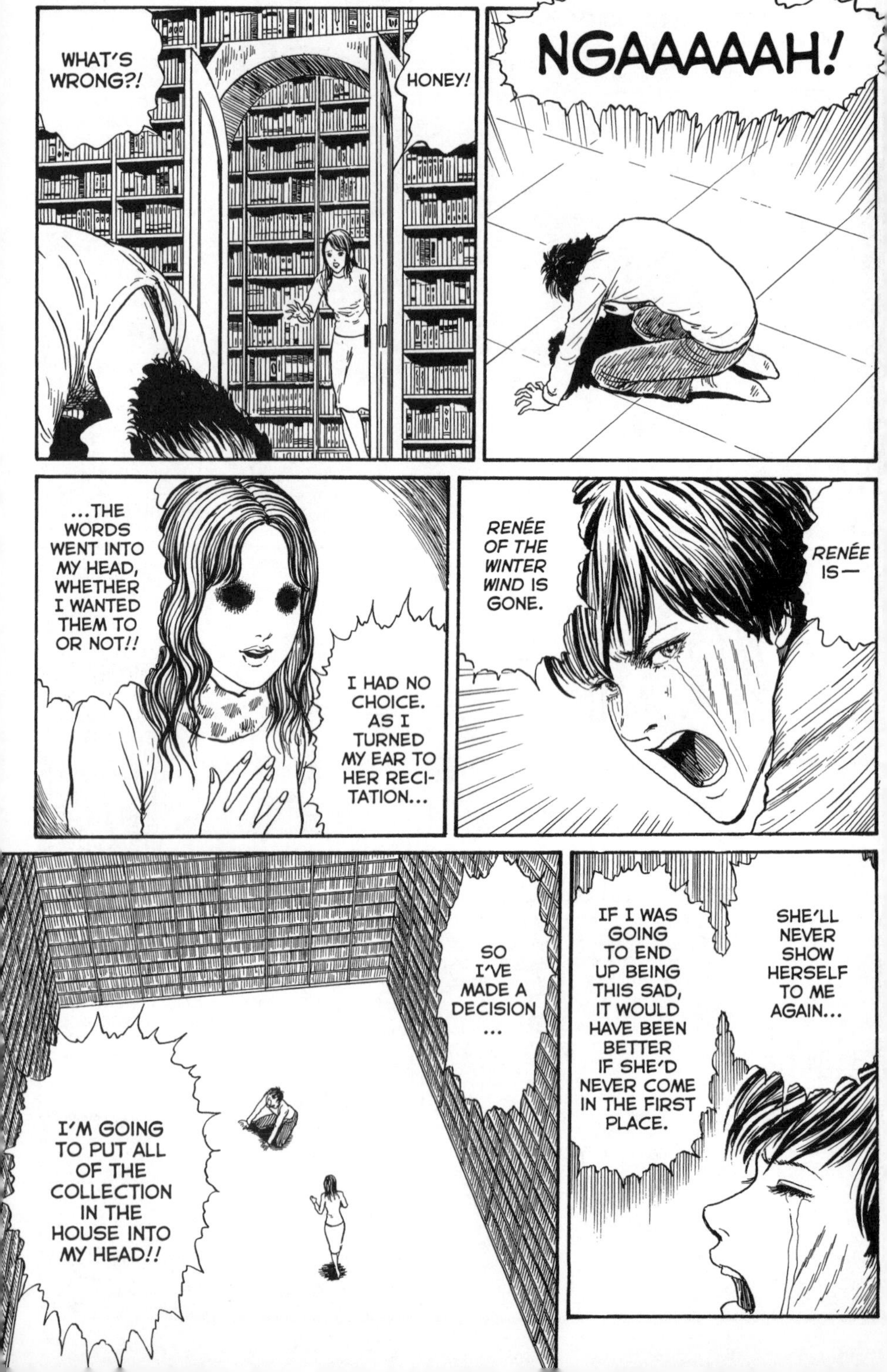
NGAAAAAH!
HONEY!
WHAT'S WRONG?!
RENÉE IS—
RENÉE OF THE WINTER WIND IS GONE.
I HAD NO CHOICE. AS I TURNED MY EAR TO HER RECITATION...
...THE WORDS WENT INTO MY HEAD, WHETHER I WANTED THEM TO OR NOT!!
SHE'LL NEVER SHOW HERSELF TO ME AGAIN...
IF I WAS GOING TO END UP BEING THIS SAD, IT WOULD HAVE BEEN BETTER IF SHE'D NEVER COME IN THE FIRST PLACE.
SO I'VE MADE A DECISION...
I'M GOING TO PUT ALL OF THE COLLECTION IN THE HOUSE INTO MY HEAD!!

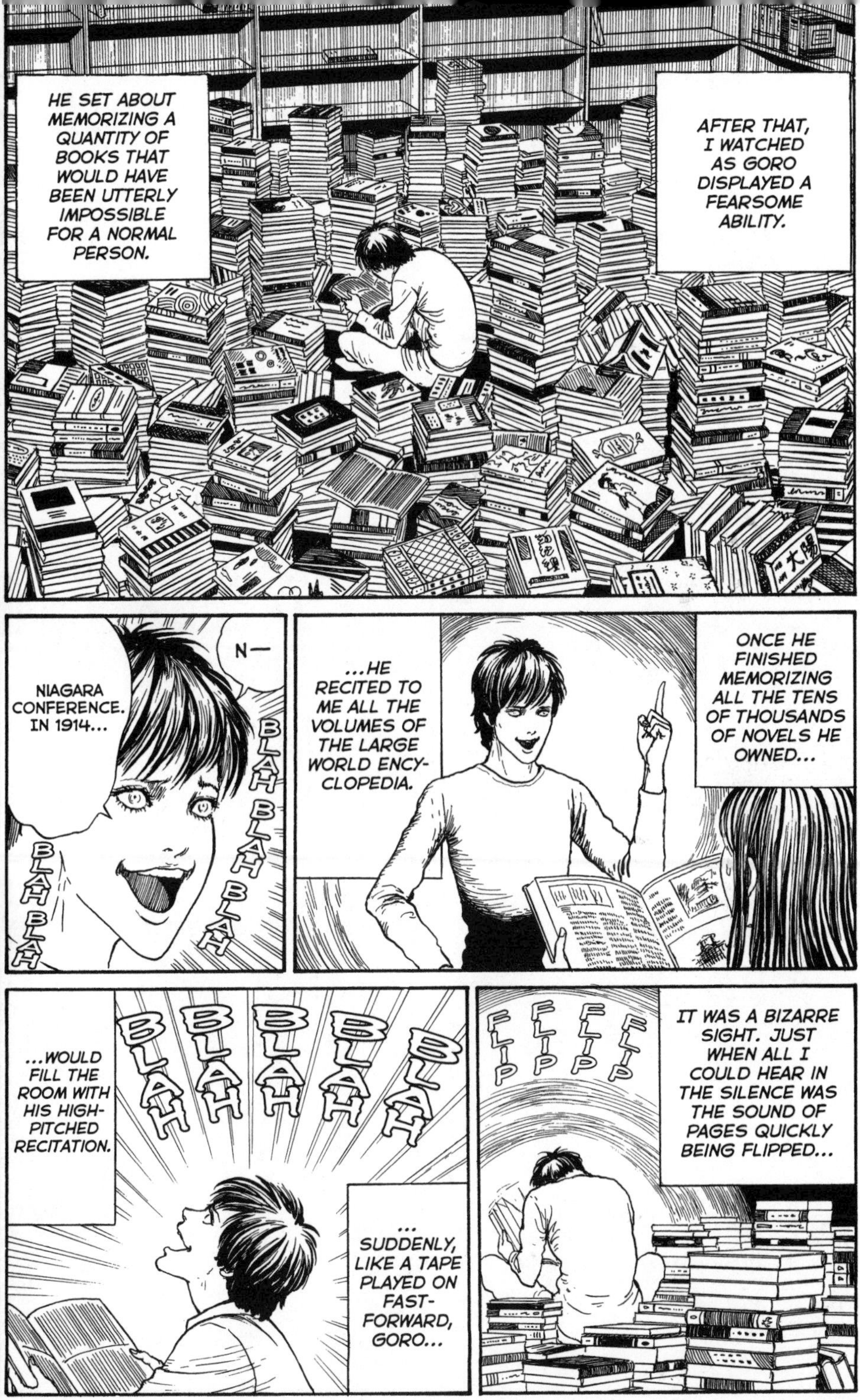
AFTER THAT, I WATCHED AS GORO DISPLAYED A FEARSOME ABILITY.
HE SET ABOUT MEMORIZING A QUANTITY OF BOOKS THAT WOULD HAVE BEEN UTTERLY IMPOSSIBLE FOR A NORMAL PERSON.
ONCE HE FINISHED MEMORIZING ALL THE TENS OF THOUSANDS OF NOVELS HE OWNED...
...HE RECITED TO ME ALL THE VOLUMES OF THE LARGE WORLD ENCY-CLOPEDIA.
N—
NIAGARA CONFERENCE. IN 1914...
BLAH BLAH BLAH
BLAH BLAH BLAH
BLAH BLAH
IT WAS A BIZARRE SIGHT. JUST WHEN ALL I COULD HEAR IN THE SILENCE WAS THE SOUND OF PAGES QUICKLY BEING FLIPPED...
FLIP FLIP FLIP FLIP
... SUDDENLY, LIKE A TAPE PLAYED ON FAST-FORWARD, GORO...
BLAH BLAH BLAH BLAH BLAH
...WOULD FILL THE ROOM WITH HIS HIGH-PITCHED RECITATION.

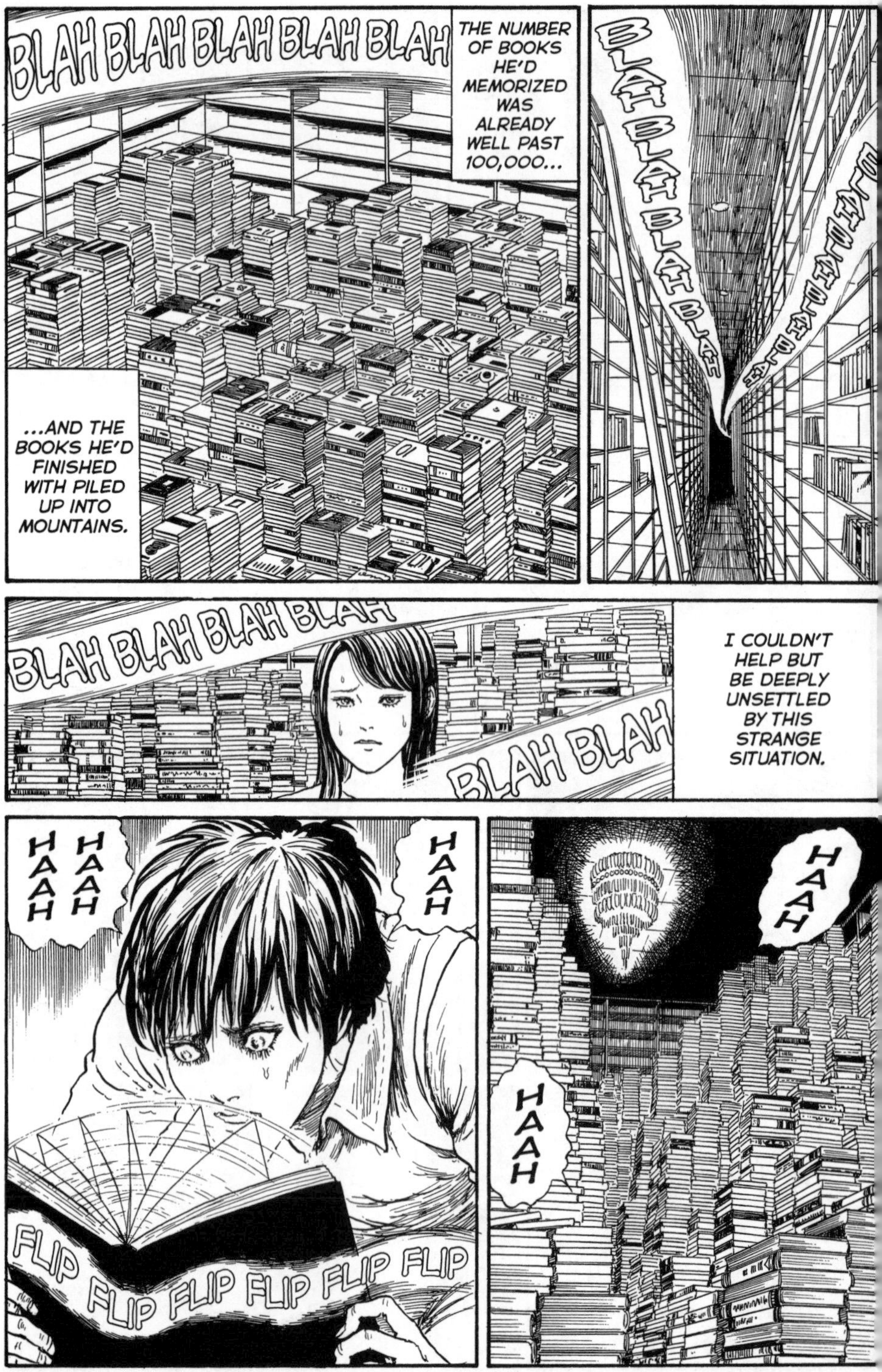

BLAH BLAH BLAH BLAH
THE NUMBER OF BOOKS HE'D MEMORIZED WAS ALREADY WELL PAST 100,000...
BLAH BLAH BLAH BLAH BLAH
...AND THE BOOKS HE'D FINISHED WITH PILED UP INTO MOUNTAINS.
I COULDN'T HELP BUT BE DEEPLY UNSETTLED BY THIS STRANGE SITUATION.
BLAH BLAH
BLAH BLAH BLAH BLAH
HAAH
HAAH
HAAH
HAAH HAAH
FLIP FLIP FLIP FLIP FLIP FLIP

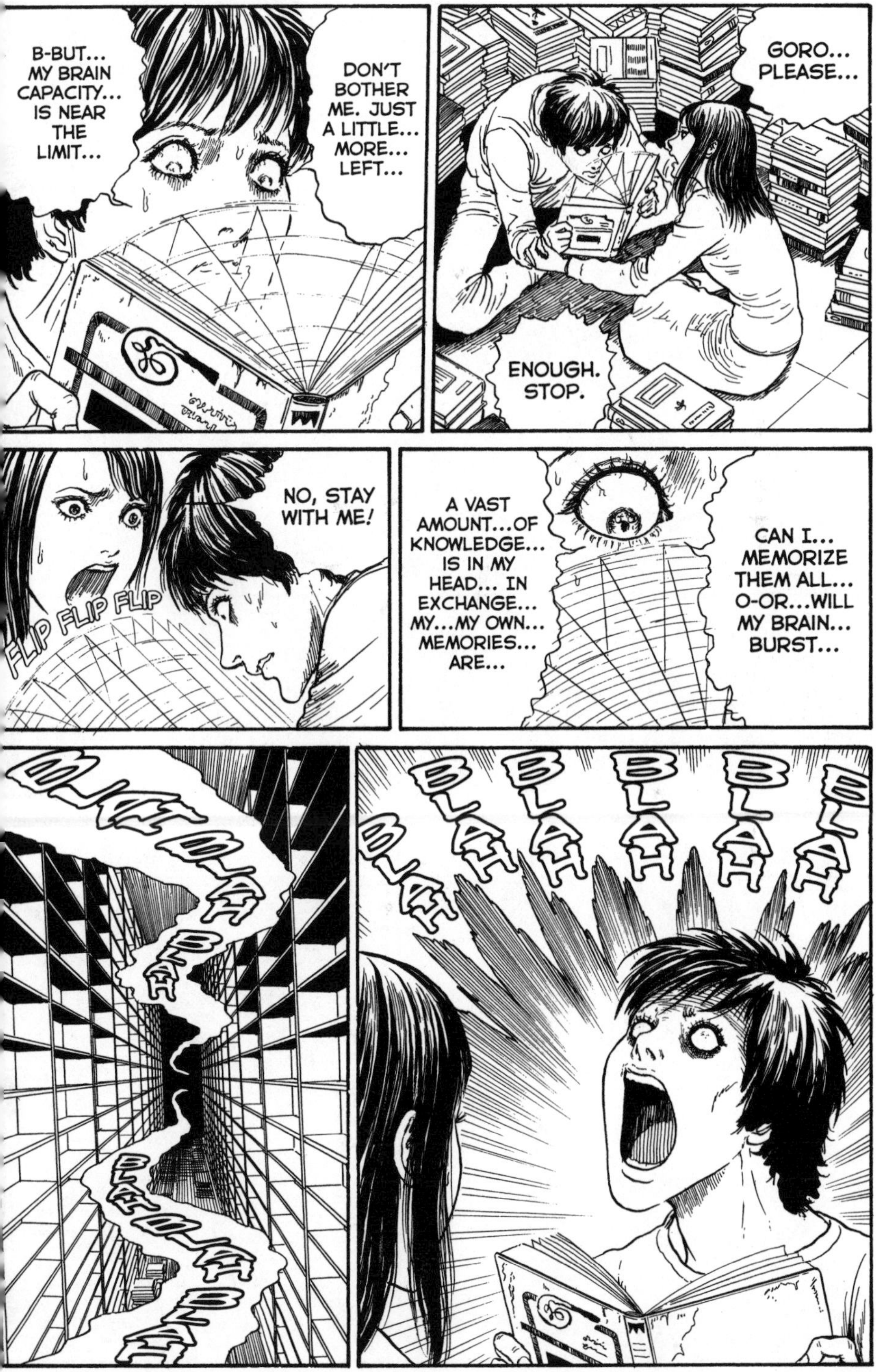
GORO... PLEASE...
ENOUGH. STOP.
DON'T BOTHER ME. JUST A LITTLE... MORE... LEFT...
B-BUT... MY BRAIN CAPACITY... IS NEAR THE LIMIT...
CAN I... MEMORIZE THEM ALL... O-OR...WILL MY BRAIN... BURST...
A VAST AMOUNT...OF KNOWLEDGE... IS IN MY HEAD... IN EXCHANGE... MY...MY OWN... MEMORIES... ARE...
NO, STAY WITH ME!
FLIP FLIP FLIP
BLAH BLAH BLAH BLAH BLAH BLAH
BLAH

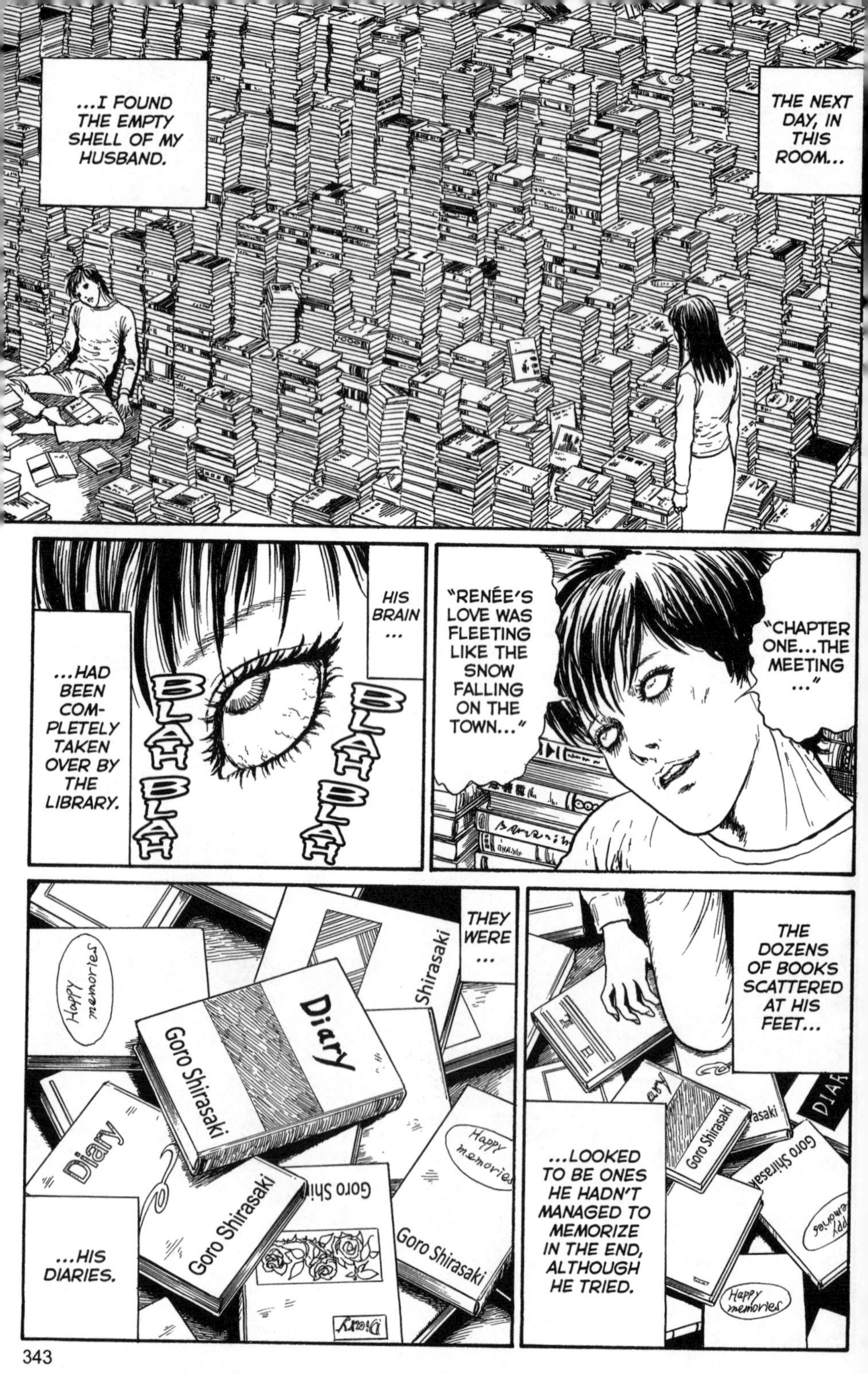
THE NEXT DAY, IN THIS ROOM...
...I FOUND THE EMPTY SHELL OF MY HUSBAND.
"CHAPTER ONE...THE MEETING..."
"RENÉE'S LOVE WAS FLEETING LIKE THE SNOW FALLING ON THE TOWN..."
HIS BRAIN ...
BLAH BLAH
BLAH BLAH
...HAD BEEN COMPLETELY TAKEN OVER BY THE LIBRARY.
THE DOZENS OF BOOKS SCATTERED AT HIS FEET...
Diary
Goro Shirasaki
Happy memories
...LOOKED TO BE ONES HE HADN'T MANAGED TO MEMORIZE IN THE END, ALTHOUGH HE TRIED.
THEY WERE ...
Happy memories
Shirasaki
Diary
Goro Shirasaki
Diary
Goro Shirasaki
Happy memories
Goro Shirasaki
...HIS DIARIES.

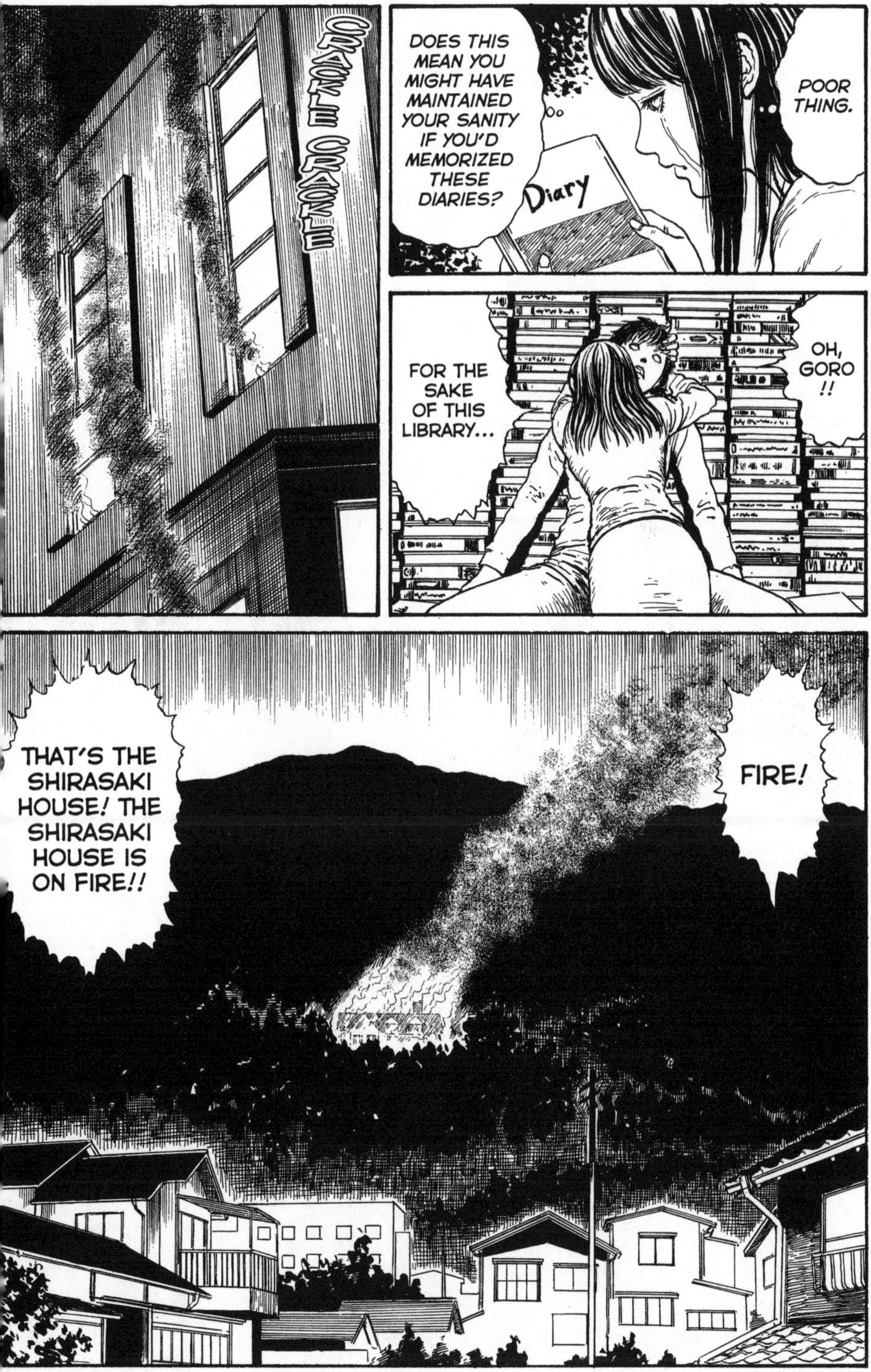
POOR THING.
DOES THIS MEAN YOU MIGHT HAVE MAINTAINED YOUR SANITY IF YOU'D MEMORIZED THESE DIARIES?
Diary
OH, GORO!!
FOR THE SAKE OF THIS LIBRARY...
CRACKLE CRACKLE
FIRE!
THAT'S THE SHIRASAKI HOUSE! THE SHIRASAKI HOUSE IS ON FIRE!!

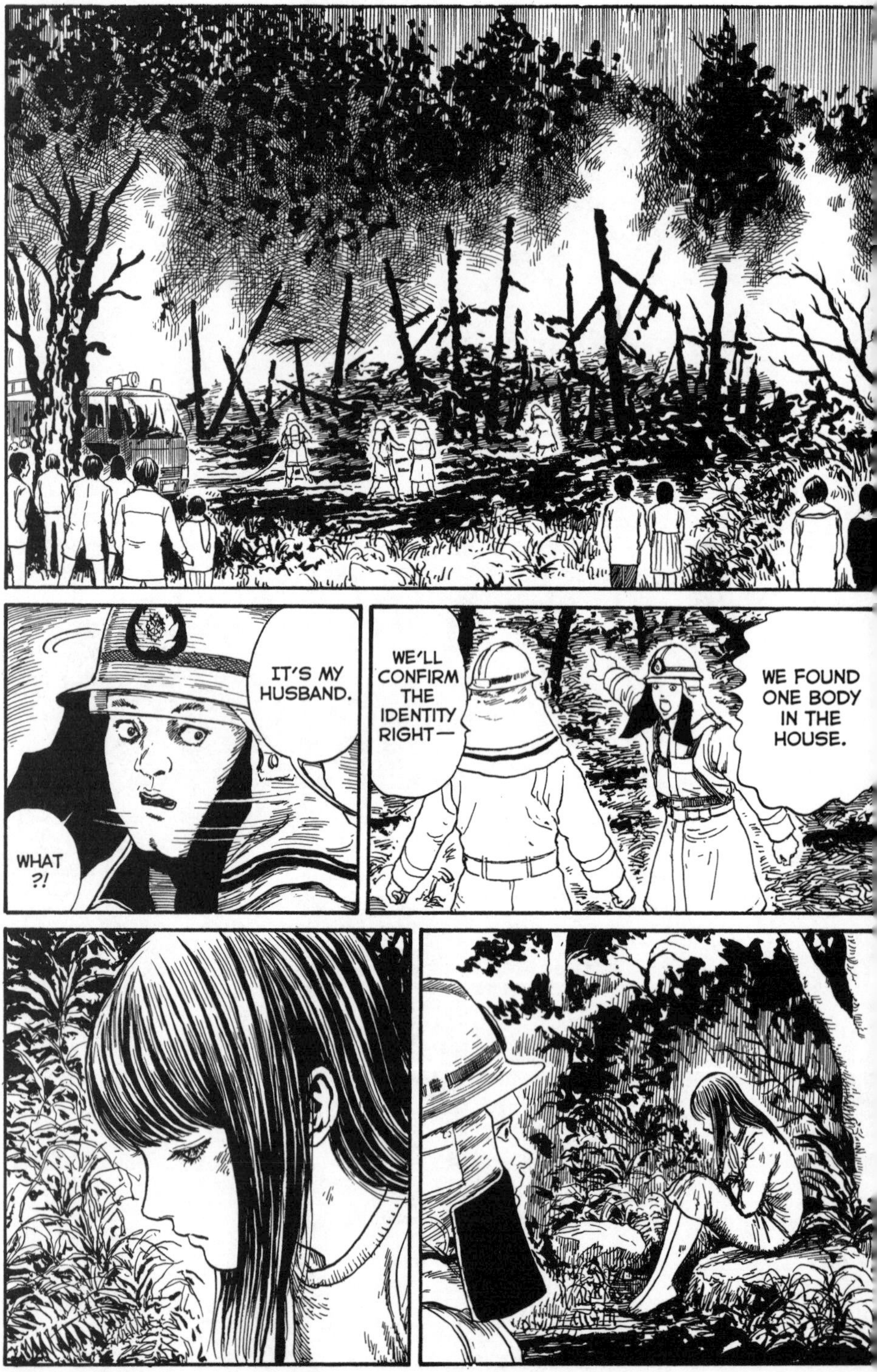
WE FOUND ONE BODY IN THE HOUSE.
WE'LL CONFIRM THE IDENTITY RIGHT—
IT'S MY HUSBAND.
WHAT ?!

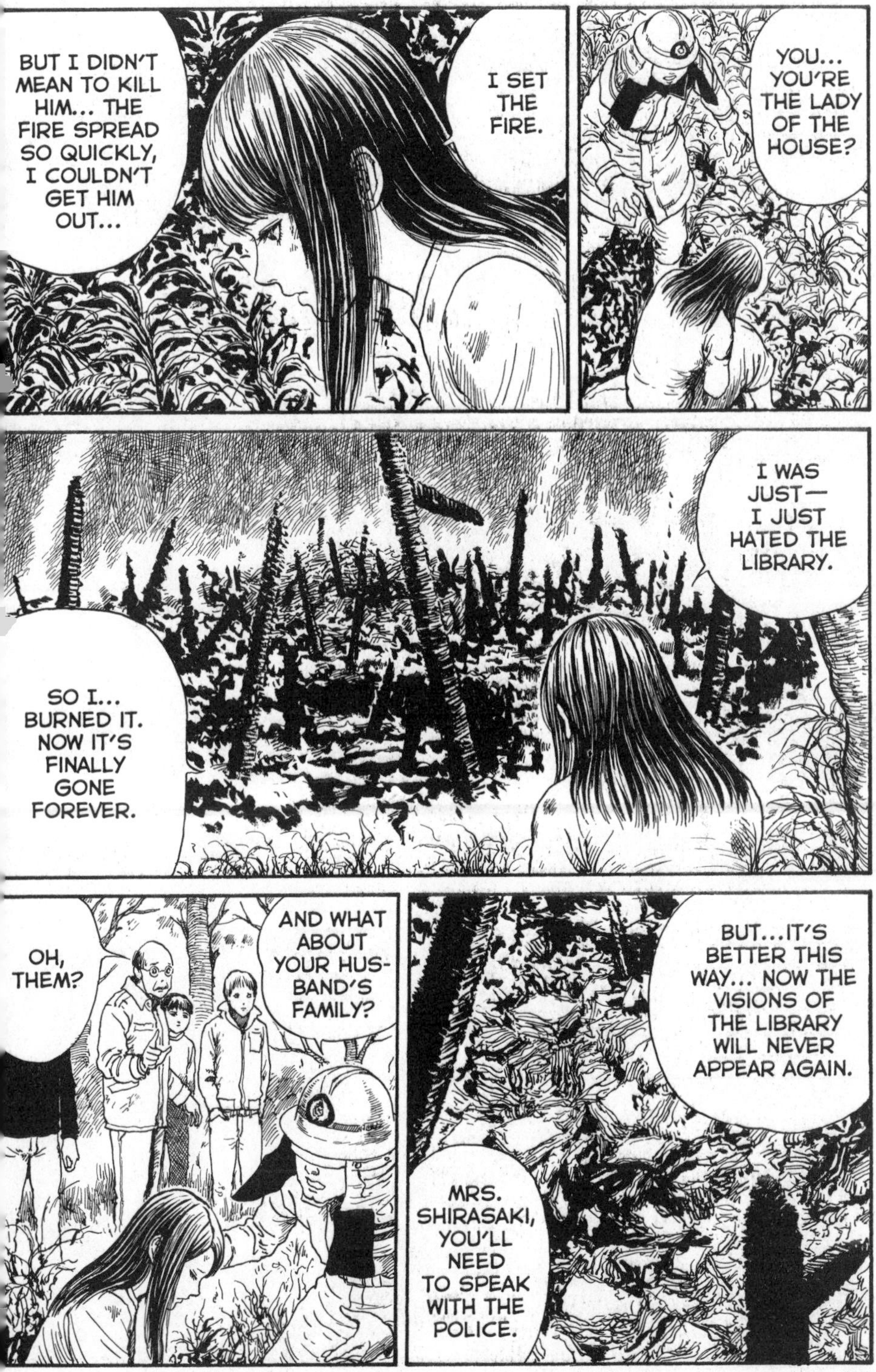
YOU... YOU'RE THE LADY OF THE HOUSE?
I SET THE FIRE.
BUT I DIDN'T MEAN TO KILL HIM... THE FIRE SPREAD SO QUICKLY, I COULDN'T GET HIM OUT...
I WAS JUST— I JUST HATED THE LIBRARY.
SO I... BURNED IT. NOW IT'S FINALLY GONE FOREVER.
BUT...IT'S BETTER THIS WAY... NOW THE VISIONS OF THE LIBRARY WILL NEVER APPEAR AGAIN.
MRS. SHIRASAKI, YOU'LL NEED TO SPEAK WITH THE POLICE.
AND WHAT ABOUT YOUR HUS-BAND'S FAMILY?
OH, THEM?

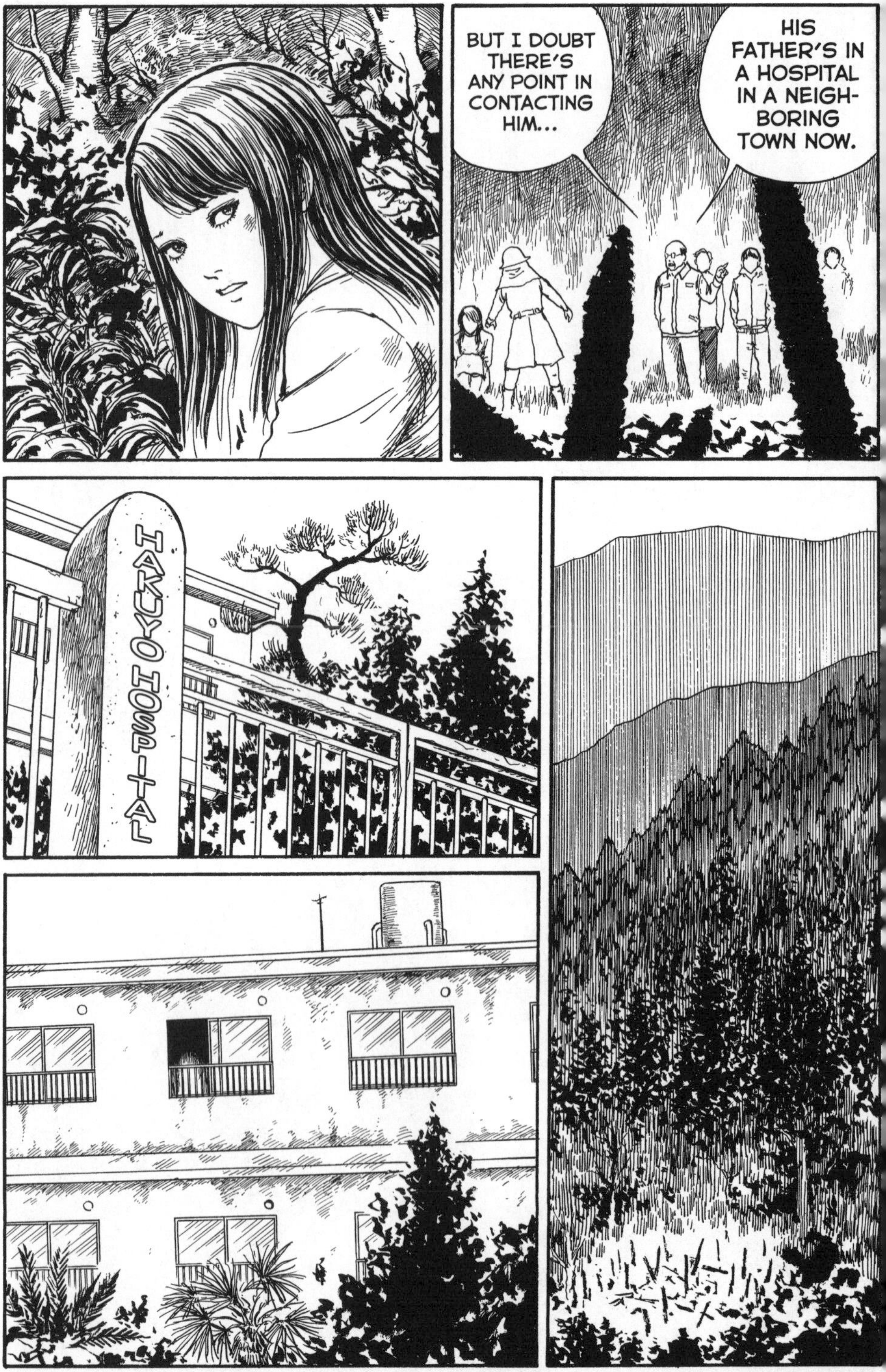
HIS FATHER'S IN A HOSPITAL IN A NEIGH-BORING TOWN NOW.
BUT I DOUBT THERE'S ANY POINT IN CONTACTING HIM...
HAKUYO HOSPITAL

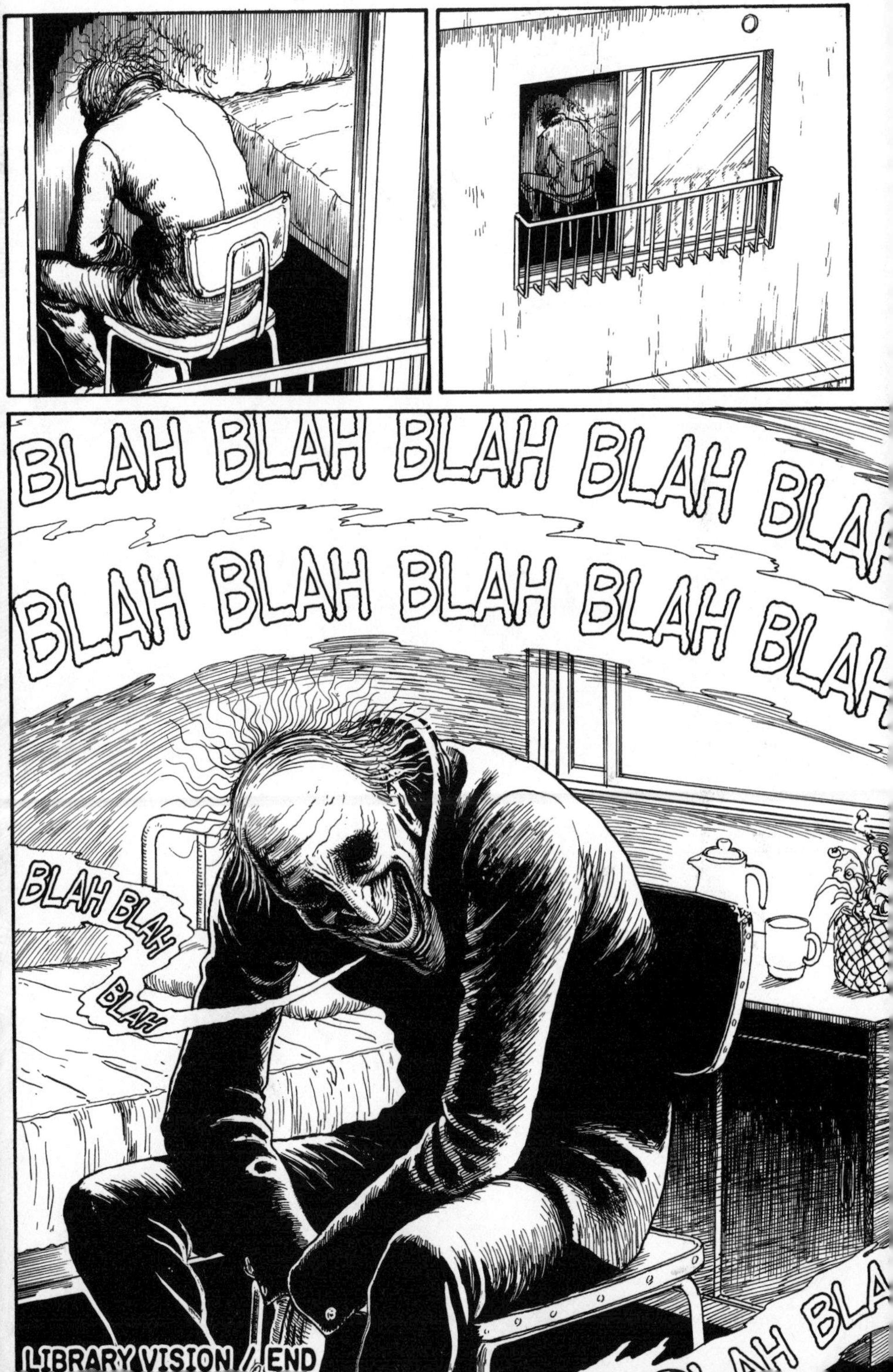
BLAH BLAH BLAH BLAH BLA
BLAH BLAH BLAH BLAH BLAH
BLAH BLAH BLAH
AH BLA
LIBRARY VISION / END

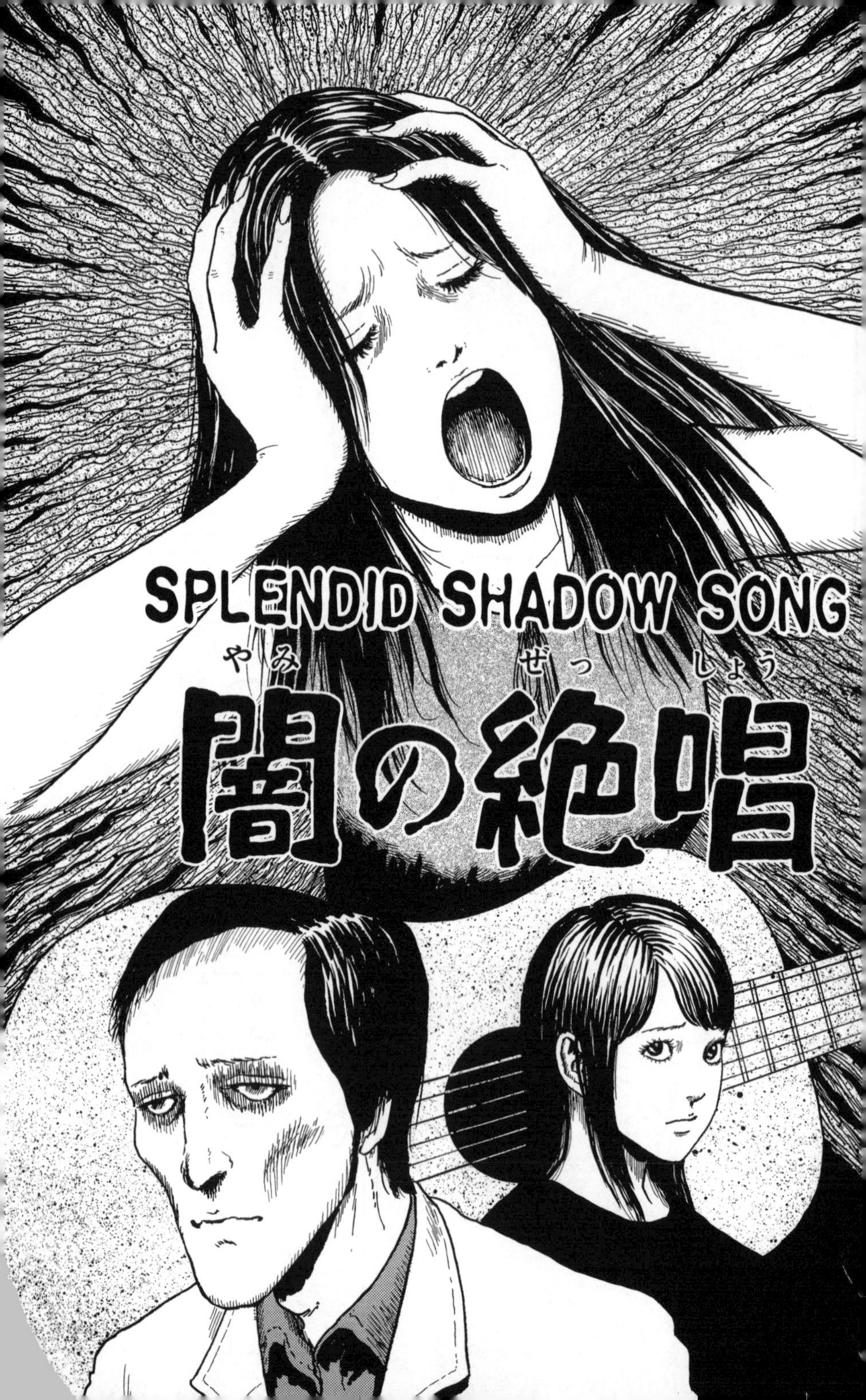
SPLENDID SHADOW SONG
闇の絶唱

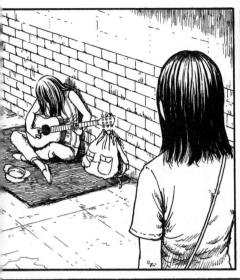
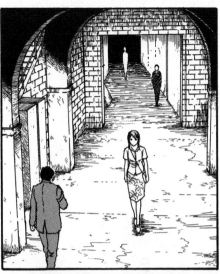
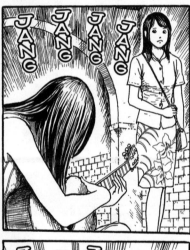
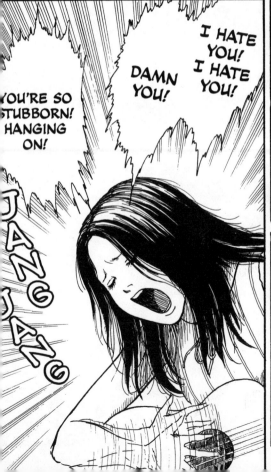
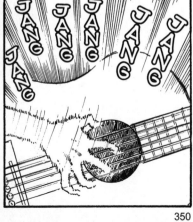

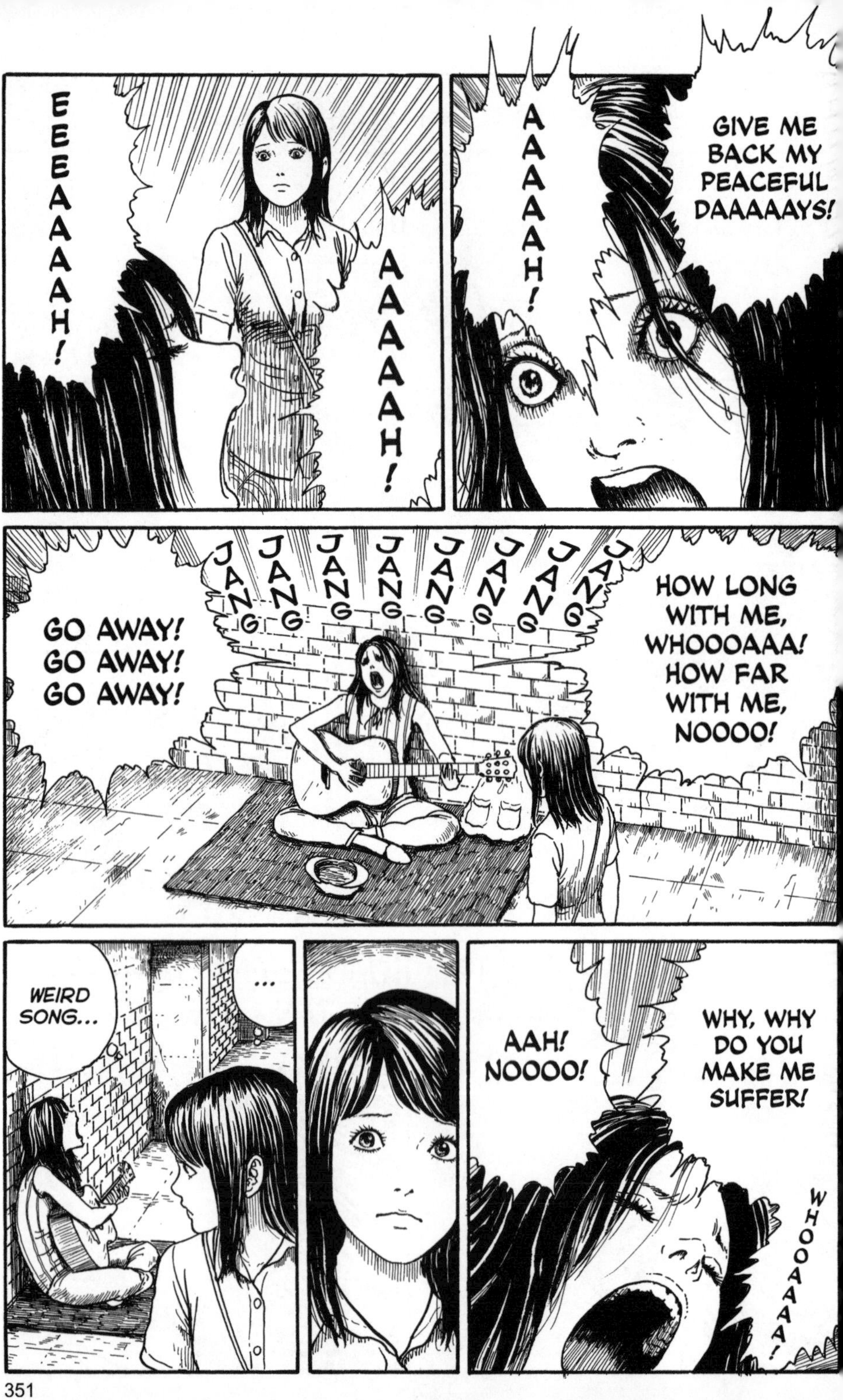
GIVE ME BACK MY PEACEFUL DAAAAAYS!
AAAAAH!
AAAAAAH!
EEEAAAAH!
HOW LONG WITH ME, WHOOOAAA! HOW FAR WITH ME, NOOOO!
JAN
JANG
JANG
JANG
JANG
JANG
JANG
JANG
GO AWAY! GO AWAY! GO AWAY!
WHY, WHY DO YOU MAKE ME SUFFER!
AAH! NOOOO!
WHOOAAAA!
...
WEIRD SONG...

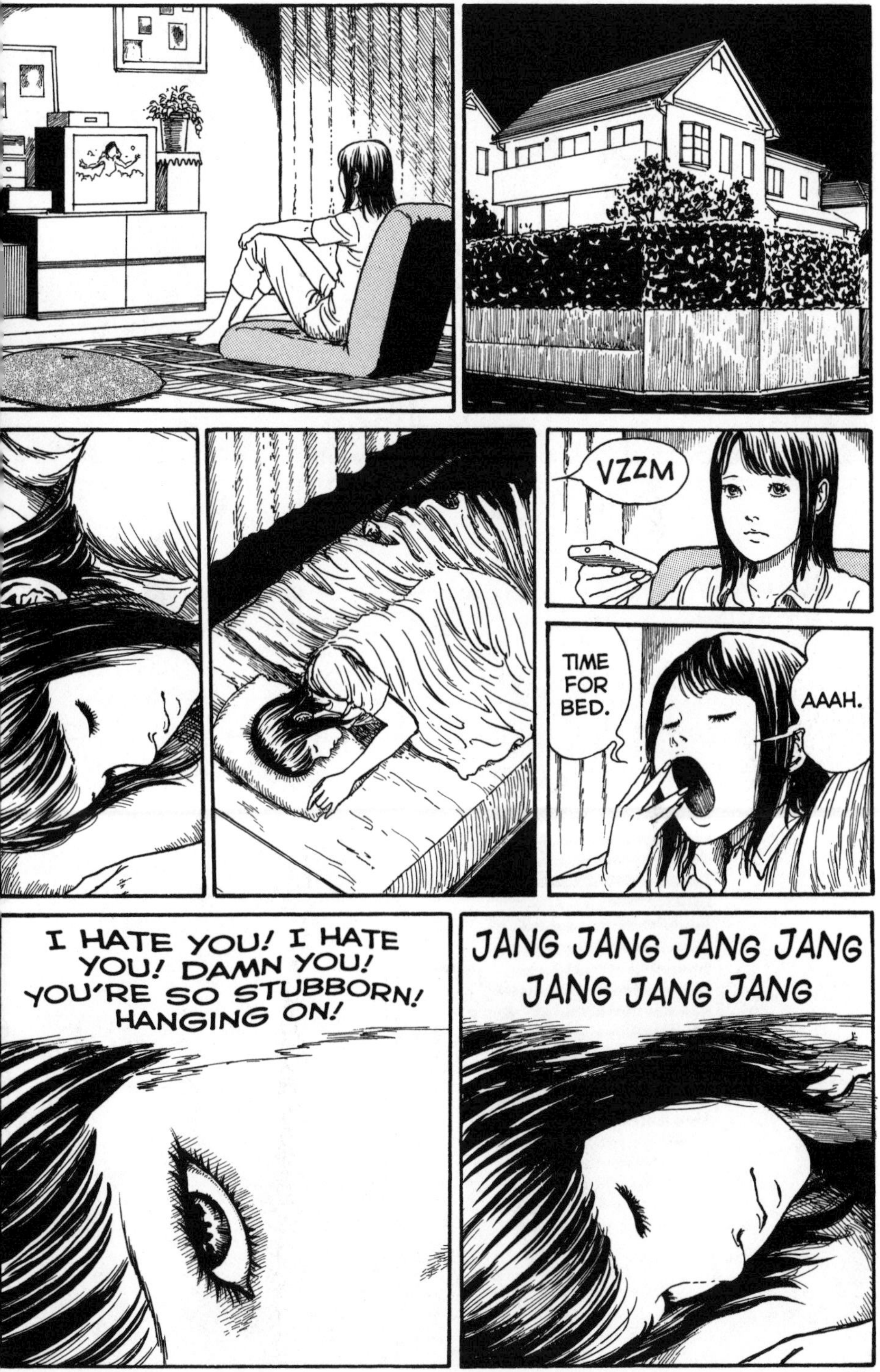
VZZM
AAAH.
TIME FOR BED.
JANG JANG JANG JANG JANG JANG JANG
I HATE YOU! I HATE YOU! DAMN YOU! YOU'RE SO STUBBORN! HANGING ON!

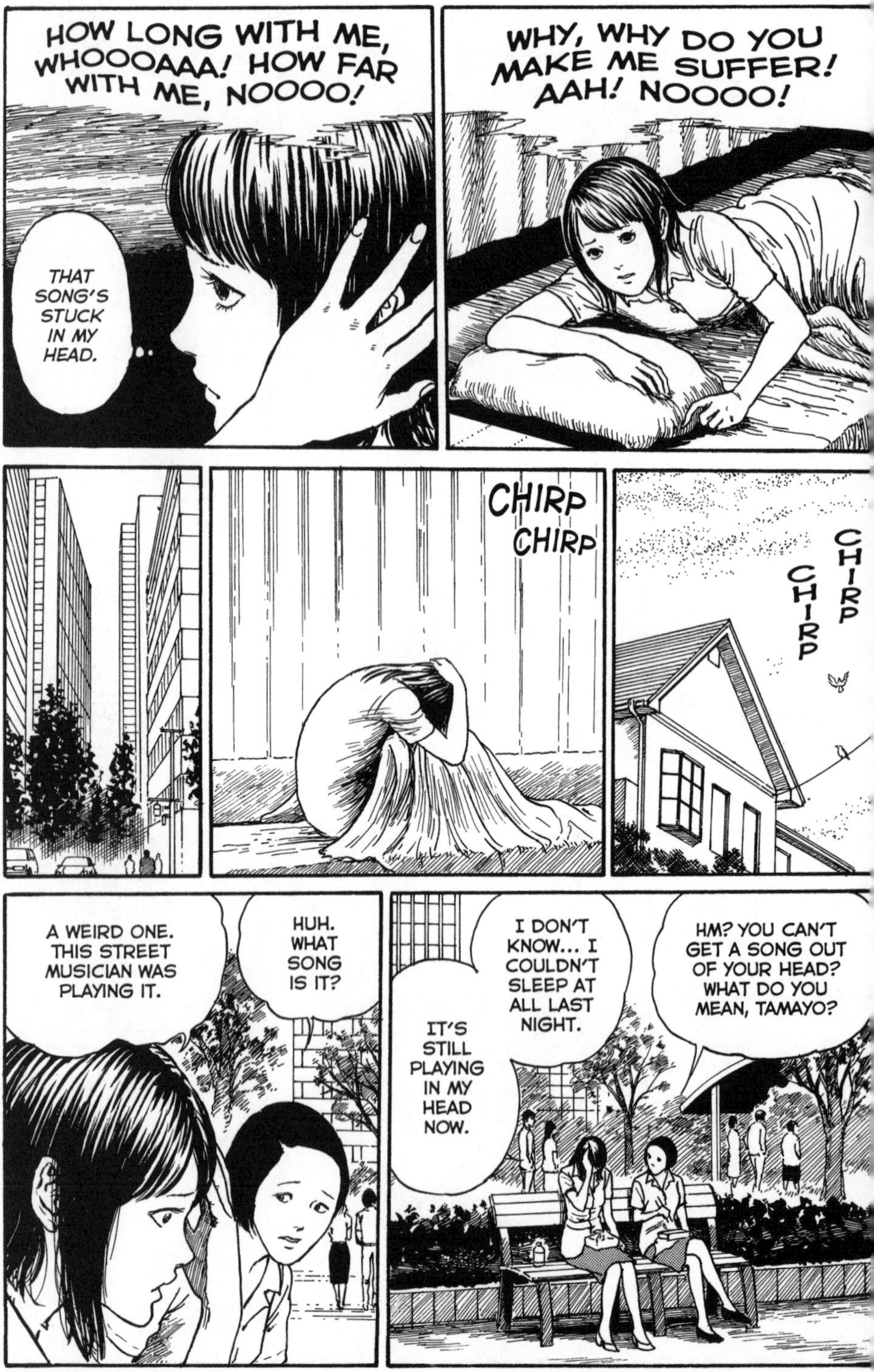
WHY, WHY DO YOU MAKE ME SUFFER! AAH! NOOOO!
HOW LONG WITH ME, WHOOOAAA! HOW FAR WITH ME, NOOOO!
THAT SONG'S STUCK IN MY HEAD.
CHIRP
CHIRP
CHIRP
CHIRP
HM? YOU CAN'T GET A SONG OUT OF YOUR HEAD? WHAT DO YOU MEAN, TAMAYO?
I DON'T KNOW... I COULDN'T SLEEP AT ALL LAST NIGHT.
IT'S STILL PLAYING IN MY HEAD NOW.
HUH. WHAT SONG IS IT?
A WEIRD ONE. THIS STREET MUSICIAN WAS PLAYING IT.

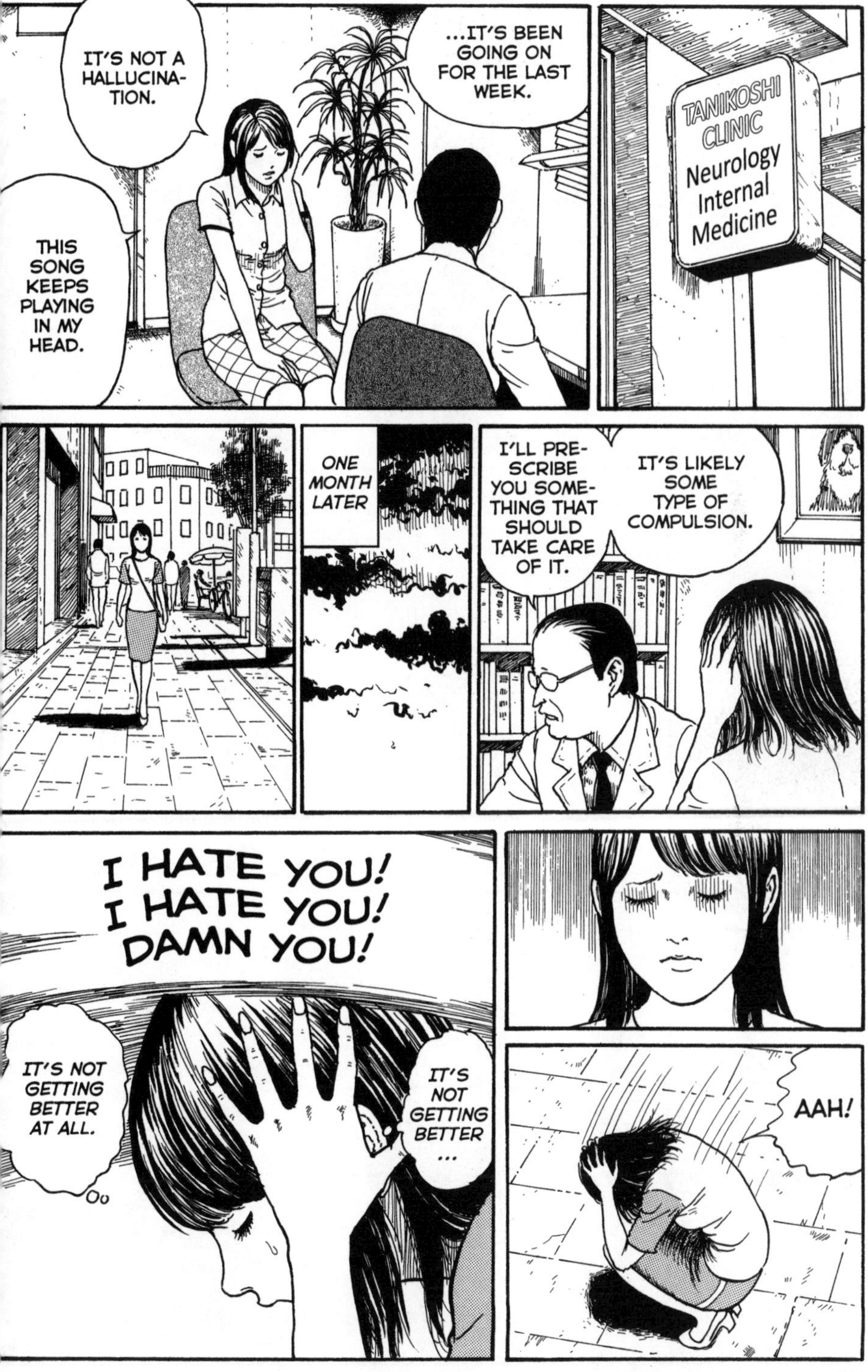
TANIKOSHI CLINIC
Neurology Internal Medicine
...IT'S BEEN GOING ON FOR THE LAST WEEK.
IT'S NOT A HALLUCINATION.
THIS SONG KEEPS PLAYING IN MY HEAD.
IT'S LIKELY SOME TYPE OF COMPULSION.
I'LL PRESCRIBE YOU SOMETHING THAT SHOULD TAKE CARE OF IT.
ONE MONTH LATER
AAH!
I HATE YOU! I HATE YOU! DAMN YOU!
IT'S NOT GETTING BETTER ...
IT'S NOT GETTING BETTER AT ALL.

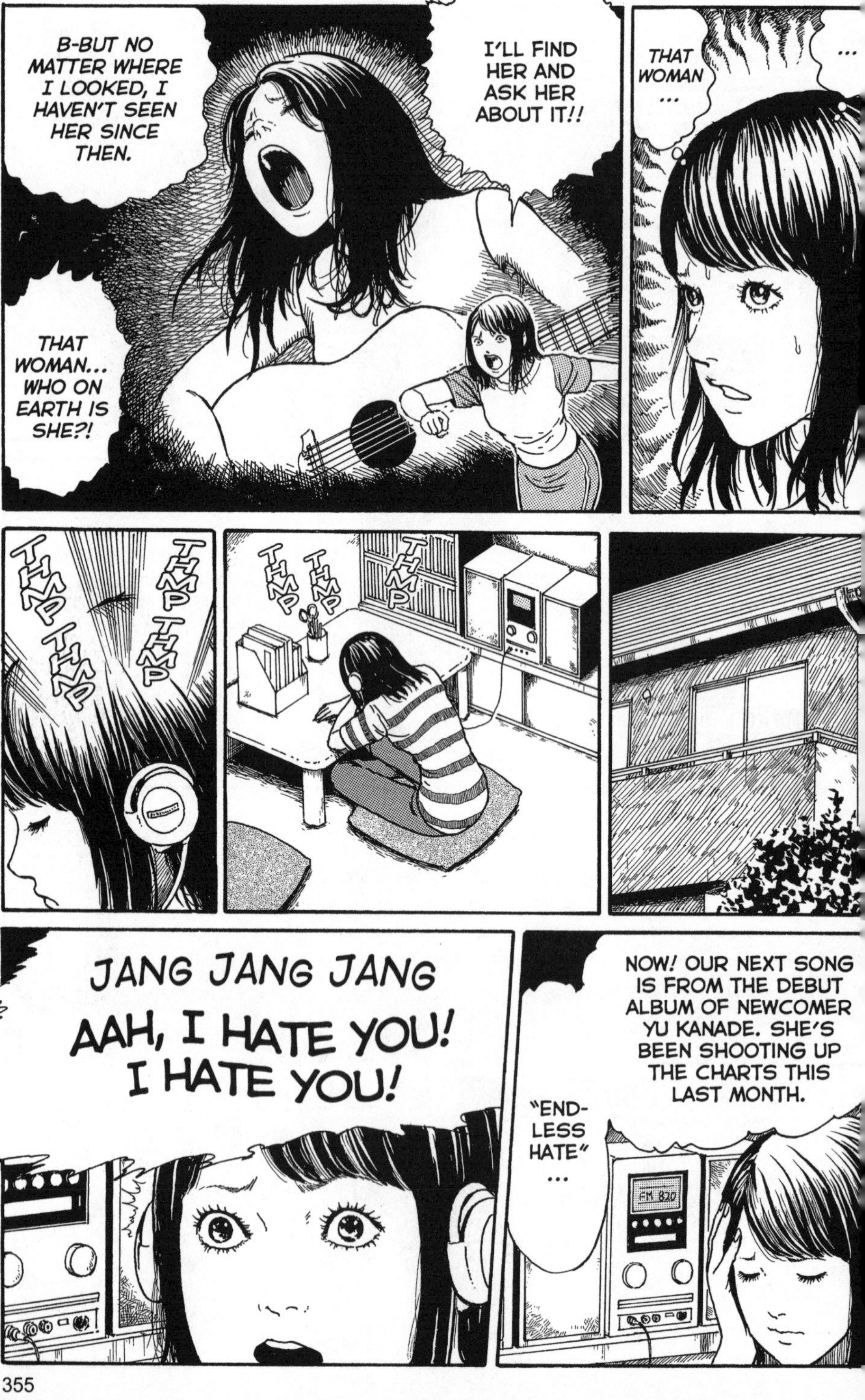
...
THAT WOMAN ...
I'LL FIND HER AND ASK HER ABOUT IT!!
B-BUT NO MATTER WHERE I LOOKED, I HAVEN'T SEEN HER SINCE THEN.
THAT WOMAN... WHO ON EARTH IS SHE?!
THMP THMP THMP
THMP THMP THMP THMP
NOW! OUR NEXT SONG IS FROM THE DEBUT ALBUM OF NEWCOMER YU KANADE. SHE'S BEEN SHOOTING UP THE CHARTS THIS LAST MONTH.
"END-LESS HATE" ...
FM 82.0
JANG JANG JANG
AAH, I HATE YOU! I HATE YOU!

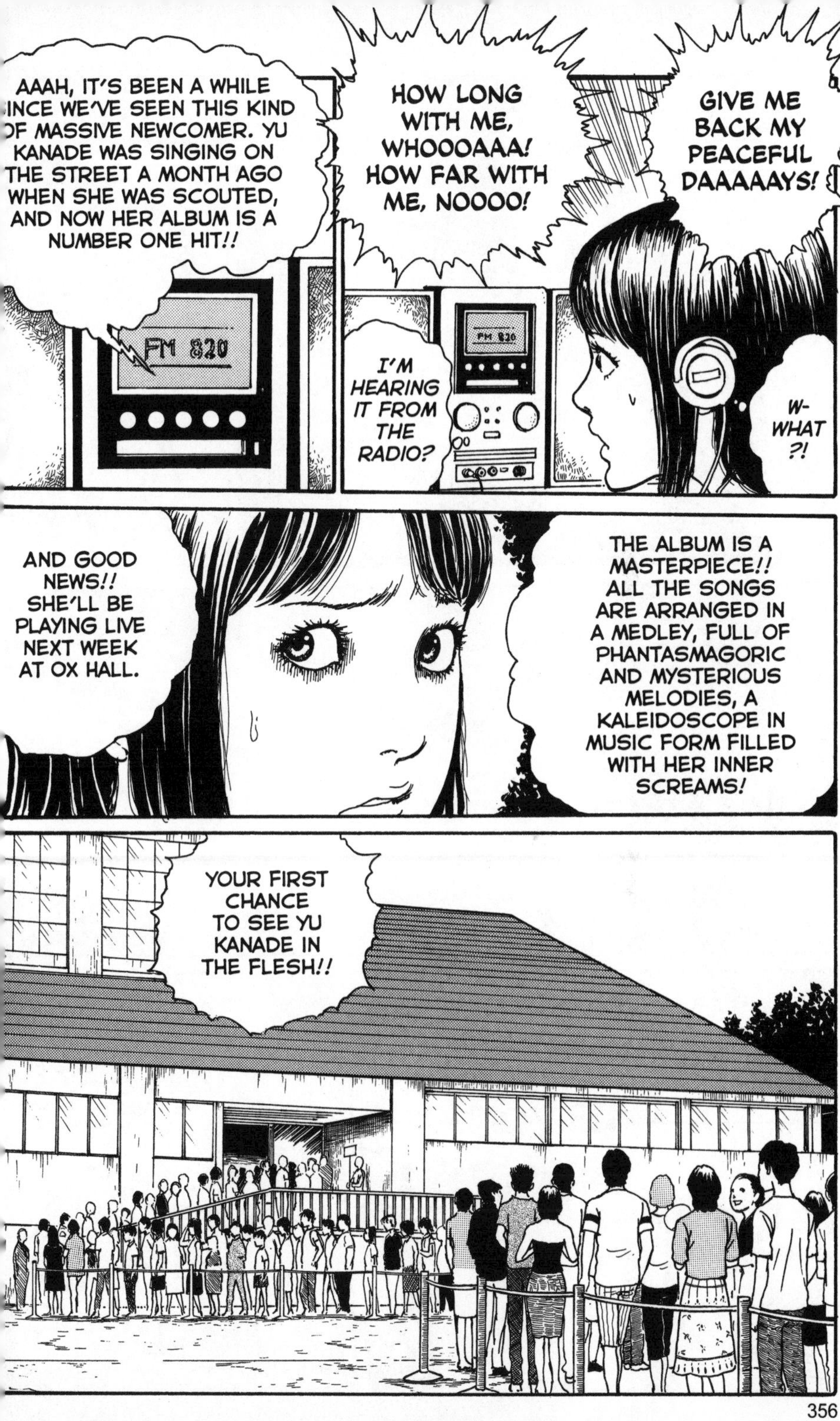
GIVE ME BACK MY PEACEFUL DAAAAAYS!
HOW LONG WITH ME, WHOOOAAA! HOW FAR WITH ME, NOOOO!
W-WHAT?!
I'M HEARING IT FROM THE RADIO?
FM 820
AAAH, IT'S BEEN A WHILE INCE WE'VE SEEN THIS KIND OF MASSIVE NEWCOMER. YU KANADE WAS SINGING ON THE STREET A MONTH AGO WHEN SHE WAS SCOUTED, AND NOW HER ALBUM IS A NUMBER ONE HIT!!
FM 820
THE ALBUM IS A MASTERPIECE!! ALL THE SONGS ARE ARRANGED IN A MEDLEY, FULL OF PHANTASMAGORIC AND MYSTERIOUS MELODIES, A KALEIDOSCOPE IN MUSIC FORM FILLED WITH HER INNER SCREAMS!
AND GOOD NEWS!! SHE'LL BE PLAYING LIVE NEXT WEEK AT OX HALL.
YOUR FIRST CHANCE TO SEE YU KANADE IN THE FLESH!!

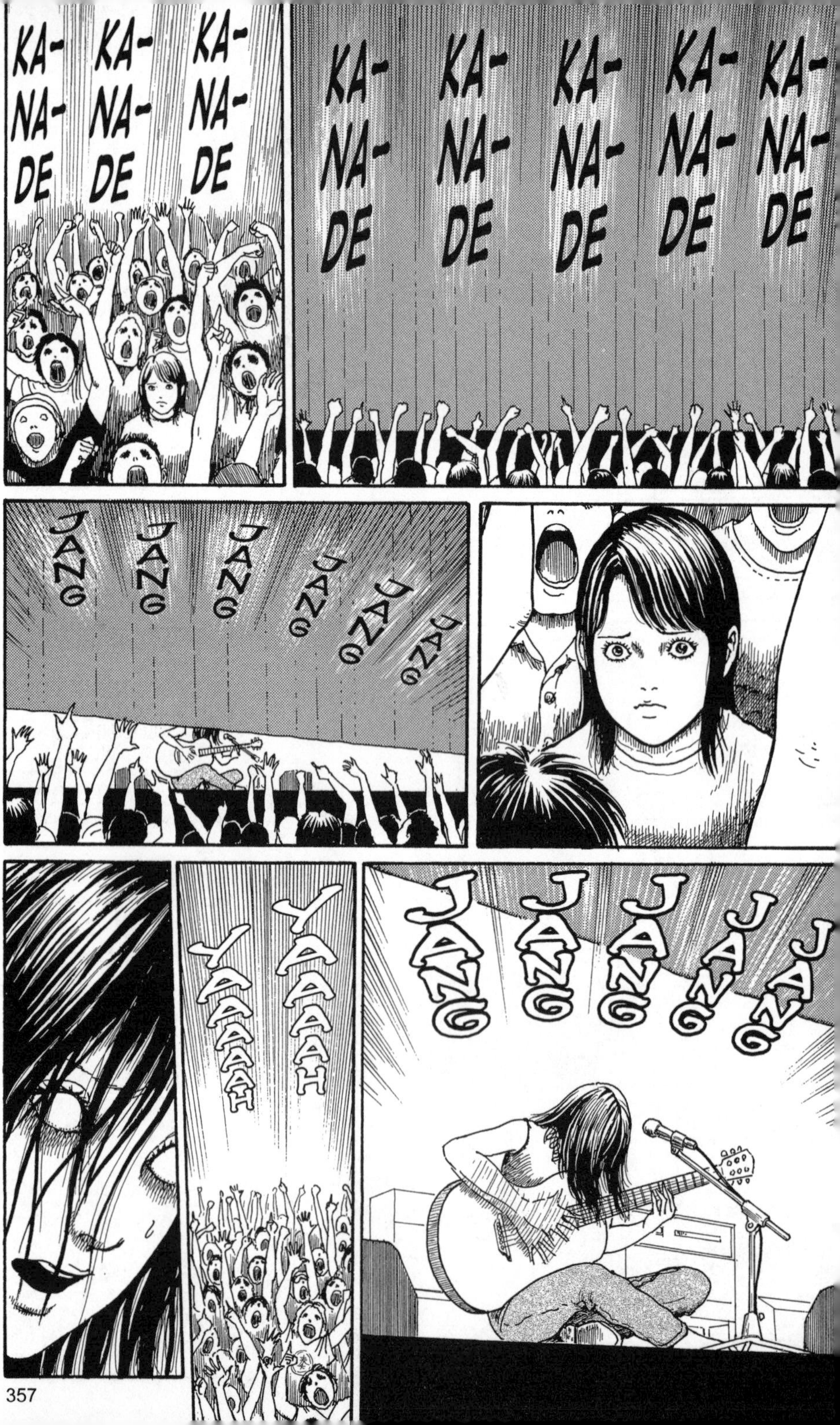
KA-NA-DE
KA-NA-DE
KA-NA-DE
KA-NA-DE
KA-NA-DE
KA-NA-DE
KA-NA-DE
KA-NA-DE
JANG
JANG
JANG
JANG
JANG
JANG
JANG
JANG
JANG
JANG
JANG
YAAAAH
YAAAAAH

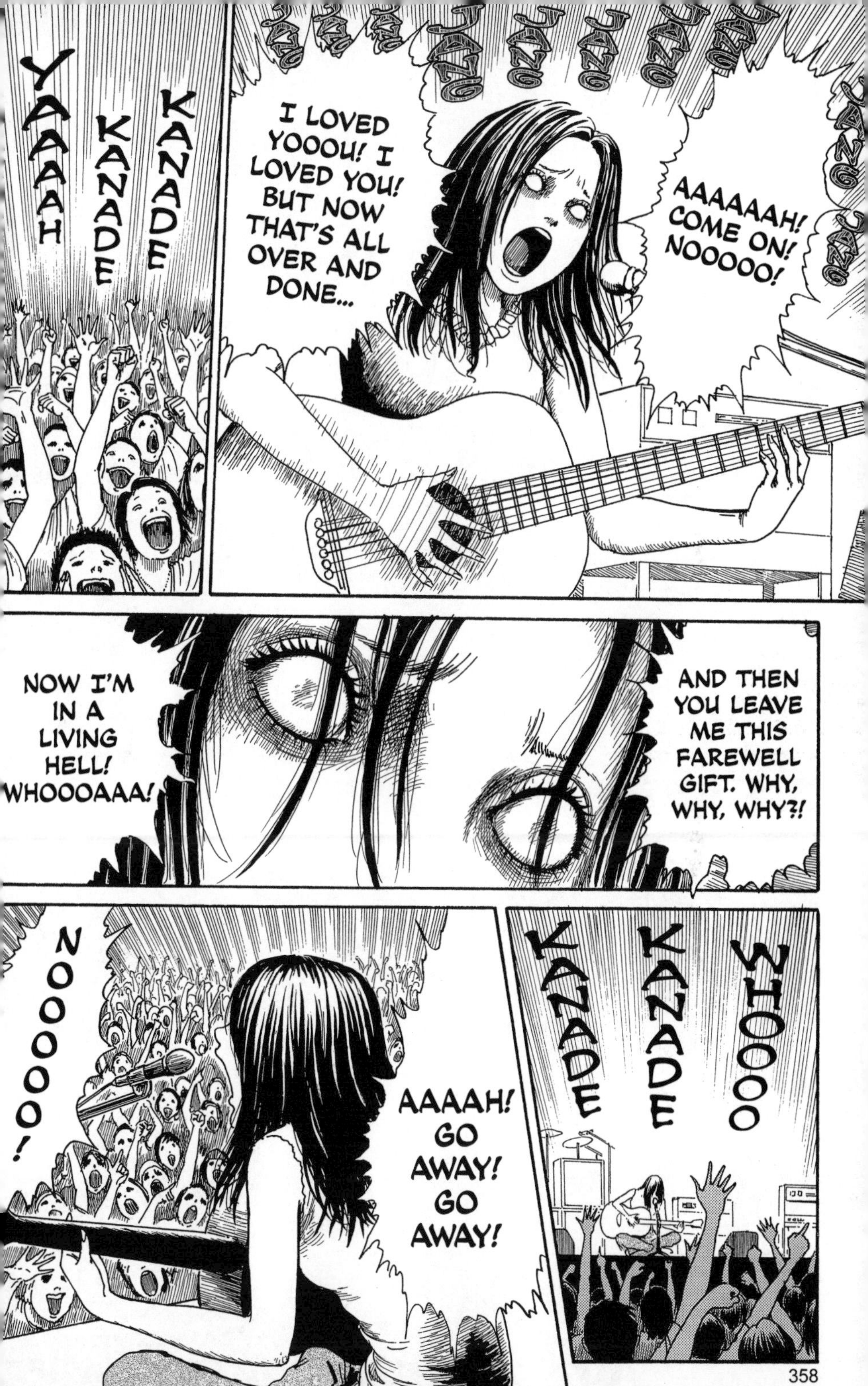
JANG JANG JANG JANG
JANG JANG
AAAAAAH! COME ON! NOOOOO!
I LOVED YOOOU! I LOVED YOU! BUT NOW THAT'S ALL OVER AND DONE...
KANADE
KANADE
YAAAAH
AND THEN YOU LEAVE ME THIS FAREWELL GIFT. WHY, WHY, WHY?!
NOW I'M IN A LIVING HELL! WHOOOAAA!
WHOOOO
KANADE
KANADE
AAAAH! GO AWAY! GO AWAY!
NOOOOOO!

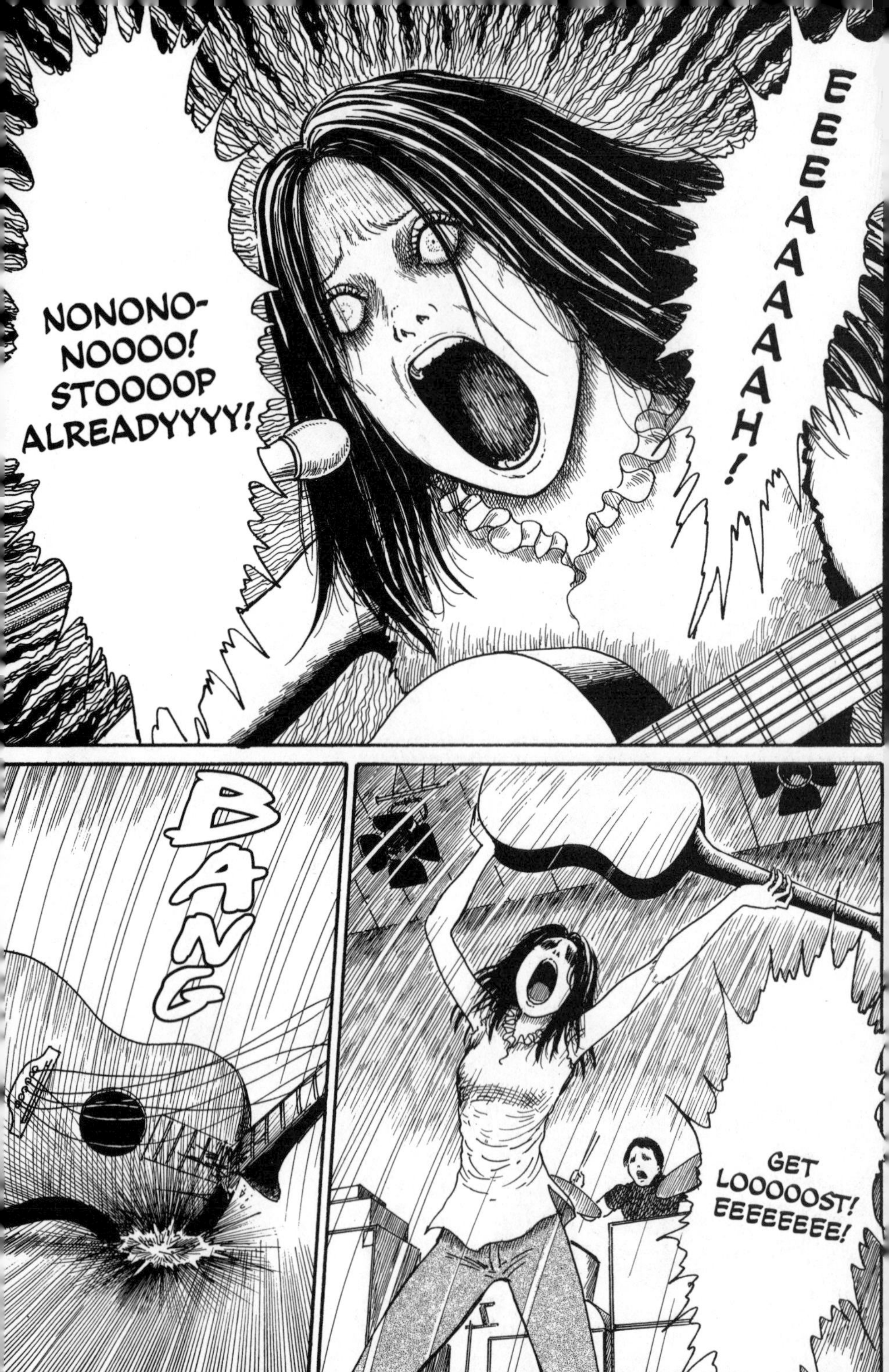
EEEAAAAAH!
NONONO-NOOOO! STOOOOP ALREADYYYY!
GET LOOOOOST! EEEEEEEE!
BANG

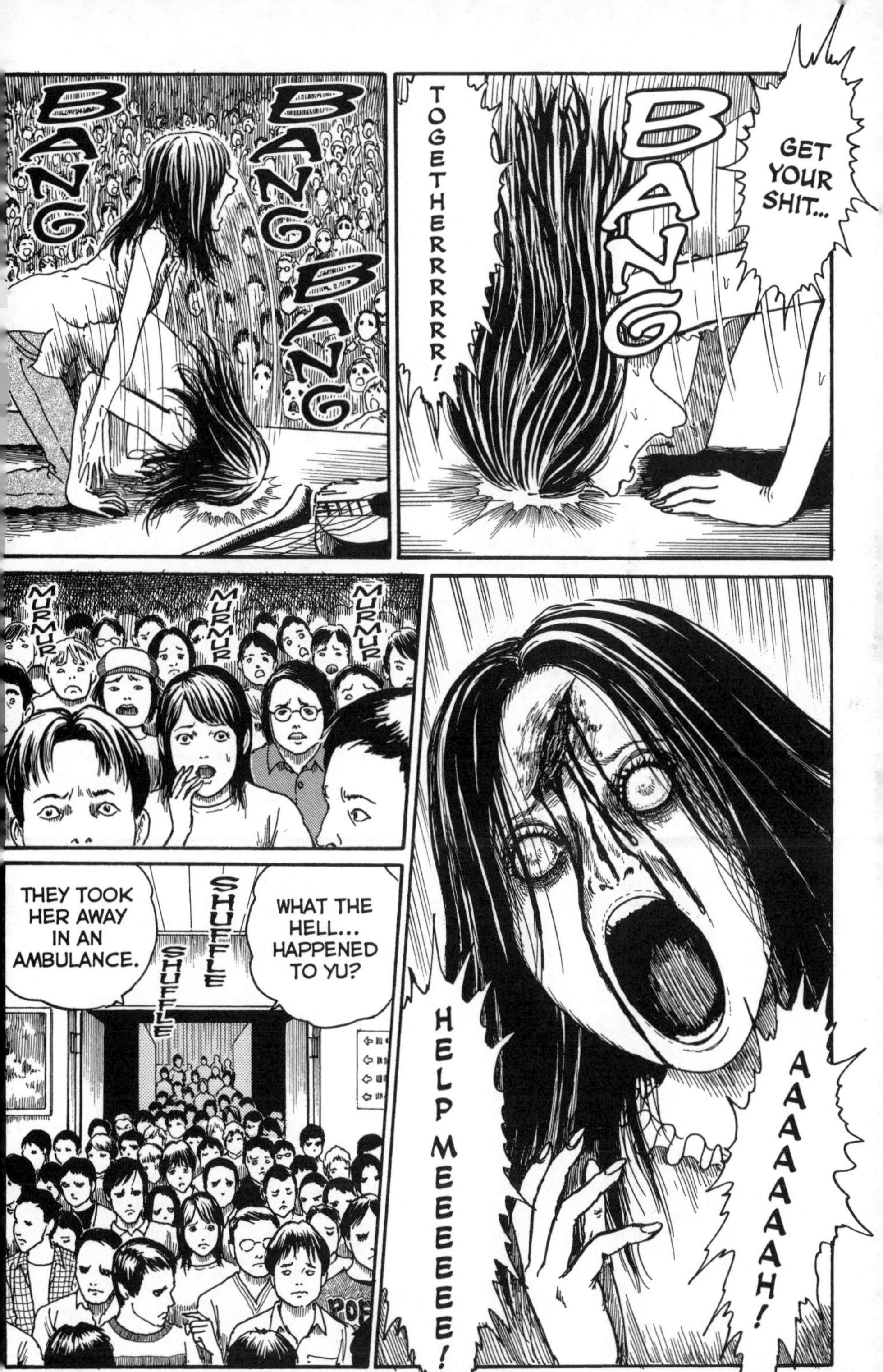
GET YOUR SHIT...
BANG
TOGETHERRRRRR!
BANG
BANG
BANG
BANG
AAAAAAAH!
HELP MEEEEEE!
MURMUR
MURMUR
MURMUR
WHAT THE HELL... HAPPENED TO YU?
SHUFFLE
SHUFFLE
THEY TOOK HER AWAY IN AN AMBULANCE.

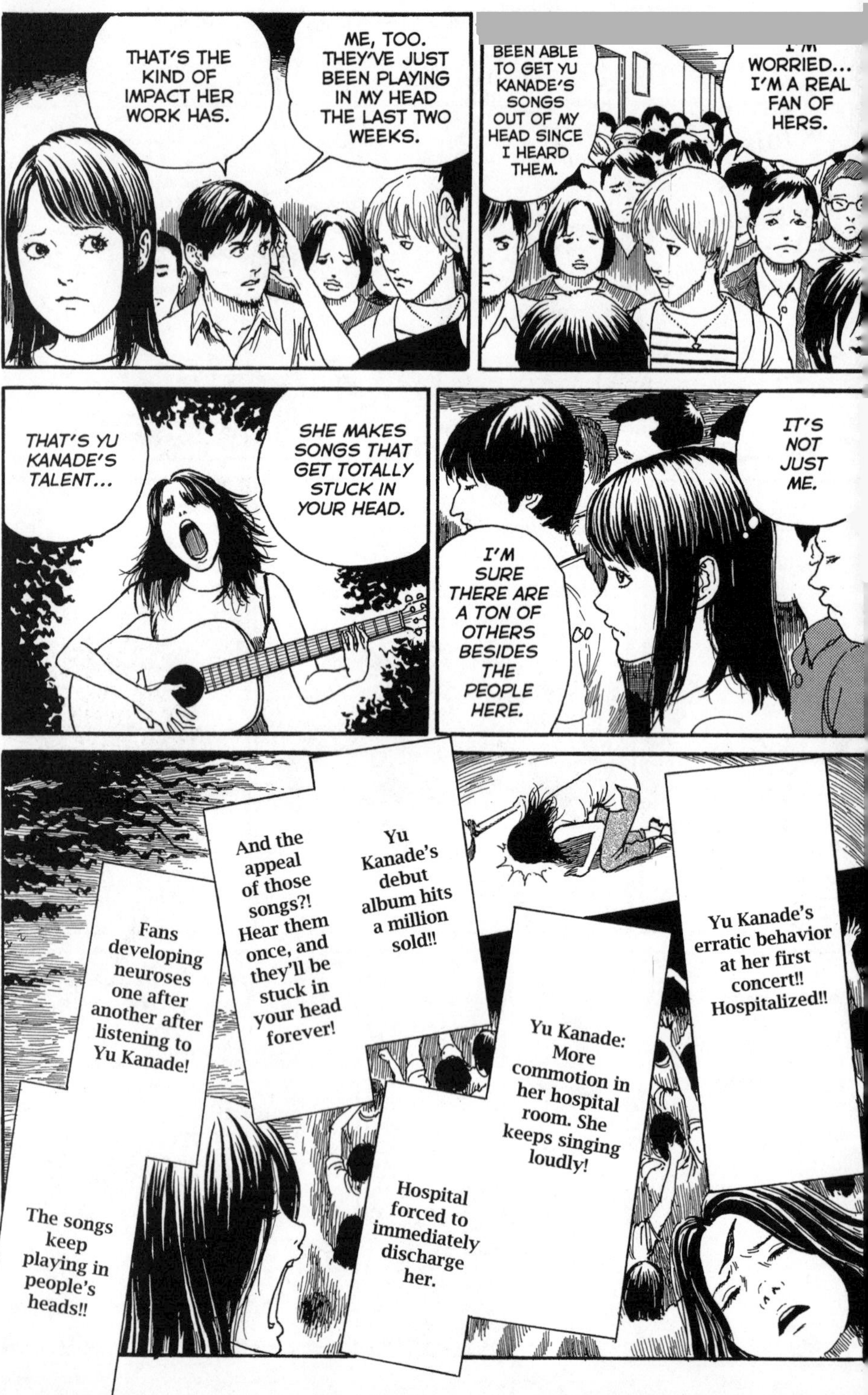
WORRIED... I'M A REAL FAN OF HERS.
BEEN ABLE TO GET YU KANADE'S SONGS OUT OF MY HEAD SINCE I HEARD THEM.
ME, TOO. THEY'VE JUST BEEN PLAYING IN MY HEAD THE LAST TWO WEEKS.
THAT'S THE KIND OF IMPACT HER WORK HAS.
IT'S NOT JUST ME.
I'M SURE THERE ARE A TON OF OTHERS BESIDES THE PEOPLE HERE.
SHE MAKES SONGS THAT GET TOTALLY STUCK IN YOUR HEAD.
THAT'S YU KANADE'S TALENT...
Yu Kanade's erratic behavior at her first concert!! Hospitalized!!
Yu Kanade's debut album hits a million sold!!
And the appeal of those songs?! Hear them once, and they'll be stuck in your head forever!
Yu Kanade: More commotion in her hospital room. She keeps singing loudly!
Fans developing neuroses one after another after listening to Yu Kanade!
Hospital forced to immediately discharge her.
The songs keep playing in people's heads!!

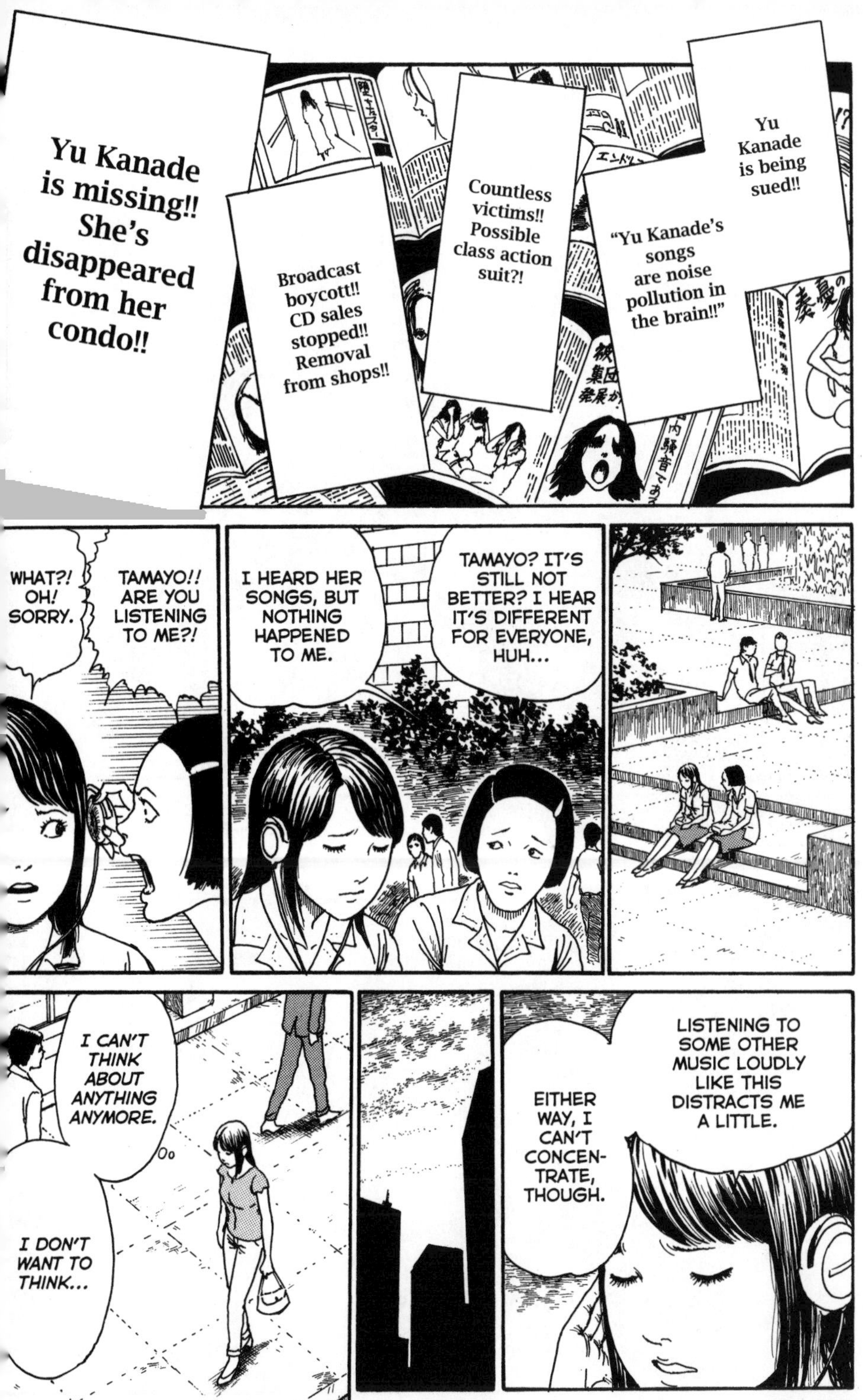
Yu Kanade is being sued!!
"Yu Kanade's songs are noise pollution in the brain!!"
Countless victims!! Possible class action suit?!
Broadcast boycott!! CD sales stopped!! Removal from shops!!
Yu Kanade is missing!! She's disappeared from her condo!!
TAMAYO? IT'S STILL NOT BETTER? I HEAR IT'S DIFFERENT FOR EVERYONE, HUH...
I HEARD HER SONGS, BUT NOTHING HAPPENED TO ME.
TAMAYO!! ARE YOU LISTENING TO ME?!
WHAT?! OH! SORRY.
LISTENING TO SOME OTHER MUSIC LOUDLY LIKE THIS DISTRACTS ME A LITTLE.
EITHER WAY, I CAN'T CONCENTRATE, THOUGH.
I CAN'T THINK ABOUT ANYTHING ANYMORE.
I DON'T WANT TO THINK...

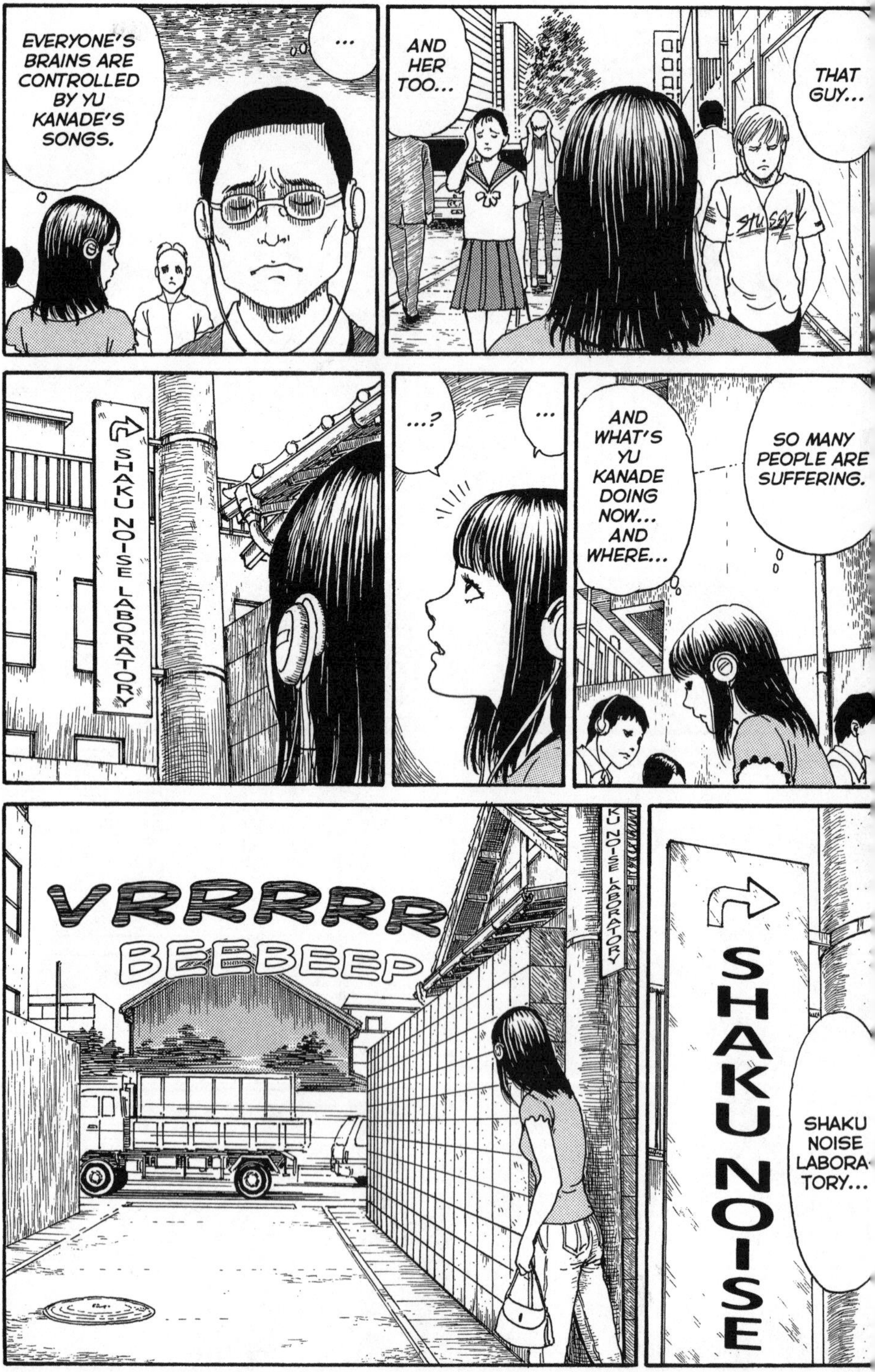
THAT GUY...
AND HER TOO...
...
EVERYONE'S BRAINS ARE CONTROLLED BY YU KANADE'S SONGS.
SO MANY PEOPLE ARE SUFFERING.
AND WHAT'S YU KANADE DOING NOW... AND WHERE...
...
...?
SHAKU NOISE LABORATORY
SHAKU NOISE
SHAKU NOISE LABORATORY...
KU NOISE LABORATORY
VRRRRR
BEEBEEP

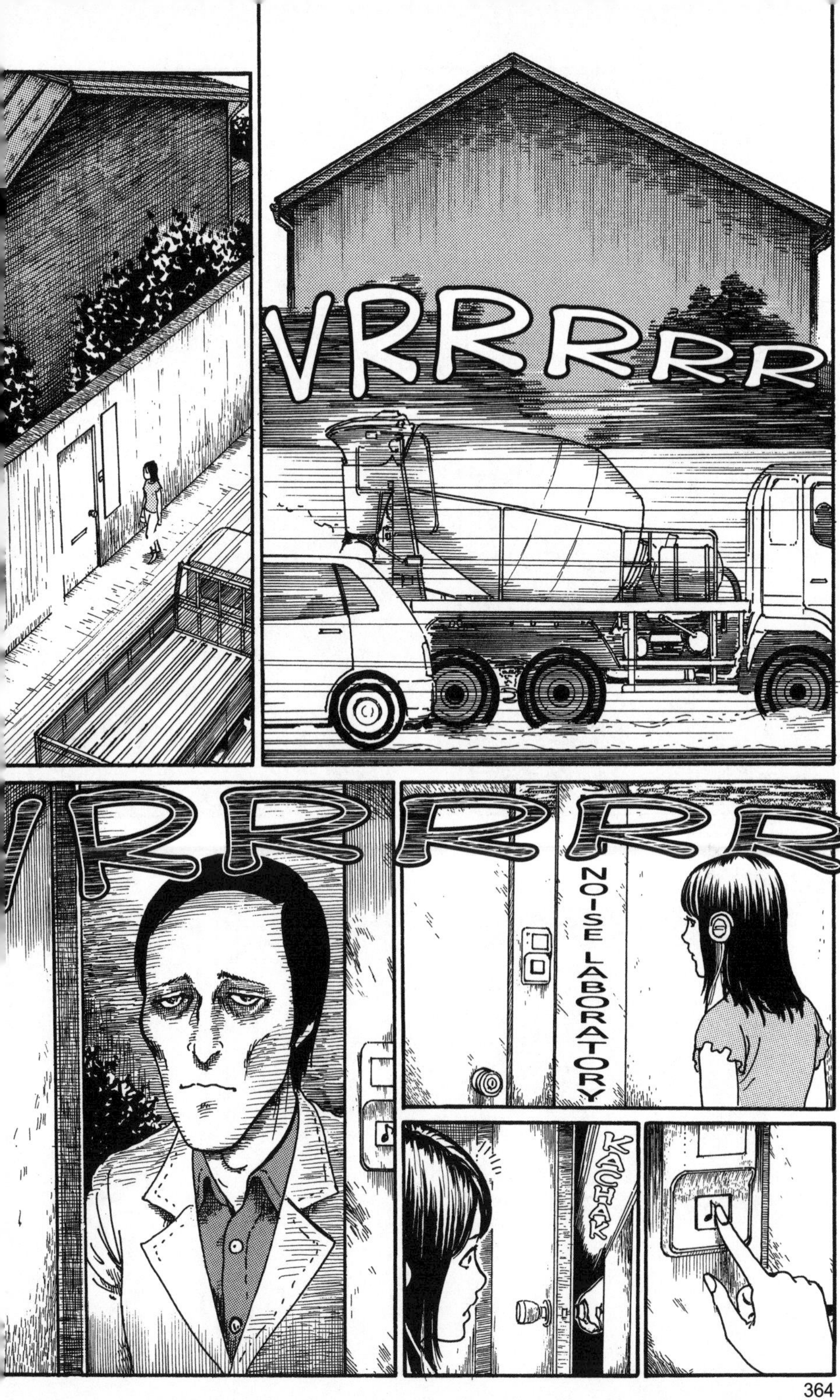
VRRRRRR
RRRRR
NOISE LABORATORY
KACHAK

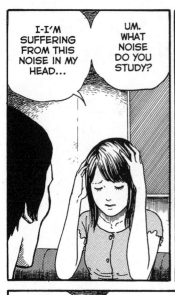

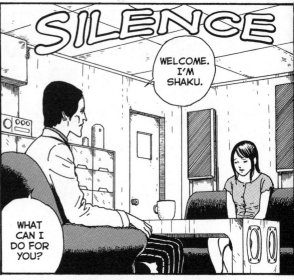

SILENCE
WELCOME. I'M SHAKU.
WHAT CAN I DO FOR YOU?
UM. WHAT NOISE DO YOU STUDY?
I-I'M SUFFERING FROM THIS NOISE IN MY HEAD...
OH HO... THE BRAIN NOISE EVERY-ONE'S TALKING ABOUT THESE DAYS.
IN MY RESEARCH, I STUDY METHODS OF DEALING WITH ALL KINDS OF NOISE.
BRAIN NOISE IS NO EXCEPTION THERE!!
STRANGELY ENOUGH, I'VE BEEN STUDYING BRAIN NOISE SINCE LAST YEAR!!
AND THAT RESEARCH IS NEARLY AT THE STAGE OF COMPLETION!!
EEAAAAAH

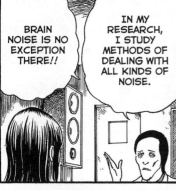

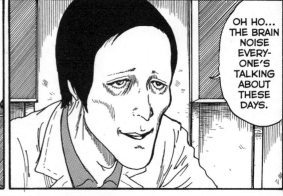

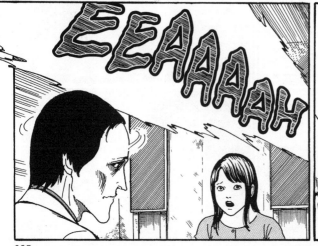

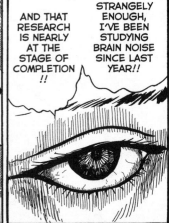

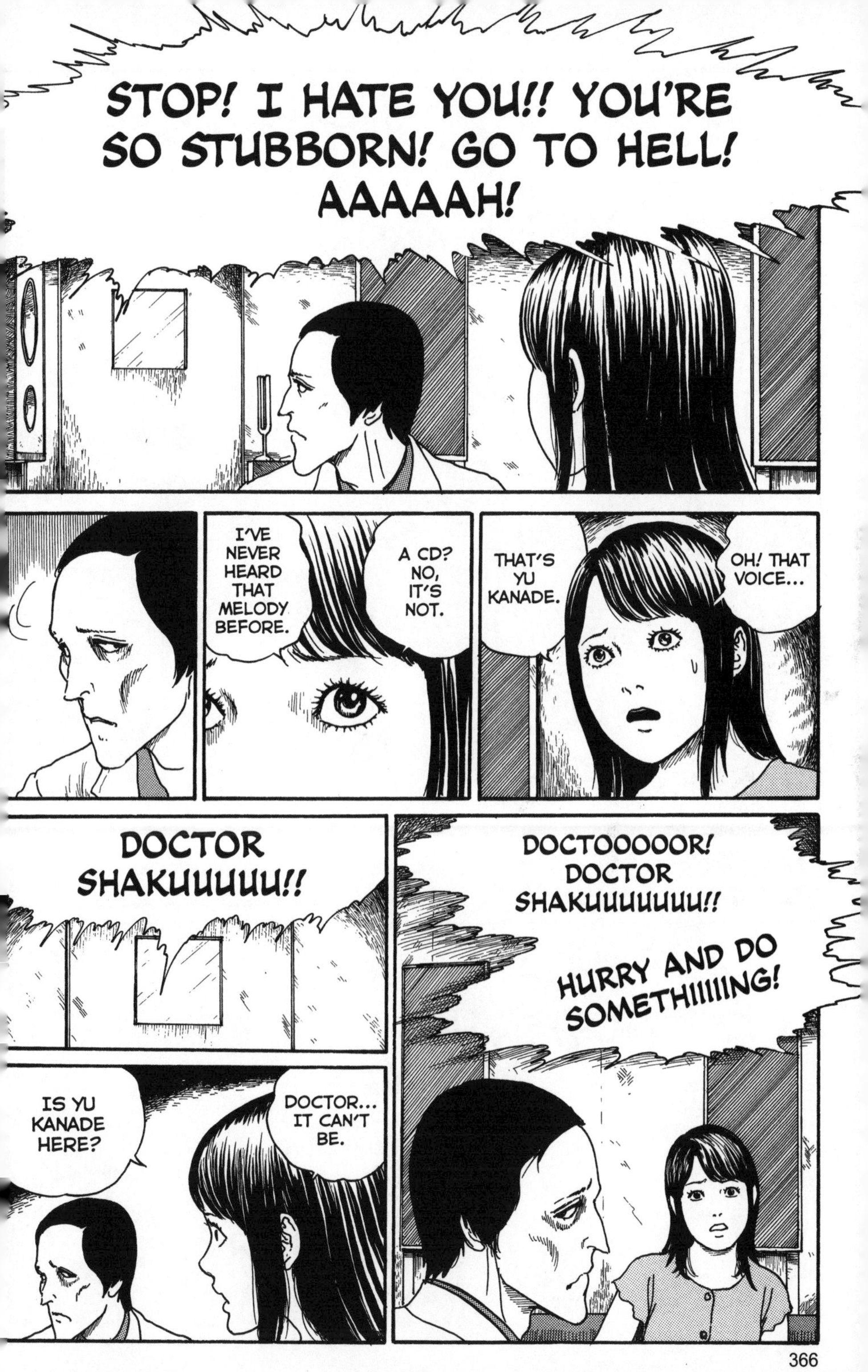
STOP! I HATE YOU!! YOU'RE SO STUBBORN! GO TO HELL! AAAAAH!
OH! THAT VOICE...
THAT'S YU KANADE.
A CD? NO, IT'S NOT.
I'VE NEVER HEARD THAT MELODY BEFORE.
DOCTOOOOOR! DOCTOR SHAKUUUUUUU!!
HURRY AND DO SOMETHIIIIING!
DOCTOR SHAKUUUUUU!!
DOCTOR... IT CAN'T BE.
IS YU KANADE HERE?

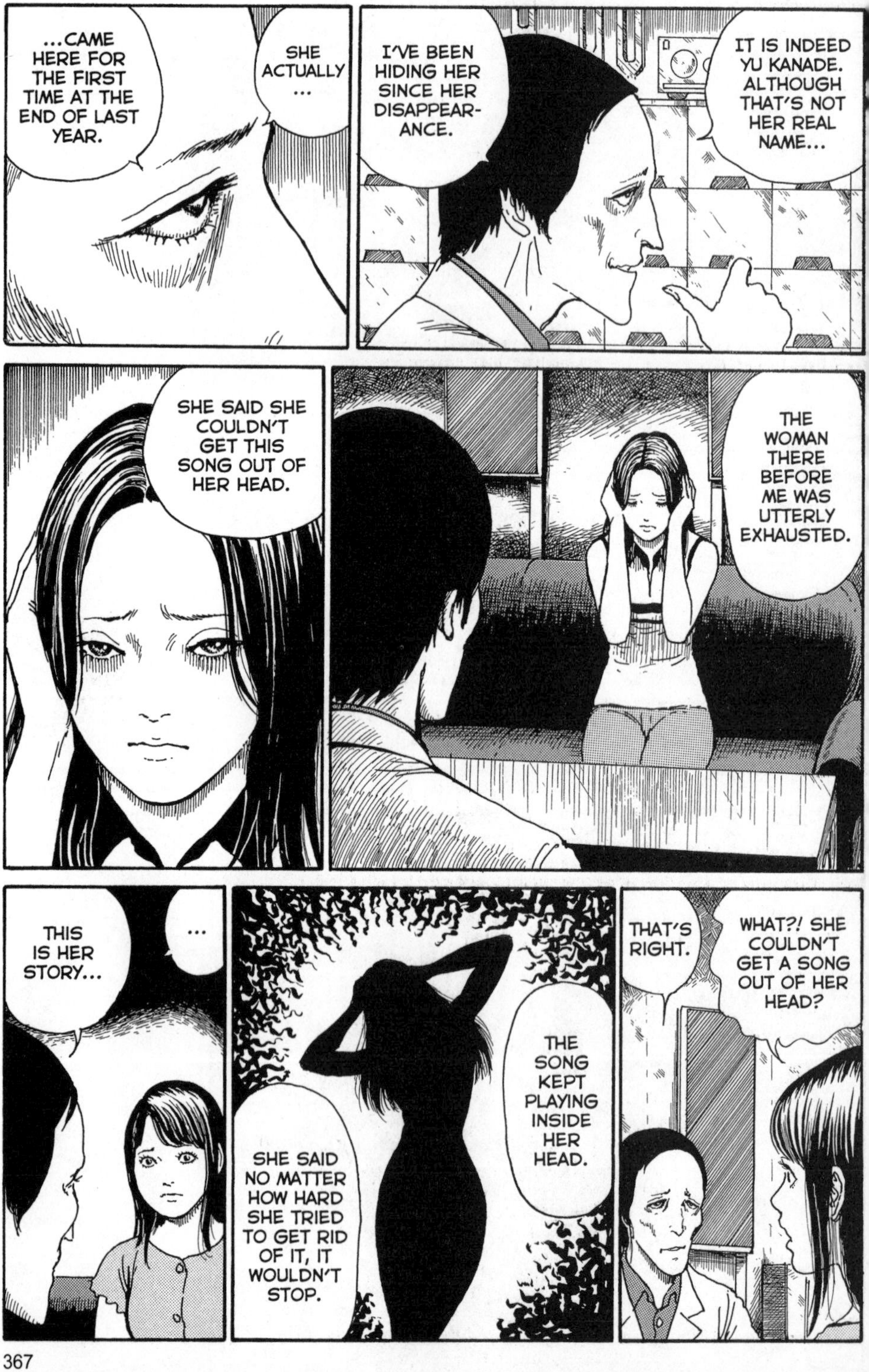
IT IS INDEED YU KANADE. ALTHOUGH THAT'S NOT HER REAL NAME...
I'VE BEEN HIDING HER SINCE HER DISAPPEARANCE.
SHE ACTUALLY ...
...CAME HERE FOR THE FIRST TIME AT THE END OF LAST YEAR.
THE WOMAN THERE BEFORE ME WAS UTTERLY EXHAUSTED.
SHE SAID SHE COULDN'T GET THIS SONG OUT OF HER HEAD.
WHAT?! SHE COULDN'T GET A SONG OUT OF HER HEAD?
THAT'S RIGHT.
THE SONG KEPT PLAYING INSIDE HER HEAD.
SHE SAID NO MATTER HOW HARD SHE TRIED TO GET RID OF IT, IT WOULDN'T STOP.
...
THIS IS HER STORY...

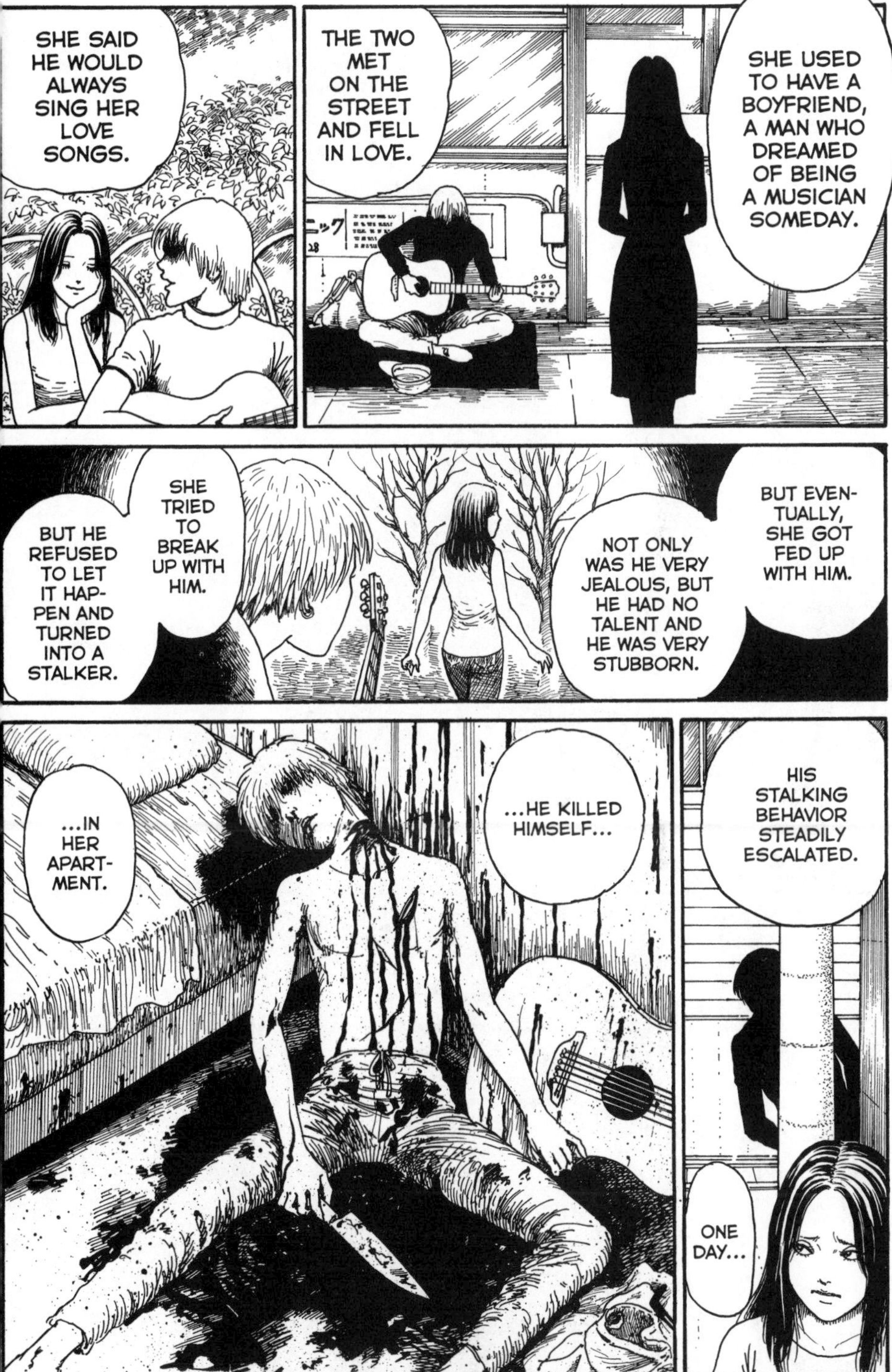
SHE USED TO HAVE A BOYFRIEND, A MAN WHO DREAMED OF BEING A MUSICIAN SOMEDAY.
THE TWO MET ON THE STREET AND FELL IN LOVE.
SHE SAID HE WOULD ALWAYS SING HER LOVE SONGS.
BUT EVENTUALLY, SHE GOT FED UP WITH HIM.
NOT ONLY WAS HE VERY JEALOUS, BUT HE HAD NO TALENT AND HE WAS VERY STUBBORN.
SHE TRIED TO BREAK UP WITH HIM.
BUT HE REFUSED TO LET IT HAPPEN AND TURNED INTO A STALKER.
HIS STALKING BEHAVIOR STEADILY ESCALATED.
ONE DAY...
...HE KILLED HIMSELF...
...IN HER APARTMENT.

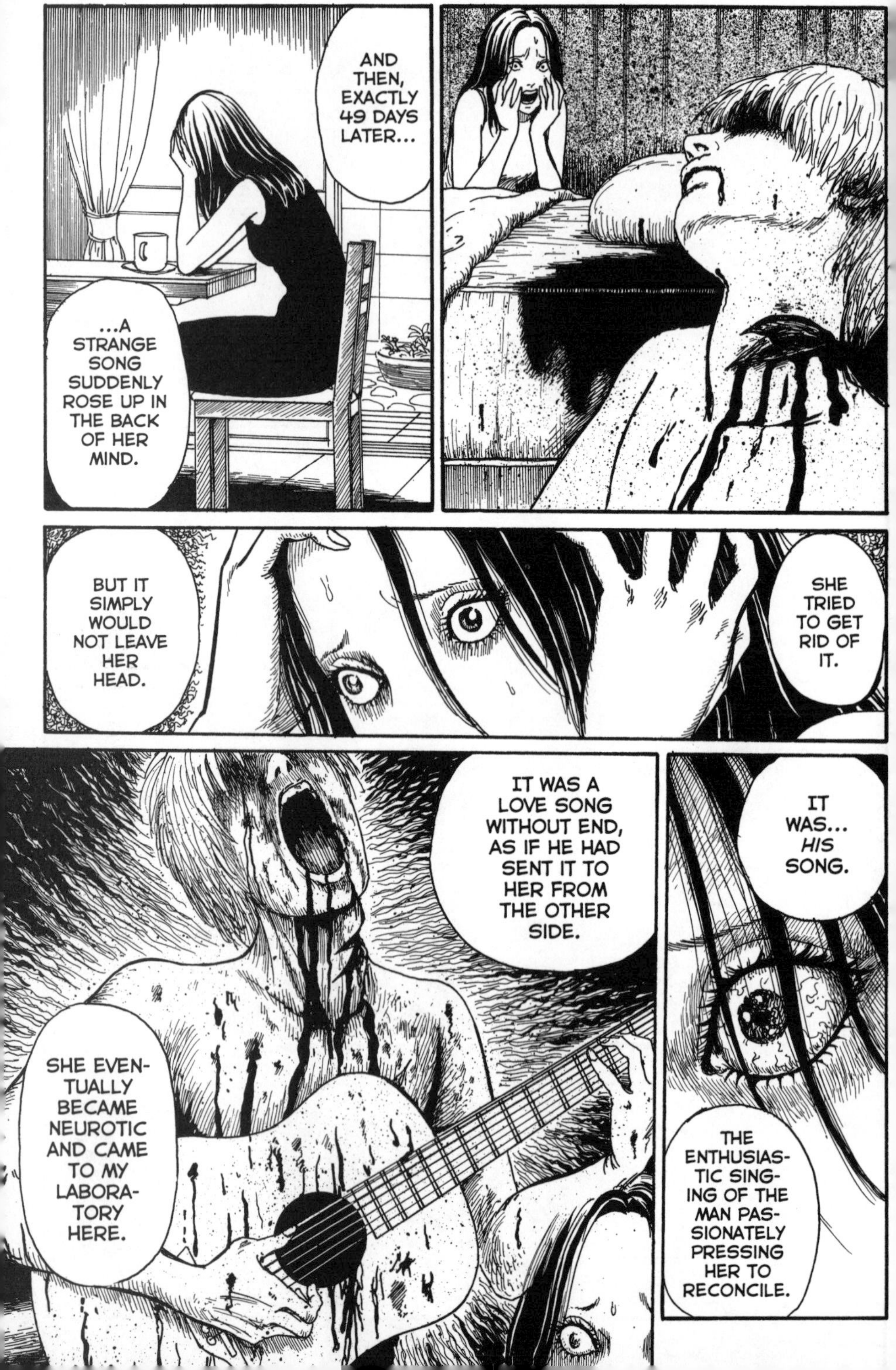
AND THEN, EXACTLY 49 DAYS LATER...
...A STRANGE SONG SUDDENLY ROSE UP IN THE BACK OF HER MIND.
SHE TRIED TO GET RID OF IT.
BUT IT SIMPLY WOULD NOT LEAVE HER HEAD.
IT WAS... *HIS* SONG.
THE ENTHUSIASTIC SINGING OF THE MAN PASSIONATELY PRESSING HER TO RECONCILE.
IT WAS A LOVE SONG WITHOUT END, AS IF HE HAD SENT IT TO HER FROM THE OTHER SIDE.
SHE EVENTUALLY BECAME NEUROTIC AND CAME TO MY LABORATORY HERE.

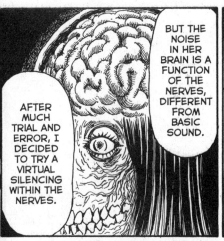

I'VE DEALT WITH A VARIETY OF NOISES.
AND I INDE-PENDENTLY DEVELOPED ACTIVE NOISE CONTROL TECHNOLOGY TO CANCEL OUT SOUND WITH SOUND TO GOOD RESULTS.
BUT THE NOISE IN HER BRAIN IS A FUNCTION OF THE NERVES, DIFFERENT FROM BASIC SOUND.
AFTER MUCH TRIAL AND ERROR, I DECIDED TO TRY A VIRTUAL SILENCING WITHIN THE NERVES.
CASES IN WHICH STIMULATION OF A CERTAIN PART OF THE BRAIN CAUSED THE PATIENT TO HEAR MUSIC PROVIDED A CLUE.
BY STIMULATING HER BRAIN WITH A SOUND AT THE EXACT OPPOSITE FREQUENCY OF THE SOUND PLAYING IN IT, I COULD KNOCK OUT THAT MAN'S SONG!
THE BIGGEST ISSUE WAS THAT THE SONG WAS PRODUCED BY HER NERVES AND DIDN'T ACTUALLY EXIST, MEANING I WOULD HAVE TO ANALYZE AND CORRECTLY READ THE SONG FROM HER BRAIN WAVES.
SIMPLY ANALYZING SOUND INSIDE THE BRAIN IS A NEXT-TO-IMPOSSIBLE UNDERTAKING.
AND SHE SAID THAT HIS SONG WAS COMPLEX AND CHANGED FROM MOMENT TO MOMENT.
SPECIAL MEASURES WOULD BE NEEDED TO HANDLE THIS COMPLEXITY AND THE CHANGES.

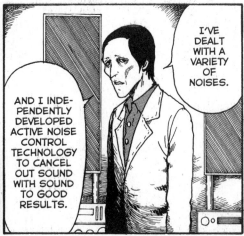

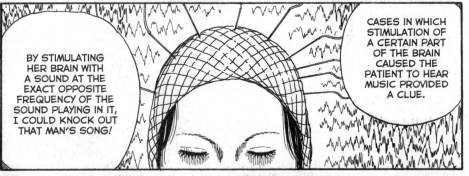

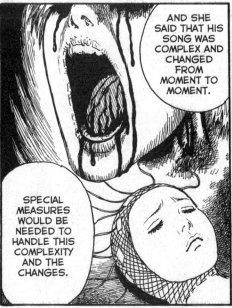

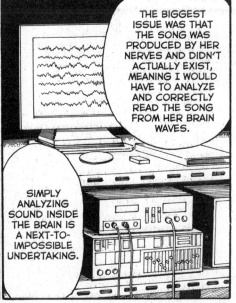

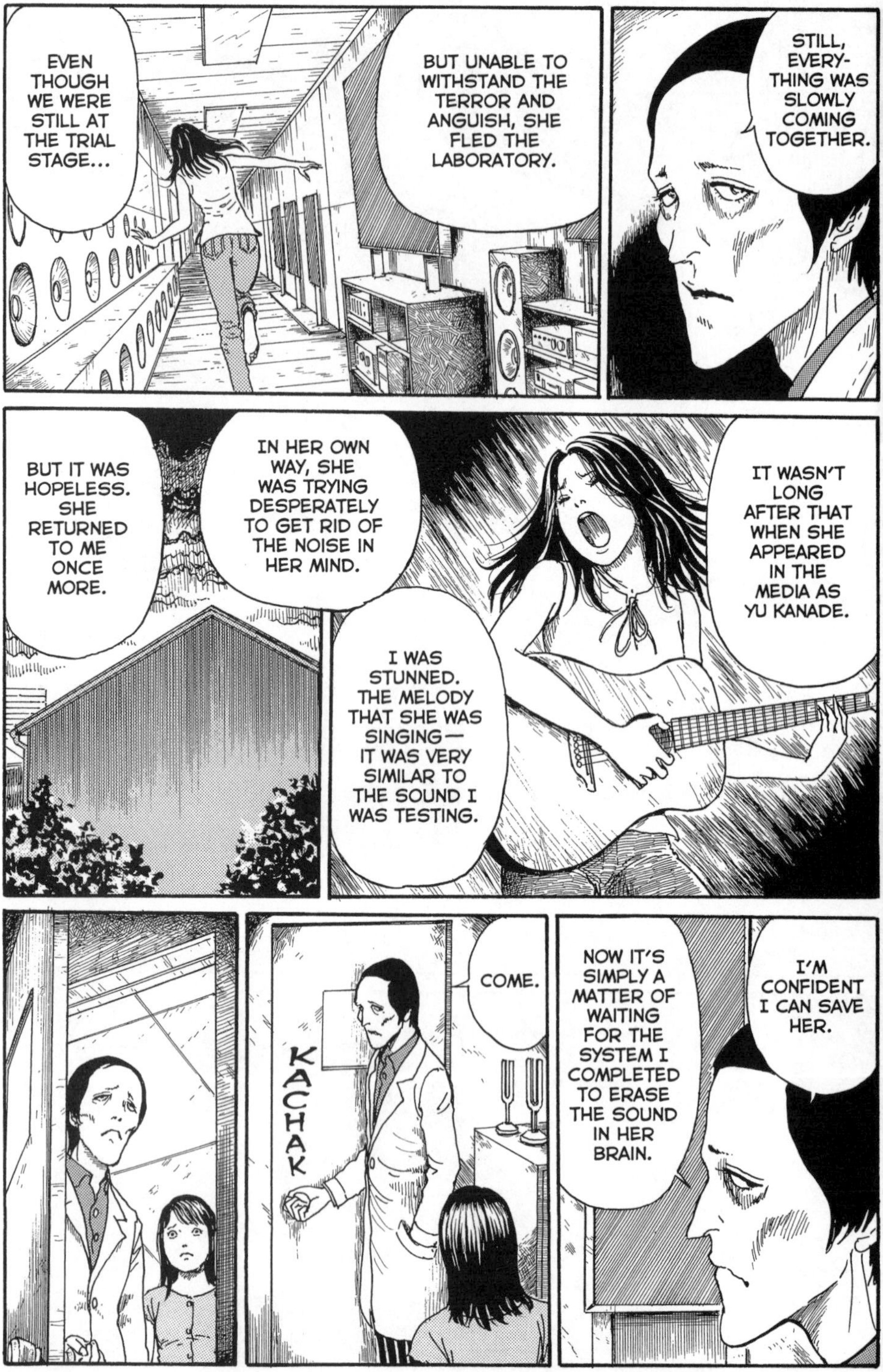
STILL, EVERY-THING WAS SLOWLY COMING TOGETHER.
EVEN THOUGH WE WERE STILL AT THE TRIAL STAGE...
BUT UNABLE TO WITHSTAND THE TERROR AND ANGUISH, SHE FLED THE LABORATORY.
IT WASN'T LONG AFTER THAT WHEN SHE APPEARED IN THE MEDIA AS YU KANADE.
I WAS STUNNED. THE MELODY THAT SHE WAS SINGING— IT WAS VERY SIMILAR TO THE SOUND I WAS TESTING.
IN HER OWN WAY, SHE WAS TRYING DESPERATELY TO GET RID OF THE NOISE IN HER MIND.
BUT IT WAS HOPELESS. SHE RETURNED TO ME ONCE MORE.
I'M CONFIDENT I CAN SAVE HER.
NOW IT'S SIMPLY A MATTER OF WAITING FOR THE SYSTEM I COMPLETED TO ERASE THE SOUND IN HER BRAIN.
COME.
KACHAK

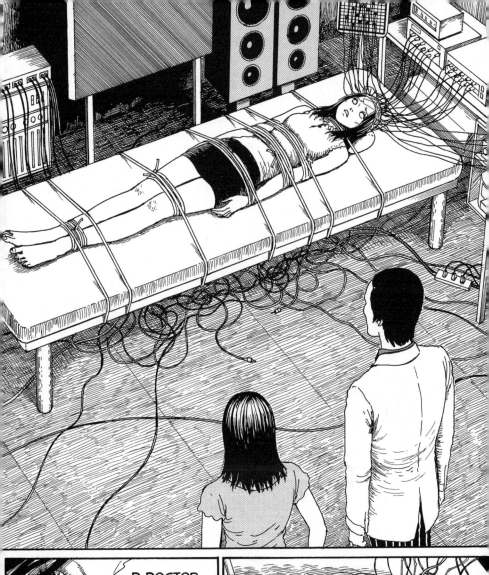

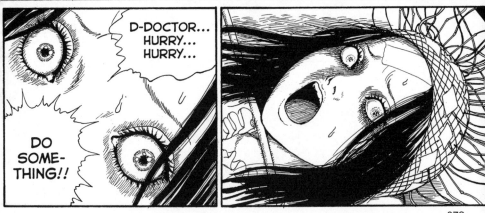

D-DOCTOR... HURRY... HURRY...

DO SOME-THING!!

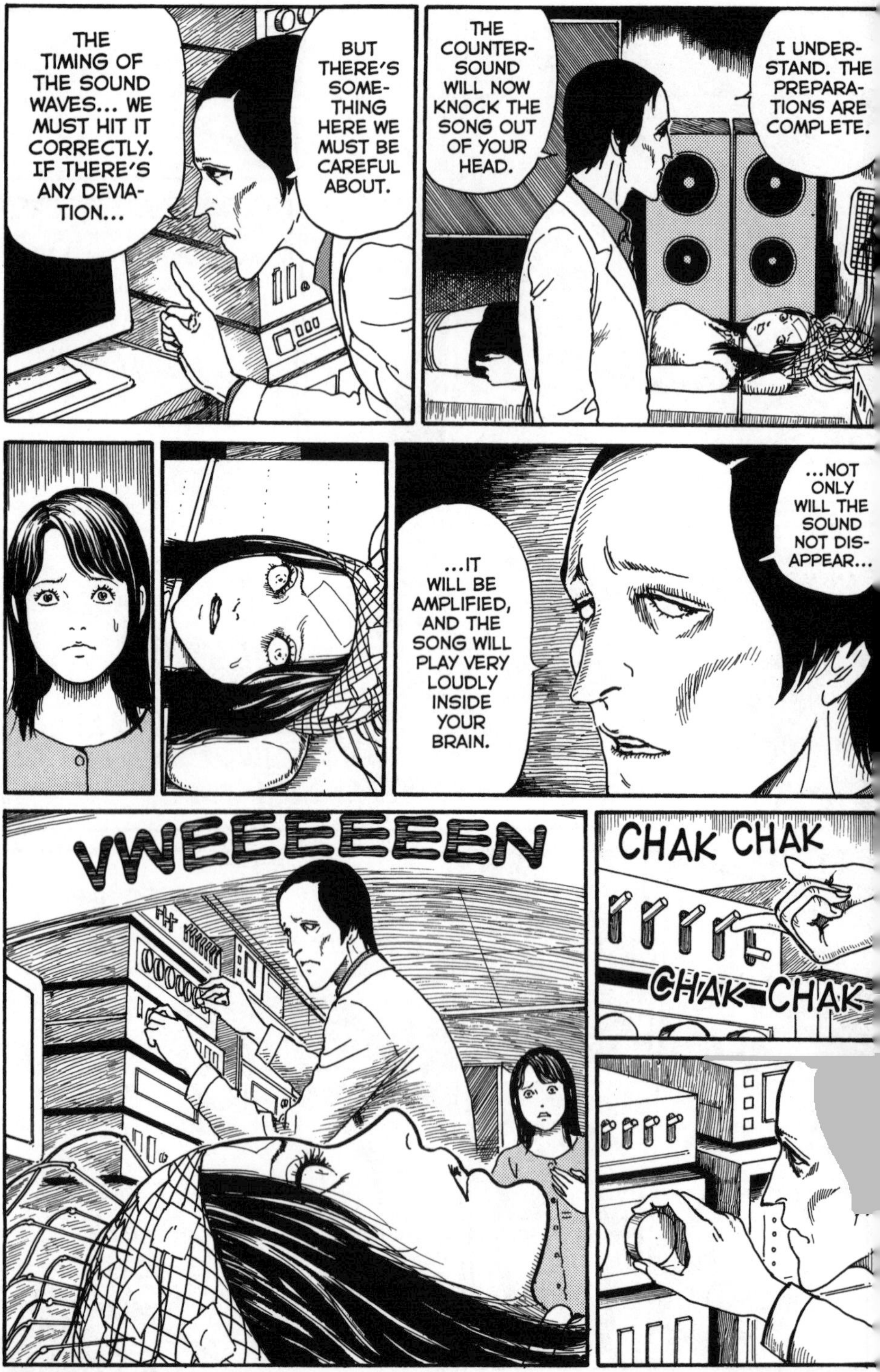
I UNDERSTAND. THE PREPARATIONS ARE COMPLETE.
THE COUNTER-SOUND WILL NOW KNOCK THE SONG OUT OF YOUR HEAD.
BUT THERE'S SOMETHING HERE WE MUST BE CAREFUL ABOUT.
THE TIMING OF THE SOUND WAVES... WE MUST HIT IT CORRECTLY. IF THERE'S ANY DEVIATION...
...NOT ONLY WILL THE SOUND NOT DISAPPEAR...
...IT WILL BE AMPLIFIED, AND THE SONG WILL PLAY VERY LOUDLY INSIDE YOUR BRAIN.
CHAK CHAK
CHAK CHAK
VWEEEEEEN

VWEEEEEE
VWEEEEEEE
D-DOCTOR...
DOCTOR!!
IT'S GONE!! ...IT DISAPPEARED!!
I CAN'T HEAR THE SONG ANYMORE!!
I'M SO HAPPY... DOCTOR, I'M FINALLY FREE!!
THANK YOU, DOCTOR!!
?!

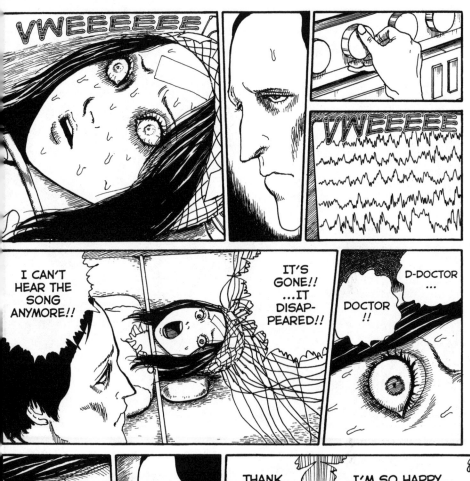

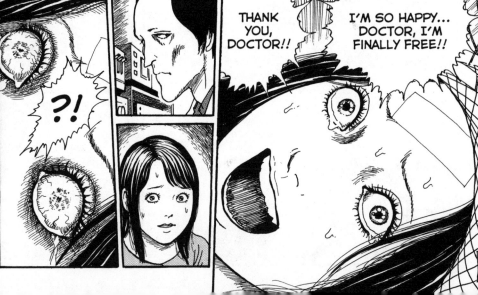

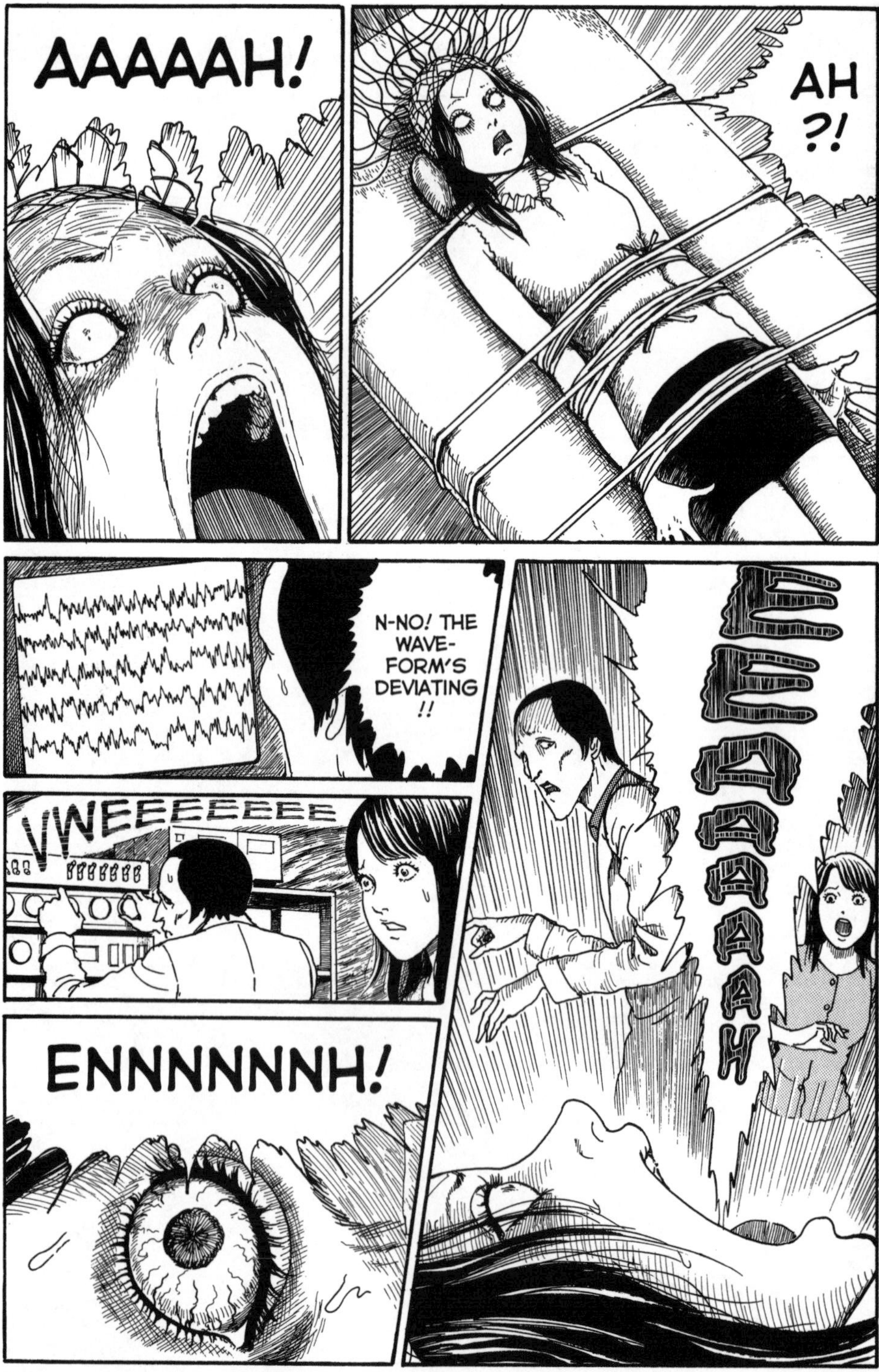
AH ?!
AAAAAH!
EEAAAAAH
N-NO! THE WAVE-FORM'S DEVIATING!!
VWEEEEEEEE
ENNNNNNH!

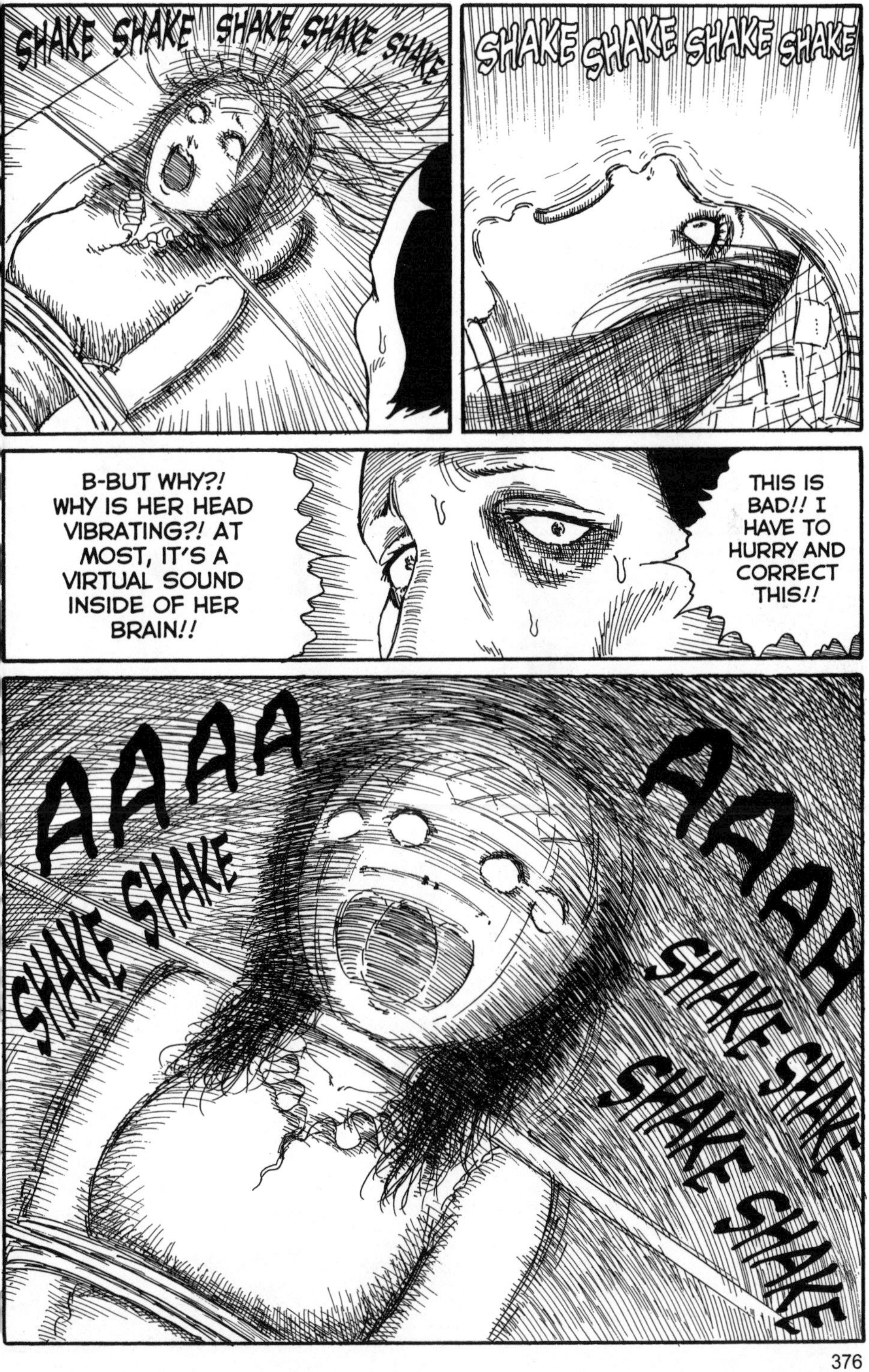
SHAKE SHAKE SHAKE SHAKE
SHAKE SHAKE SHAKE SHAKE SHAKE
THIS IS BAD!! I HAVE TO HURRY AND CORRECT THIS!!
B-BUT WHY?! WHY IS HER HEAD VIBRATING?! AT MOST, IT'S A VIRTUAL SOUND INSIDE OF HER BRAIN!!
AAAAH
SHAKE SHAKE SHAKE SHAKE
AAAA
SHAKE SHAKE

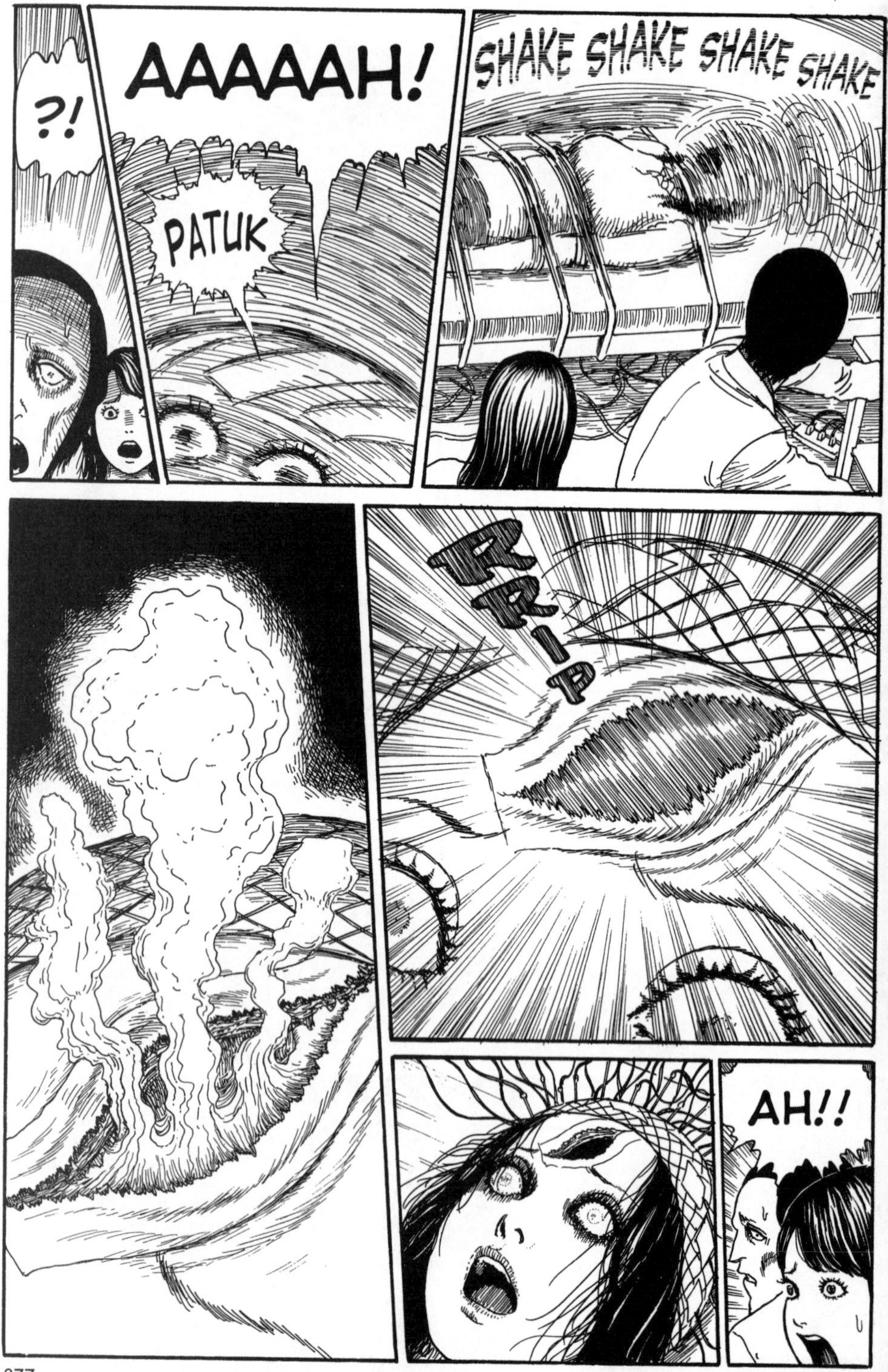
SHAKE SHAKE SHAKE SHAKE
AAAAAH!
PATUK
?!
RRIP
AH!!

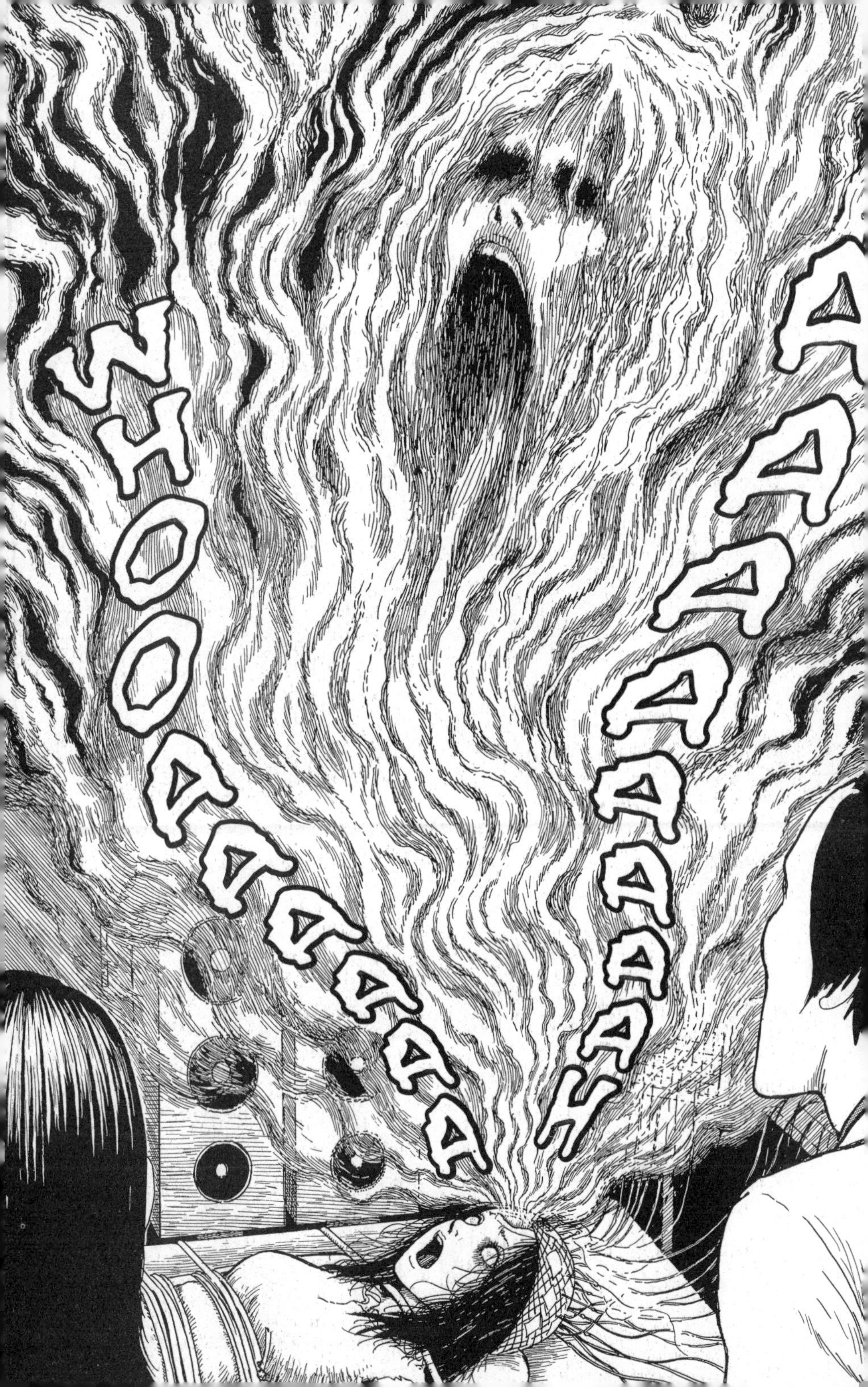
AAAAAAAAAH
WHOOAAAAAA

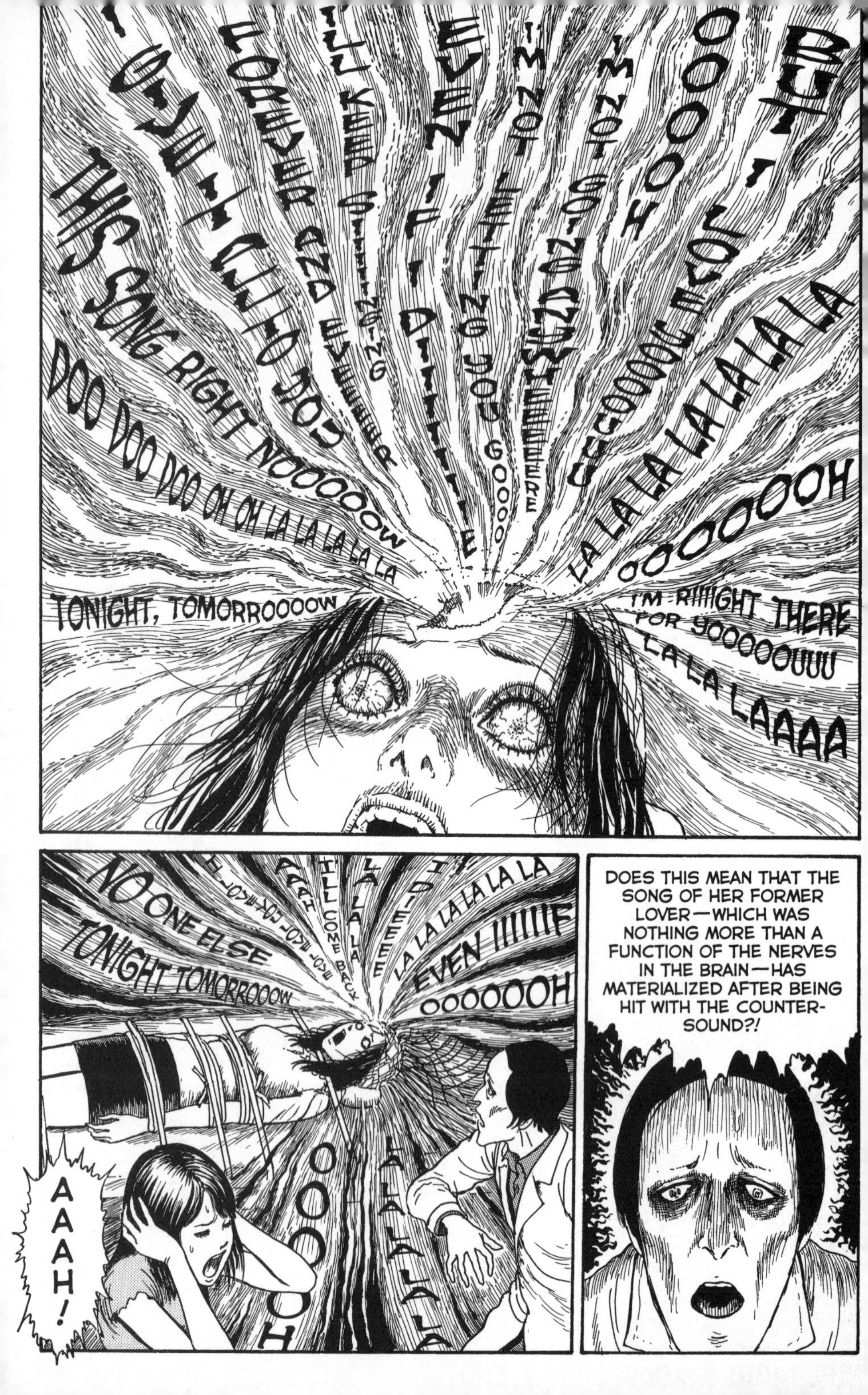
BUT I LOVE YOOOOOOUUU
OOOOOOOH
I'M NOT GOING ANYWHEEEERE
I'M NOT LETTING YOU GOOOO
EVEN IF I DIIIIIIIE
I'LL KEEP SIIIIIINGING
FOREVER AND EVEEEEER
THIS SONG RIGHT NOOOOOOW
DOO DOO DOO OH OH LA LA LA LA LA
LA LA LA LA LA LA LA LA LA
OOOOOOOOH
I'M RIIIGHT THERE FOR YOOOOOOUUU
LA LA LAAAA
TONIGHT, TOMORROOOOW
DOES THIS MEAN THAT THE SONG OF HER FORMER LOVER—WHICH WAS NOTHING MORE THAN A FUNCTION OF THE NERVES IN THE BRAIN—HAS MATERIALIZED AFTER BEING HIT WITH THE COUNTER-SOUND?!
I DIEEEE
LA LA LA LA LA LA LA
EVEN IIIIIIF
OOOOOOH
LA LA LA
I'LL COME BACK
AAAH
NO ONE ELSE
TONIGHT TOMORROOOW
OOOOOH
LA LA LA LA LA
AAAH!

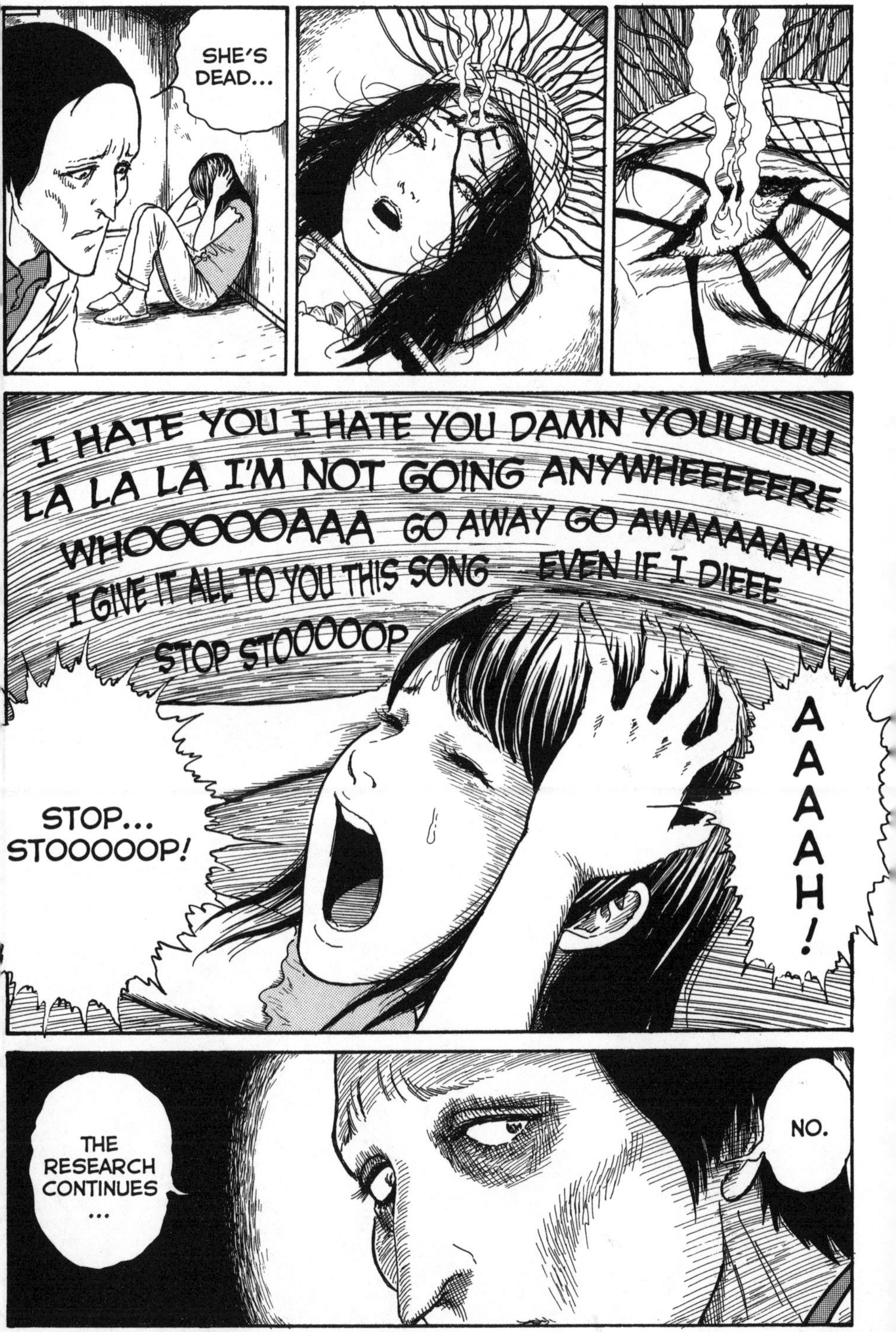
SHE'S DEAD...
I HATE YOU I HATE YOU DAMN YOUUUUU
LA LA LA I'M NOT GOING ANYWHEEEEEERE
WHOOOOOOAAA GO AWAY GO AWAAAAAAY
I GIVE IT ALL TO YOU THIS SONG EVEN IF I DIEEE
STOP STOOOOOP
AAAAH!
STOP... STOOOOOP!
NO.
THE RESEARCH CONTINUES ...

SPLENDID SHADOW SONG / END

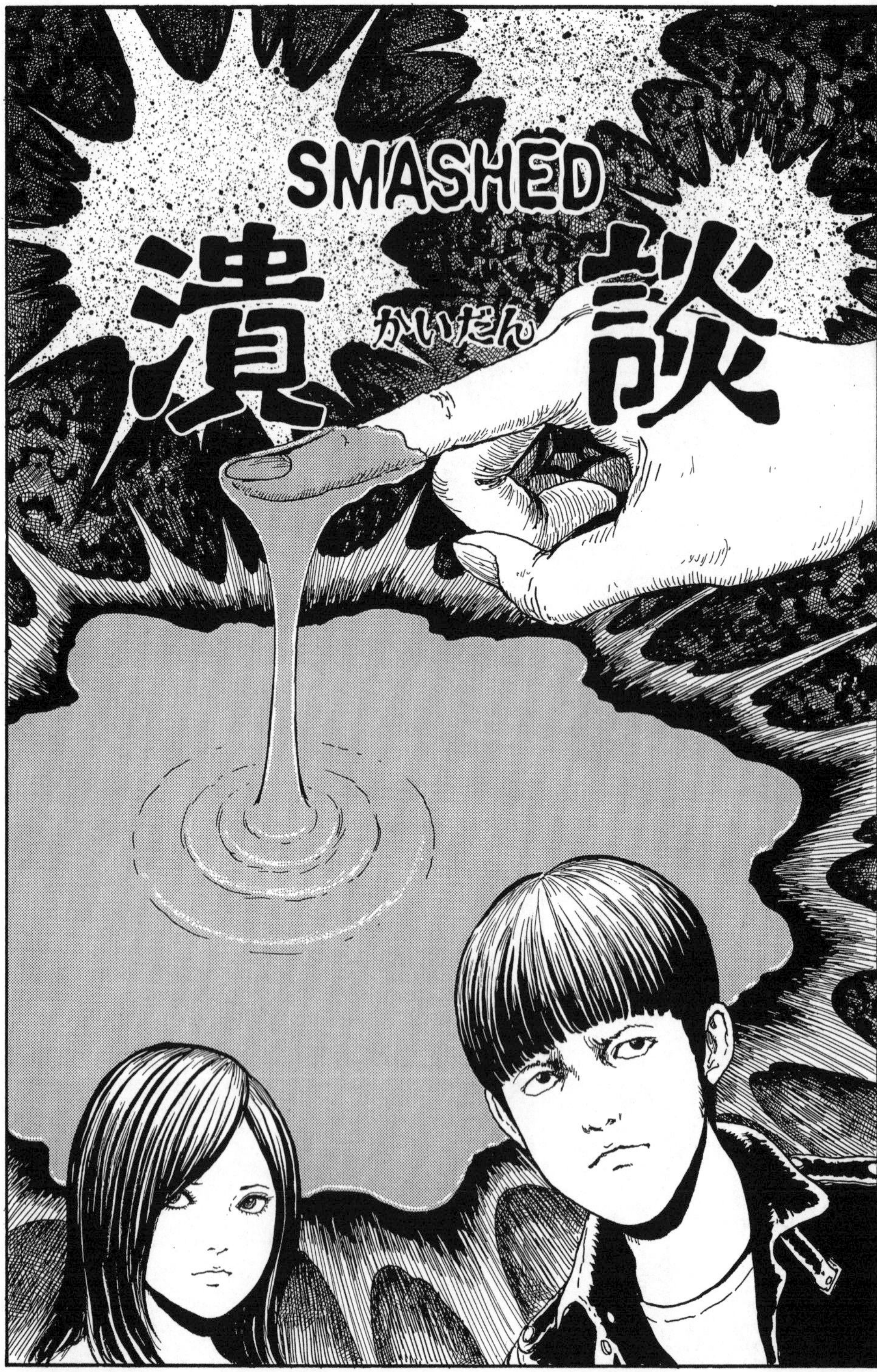
SMASHED
潰談
かいだん

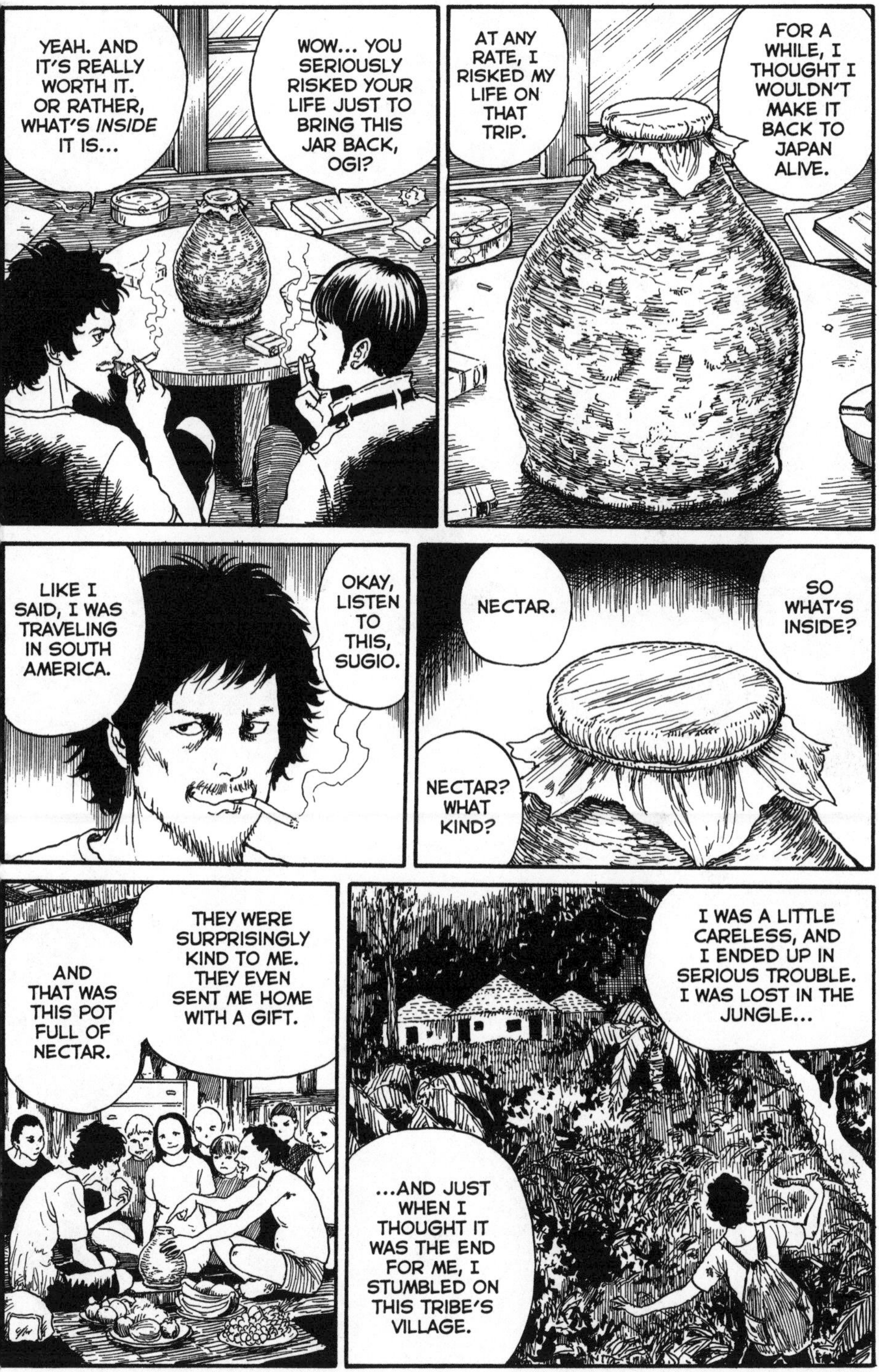
FOR A WHILE, I THOUGHT I WOULDN'T MAKE IT BACK TO JAPAN ALIVE.
AT ANY RATE, I RISKED MY LIFE ON THAT TRIP.
WOW... YOU SERIOUSLY RISKED YOUR LIFE JUST TO BRING THIS JAR BACK, OGI?
YEAH. AND IT'S REALLY WORTH IT. OR RATHER, WHAT'S *INSIDE* IT IS...
SO WHAT'S INSIDE?
NECTAR.
NECTAR? WHAT KIND?
OKAY, LISTEN TO THIS, SUGIO.
LIKE I SAID, I WAS TRAVELING IN SOUTH AMERICA.
I WAS A LITTLE CARELESS, AND I ENDED UP IN SERIOUS TROUBLE. I WAS LOST IN THE JUNGLE...
...AND JUST WHEN I THOUGHT IT WAS THE END FOR ME, I STUMBLED ON THIS TRIBE'S VILLAGE.
THEY WERE SURPRISINGLY KIND TO ME. THEY EVEN SENT ME HOME WITH A GIFT.
AND THAT WAS THIS POT FULL OF NECTAR.

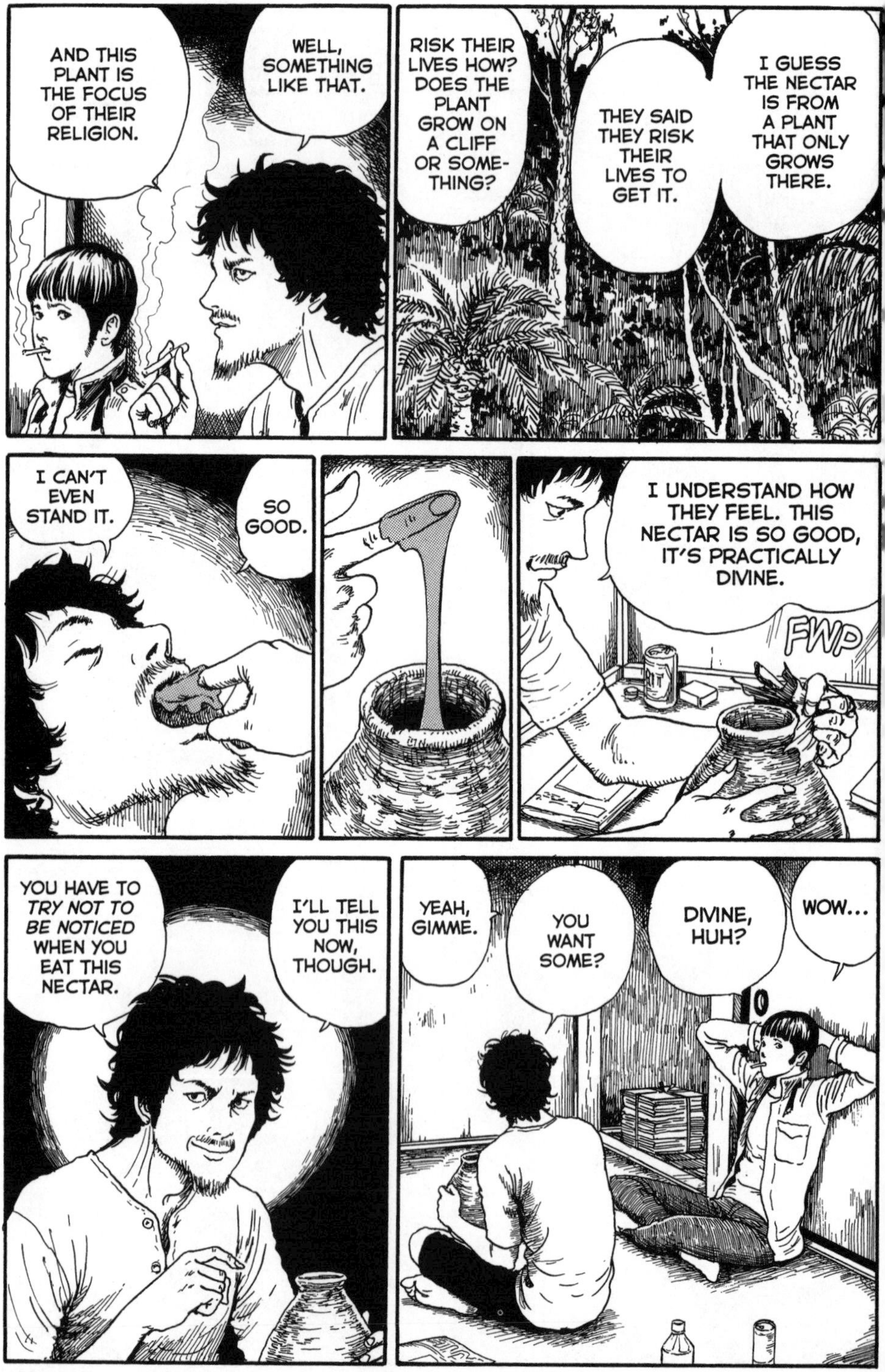
I GUESS THE NECTAR IS FROM A PLANT THAT ONLY GROWS THERE.
THEY SAID THEY RISK THEIR LIVES TO GET IT.
RISK THEIR LIVES HOW? DOES THE PLANT GROW ON A CLIFF OR SOME-THING?
WELL, SOMETHING LIKE THAT.
AND THIS PLANT IS THE FOCUS OF THEIR RELIGION.
I UNDERSTAND HOW THEY FEEL. THIS NECTAR IS SO GOOD, IT'S PRACTICALLY DIVINE.
FWP
SO GOOD.
I CAN'T EVEN STAND IT.
WOW...
DIVINE, HUH?
YOU WANT SOME?
YEAH, GIMME.
I'LL TELL YOU THIS NOW, THOUGH.
YOU HAVE TO *TRY NOT TO BE NOTICED* WHEN YOU EAT THIS NECTAR.

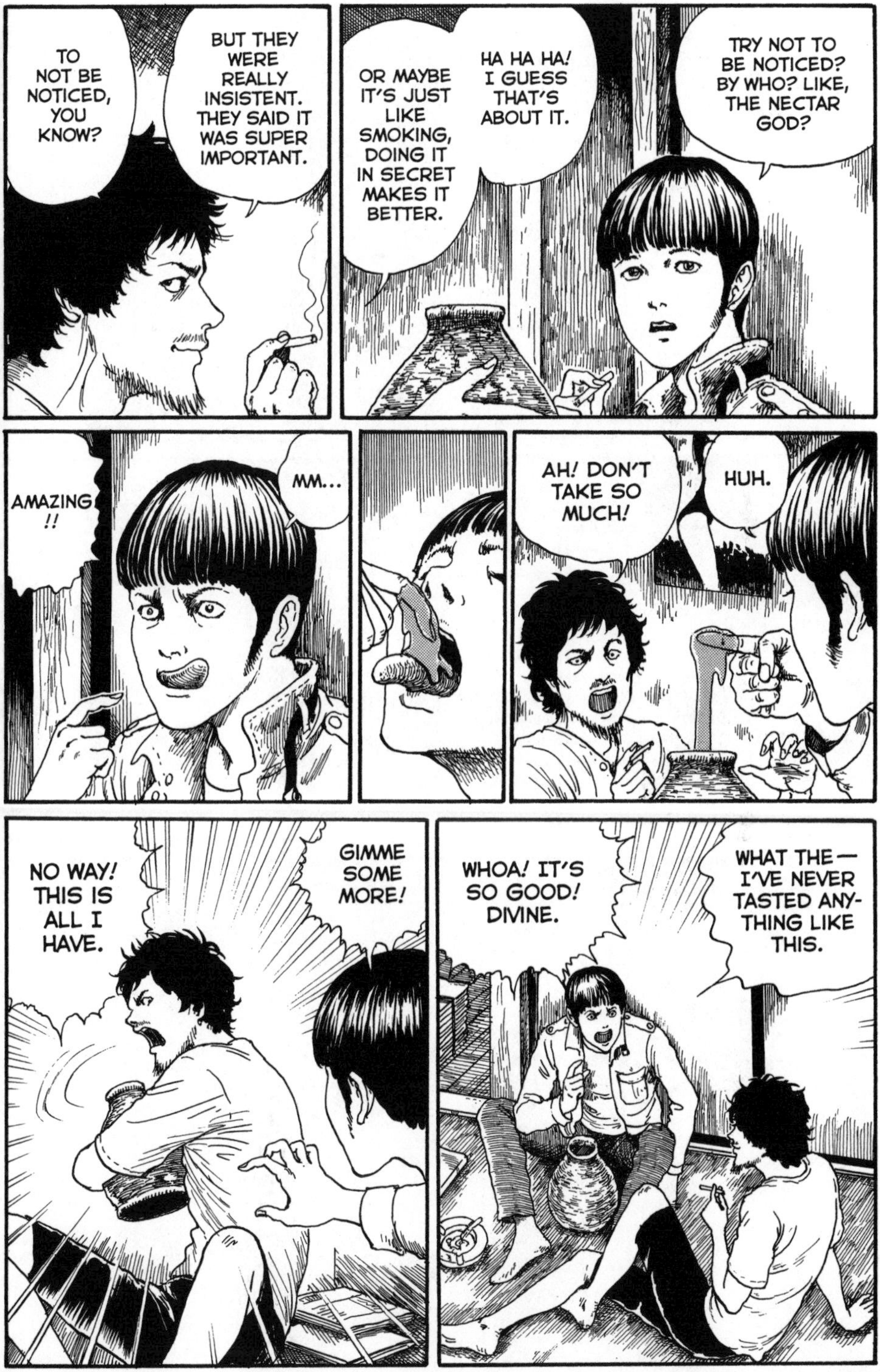
TRY NOT TO BE NOTICED? BY WHO? LIKE, THE NECTAR GOD?
HA HA HA! I GUESS THAT'S ABOUT IT.
OR MAYBE IT'S JUST LIKE SMOKING, DOING IT IN SECRET MAKES IT BETTER.
BUT THEY WERE REALLY INSISTENT. THEY SAID IT WAS SUPER IMPORTANT.
TO NOT BE NOTICED, YOU KNOW?
HUH.
AH! DON'T TAKE SO MUCH!
MM...
AMAZING!!
WHAT THE— I'VE NEVER TASTED ANY-THING LIKE THIS.
WHOA! IT'S SO GOOD! DIVINE.
GIMME SOME MORE!
NO WAY! THIS IS ALL I HAVE.

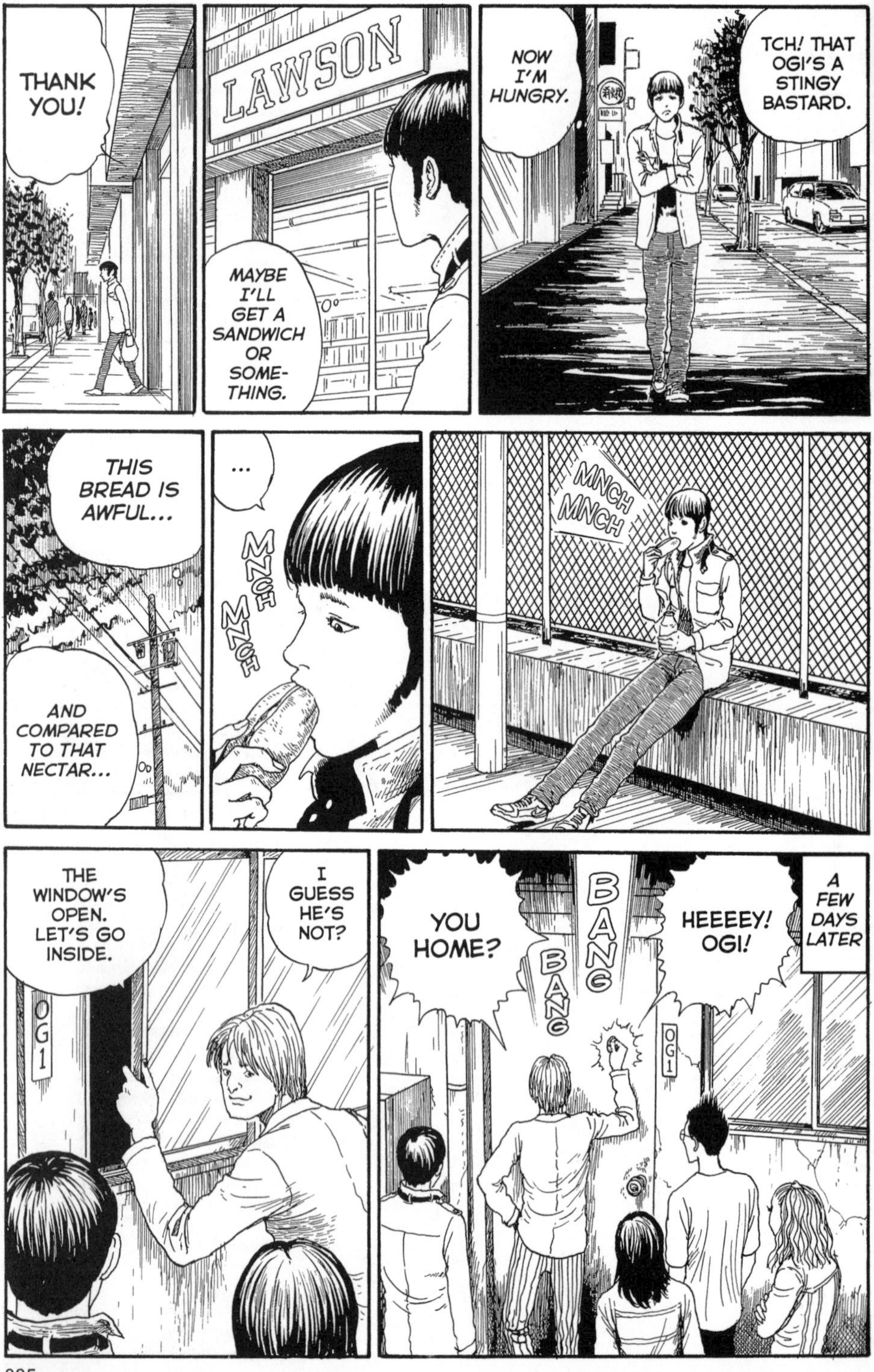
TCH! THAT OGI'S A STINGY BASTARD.
NOW I'M HUNGRY.
LAWSON
MAYBE I'LL GET A SANDWICH OR SOMETHING.
THANK YOU!
MNCH MNCH
...
MNCH MNCH
THIS BREAD IS AWFUL...
AND COMPARED TO THAT NECTAR...
A FEW DAYS LATER
HEEEEY! OGI!
BANG
BANG
YOU HOME?
OG1
I GUESS HE'S NOT?
THE WINDOW'S OPEN. LET'S GO INSIDE.
OG1

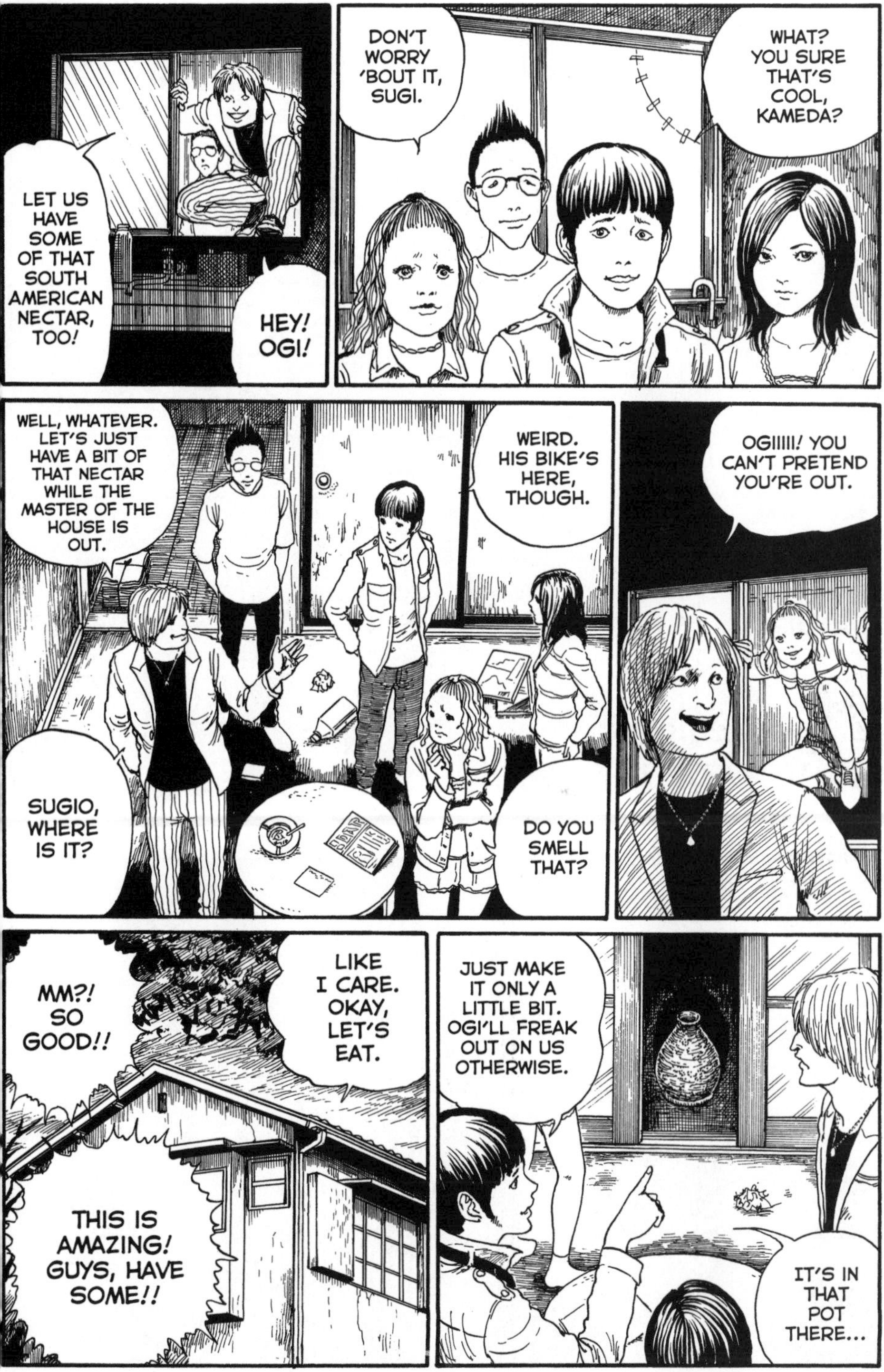
WHAT? YOU SURE THAT'S COOL, KAMEDA?
DON'T WORRY 'BOUT IT, SUGI.
HEY! OGI!
LET US HAVE SOME OF THAT SOUTH AMERICAN NECTAR, TOO!
OGIIIII! YOU CAN'T PRETEND YOU'RE OUT.
WEIRD. HIS BIKE'S HERE, THOUGH.
WELL, WHATEVER. LET'S JUST HAVE A BIT OF THAT NECTAR WHILE THE MASTER OF THE HOUSE IS OUT.
DO YOU SMELL THAT?
SUGIO, WHERE IS IT?
IT'S IN THAT POT THERE...
JUST MAKE IT ONLY A LITTLE BIT. OGI'LL FREAK OUT ON US OTHERWISE.
LIKE I CARE. OKAY, LET'S EAT.
MM?! SO GOOD!!
THIS IS AMAZING! GUYS, HAVE SOME!!

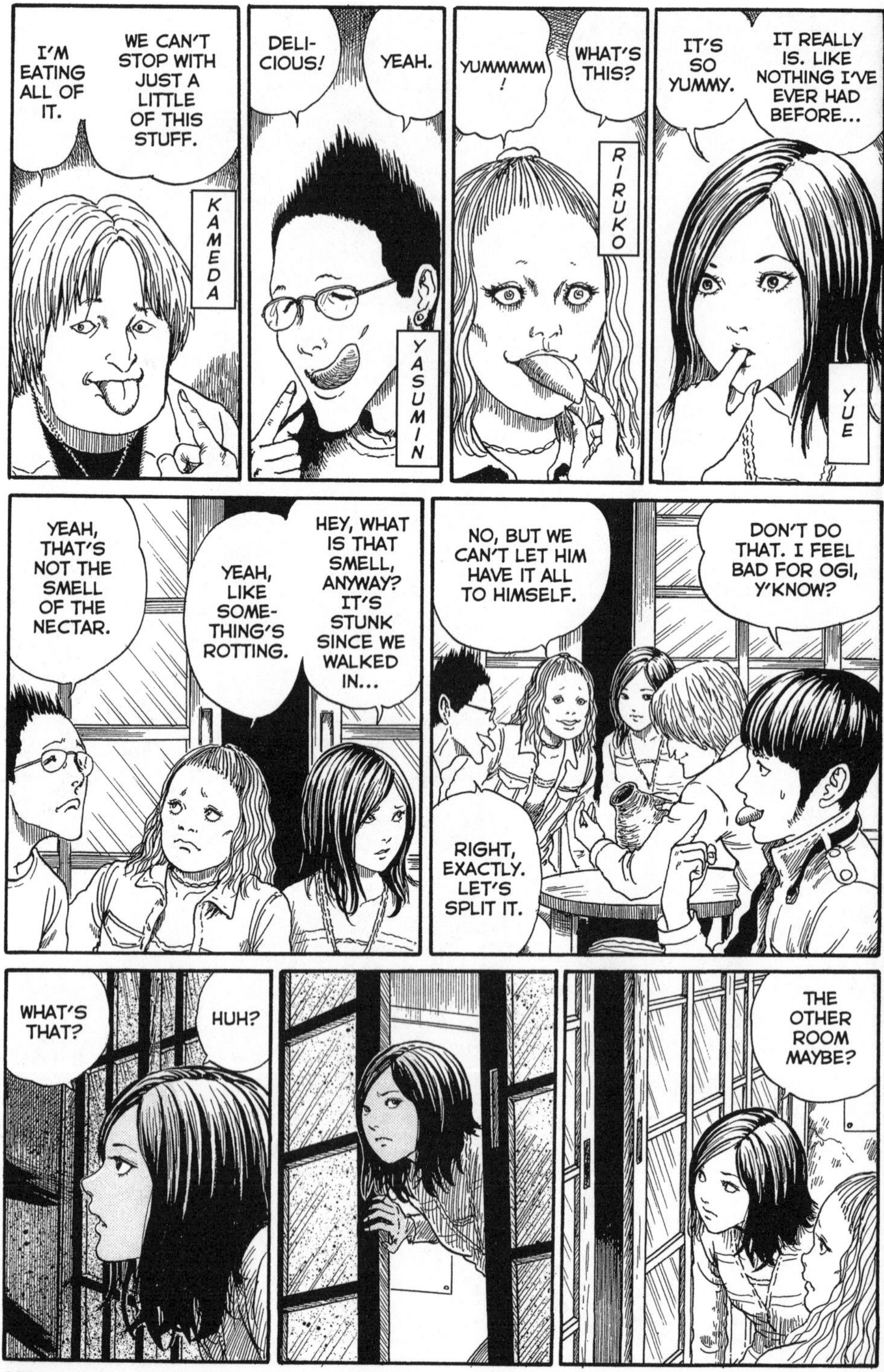
IT REALLY IS. LIKE NOTHING I'VE EVER HAD BEFORE...
IT'S SO YUMMY.
YUE
WHAT'S THIS?
YUMMMMM!
RIRUKO
YEAH.
DELICIOUS!
YASUMIN
WE CAN'T STOP WITH JUST A LITTLE OF THIS STUFF.
I'M EATING ALL OF IT.
KAMEDA
DON'T DO THAT. I FEEL BAD FOR OGI, Y'KNOW?
NO, BUT WE CAN'T LET HIM HAVE IT ALL TO HIMSELF.
RIGHT, EXACTLY. LET'S SPLIT IT.
HEY, WHAT IS THAT SMELL, ANYWAY? IT'S STUNK SINCE WE WALKED IN...
YEAH, LIKE SOMETHING'S ROTTING.
YEAH, THAT'S NOT THE SMELL OF THE NECTAR.
THE OTHER ROOM MAYBE?
HUH?
WHAT'S THAT?

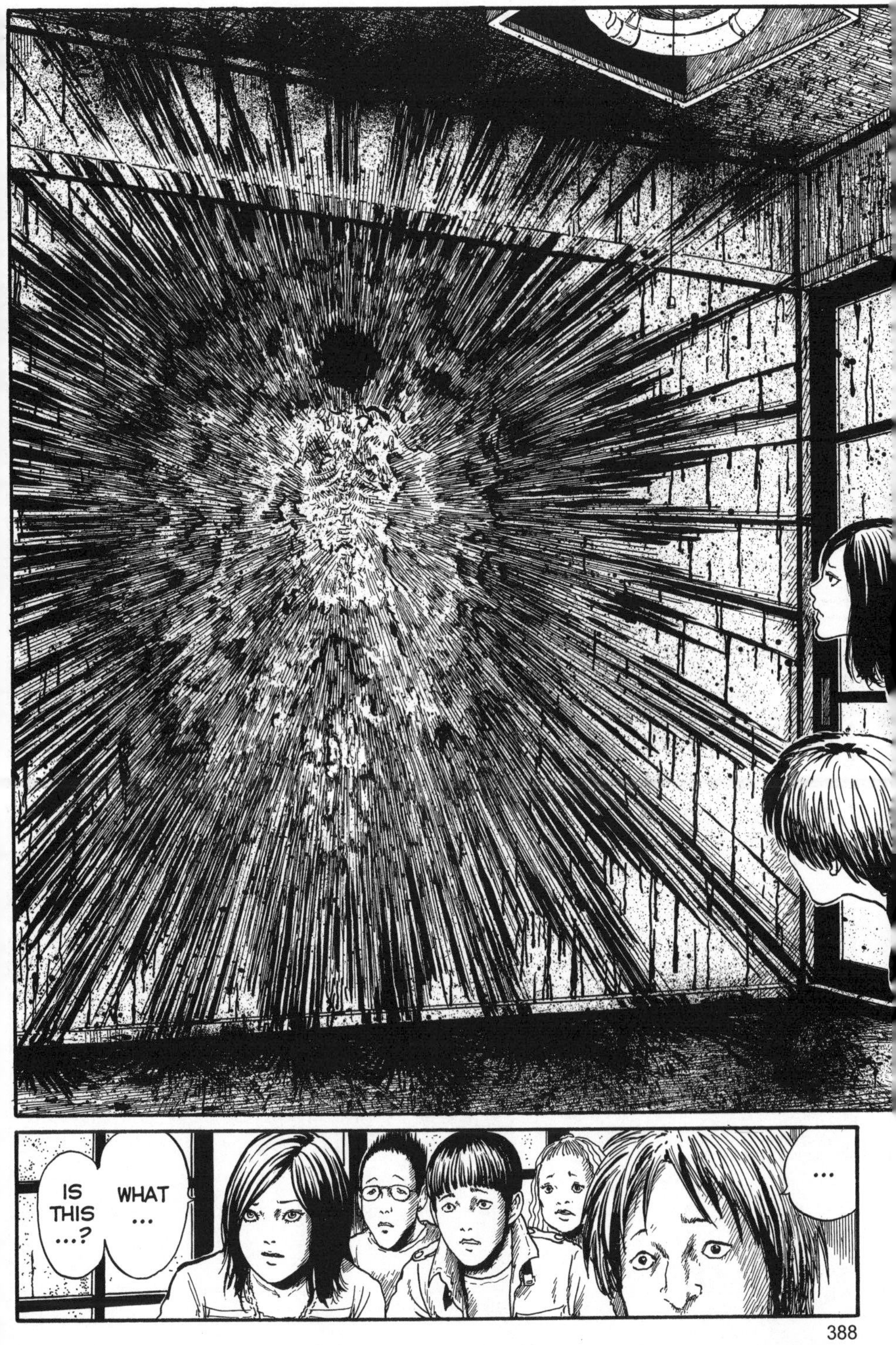
...
WHAT ...
IS THIS ...?

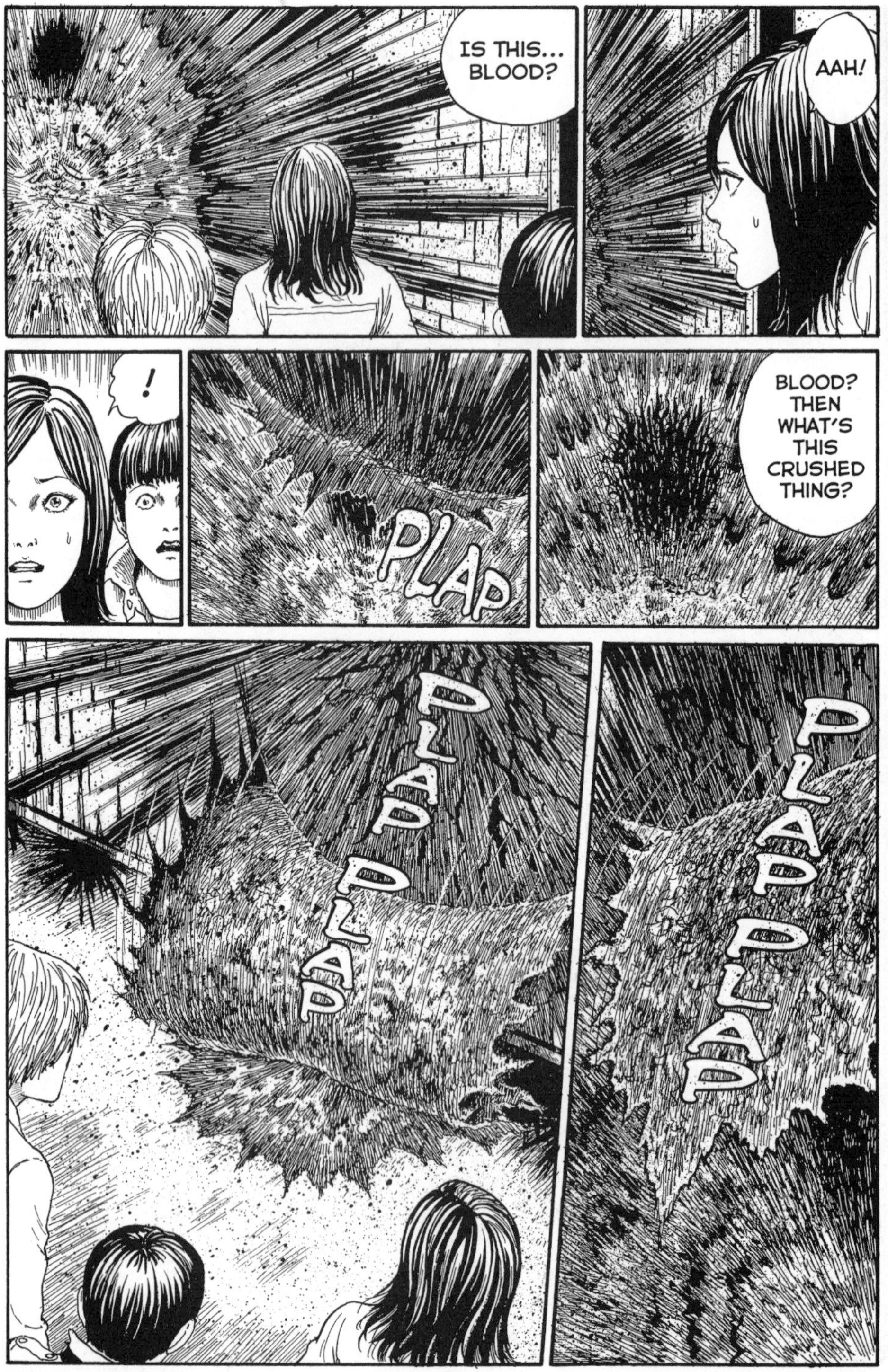
AAH!
IS THIS... BLOOD?
BLOOD? THEN WHAT'S THIS CRUSHED THING?
PLAP
!
PLAP PLAP
PLAP PLAP

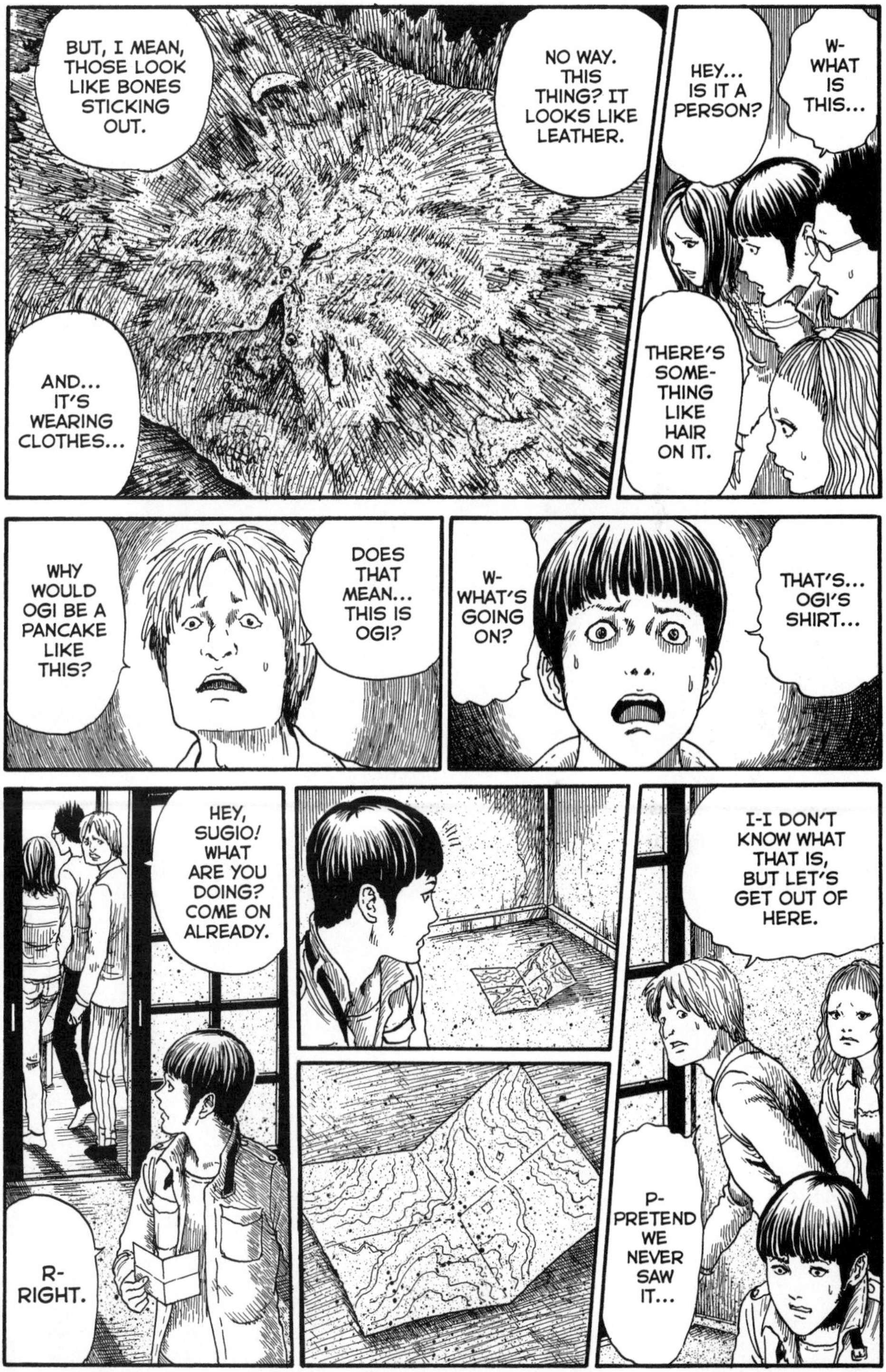
W- WHAT IS THIS...
HEY... IS IT A PERSON?
THERE'S SOMETHING LIKE HAIR ON IT.
NO WAY. THIS THING? IT LOOKS LIKE LEATHER.
BUT, I MEAN, THOSE LOOK LIKE BONES STICKING OUT.
AND... IT'S WEARING CLOTHES...
THAT'S... OGI'S SHIRT...
W- WHAT'S GOING ON?
DOES THAT MEAN... THIS IS OGI?
WHY WOULD OGI BE A PANCAKE LIKE THIS?
I-I DON'T KNOW WHAT THAT IS, BUT LET'S GET OUT OF HERE.
P- PRETEND WE NEVER SAW IT...
HEY, SUGIO! WHAT ARE YOU DOING? COME ON ALREADY.
R- RIGHT.

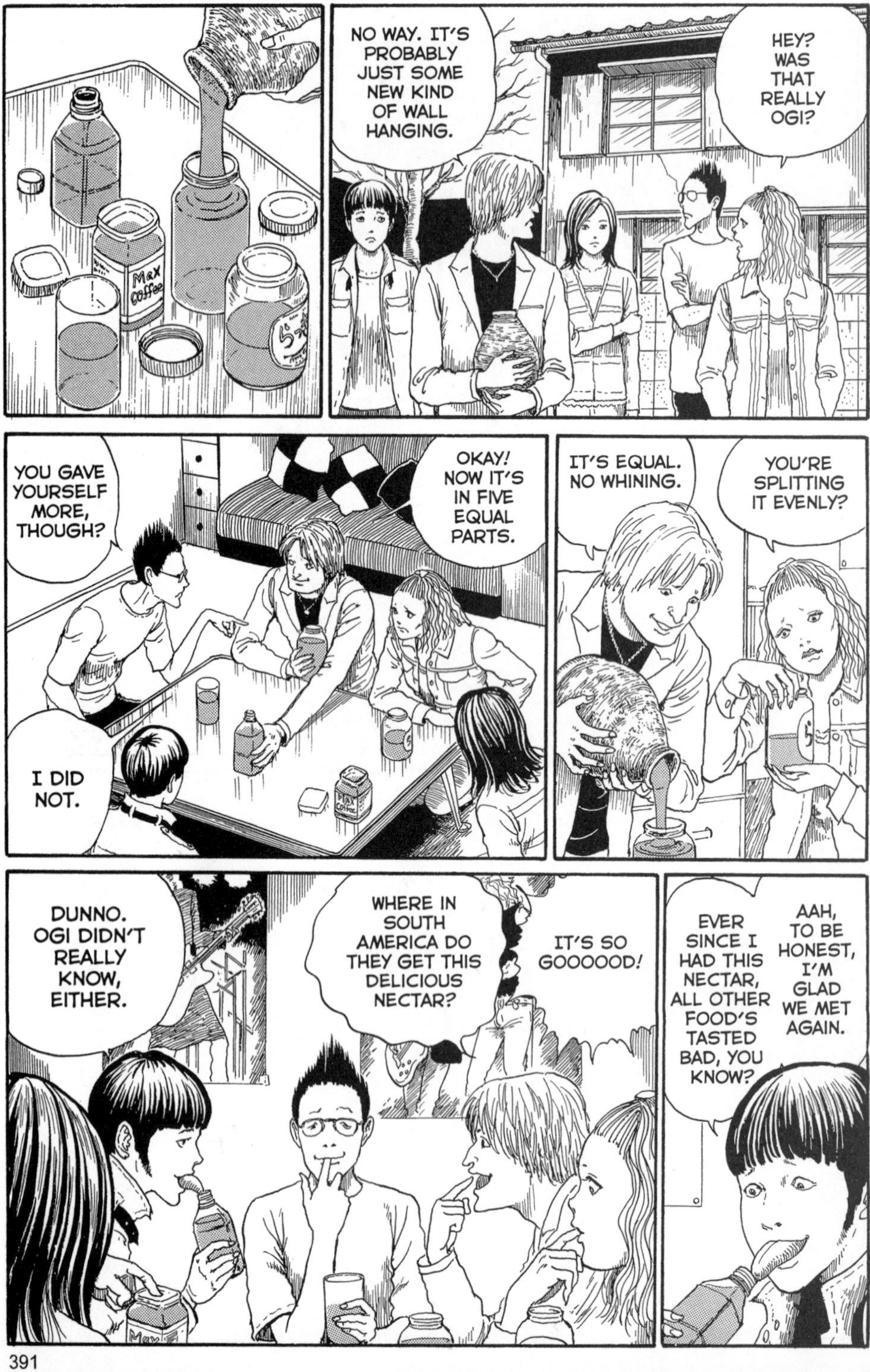
HEY? WAS THAT REALLY OGI?
NO WAY. IT'S PROBABLY JUST SOME NEW KIND OF WALL HANGING.
Max Coffee
YOU'RE SPLITTING IT EVENLY?
IT'S EQUAL. NO WHINING.
OKAY! NOW IT'S IN FIVE EQUAL PARTS.
YOU GAVE YOURSELF MORE, THOUGH?
I DID NOT.
AAH, TO BE HONEST, I'M GLAD WE MET AGAIN.
EVER SINCE I HAD THIS NECTAR, ALL OTHER FOOD'S TASTED BAD, YOU KNOW?
IT'S SO GOOOOOD!
WHERE IN SOUTH AMERICA DO THEY GET THIS DELICIOUS NECTAR?
DUNNO. OGI DIDN'T REALLY KNOW, EITHER.

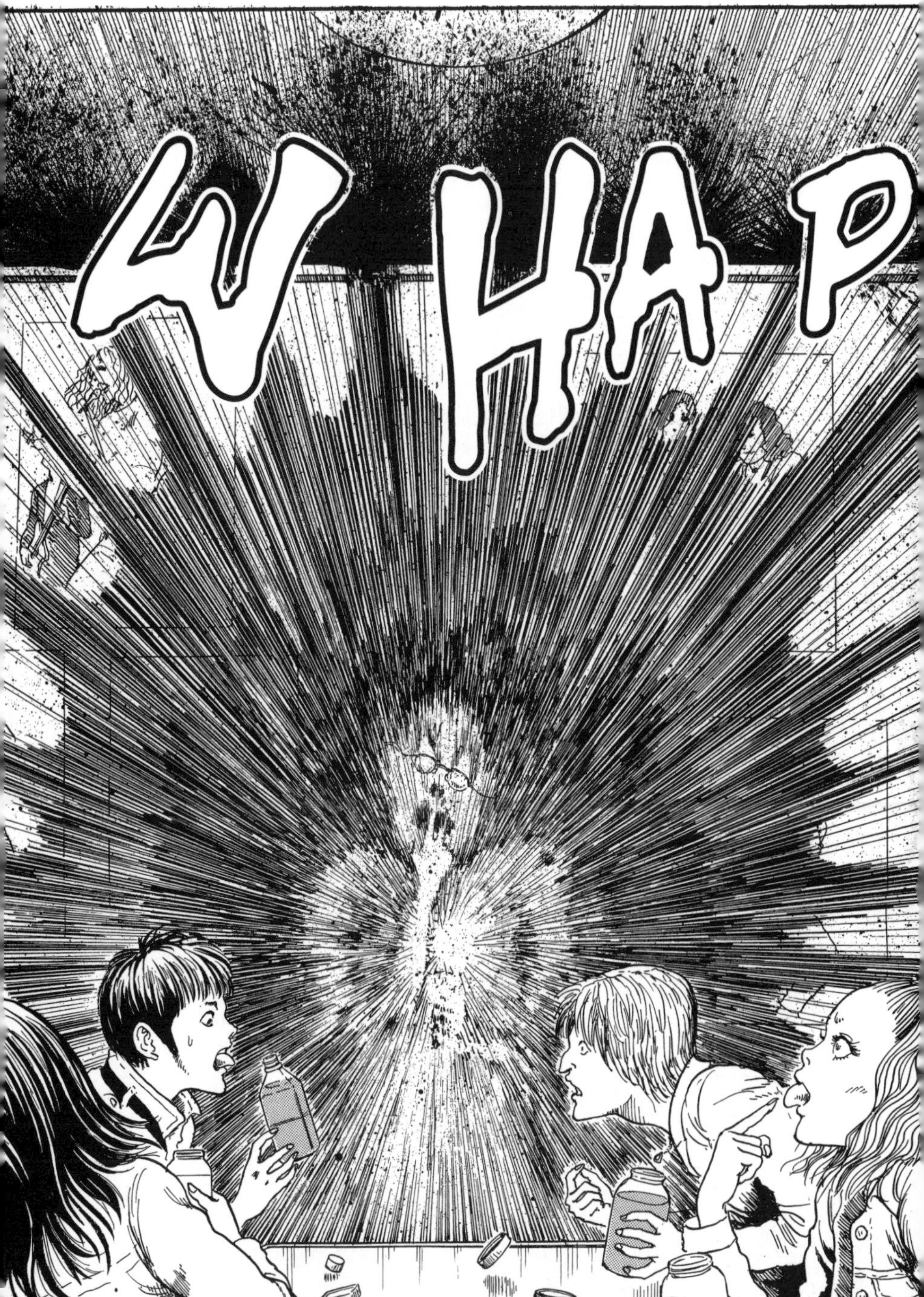
WHAP

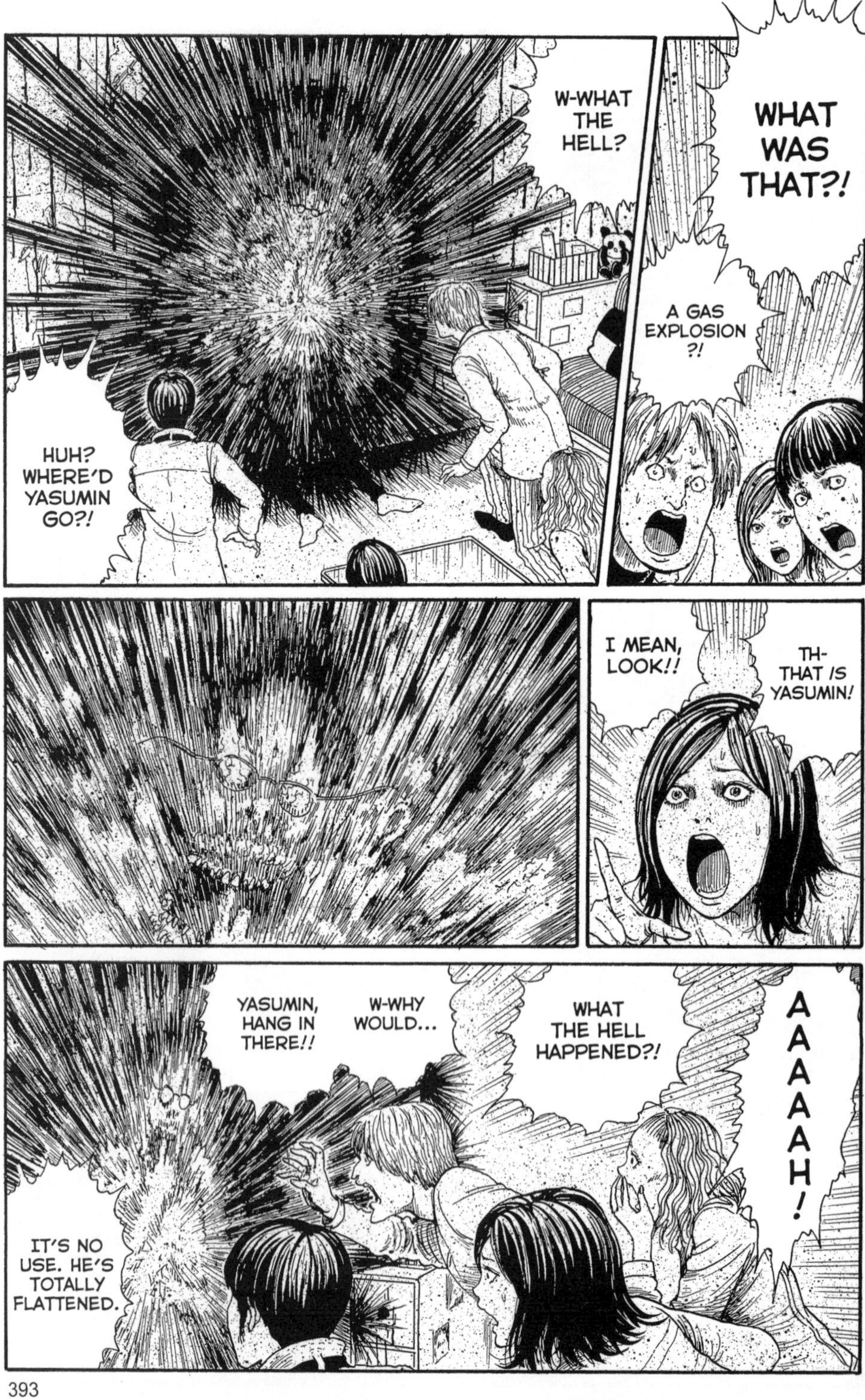
WHAT WAS THAT?!
A GAS EXPLOSION ?!
W-WHAT THE HELL?
HUH? WHERE'D YASUMIN GO?!
TH- THAT *IS* YASUMIN!
I MEAN, LOOK!!
AAAAAAH!
WHAT THE HELL HAPPENED?!
W-WHY WOULD...
YASUMIN, HANG IN THERE!!
IT'S NO USE. HE'S TOTALLY FLATTENED.

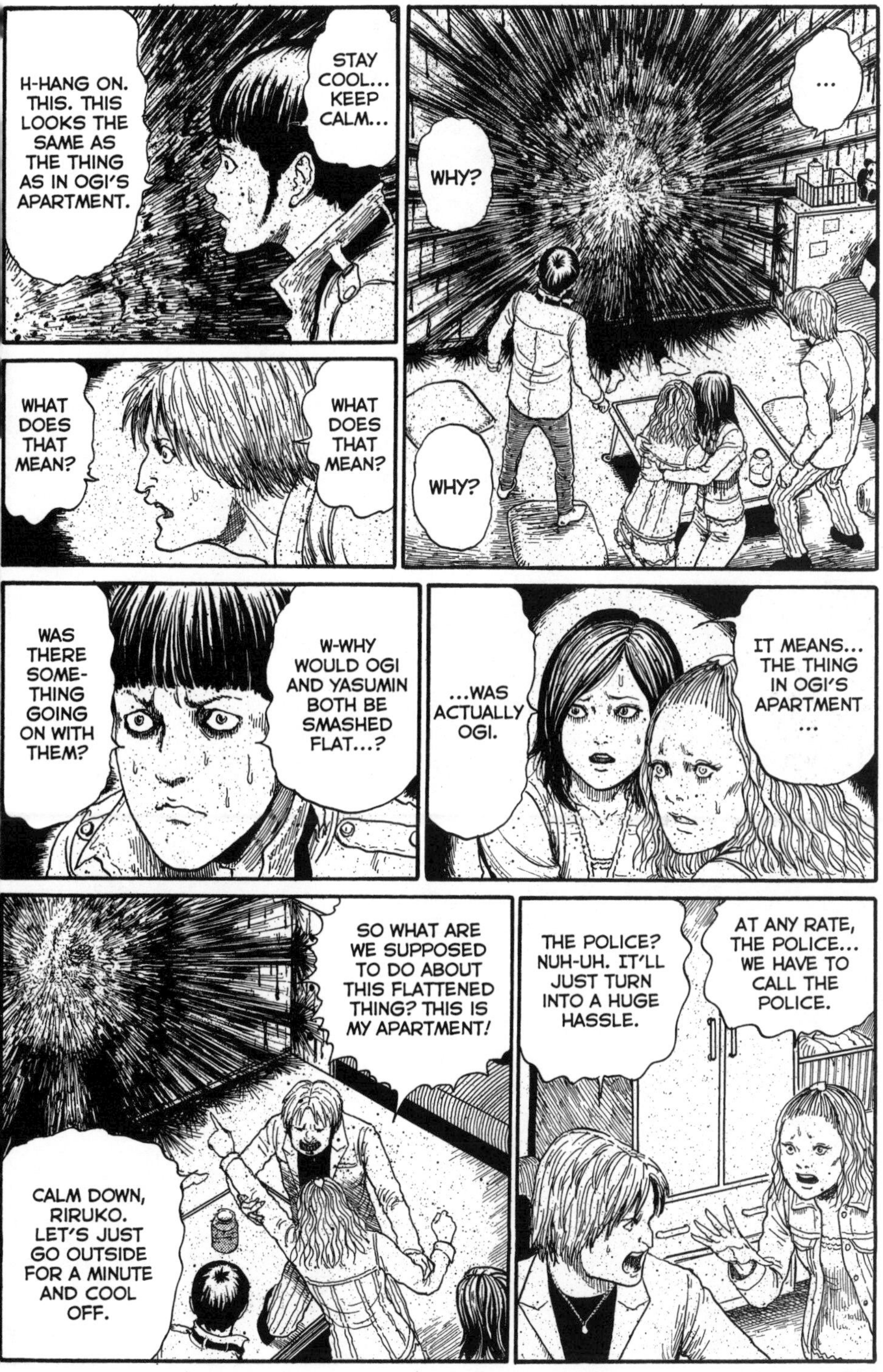
...
WHY?
WHY?
STAY COOL... KEEP CALM...
H-HANG ON. THIS. THIS LOOKS THE SAME AS THE THING AS IN OGI'S APARTMENT.
WHAT DOES THAT MEAN?
WHAT DOES THAT MEAN?
IT MEANS... THE THING IN OGI'S APARTMENT ...
...WAS ACTUALLY OGI.
W-WHY WOULD OGI AND YASUMIN BOTH BE SMASHED FLAT...?
WAS THERE SOME-THING GOING ON WITH THEM?
AT ANY RATE, THE POLICE... WE HAVE TO CALL THE POLICE.
THE POLICE? NUH-UH. IT'LL JUST TURN INTO A HUGE HASSLE.
SO WHAT ARE WE SUPPOSED TO DO ABOUT THIS FLATTENED THING? THIS IS MY APARTMENT!
CALM DOWN, RIRUKO. LET'S JUST GO OUTSIDE FOR A MINUTE AND COOL OFF.

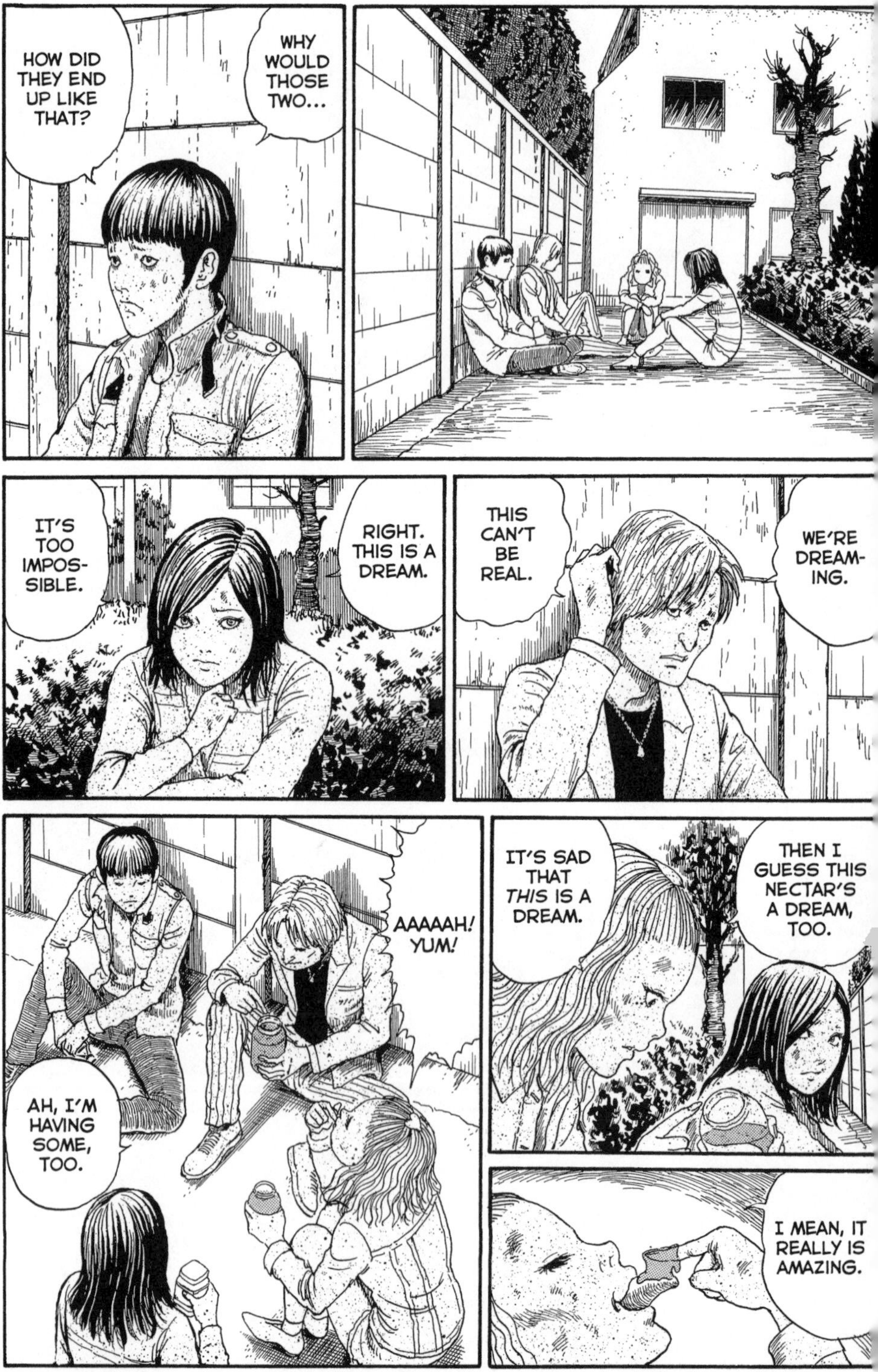
WHY WOULD THOSE TWO...
HOW DID THEY END UP LIKE THAT?
WE'RE DREAMING.
THIS CAN'T BE REAL.
RIGHT. THIS IS A DREAM.
IT'S TOO IMPOSSIBLE.
THEN I GUESS THIS NECTAR'S A DREAM, TOO.
IT'S SAD THAT *THIS* IS A DREAM.
I MEAN, IT REALLY IS AMAZING.
AAAAAH! YUM!
AH, I'M HAVING SOME, TOO.

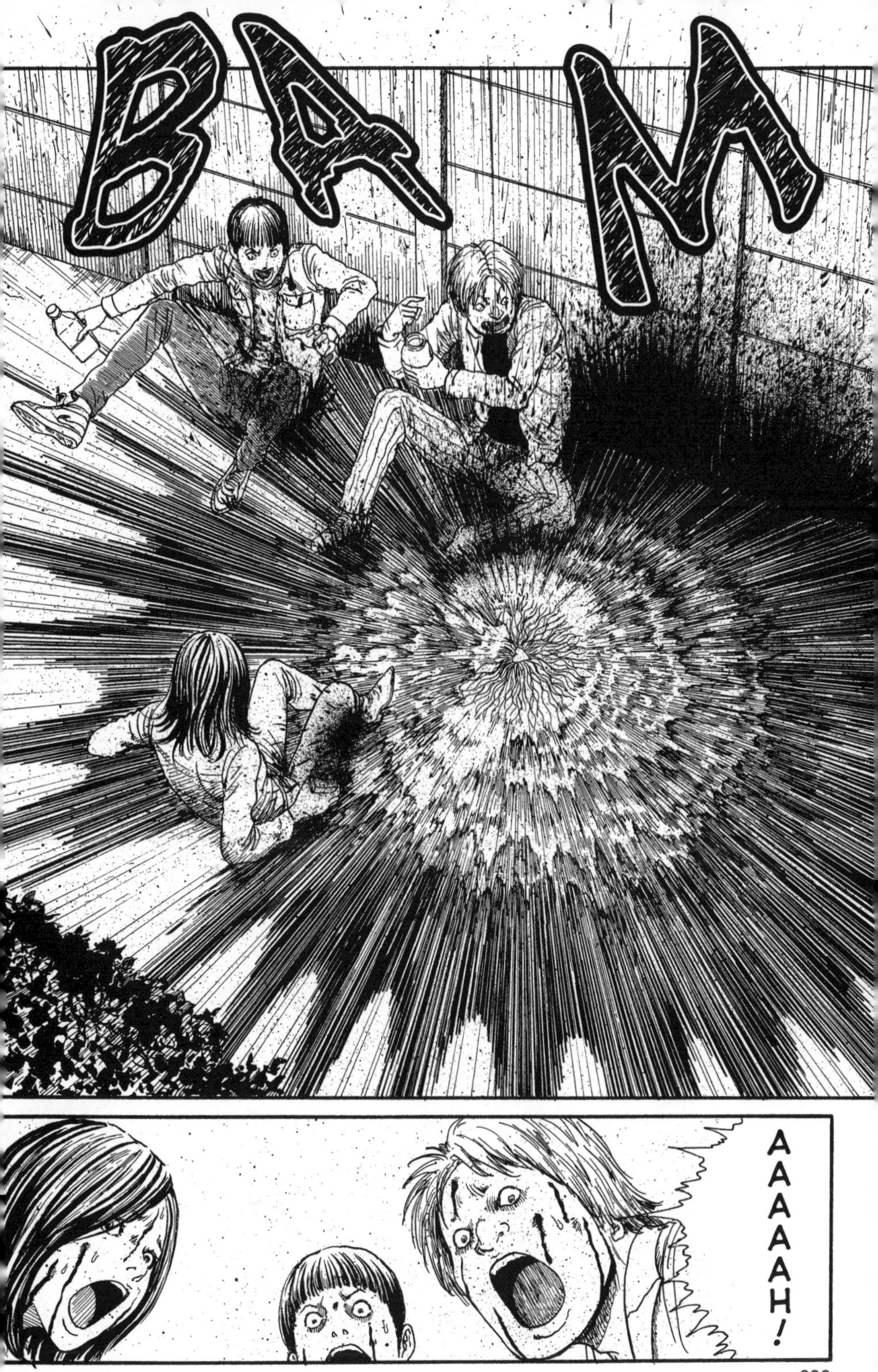
BAM
AAAAAH!

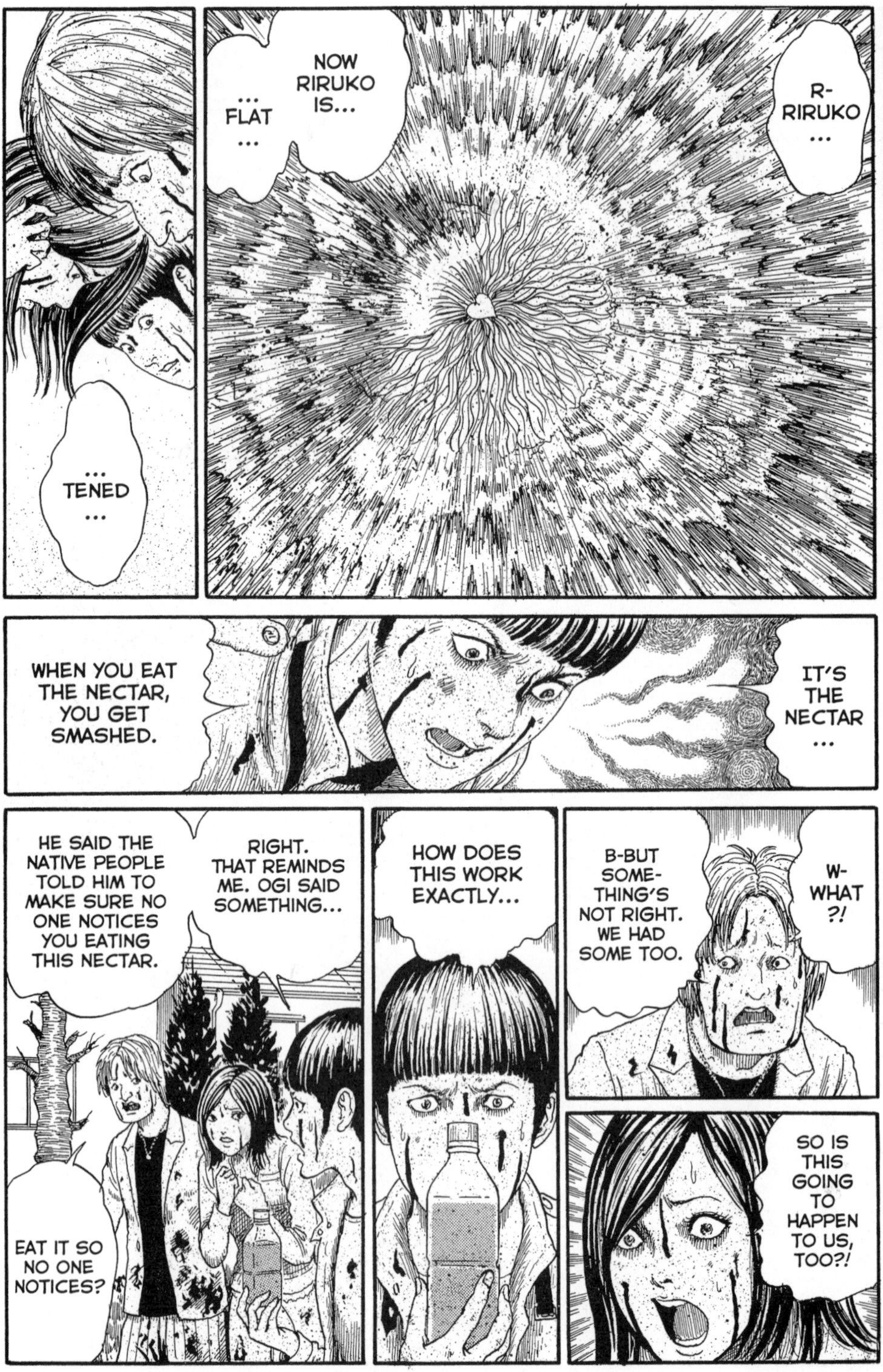
R- RIRUKO ...
NOW RIRUKO IS...
... FLAT ...
... TENED ...
IT'S THE NECTAR ...
WHEN YOU EAT THE NECTAR, YOU GET SMASHED.
W- WHAT ?!
B-BUT SOME- THING'S NOT RIGHT. WE HAD SOME TOO.
SO IS THIS GOING TO HAPPEN TO US, TOO?!
HOW DOES THIS WORK EXACTLY...
RIGHT. THAT REMINDS ME. OGI SAID SOMETHING...
HE SAID THE NATIVE PEOPLE TOLD HIM TO MAKE SURE NO ONE NOTICES YOU EATING THIS NECTAR.
EAT IT SO NO ONE NOTICES?

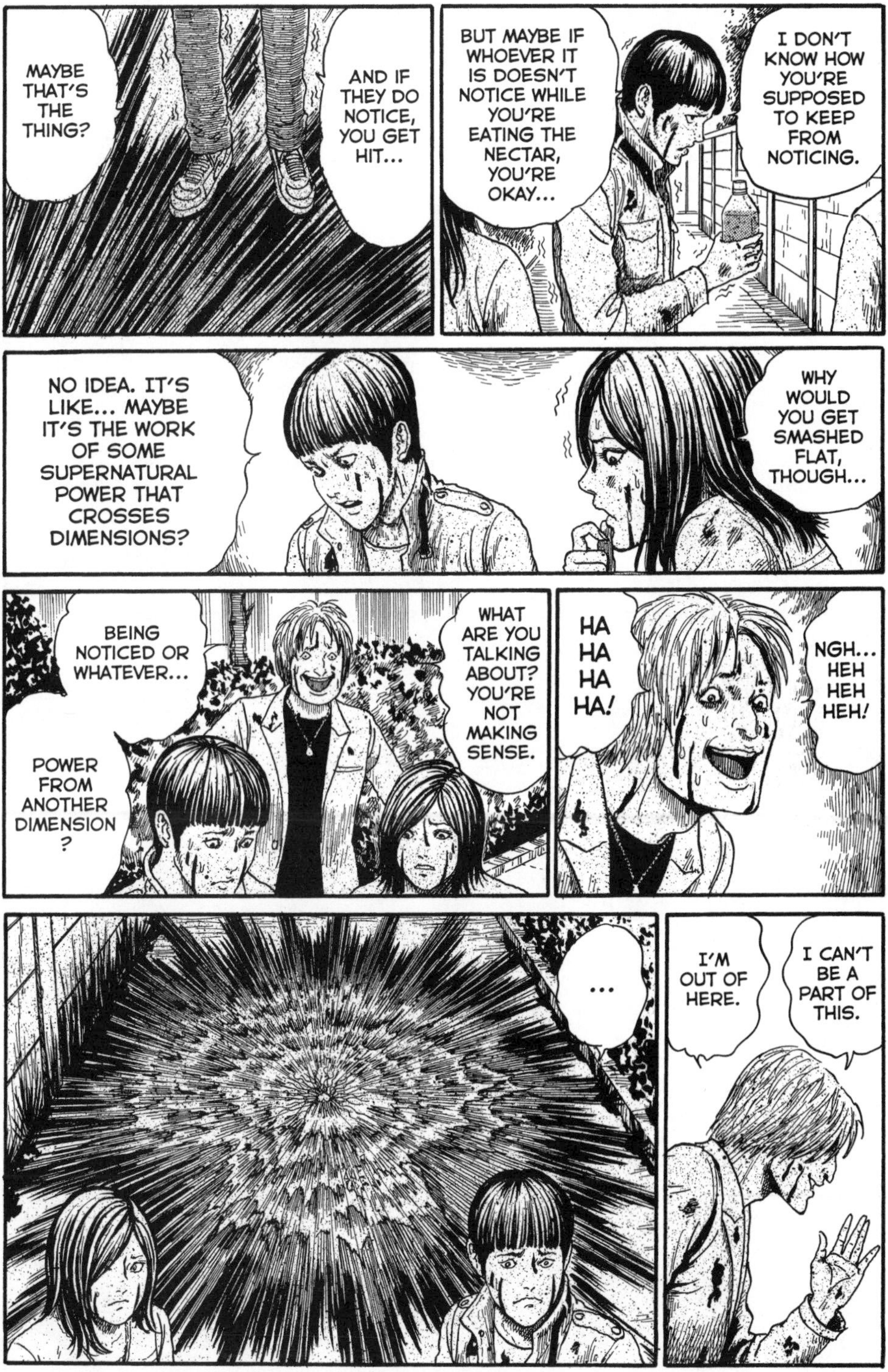
I DON'T KNOW HOW YOU'RE SUPPOSED TO KEEP FROM NOTICING.
BUT MAYBE IF WHOEVER IT IS DOESN'T NOTICE WHILE YOU'RE EATING THE NECTAR, YOU'RE OKAY...
AND IF THEY DO NOTICE, YOU GET HIT...
MAYBE THAT'S THE THING?
WHY WOULD YOU GET SMASHED FLAT, THOUGH...
NO IDEA. IT'S LIKE... MAYBE IT'S THE WORK OF SOME SUPERNATURAL POWER THAT CROSSES DIMENSIONS?
NGH... HEH HEH HEH!
HA HA HA HA!
WHAT ARE YOU TALKING ABOUT? YOU'RE NOT MAKING SENSE.
BEING NOTICED OR WHATEVER...
POWER FROM ANOTHER DIMENSION?
I CAN'T BE A PART OF THIS.
I'M OUT OF HERE.
...

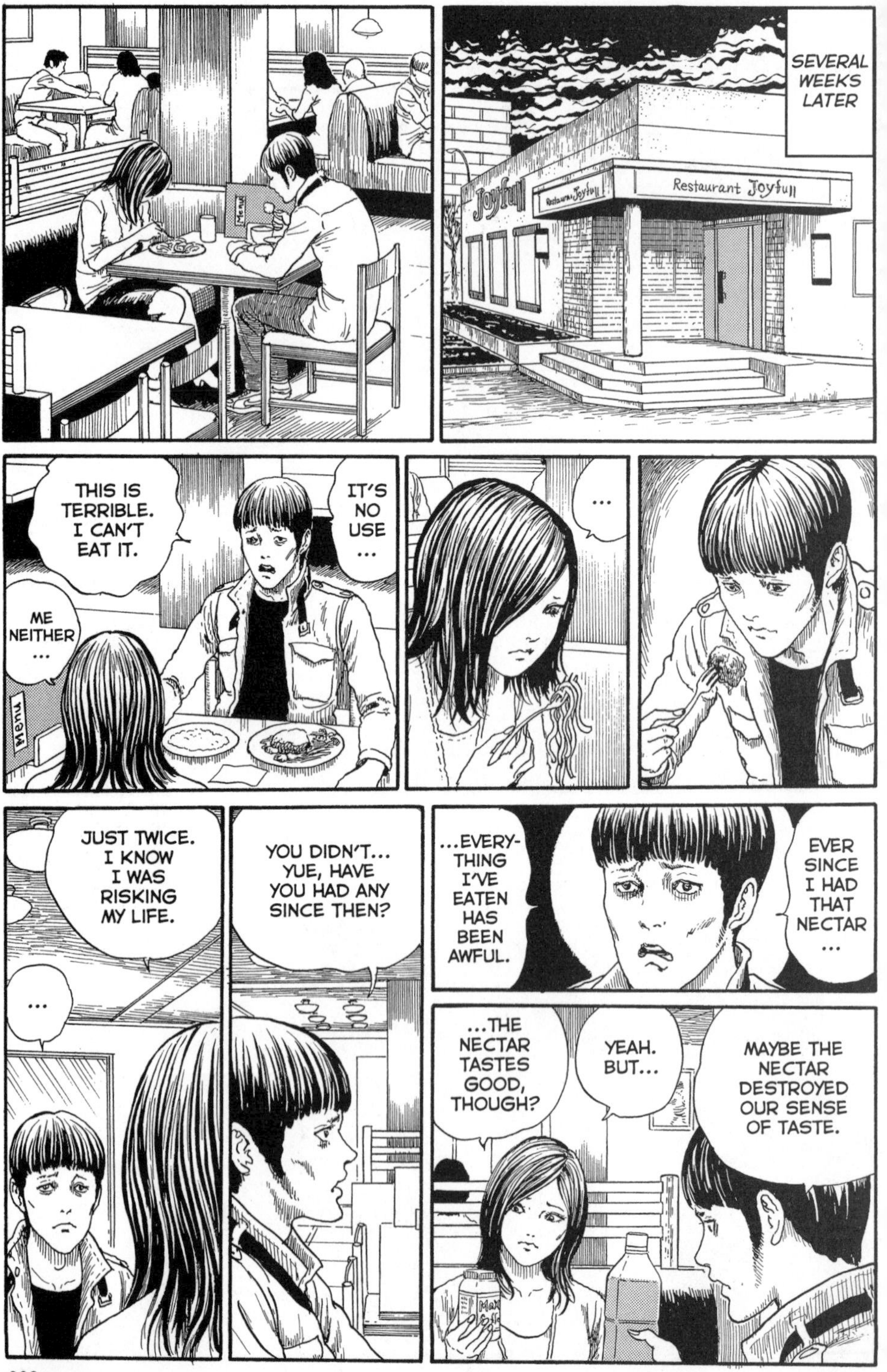
SEVERAL WEEKS LATER
Joyfull
Restaurant Joyfull
Restaurant Joyfull
Menu
...
IT'S NO USE ...
THIS IS TERRIBLE. I CAN'T EAT IT.
ME NEITHER ...
Menu
EVER SINCE I HAD THAT NECTAR ...
...EVERY-THING I'VE EATEN HAS BEEN AWFUL.
MAYBE THE NECTAR DESTROYED OUR SENSE OF TASTE.
YEAH. BUT...
...THE NECTAR TASTES GOOD, THOUGH?
YOU DIDN'T... YUE, HAVE YOU HAD ANY SINCE THEN?
JUST TWICE. I KNOW I WAS RISKING MY LIFE.
...

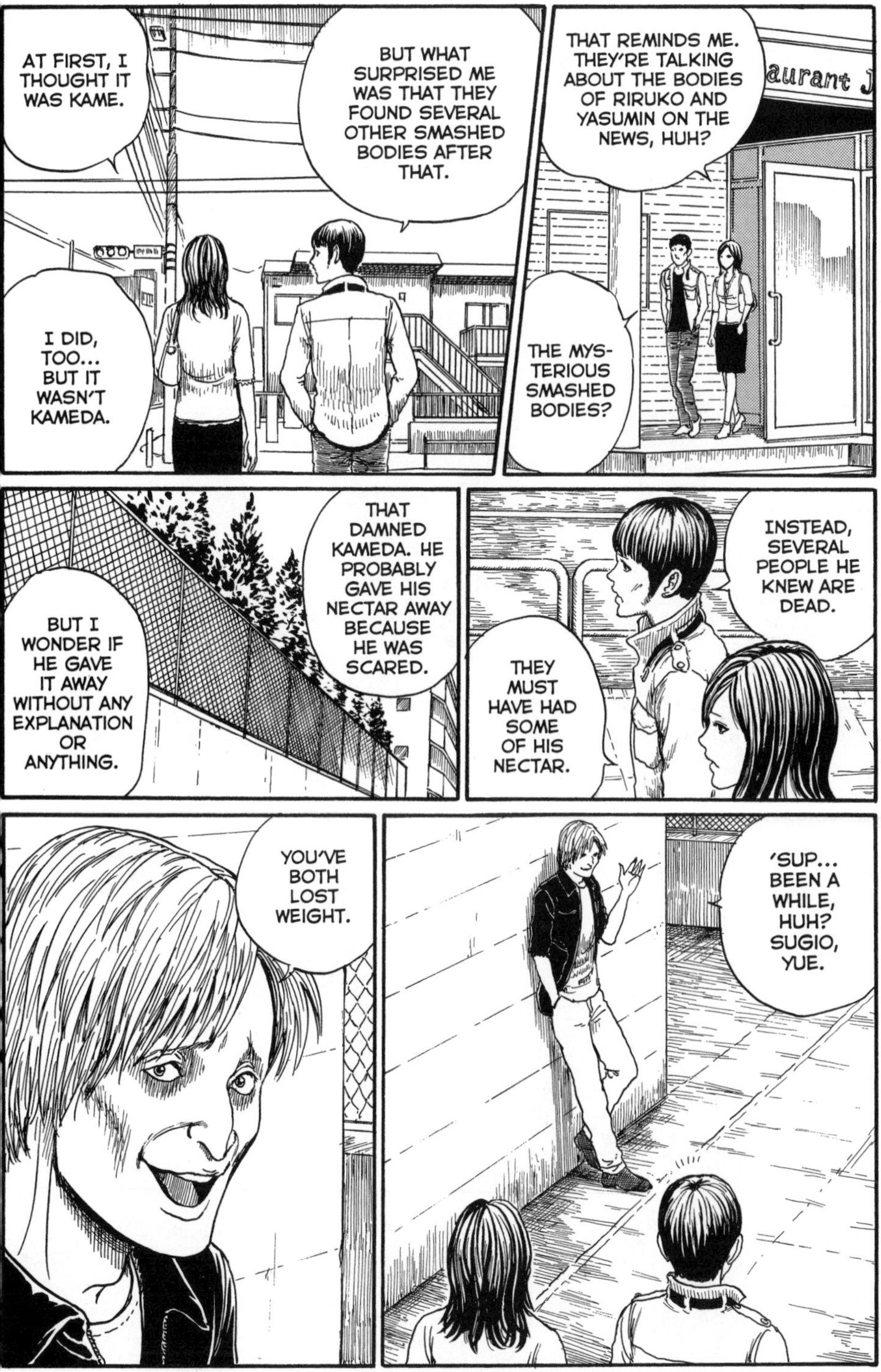
THAT REMINDS ME. THEY'RE TALKING ABOUT THE BODIES OF RIRUKO AND YASUMIN ON THE NEWS, HUH?
THE MYS-TERIOUS SMASHED BODIES?
BUT WHAT SURPRISED ME WAS THAT THEY FOUND SEVERAL OTHER SMASHED BODIES AFTER THAT.
AT FIRST, I THOUGHT IT WAS KAME.
I DID, TOO... BUT IT WASN'T KAMEDA.
INSTEAD, SEVERAL PEOPLE HE KNEW ARE DEAD.
THEY MUST HAVE HAD SOME OF HIS NECTAR.
THAT DAMNED KAMEDA. HE PROBABLY GAVE HIS NECTAR AWAY BECAUSE HE WAS SCARED.
BUT I WONDER IF HE GAVE IT AWAY WITHOUT ANY EXPLANATION OR ANYTHING.
'SUP... BEEN A WHILE, HUH? SUGIO, YUE.
YOU'VE BOTH LOST WEIGHT.

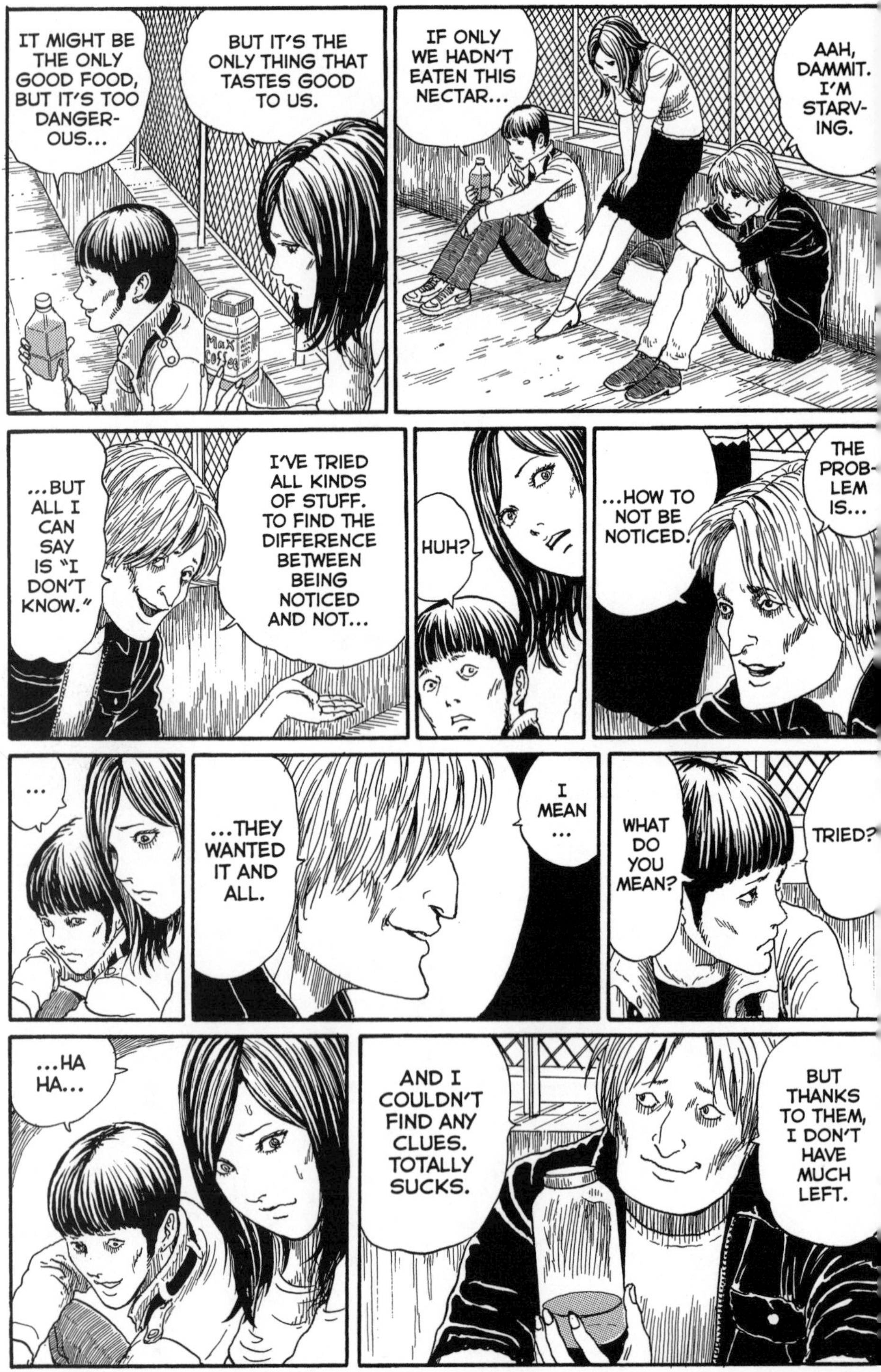
AAH, DAMMIT. I'M STARVING.
IF ONLY WE HADN'T EATEN THIS NECTAR...
BUT IT'S THE ONLY THING THAT TASTES GOOD TO US.
IT MIGHT BE THE ONLY GOOD FOOD, BUT IT'S TOO DANGEROUS...
THE PROBLEM IS...
...HOW TO NOT BE NOTICED.
HUH?
I'VE TRIED ALL KINDS OF STUFF. TO FIND THE DIFFERENCE BETWEEN BEING NOTICED AND NOT...
...BUT ALL I CAN SAY IS "I DON'T KNOW."
TRIED?
WHAT DO YOU MEAN?
I MEAN ...
...THEY WANTED IT AND ALL.
...
BUT THANKS TO THEM, I DON'T HAVE MUCH LEFT.
AND I COULDN'T FIND ANY CLUES. TOTALLY SUCKS.
...HA HA...

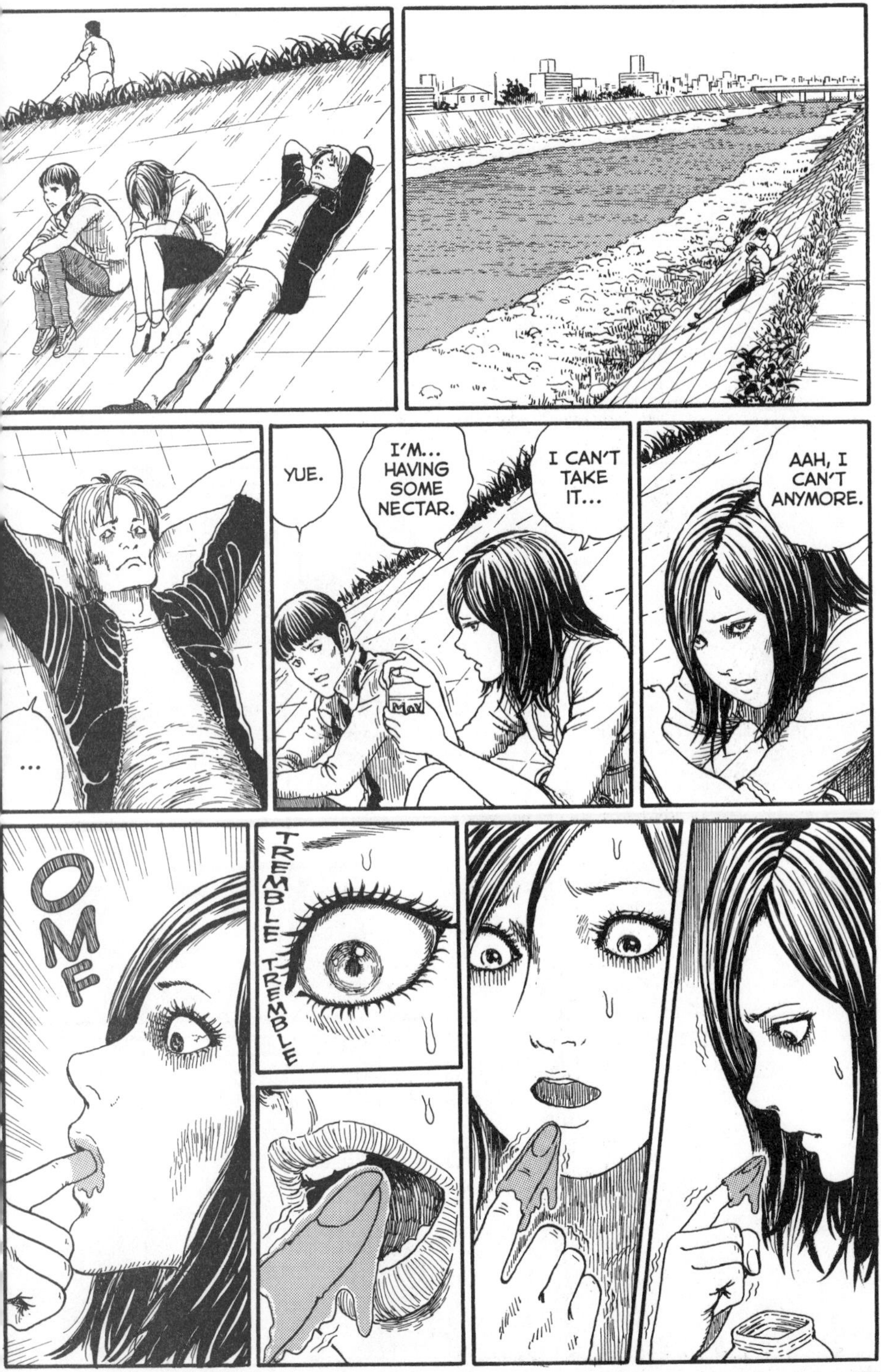
AAH, I CAN'T ANYMORE.
I CAN'T TAKE IT...
I'M... HAVING SOME NECTAR.
YUE.
...
TREMBLE TREMBLE
OMF

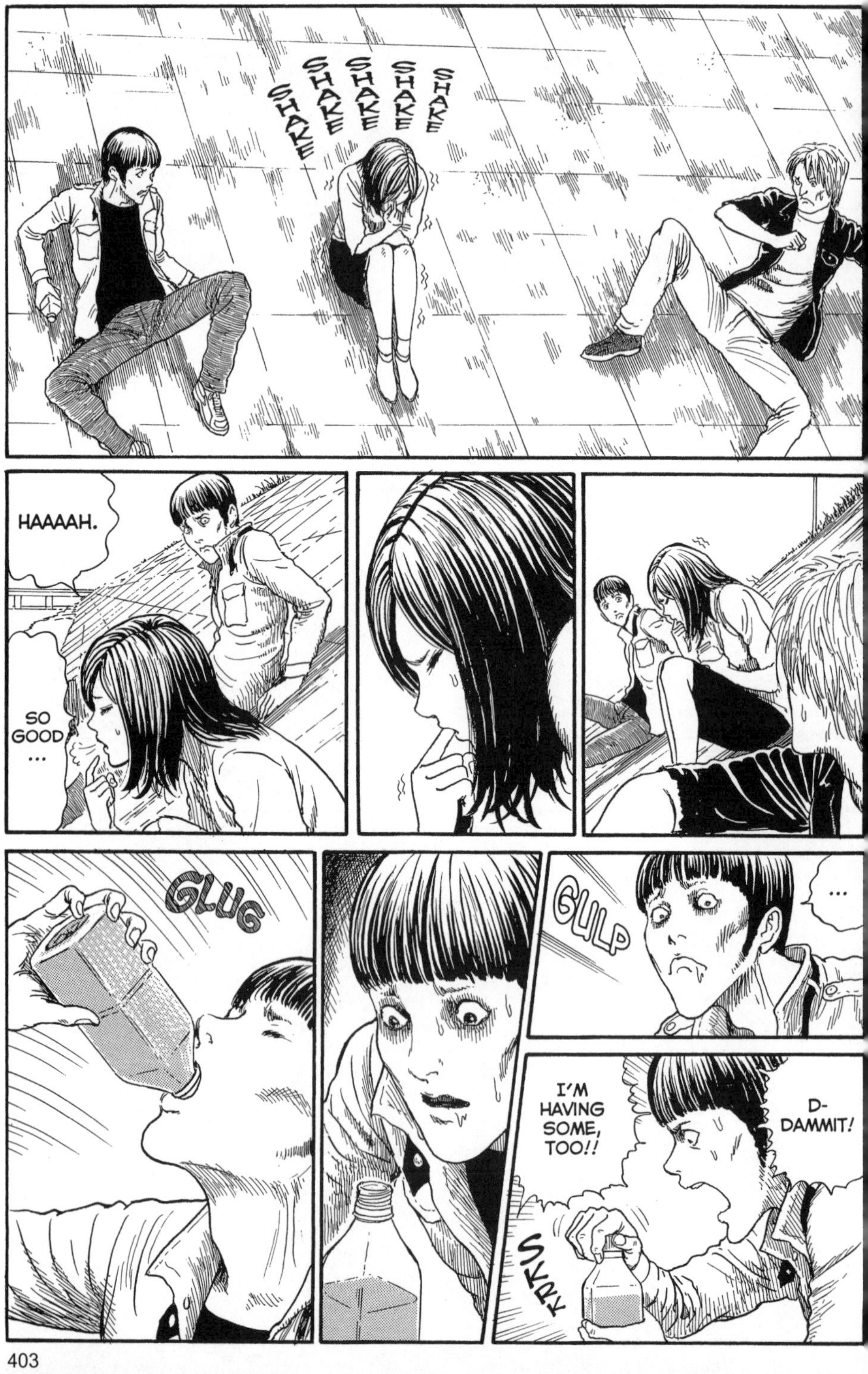
SHAKE SHAKE SHAKE SHAKE SHAKE
HAAAAH.
SO GOOD ...
...
GULP
D-DAMMIT!
I'M HAVING SOME, TOO!!
SKRK
GLUG

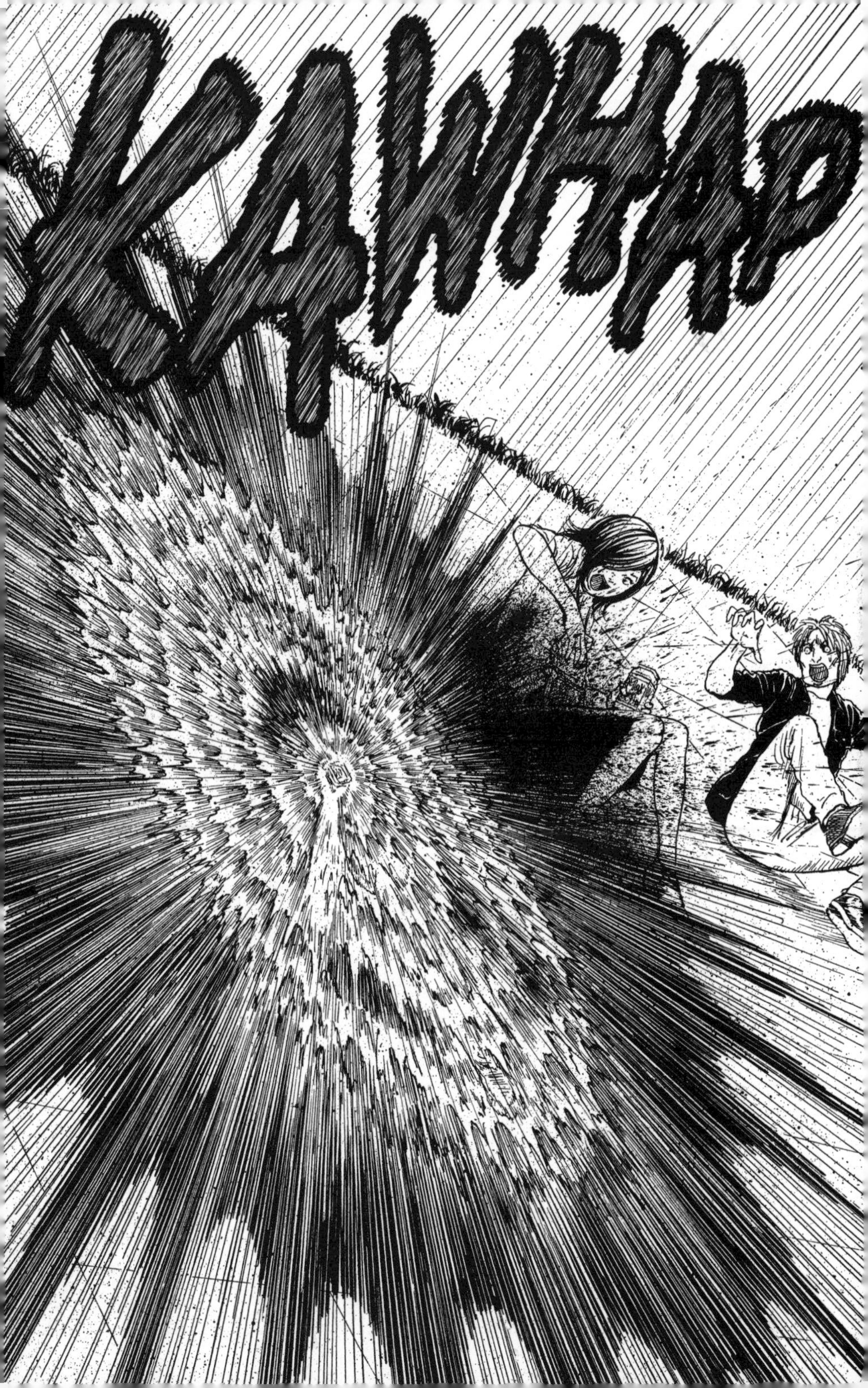
KAWHAP

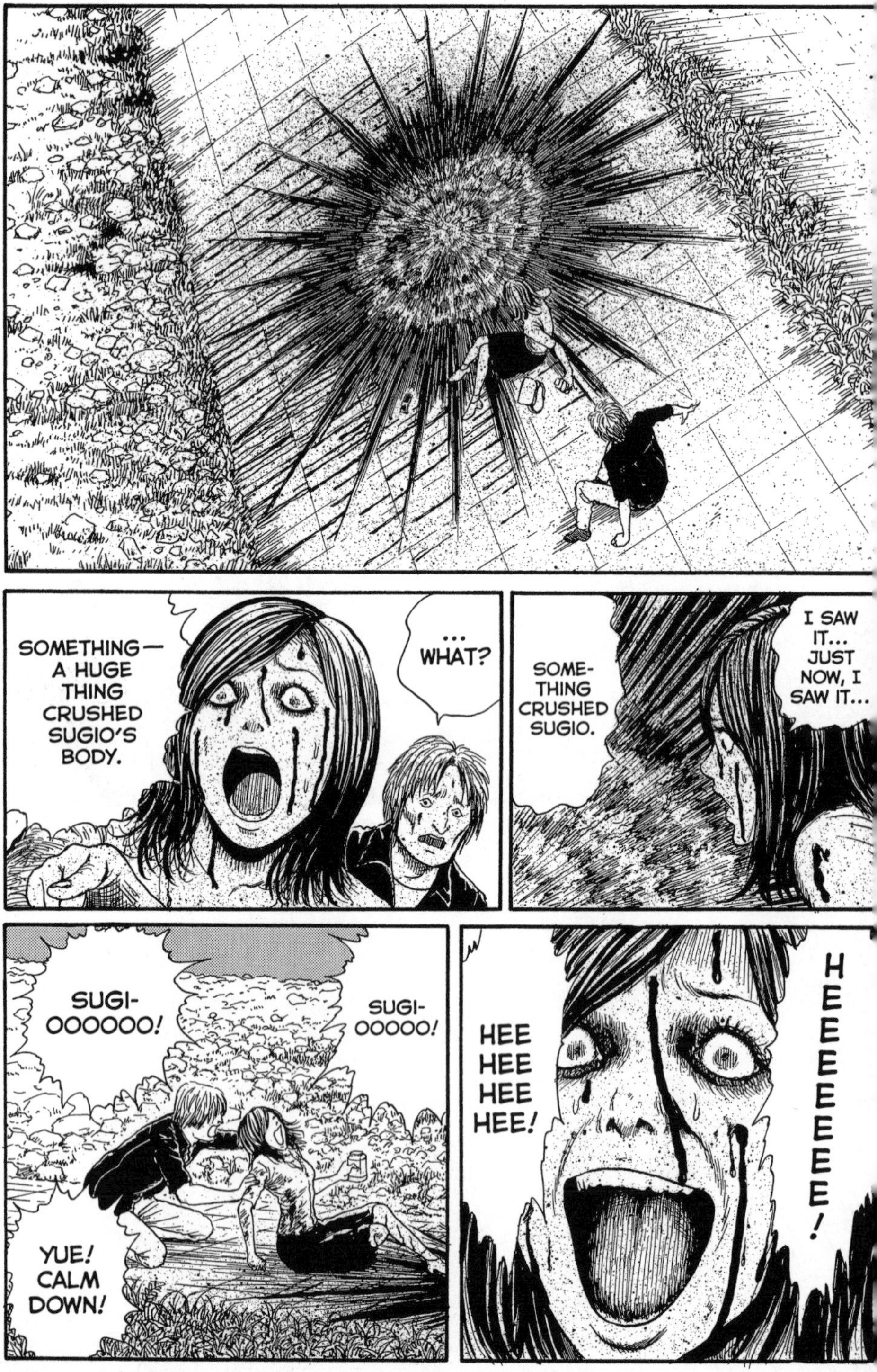
I SAW IT... JUST NOW, I SAW IT...
SOME-THING CRUSHED SUGIO.
... WHAT?
SOMETHING— A HUGE THING CRUSHED SUGIO'S BODY.
HEEEEEEEE!
HEE HEE HEE HEE!
SUGI-OOOOO!
SUGI-OOOOOO!
YUE! CALM DOWN!

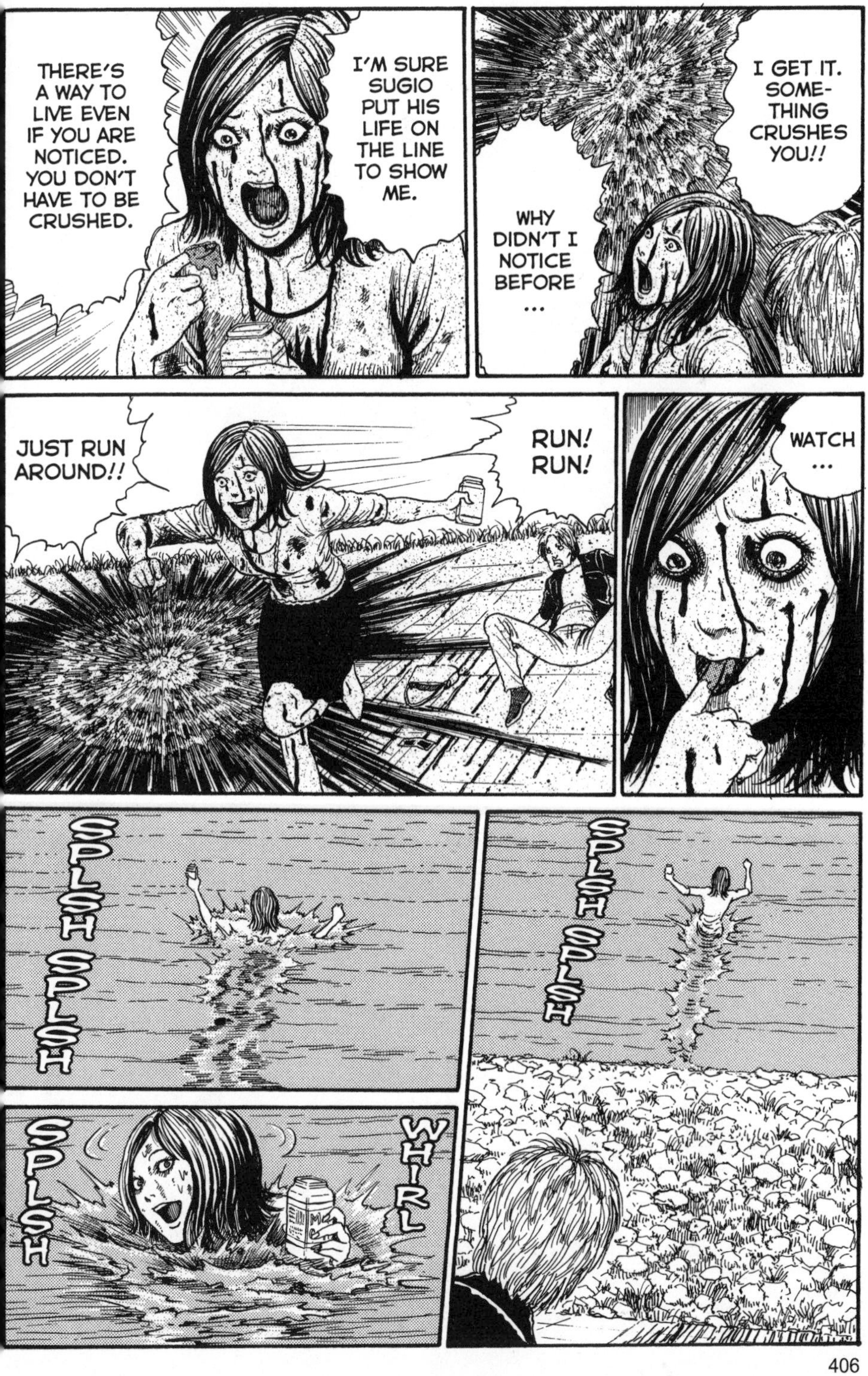
I GET IT. SOME-THING CRUSHES YOU!!
WHY DIDN'T I NOTICE BEFORE ...
I'M SURE SUGIO PUT HIS LIFE ON THE LINE TO SHOW ME.
THERE'S A WAY TO LIVE EVEN IF YOU ARE NOTICED. YOU DON'T HAVE TO BE CRUSHED.
WATCH ...
RUN! RUN!
JUST RUN AROUND!!
SPLSH SPLSH
SPLSH SPLSH
WHIRL
SPLSH

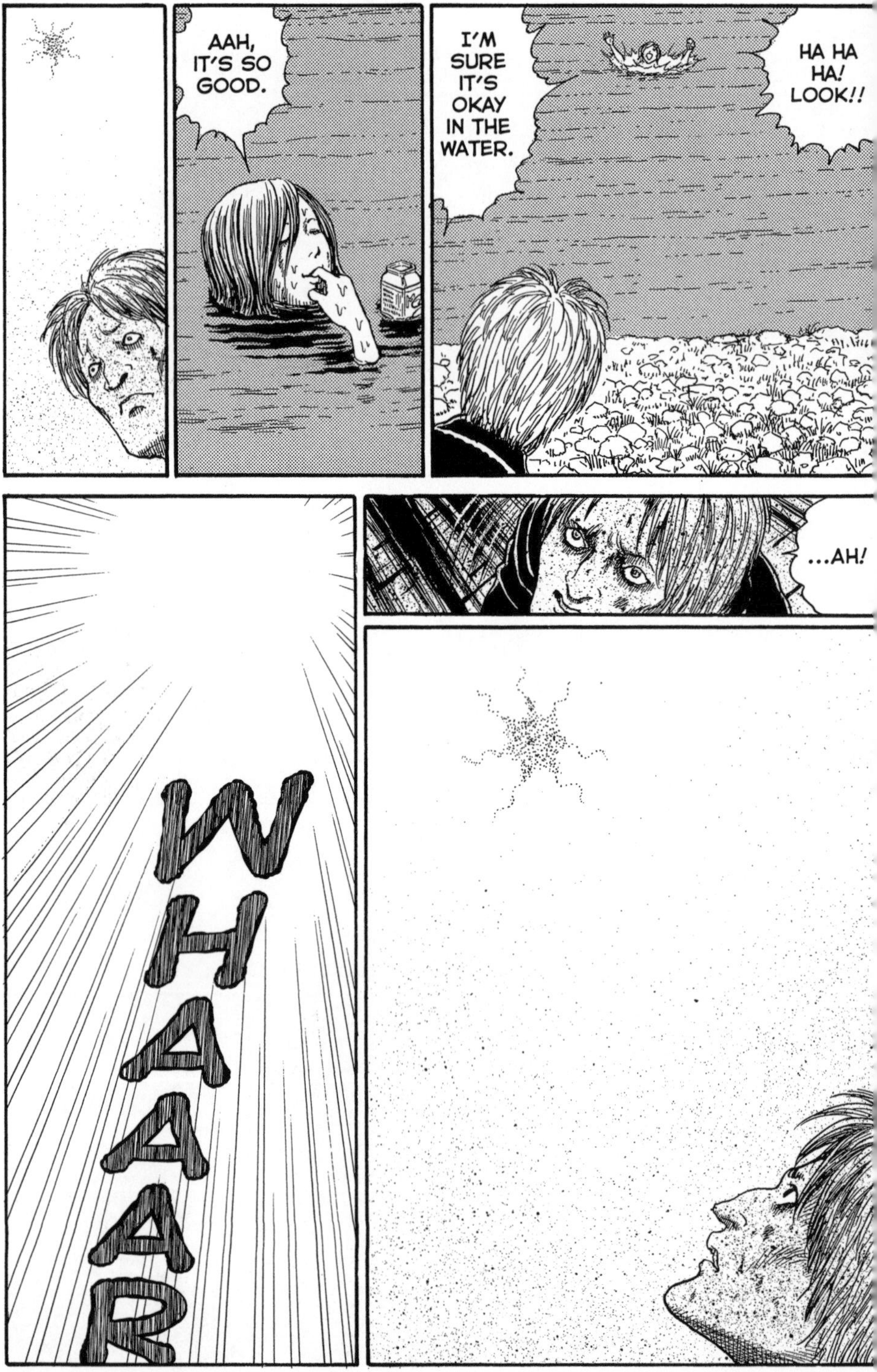
HA HA HA! LOOK!!
I'M SURE IT'S OKAY IN THE WATER.
AAH, IT'S SO GOOD.
...AH!
WHAAAR

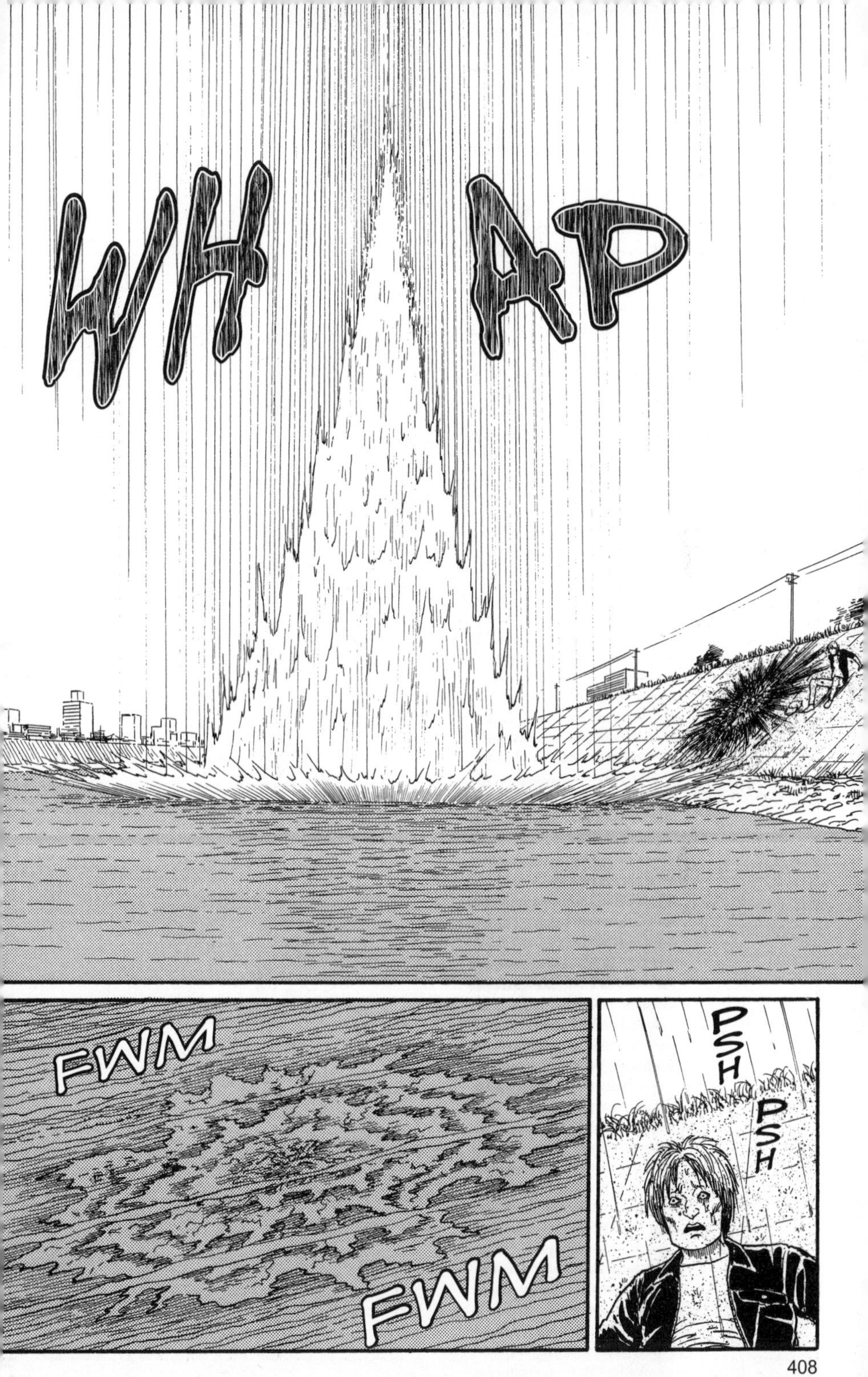
WHAP
PSH
PSH
FWM
FWM

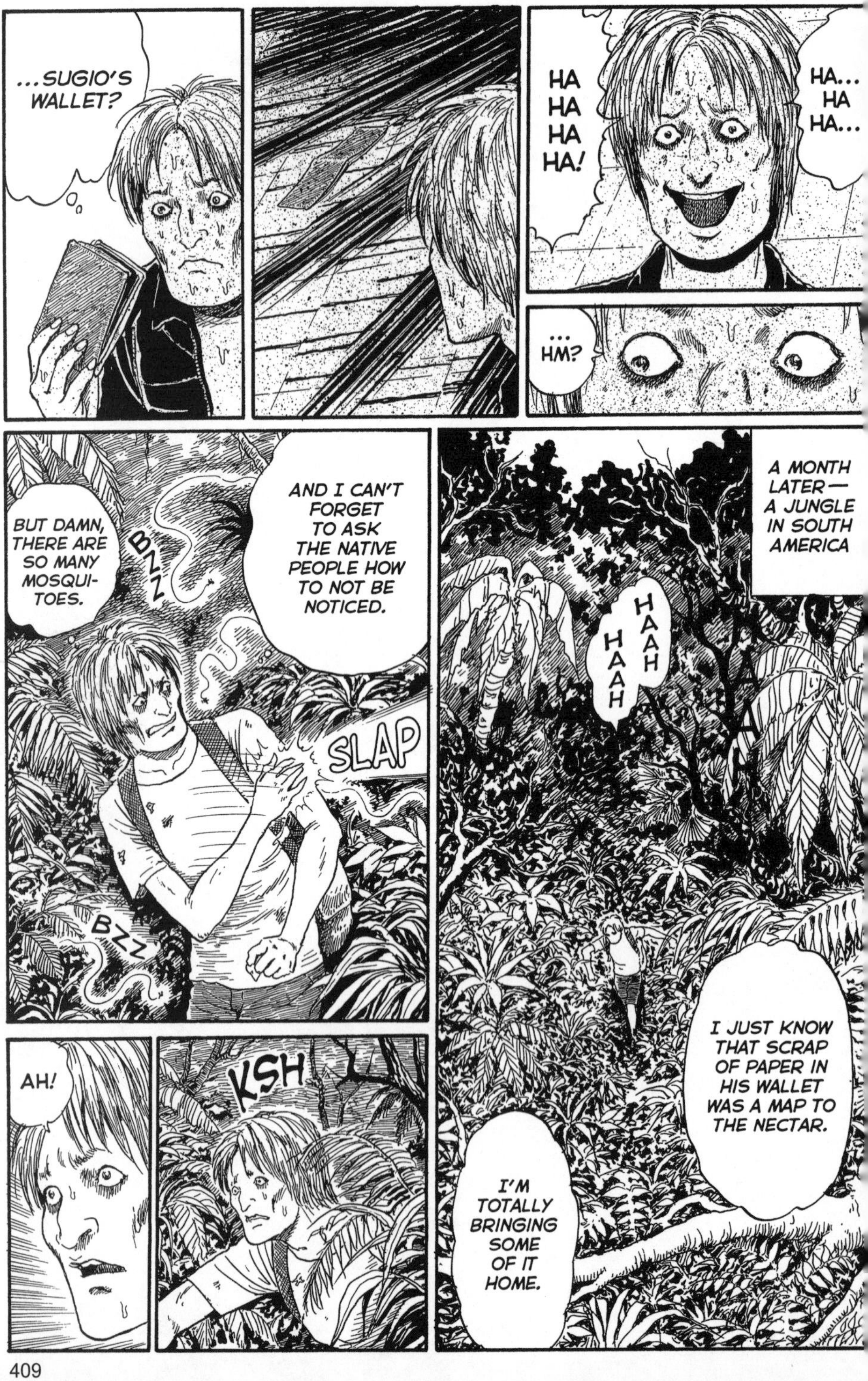
HA... HA HA...
HA HA HA HA!
... HM?
...SUGIO'S WALLET?
A MONTH LATER— A JUNGLE IN SOUTH AMERICA
HAAH
HAAH
I JUST KNOW THAT SCRAP OF PAPER IN HIS WALLET WAS A MAP TO THE NECTAR.
I'M TOTALLY BRINGING SOME OF IT HOME.
AND I CAN'T FORGET TO ASK THE NATIVE PEOPLE HOW TO NOT BE NOTICED.
BZZ
SLAP
BUT DAMN, THERE ARE SO MANY MOSQUI-TOES.
BZZ
KSH
AH!

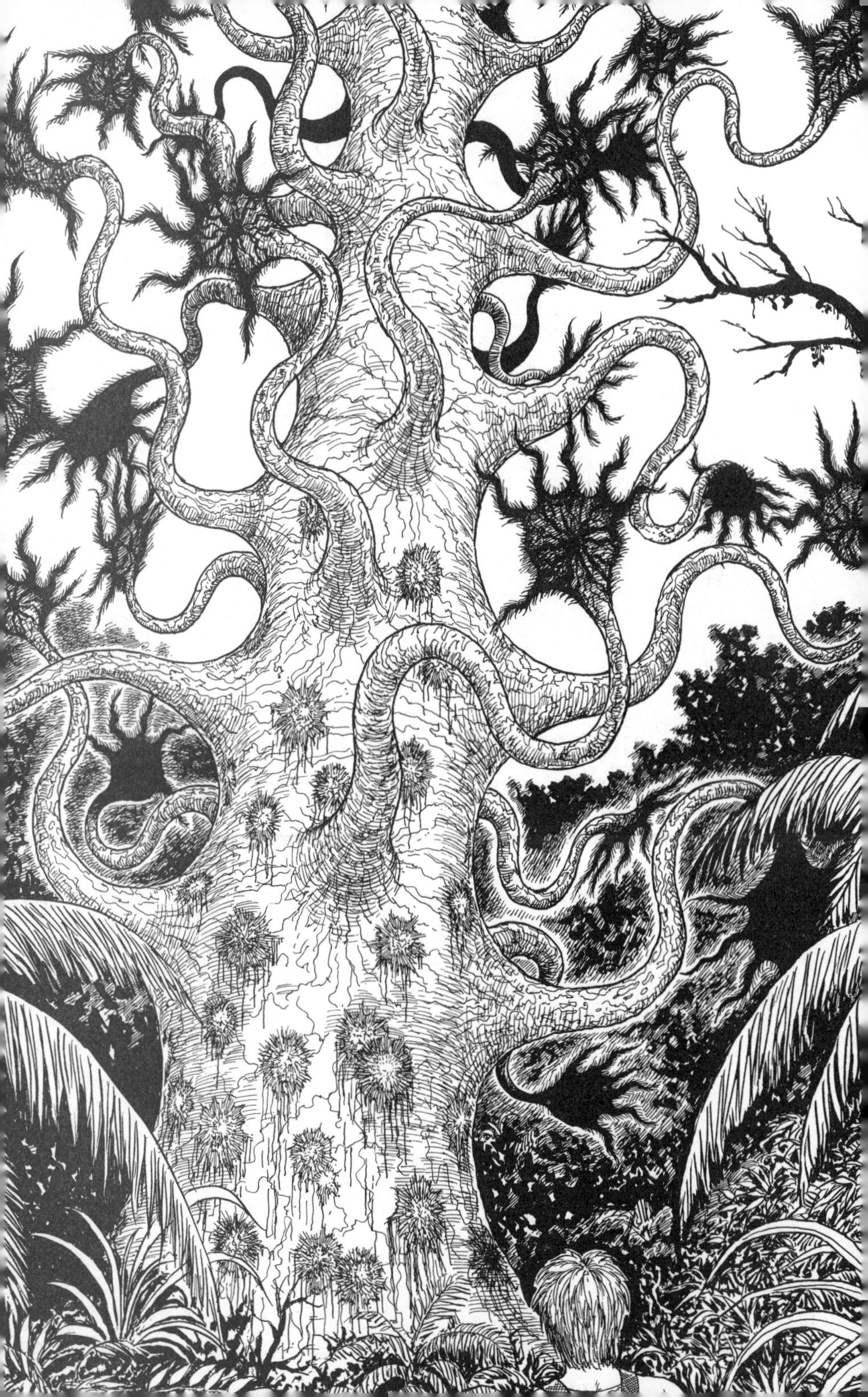

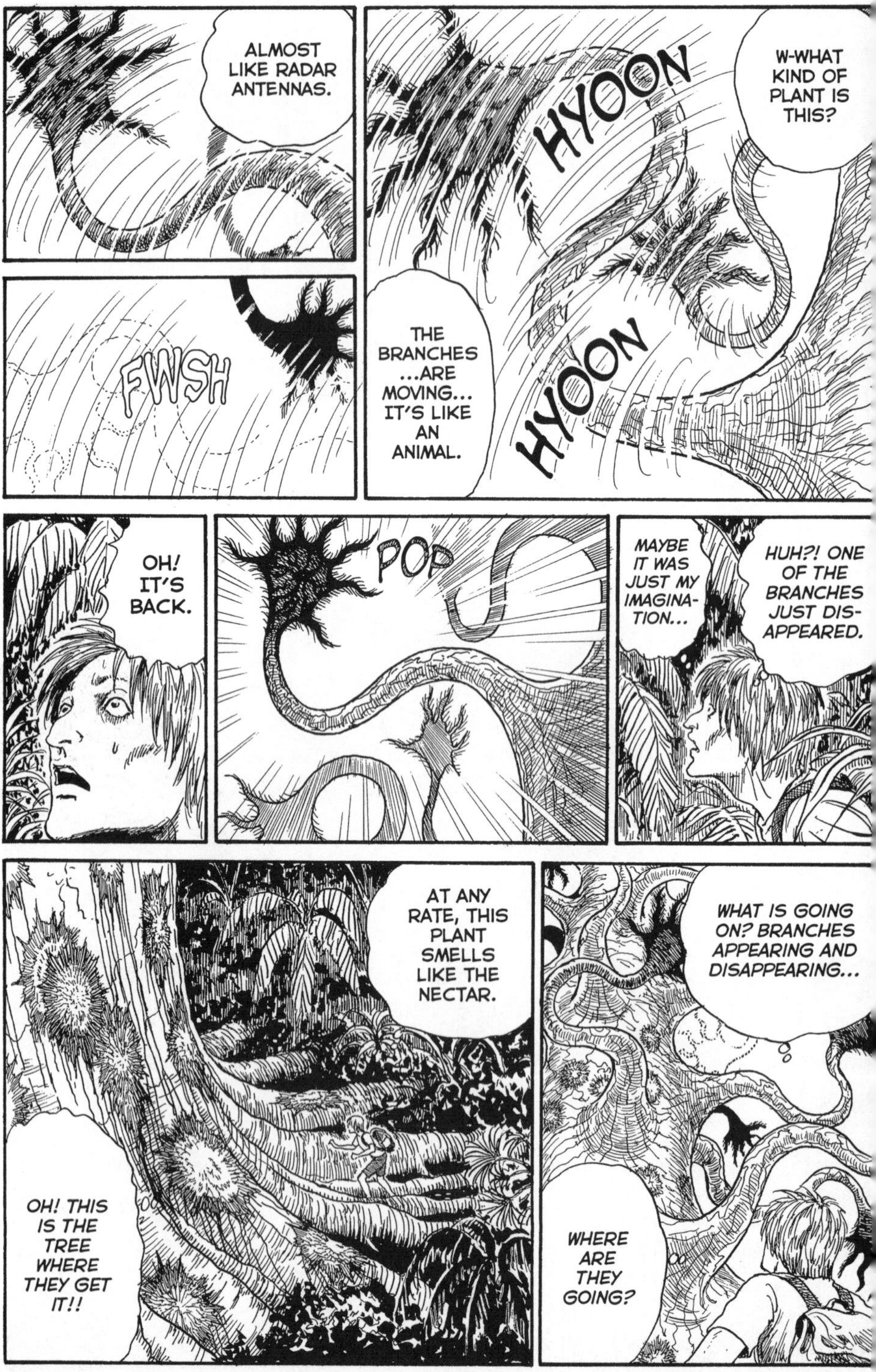

W-WHAT KIND OF PLANT IS THIS?
HYOON
HYOON
THE BRANCHES ...ARE MOVING... IT'S LIKE AN ANIMAL.
ALMOST LIKE RADAR ANTENNAS.
FWSH
HUH?! ONE OF THE BRANCHES JUST DISAPPEARED.
MAYBE IT WAS JUST MY IMAGINATION...
POP
OH! IT'S BACK.
WHAT IS GOING ON? BRANCHES APPEARING AND DISAPPEARING...
WHERE ARE THEY GOING?
AT ANY RATE, THIS PLANT SMELLS LIKE THE NECTAR.
OH! THIS IS THE TREE WHERE THEY GET IT!!

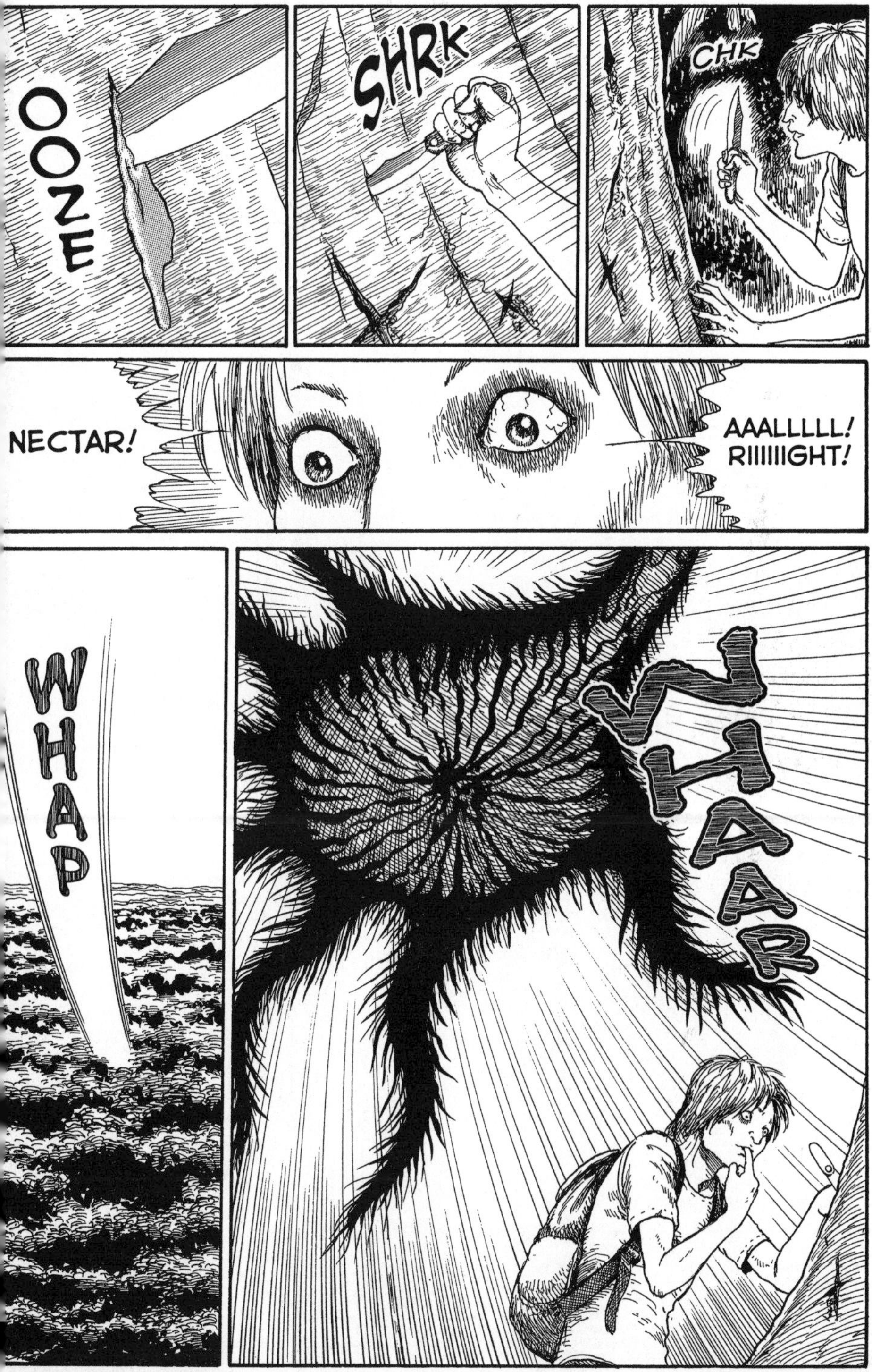
CHK
SHRK
OOZE
AAALLLLL! RIIIIIIGHT!
NECTAR!
WHAP
WHAP

SMASHED / END

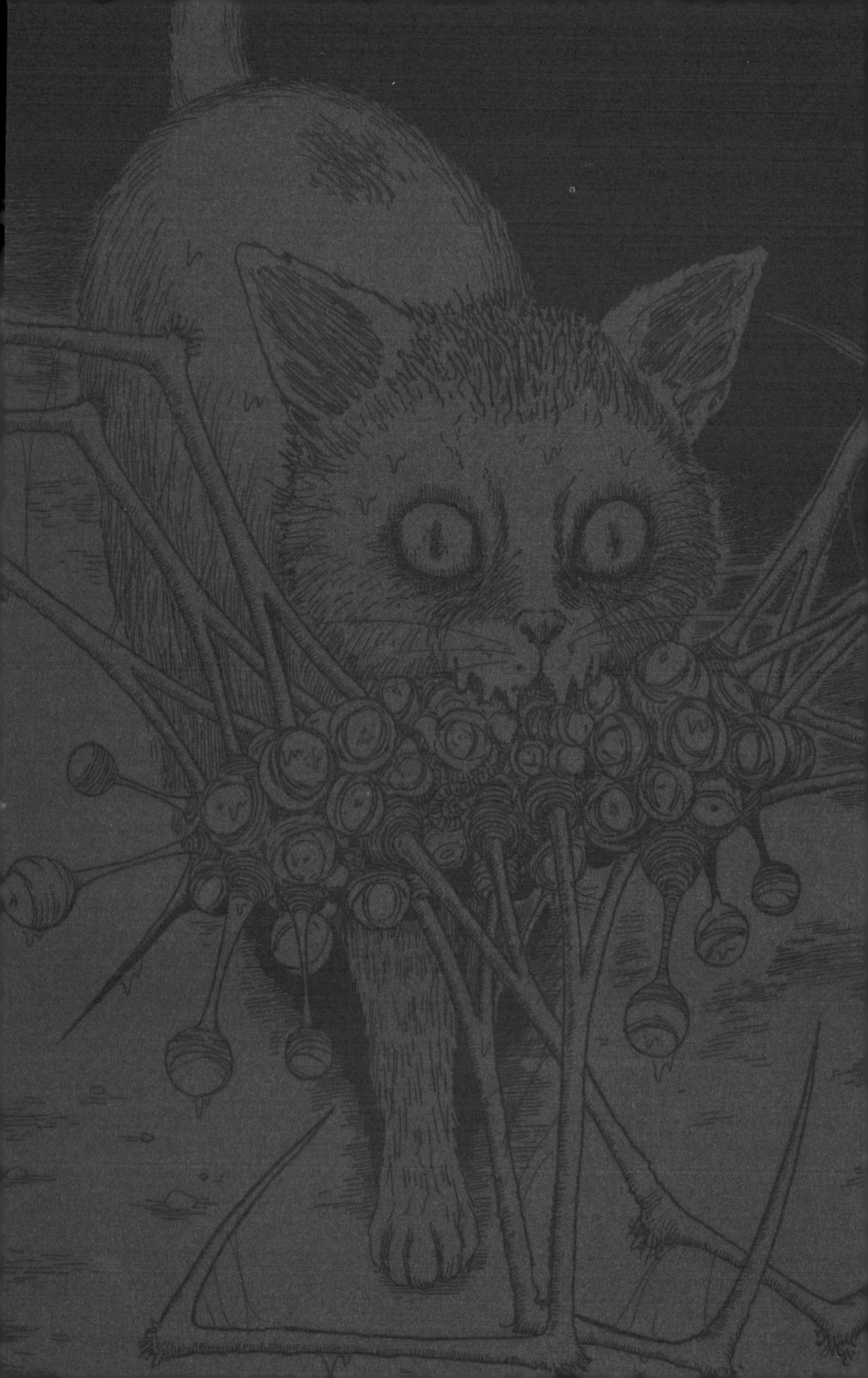

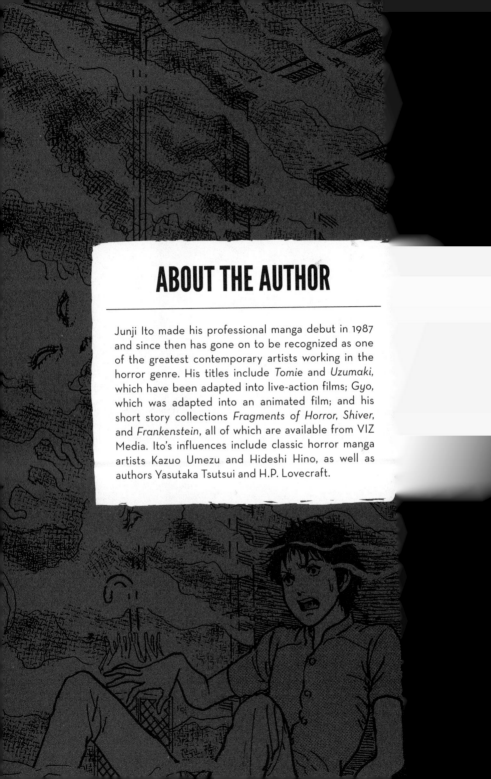

ABOUT THE AUTHOR

Junji Ito made his professional manga debut in 1987 and since then has gone on to be recognized as one of the greatest contemporary artists working in the horror genre. His titles include *Tomie* and *Uzumaki*, which have been adapted into live-action films; *Gyo*, which was adapted into an animated film; and his short story collections *Fragments of Horror*, *Shiver*, and *Frankenstein*, all of which are available from VIZ Media. Ito's influences include classic horror manga artists Kazuo Umezu and Hideshi Hino, as well as authors Yasutaka Tsutsui and H.P. Lovecraft.

SMASHED

JUNJI ITO STORY COLLECTION

Story & Art by Junji Ito

Ito Junji Kessakushu 11: Kaidan

Originally published in Japan in 2013 by Asahi Shimbun Publications Inc., Tokyo. English translation rights arranged with Asahi Shimbun Publications Inc., Tokyo through TOHAN CORPORATION, Tokyo.

Translation & Adaptation: Jocelyne Allen
Touch-Up Art & Lettering: Eric Erbes
Cover & Graphic Design: Adam Grano
Editor: Masumi Washington

Printed in the U.S.A.

Published by VIZ Media, LLC
P.O. Box 77010
San Francisco, CA 94107

10 9 8 7 6 5
First printing, April 2019
Fifth printing, April 2021

VIZ SIGNATURE

PARENTAL ADVISORY
SMASHED is rated T+ for Older Teen and is recommended for ages 16 and up. This volume contains graphic violence and mature themes.

VIZ MEDIA
viz.com

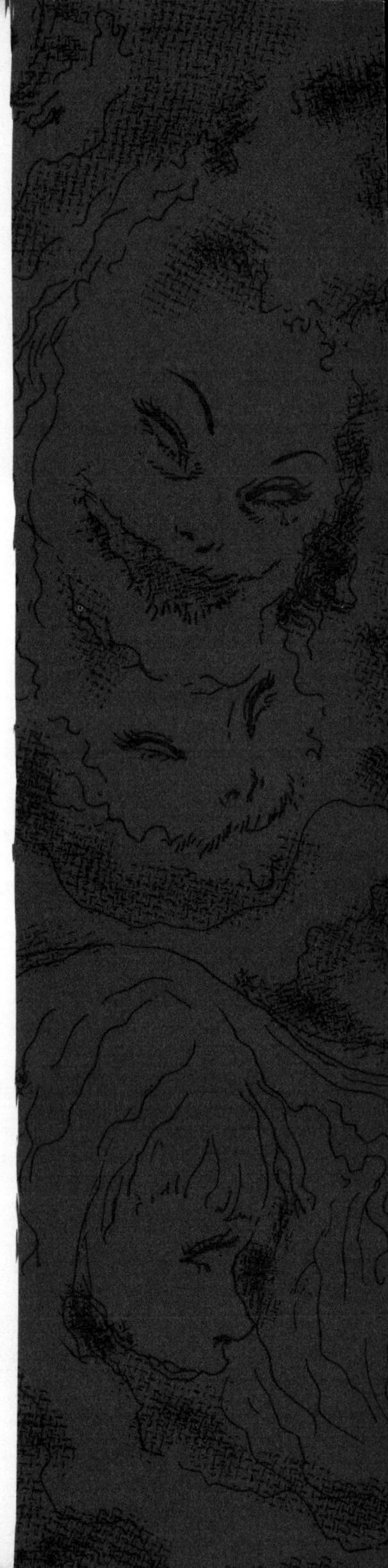

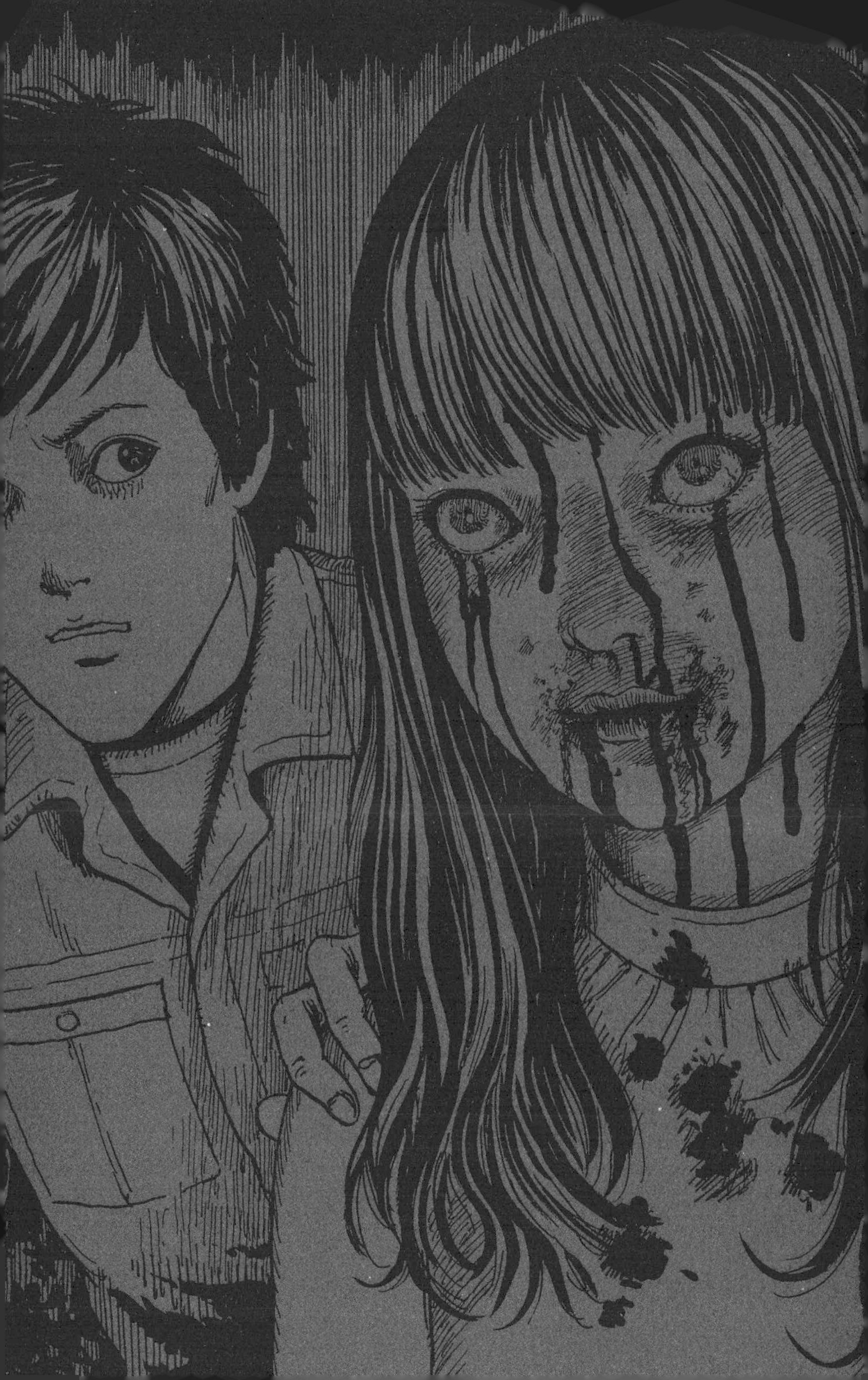